The Oxford Handbook of
Internet
Psychology

The Oxford Handbook of
Internet
Psychology

Edited by

Adam N. Joinson
School of Management,
University of Bath, UK

Katelyn Y.A. McKenna
Ben-Gurion University of the Negev, and the
Interdisciplinary Center, Herzliya, Israel

Tom Postmes
Department of Psychology, University of Exeter, UK

Ulf-Dietrich Reips
Department of Psychology, University of Zurich,
Switzerland

OXFORD
UNIVERSITY PRESS

OXFORD

UNIVERSITY PRESS

Great Clarendon Street, Oxford OX2 6DP

Oxford University Press is a department of the University of Oxford.
It furthers the University's objective of excellence in research, scholarship,
and education by publishing worldwide in

Oxford New York

Auckland Cape Town Dar es Salaam Hong Kong Karachi
Kuala Lumpur Madrid Melbourne Mexico City Nairobi
New Delhi Shanghai Taipei Toronto

With offices in

Argentina Austria Brazil Chile Czech Republic France Greece
Guatemala Hungary Italy Japan Poland Portugal Singapore
South Korea Switzerland Thailand Turkey Ukraine Vietnam

Oxford is a registered trade mark of Oxford University Press
in the UK and in certain other countries

Published in the United States
by Oxford University Press Inc., New York

© Oxford University Press, 2007

British Library Cataloguing in Publication Data

Data available

Library of Congress Cataloguing in Publication Data

Data available

ISBN 978-0-19-856800-1 (Hbk.)

ISBN 978-0-19-956180-3 (Pbk.)

10 9 8 7 6 5 4 3 2 1

Typeset in Minion
by Cepha Imaging Pvt Ltd, Bangalore, India
Printed in Great Britain
on acid-free paper by
CPI Antony Rowe

Contents

Part 4 Psychological Aspects of Internet Use

Part 5 Internet-Based Research

List of Contributors

Yair Amichai-Hamburger, Bezeq International Research Center for Internet Psychology, IDC Herzliya, Israel

Yaron Ariel, Graduate School of Business Administration, University of Haifa, Israel

Azy Barak, Department of Education, University of Haifa, Israel

Victoria Bellotti, Stanford University, USA

Michael H. Birnbaum, Department of Psychology, C.S.U.F, Fullerton, USA

David P. Brandon, Department of Psychology, University of Illinois UIUC, USA

Di Bretherton, Department of Psychology, RMIT University, Melbourne, Australia

Pam Briggs, School of Psychology and Sports Sciences, Northumbria University, Newcastle–upon–Tyne, UK

Tom Buchanan, Department of Psychology, University of Westminster, London, UK

Andrea Chester, Department of Psychology, RMIT University, Melbourne, Australia

Leah M. Christian, Pew Research Center for people and the press, Washington DC, USA

Don A. Dillman, Social & Economic Sciences Research Center, Washington State University, Pullman, USA

Karen M. Douglas, School of Psychology, University of Kent, UK

William H. Dutton, Department of Communication, Center for Film, Television & New Media, University of California, USA

Ame Elliott, Stanford University, USA

Charles Ess, Interdisciplinary Studies Center, Drury University, Springfield, USA

Anja S. Goritz, Erlangen-Nurnberg, Germany

Melanie C. Green, Department of Psychology, University of Pennsylvania, Philadelphia, USA

Jeffrey T. Hancock, Department of Communication, Cornell University, Ithaca, USA

Caroline Haythornthwaite, Graduate School of Library & Information Science, University of Illinois at Urbana-Champaign, USA

Claire Hewson, Department of Psychology, The Open University, Milton Keynes, UK

Andrea B. Hollingshead, Department of Psychology, University of Illinois UIUC, USA

Kai J. Jonas, Department of Social Psychology, Friedrich Schiller University, Jena, Germany

James E. Katz, Department of Communication, Center for Film, Television and New Media, University of California, USA

Martin Lea, Department of Psychology, University of Manchester, UK

John D. McCarthy, LIDA, London, UK

Janet Morahan-Martin, Department of Applied Psychology, Bryant University, Smithfield, USA

Carina B. Paine, Institute of Educational Technology, The Open University, UK

Sheizaf Rafaeli, Graduate School of Business Administration, University of Haifa, Israel

Ronald E. Rice, Department of Communication, Center for Film, Television and New Media, University of California, USA

Jens Riegelsberger, Multimedia Laboratory, Department of Computer Science, University College London, UK

M. Angela Sasse, Multimedia Laboratory, Department of Computer Science, University College London, UK

Kai Sassenberg, Department of Social Psychology, Friedrich Schiller University, Jena, Germany

Diane J. Schiano, Consultant, Stanford University, USA

William C. Schmidt, Department of Psychology, SUNY, New York, USA

Adrian Shepherd, Department of Communication, Center for Film, Television and New Media, University of California, USA

Elizabeth Sillence, School of Psychology and Sports Sciences, Northumbria University, Newcastle–upon–Tyne, UK

Jolene D. Smyth, Survey Research and Methodology Program and the Department of Sociology, University of Nebraska-Lincoln, Lincoln, NE, USA

S. Shyam Sundar, Media Effects Research Laboratory, Penn State University, USA

Russell Spears, School of Psychology, Cardiff University, UK

Martin Tanis, Vrije Universiteit, Faculteit der Sociale Wetenschappen, Amsterdam, The Netherlands

Monica Whitty, School of Psychology, Queens' University Belfast, UK

Adam Joinson, Senior Lecturer, Institute of Educational Technology, The Open University, Milton Keynes, UK

Katelyn McKenna, Senior Lecturer, Ben-Gurion University of the Negev, Israel and the Interdisciplinary Center, Herzliya, Israel

Tom Postmes, Department of Psychology, University of Exeter, UK

Ulf Dietrich-Reips, Department of Psychology, University of Zurich, Switzerland

CHAPTER 1

Introduction to the Handbook

Adam N. Joinson, Katelyn Y. A. McKenna, Tom Postmes and Ulf-Dietrich Reips

It feels like the Internet has always been here. It's difficult, as editors, to imagine a world where we couldn't email authors of chapters, host draft chapters on web pages, or use a wiki to co-edit work. Reviewers can be sent electronic copies of draft chapters instantaneously. The Internet is also changing where we work – no longer need we be based exclusively in a particular physical location. For example, the process of conducting research on the Internet, one of the foci of this book, has freed many of us from the need to be physically co-present with participants.

This change in how we do things, as well as where we do them, is, we would argue, a sign of a truly transforming technology akin to the automobile or telephone. Travel and commuting should reduce as people increasingly work at home, university campuses will empty as students learn and socialize online, and the peer review process in academia will speed considerably without the delays caused by 'snail mail'.

Except, of course, that none of the above are happening yet, nor are they likely to happen in the near future. Congestion worsens, campuses continue to be filled, and peer review is still often a tortuously slow process. How can it be that something that has seeped into so many areas of our lives, and has the potential to transform how we shop, socialize, work and learn, leaves us fundamentally unchanged as humans? We believe that the field of Internet Psychology, and this Handbook, will provide some of the answers. From the many chapters included in this volume, we believe that a number of key themes emerge.

First, regardless of what media people use to communicate, basic human motivations and emotions remain. In Chapter 13, Yair Amichai-Hamburger discusses personality and Internet use, and outlines some of the motivations that might dictate how people act online. Motivation is also discussed in the context of deception by Jeffery Hancock in Chapter 19, and privacy by Adam Joinson and Carina Paine in Chapter 16. Conversely, in Chapter 17 Spears, Lea, and Postmes focus not on an individual's personal motivations, but rather on their group-related behaviour during computer-mediated communication. All the examples above (and there are many others in the Handbook) argue that while the Internet is not transforming the basics of human behaviour it is enabling new forms of more traditional processes.

This approach, which is adopted by many of the authors, discourages the 'scorched earth' approach to understanding new technology – the idea that new media warrant a new psychology – by emphasizing the importance of existing, related theories and approaches within psychology. For instance, Martin Tanis combines the existing literature on social support with work on computer-mediated communication in Chapter 10 to illuminate the dynamics and pros and cons of online social support. Similarly, in Chapter 3 Monica Whitty draws parallels between pre-Internet dating rituals and online romance, arguing that to understand present day cyber romance we must examine pre-Internet techniques such as letter writing. In Chapter 12 Tom Postmes argues that although the Internet offers radically different forms of achieving collective goals, the processes involved in collective action are fundamentally unchanged. This approach is supported by the work of Ronald Rice and colleagues who argue in Chapter 2 that social interaction on the Internet supplements rather than displaces more traditional modes of interaction.

This approach to understanding psychological aspects of Internet behaviour should not be taken to mean that there is nothing new about the Internet. Indeed, the very fact that what we can encounter on the Internet can be very much the same as we knew before highlights the special status of the Internet for psychology. After all, the widespread expectation that the Internet would introduce rapid social transformations was based on established understandings of personality and self, relationships and interactions, groups and communities. That the Internet would transform these seemed inevitable, given what we understood about them: in fact, as demonstrated in these chapters, the Internet can be used successfully to achieve intimacy, relationship formation, social influence or the formation of communities. The very possibility of such uses undermines existing theories that assume that physical co-location and direct visual contact are necessary for such things to occur. Given the prominence of implicit and explicit assumptions that there is a 'magic touch' and that 'the eyes have it', this increasingly necessitates a reconsideration of established thinking.

Examples of this can be found in the Chapter 9 by Caroline Haythornthwaite, which re-examines traditional conceptions of community, making the case that the online community is no more than an extension of existing and long-emerging community practices. Andrea Chester and

Di Bretherton make similar points in Chapter 15 in discussing impression formation. Regardless of the medium, they argue that many of the same psychological processes occur.

A different set of chapters focuses on the ways that the Internet doesn't just reapply a psychological process to a new context – instead, it transforms what it means to be a member of a group or community or even what it means to be 'ourselves'. For instance, in Chapter 14 Katelyn McKenna argues that CMC may enable people to be their 'true selves' – something not possible in many face-to-face situations, while in Chapter 20 Azy Barak argues that the Internet might encourage the experience of 'phantom emotions' – seemingly real experiences that have little or no foundation in reality.

The final section of the handbook, which focuses primarily on the use of the Internet as a research tool, illustrates perfectly these shared themes and approaches. The Internet enables researchers to do things simply not possible using more traditional methods – Ulf-Detirich Reips shows this for Internet-based experiments in Chapter 24, Michael Birnbaum for Internet-based study designs in Chapter 25, and Anja Göritz for online panels in Chapter 30. At the same time, many of the same processes, concerns and considerations of face-to-face research also exist online, for example in qualitative research and multimethod approaches (Claire Hewson, Chapter 26), regarding context effects in surveys (Jolene Smyth, Don Dillman and Leah Christian, Chapter 27), and in research ethics (Charles Ess, Chapter 31). Using a different medium may have an impact on people's behaviour and the results of personality research using the Internet, as discussed in Chapter 28 by Tom Buchanan. Many, sometimes simple, issues need to be observed and learned about in Internet-based research, even just on the level of the technologies involved in the Internet (William Schmidt, Chapter 29).

Of course, part of the problem is that there is no one 'Internet', no single effect of the Internet on behaviour, and no simple link between an individual and how they choose to use the Internet. Instead, we shape the Internet in accordance with our needs and desires, and in turn the Internet shapes us. Some examples of this are examined in Chapter 23 by Diane Schiano and colleagues on the use of mobile technology,

Chapter 19, by Jeffrey Hancock on deception and Karen Douglas (Chapter 11) on hate groups and the chapters on trust and interactivity. We hope that this Handbook begins the process of consolidating our understanding of how these myriad interactions operate.

Acknowledgements

We are grateful to Martin Baum and Carol Maxwell of Oxford University Press for their support of this project, and for the anonymous reviewers of the original proposal for their valuable comments and insights. We are also indebted to our many colleagues who reviewed the chapters of this book, including Zachary Birchmeier, Pam Briggs, Scott Caplan, Nicola Döring, Waldemar Dzeyk, Jan Eichstaedt, Gunther Eysenbach, Immo Fritsche, Mark Griffiths, Dirk Heerwegh, Thomas Koenig, Yuliang Liu, Germán Loewe, David Nicholas, Norbert Schwarz, S.Shyam Sundar, Rhonda Swickert, Tracy Tuten Ryan, Monica Whitty, and others who wish to remain anonymous.

Adam Joinson is Senior Lecturer of Information Systems at the School of Management at the University of Bath. His research interests include computer-mediated communication, e-social science, privacy and disinhibition online. He is the author of *Understanding the Psychology of Internet Behavior* (2003, Palgrave), *Truth, Lies and Trust on the Internet* (with Monica Whitty, Psychology Press, 2007), and has published over 50 journal articles, book chapters and conference proceedings in the field.

Katelyn Y. A. McKenna (Yael Kaynan) is a Senior Lecturer at Ben-Gurion University of the Negev and at The Interdisciplinary Center Herzliya in the Department of Communication. Her research interests are in the areas of relationship cognition, the self, and social identity, particularly in terms of their applicability to Internet interactions.

Tom Postmes is Professor of Communication and Social Psychology at the University of Exeter. His research interests are group processes and communication, in particular on the topics of social influence, the formation of group norms, collective action, intergroup conflict, perceptions of discrimination and oppression. His work has been published in over 40 journal articles, more than a dozen book chapters and several other publications.

Ulf-Dietrich Reips is an Assistant Professor in the Department of Psychology, University of Zurich. Reips' research interests include methods, tools, and techniques of Internet-based research, in particular Internet-based experimenting, e-/i-learning and -teaching, online privacy and self-disclosure, Internet-based data mining and log file analysis, cognition, social psychology, and e-health. Reips is founding editor of the *International Journal of Internet Science*, and has published over 60 journal articles, book chapters and books in the field, including *Dimensions of Internet Science* (with Michael Bosnjak, 2001) and *Online Social Sciences* (with Bernard Batinic and Michael Bosnjak, 2002).

PART 1

Interaction and Interactivity

CHAPTER 2

Social interaction and the Internet

A comparative analysis of surveys in the US and Britain

Ronald E. Rice, Adrian Shepherd, William H. Dutton and James E. Katz

The Internet has been a major social and technical innovation, ranging from household use of the Web for electronic messaging to accessing information and operating one's financial affairs. This worldwide multimedia computer and transmission network of networks is altering access to important intellectual resources and dramatically changing lives and social arrangements in many places around the world. In the decade since the Internet became available to both public and commercial interests and was made much more accessible through the Web and browsers, nearly two-thirds of the adult population in the US and over half the adult population in Britain has used the Internet to seek and receive information and communicate with others both known and unknown (Rice and Katz 2003). This chapter examines a central question raised by this growth in Internet use: is Internet use associated with increased or decreased social interaction?

First, the chapter reviews relevant prior literature and research on the digital divide in general and the relationships of Internet use with social interaction. This overview grounds four research questions, namely what can be learned by: comparing users and non-users; comparing users with more and less offline interpersonal and mediated social interaction; assessing changes in social networks; and comparing US and British Internet users. We then identify possible answers to these questions based on results from national surveys in the US in 1995 and 2000 and Britain in 2003.

The Internet, digital divides and social interaction

Digital divides

The 'digital divide' is a critical social issue because it tends to represent and reinforce socio-economic divides, including social interaction.

Individuals can participate in, or be excluded from, networks of information and communication by virtue of which side of the digital divide they are on (Katz and Aspden 1997a, b, 1998; Rice *et al.* 2001). In the US, racial and sex differences in access to the Internet have diminished, and most remaining differences can be explained by other basic demographic/socio-economic factors such as income, age, education and, in the case of race, awareness of the Internet (Hoffman 1998; Katz and Aspden 1997b, 1998; Katz and Rice 2002; Net users 2001; NTIA 2002; Walsh *et al.* 2001). Still, as a 2002 NTIA report shows, there is a persistent large and in some cases, increasing, disparity (The Children's Partnership 2002). More complex forms of divide exist, such as those based on conceptualizations of access (Liff and Shepherd 2004), kinds of usage (Net users 2001), differences in use by sex within ethnic groups (Shade 2004) or by race within low-income groups (Mossberger *et al.* 2003), by those with sight, hearing or mobility disabilities (NTIA 2002) and across national boundaries (Anderson and Tracey 2002: 144–146; Chen *et al.* 2002: 84; Rose 2004). Thus any study of Internet use and social interaction must control for socio-demographic influences on usage.

Internet and social interaction

Considerable significance has been accorded to the question of whether Internet use is associated with more, or less, social interaction, in various forms (*American Behavioral Scientist* 2001; DiMaggio *et al.* 2001; Rice 2002; Wellman and Haythornthwaite 2002). Social interaction issues are particularly significant because they are central to notions of how the Internet might reconfigure access to information, people, services and technologies, such as in changing personal relationships with family and friends (Dutton 1999, 2004). This may affect social capital through decreased or increased social interaction with others. Thus there is a need to understand in what ways, within different contexts, the Internet might reduce, maintain or increase current forms of social interaction and expression, or foster new forms. (Hiltz and Turoff 1995; Parks and Floyd 1996; Turkle 1996).

On the one hand, some researchers have argued that information and communication technologies (ICTs) are inherently impersonal and mediating and enable deception and misinformation, which could undermine their role in enabling the formation of meaningful interpersonal relationships (Stoll 1995; Turkle 1996). From this perspective, the Internet detracts from meaningful real-world communities and reduces social capital (Beniger 1987; Gergen 1991; Kiesler *et al.* 1984; Nie 2001), for example because spending more time on the Internet 'crowds out' more meaningful relationships and higher quality communications and decreases meaningful social interaction and social integration (Kraut *et al.* 1998; Selnow 1994; Putnam 2000). There is some evidence that Internet use is associated with social withdrawal, such as the way it can provide some protection from anxiety by those who are shy (Birnie and Horvath 2002). Riphagen and Kanfer's (1997) survey showed that email users and non-users had similar numbers of relationships, but users had more distant relationships, suggesting those came at the cost of local interactions.

The Carnegie-Mellon HomeNet study (Kraut *et al.* 1998) provided one of the earliest quantitative field surveys of Internet use which found negative effects of Internet use on social interaction. They recruited 96 volunteer families and provided them with computers and dial-up Internet access and then surveyed these novice users for three years. At the midpoint, those who used the Internet most reported lower levels of family face-to-face communication and interaction in social circles, as well as greater loneliness, depression and stress. The authors concluded that Internet use displaces interactions with close social ties. Nie and Hillygus (2002) also found, through a cross-sectional time diary study, that interactions with family members decrease with more Internet use.

However, others have argued that yet another context for social interaction, creativity and emotional and informational support, is provided by the Internet, including through the use of discussion lists and newsgroups; health and psychological support groups; Internet Relay Chats; Multi-User Dungeons (MUDs) and online dating services (Baym 1995; Katz and Rice 2002; Matei and Ball-Rokeach 2001; Rice 1987a, b; Rice 2001). Partially, this is due to the increased opportunities to interact with both known and unknown others based on similar interests, networks of relationships and mere chance. For example, looking at 1995 data, Katz and Aspden (1997a), in apparently the first national random study of users and non-users, found that there was no social deficit for users compared to non-users (these data are analysed along with several other series in this chapter). Looking at this subject but with different data several years later, Robinson et al. (2000) concluded that Internet users engage in more telephone and face-to-face communication with friends and family than non-users. Also, to the degree that email and Internet communication masks some interpersonal behaviours and cues, it may well foster more honest and insightful online friendships (McKenna and Bargh 2002). The Internet may enable diverse people to share information, interests and support (Kavanaugh and Patterson 2001; Sullivan et al. 2002; Wellman et al. 2001), but also reconfigure patterns of communication, reshaping not only who people know and communicate with but also how they access services and other technologies (Dutton 1999, 2004; Rheingold 1993). People who move can use the Internet to maintain their prior social relationships and associated social support and consequent psychological well-being, as well as to communicate with others in the new location to reduce uncertainty (Shklovski et al. 2005). However, Shklovski et al. suggest that using the Internet both to maintain those prior relationships and for entertainment to escape the stress from moving may delay developing new relationships, thereby leading to lower psychological well-being.

Indeed, those who communicate more and have broader social networks are likely to use the Internet for the same purposes: Birnie and Horvath's (2002) survey of undergraduates found that frequency and intimacy of Internet communication were positively associated with frequency and intimacy of face-to-face and telephone communication. A poll conducted by the Pew Research Center for the Pew Internet and American Life Project (2000) reported that Internet users indicated email had improved their social and kinship connections and more so for those who had used the Internet longer and more frequently. Indeed, there were fewer social isolates among users than non-users and users had a greater number of recent social contacts and greater access to social support. Parks and Floyd (1996) and Parks and Roberts (1998) found evidence of intimate and well-developed online relationships, often leading to real-world interactions.

Boase et al. (2006) assessed this fundamental question in a somewhat different way through a Pew nationally representative survey in 2004 about the role of the Internet and social ties. This study distinguished two types of relations: 'core ties' (very close relationships involving frequent contact, important matters, or help) and 'significant ties' (lower levels of these relationships). People who keep in contact with most of their core ties via email also keep in touch with 25 per cent more of their core ties by telephone than non-emailers and people who keep in contact with most of their significant ties via email also keep in touch with 50 per cent more by in-person contact. Controlling for other factors, such as income, education, network size, or more diverse occupational networks, Internet users were also more likely to get help on up to eight issues from their core as well as significant ties (such as in caring for someone with a major illness, finding a new place to live, changing jobs, deciding for whom to vote, etc.) compared to non-users and for more issues. Further, Internet users have more significant ties (though not more core ties) and 31 per cent report that using the Internet increased the number of their significant ties and 28 per cent said core ties increased. They conclude that Internet use supplements and complements in-person and telephone communication; helps maintain social networks including those who do not live nearby; allows users to seek medical, financial, or other support from others in their networks; and shifts major sources of social capital from a physical community to diverse people and resources.

Later evidence from the HomeNet study (Kraut et al. 2002) shifted from its initial conclusion that heavy Internet use caused isolation and depression to stating that, after three years, the heaviest Internet users were happier and had more social contacts, including increased social interaction with family members increased. Likewise, Gershuny's (2002) study of parents' and kids' diaries from 1,000 randomly chosen households concluded that Internet users were involved in as much social activity as non-users and that new users actually increased the time they devoted to social and leisure activities. Howard's (2004) analysis of the Pew Internet and American Life Project surveys found that people who had more experience using the Internet were more likely to have called a friend or relative 'yesterday' just to talk and also turn to more people for help. In addition, controlling for demographic variables, Internet experience was significantly associated with perceived increases in those users' connection with friends and family and their ability to meet new people (Howard 2004: 15–16).

Copher, Kanfer and Walker's (2002) analysis of a week's worth of around-the-clock communication diaries by 45 community leaders in a US found that 'heavy' email users had more communication, a higher percentage of communication and spent more time communicating than 'light' users. There was little difference in proportionate use of each of the other communication media mentioned, with exceptions such as slightly less phone use or, as also found in the World Internet Project, less television watching (Dutton and Shepherd 2003). Boneva et al. (2001) looked specifically at gender differences in relationships between Internet use and social interaction (among a small sample from Pittsburgh), which seem to reflect some gender differences in interpersonal communication. For example, women tend to use email to support family relationships (elderly parents, siblings, extended family), keep in touch with distant people and enjoy email more than do men for such purposes. The paradox here is that the authors conclude that email better fits women's 'expressive style,' involving 'emotional intimacy and sharing of personal information' not usually considered as indicators of isolation, depression and depersonalization attributed to Internet use.

A meta-research project reviewed the results of 16 studies involving 35,578 respondents and 48 relationships between Internet use and social involvement (Shklovski et al. 2006; IT & Society 1(1)). Shklovski et al. concluded that Internet use is not associated with social interaction with family members and found contradictory evidence concerning social interaction with friends. Of 74 relationships examined 10 (from 5 studies) were significantly positive (e.g., increased time with friends, face-to-face communication) and 12 (from 6 studies) were significantly negative (e.g., decreased time with family, social visits). They argue that research design contributes somewhat to different results, with cross-sectional studies sometimes indicating decreased interactions with friends while longitudinal studies sometimes show greater interactions with friends. Additional influences on divergent findings include different measures for Internet use (for instance, system logs of actual use vs. self-report; frequency, breadth, or history of use; activities and information searching vs. communication) and for social interaction (for instance, friends vs. family).

For example, the Nie and the HomeNet studies have been criticized for biased samples, atypical technology and possibly intrusive interventions. When LaRose et al. (2001) analysed a survey replication of the HomeNet data with different causal assumptions, they found no direct influence of Internet use on depression. Rather, that relationship was mediated by self-efficacy and expectations of experiencing stressful situations on the Internet and email was used to communicate with close associates to obtain social support which helped to reduce depression. Thus, they argue, increased depression among the novice users in the HomeNet study arose because they did not have enough self-efficacy to handle sufficiently the stresses of using the new technology in their home. Across all 48 relationships (using effect sizes, but removing three outliers all from one six-hour diary study), there was no statistically significant relationship between Internet use and social interaction. Relationships involving social interaction with friends were less positive than with unspecified close relationships but, when using hierarchical linear modelling to control for whether multiple effect sizes come from the same study, there was a slight positive association of Internet use and social interactions with friends. Longitudinal design differed from survey design only by tending to find positive effects with friends and none with others (and no influence on family interactions). The authors interpret all these results as the effect of reducing costs and inconvenience of communicating with friends, or the Internet playing a role as a sort of reminder of friendships outside of home or work; in both cases, family relationships are more stable, enduring and available).

They also argue that longitudinal studies have greater validity in asserting causal influences of Internet use on social interaction and that personality factors should be included in more such studies, as baseline controls for, moderators of and direct influences on Internet use and social interaction. Shklovski *et al.* (2004) followed their own advice and analysed year-long panel data (2000 and 2001) from the Pew Internet and American Life Project that included measures of social support and extroversion for 1,501 respondents (42 per cent of the 2000 sample of 3,533). Considering only the 2001 data, family visits, telephone calls and email were all moderately intercorrelated, which could be interpreted as Internet use positively influencing physical and mediated social interaction, but the longitudinal analysis found that Internet use is related to decreases in visiting family the prior day (with greater effects for more extroverted users). Among the 493 relevant respondents, telephone calls increase visits, visits increase email and email does not influence either phone or visits. Overall, then, Internet use led to decreased family visits, but no changes in phoning friends and family, or perceived social support – regardless of the three measures of Internet use – and email is a weaker form of social interaction than face-to-face visits or telephone calls. Methodologically, the meta-analysis and this longitudinal analysis question both causal claims and directional results of cross-sectional studies.

Physical communities and Internet use

In line with this thesis, some studies have analysed how community access to the Internet is associated with social interaction measures such as network density, visits or mediated communication with friends and family (Wellman *et al.* 2001). The Camfield Estates–MIT Creating Community Connections Project applied community technology and community-building concepts to 80 new low to moderate income housing units in the Roxbury area of Boston (Pinkett and O'Bryant 2003). In late 2000, the project provided each family who had at least one member complete an introductory course with a home computer which had high-speed connectivity and the community with a technology center and community web content. After less than one year, for those 26 families who took the introductory course and participated in both surveys, the following changes in social interaction were found: strengthened and expanded local ties (visiting others' homes, talking to others, recognition of others, emailing other residents, phoning other residents, greater connection to friends and family in the area); being better informed about local activities, including increased communication flow in the development (such as calendars of events and discussion forums); increased motivation to be informed locally, nationally and internationally and increased confidence in themselves and their ability to learn (transition to a sense of competency and activeness and awareness of skills and abilities of the community).

A three-year multimethod study of high-speed access to the Internet in a new wired suburb in Toronto also found that, over time, more neighbours were known and chatted with (although they were more geographically dispersed around the suburb) and an increase in neighbourhood interaction, discussion and mobilization around local issues increased (Hampton and Wellman 2003). Of the 109 housing units, only 64 were connected (due to miscommunication with the developers and insufficient developer resources) and 46 of those homes participated in the study. A natural control group of 21 non-connected households was also studied, enabling the researchers to show that these changes were associated with being among the wired participants. Controlling for gender, age, education and length of residence, being wired still showed increased presence of weak ties, in terms of having being 'recognized' and 'talked with' other community members. This increased social interaction also shaped other social behaviour, such as enabling the community to pressure the developer to fix various problems.

The Internet and social interaction in the US and Britain

The research questions addressed

The kind of social research on the Internet summarized above identifies four general questions related to the central issue of whether Internet use is associated with increased social isolation or interaction:

1. To what extent are Internet users, compared to non-users, more likely to engage in social interaction?

2. Do people with greater offline interpersonal and mediated social interaction engage in greater online social interaction?

3. Do Internet users reconfigure their social networks in more complex ways? And

4. Do these relationships differ between US and British Internet users?

The study reported below focuses on a small set of social interaction measures (offline interpersonal interaction, offline mediated inter-action and online interaction) in considering how Internet use enables people to reconfigure the networks in which they interact, compares results across time (but without using longitudi-nal, panel data) and compares results across two English-speaking countries with similar Internet adoption rates.

The surveys, sample and analyses

This comparative study analyses two datasets, one from the US and one from Britain. These included many of the same or similar measures, thus allowing for a cross-national comparison of relationships (detailed descriptive and correla-tion tables are available from the authors). The US data source is the Syntopia project, which has compared Internet users to non-users (and former users, or dropouts) throughout the formative years of the Internet (1995–1997 and 2000) using nationally representative random-digit telephone dialling surveys of US adults (Katz and Rice 2002). The present analyses use data from 1995 and 2000, as those two surveys included measures of social interaction.

The second data source is the 2003 Oxford Internet Survey (OxIS) carried out by the Oxford Internet Institute. This multi-stage random sam-ple of Britons aged 14 and older interviewed par-ticipants face to face at their residences, between May 23 and June 28 of 2003 (Rose 2003). First, a random sample of 175 paired Enumeration Districts (EDs) with a combined population of 60

or more, which are stratified and proportional within the main governmental regions, were selected by random start and fixed sampling interval from a list of EDs ordered by income. Within each ED, a random sample of 10 addresses was selected from the British Postal Address File. Of the 3,077 addresses visited 2030 (66 per cent) provided a complete interview, in almost all cases by the available resident with the next birthday. Each potential interview participant was told that 1 British pound would be con-tributed to the Red Cross for each successful interview.

Internet users were 8.1 per cent of the US sample ($n = 2500$) in 1995 and 59.7 per cent in 2000 ($n = 1305$) and 59.3 per cent of the British 2003 sample ($n = 2025$). Of the US respon-dents, 7.8 per cent of were dropouts in 1995 and 10.5 per cent in 2000, compared with 6.0 per cent of the British respondents. Anderson and Tracey (2002) reported a similar level of dropouts, as 5.6 per cent of their sample of 1,075 UK respon-dents had stopped their Internet connection between 1999 and 2000 (see also Katz and Aspden 1998; Katz and Rice 2002).

The analyses are based on the most general and conservative approach to coding, using three main approaches. First, by dichotomizing both continuous and categorical variables in order to enable comparisons both across time and across the US and Britain, as well as with other surveys. Although this was at the cost of loss of variance and an inability to test for curvilinear relationships, appropriate binary logistic regression was used. Secondly, through including relevant socio-demographic and indi-vidual control variables. Thirdly, using either chi-square associations for cross-tabulation tables or logistic binary regressions for multivariate analyses.

Internet users are defined here as those who were currently (as of the survey dates) using the Internet; thus dropouts are not included. We also asked users the year they started using the Internet, enabling us to analyse users both as of the year the survey was conducted, as well as how experienced or 'veteran' (as opposed to 'recent') they were. And we asked them to rate their expertise. Thus there are three primary Internet usage measures: non-user/user;

recent/veteran (recent, since 1997, vs. long-term, before 1997); and novice/expert.

Conceptualizations of social interaction

Social interaction is a broad concept, with many different components. These surveys incorporated a small set of variables that represent three main dimensions of social interaction: offline interpersonal; offline mediated; and online interaction. In addition, a few individual traits that might influence general social interaction were included, such as sense of belonging, shyness and innovativeness (see Table 2.1) (Katz and Aspden 1997a; Kraut *et al.* 1998; McKenna and Bargh 2000; Birnie and Horvath 2002).

Socio-demographic aspects of the digital divide in the US and Britain

In 1995, significant unique (from multiple logistic binary regressions) demographic associations with Internet use in the US were: male, younger, higher income and higher education (16 per cent variance explained, 90 per cent of the 1651 cases correctly predicted). In 2000, significant unique explanations of usage were: younger, higher income and higher education (46 per cent variance, 80.4 per cent of 922 cases correctly predicted). In the 2003 British sample, the significant unique predictors of Internet usage were: male, younger, higher socio-economic status and a higher level of education (explaining 37 per cent variance and 75.2 per cent of 2,030 cases correctly predicted). Descriptive analyses of changes in the US data from 1995 to 2000 and in the cohort data from all three surveys show that the digital divide is being narrowed, if not bridged, on sex, age, household income, education and race.

Divides do remain. Many people are not online and both the US and British surveys identify a noticeable percentage of respondents who are Internet dropouts. However, as the digital divide narrows, more of the public in both countries are able to use the Internet, thus highlighting both positive and negative potential consequences for social interaction.

The US case

Offline interpersonal social interaction

The 1995 survey asked interviewees about two kinds of interpersonal social interaction: how many of their 10 closest neighbours they know (dichotomized at six or more) and how many times in the last week did you meet with friends (dichotomized at three or more).

In 1995, long-term and recent Internet users were more likely to know fewer of their 10 closest neighbours. Internet users know fewer of their 10 closest neighbours (44.0 per cent knew 6 or more) than do those who have never used the Internet (52.0 per cent) (chi-square = 4.6, $p < 0.05$). Of non-users who had not heard of the Internet, 37 per cent reported knowing the 10 people living closest to their home and 31 per cent reported knowing 4–9 of the 10 closest people. Similarly, of non-users who had heard of the Internet, 33 per cent reported knowing the 10 closest people and 36 per cent knowing 4–9 of the 10 closest people. Former users reported knowing slightly fewer neighbours (28 per cent reported knowing the 10 closest people and 42 per cent knowing 4–9 of the 10 closest people). They were followed by long-time users (28 per cent reported knowing the 10 closest people and 37 per cent knowing 4–9 of the 10 closest people). Recent users reported knowing the fewest neighbours (21 per cent reported knowing the 10 closest people and 43 per cent knowing 4–9 of the 10 closest people). These results imply that users' social communities are larger and more physically dispersed than non-users'.

However, Internet use and longer-term use are both associated with more, not less, interpersonal social interaction with friends. Internet users meet with friends more (71.0 per cent at least three times per week) than do non-users (58.5 per cent) (chi-square = 11.7, $p < 0.001$). In the week prior to the 1995 survey, 38 per cent of long-time users (having adopted the Internet more than a year before) met 1–3 times with friends and 54 per cent met four or more times. Of recent users, 40 per cent met 1–3 times with friends and 48 per cent met four or more times. Nearly three-quarters (71 per cent) of current users had met with friends at least three times in

Table 2.1 Indicators of social interaction: offline interpersonal interaction, offline mediated interaction, online interaction and controls

Surveys	Offline social interaction		Online social interaction	Controls
	Interpersonal	Mediated	Internet	Sociability, media use and innovativeness
US 1995	Know how many of 10 closest neighbours No. of times met with friend in past week $U+$ Internet affect time spent with friends and family	Letters written weekly Phone calls weekly	Contacted family members online $V+$ Member of online community $V+$ Made online friend Met person they first knew online	Innovativeness (mean of 'like to do things that are a little dangerous' and 'first among friends to go out and try a new thing'; $\alpha = 0.65$ 1–5) $V+$
US 2000		Letters written weekly Phone calls weekly	Contacted family members online Member of online community $E+$ Made online friend $E+$ Met person first knew online $V+ E+$	Belonging (mean of 'there are people you feel close to,' and 'you feel part of a group of friends'; $\alpha = 0.56$ 1–5) $U+ V+$ Like listening to radio Like watching TV Like reading newspaper (mean for news, for entertainment; $\alpha = 0.56$ 1–5)
Britain 2003	Meet friends/family who live 'close but not within walking distance' $U-$ or 'in another country or city' People outside your household you can confide in Time spent meeting with friends	Write to friends/ family who live 'close but not within walking distance' or 'in another country or city' $U-$ Phone friends/family who live 'close but not within walking distance' or 'in another country or city'	Email friends/family who live 'close but not within walking distance' $V+ E+$ or 'in another country or city' $V+ E+$	Shyness (I am a shy person 1–2) $U-$ Innovativeness (when new services are invented it is a good idea to try them 1–5) $U+$

Note: Summary multivariate Internet influences: U = Internet usage; V = Veteran users; E = expert users; $+$ = positive association; $-$ = negative association.

the past week compared to 58.5 per cent for those who had never used the Internet.

In an overall logistic regression predicting Internet usage (Nagelkerke R-sq = 0.11, chi-square = 86.7, $p < 0.001$), knowing 10 closest neighbours became marginally non-significant (beta = –0.31, $p = 0.07$), but the number of times they get together with friends remained significant (beta = 0.46, $p < 0.01$) when the significant influences of education (beta = 0.94, $p < 0.001$), income (0.77, $p < 0.001$) and innovativeness (0.62, $p < 0.001$) were controlled (see left side of Table 2.2, for 1995).

Offline mediated social interaction

In 1995, both users and non-users were asked about their offline mediated social interaction. There was no difference in the number of letters written weekly (54.3 per cent of users and 52.3 per cent of non-users reported writing at least one) but users made significantly more phone calls weekly (82.9 per cent making more than 10, vs. 72.8 per cent for non-users, chi-square = 9.6, $p < 0.01$). In 2000, only users were asked these two questions: 33.2 per cent had written at least one letter and 60.4 per cent had made 10 or more phone calls, in the last week. For letter writing, there were no significant differences between recent Internet users (those who began using in the year prior to the respective survey) vs. long-term users and in novices vs. those with at least average Internet expertise. For telephone calling, long-term users did make more calls (92.0 per cent vs. 79.9 per cent), but there was no difference between novice and expert users.

The left side of Table 2.2 provides logistic regressions predicting offline mediated social interaction (letters, phone calls) for 1995 and 2000, showing any significant influences from demographic factors or the appropriate kinds of Internet usage measures. In the overall logistic regressions for 1995, letter writing was not significantly explained by Internet usage, after controlling for the significant influences of greater education and being male. Making more phone calls was no longer explained by Internet usage, once the significant influences of income and age are taken into account. In the overall logistic regression for 2000, there were no significant influences of veteran usage or Internet expertise

on letter writing, after the significant influences of sex and work status were controlled. And there were no significant influences of veteran usage or expertise on telephone calls after controlling for the significant influence of younger age.

Online social interaction

Internet users were asked about the extent of four kinds of online social interaction: contacting family members online, being a member of at least one online community, making a friend through online interaction, or physically meeting a person (not necessarily a friend) whom they had met first online. All of these, except making an online friend, were lower in 2000. This possibly indicates that later adopters are more likely to be drawn to the Internet for informational than interaction purposes.

Communicating with family members online

In 1995, 42 per cent of users indicated they had contacted family members online, compared to 22.6 per cent in 2000. In 1995, longer-term users were much more likely than recent users to do so (56.0 vs. 26.7 per cent), but level of expertise made no difference. In the overall logistic model, the influence of being a long-term user persisted after controlling for the significant influence of greater income. In the 2000 survey, a smaller proportion of users (20.5 per cent) reported contacting family members online at least several times a year, but there were no differences by recent or long-term status or level of expertise. The overall logistic regression model was not significant.

Member of online communities

Membership in online communities declined as a percentage of users between 1995 and 2000. In the 1995 survey 25.5 per cent of users reported being a member of at least one Internet community. This percentage was significantly higher (48.0 per cent) among long-term users vs. recent users (18.0 per cent) and for those with at least average expertise (33.3 per cent) vs. novices (16.8 per cent). This difference persisted in the overall regression, as shown in the right-hand side of Table 2.2. In 2000, a smaller proportion of users (10.4 per cent) reported being a member of at least one online community. There were significantly more long-term users

Table 2.2 Logistic regressions explaining offline media use and online interactions, US 1995 and 2000

| 1995 | Users and non-users | | | | Users only | | | | | |
| | Letters weekly | | Phone calls weekly | | Contact family members online | | Member of Internet community | | Know Internet-only friends | |
	B	Exp (B)	B	Exp (B)	B	Exp (B)	B	Exp (B)	B	Exp (B)
Education 0 < BA 1 >= BA	0.43**	1.5								
Income 0 <35K 1 >35K			0.61**	1.8	1.3**	3.6				
Sex 0 = M 1 = F	-0.36***	0.70								
Age 0 < 40 1 > 40			-0.47***	0.62						
Race 0 = AA 1 = WnonH									-1.5*	0.22
User 0 = non 1 = user	0.04	1.0	0.32	1.4	–		–		–	
Veteran user 0 = recent user 1 = long-term	–		–		1. ***	3.6	1.4***	4.2	-0.20	0.82
Expert 0 = novice 1 = more expert	–		–		–					
Chi-sq	30.8***		41.5***		23.9***		16.5***		4.7***	
−2log likelihood	2609		1688		191		210		121	

	Nagelkerke R-sq	Correctly assigned	N
	0.02	56%	1908
	0.04	75%	1539
	0.19	71%	166
	0.12	75%	200
	0.05	89%	179

	Users and non-users				Users only					
2000	Letters Weekly		Phone calls weekly		Contact family members online		Member of Internet community		Know Internet-only friends	
	B	Exp (B)	B	Exp (B)	B	Exp (B)	B	Exp (B)	B	Exp (B)
Education 0 < BA 1 > = BA									−0.54**	0.59
Sex 0 = M 1 = F	0.39**	1.48	0.29***	1.33						
Age 0 < 40 1 > 40			−0.83***	0.44						
Work 1 = full time 2 = other	0.34*	1.4								
Children 0 = none 1 = any										
User 0 = none 1 = user	—		—		—		—		—	
Veteran user 0 = recent user 1 = long-term										

Continued

Table 2.2 Logistic regressions explaining offline media use and online interactions, US 1995 and 2000 cont.

| | Users and non-users | | | | | | Users only | | | |
| | Letters Weekly | | Phone calls weekly | | Contact family members online | | Member of Internet community | | Know Internet-only friends | |
2000	B	Exp (B)	B	Exp (B)	B	Exp (B)	B	Exp (B)	B	Exp (B)
1 = more expert										
Expert 0 = novice	–	–	–	–			1.2**	3.2	1.3***	3.6
Chi-sq		16.4***				41.8***	ns		17.8****	20.8***
−2log likelihood		1256		1270				547		660
Nagelkerke R-sq		0.02		0.06				0.04		0.04
Correctly assigned		66.7%		61.9%				89.6%		86.2%
N		1000		976		1405		800		850

* p < 0.05; ** p < 0.01; *** p < 0.001.

(11.7 vs. 5.8 per cent for recent users) and those with greater expertise (11.8 vs. 3.9 per cent). In the overall logistic regression, only having greater Internet expertise persisted as an influence on belonging to online communities.

Developing online friendships

In 1995 11.5 per cent and in 2000 13.8 per cent, of users who responded to the question had established friendships via the Internet, presumably people they would not otherwise meet. In 1995, there were no significant differences between recent and long-term users, or between novices and those with more expertise. In the overall regression (right-hand side of Table 2.2), the only significant influence was being African-American. In 2000, however, those with greater Internet expertise were significantly more likely to have developed at least one online friendship (15.7 vs. 5.2 per cent for novices) and this difference persisted in the overall regression after controlling for the significant influence of having less education.

Meeting online friends or acquaintances

In 1995 17 per cent of users who responded to the question reported that they had met face-to-face at least one of the friends they had first met online, with no significant differences by level of usage or experience. In 2000 10.1 per cent of users met an Internet acquaintance (in 2000, the question was not about online friends, but simply anyone they had met first online); they were more likely to do so if they were a long-term (11.4 vs. 5.8 per cent) or more expert user (11.6 vs. 3.2 per cent). Of the 67 people responding to the question asking about whether the most recent meeting with someone they had first met online was a positive experience, 47.8 per cent strongly agreed, 35.8 per cent agreed 10.4 per cent were neutral, 4.5 per cent disagreed and 1.5 per cent strongly disagreed. While the relevant subsample size is too small to assess overall influences on meeting Internet acquaintances, nearly 85 per cent felt it was a positive experience.

Offline interaction associations with online social interaction in 1995

We examined whether those who are more sociable offline are also more sociable online.

With the 1995 survey, we were able to test for associations between two indicators of offline interpersonal social interaction (the number of their 10 closest neighbours the respondent knew and the number of times the respondent got together with friends in the prior week) and three measures of online interaction (contacting family members online; membership in online communities; and developing friendships with people met only on the Internet). In overall logistic regressions, neither of the two forms of offline social interaction was significantly associated with any of the three forms of online social interaction, after controlling for significant demographic influences and after including the two usage measures (recent vs. long-term user and novice vs. more expert user). Additionally, in 1995, 88 per cent of both long-time and recent users felt that use of the Internet did not affect the time they spent with friends and family face-to-face or by phone. The same proportion of users (6 per cent) reported they spent more time with friends and family face-to-face or by phone as the percentage reporting that they spent less time. This reveals that the 1995 US data indicates that engaging in more online social interaction is not related to engaging in more offline social interaction in general.

Offline interaction associations with online social interaction in 2000

The 2000 survey contained some items not on the 1995 survey, enabling us to control for some individual factors related to social interaction and media use. One set of items represented 'belonging' (the mean of 'There are people you feel close to' and 'You feel part of a group of friends'). A related sociability variable (intro-version/extroversion), was also measured, but played no significant bivariate or multivariate role, so is not reported here. The second set of items represented media use (the extent to which respondents liked listening to the radio, or liked watching TV) and two items about liking to read the newspaper ('to find out what is going on' and for 'entertainment') that were combined into a mean scale. Cross-tabulations indicated that Internet users were more likely to have a greater sense of 'belonging', especially for long-term users but not for expert users; to be less interested in watching TV; and to like listening to the radio more. When controlling for the significant socio-demographic influences of age (younger – standardized $beta = -1.3$, $p < 0.001$), education (1.1, $p < 0.001$) and income (1.2, $p < 0.001$), the greater sense of belonging persisted as being associated with Internet use (0.46, $p < 0.05$), while the two media variables did not (overall chi-square = 150, Nagelkerke R-square = 0.27, $n = 720$).

The British case

Associations were tested between Internet usage/non-usage and four offline interpersonal mediated and mediated social interaction activities (meeting, telephoning, emailing, writing letters to friends/family) at two levels of physical proximity (either with those who are close but not within walking distance, or with those who live in another country or city). Internet users (17.9 per cent) are significantly less likely than non-users (29.9 per cent) to write letters to friends and family who live far away (chi-square = 29.7, $p < 0.001$), but are significantly (though only slightly) more likely (72.0 per cent) to actually meet with those far-away friends and family than are non-users (67.3 per cent) (chi-square = 3.7, $p < 0.05$). None of the other six measures differed by Internet usage.

Table 2.3 provides the results from the eight regressions, explaining the four interpersonal and mediated offline social interactions, nearby and far away. The significant socio-demographic influences were: sex (females were more likely to meet, phone and write nearby and phone and write far away); age (younger users were more likely to meet and phone nearby but older users more likely to write nearby and telephone far away); socio-economic status (higher status users were more likely to meet people far away); education (those with more schooling were more likely to email people far away); and employment (those not employed full-time were more likely to write to those nearby and far away). The veteran users (using the Internet more than one year) and experts (who rated their ability to use the Internet as excellent or good) were more likely to email friends and family who live close and those who live far away. There were no significant influences of veteran usage and Internet expertise in using the

telephone, meeting face-to-face, or writing letters. Generally, Internet users are less likely to meet friends or family members nearby, or write to friends or family far away. Shyness, at least in this study, is not associated with use of the Internet, but shy people are less likely to phone nearby friends or family or email those who live far away.

Internet users in Britain were more likely to have more than one person outside their household whom they can confide in (69.8 vs. 57.2 per cent for non-users, chi-square = 30.0, $p < 0.001$), spend eight hours or more meeting with friends (55.9 vs. 47.2 per cent, chi-square = 13.3, $p < 0.001$) and be more innovative (79.0 per cent agree or strongly agree vs. 47.1 per cent, chi-square = 204.0, $p < 0.001$). The two interpersonal interaction measures were found to be no longer significantly associated with Internet use in a logistic regression (chi-square = 613.5, $p < 0.001$, Nagelkerke R-square = 0.38) controlling for the significant influences of higher education, higher working class, lower age, full-time employment and innovativeness.

Summary and discussion

The evidence presented here, in particular from the specific US and British studies highlighted, suggest that, after controlling for primary socio-demographic differences relating to Internet use and some indicators of sociability and innovativeness, Internet use is associated with some increased offline interpersonal interaction (meeting friends) but not with traditional offline mediated interaction (letters, telephone calls), as well as with online social interaction (contacting or emailing friends or family) including some new forms (being a member of online communities, making friends online).

Of course, there are other factors that could and should be examined to fully understand patterns of social interaction. This is empirically suggested in that few of the analyses explained much variance. It is also theoretically likely, in that research can identify many additional factors, such as personality attributes, cultural preferences and use contexts (both social and technological) which influence social interaction. Moreover, it is important to note that as the US and British datasets in the current study were

Table 2.3 Logistic regressions explaining interpersonal, mediated and online social interactions, Britain 2003

	Offline interpersonal		Offline mediated				Online	
	Meet friends/family who live close but not within walking distance		Telephone friends/family who live close but not within walking distance		Write to friends/family who live close but not within walking distance		Email friends/family who live close but not within walking distance (users only)	
Variables	B	Exp (B)	B	Exp (B)	B	Exp (B)	B	Exp (B)
Education 0 < BA 1 >= BA								
Working class A, B, C1 = 0, C2, D, E = 1								
Sex 0 = M 1 = F	0.24*	1.27	0.39***	1.47	0.55***	1.74		
Age 0 = 40 1 = > 40	-0.41***	0.66	-0.37**	0.69	0.63***	1.87		
Full-time employment 0 = n 1 = y					-0.36*	0.70		
'I am a shy person' 0 = not shy 1 = shy			-0.33**	0.72				
User 0 = n 1 = y	-0.29 *	0.75	-0.21	0.81	0.17	1.19	–	–

Continued

Table 2.3 Logistic regressions explaining interpersonal, mediated and online social interactions, Britain 2003 cont.

	Offline interpersonal	Offline mediated		Online	
	Meet friends/family who live close but not within walking distance	Telephone friends/family who live close but not within walking distance	Write to friends/family who live close but not within walking distance	Email friends/family who live close but not within walking distance (users only)	
Veteran user 0 = n 1 = y	—	—	—	0.35*	1.43
Expert user 0 = n 1 = y	—	—	—	1.24***	3.47
Chi-sq	24.0***	28.8***	45.9***	42.1***	
−2log likelihood	1885	1782	1300	1100	
Nagelkerke R-sq	0.02	0.03	0.05	0.07	
Correctly assigned	60.8%	67.3%	81.3%	64.3%	
N	1415	1424	1397	855	

Variables	Offline interpersonal		Offline mediated				Online	
	Meet friends/family who live in another country or city		Telephone friends/family who live in another country or city		Write friends/family who live in another city or country		Email friends/family who live in another country or city (users only)	
	B	Exp (B)	B	Exp (B)	B	Exp (B)	B	Exp (B)
Education 0 < BA 1 > = BA	–						0.66***	1.93
Working class A, B, C1 = 0, C2, D, E = 1	0.33**	0.72						
Sex 0 = M 1 = F			0.49***	1.63	0.49***	1.63		
Age 0 = 40 1 = >40			0.37**	1.45	0.60***	1.82		
Full-time employment 0 = n 1 = y					-0.44**	0.64		
'I am a shy person' 0 = not shy 1 = shy							-0.35*	0.70
User 0 = n 1 = y	-0.02	0.99	-0.08	0.93	-0.38**	0.68	–	
Veteran user 0 = n 1 = y	–		–		–		0.43*	1.54

Continued

Table 2.3 Logistic regressions explaining interpersonal, mediated and online social interactions, Britain 2003 cont.

	Offline interpersonal	Offline mediated		Online
	Meet friends/family who live in another country or city	Telephone friends/family who live in another country or city	Write friends/family who live in another city or country	Email friends/family who live in another country or city (users only)
Expert user	–	–	–	1.05*** 2.85
0 = n 1 = y				
Chi-sq	18.0*	27.2***	80.2***	51.2***
–2log likelihood	1870	1340	1515	1211
Nagelkerke R-sq	0.02	0.03	0.08	0.07
Correctly assigned	68.6%	83.5%	78.0%	60.9%
N	1518	1424	1514	914

Note: The same analyses as above for meeting, telephone calling and writing letters were run for *Internet users only*. In none of those analyses were the Veteran user or Expert user variables significant.

* *p* < 0.05; ** *p* < 0.01; *** *p* < 0.001.

cross-sectional, no tests of causality can plausibly be performed on them. Nonetheless, this study has tested for typical biases and major competing explanations. It has done so through the use of nationally representative samples in the two countries, comparison of non-users to users, trends across time and statistical controls for socio-demographic and individual factors.

In the US, considering only unique influences that persist in multivariate regressions, Internet users tend to meet more with their friends than do non-users. Among those on the Internet, somewhat more than one in ten users have become friends with others online, have met a notable percentage of them and belong to online communities. Earlier Internet adopters in 1995 tended to engage in more online social interactions, while in 2000 those with greater Internet expertise did so. Internet users in 2000 were more likely to have a greater sense of belonging. The fundamental indicators of the digital divide (age, education and income) tended to persist and even dominate nearly all of the analyses.

The 2003 British data show that Internet users are slightly less likely to meet friends or family who live close by than are non-users, in addition to being less likely to write to friends or family who live in another city or country. This suggests that Internet users do socialize less via other media than do non-users, but only relative to these two contexts (meeting close by and writing far away). In other contexts, both veteran and expert users employ email to interact with friends and family more, both close and far away. Expert and experienced users do not use media other than the Internet less to socialize than do new users, but they do use email more to socialize. This suggests that they socialize overall more than new users, indicating that experience tends to foster more use of the Internet for social relations.

Conclusion

Key findings different from previous studies

The research reported in this chapter does not purport to be a consistent over-time or cross-cultural replication. But the significant multivariate influences summarized in Table 2.1 do provide some possible explanations in four

main areas as to the diverging results compared to prior studies.

First, there are some clear positive associations between Internet use and sociability. However, after controlling for major socio-demographic variables, most analyses show that Internet use is not associated (either positively or negatively) with offline interpersonal or mediated social interaction, which is better accounted for by the socioeconomic and demographic characteristics of users.

Secondly, there seems to be some shift over the time span covered in the US sample. In the earlier stages (1995) of Internet diffusion, earlier adopters (who had been using the Internet for at least one year at the time of the survey) were more likely to engage in more and new social interactions, such as with members of their family or through online communities. In the later stages of Internet diffusion (2000), expertise rather than experience in Internet use was the primary influence.

Thirdly, as the percentage of Internet adopters in the US in 2000 was almost exactly the same (59.7 per cent) as in the 2003 British samples (59.3 per cent), we might expect quite similar relationships. This was confirmed by the finding in both samples of a positive association between both veteran and expert usage levels with online social interaction.

Fourth, it seems that meeting with friends or family is associated in opposite directions with Internet use in certain contexts. For instance, there is a positive association in the 1995 US data but a negative connection in the 2003 British sample, indicating either adoption stage differences or national/cultural differences. However, a more consistent interpretation can be provided by integrating the related measures: of knowing one's 10 closest neighbours; meeting friends in the past week; meeting friends/family who are close; and meeting friends/family who are distant. Internet use seems to be employed to maintain or enhance more diverse and dispersed social interaction, while possibly reducing very proximate social interaction (as Mesch and Talmud 2004 found in their Israeli study). Local social capital might be reduced, while more general, kin-related, or varied social capital might be increased (Birnie and Horvath 2002; Katz and Rice 2002; Robinson, et al. 2000; Wellman et al. 2001).

Digital divides and choices reconfiguring access

Both the US and the British data show that the most important effect of the Internet is not to increase or decrease the overall level of contact in any one direction in all, or most, circumstances, but to reconfigure access. That is, it helps to change who users interact with and what medium they use to conduct that interaction, for example in relation to friends living further away or with new online friends. This is not a wholesale change in one's social relations, but a change at the margins that can significantly affect who one has access to and who one gets to know. Anecdotal and more systematic research on activities such as online dating provide vivid examples of the significance of reconfiguring access (Dutton 2004, 2005).

With respect to digital divides in the US and Britain, a simple formulation of divides, such as based on gender or race, no longer seems to hold as much explanatory power. However, there are still significant, albeit more nuanced, divides. In Britain, for example, there is some evidence of differential usage patterns and intensity when one looks beyond mere adoption of the Internet (Liff and Shepherd 2004). In the US, except for elderly women, there are few statistically significant differences by gender in Internet adoption and very few related to usage profiles (Pew Internet and American Life Project 2005). While there are divergent usage profiles by gender, similar to those in the UK, such divergences may be smaller for Internet users than they are for users of other communication technologies about which there is much less discussion concerning digital divides. These include, for instance, television content choices and viewing practices, letter writing, book reading and telephone call initiation, answering and duration (Katz 1999).

In terms of race and ethnicity, differential patterns of adoption remain. Yet such differences are not a simple matter of a so-called privileged group enjoying more access. The argument that there is a race component different from an income component in the digital divide is problematical. At least insofar as the US is concerned, there is markedly higher Internet use among those of Asian-American ethnicity (Pew Internet and American Life Project 2001), who also have the highest income of any US ethnic group as measured by the US Census Bureau (US Census Bureau 2005). Neither is it clear that all of those who are not online are being held back against their preference or are otherwise impeded. For instance, a 2005 study of 1,000 Americans who were not online shows very little interest among them in going online and thereby ending their status on the deprived side of the digital divide (Parks Associates 2006). Moreover, even the subsample of those without Internet access but who already had a PC in their household (about 1 out of 5) said they would not subscribe to the Internet regardless of the cost.

The contrast to the mobile phone is instructive (for a comparison of Internet and mobile phone adoption, see Rice and Katz [2003]). In contrast to the Internet, the poorest and least educated people in the US, Britain and the rest of the world are among the most enthusiastic adopters of the cell phone. The monthly costs of the two technologies are not much different (and may be higher for the cell phone), but the cell phone seems to better suit the needs of users with less education and lower income. In sum, those looking for data that would justify 'doing something' about reducing Internet digital divides among various social groupings will find little unalloyed support in recent data, save among the elderly. Policy might therefore better focus on shaping what Dutton and others (forthcoming) have called the 'digital choice' – generating opportunities to experience the Internet among those predisposed against, or uninterested in, the Internet (see also Compaine 2001).

Future research directions

An important aspect that should be considered regarding our research findings is that the Internet is neither a stable nor a unitary technology. Hence, the clarity of claims that can be made about the Internet's uses and consequences depart importantly from those that have historically come from studies of earlier mass and personal mediated communication systems. These earlier systems were relatively contained and uniform, such as the cinema and TV broadcasting (until the video recorder) in mass communication or the telephone (until the answering machine) and postcard in personal mediated communication. Hence, it was easier to make claims about the consequences of such reasonably consistent technologies in different places, subcultures and times. The Internet is very different in this regard: its rapid changes in functionality, integration of digital modes, accessibility and ease of user customization make it hard to generalize about its purported monadic qualities and social consequences. For example, the uses and usability profiles in the 1995 US dataset reported here are quite different from those of nearly a decade later in the UK, even though both activities may be called 'being online.' The introduction of mobile access, instant-messaging, multi-player gaming, location services, social networking, mobile digital music (iPods most typically) and multimedia sharing further blur the notion of online versus offline. In addition, the spread of modes of Internet accessibility, which now range from mobile phones to Internet cafes and schools and libraries, exacerbate the challenge of speaking about social consequences.

The ability to track one pre-selected group over time, as some researchers have done, certainly adds a new and valuable dimension to understanding in the areas examined in this chapter. However, without prior random assignment of a representative sample to conditions of being online or offline, or of heavy or light usage (and a proliferating host of other possible controls), it is not always clear that the subsequent claims of longitudinal studies are really stronger than those based on surveys that rely on comparative cross-sectional sampling over time with post hoc statistical controls. Both are needed, but what is clear from our research and that of many others is that those who are online typically do not suffer significant social interaction deficits. There are important exceptions, such as instances of heavy Internet use by social isolates, Internet addiction (Griffiths 2000) and use the Internet for deceptive and harmful purposes. Similar phenomena arise in people's use of letter-writing, telephone conversations and television programming (Katz 1999). This strongly indicates that research might usefully move away from a focus on any deterministic effect of the Internet in reducing or increasing social interaction. Instead, it might be of more value to see the Internet as a medium that can complement, and in some cases extend, social interaction (e.g. Anderson and Tracey 2002; Copher et al. 2002; Katz and Rice 2002). That is, people seem to use the Internet for many of the same purposes they participate in other forms of interaction – a syntopian perspective rather than either a dystopian or a utopian perspective (Katz and Rice 2002). Most generally, the Internet could tend to reconfigure social interaction, for better or worse (Dutton 2004, 2005). In turn, this could contribute to the transformation of who we know, who we maintain relationships with, who we meet online and offline and many other aspects central to the lives of people around the world.

Humans are social and communicative beings and are generally able to use a (still) primarily text-based computer-based communication medium like the Internet to exercise and expand that need and ability. Thus, persisting digital divides and their socio-demographic influences, also represent decreased opportunities for online as well as offline social interaction (both interpersonal and mediated), especially outside one's local network.

Author's note

An earlier version of this chapter was presented at the Association of Internet Researchers International Conference, Sussex, Brighton, September 2004. We thank the Markle Foundation and the Robert Wood Johnson Foundation for their support of the US surveys and the Higher Education Foundation for England, Ofcom and Wanadoo for their support of the 2003 Oxford Internet Survey. We also thank Malcolm Peltu, editor Adam Joinson and several anonymous reviewers for their helpful comments.

References

American Behavioral Scientist (2001). Special issue on Internet use and everyday life, 45(3). (Note: articles from this special issue that appear in this reference list also appear in extended form in Wellman and Haythornthwaite 2002, along with additional chapters.)

Anderson, B. and Tracey, K. (2002). Digital living: the impact (or otherwise) of the Internet on everyday British life. In B. Wellman and C. Haythornthwaite (eds), The internet in everyday life (pp. 139–163). Oxford, UK: Blackwell Publishers.

Baym, N. K. (1995). The emergence of community in computer-mediated communication. In S. G. Jones (ed.), *Cybersociety: Computer-mediated communication and community* (pp. 138–163). Thousand Oaks, CA: Sage.

Beniger, J. (1987). The personalization of mass media and the growth of pseudo-community. *Communication Research 14*(3), 352–371.

Birnie, S. and Horvath, P. (2002). Psychological predictors of Internet social communication. *Journal of Computer-Mediated Communication, 7*(4), available at http://www.ascusc.org/jcmc/vo17/issue4/horvath.html

Boase, J., Horrigan, J., Wellman, B. and Rainie, L. (2006). The strength of Internet ties: the Internet and email aid users in maintaining their social networks and provide pathways to help when people face big decisions. Pew Internet and American Life Project. Accessed 20 February 2006 at http://www.pewinternet.org.

Boneva, B., Kraut, R. and Frohlich, D. (2001). Using e-mail for personal relationships: the difference gender makes. *American Behavioral Scientist 45*(3), 530–549.

Chen, W., Boase, J. and Wellman, B. (2002). The global villagers: comparing Internet users and uses around the world. In B. Wellman and C. Haythornthwaite (eds), *The internet in everyday life* (pp. 45–73). Oxford, UK: Blackwell Publishers.

The Children's Partnership (2002). 'A nation online' – who's not online and why it matters. Available at http://www.techpolicybank.org/2002commercereport.html.

Compaine, B. (ed.) (2001). *The digital divide: Facing a crisis or creating a myth?* Cambridge, MA: The MIT Press.

Copher, J., Kanfer, A. and Walker, M. (2002). Everyday communication patterns of heavy and light email users. In B. Wellman and C. Haythornthwaite (eds), *The Internet in everyday life* (pp. 263–288). Oxford, UK: Blackwell Publishers.

DiMaggio, P., Hargittai, E., Neuman, W. R. and Robinson, J. (2001). Social implications of the Internet. *American Review of Sociology 27*, 207–336.

Dutton, W. H. (1999). *Society on the line.* Oxford: Oxford University Press.

Dutton, W. H. (2004). *Social transformation in the Information society.* Paris: UNESCO Publications for the World Summit on the Information Society. Available at http://portal.unesco.org/ci/en/file_download.php/7364b6dd37bccc23a9038e48cb7f956dcorpus-1–144.pdf.

Dutton, W. H. (2005). The Internet and social transformation. In W. H. Dutton, B. Kahin, R. O'Callaghan and A. W. Wyckoff (eds), *Transforming enterprise* (pp. 375–398). Cambridge, MA: MIT Press.

Dutton, W. H. and Shepherd, A. (2003). *Society and the Internet: themes of the world Internet project.* Paper presented at the e-Living Conference, Essen, Germany. Available at http://www.worldinternetproject.net.

Dutton, W. H., Shepherd, A. and di Gennaro, C. (2007). Digital divides and choices reconfiguring access: national and cross-national patterns of Internet diffusion and use. In B. Anderson, M. Brynin and Y. Raban (eds), *Information and communication technologies in society.* (in press). London: Routledge.

Gergen, K. (1991). *The saturated self: dilemmas of identity in contemporary life.* New York, Harper Collins.

Gershuny, J. (2002). *Web-use and net-nerds: a neo-functionalist analysis of the impact of information technology in the home.* Working papers of the Institute for social and economic research, #2002–1. Colchester, United Kingdom: University of Essex. Available at http://www.iser.essex.ac.uk/pubs/workpaps/2002–01.php.

Griffiths, M. (2000). Internet addiction – time to be taken seriously? *Addiction Research 8*, 413–418.

Hampton, K. and Wellman, B. (2003). Neighboring in Netville: how the Internet supports community and social capital in a wired suburb. *City and Community 2*(4), 277–311.

Hiltz, S. R. and Turoff, M. (1995). *Network nation* (revised edn). Cambridge, MA: MIT Press.

Hoffman, N. (1998). Bridging the racial divide on the Internet. *Science 280*, 390–391.

Howard, P. (2004). Embedded media: who we know, what we know and society online. In P. Howard and S. Jones (eds), *Society online: The Internet in context* (pp. 1–27). Thousand Oaks, CA: Sage.

IT&Society—A Web Journal Studying How Technology Affects Society. http://www.stanford.edu/group/siqss/itandsociety/

Katz, J. E. (1999). *Connections: Social and cultural studies of the telephone in American life.* New Brunswick, NJ: Transaction.

Katz, J. E. and Aakhus, M. (2002). *Perpetual contact: Mobile communication, private talk and public performance.* Cambridge: Cambridge University Press.

Katz, J. E. and Aspden, P. (1997a). A nation of strangers. *Communications of the ACM 40*(12), 81–86.

Katz, J. E. and Aspden, P. (1997b). Motivations for and barriers to Internet usage: results of a national public opinion survey. *Internet Research: Electronic Networking Applications and Policy 7*(3), 170–188.

Katz, J. E. and Aspden, P. (1998). Internet dropouts in the USA: the invisible group. *Telecommunications Policy 22*(4/5), 327–339.

Katz, J. E. and Rice, R. E. (2002). *Social consequences of Internet use: Access, involvement and interaction.* Cambridge, MA: The MIT Press.

Kavanaugh, A. and Patterson, S. (2001). The impact of community computer networks on social capital and community involvement. *American Behavioral Scientist 45*(3), 496–509.

Kiesler, S., Siegel, H. and McGuire, T. W. (1984). Social psychological aspects of computer-mediated communication. *American Psychologist 39*(10) 1123–1134.

Kraut, R., Kiesler, S., Boneva, B., Cummings, J., Helgeson, V. and Crawford, A. (2002). Internet paradox revisited. *Journal of Social Issues 58*(1), 49–74.

Kraut, R., Patterson, M., Lundmark, V., Kiesler, S., Mukhopadhyay, T. and Scherlis, W. (1998). Internet paradox: a social technology that reduces social involvement and psychological well-being? *American Psychologist 53*(9) 1017–1031.

Liff, S. and Shepherd, A. (2004). *Internet issue brief No. 2.* Oxford, UK: Oxford Internet Institute. http://www.oii.ox.ac.uk/resources/.

LaRose, R., Eastin, M. and Gregg, J. (2001). Reformulating the Internet paradox: social cognitive explanations of Internet use and depression. *Journal of Online Behavior* 1(2). Accessed 20 February 2006 at http://www.behavior.net/JOB/v1n1/paradox.html.

Matei, S. and Ball-Rokeach, S. (2001). Real and virtual ties: connection in the everyday lives of seven ethnic neighborhoods. *American Behavioral Scientist* 45(3), 550–564.

McKenna, K. Y. and Bargh, J. (2002). Plan 9 from cyberspace: The implications of the Internet for personality. *Personality and Social Psychology Review* 4(1), 57–75.

Mesch, G. and Talmud, I. (2004). *Homo hily and social networks in computer-mediated communication: A study of adolescents in Israel.* Paper presented at the Annual Meeting of the Association of Internet Researchers, Sussex, Brighton, UK, 21 September.

Mossberger, K., Tolgert, C. and Stansbury, M. (2003). *Virtual inequality: Beyond the digital divide.* Washington, DC: Georgetown University Press.

USA Today (2001). Net users mirror nation's gender breakdown. 15 June. Available at http://www.usatoday.com/life/cyber/nb/nb5.htm.

Nie, N. (2001). Sociability, interpersonal relations and the Internet. *American Behavioral Scientist* 45(3), 420–435.

Nie, N. and Hillygus, S. (2002). The impact of Internet use on sociability: time diary findings. *IT and Society* 1(1) 1–20.

NTIA (2002). *A nation online: How Americans are expanding their use of the Internet.* Washington, DC: US Department of Commerce, National Telecommunications and Information Administration.

Parks Associates (2006). *Internet finding few newcomers in 2006.* Accessed 27 February 2006 at http://www.parksassociates.com/press/press_releases/2006/nat-scan_pr1.html.

Parks, M. and Floyd, K. (1996). Making friends in cyberspace. *Journal of Communication* 46, 80–97.

Parks, M. and Roberts, L. (1998). 'Making MOOsic': the development of personal relationships online and a comparison to their off-line counterparts. *Journal of Social and Personal Relationships* 15, 519–537.

Pew Internet and American Life Project (2000). Tracking online life: how women use the Internet to cultivate relationships with family and friends. http://www.pewinternet.org/reports/toc.asp?Report = 11.

Pew Internet and American Life Project (2001). *Asian-Americans are prolific Internet users.* Accessed 27 February 2006 at http://www.pewinternet.org/PPF/r/35/press_release.asp.

Pew Internet and American Life Project (2005). *How women and men use the Internet.* Accessed 27 February 2006 at http://www.pewinternet.org/PPF/r/171/report_display.asp.

Pinkett, R. and O'Bryant, R. (2003). Building community, empowerment and self-sufficiency: early results from the Camfield Estates-MIT creating community connections project. *New Media and Society* 6(2) 187–210.

Putnam, R. D. (2000). *Bowling alone.* New York: Simon and Schuster.

Rheingold, H. (1993). *The virtual community: Homesteading on the electronic frontier.* Reading, MA: Addison Wesley.

Rice, R. E. (1987a). New patterns of social structure in an information society. In J. Schement and L. Lievrouw (eds), *Competing visions, complex realities: Social aspects of the information society* (pp. 107–120). Norwood, NJ: Ablex.

Rice, R. E. (1987b). Computer-mediated communication and organizational innovation. *Journal of Communication* 37, 65–94.

Rice, R. E. (2001). The Internet and health communication: a framework of experiences. In R. E. Rice and J. E. Katz (eds), *The Internet and health communication: Experiences and expectations* (pp. 5–46). Thousand Oaks, CA: Sage.

Rice, R. E. (2002). Primary issues in Internet use: access, civic and community involvement and social interaction and expression. In L. Lievrouw and S. Livingstone (eds), *Handbook of new media* (pp. 105–129). London: Sage. Updated version: Rice, R. E. and Haythornthwaite, C. (2006). Perspectives on Internet use: access, involvement and interaction. In L. A. Lievrouw and S. Livingstone (eds), *Handbook of new media: Social shaping and social consequences of ICTs* (Updated student edition) (pp. 92–113). London: Sage.

Rice, R. E. and Katz, J. E. (2003). Comparing internet and mobile phone usage: digital divides of usage, adoption and dropouts. *Telecommunications Policy* 27(8/9), 597–623.

Rice, R. E., McCreadie, M. and Chang, S-J. (2001). *Accessing and browsing information and communication.* Cambridge, MA: The MIT Press.

Riphagen, J. and Kanfer, A. (1997). How does e-mail affect our lives? National Center for Supercomputing Applications. http://www.ncsa.uiuc.edu/edu/trg/e-mail/index.html.

Robinson, J., Kestnbaum, M., Neustadtl, A. and Alvarez, A. (2000). Mass media use and social life among Internet users. *Social Science Computer Review* 18(4), 490–501.

Rose, R. (2003). *Oxford Internet survey.* Report. http://users.ox.ac.uk/~oxis/index.html.

Rose, R. (2004). Governance and the Internet. In S. Yusuf, M. A. Altaf and K. Nabeshima (eds), *Global change and East Asian policy initiatives* (Chapter 8). New York: World Bank.

Selnow, G. W. (1994). *High-tech campaigns: Computer technology in political communication.* New York: Praeger.

Shade, L. R. (2004). Bending gender into the net: feminizing content, corporate interests and research strategy. In P. Howard and S. Jones (eds), *Society online: The Internet in context* (pp. 57–70). Thousand Oaks, CA: Sage.

Shklovski, I., Kiesler, S. and Kraut, R. E. (2006). The Internet and social interaction: a meta-analysis and critique of studies 1995–2003. In R. Kraut, M. Brynin and S. Kiesler (eds), *Computers, phones and the Internet: domesticating information technology* pp. 251–264. New York: Oxford University Press.

Shklovski, I., Kraut, R. E. and Cummings, J. (2005). Residential mobility, technology use and social ties. Paper presented to Internet Research Conference 6.0: Internet Generations. Accessed 21 February 2006 at http://conferences.aoir.org/viewabstract.pho?id = 263andcf = 3.

Shklovski, I., Kraut, R. E. and Rainie, L. (2004). The Internet and social participation: contrasting cross-sectional and longitudinal analyses. *Journal of Computer-Mediated Communication 10*(1). Accessed 20 February 2006 at http://jcmc.indiana.edu/vol10/issue1/shklovski_kraut.html.

Stoll, C. (1995). *Silicon snake oil.* New York: Doubleday.

Sullivan, J., Borgida, E., Jackson, M., Riedel, E., Oxendine, A. and Gangl, A. (2002). Social capital and community electronic networks. *American Behavioral Scientist 45*(5), 868–886.

Turkle, S. (1996). Virtuality and its discontents: searching for community in cyberspace. *The American Prospect 24*, 50–57.

US Census Bureau (2005). *Income stable, poverty rate increases, percentage of Americans without health insurance unchanged.* 30 August. Accessed February 27 2006 at http://www.census.gov/Press-Release/www/releases/archives/income_wealth/005647.html.

Walsh, E., Gazala, M. and Ham, C. (2001). The truth about the digital divide. In B. Compaine (ed.), *The digital divide: Facing a crisis or creating a myth?* (pp. 279–284). Cambridge, MA: The MIT Press.

Wellman, B., Haase, A., Witte, J. and Hampton, K. (2001). Does the Internet increase, decrease, or supplement social capital? Social networks, participation and community commitment. *American Behavioral Scientist 45*(3), 436–455.

Wellman, B. and Haythornthwaite, C. (eds) (2002). *The Internet in everyday life.* Oxford, UK: Blackwell Publishers.

CHAPTER 3

Love letters

The development of romantic relationships throughout the ages

Monica Whitty

I hold this letter in my hand
A plea, a petition, a kind of prayer
I hope it does as I have planned
Losing her again is more than I can bear
I kiss the cold, white envelope
I press my lips against her name
Two hundred words. We live in hope
The sky hangs heavy with rain.

(Nick Cave and the Bad Seeds 2001)

This chapter considers the history of dating throughout the ages and compares how previous forms of dating might compare to the way individuals initiate and develop relationships in cyberspace. Although theorists are currently fascinated with the ways individuals meet online, it is important to note that face-to-face settings have not been the only way that relationships have begun prior to the existence of the Internet. Similarities between the ways individuals in the past developed relationships using the telegraph and love letters are elucidated in this chapter. Some important differences between the Internet and these spaces are also presented. While early theories on computer-mediated relating (CMR) presented a rather negative view of online relationships, later theorists argued that the Internet provides a unique way to get to know others as well as to self-disclose to others. While it is fairly widely accepted by researchers today that real relationships can be formed online and successfully move offline, it is argued here that the ways individuals go about developing these relationships varies according to which space the relationship is initiated in cyber space. Comparisons are made between the ways individuals develop romantic relationships via newsgroups with the ways relationships are developed via on online dating site. Finally, suggestions for how online dating might look in the future is considered.

Courting: where has it traditionally taken place?

The places and the ways potential mates have been introduced to one another have varied over time. Sometimes this was more pragmatic and at other times more romantic. In the main, the men did the asking out – but this has not always been the case. With the availability and affordability of the Internet we have more options and ways to meet individuals – but are these ways of meeting so different to the past? This chapter now turns to consider a brief history of the courting process in Western culture (see Whitty and Carr, 2006, for a more extensive overview).

If we consider as far back as the early nineteenth century, marriages in Europe were arranged. During these times there was little emphasis on romantic attraction (Murstein 1974; Rice 1996): matches were made based on the desire to merge property and to continue the good name of the families (Rice 1996). Cate and Lloyd (1992) and Murstein (1974) tell us that the choice of a partner was based more on reason than love or affection. For instance, it was important for the man to demonstrate that he could support his wife and family financially, that the couple was of similar social standing, and that the families approved of the choice in partner. Individuals met in social settings, such as church, and parents would give the young couple privacy.

Despite the desire to continue good economic well-being, young people in America were still given some choice as to who their spouse would be. Cate and Lloyd (1992) explain that during this time some individuals engaged in the colonial practice of bundling. As they describe it:

Bundling consisted of a young woman inviting a suitor to go to bed with her, fully clothed, in some cases with a board placed between their bodies (Murstein 1974; Stiles 1871). Bundling was a privilege of the woman to bestow upon a favorite suitor (Rothman 1984) and in situations where there was little room for privacy of the couple, bundling served as a time for the young people to get to know one another (Murstein 1974). Bundling obviously must have taken place with the sanction of the young women's parents.

(Cate and Lloyd 1992: 15)

In the mid nineteenth century, men and women's social roles in America had changed: women were back in the home and their domesticity was highly valued (Cate and Lloyd 1992). It was at this time that the formal wedding ceremony emerged, together with the white wedding dress to symbolize the purity of the bride. This was also a time when romantic love began to flourish.

Romantic love contained elements of passion as well as mutuality, communion, sympathy, and candor (Coontz 1988; Rothman 1984); romantic love was very emotionally intimate and at the same time mysterious and unexplainable (Lystra 1989). Romantic love centered around the concept of the 'ideal self' (Lystra 1989). The true inner person was to be revealed through extensive self-disclosure and honesty with the loved one; thus romantic love embodied total self-revelation and open communication.

(Cate and Lloyd 1992: 18)

Towards the end of the nineteenth century and at the beginning of the twentieth century courtship in America became increasingly more formalized and began in the woman's home. The spheres between men and women widened further during this time.

A young man and young woman had to be formally introduced before they were allowed to speak to one another (Waller 1951). After such an introduction, the young women's mother would ask the young man to call upon her daughter; later on the young lady could do the asking (Bailey 1988).

(Cate and Lloyd 1992: 20–21)

In the early twentieth century, courtship moved again to outside the home. Although surveillance of the couple was still important, this was more informal through community control (Koller 1951; Cate and Lloyd 1992). Towards the mid twentieth century dating become even more informal, and the rules of dating were established by the peer group (Cate and Lloyd 1992). Mongeau *et al.* (1993) have contended that, from around the turn of the twentieth century, men began to initiate the courtship, generally because they had to pay for the date and arrange transportation. Hence these theorists, amongst others, argue that this altered who was in more control. As Cate and Lloyd (1992: 23) explain: 'When courtship was centered in the home, the woman was more in control, but as courtship shifted to the public sphere and the need for money arose, control also shifted to the man.' Interestingly, Cate and Lloyd (1992) make the claim that courting was more about competition than love at this time in history.

From the mid twentieth century to the 1960s love was still the main reason for marriage

(Cate and Lloyd 1992). However, in the postwar era, according to Cate and Lloyd (1992), women became more passive in the courting process. Of course, the sexual revolution in the 1960s changed the courting process again for both men and women. Moreover, the end goal was not necessarily marriage, and cohabitation began to become a popular choice. Concern over HIV arose in the 1980s and monogamous sexual relationships were valued, probably more than they were in the 1960s.

The above summary demonstrates how we have changed our practices in Western society and even the places we have initiated romantic relationships throughout time. Who watches over the interaction, who decides the meeting should take place in the first instance, who decides it should continue and where courting takes place have changed over time. The reason for pairing up has also varied. Sometimes this was the result of 'romantic love', while at other times it was more pragmatic. Moreover, once a relationship was established, how this relationship developed, the pace at which it is developed and whether it would result in marriage also altered over time. So how does this compare with how we initiate relationships in cyberspace?

Initiating a relationship in the home might seem old-fashioned, but as our brief history of American dating shows, this was how courtship initiated in the mid nineteenth century. Nonetheless, these days we are now moving back into the home (as well as other spaces, such as cafes, libraries and offices) and logging onto our computers to initiate romantic relationships. Hence, in considering the history of courtship the home is not a unique place to initiate relationships. However, how we go about this and our motivations for doing so is considerably different.

Throughout history, couples have had the concern of those who monitor their courting behaviours and who has a say in who they see and who they ought to marry. Such concerns for who has a stake in the match do not seem as important in our current times (at least in Western society). Parents are more concerned that their children find someone who makes them happy – although, of course, concerns about social class are an issue for some. Cyberspace can potentially provide a space for individuals to be more private and have their dating activities far less

monitored than they would be in more traditional spaces. Nonetheless, it is interesting that some individuals have a desire to include others in this dating process. Moreover, others have family and friends who want to be involved in their online dating experiences. For example, some of the participants interviewed, in Whitty's study (see Whitty and Carr, 2006), from an Australian online dating site purported that they included their family and friends in this online dating process. Some asked their family (including their own children) for advice on how to present themselves online, while others also asked for advice on appropriate candidates for their affection.

As highlighted earlier in this chapter, which gender made the first move when it comes to relationship development has varied throughout time – although in the main, it has typically been the male's role to do the asking out. Theorists such as Sherry Turkle (1995) have argued that cyberspace provides an opportunity for individuals to experiment with identity and transcend their traditional roles. Therefore, we might expect that men and women equally do the asking out online. However, empirical evidence does not convincingly support this notion. For example, Whitty (2004) has found that the ways individuals flirt in chat rooms is in many ways the same ways men and women flirt offline. She found that women were more likely than men to cyber-flirt by utilizing non-verbal substitutes, such as laughing and emphasizing physical attractiveness. Men, in this study, were also more likely than women to initiate contact with women they were attracted to online.

Cyberspace – a space prior to the advent of the Internet

The above brief history provides details about how relationships are initiated and maintained in face-to-face: however, relationships were originated and developed in cyberspace long before the Internet. Before providing examples of these types of relationships, a definition of cyberspace is required.

The science fiction writer, William Gibson (1986) is credited with coining the phrase 'cyberspace' in his novel *Neuromancer*. Within Gibson's matrix, entities attain a 'hyperreality'. When he wrote the book he had little knowledge of computers or how interactions might actually occur in cyberspace: nevertheless, his fictional writing has had some influence on our non-fictional perceptions about interactions over the Internet. Although it is generally understood that cyberspace is the space generated by software within a computer that produces a virtual reality, an alternative view is that cyberspace existed before the origins of the Internet, via the space produced in telephone calls (Stratton 1987; Whitty 2003).

Standage (1998) has made some interesting parallels between the telegraph and the Internet. He contends that although the Internet and the telegraph differ in respect to technology, the impact that the telegraph has had on people's lives is very similar. He calls the telegraph the Victorian Internet. This is how he describes the telegraph:

> During Queen Victoria's reign, a new communications technology was developed and allowed people to communicate almost instantly across distances, in effect shrinking the world faster and further than ever before. A worldwide communications network whose cables spanned continents and oceans, it revolutionized business practice, gave rise to new forms of crime, and inundated its users with a deluge of information. Romances blossomed over the wires. Secret codes were devised by some users and cracked by others. The benefits of the network were relentlessly hyped by its advocates and dismissed by the sceptics. Governments and regulators tried and failed to control the new medium. Attitudes toward everything from news gathering to diplomacy had to be completely rethought. Meanwhile, out on the wires, a technological subculture with its own customs and vocabulary was establishing itself.
>
> (Standage 1998: vii–viii)

In his book, *The Victorian Internet*, Standage (1998) also provides examples of romances that blossomed in this more 'old-fashioned cyberspace'. One such story is an online wedding that took place via Morse code:

> The daughter of a wealthy Boston merchant had fallen in love with Mr. B., a clerk in her father's counting house. Although her father had promised her hand to someone else, she decided to disregard his intentions and marry Mr. B. instead. When her father found out, he put the young man on a ship and sent him away on business to England.
>
> The shop made a stopover in New York, where the young woman sent her intended a message, asking him to present himself at the telegraph office with a magistrate at an agreed-upon time. At the appointed hour she was at the other end of the wire in the Boston telegraph office, and, with the telegraph operators relaying their words to and fro in Morse code, the two were duly wed by the magistrate.
>
> (Standage 1998: 128)

Love via the telegraph has also featured in romantic novels. For example, in 1880 Ella Cheever Thayer wrote a book entitled *Wired Love: A Romance of Dots and Dashes*, a romance novel in which a telegrapher falls in love with someone via the telegraph. The lovers meet 'online' and chat for a while, attempting to guess the other's gender. The story also describes how the couple flirt in this cyberspace. It sounds very similar to the more recent film *You've got mail* – which is story about a couple who meet on the Internet. They also flirt in this space, while oblivious to their offline connection.

> Received your most wonderful letter to-day, and it was the best I had ever had . . . Good night my love and dream pleasant dreams. I shall be thinking of you always and loving you more every day.
>
> (Louise Upchurch, cited in Tennies and Rauhauser 2005)

Love letters are another way that relationships have been developed and/or maintained. For example, love letters were in abundance during wartime. The above extract is from a letter written by Louise Upchurch to Robert Zartman during the time he was serving the army during 1943–1945. The couple met while Robert was stationed at Camp Mackall and they developed their relationship through letters during the war. They married two years later in 1947 (Tennies and Rauhauser 2005). While this was long before the origins of the Internet, this example sounds very similar to relationships developed on the Internet that successfully move to face-to-face.

> Good evening sir! It's a nasty raw windy night and I wish that you were here. We'd have a big blazing fire in the living room, and you'd throw yourself

down on the davenport, and I'd curl up beside you with my 'head tucked under your wing'.

(Elizabeth Miller, cited in Tennies and Rauhauser 2005)

The extract came from a letter written during the First World War, by Elizabeth Miller to her husband Robert Everts Miller in 1918. The couple had married two years prior to Miller enlisting in the US Army Aviation Signal Corps (Tennies and Rauhauser 2005). The above extract sounds very similar to the following email:

Very quietly, because the night is so very quiet a hundred miles from all other humans, on the lake. We lean up against each other for warmth, I have my arm around you to hold you close. The sense of waiting becomes almost intolerable . . . . We reach out to touch the reflections and our hands meet in the sparkling water. Breathless from the transformation of night to day, I turn to you and our lips meet . . .

(Gwinnell 1998: 59)

Love letters featured in the development of relationships long before World War I. Diana O'Hara writes that in the sixteenth century in England, the making of marriage was regarded 'as an extended and complex process of communication, signalled with gifts from beginning to end, wherein the language of tokens embodied an ambiguous interplay of emotions and behaviour' (O'Hara 2000: 64). Interestingly, she also tells us that 'attitudes expressed in the giving and receipt of gifts and tokens, on an individual level, and in the public face, affected the progress of relationships. The suitor's expectation was to elicit a response as a starting point for further negotiations and renegotiations' (2000: 67). One of these types of gifts she talks about is the exchange of letters. O'Hara reports that during these times, the less literate might employ professionals to write love letters; however, she admits that the practice of sending such letters was associated more with individuals from higher social status as well as the better educated, or were used by people who were forming relationships over a long distance. Hence, before we had the Internet, there is evidence that some relationships, even many centuries ago, developed (at least in part) through text.

Cyberspace and courtly love

Similarities between letter writing and the telegraph and developing relationships on the Internet are not the only parallels that can be made. In previous work, it has been argued that cyber-flirting is in many ways akin to courtly love (Whitty and Carr 2003; Whitty and Carr 2006). In courtly love

the male lover presents himself as engrossed in a yearning desire for the love of an exceedingly beautiful and perfect woman whose strange emotional aloofness and high social status make her appear hopelessly distant. But the frustrated and sorrowful lover cannot overcome his fascination and renders faithful 'love service' to this 'high-minded' and exacting lady who reciprocates in a surprising manner: She does not grant him the amorous 'reward' which he craves, but she gives him what immeasurably increases his 'worth': She rewards him with approval and reassurance.

(Moller 1959: 137)

Courtly love is said to have its origins in the twelfth century, and was a luxury of the aristocrats (Askew 1965). Andreas Capellanus attempted to systematically record the rules of Courtly love in his book *The Art of Courtly Love* (1960). He describes idealized relationships that could not exist within the context of a *real life* marriage. Courtly lovers apparently spent a great deal of time talking to each other, mostly about the nature of love. They could not physically act out their passions, and if made public this love rarely endured. Finding it to be extremely oppressive to women, it may be of little surprise that feminist theorists are completely 'opposed' to courtly love (Baruch 1991). Nonetheless, there are some similar aspects between courtly love and cyber-flirting that ought to be highlighted. For instance, cyber-flirting is unlike a real-life marriage while it remains solely online. Conversations can abound about love online, but in a real physical sense cannot be consummated. Online relationships can also seem hopelessly distant, as with courtly love. Moreover, it is possibly easier to idealize someone in cyberspace (Whitty and Carr, 2005 a, b). Walther *et al.* (2001) have argued that under certain conditions individuals idealize their virtual partners. They observed interactions between people with and without photographs online. These researchers believed that their results suggest that idealization and selective self-presentation is more likely to occur online when there is no photograph present.

Real relationships in cyberspace

Given the parallels that can be made between developing relationships on the Internet and other spaces, it is perhaps a little surprising that in the earlier days of research into cyber-relationships, some theorists contended that the lack of non-verbal cues online (that are typically present in face-to-face encounters) make cyber-space a relatively impersonal medium. The early theorists considered what was lacking in cyber-space and argued that this lack meant that 'real', genuine, relationships could not be formed in such a space. For example, the social context cues theory, first proposed by Sproull and Kiseler (1986) states that online and face-to-face communication differ in the amount of social information available. Sproull and Kiesler (1986) argued, at the time, that because these social context cues are absent online there is an increase in excited and uninhibited communication online (e.g., in the form of flaming). Another example is social presence theory, which although was first devised to explain interactions via telecon-ferencing, it was later adapted to explain computer-mediated communication (CMC). This theory contends that social presence is the feeling that one has that other individuals are involved in a communication exchange. Since CMC involves less non-verbal cues (such as facial expression, posture, dress and so forth) and auditory cues in comparison to face-to-face communication, it is said to be extremely low in social presence (Hiltz *et al.* 1986; Rice and Love 1987). According to this theory, as social presence declines communication becomes more impersonal. In contrast, more information in regards to physical appearance leads to greater positive regard. Hence, given that there is less social presence online compared to other medians (including videoconferencing), according to this theory, CMC is less personal and intimate.

Despite these early claims, the evidence does rather convincingly suggest that real relationships

do initiate online and can successfully progress to an offline setting. Parks and Floyd (1996), for instance, found in their research on news-groups that almost two-thirds of their sample (60.7 per cent) admitted to forming a personal relationship with someone they had met for the first time in a newsgroup. Of these, 7.9 per cent stated that this was a romantic relationship. In 1998 Parks and Roberts attempted to replicate the results yielded in the Parks and Floyd (1996) study by investigating a different space online. Instead, these researchers examined relationships initiated and developed in MOOs (multi-object orientation). They found that most of the partici-pants they surveyed (93.6 per cent) reported forming at least one ongoing personal relation-ship during their time on MOOs. A variety of kinds of relationships were identified, including, close friendships (40.6 per cent), friendships (26.3 per cent) or romantic relationships (26.3 per cent). Parks and Roberts remark that 'the forma-tion of personal relationships on MOOs can be seen as the norm rather than the exception' (1998: 529). In Utz's (2000) study of MUD (multi-user dimension) users she found that 76.7 per cent of her respondents reported forming a relationship online that developed offline, of which 24.5 per cent stated this was a romantic relationship.

Differences between the Internet and love letters

Although it is helpful to seek out the similarities between relationships developed on the Internet and relationships developed via the telegraph and through love letters there are nonetheless some essential differences that ought to be considered. For example, the Internet is more accessible and affordable than the telegraph. Communication on the Internet can be synchronous or asynchro-nous. Individuals are not restricted to commu-nicating only through text. Instead, people can use web cams, display photographs, pictures, videos and so forth. Moreover there are a range of different types of spaces online – some where strangers can meet (e.g., chat rooms), some where offline friends can meet up (e.g., Instant Messenger), and other spaces are specifically designed for individuals to seek out a mate (e.g., online dating sites). When we consider the way relationships are initiated and developed online, it is vital that we do not consider cyberspace as one generic space (Whitty and Carr 2003). This chapter now considers the different ways individuals might initiate and develop online relationships as well as how they might take these relationships offline.

Different spaces on the Internet

Many of the theories developed to explain how relationships are formed online make the assumption that individuals are anonymous on the Internet. Lea and Spears, for instance, state that 'the visual anonymity of the communicators and the lack of co-presence – indeed the physical isolation – of the communicators add to the interaction possibilities, and for some this is the 'magic' of on-line relationships' (1995: 202). Other theorists have also made the claim that the anonymous nature of the Internet provides a space to feel more comfortable to self-disclose information about themselves (e.g., Joinson 2001; Parks and Roberts 1998). Parks and Roberts (1998) compare this phenomenon to Thibaut and Kelley's (1959) 'stranger-on-the-train' theory; whereby people feel more comfortable disclosing to someone that they will probably never meet again.

Turkle (1995) also talked about how individuals take advantage of the anonymous nature of the Internet. Turkle presents us with a utopian view of cyberspace – a place where one can excogitate new identities. She envisaged the Internet as a place where people can take on any identity they choose.

> I am not implying that MUDs or computer bulletin boards are causally implicated in the dramatic increase of people who exhibit symptoms of multiple personality disorder (MPD), or that people on MUDs have MPD, or that MUDing is like having MPD. What I am saying is that the many manifestations of multiplicity in our culture, including the adoption of online personae, are contributing to a general reconsideration of traditional, unitary notions of identity.
>
> (Turkle 1995: 260)

It is important to note that Turkle devised this theory after observing and participating herself in MUDs and MOOs. These are places, like dungeons and dragons, set up for people to role play. Therefore, it makes sense that we would witness individuals trying on different identities in this place, given that they are encouraged to do so. However, we need to be cautious about assuming that all of cyberspace is a place where individuals play with different identities or a place where they feel completely liberated.

Some researchers have now come to appreciate that depending on the place individuals interact online and the ways they choose to interact can alter the types of relationships formed. Joe Walther is one such theorist. After conducting numerous social experiments, Walther has devised a 'hyperpersonal' communication framework. In this theory he and his colleagues posit that 'CMC users sometimes experience intimacy, affection, and interpersonal assessments of their partners that exceed those occurring in parallel FTF (face-to-face) activities or alternative CMC contexts' (Walther et al. 2001: 109). As mentioned earlier in this chapter, Walther and his colleagues believe that in some situations CMC users idealize their virtual partners. This theory also stresses that CMC users may be selective in their self-presentations. While of course we know that individuals do tend to be strategic in their presentation of self offline, Walther and his colleagues believe that in CMC impression management is more controllable and fluid. Hence, these researchers claim that 'online communicators may exploit the capabilities of text-based, nonvisual interaction to form levels of affinity that would be unexpected in parallel offline interactions' (Walther et al. 2001: 110).

According to this hyperpersonal communication framework, displaying of affiliative behaviours depends on whether the individual anticipates a long-term or short-term commitment with their partners. In addition, these hyperbolic projections are altered by the presence of a photograph. Walther and his colleagues found that the presence of a photograph prior to and during CMC had a positive effect on intimacy /affection and social attractiveness for short-term CMC partners. Moreover, CMC partners who met online felt less intimacy/affection and social attraction once a photograph was introduced compared to individuals with long-term

CMC partners who never saw each others' picture. Hence, they purport that ironically the same photographs 'that help defeat impersonal conditions also dampen hyperpersonal ones' (Walther *et al.* 2001: 122). It is also noteworthy that this result does not occur for ratings of physical attractiveness. However, these researchers did find that when there was no photograph present, physical attractiveness perceptions depended on the success of one's self-presentation: when photographs were present self-presentation was negatively related to physical attractiveness and familiarity had a positive effect on physical attractiveness.

> It appears that when partners' photographs are shown, the less physically attractive they are, the more they engage in successful self-presentation, perhaps in a compensatory manner. Or, the more physically attractive partners are, the less successful they believe their impression management efforts are. (Or they are wrong about their perceived success at self-presentation, and the more successfully they believe they self-presented, the less physically attractive they were rated.)
>
> (Walther *et al.* 2001: 123–124)

Presenting different selves in online spaces

John Bargh, Katelyn McKenna and their colleagues have considered which aspects of the self individuals are more likely to present in newsgroups. These researchers have drawn from Rogers' and Higgins' work on personality to come up with two aspects of self that they believe are important to consider when focusing on the development of relationships online – 'true' selves and 'actual' selves (Bargh *et al.* 2002; McKenna *et al.* 2002). Bargh *et al.* (2002) and McKenna *et al.* (2002) drew from Rogers' work (1951), to define the *true* self (or what they also refer to as the '*Real Me*') as traits or characteristics that individuals posses and would like to but are not usually able to express. In contrast, drawing from Higgins' (1987) research, they defined the *actual* self as traits or characteristics that individuals possess and express to others in social settings. In line with Higgins, these researchers claim that as one develops trust and

intimacy with one's partner they are more likely to disclose aspects of themselves that are not widely known to others.

Based on previous theoretical and empirical work that suggests that the Internet provides a safer space to disclose intimate aspects about one's self, McKenna *et al.* reasoned that

> we would expect people who are lonely or are socially anxious in traditional, face-to-face interaction settings to be likely to feel better able to express their true self over the Internet and so to develop close and meaningful relationships.
>
> (McKenna *et al.* 2002: 12)

These researchers have argued that individuals who are more likely to express their true self online will consider the relationships they form in this space to be more identity-important compared to those individuals who are more likely to express their true selves in non-Internet relationships.

> Those who locate their true selves on-line, as opposed to off-line, will feel that their on-line relationships develop much more quickly than do their non-Internet relationships, these relationships will be close and meaningful, and they will be motivated to move these relationships into their face-to-face lives through a series of stages. These close relationships should also be durable and stable over time.
>
> (McKenna *et al.* 2002: 13)

To test out the above ideas, Bargh, McKenna and their colleagues conducted a number of experiments. They revealed that the individuals' true selves were more accessible in memory after interacting with a stranger online compared to face-to-face. Moreover, they found that participants tended to like each other more when they meet first online compared to face-to-face.

Taking this work a step further, McKenna *et al.* (2002) were interested in whether individuals who are better able to disclose their 'true' selves online than offline were more equipped to form close relationships online and then take these relationships offline successfully. They randomly selected 20 Usenet newsgroups to include in their study. Their first study found that when people convey their 'true' self online they develop strong Internet relationships and bring these relationships into their 'real' lives. Two years after this initial study 354 of the 568 participants were emailed a follow-up survey (the remainder of the sample had email addresses that were no longer valid). In line with these researchers' prediction, these relationships remained relatively stable and durable over the two-year period. In this same research, McKenna *et al.* (2002) found that participants who were more socially anxious and lonely were somewhat more likely to believe they could express their true selves with others online than they could with people they knew offline. They conclude from this research that:

> rather than turning to the Internet as a way of hiding from real life and from forming real relationships, individuals use it as a means not only of maintaining ties with existing family and friends but also of forming close and meaningful new relationships in a relatively nonthreatening environment. The Internet may also be helpful for those who have difficulty forging relationships in face-to-face situations because of shyness, social anxiety, or a lack of social skills.

(McKenna *et al.* 2002: 30)

Although Bargh, McKenna and their colleagues discuss these results as if they would apply to all spaces online, recent research suggests this is not the case (see Whitty and Carr, 2006). In Whitty's research on online daters, individuals were very strategic and very conscious of their presentations of self online. On an online dating site individuals are required to construct a profile. Typically they include their photograph and are required to answer questions in regards to their physical descriptions, work situation, relationship status and so forth. They are also given the opportunity to write about who they are and the sort of partner they would like to meet.

Unlike the relationships Bargh and McKenna observed being developed in newsgroups, the 60 online daters Whitty interviewed did not spend a great deal of time getting to know one another online (see Whitty and Carr, 2006). In fact, 65 per cent of the sample stated that they typically meet their date within a week of first making contact online. Therefore, while these individuals might exchange emails, phone numbers and chat for a short period of time using the site's IM (Instant Messenger), the objective is typically to move offline as quickly as possible. The explanations given for meeting people so quickly included; a need to establish if there is any 'physical

chemistry', a desire to not waste time and to move new profiles if the date did not work out, a lack of trust in people's profiles and a desire to get to know the 'real' person behind the profile as quickly as possible. The process and the reasons given are illustrated in the following extracts:

R First of all it was the kiss [an automatic statement that one can choose that is delivered through the site to say they are interested in someone], she sent a kiss reply saying she was interested and would like to receive an email from me to which I sent an email and told her a little bit more about myself. And then she emailed back and told me a little bit more about her and then we arranged to meet. I asked if she would like to have coffee somewhere and meet in town. She agreed and we met and it went quite well.

I How long did all that take and in what stages? How long were you doing email?

R Just a week.

(Robbie)

J I had learnt from a few very early test runs that too many emails and phone calls before actually meeting over coffee or whatever can be a big mistake. Well at least for me, because although you start to develop a sort of friendship and a certain intimacy if there is no chemistry and you don't want to retain them as a friend it feels very awkward. So I make it a rule that ... I don't sort of become emotionally close to someone I don't actually, I haven't seen in the flesh, because it is disappointing for both parties and it can feel quite strange.

(Jenny)

Interestingly, 53 per cent of the sample talked about being attracted to genuine and honest people. They believed it was very important that the individual matched up in face-to-face with the online profile. While they were savvy enough to know that their potential dates might present a picture of who they would like to be and a profile that presented their best points, individuals were insistent about meeting others who presented a profile of who they 'actually' are in day-to-day settings. They also pointed out how unattractive some of the stereotypical or clichéd profiles were. To give an example:

> If you run through the profiles every girl wants to sit by an open fire with a glass of red wine or walk

along a beach. I mean it just repeats itself. If you find someone who's put a bit of thought into it, more particular about what they're all about and they vary it a bit you think well there's someone a bit different there. They tend to all be run of the mill in what they say they want. They put in the obvious, good sense of humour well you wouldn't put in you had a bad sense of humour.

(Grant)

The process of getting to know one another through an online dating site was very different to getting to know someone via a newsgroup. Individuals did not want to spend time unravelling their personality in cyberspace. Moreover, rather than gradually self-disclosing as one would typically do in face-to-face or other places online, such as newsgroup and chat rooms, individuals on an online dating site provide a gamut of information about themselves on their profiles – information they might take a few dates to self-disclose to another.

Social penetration theory, initially proposed by Altman and Taylor (1973) essentially argues that relationships move from less intimate to more intimate involvement over time. The process has been described using an onion analogy, arguing that people self-disclose deeper and deeper aspects about themselves as the relationship progresses. This theory discusses depth and breadth. According to social penetration theory, in the early phases of relationship development one moves with caution, discussing less intimate topics and checking in the conversations for signs of reciprocity. Gradually one feels safer to admit to other aspects of themselves. If you consider the process of online dating, there is far less opportunity for relationships to develop in this way. The profiles are set up in such as way to reveal both depth and breadth. They are encouraged on these sites to open up about all aspects of themselves online – so that they will attract the most appropriate person. Therefore, online dating is arguably even more removed from what people are used to when it comes to developing a relationship. There is no any real opportunity to test the waters gradually and check for reciprocity, instead, reciprocity is determined prior to communication with the individual.

Participants were asked to reflect on their own experiences of constructing their own profiles.

In the interviews they admitted to the difficulties they had in developing a profile. They were consciously aware of trying to attract people, but at the same time wanting to present themselves as 'real' people. Writing a profile was a *dynamic process*. Online daters would monitor who responded to their profile and accordingly alter their profile to either attract more people, attract a different type or person or to filter out too many people from responding. Many would also have a few profiles at the same time to see which ones attracted what types of people.

The participants in Whitty's research seemed to be trying to create a balance between keeping their profiles real (actual self) as well as selling themselves (true self). Hence, unlike McKenna and Bargh's research, participants do not gradually reveal a true self online – nor was the presentation of a true self online likely to lead to a successful offline relationship. Online daters were aware from previous experience on the site that they did not want to disappoint their dates once they were exposed face-to-face, but at the same time they were wanting to attract a decent number of individuals to select from. Wayne explains quite well how writing his profile was a way to sell himself.

W   The other thing for me personally is I'm great at writing trade manuals for someone, but when it comes to writing about yourself and trying to sell yourself it's a very different story. I don't know whether that's more of a male trait than a female trait. It depends how good you want to try selling yourself too isn't it?

(Wayne)

Many of the online daters also recruited friends and family to assist them in constructing their profiles. Some were self-aware enough to know that their own view of who they are is not necessarily how others view them. Therefore, friends and family were helpful in constructing a profile that reflected how the individual is typically in everyday situations, as Danny tells us:

D   The accuracy of the information is something I put ahead of everything else. I took forever to put up that profile, I didn't just stick up a photo and put up a profile. Have you seen my profile?

I   No, No, I haven't mate.

D   OK that is fine. I laboured and drafted and sent across to a friend for clarification, I then re-drafted.

(Danny)

The future of online dating

Although the Internet was not designed to develop relationships with others, it did not take long for individuals to find this is an attractive space to meet people. The ways we do this, however, are constantly changing. Online dating sites have increased in popularity and will no doubt continue to do so. The increase in numbers of online dating sites worldwide is testament to this. Brym and Lenton (2003), who examined the rise of online dating in Canada identified four main social forces that have driven the growth of online dating. These include:

- an increasing number of singles in the population (especially because people are leaving marriage until later in life)
- given that career and time pressures are increasing, people are looking for more efficient ways of meeting others for intimate relationships
- single people are more mobile due to demands of the job market, so it is more difficult for them to meet people for dating
- workplace romance is on the decline due to growing sensitivity about sexual harassment.

What is also interesting about online dating is the way these sites are developing more effective ways to match individuals. Online dating sites typically have search tools, where people put in categories of the person they are searching for: a program has been written to match the most appropriate people. This is not solely based on demographic characteristics (e.g. socio-economic status, number of children, attractiveness) but also on personality characteristics. These programmes have been written to assist the online dater in their quest to seek out the most appropriate partner. Therefore, online dating is becoming quite scientific. Various companies, like eharmony.com, boast about having the best matching tools available on their site. This is not just a question that people running the companies are concerned with. Academics are also now starting to question the logistics of these compatibility services. For instance, Houran, Lange, Rentfrow

and Bruckner (2004) critique some of these computer programmes, arguing that matchmaking is not necessarily all about *similarity* and that sometimes *complementarity* is an important notion to consider (an aspect often neglected by the matchmaking programmes on these sites).

Conclusions

It would seem that online dating is here to stay. However, the way people use the Internet and the ways online dating sites will be constructed in the future will no doubt change. Other technologies will be incorporated with the Internet for future online dating – for example, Bluetooth technology is starting to take off as a way to meet a partner. Despite the relative newness of the Internet, it is important that we do not forget the past when it comes to dating. As this chapter has demonstrated, there are some obvious similarities between developing a relationship on the Internet and other spaces – such as the telegraph and letter writing. Moreover, it is critical that we do not treat cyberspace as one generic space. Rather the ways individuals present themselves and the ways relationships are developed and maintained do vary depending on which space online we are referring to.

References

Altman, I. and Taylor, D. A. (1973). *Social penetration: The development of interpersonal relationships.* New York: Holt, Rinehart and Winston.

Askew, M. W. (1965). Courtly love: neurosis as institution. *The Psychoanalytic Review 52*(1), 19–29.

Bargh, J. A., McKenna, Y. A., Fitzsimons, G. M. (2002). Can you see the real me? Activation and expression of the 'true self' on the Internet. *Journal of Social Issues 58*(1), 33–48.

Baruch, E. H. (1991). *Women, love, and power: Literary and psychoanalytic perspectives.* New York: New York University.

Brym, R. J. and Lenton, R. L. (2003). Love at first byte: Internet dating in Canada. Retrieved 25 March 2005 from http://www.societyinquestion4e.nelson.com/Chapter33Online.pdf.

Capellanus, A. (1969). *The art of courtly love* (J. Parry, Trans.). New York: Norton. (Original work published around 1174.)

Cate, R. M. and Lloyd, S. A. (1992). *Courtship.* Newbury Park, CA: Sage Publications, Inc.

Gibson, W. (1986). *Neuromancer.* London: Grafton Books.

Gwinnell, E. (1998). *Online seductions: Falling in love with strangers on the Internet.* New York: Kodansha International.

Hiltz, S. R., Johnson, M. and Turoff, M. (1986). Experiments in group decision making: communication process and outcome in face-to-face versus computerized conferences. *Human Communication Research 13*, 225–252.

Houran, J., Lange, R., Rentfrow, P. J. and Bruckner, K. H. (2004). Do online matchmaking tests work? An assessment of preliminary evidence for a publicized 'predictive model of marital success'. *North American Journal of Psychology 6*(3), 507–526.

Joinson, A. N. (2001). Self-disclosure in computer-mediated communication: the role of self-awareness and visual anonymity. *European Journal of Social Psychology 31*, 177–192.

Koller, M. R. (1951). Some changes in courtship behavior in three generations of Ohio women. *American Sociological Review 16*, 266–370.

Lea, M. and Spears, R. (1995). Love at first byte? Building personal relationships over computer networks. In J. T. Wood and S. W. Duck (eds), *Understudied relationships: Off the beaten track* (pp. 197–233). Newbury Park, CA: Sage.

McKenna, K. Y. A., Green, A. S. and Gleason, M. E. J. (2002). Relationship formation on the internet: what's the big attraction? *Journal of Social Issues 58*(1), 9–31.

Moller, H. (1959). The causation of the courtly love complex. *Comparative Studies in Society and History 1*, 137–163.

Mongeau, P. A., Hale, J. L., Johnson, K. L. and Hillis, J. D. (1993). Who's wooing whom? An investigation of female initiated dating. In P. J. Kabfleisch (ed.), *Interpersonal communication: Evolving interpersonal relationships* (pp. 51–68). Hillsdale, NJ: Lawrence Erlbaum Associates, Inc.

Murstein, B. I. (1974). *Love, sex and marriage through the ages*. New York: Springer.

Nick Cave and the Bad Seeds. (2001). Love Letters. *No more shall we part* [CD]. Australia: EMI Music Group Australia.

O'Hara, D. (2000). *Courtship and constraint: Rethinking the making of marriage in Tudor England*. Manchester: Manchester University.

Parks, M. R. and Floyd, K. (1996). Making friends in cyberspace. *Journal of Communication 46*, 80–97.

Parks, M. R. and Roberts, L. D. (1998). 'Making MOOsic': the development of personal relationships online and a comparison to their off-line counterparts. *Journal of Social and Personal Relationships 15*, 517–537.

Rice, F. P. (1996). *Intimate relationships, marriages, and families*. Mountain View, CA: Mayfield Publishing Company.

Rice, R. E. and Love, G. (1987). Electronic emotion: socioemotional content in a computer mediated communication network. *Communication Research 14*, 85–108.

Sproull, L. and Kiesler, S. (1986). Reducing social context cues: electronic mail in organizational communication. *Management Science 32*, 1492–1512.

Standage, T. (1998). *The Victorian internet*. New York: Walker and Company.

Stratton, J. (1987). Not really desiring bodies: the rise and rise of email affairs. *Media International Australia 84*, 28–38.

Tennies, H. S. and Rauhauser, B. R. (2005). Love letters: an intimate look at love in Lancaster County. Retrieved 28 March 2005 from http://www.lancasterhistory.org/collections/exhibitions/loveletters/LoveLettersCredit.htm.

Thayer, E. C. (1880). *Wired love: A romance of dots and dashes*. New York: W. J. Johnson.

Turkle, S. (1995). *Life on the screen: Identity in the age of the Internet*. London: Weidenfeld and Nicolson.

Utz, S. (2000). Social information processing in MUDs: the development of friendships in virtual worlds. *Journal of Online Behavior 1*(1), Retrieved 7 February 2005 from http://www.behavior.net/JOB/v1n1/utz.html.

Walther, J. B., Celeste, L. S. and Tidwell, L. C. (2001). Is a picture worth a thousand words? Photographic images in long-term and short-term computer-mediated communication. *Communication Research 28*(1), 105–134.

Whitty, M. (2004). Cyber-flirting: an examination of men's and women's flirting behaviour both offline and on the Internet. *Behaviour Change 21*, 115–126.

Whitty, M. T. (2003). Cyber-flirting: playing at love on the Internet. *Theory and Psychology 13*, 339–357.

Whitty, M. T. and Carr, A. N. (2003). Cyberspace as potential space: considering the web as a playground to cyber-flirt. *Human Relations 56*, 861–891.

Whitty, M. T. and Carr, A. N. (2006). *Cyberspace romance: the psychology of online relationships*. Basingstoke: Palgrave Macmillan.

Whitty, M. T. and Carr, A. N. (2005). Taking the good with the bad. In F. Piercy, J. Wetchler and K. Hertlein (eds), *Handbook on treating infidelity* (pp. 103–115). Haworth Press.

Whitty, M., T. and Carr, A. N. (2005). Taking the good with the bad: applying Klein's work to further our understanding of cyber-cheating. *Journal of Couple and Relationship Therapy: Special issue on Treating infidelity 4*(2 and 3) 103–115.

CHAPTER 4

Trust and social interaction on the Internet

Melanie C. Green

Trust, both specific and generalized, is an important ingredient in smoothly functioning relationships. An emerging area of investigation is the development of trust in computer-mediated or online relationships. Although existing relationships may be supplemented with online interaction – family members keeping in touch with relatives in faraway cities via email; teenagers chatting with school friends on Instant Messenger (IM) – the primary focus of this chapter is interactions and relationships that start on the Internet. Relationships that begin online pose unique challenges: false identities are easy to create and difficult to verify (see, for example, Van Gelder 1985; Turkle 1995). Visual and non-verbal cues are typically absent, despite the technical possibilities for video and audio transmissions. Because individuals communicating online are likely to be geographically distant from one another, it is often impossible to rely on mutual acquaintances to vouch for the trustworthiness of a person.

On some level, individuals may feel less vulnerable when interacting on the Internet, because in most cases the individual is physically in the privacy and safety of his or her own home or workplace. An individual can easily exit from online interactions and does not have to worry about stumbling over words or appearing awkward, as might happen in a face-to-face conversation: these features make the Internet appealing to individuals who wish to avoid interpersonal risk

(Green and Brock, under review). However, Internet interactions have the potential to have costs to one's privacy, emotional well-being and perhaps even physical safety (if a dangerous individual learns where a person lives, for example, or if an in-person meeting is arranged.) Interactions on the Internet, as with other forms of interpersonal contact, are a domain where more trust is not always better. An optimal level of trust is one in which the person is open to gaining deep and fulfilling relationships, but is not gullible enough to be cheated or taken advantage of (Rotter 1980; Yamagishi 2001).

Unique features of computer-based communication – the ease and speed of sending messages, the absence of non-verbal feedback, the increased anonymity and different norms and standards of etiquette – may alter the kinds of interactions that occur via the Internet (Kiesler et al. 1984). Trust or lack of trust may be a key factor in determining whether online relationships will thrive and move to deeper levels, providing reliable social support, or whether they will remain weak ties that provide little benefit to the individual and do little to build social capital (Green and Brock 1998).

Defining trust

Trust has been studied in a variety of different disciplines – philosophy, economics, marketing and psychology, to name a few – and researchers have not always shared a common understanding of this abstract concept. Though there is continuing discussion about the definition of trust, from a psychological perspective it can be broadly defined as 'confident expectations of positive outcomes from an intimate partner' (Holmes and Rempel 1989: 188). More specifically, trust can be conceptualized as a three-part relation, involving two individuals and an action: a person trusts another person to do (or not do) a specific action (Hardin 2001).

On the Internet, a primary form of trust may involve sharing information. Individuals may trust others to provide honest and accurate information, or to keep private information confidential. This trust may expand to include in-person meetings or other responsibilities.

Risk

Many definitions of trust include the concept of risk (e.g., Deutsch 1962): if there is no possibility of a negative outcome, trust is not necessary. As mentioned above, risks in Internet relationships – as in offline relationships – include the possibility of emotional betrayal, violations of privacy, or in more extreme cases, physical harm. Another form of risk takes place when individuals follow advice that they receive online; if this information is inaccurate, a variety of costs may be incurred, depending on the domain of the advice (health, travel, finances, etc.).

Individuals appear to recognize these risks and may even be more concerned about them than they are about the risks of in-person relationships, even though con artists, stalkers and the like do not limit their activities to online targets. Internet relationships start at some disadvantage as a result of lowered general trust due to the medium of communication: in response to standard trust questions such as 'Generally speaking, would you say that most people [on the Internet] can be trusted, or can't you be too careful?', people reported significantly less trust in people on the Internet than they did about people more generally (Green 2005). A similar result has emerged in bargaining settings; online negotiators have lower pre-negotiation levels of trust relative to in-person negotiators (Naquin and Paulson 2003).

Opportunity

Individuals are willing to take the risks of trusting others because of the opportunity to gain benefits from the interactions. Benefits such as entertainment or passing time can be gained without trust; individuals can drop in on a chatroom without revealing any personal information, or 'lurk' on newsgroups or website message boards (that is, read prior messages but not post new messages of one's own). Deeper benefits such as emotional support require the individual to open up to others, however, trusting them to respond with kindness. Engaging in collective or cooperative action with online partners may also entail some risk, but can lead to accomplishing tasks that might be difficult or impossible to do alone. Sometimes Internet relationships can even yield tangible rewards. For example, authors of popular weblogs (online personal journals or diaries) occasionally receive gifts or donations from readers.

Global versus specific trust

Interestingly, research suggests that trust in Internet friendships or romantic relationships is a global feeling towards the Internet partner (Green 2005). In a set of survey studies, participants who had formed a relationship online were asked how much they trusted their partner. They also answered a series of questions about how much they trusted their partner in specific domains: emotional support, honesty in interactions, keeping a secret, with physical safety, lending money, expectation of repayment of money and inviting the person to one's home. Results revealed that responses to these items were highly intercorrelated and formed a reliable trust scale. If a partner was trusted for emotional support, that partner also tended to be trusted to not harm the person physically and to repay money lent to him or her. The relationships examined in this study were relatively enduring ones, lasting on average a year or more. However, similar results emerged when people in an experimental study were asked to imagine meeting someone online. (Of course, these findings carry the caveat that individuals' self-reported trust or responses to hypothetical situations may differ from their actual behaviour; further research is needed to confirm the extent to which reported trust corresponds with actions such as lending money, extending invitations and the like.)

Trust can take a more specific form when individuals follow advice given by others online (Constant *et al.* 1996). Such individual advice may supplement or replace information from professional or official sources. A person may trust and act on an online acquaintance's opinion about a new band, automotive repairs, or travel destinations, but would not consider sharing a secret with that person or lending him or her money. This type of trust may be based solely on judgements of expertise and sincerity. Cues to expertise might include specific statements about relevant experience ('I worked in the cruise industry for twenty years') or messages that convey knowledge through details or the use of appropriate technical terms; alternatively, individuals who have been part of a community (a newsgroup or message board) over time may establish reputations for giving especially useful information. Although these interactions may lead to deeper relationships, as when regulars on a particular chat room or message board come to know more information about each other's lives, in many instances there is not necessarily an expectation of continued interaction.

Development of trust

Trust moves through stages as relationships develop (Holmes and Rempel 1989). Some of these stages are likely to be similar in face-to-face and Internet relationships, but others may differ. For example, revealing personal appearance and other identity details typically takes place later in an Internet relationship (although this progression may change with new technological developments and usage patterns; dating sites, for example, typically include photographs along with personal profiles and personal websites often include a wealth of detail). Typically, one of those stages is also moving to different modes of communication, such as the telephone (e.g., McKenna *et al.* 2002).

There is some evidence that in-person friendships are higher in quality than online friendships in the early stages, but that these differences are diminished in relationships lasting a year or more (Chan and Cheng 2004).[1] However, other research suggests that Internet relationships can progress to intimate levels more quickly than in-person relationships (Walther 1996; McKenna *et al.* 2002). Like talking to a stranger on a train, individuals may be willing to share more intimate information with online partners, because those partners are not connected with the person's existing social circle and thus cannot pass sensitive information along to those individuals (cf. Derlega and Chaikin 1977). Disclosure is associated with trust, so conditions that foster high disclosure may also be those that evoke greater trust.

Different terms have been used to describe stages of trust, but a broad distinction seems to exist between an initial willingness to take risks and a more mature, grounded trust that arises over time and with increased experience with the interaction partner. In work groups, this has been termed 'swift trust' versus 'slow trust' (Meyerson *et al.* 1996). Early levels of trust may be characterized by smaller risks or relying on systems of rewards and punishments, while more developed levels of trust involve an expectation that the partner will have the person's best interests in mind (Corritore *et al.* 2003). Longitudinal studies of Internet relationship development would be particularly helpful in understanding how these processes are influenced by the online context.

'On the Internet, nobody knows you're a dog'

Peter Steiner's famous *New Yorker* cartoon – a dog sitting in front of a computer, telling another canine that 'On the Internet, nobody knows you're a dog' – sums up the key dilemma facing people trying to form relationships on the Internet. Dramatic cases of online deception have rocked Internet communities and grabbed media headlines. In one such case, a male psychiatrist pretended to be a young disabled woman (van Gelder 1985); in another, a person invented a fictitious daughter (Kaycee Nicole)

---

[1] The measures of quality in Chan and Cheng (2004) did not include trust, but did include measures such as interdependence, commitment and understanding, which are likely correlated with trust.

who was dying of leukemia and documenting her life on a weblog. In both of these instances, people felt that they had formed real friendships with the fictitious personas and were stunned when the betrayal was revealed. Of course, even more serious misrepresentations can occur, as when sexual predators pose as children or teens online in order to lure young victims.

Because presenting a false persona is relatively easy online, one of the most important elements of trust in online relationships appears to be identity verification, a step that is usually taken for granted in in-person relationships. People might verify information provided by another person through mutual friends, through website information (for example, a listing on an employer's web page), or through meeting in person (although this method of verification may already imply a higher level of trust). In some instances, people can use other sources, such as newspaper reports or other factual information to prove or disprove claims. The Kaycee Nicole deception was uncovered in part because the mother was unwilling to provide information about a funeral and no obituary appeared in local newspapers (see the Kaycee Nicole Swenson FAQ; http://www.rootnode.org/article.php?sid=26 for more information).

Not only does identity verification provide a 'main effect' boost to trust, but it also interacts with other trust-relevant factors. It appears that not being certain of a person's identity in an online relationship leads to lowered confidence in the information provided. This lack of confidence leads to lowered trust, or to a form of trust that may be tempered by scepticism (perhaps analogous to a weak attitude). Standard predictors of trust such as similarity, friendliness and other variables are more predictive of trust in an online partner once individuals have verified the partner's identity (Green 2005).

Despite the potential negative impact on trust, the ability to 'hide behind the screen' may have some positive aspects as well. Anonymity may reduce the perceived risks of self-disclosure (Derlega and Chaikin 1977; Bargh and McKenna 2004). Individuals may not need to develop a high degree of trust to be willing to disclose information about themselves. Similarly, under some circumstances, anonymity could also have benefits for more trusting relationships in an intergroup context by removing salient cues to group differences. Walther suggests that a fruitful area for future research is 'when the turban and the yarmulke need not be visible during interactions, can commonalities be made more salient than differences?' (2004: 393).[2]

Perhaps in response to concerns about identity verification, new web services have emerged that draw upon existing social networks. For example, Friendster links people with their existing (offline) friends and friends of those friends. People are thus able to expand their social circles with the assurance that there is a link to an already-trusted friend or acquaintance who knows the new person in real life; indeed, the service is explicitly advertised as 'safe'. Similarly, Facebook.com allows college students to meet or learn about other students from their own universities. Limiting access to those within a particular institution gives users some additional confidence in the information provided.

Lying on the net

Online deception itself may sometimes be a product of a lack of trust. Individuals (particularly women) concerned about their safety may be reluctant to reveal their real names, ages, or other personal details that may make them vulnerable (e.g., Whitty and Gavin 2001). Individuals low in generalized trust are more likely to use false identities online (Uslaner 2004). Of course, online deception may have other roots as well, including psychiatric illness, identity play, or the desire to reveal a true or ideal self (see Joinson and Dietz-Uhler 2002, for a discussion).

In a study of over one hundred students who had formed relationships online, reports of lying were relatively infrequent (Green 2005). Deception was more frequent from the respondents than from their partners (though most participants claimed this dishonesty was

---

[2] In contrast to this optimistic perspective, however, research on the Social Identity Model of Deindividuation by Postmes, Spears and their colleagues suggests that under some circumstances group norms may become even more important when individuals are depersonalized, as opposed to individually identifiable, online (e.g., Postmes et al. 1998).

relatively infrequent, either only once or a few times). Somewhat surprisingly, partner lying was unrelated to trust, but respondent lying was negatively related to trust. People who lied to their Internet partner trusted that partner less (for similar findings in non-Internet relationships, see Sagarin *et al.* [1998]). This relationship may be bidirectional – people may be reluctant to tell the truth to partners that they suspect may be untrustworthy. Although the study did not investigate the nature of the lies, the timing and severity of the deception may influence the effect of lies on trust. A small lie early in a relationship is likely more easily forgiven than a lie told in a more advanced stage of the relationship, or about a more serious matter (for instance, claiming to be single when one is actually married).

Individuals are not particularly good at detecting deception even in face-to-face contexts, however; studies have shown accuracy only slightly greater than chance (e.g., DePaulo 1994). Online deception may be even more difficult to detect because non-verbal and paralinguistic cues to deception are eliminated. For instance, in an online game where one person presented themselves as either their own gender or the opposite gender and the participant's job was to guess the person's real gender, high rates of error occurred. Even when players knew that deception was likely to be common, they were swayed by answers that employed gender-stereotypic content, rather than attending to more subtle aspects of linguistic style (Herring and Martinson 2004).

An additional complexity arises when individuals have a choice of communication modes. People may use the Internet strategically for deception in order to avoid sending non-verbal signals of deceit. Individuals may generally trust an interaction partner, but may become suspicious of a particular communication (e.g., 'why did he email to cancel our meeting rather than calling me?') Future research could explore the influence of suspicion about discrete events or statements on overall trust.

Personal factors

Experience and time spent online

Experience with computers and with online technology may influence trust. More time spent online (both in number of years using the Internet and number of hours used per day or week) may make people less wary of the technology itself, as people gain a greater understanding of how various aspects of the Internet work and this comfort may extend to the interactions that take place on the Internet. Of course, a longer amount of time spent online also provides more time for relationships to develop. For example, a study of chat room users suggested that the more time individuals spent in chat rooms, the more likely they were to have received emotional support from them. Conversely, people who spent few hours per week on chat rooms were more likely to have lied in chats (Whitty 2002). Although trust was not directly measured in the study, these measures are likely to be related to trust. Furthermore, with increasing experience in the relatively low-information environment of the Internet, individuals may learn to identify or seek out more accurate cues to trustworthiness.

Dispositional tendencies

All else being equal, individuals may be relatively more or less trusting due to differing dispositional levels of trust (chronic optimistic or pessimistic outlooks established by temperament or early experience). Dispositional trust may have the main effect of making the individual more open to interpersonal risks online just as they would be in traditional social settings, but there is no reason to expect that dispositional trust would interact in a particular way with the online context.

Partner factors

Not surprisingly, other factors influencing trust in online relationships are the same as those that affect trust in traditional social relationships. Partner characteristics such as integrity or honesty can inspire trust. The presence of negative qualities, such as inconsistency, unreliability, or the use of threats may undermine trust.

Perceptions of an Internet partner's personality – particularly their degree of friendliness and secondarily their intelligence – are positively related to trust (Green 2005). As expected, people who are bright and kind inspire trust. Similarity also matters, though similarity in values and personality is more important than similarity in background. Although people in longer relationships are generally aware of their partner's race, trust does not seem to be significantly affected by being a member of the same or a different ethnic group (Green 2005). This may be a key difference between relationships formed online rather than in person: similarity may be based on internal, psychological similarities rather than more categorical or superficial ones (see also Bargh *et al.* 2002).

A key area for future research is the type of cues that individuals use to make these determinations. The content, tone and frequency of the communications likely matter; more subtle stylistic features may also play a role. The different methods of information transmission may also influence trust decisions. Email provides time for reflection and longer messages, whereas Instant Messenger does not (e.g., Green *et al.* 2005). Furthermore, research suggests that observers can make fairly accurate assessments of personality by viewing personal websites (Vazire and Gosling 2004). However, email and Instant Messenger communications are often not explicitly designed to convey information about the self.

Beliefs about characteristics of trustworthy partners

Individuals have intuitive theories about the kinds of information that would lead them to trust or distrust a person encountered online. To explore these intuitions, we gave participants a list of nineteen characteristics of potential Internet partners and asked them to rate each characteristic for whether it would make them trust the person more, less, or would not affect their trust for the person (Green 2005). Examples included perceptions of the person's intelligence, presence of deception and characteristics of the person's online persona, such as whether their email address was from an employer or an educational institution.

The three items that participants believed were most likely to inspire trust were: the person is a friend of one of your real-life (in person) friends, you have communicated with the person

for a year or more, and after first talking on the Internet, you met the person in real life (in person). These findings are consonant with other research in this domain, but of course, some of these elements might also be consequences or indicators of trust.

The three items that were most likely to make people trust a partner less were finding out the person lied to you about what gender they are, finding out that the person lied to you about minor details of their life and that the person has terrible spelling and grammar online. These findings are intuitive, but somewhat inconsistent with the fact that partner deception was not a strong predictor of trust in a study of individuals who had formed online relationships. There are two possibilities for this disconnect. First, it is possible that finding out a person lied about their gender or aspects of their life would lead individuals to discontinue contact with the person, so that a relationship never really began. In other words, relationships that the survey study respondents reported on had already overcome these barriers. A second alternative is that individuals' ideas about what would make them distrust a person online do not reflect the actual cues that they use. People in hypothetical situations cannot always accurately predict real behaviour. Future research should explore these possibilities.

Types of relationships: acquaintances, friends, romantic partners

Acquaintanceships on the Internet are likely a starting point for other forms of relationships. Individuals may become acquainted by frequenting the same chat rooms, newsgroups, or website message boards. Little trust may be required to maintain these weak bonds, as the expectations for partners may not go beyond maintaining civility and appropriate conversation.

When individuals begin interaction on a more personal level or moving to one-on-one communication, they shift to defining the relationship as a friendship. Friendship is perhaps the most common form of Internet relationship (Parks and Roberts 1998) and most of the trust issues discussed already in this chapter apply most readily to friendships.

Romantic or sexual relationships online may range from flirtatious email or chat room messages to cybersex to deep emotional commitments. Much of the existing research on Internet sexual attachments has focused on the problematic aspects of these contacts, such as sexual addictions, pornography viewing and the use of the Internet for marital infidelity. Interactions in which the primary goal is physical satisfaction (and in which there may be little or no expectation of future offline contact) likely do not implicate trust.

There are at least two main differences between romantic relationships and friendships. First, while friendships may be maintained completely in the online world, romantic relationships are expected to progress to in-person meetings. Second, appearance matters more for romantic or sexual relationships. A spark of physical attraction is part of maintaining these connections. Appearance may affect the progress of the relationship; if one partner finds the other unappealing, the romance is unlikely to continue. However, learning about a person's appearance should not affect trust per se, unless it reveals some deception (e.g., a person turns out to be a different weight, age, or gender than advertised).

In romantic relationships (at least those that progress beyond flirtation or titillation), the risk is also increased, just as in relationships that begin face-to-face. Individuals can be disappointed or betrayed by a friend, but a romantic partner can inflict even deeper emotional wounds. Because the risk is greater, higher levels of trust are also required.

While some romantic relationships may grow out of other kinds of contact (friendships or acquaintanceships), the use of Internet dating or matchmaking services (such as Match.com or eHarmony) has become increasingly common, even among individuals who do not otherwise use the Internet for interaction with strangers. Because these relationships are expected to progress relatively quickly from an initial email contact to an in-person meeting, the development of trust may follow a different pattern. Indeed, users are cautioned against being too trusting. Standard recommendations include meeting at a public place,

telling a friend where they will be and exiting the situation if they feel uncomfortable.

Reputation systems

The Internet is frequently used for commercial or financial transactions. Although a growing body of research has been exploring factors that affect trust in particular websites or willingness to give financial information (such as credit card numbers) online, a review of that literature is beyond the scope of the current discussion.[3] However, some financial transactions have a somewhat more social flavour; in particular, individual transactions facilitated through auction sites. The feedback systems developed by auction websites such as Ebay, where individuals earn a score based on the number of positive or negative comments from individuals with whom they have previously conducted transactions, serve as a proxy for real-world reputation (e.g., Dellarocas 2003; Resnick et al. 2000). These systems can be a powerful means of creating trust. Indeed, feedback systems are used on some purely discussion-based message boards where users rate the qualities of each other's posts. Users can then gain 'trusted' or 'distrusted' status in the community.

Effect of Internet interactions on generalized trust

Researchers have also been interested in how the Internet affects social capital and social networks more broadly and in particular, whether Internet use leads to a more or less trusting outlook on the world (e.g., Putnam 2000). Although this issue remains somewhat controversial, research by Uslaner (2004) using large survey samples suggests that Internet use neither increases nor decreases general trust in others (but see Kraut et al. [2002] for evidence of positive effects of Internet use on generalized trust and Wellman et al. [2001] for evidence that Internet use supplements

---

[3] The *International Journal of Human–Computer Studies* special issue on Trust and Technology, 58(6), is a good starting point for readers interested in the role of trust in ecommerce.

other forms of communication rather than replacing it, thus increasing social connectedness).[4]

Beyond trust

Of course, there are other facets of relationships that must be developed for Internet bonds to be strong ties. Parks and Floyd (1996), for example, identify interdependence, breadth of interaction and commitment as other measures of relationship strength. Trust is likely a precursor of some of these additional relationship dimensions.

Future directions

Although text-based communications such as email and Instant Messages remain the most common forms of online communication, the evolution of the Internet and interactive technology will present new challenges and opportunities for individuals attempting to make trust decisions. For example, the rise of text messaging on cell phones blurs the line between Internet and telephone communication, but at the same time limits the amount of information that can be conveyed in each message. This minimal-information environment may not present problems for individuals who already know each other well, but may affect trust-related judgements of individuals who are not well-acquainted. On the other hand, systems based on existing social networks (such as Friendster) or word-of-mouth (reputation systems), may become increasingly useful aids to establishing trust online.

Regardless of the technological advances ahead, two important future directions for work on Internet trust are to increase understanding of the cues that people use to determine whether others are trustworthy (and whether such cues are accurate) and to trace the development of trust in online relationships. Of course, an underlying question is to what extent these processes differ from those that occur in more traditional social relationships.

---

[4] Some research suggests that individuals who are low in generalized trust may be especially drawn to Internet interaction, at least under some circumstances (e.g., Green and Brock 1998; Uslaner 2004).

References

Bargh, J. A. and McKenna, K. Y. A. (2004). The Internet and social life. *Annual Review of Psychology 55*, 573–590.

Bargh, J. A., McKenna, K. Y. A. and Fitzsimons, G. M. (2002). Can you see the real me? Activation and expression of the 'true self' on the Internet. *Journal of Social Issues 58*(1), 33–48.

Chan, D. K. S. and Cheng, G. H. L. (2004). A comparison of offline and online friendship qualities at different stages of relationship development. *Journal of Social and Personal Relationships 21*(3), 305–320.

Constant, D., Sproull, L. and Kiesler, S. (1996). The kindness of strangers: the usefulness of electronic weak ties for technical advice. *Organization Science 7*, 119–135.

Corritore, C. L., Kracher, B. and Weidenbeck, S. (2003). Online trust: concepts, evolving themes, a model. *International Journal of Human–Computer Studies 58*, 737–758.

Dellarocas, C. (2003). The digitization of word of mouth: promise and challenges of online feedback mechanisms. *Management Science 49*(10), 1407–1424.

DePaulo, B. (1994). Spotting lies: can humans learn to do better? *Current Directions in Psychological Science 3*(3), 83–86.

Derlega, V. J. and Chaikin, A. L. (1977). Privacy and self-disclosure in social relationships. *Journal of Social Issues 33*(3), 102–115.

Deutsch, M. (1962). Cooperation and trust: some theoretical notes. *Nebraska Symposium on Motivation 10*, 275–318.

Green, M. C. (2005). Trust in Internet relationships. Unpublished manuscript.

Green, M. C. and Brock, T. C. (1998). Trust, mood and outcomes of friendship predict preferences for real versus ersatz social capital. *Political Psychology 19*(3), 527–544.

Green, M. C. and Brock, T. C. Antecedents and civic consequences of choosing real versus ersatz social activities. Manuscript under review.

Green, M. C., Hilken, J., Friedman, H., Grossman, K., Gasiewski, J., Adler, R. and Sabini, J. P. (2005). Communication via instant messenger: short and long-term effects. *Journal of Applied Social Psychology 35*(3), 445–462.

Hardin, R. (2001). Conceptions and explanations of trust. In K. S. Cook (ed.), *Trust in Society* (pp. 3–39). New York: Russell Sage Foundation.

Herring, S. C. and Martinson, A. (2004). Assessing gender authenticity in computer-mediated language use: Evidence from an identity game. *Journal of Language and Social Psychology 23*(4), 424–446.

Holmes, J. G. and Rempel, J. K. (1989). Trust in close relationships. In C. Hendrick (ed.), *Close Relationships* (pp. 187–220). Thousand Oaks, CA: Sage.

Joinson, A. N. and Dietz-Uhler, B. (2002). Explanations for the perpetration of and reactions to deception in a virtual community. *Social Science Computer Review 20*(3), 275–289.

Kiesler, S., Siegel, J. and McGuire, T. W. (1984). Social psychological aspects of computer-mediated communication. *American Psychologist 39*(10), 1123–1134.

Kraut, R., Kiesler, S., Boneva, B., Cummings, J., Hegelson, V. and Crawford, A. (2002). Internet paradox revisited. *Journal of Social Issues 58*(1), 49–74.

McKenna, K. Y.A, Green, A. S. and Gleason, M. J. (2002). Relationship formation on the Internet: what's the big attraction? *Journal of Social Issues 58*(1), 9–31.

Meyerson, D., Weick, K. E. and Kramer, R. M. (1996). Swift trust and temporary groups. In R. M. Kramer and T. R. Tyler (eds), *Trust in organizations: Frontiers in theory and research* (pp. 166–195). Thousand Oaks, CA: Sage.

Naquin, C. E. and Paulson, G. D. (2003). Online bargaining and interpersonal trust. *Journal of Applied Psychology 88*(1), 113–120.

Parks, M. and Floyd, K. (1996). Making friends in cyberspace. *Journal of Computer-Mediated Communication 4*(1).

Parks, M. R. and Roberts, L. D. (1998). Making MOOsic: the development of personal relationships online and a comparison to their off-line counterparts. *Journal of Social and Personal Relationships 15*, 517–537.

Postmes, T., Spears, R. and Lea, M. (1998). Breaching or building social boundaries? SIDE-effects of computer-mediated communication. *Communication Research 25*, 689–715.

Putnam, R. D. (2000). *Bowling alone*. New York: Simon and Schuster.

Resnick, P., Zeckhauser, R., Friedman, E. and Kuwabara, K. (2000). Reputation systems. *Communications of the ACM 43*(12), 45–48.

Rotter, J. B. (1980). Interpersonal trust, trustworthiness and gullibility. *American Psychologist 35*(1), 1–7.

Sagarin, B. J., Rhoads, K. and Cialdini, R. B. (1998). Deceiver's distrust: denigration as a consequence of undiscovered deception. *Personality and Social Psychology Bulletin 24*, 1167–1176.

Turkle, S. (1995). *Life on the screen: Identity in the age of the Internet*. New York: Touchstone.

Uslaner, E. M. (2004). Trust, civic engagement and the Internet. *Political Communication 21*, 223–242.

Van Gelder, L. (1985). The strange case of the electronic lover: a real-life story of deception, seduction and technology. *Ms 14*(4), 94, 99, 101–104, 117, 123, 124.

Vazire, S. and Gosling, S. D. (2004). E-perceptions: personality impressions based on personal websites. *Journal of Personality and Social Psychology 87*(1), 123–132.

Walther, J. B. (1996). Computer-mediated communication: impersonal, interpersonal and hyperpersonal interaction. *Communication Research 23*(1), 3–43.

Walther, J.B. (2004). Language and communication technology: introduction to the special issue. *Journal of Language and Social Psychology, 23*, 384–396.

Wellman, B., Haase, A. Q., Witte, J. and Hampton, K. (2001). Does the Internet decrease, increase, or supplement social capital? *American Behavioral Scientist 45*(3), 436–455.

Whitty, M. (2002). Liar, liar! An examination of how open, supportive and honest people are in chat rooms. *Computers in Human Behavior 18*(4), 343–352.

Whitty, M. and Gavin, J. (2001). Age/sex/location: uncovering social cues in the development of online relationships. *Cyberpsychology and Behavior 4*(5), 623–630.

Yamagishi, T. (2001). Trust as a form of social intelligence. In K. S. Cook (ed.), *Trust in society* (pp. 121–147). New York: Russell Sage Foundation.

CHAPTER 5

Trust in mediated interactions

Jens Riegelsberger, M. Angela Sasse and John D. McCarthy

Introduction

Examples of trust issues in mediated interactions range from potential e-commerce customers staying away from a technology for fear of being defrauded (Consumer Web Watch 2002) to virtual organizations struggling because *'trust requires touch'* (Handy 1995). Hence, there has been a surge in online trust research in the field of human–computer interaction (HCI). This research mainly addresses two areas: trust in websites, in particular those of business to customer (B2C) e-commerce vendors, and trust in other people with whom one interacts via online technologies (e.g. email, instant messaging, video-conferencing) in virtual team settings. The findings of this research are highly relevant for companies providing such technologies and services, but also for regulators, consumer protection agencies and researchers who are concerned about the social transformations induced by new technologies.

However, HCI trust research lacks an agreed theoretical basis in terms of concepts and research methodologies. This has led to a situation where many researchers who claim to investigate trust in online interactions are in fact studying rather distinct aspects of trust. Unsurprisingly, many apparently contradictory findings have been reported and it is difficult to reconcile them without a common terminology and a common frame of reference.

In this chapter, we present a brief overview on the background of trust research and its relevance. We then introduce a framework for trust in mediated interactions that draws on existing models and findings and applies to human trust in other humans, organizations (e.g. e-commerce vendors) and technology (e.g. websites). Beyond incorporating variables related to the trusting and the trusted actor, the framework accommodates key contextual factors. Rather than treating trustworthiness as a relatively stable attribute of the trusted actor, the framework considers how trustworthiness is influenced by these contextual factors. We believe that this framework will help researchers in aligning disparate research findings and that it can be a step towards building a theory of trust in human–computer interactions. For designers, the benefit lies in helping them to fully explore the available design space of systems fostering trust in mediated interactions.

After a short introduction to the background of trust research, this chapter outlines the framework and applies it to research findings on trust in e-commerce and trust in virtual teams. A more detailed version of the framework can be found in Riegelsberger *et al.* (2005).

Trust

The term *trust* is used in everyday language, but its meaning is only loosely defined and varies considerably with context. In the scientific community, the situation is unfortunately not very different. Trust has been studied for many years in many disciplines and there is a plethora of trust definitions researchers can choose from (Corritore *et al.* 2003). The definitions contrast on various dimensions and consider trust in different situational contexts. In addition, the empirical methods used range from social dilemma games via self-report questionnaires to ethnographic studies – again with ample differences in the constructs that are measured or the phenomena observed. The sociologist Uslaner (2002) concedes that it 'works somewhat mysteriously' (2002: 1). There is no widely accepted theory of trust – rather research is fragmented across several disciplines, divided by conceptual and methodological boundaries (Gambetta 1988).

While the definition and measurement of trust are subject to much disagreement, the relevance of trust is rarely disputed. Trust reduces the need for costly control structures, thus enabling exchanges that could otherwise not take place, and makes social systems more adaptable (Uslaner 2002). Not surprisingly, generalized trust correlates well with macro-economic indicators such as productivity or health (Fukuyama 1999; Putnam 2000 O'Neill 2002; Uslaner 2002). Empirical studies by economists did also find a positive effect of trust on productivity in joint ventures and within work teams (Sitkin and Roth 1993; Fukuyama 1995; Uslaner 2002). In research on consumer decision-making, trust in the vendor and the product has been identified as an important factor for purchasing decisions (Aaker 1996; Kotler 2002).

Trust permeates most of our actions, because modern life is characterized by a high dependency on others' actions (Giddens 1990). As an example, making ourselves dependent on others allows us to focus on specialized professional activities, while others ensure the safety of our possessions, the supply of food, or the education of our children. Relinquishing direct control of critical activities by externalizing them to others frees resources for activities at which we are more productive. In many situations trust will be given so fully and habitually that it is not recognized as such, but is experienced as mere 'expectation of continuity' (Luhmann 1979).

Most researchers, however, agree that the question of trust is experienced in situations in which there is some level of experienced uncertainty regarding the outcome and where this outcome has some value to the individual, i.e. if there is some risk (Luhmann 1979; Mayer *et al.* 1995). Uncertainty arises from the dependence of the outcome on the actions of actors in whose reasoning or functioning the trusting individual has only limited insight (Giddens 1990).

The discourse on trust, held within the field of HCI with a view to optimizing design, should also be seen within the wider sociological debate on the effects of technology on society and – more specifically – *social capital*.[1] Several researchers have argued that the drop in indicators of social capital seen in modern societies in recent years can partially be attributed to the transformations of social interactions brought about by advances in communication technologies (Putnam 2000). Interactions that used to be based on long-established personal relationships and face-to-face interaction, goes the argument, are now conducted over distance or with automated systems – a process also described by Giddens (1990) as *disembedding*. From this point of view, by conducting more interactions over distance or with computers rather than with humans, we deprive ourselves of opportunities for trust building. A similar perspective can be found in the field of organizational theory. Some authors claim that reported failures of systems to yield the expected productivity gains in organizations (Landauer 1996) partially stem from a reduction in opportunities to build social capital that came with their introduction (Resnick 2002). Trust, goes the argument, can be formed as a by-product of informal exchanges, but if new technologies make many such exchanges obsolete through automation, trusting relations between humans may not be formed.

While this view is not universally shared (systems may, for example, be designed in such a way that they encourage personal interaction; Resnick [2002]), it suggests that trust is a highly relevant subject for the design of systems that support

---

[1] 'Social capital inheres in the structure of relations between actors and among actors' (Coleman 1988: S98). Social capital becomes manifest in obligations and expectations, information channels and social norms. Trust is an important factor of social capital (Coleman 1988; Fukuyama 1995; Glaeser *et al.* 2000).

mediated interactions. Several researchers responded to this situation by creating models of trust in mediated interactions (e.g. Friedman *et al.* 2000; McKnight and Chervany 2000, 2001; Tan and Thoen 2000; Corritore *et al.* 2003, Fogg 2003; Johnston and Warkentin 2004)[2]. Most of these models focus on the factors that contribute to the perception of trustworthiness. Our framework outlined in the next section references these models, but it broadens the focus to include factors that motivate trustworthy behaviour. Signals for trustworthiness are then considered in a second step.

Framework for trust in mediated interactions

The basic model

We develop the framework from the sequential interaction between two actors, the *trustor* (trusting actor) and the *trustee* (trusted actor) – e.g. a human or an e-commerce vendor and its technology. Figure 5.1 shows a model of a prototypical trust-requiring situation.[3] Both actors can realize some gain by conducting an exchange. Prior to

the exchange, trustor and trustee perceive signals (1) from each other and the context. The trustor's level of trust will be influenced by the signals perceived. Depending on her level of trust and other factors (e.g. the availability of outside options), the trustor will either engage in trusting action (2a), or withdraw from the situation (2b). *Trusting action* is defined as a *behaviour that increases the vulnerability of the trustor* (Corritore *et al.* 2003). This can apply to anything of value to the actors: money, time, personal information, or psychological gratification. A trustor will engage in trusting action if they can realize a gain when the trustee fulfils his part of the exchange (3a). However, the trustee may lack the *motivation* to fulfil and decide to exploit the trustor's vulnerability, or he might simply not have the *ability* (Deutsch 1958). Both possibilities result in non-fulfilment (3b).

In the hypothetical absence of any other motivating factors, being trusted and then refusing to fulfil (3b) is the outcome with the highest gain for the trustee. However, in most real-world situations, we observe trusting actions and fulfilment in spite of incentives to the contrary: vendors deliver goods after receiving payment, banks pay out savings, individuals do not sell their friends' phone numbers to direct marketers. In many such cases, trustees' actions are motivated by *trust-warranting properties* (Bacharach and Gambetta 2003), i.e. intrinsic or contextual factors that provide incentives for fulfilment. Identifying and reliably signalling trust-warranting properties is

[2] See Grabner-Kraeuter and Kaluscha (2003) for a review of additional models and studies that focus on user trust in e-commerce.

[3] This situation is captured by the Trust Game (Berg *et al.* 2003; Bacharach and Gambetta, 2003).

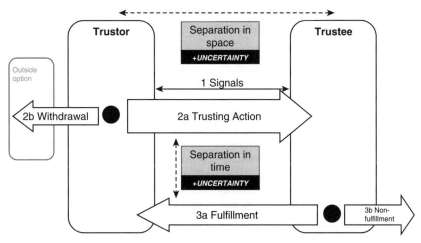

Figure 5.1 The trust-requiring situation.

the key concern for the emergence of trust and trustworthy behaviour.

If we had accurate insight into the trustee's reasoning or functioning, trust would not be an issue (Giddens 1990). Uncertainty, and thus the need for trust, stems from the lack of detailed knowledge about the trustee's trust-warranting properties. Information about these is only available in the form of signals (1). If trustor and trustee are separated in space, their interactions are mediated (e.g. by mail, email, telephone) and some of the signals that are present in face-to-face encounters may not be available or become distorted. This effect is captured in communication theory by models of *channel reduction* (Döring 1998). These include *social presence* (Short *et al.* 1976), *presence* (Lombard and Ditton 1997; Biocca *et al.* 2003) and *media richness* (Daft and Lengel 1986; Rice 1992). This loss of information is often considered to increase uncertainty and result in lower trust (e.g. Handy 1995). However, such channel reduction models have also been criticized because they do not account for the ability of technology to supply information that otherwise would not be available in a face-to-face situation (e.g. reputation rating scores; see p. 57) (Döring 1998). Mediation may also increase the delay between trusting action (2a) and fulfilment (3a), for example if an exchange relies on the postal system. This separation in time prolongs the period of uncertainty for the trustor. Thus, temporal as well as spatial separation of trusting action and fulfilment can increase uncertainty and thus the need for trust (Giddens 1990; Brynjolfsson and Smith 2000).

Signalling trustworthiness: symbols and symptoms

Signals from the trustee and the context allow the trustor to form expectations of behaviour. A stable identity (e.g. provided by facial recognition) is an example of an important signal for the assessment of trustworthiness in a given situation, as it allows the trustor to form expectations based on previously observed behaviour.

As many mediated interactions are relatively novel, the observed lack of trust may partially be explained by a lack of experience in decoding signals and making inferences about baseline probabilities of untrustworthy behaviour (Riegelsberger and Sasse 2001). Lack of trust is also a result of

mimicry (Bacharach and Gambetta 2003): non-trustworthy actors trying to *appear trustworthy* in order to obtain the benefits. In the view of many consumers, moving interactions online makes mimicry easier (Riegelsberger and Sasse, 2001). To understand how mimicry can operate we draw on semiotics and distinguish between two types of signals: symbols and symptoms (Bacharach and Gambetta 2003; Riegelsberger *et al.* 2003b).

Symbols of trustworthiness

Symbols have an arbitrarily assigned meaning, they are specifically created to signify the presence of trust-warranting properties: examples of symbols for such properties are e-commerce trust seals. Symbols can be protected by making them very difficult to forge, or by threatening sanctions in the case of misuse. They are a common way of signalling trustworthiness, but their usability is currently limited. Because they are created for specific settings, the trustor has to know about their existence and how to decode them. At the same time, trustees need to invest in emitting them and in getting them known (Bacharach and Gambetta 1997).

Symptoms of trustworthiness

Symptoms are not specifically created to signal trust-warranting properties; rather, they are given off as a by-product of trust warranting properties. Symptoms come at no cost to trustworthy actors, but mimicking them requires some effort from untrustworthy actors. Interpersonal cues (e.g. eye gaze) are often considered to be symptomatic of emotional states and thus thought to give insight into people's trustworthiness (Baron and Byrne 2004). However, this widely held belief is only partially supported by research in social psychology and will be discussed in more depth in the section *Intrinsic properties*.

Trust-warranting properties

Having established the terminology to describe trust-requiring situations, we introduce the factors that support trustworthy behaviour. In the interest of creating a parsimonious framework, we will delineate the main classes of trust-warranting properties, rather than describing all specific motivational factors or attributes of ability.

Contextual properties

Raub and Weesie (2000b) identified three categories of factors that can lead trustees to fulfil. These are *temporal*, *social* and *institutional embeddedness* (see Figure 5.2). These contextual properties allow trustors to make themselves vulnerable, even if they know very little about the personal attributes of the trustee.

Temporal embeddedness

If trustees have reason to believe that they will interact again with a given trustor in a situation where they are recognizable (i.e. have stable identities), fulfilment can become preferable. While a trustee could realize a large gain from non-fulfilment, he also knows that the trustor would not place trust in future encounters. Non-fulfilment in the present encounter thus prevents gains that could be realized in future exchanges (Friedman 1977; Axelrod 1980). In a more trustor-centric view of *temporal embeddedness*, repeated interactions also allow the trustor to accumulate knowledge about the trustee and thus to make better predictions about his future behaviour. Hence, assuming stability of a trustee's attributes, repeated interactions can decrease uncertainty. By extrapolating from past behaviour, trust in future encounters can be won (Luhmann 1979).

Social embeddedness

This property is included in many models of trust in the form of reputation (e.g. Corritore *et al.* 2003; Fogg 2003). From the perspective of these models reputation is historic information about trustors' attributes such as *honesty*, *reliability*, or *dependability* (McKnight and Chervany 2000; Sapient and Cheskin 1999; Corritore *et al.* 2003; Friedman *et al.* 2000; see below). Assuming stability of such attributes across time and context, they can form the basis of trust in present encounters. However, trust based on reputation alone is vulnerable to strategic misuse, as inherently untrustworthy actors can build up a good reputation to 'cash in' by not fulfilling in the final transaction. Anecdotal evidence of such behaviour exists for online-auction sites (Lee 2002), but it has also been shown in laboratory experiments with social dilemma games (e.g. Bohnet *et al.* 2003). Reputation also has a second function, as the trustor's ability to tarnish the trustee's reputation provides an incentive to fulfil. Reputation can thus act as a *'hostage'* in the hands of socially well-embedded trustors (Raub and Weesie 2000a; Einwiller 2001).

Factors that influence the effect of reputation are *identifiability* and *traceability*, the *social connectedness* of the trustor (Glaeser *et al.* 2000), the topology of the *social network* (Granovetter 1973), the cost of capturing and disseminating *reliable past information* and the degree to which such information itself can be trusted to be truthful (Bacharach and Gambetta 2003).

Institutional embeddedness

Institutions often take the form of organizations that influence the behaviour of individuals or other organizations. Examples of institutions are law enforcement agencies, judicial systems, trade organizations, or companies. Institutions are often embedded in wider networks of trust where one institution acts as guardian of trust for another one (Shapiro 1987). As most everyday interactions are conducted within a web of institutional embeddedness, the effect of institutions often does not come to mind as long as a situation conforms a template of *situational normality* (Shapiro 1987; Rousseau *et al.* 1998; McKnight and Chervany 2000). When new technologies transform the way in which people interact, their templates of situational normality may not apply any more. Additionally, if technology increases the spatial distance between the actors, the trustee may be based in a different society or culture and consequently the trustor may be less familiar with the institutions that govern his behaviour (Jarvenpaa and Tractinsky 1999; Brynjolfsson and Smith 2000).

In summary, contextual properties provide incentives for the trustee to behave in a trustworthy manner. Their presence allows trustors to engage in trusting action without detailed knowledge of the trustee. However, trust – some would say reliance (see Forms of trust) – when solely based on these properties – is bound to break down in their absence.

Intrinsic properties

While contextual properties can motivate trustees to fulfil, they do not fully explain how actors behave empirically (Riegelsberger *et al.* 2003b). Contextual properties are complemented by intrinsic properties, which we define as relatively stable attributes of a trustee that provide the ability and intrinsic motivation for fulfilment (Deci 1992).

Ability

This property is the counterpart to motivation in Deutsch's (1958) classic definition of trustworthiness. Mayer *et al.* (1995: 707) define ability for human and institutional actors as a 'group of skills, competencies and characteristics that enable a party to have influence within some specific domain'. Ability also applies to technical systems in the form of confidentiality, integrity (accuracy, reliability), authentication, non-repudiation, access-control and availability (Ratnasingam and Pavlou 2004).

Internalized norms

Granovetter's (1985) classic example of the economist, who – against all economic rationality – leaves a tip in a roadside restaurant far from home[4] illustrates the effect of *internalized norms*. In many cases, norm compliance will be internalized to such an extent that it becomes habitual (Fukuyama 1999). The foundation is laid in individuals' socialization, in which they are 'culturally embossed' with basic social norms of their culture (Brosig *et al.* 2002). However, social norms differ across groups and cultures, they have to evolve over time and triggering them may depend on the trustor's signalling of group membership (Fukuyama 1999). Not all norms are desirable per se, as strong in-group reciprocity may come at the cost of hostility or aggression towards non-members (Fukuyama 1999).

Benevolence

The intrinsic property *benevolence* captures the trustee's gratification from the trustor's well-being and his company. Hence, it is different from the expectation of future returns that is the source of motivation arising from the contextual property temporal embeddedness. The capacity for benevolence is an attribute of the trustee, but the specific level of benevolence in a trust-

requiring situation is an attribute of the relationship between trustor and trustee. A trustee may act benevolently towards one trustor, but not towards another one. Strong benevolence is typical for long-standing or romantic relationships (Rempel *et al.* 1985), but it can also be present – to a lesser degree – among work colleagues or business partners (Macauley 1963; Granovetter 1985).

Interpersonal cues and intrinsic properties

Interpersonal cues play a special role in signalling and triggering intrinsic trust-warranting properties in interactions between humans. As mediating face-to-face interactions or replacing them with human–computer interaction often leads to the loss of some interpersonal cues (Döring 1998), their role merits a brief discussion.

The presence of intrinsic trust-warranting properties is widely believed to manifest itself through interpersonal cues (Goffman 1959; Bacharach and Gambetta 2003). The symptomatic nature of interpersonal cues is supported by empirical studies (Hinton 1993; Baron and Byrne 2004) – but these also found that such cues can be subject to impression management (Hinton 1993), i.e. trustees' deliberate use of interpersonal cues to create the desired impressions. Interpersonal cues can create some level of affective trust, even if there is no rational basis for such trust attributions. Reeves and Nass (1996), in their studies with computers as social actors, provide examples of this effect: even a synthetic animated character that exhibited only very simplistic interpersonal cues was found to increase trust (Rickenberg and Reeves 2000).

In summary, intrinsic properties provide motivation and the ability for trustworthy behaviour that is independent from contextual incentives. Interpersonal cues are widely believed to give information about intrinsic properties, but there is only limited empirical evidence. Figure 5.2 shows the framework, based on the abstract situation introduced in Figure 5.1, with contextual and intrinsic properties added.

Forms of trust

In this section we discuss how the different types of trust identified by other researchers can be accommodated by the framework. Each type of trust relates to a belief about a specific

---

[4] This situation is not embedded temporally (he will not visit the restaurant again), socially (the waiter cannot tell relevant others about his behaviour), or institutionally (there is no formal way of enforcing tipping).

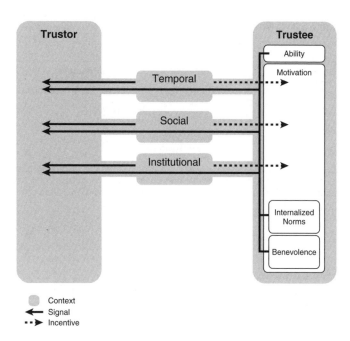

Figure 5.2 The complete framework.

Context
Signal
Incentive

configuration of trust-warranting properties. Subsequently, types of trust differ in the way trustworthiness is signalled and perceived, in their stability over time, how wide their scope is and what types of vulnerabilities are normally covered by them (Corritore *et al.* 2003). Our fundamental distinction between contextual and intrinsic properties is reflected in the discussion of other researchers.

Contextual properties

Trust based on contextual properties is also called *reliance* or *assurance-based trust* (Yamagishi and Yamagishi 1994; Lahno 2002). Describing a similar concept, Rousseau *et al.* (1998) and Koehn (2003) use the terms *calculus-based trust* or *calculative trust*, respectively. Other terms that have been coined are *guarded trust* (Brenkert 1998; Corritore *et al.* 2003), *deterrence-based trust* (Lewicki and Bunker 1996; Lewis and Weigert 1985) and *control trust* (Tan and Thoen 2000). *Institutional trust* (Lahno 2002) specifically captures the effect of the contextual property *institutional embeddedness*. Rousseau *et al.* (1998) see it as a backdrop that envelops and safeguards our everyday interactions, thus closely matching McKnight and Chervany's (2000) concept of *situational normality*.

Technology trust (Ratnasingam and Pavlou 2004) and *Internet trust* (Lee and Turban 2001) are largely based on the *ability* of a technology to support interactions as expected by the user. However, as they are embedded in socio-technical systems, technology trust commonly also entails other types of trust in organizations or institutions that safeguard technology.

Intrinsic properties

Types of trust that are mainly based on intrinsic properties of the trustee are *relational* (Rousseau *et al.* 1998), *party* (Tan and Thoen 2000), *partner* (Ratnasingam and Pavlou 2004), *knowledge-based* (Koehn 2003), or *respect-based trust* (Koehn 2003). Types of trust that rely on intrinsic properties develop over time and are founded on a history of successful exchanges. They have a higher *bandwidth* (Rousseau *et al.* 1998; Corritore *et al.* 2003), i.e. ensures risk-taking across a wider range of situations. Table 5.1 maps types of trust to the level of acquaintance.

Trust in e-commerce websites

This section provides an overview of research into the trustworthiness of websites. While some

Table 5.1 Different types of trust linked to levels of acquaintance

Level			Source
Early	Medium	Mature	
Deterrence-based	Knowledge-based	Identification-based	Lewicki and Bunker (1996)
Calculus-based	Relational		Rousseau *et al.* (1998)
Basic/guarded	Extended		Corritore *et al.* (2003)
Swift			Meyerson *et al.* (1996)
Calculative	Knowledge-based, respect-based		Koehn (2003)
Mainly based on contextual properties	Mainly based on intrinsic properties		

researchers looked at trust in health information sites (Sillence *et al.* 2004) and into the credibility of news sites (Schweiger 1999; Fogg *et al.* 2001), the majority of website trust research addresses user trust in e-commerce sites. This section first discusses how the framework can be used to structure an analysis of signifiers of trustworthiness in e-commerce and then gives an overview on existing design guidelines.

Applying the framework

E-commerce transactions are subject to several risks such as loss of privacy, interception of financial data, lack of fulfilment, etc. (Egger 2001; Riegelsberger and Sasse 2003a). While not all of these risks are related to the actions of e-commerce vendors, we focus our discussion on activities that can be undertaken by individual vendors to build user trust.

Temporal embeddedness

Vendors can indicate that they are interested in continued interactions. This may be achieved by showing that the company has been in business for a long time, or that it is linked to a long-standing off-line brand, or even by making clear that considerable investment has been made in the site or the brand (e.g. through advertising). Another way to show trustworthiness in terms of temporal embeddedness is customer relationship management (Egger 2001). Vendors can demonstrate an interest in a continued relationship by giving first-time purchase price incentives (e.g. Amazon's first-time visitor's voucher), by eliciting feedback

(e.g. publicly, as does Amazon.com on its site), or by offering loyalty schemes (Egger 2001).

Social embeddedness

This property is an important factor for purchase decisions. Users – in particular first-time ones – pay much attention to their friends' and families' recommendations when deciding where to shop online (Murray 1991; Kotler 2002; Riegelsberger and Sasse 2003a). Recognizing this process, several marketing methods have sprung up that aim to influence the dissemination of reputation information in informal networks. These include viral marketing and targeting opinion leaders (Kotler 2002). The Internet itself can be used to facilitate the formation and dissemination of reputation information in informal networks: services such as Epinions[5] or Bizrate[6] that collect customer feedback on many products and services. Amazon's affiliate programme is another example of using the Internet to communicate reputation information. An individual vendor can display social embeddedness through endorsements (e.g. from well-known experts), or through positive customer comments.

Institutional embeddedness

Trust seal programmes (Sapient and Cheskin 1999) are an example of a prominent institutional approach to building trust in e-commerce.

[5] http://www.epinions.com.

[6] http://www.bizrate.com.

Such programmes work by establishing rules of conduct (e.g. with regard to security technology or privacy policies) and checking their members' performance against these rules. Complying members are awarded trust seals: small icons they can display on their site. These seals are commonly linked to the certifying body's site to enable checking their veracity. The disadvantage of many such programmes is that the certifying organizations are not well known and thus have no trust they could transfer (Riegelsberger and Sasse 2003a). Trust seals given by well-known organizations that 'sublet' their trust by endorsing unknown vendors are more promising, because they put their established reputation at stake. Amazon's zShops go beyond giving seal-based endorsements by hosting independent vendors and enforcing codes of conduct.

Ability

This property takes the shape of professionalism in the context of e-commerce. Professionalism in site design can be seen as a symptom for competence or ability to fulfil (Egger 2001). To appear professional, a vendor needs to comply with offline business standards, for example consistent graphic design, absence of technological failures, clear assignment of responsibilities, upfront disclosure of terms and conditions, shipping costs and availability, and with web standards, for example an easy to remember URL, good usability, privacy policy, similarity in interaction design to well known sites (Egger 2001) (see Table 5.2).

Internalized norms

This property is easily identified in the case of human trustees: with an e-commerce vendor, however, the mapping is more difficult. An organization can aim to influence the internalized norms of its employees by promoting appropriate values, norms and performance targets through mission statements, training programmes and selection processes (Kotler 2002). These intrinsic properties can then be communicated in the form of advertising, public relations activities, but also through the e-commerce interface. However, potential users are unlikely to read corporate mission statements or philosophies in detail. Hence, the interface design must communicate these by allowing users to experience them while they are fulfiling their task. This can be achieved through

visual design, through the use of language and through appropriate conceptual modelling. As an example, the way in which a system responds to incorrect customer entries gives much information about an organization's attitude towards its customers (Cooper and Reimann 2003).

Benevolence

Strong benevolence as identified in long-standing relationships between humans does not apply to e-commerce. However, with a continued business relationship, a form of benevolence between vendor and customer can grow in the shape of strong brand loyalty (Riegelsberger and Sasse 2002).

Interpersonal cues and intrinsic properties

In the context of e-commerce, marketing photos or other media representations of 'friendly people' are often used with the aim to build trust. This approach harnesses the immediate visceral effect such interpersonal cues have – even in mediated form. Empirical evidence suggests that this approach can sway superficial impressions – but there is also evidence for negative effects on the usability of e-commerce systems (Fogg *et al.* 2001; Riegelsberger and Sasse 2002; Steinbrueck *et al.* 2002).

Existing guidelines for trust in e-commerce

HCI research on trust in e-commerce is largely focused on creating interface design guidelines that are derived from user interviews or observations. The resulting guidelines have been very helpful for designers of e-commerce sites. However, they have also been criticized for focusing too narrowly on increasing trust, rather than aiming to support correctly placed trust (Riegelsberger *et al.* 2005).

In one of the earliest studies on consumer trust in e-commerce, Jarvenpaa and Tractinsky (1999) identified perceived size and reputation of existing e-commerce vendors as predictors of trust and willingness to buy. These findings, however, were not linked to specific e-commerce design elements. One of the earliest studies that focused exclusively on the effect of interface elements on consumer trust was conducted by Sapient and

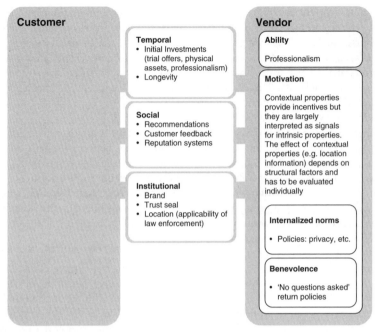

Figure 5.3 The framework applied to trust in consumer e-commerce.

Cheskin (1999). The fundamental building blocks of trust identified in this study were *seals of approval, quality of presentation, navigation, branding, fulfilment* and *use of secure, error-free technology*. The findings related to interface elements are included in Table 5.2. The most comprehensive e-commerce trust model linked to interface design guidelines has been developed by Egger (2001). Factors in his MoTEC model include:

◆ *Pre-interactional* filters refer to factors that affect a new customer's a priori trust. These are personal propensity to trust, knowledge about the industry and the brand and trust transferred via recommendations.

◆ *Interface properties* are those surface cues that determine the first impression of a website; they are included in Table 5.2.

◆ *Informational content* refers to interface surface cues that require a more detailed exploration of the site, such as policies and company information – they are also included in Table 5.2.

◆ *Relationship management* refers to the vendor's actions after a transaction incurred. Here, trust-building activities include various channels of

contact, rapid turnaround for questions and order tracking.

Table 5.2 summarizes the key elements from Egger's (2001) and Sapient and Cheskin's (1999) models and adds findings from guidelines and reviews that were subsequently published. It also shows which trust-warranting properties are addressed by individual design recommendations.

In summary, the research on trust in e-commerce vendors has resulted in a large number of guidelines detailing interface elements and constructs that have been named by users as signifiers of trustworthiness. Using the framework, these elements can be interpreted as signals for the underlying contextual and intrinsic properties. This approach abstracts from the specific technical implementations and thus provides guidelines that are transferable to other technologies.

Trust in virtual teams

While many studies in social psychology looked at trust as one of several aspects of interpersonal perception in mediated communications, only a

Table 5.2 Elements of trustworthy interface design

Recommendation	Property addressed	Source
Absence of errors (absence of outdated information)	Ability	Nielsen (1999), Sapient (1999)
Aesthetic design	Ability, norms	Nielsen (1999), Egger (2001), Dayal et al. (2001), Sapient (1999)
Affiliations (linking to others, link backs, cooperating with trusted brands, customer references, third party endorsements, trust seals, testimonials)	Social, institutional embeddedness	Nielsen (1999), Dayal et al. (2001), IBM (2003), Shneiderman (2000), Bailey et al. (2001), Grabner-Kraeuter and Kaluscha (2003), de Ruyter et al. (2001), Ratnasingam and Pavlou (2004), Jarvenpaa and Tractinsky (1999)
Branding	Institutional embeddedness	Egger (2001), Bailey et al. (2001), Sapient and Cheskin (1999)
Detailed product information	Ability	Dayal et al. (2001), Egger (2001), Nielsen et al. (2000)
Information about past performance	Temporal embeddedness	Shneiderman (2000)
Openness/transparency (providing background on company, contact information, photographs)	Ability, norms, benevolence	IBM (2003), Egger (2001), Nielsen et al. (2000), Grabner-Kraeuter et al. (2003), Gefen (2005), de Ruyter et al. (2001)
People and social presence (showing staff, customers – giving interpersonal cues	Interpersonal cues to signal intrinsic properties	Grabner-Kraeuter et al. (2003), Egger (2001), Nielsen et al. (2000)
Physical assets (showing or describing company's buildings, offices)	Institutional embeddedness, temporal embeddedness	Grabner-Kraeuter et al. (2003), Gefen (2005), de Ruyter et al. (2001)
Privacy policy	Norms	Egger (2001), Cranor et al. (1999)
Security (e.g. encryption)	Ability (technological)	IBM (2003), Egger (2001), Sapient and Cheskin (1999), Nielsen et al. (2000)
Size (perceived size of the site/ organization)	Temporal Embeddedness, Ability	Jarvenpaa and Tractinsky (1999), Bailey et al. (2001), Grabner-Kraeuter et al. (2003)
Trials (low-risk initial interactions)	Benevolence, reduction of risks Riegelsberger et al. (2003a)	Dayal et al. (2001)
Upfront disclosure (privacy policy, shipping cost, corporate philosophy)	Norms, benevolence	Nielsen (1999), IBM (2003), Shneiderman (2000), Egger (2001), Bailey et al. (2001), Nielsen et al. (2000)
Usability (good navigation)	Ability	Nielsen (1999), Egger (2001), Bailey et al. (2001), Sapient and Cheskin (1999) Grabner-Kraeuter et al. (2003), Lee and Turban (2001)

Continued

Table 5.2 Elements of trustworthy interface design *cont.*

Recommendation	Property addressed	Source
User control over information (giving reasons/benefits for and control over captured personal information)	Reduction of risks Riegelsberger *et al.* (2003a)	Nielsen (1999), IBM (2003), Egger (2001), Dayal *et al.* (2001)
Warranty policy	Norms	Grabner-Kraeuter *et al.* (2003), Jarvenpaa and Tractinsky (1999) de Ruyter *et al.* (2001), Lee and Turban (2001), Ratnasingam and Pavlou (2004), Kim (1996)

few specifically investigated trust. Most of the studies in the field of HCI that specifically focused on trust explored media effects on cooperation (i.e. on trust *and* trustworthy behaviour) in virtual teams with social dilemma games. They compared cooperation in representations such as video, audio, email, or text-chat. They thus focused on the effect of mediating interactions on the visibility of interpersonal cues (see the section Intrinsic properties). Due to the relatively narrow focus of these studies, the discussion in this section is mainly concerned with demonstrating how the framework can be used to incorporate further aspects of interpersonal trust in mediated interactions. First, however, the findings of these studies are briefly summarized.

Studies on media representations and trust

Video

Studies on team cooperation found that video resulted in the highest rate of cooperation compared to the other media researched (Bos *et al.* 2002; Brosig *et al.* 2002). In the study by Brosig *et al.* (2002) video with audio, reached levels of cooperation that were similar to those reached in face-to-face (ftf) communication. They are, however, reached after a longer time than in face-to-face interaction. Furthermore, cooperation was less stable without face-to-face communication (Bos *et al.* 2002).

Audio

The studies on cooperation in teams, yielded – in line with media richness models – that audio-only communication resulted in levels of cooperation that were lower than those for video (Bos *et al.* 2002), but higher than those found for text-only communications (Jensen *et al.* 2000; Bos *et al.* 2002; Davis *et al.* 2002; Olson *et al.* 2002). Even synthetic speech was found to reduce uncooperative behaviour compared to text chat (Jensen *et al.* 2000; Davis *et al.* 2002).

Photos

Out of the studies reported in Table 5.3, only Olson *et al.* (2002) looked specifically at the effect of exposure to a photo; they found a marginal positive effect on cooperation. Similarly, Bohnet and Frey (1999) found that silent mutual identification prior to making decisions in a social dilemma game with no communications increased cooperation, even though a photo or silent identification do not carry any information specific to the task at hand (e.g. intentions and strategies in a social dilemma game). These findings are not in line with those of a longitudinal study by Walther *et al.* (2001) on his earlier concept of hyperpersonal interaction: in the long run, groups communicating without seeing photos of each other rated their partners more positively than those that had been given photos of each other.

Text

Text-only communication was used by many of the studies discussed for baseline comparisons. Text-only communication led to lower cooperation than richer channels such as ftf or video (Jensen *et al.* 2000; Bos *et al.* 2002; Brosig *et al.* 2002). These findings are corroborated by Frohlich and Oppenheimer (1998), who compared text-only to ftf communications. In one of the few longitudinal studies in this field, Jarvenpaa and Leidner (1998) found that collaboration via email only resulted in fragile swift trust (Meyerson *et al.* 1996, see Table 5.1). However, even text-only communication increases cooperation and trust compared to no communication. This finding is strongly supported by a review of 37 social dilemma studies conducted by Sally (1995).

Applying the framework

In this section, the framework for trust in mediated interactions is used to discuss the studies on trust in virtual teams, to show limits to their generalizability and to outline further areas for research into trust in human actors.

Structure

The studies on virtual teams used symmetric and synchronous social dilemma games, in which all actors have the same role and where decisions have to be reached at exactly the same time. These games are good models of a public good problem, where many individuals decide at the same time without knowing the others' decisions. However, they do not model many everyday trust-requiring situations, where we can identify a trustor and a trustee as actors with distinct roles. Public good models are characterized by strategic insecurity (Lahno 2002), which does not apply to conventional trust-requiring situations. In addition, symmetric games make it impossible to investigate the effect of a technology on trust and trustworthy behaviour individually, as non-cooperation can be the consequence of defensive (i.e. lack of trust) as well as defective motives (i.e. lack of trustworthiness).

Temporal embeddedness

Social dilemma studies clearly show the effect of temporal embeddedness in the form of deteriorating cooperation towards the end of the experimental games, when participants do not expect future interactions with other participants (Bos *et al.* 2002; Olson *et al.* 2002; Bohnet *et al.* 2003). One can also argue that the chosen media representation in effect determines the temporal embeddedness of a situation, as e.g. facial representations allow recognition of the experimental

partner beyond the laboratory situation, whereas participants who are e.g. represented by text-only cease to be identifiable after the experiment. However, experimental studies – varying prior acquaintance of participants aside – cannot investigate temporal embeddedness beyond the duration of one experimental session. Hence, they need to be complemented with longitudinal surveys and ethnographic studies (e.g. Jarvenpaa and Leidner 1998; Walther *et al.* 2001).

Social embeddedness

The studies on trust in teams did not investigate effects of reputation. As the Internet allows for the cheap dissemination of reputation information across a large but loosely knit network, reputation systems are increasingly receiving attention – in particular in experimental economics (e.g. at the MIT Reputation Systems Symposium: Dellarocas and Resnick [2003]; at the Symposium on 'Trust and Community on the Internet': Baurmann and Leist [2004]). However, these studies rarely compare the effect of different media representations of human trustees. Ideally, the approaches in these disciplines should be combined in future studies.

Institutional embeddedness

As indicated earlier in this chapter, this property is present in most everyday trust-requiring situations – often without the actors being aware of it. Institutional assurance, e.g. in the form of law enforcement agencies or a legal system, forms part of our template of situational normality (McKnight and Chervany 2000). Most organizations provide incentives for their members to act in specific ways through job descriptions and hierarchies. The channel used in mediated interactions conveys much information about organizational embeddedness that will influence the perception of trust. Being contacted by someone on the company's Intranet will result in a different level of a priori trust than being contacted via an Internet Relay Chat (IRC). Modelling this important aspect of trust transfer is difficult in a laboratory setting, as the experiment itself is embedded in the context of a research institution. Nonetheless, this factor will have to be explored in future studies on online trust – e.g. by conducting field experiments or ethnographic studies.

Ability

Virtual team studies investigated willingness to fulfil – they researched motivation as one factor of trustworthiness. However, following Deutsch's (1958) classic definition, trustworthiness also consists of an ability to perform as expected. In many everyday situations, questions of trust do not arise from the risk of wilful deception, but because one is uncertain about the other's ability to perform as expected (Riegelsberger *et al.* 2003b): an individual might mean well, but lack the expertise to be truly helpful.

Internalized norms and benevolence

Since interpersonal cues have been identified (see Section 2.3.2) as important triggers of these intrinsic properties, the studies on trust in virtual team can be seen as primarily investigating the effect of internalized norms and benevolence, depending on the type and number of cues transmitted. A further way of investigating these properties for human trustees would be to observe how the evolution of norms and benevolence is affected by the design of the technical environment (see Cheng, Farnham and Stone [2002] for such an longitudinal analysis in the area of online gaming communities).

In summary, it is clear that further research on online trust in human trustees is needed that systematically varies the intrinsic and contextual properties. In particular, studies other than symmetric social dilemma games are required to investigate trust and trustworthy behaviour individually. Existing studies suggest a positive effect of media richness (i.e. the number of cues transmitted) on cooperation and trust in symmetric group settings.

Summary

Trust is an integral part of coordinated action among humans. It allows actors to engage in exchanges that leave both parties better off. New technologies allow interactions between individuals who know little about each other prior to the encounter. Exchanges that have traditionally been conducted face-to-face are now mediated by technology or even executed with technology as a transaction partner. This situation has led to a surge of research in trust in e-commerce and virtual teams. We outlined a framework of trust in mediated interactions that accommodates both areas and incorporates trustor, trustee and contextual factors. We identified two types of

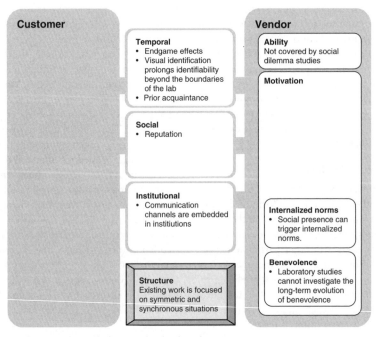

Figure 5.4 The framework applied to studies in virtual teams.

signals for trustworthiness: symbols and symptoms. Symptoms are given as by-product of behaviour. They are preferable to symbols, which are less reliable and subject to mimicry. We identified contextual (temporal, social and institutional embeddedness) as well as intrinsic properties of the trustee (ability, internalized norms and benevolence) as the basis of trustworthy behaviour and thus as the source of signals of trustworthiness. The framework was then used to discuss existing types of trust, guidelines for trust in e-commerce and studies on trust in virtual teams.

For trust in e-commerce vendors, the framework allows identifying how individual interface cues work as signifiers of trustworthiness by tying them to underlying properties. Temporal embeddedness can be signalled by elements that signal interest in future business (e.g. investments in first purchases). For social embeddedness, various forms of reputation-building and trust transfer were reviewed (e.g. affiliate programmes). Institutional embeddedness covers regulatory approaches and trust seal programmes. Intrinsic properties such as ability can be signalled by adherence to offline and online business standards. Internalized norms can be conveyed by mission statements, policy documents, or upfront disclosure of terms. Benevolence, finally, applies only with limitations to interactions between organizations and individual customers (e.g. in the form of loyalty schemes).

The discussion of HCI research on trust in virtual teams was more focused on using the framework to show how the present research agenda can be broadened to include further relevant aspects of interpersonal trust in mediated interactions. Existing studies mostly support media richness models, in the sense that the representations that conveyed the highest number of interpersonal cues resulted in the highest rate of cooperation.

While the framework discussed in this chapter can be helpful in the design of studies and for exploring design solution to the problem of trust in mediated interactions,[7] it does not suggest

that trust and trustworthy action can be 'designed into a system'. Designers can aim to create optimal environmental conditions for the emergence of trust, but they cannot fully determine users' behaviour. However, by designing technology with an awareness for the wider temporal, social and institutional factors as well as trustor and trustee factors, researchers and designers can support trustworthy behaviour and well-placed trust – and the proverbial lack of trust need not be accepted as an inherent consequence of mediated interactions.

References

Axelrod, R. (1980). More effective choice in the Prisoner's Dilemma. *Journal of Conflict Resolution 24*(3), 379–403.

Bacharach, M. and Gambetta, D. (2003). Trust in signs. In K. S. Cook, *Trust in society* (pp. 148–184). New York: Russell Sage.

Baron, R and Byrne, D. (2004). *Social psychology*, 9th edn. Boston, MA: Allyn and Bacon.

Baurmann, M. and Leist, M. (2004). *Trust and community on the Internet: opportunities and restrictions for online cooperation*. Analyse and Kritik, 1.

Berg, J., Dickhaut, J. and McKabe, K. (2003). Trust, reciprocity and social history. *Games and Economic Behaviour 10*, 122–142.

Biocca, F., Harms, C. and Burgoon, J. K. (2003). Criteria for a theory and measure of social presence. *Presence 12*(5), 456–480.

Bohnet, I., Frey, B. S. and Huck, S. (2001). More order with less law: on contract enforcement, trust and crowding. *American Political Science Review 95*, 131–144.

Bohnet, I., Huck, S. and Tyran, J. R. (2003). Instinct or incentive to be trustworthy? The role of informational institutions. In M. J. Holler *et al.*, *Jahrbuch für Neue Politische Ökonomie* (pp. 213–221) Tübingen: Mohr Siebeck.

Bos, N., Olson, J. S., Olson, G. M., Wright, Z. and Gergle, D. (2002). *Rich media helps trust development*. CHI 2002 Conference Proceedings New York: ACM Press.

Brenkert, G. G. (1998). Trust, morality and international business. *Business Ethics Quarterly 8*(2), 293–317.

Brosig, J., Ockenfels, A. and Weimann, J. (2002). The effects of communication media on cooperation. *German Economic Review 4*(2), 217–241.

Brynjolfsson, Erik and Smith, M. (2000). Frictionless commerce? A comparison of Internet and conventional retailers. *Management Science 46*(4), 563–585.

Cheng, L., Farnham, S. and Stone, L. (2002). Lessons learned: building and deploying shared virtual environments. In R. Schroeder, *The social life of avatars* (pp. 90–111). London: Springer.

Consumer Web Watch (2002). A matter of trust: what users want from web sites. Available at http://www.consumerwebwatch.org/news/report1.pdf.

---

[7] See (Riegelsberger *et al.* 2005) for examples of how the framework can be used to structure design approaches to trust in online gaming environments and (Riegelsberger, Sasse and McCarthy 2004) for an application to trust in ambient technologies.

Cooper, A. and Reimann, R. (2003). *About Face 2.0: the essentials of interaction design*. New York: John Wiley and Sons.

Corritore, C. L., Kracher, B. and Wiedenbeck, S. (2003). On-line trust: concepts, evolving themes, a model. *International Journal of Human Computer Studies 58*(6), 737–758.

Cranor, L. F, Reagle, J. and Ackerman, M. S. (1999). *Beyond concern: understanding net users concerns about on-line privacy*. Available at http://www.research.att.com/projects/privacystudy/.

Daft, R. L. and Lengel, R. H. (1986). Organizational information requirements, media richness and structural design. *Marketing Science 32*, 554–571.

Davis, J. P., Farnham, S. D. and Jensen, C. (2002). Decreasing online 'bad' behavior. In: Extended Abstracts CHI 2002 (pp. 718–719). New York: ACM Press.

de Ruyter, K., Wetzels, M. and Kleijnen, M. (2001). Customer adoption of e-services: an experimental study. *International Journal of Service Industry Management 12*(2), 184–207.

Deci, E. L. (1992). A history of motivation in psychology and its relevance for management. In V. H. Vroom E. L. and Deci, *Management and motivation* (2nd edn) (pp. 9–33). Harmondworth: Penguin Books.

Dellarocas, C. and Resnick, P. (2003). *Reputation Systems Symposium* MIT, Cambridge, MA, April 26–27 2003. Available at http://www.si.umich.edu/~presnick/reputation/symposium/.

Deutsch, M. (1958). Trust and suspicion. *Journal of Conflict Resolution 2*(3), 265–279.

Döring, N. (1998). *Sozialpsychologie des Internet*. Göttingen: Hogrefe.

Egger, F. N. (2001). Affective design of e-commerce user interfaces: how to maximize perceived trustworthiness. In M. Helander, H. M. Khalid and P. O. Tham. *Proceedings of CAHD: Conference on Affective Human Factors Design* (pp.317–324). New York: ACM Press.

Einwiller, S. (2001). The significance of reputation and brand for creating trust in the different stages of a relationship between an online vendor and its customers. In M. Schoop, M. and R. Walczuch, *Proceedings of the 8th Research Symposium on Emerging Electronic Markets* (RSEEM2001).

Fogg, B. J. (2003). *Persuasive technology. Using computers to change what we think and do*. San Francisco, CA: Morgan Kaufmann.

Fogg, BJ, Marshall, J., Kameda, T., Solomon, J., Rangnekar, A., Boyd, J. and Brown, B. (2001). Web credibility research: a method for online experiments and early study results. In CHI2001 extended abstracts (pp. 295–296). New York: ACM Press.

Friedman, J. W. (1977). *Oligopoly and the theory of games*. Amsterdam: North-Holland Publishers.

Friedman, B., Kahn, P. H. and Howe, D. C. (2000). Trust online. *Communications of the ACM 43*(12), 34–40.

Frohlich, N. and Oppenheimer, J. (1998). Some consequences of e-mail vs. face-to-face communication in experiment. *Journal of Conflict Resolution 35*, 389–403.

Fukuyama, F. (1999). Social capital and the civil society. In *The Second Conference on Second Generation Reforms*. Washington, DC: IMF.

Gefen, D. (2005). E-commerce: the role of familiarity and trust. *Omega: The International Journal of Management Science 28*, 725–737.

Giddens, A. (1990). *The consequences of modernity*. Stanford, CA: Stanford University Press.

Grabner-Kraeuter, S. and Kaluscha, E. A. (2003). Empirical research in on-line trust: a review and critical assessment. *International Journal of Human Computer Studies 58*, 783–812.

Granovetter, M. S. (1973). The strength of weak ties. *American Journal of Sociology 78*, 1360–1380.

Granovetter, M. S. (1985). Economic action and social structure: the problem of embeddedness. *American Journal of Sociology 91*, 481–510.

Handy, C. (1995). Trust and the virtual organization. *Harvard Business Review 73*(3), 40–50.

Hinton, P. R. (1993). *The psychology of interpersonal perception*. London: Routledge.

Jarvenpaa, S. L. and Leidner, D. (1998). Communication and trust in global virtual teams. *Journal of Computer Mediated Communication 3*(4).

Jarvenpaa, S. L. and Tractinsky, N. (1999). Consumer trust in an internet store: a cross-cultural validation. *Journal of Computer Mediated Communication 5*(2).

Jensen, C., Farnham, S. D., Drucker, S. M. and Kollock, P. (2000). The effect of communication modality on cooperation in online environments. In *CHI 2000 Conference Proceedings* (pp. 470–477). New York: ACM Press.

Johnston, A. C. and Warkentin, M. (2004). *The consumer online trust construct: A web merchant practitioner perspective*. Proceedings of the 2004 Southern Association of Information Systems (SAIS) (pp. 221–226), Atlanta, GA: AIS

Kim, T. (1996). *Effects of presence on memory and persuasion*. Chapel Hill, NC: University of North Carolina.

Koehn, D. (2003). The nature of and conditions for online trust. *Journal of Business Ethics 43*, 3–19.

Kotler, P. (2002). *Marketing management*, 11th edn. Englewood Cliffs, NJ: Prentice Hall.

Lahno, B. (2002). *Institutional trust: A less demanding form of trust?* http: www.uni-due.de/philosophie/personal/lahno/institutional-trust.html.

Lee, J. (2002). Making losers of auction winners. *New York Times 3* July.

Lee, M. K. O. and Turban, E. (2001). A trust model for consumer Internet shopping. *International Journal of Electronics Commerce 6*(1), 75–91.

Lewicki, R. J. and Bunker, B. B. (1996). Developing and maintaining trust in work relationships. In R. M. Kramer and T. R. Tyler, *Trust in organizations. Frontiers of theory and research* (pp. 114–136). Thousand Oaks, CA: Sage.

Lewis, J. D. and Weigert, A. (1985). Trust as a social reality. *Social Forces 63*, 967–985.

Lombard, M. and Ditton, T. (1997). At the heart of it all: the concept of presence. *Journal of Computer Mediated Communication 3*(2).

Luhmann, N. (1979). *Trust and power.* Chichester: Wiley.

Macauley, S. (1963). Non-contractual relations in business: a preliminary study. *American Sociological Review 28*(1), 55–67.

Mayer, R. C., Davis, J. H. and Schoorman, F. D. (1995). An integrative model of organizational trust. *Academy of Management Review 20*(3), 709–734.

McKnight, D. H. and Chervany, N. L. (2000). What is trust? A conceptual analysis and an interdisciplinary model. In M.H. Chung (Ed.), Proceedings at the *American Conference on Information Systems* (pp. 827–833) August 10-13, Long Beach, California, US.

Meyerson, D., Weick, K. E. and Kramer, R. M. (1996). Swift trust and temporary groups. In R. M. Kramer and T. M. Tyler, *Trust in organizations. Frontiers of theory and research* (pp. 166–195). Thousand Oaks, CA: Sage.

Murray, K. B. (1991). A test of services marketing theory: consumer information acquisition activities. *Journal of Marketing 55*, 10–25.

Nielsen, J., Molich, R., Snyder, S. and Farrell, C. (2000). *E-commerce user experience: Trust.* Fremont, CA: Nielsen Norman Group.

Olson, J. S., Zheng, J., Bos, N., Olson, G. M. and Veinott, E. (2002). Trust without touch: jumpstarting long-distance trust with initial social activities. In *CHI2002 Conference Proceedings* (pp. 141–146). New York: ACM Press.

Preece, J, Rogers, Y. and Sharp, H. (2002). *Interaction design: Beyond human–computer interaction.* New York: John Wiley and Sons.

Ratnasingam, P. and Pavlou, P. A. (2004). Technology trust in internet-based interorganizational electronic commerce. *Journal of Electronic Commerce in Organizations 1*(1), 17–41.

Raub, W. and Weesie, J. (2000a). *The management of durable relations.* Amsterdam: Thela Thesis.

Raub, W. and Weesie, J. (2000b). The management of matches: a research program on solidarity in durable social relations. *Netherland's Journal of Social Sciences 36*, 71–88.

Reeves, B. and Nass, C. (1996). *The media equation: How people treat computers, television and new media like real people and places.* Stanford, CA: CSLI Publications.

Rempel, J. K., Holmes, J. G. and Zanna, M. P. (1985). Trust in close relationships. *Journal of Personality and Social Psychology 49*(1), 95–112.

Rice, R. E. (1992). Task analyzability, use of new medium and effectiveness: a multi-site exploration of media richness. *Organization Science 3*(4), 475–500.

Rickenberg, R. and Reeves, B. (2000). The effects of animated characters on anxiety, task performance and evaluations of user interfaces. In *Proceedings of CHI 2000* (pp. 49–56). New York: ACM Press.

Riegelsberger, J. and Sasse, M. A. (2001). Trustbuilders and trustbusters: the role of trust cues in interfaces to e-commerce applications. In B. Schmid, K. Stanoevska-Slabeva and V. Tschammer, *Towards the e-society: E-commerce, e-business and e-government* (pp. 17–30). Deventer, The Netherlands: Kluwer.

Riegelsberger, J. and Sasse, M. A. (2002). Face it: photographs don't make websites trustworthy. In *CHI2002 extended abstracts* (pp. 742–743). New York: ACM Press.

Riegelsberger, J. and Sasse, M. A. (2003a). Designing e-commerce applications for consumer trust. In O. Petrovic, M. Ksela and M. Fallenboeck, *Trust in the network economy* (pp. 97–110). Wien: Springer.

Riegelsberger, J., Sasse, M. A. and McCarthy, J. (2003b). The researcher's dilemma: evaluating trust in computer-mediated communication. *International Journal of Human Computer Studies 58*(6), 759–781.

Riegelsberger, J., Sasse, M. A. and McCarthy, J. (2004). Depending on the kindness of strangers? Trust relationships in ambient societies. Available at http://www.cs.ucl.ac.uk/staff/J.Riegelsberger/ Ambient_Trust_Workshop_Riegelsberger.pdf.

Riegelsberger, J., Sasse, M. A. and McCarthy, J. (2005). The mechanics of trust: a framework for research and design. *International Journal of Human Computer Studies 62*(3), 381–422.

Rousseau, D. M., Sitkin, S. B., Burt, R. S. and Camerer, C. (1998). Not so different after all: a cross-discipline view of trust. *Academy of Management Review 23*(3), 393–404.

Sally, D. (1995). Conversation and cooperation in social dilemmas. a meta-analysis of experiments from 1958 to 1992. *Rationality and Society 7*(1), 58–92.

Sapient and Cheskin (1999). *Ecommerce trust.* Available at http://www.cheskin.com/think/studies/ecomtrust.html.

Schweiger, W. (1999). Medienglaubwuerdigkeit – Nutzungserfahrung oder Medienimage? In P. Roessler and W. Wirth, *Glaubwuerdigkeit im Internet. Fragestellungen, Modelle, empirische Befunde* (pp. 89–110). Muenchen: Reinhard Fischer.

Shapiro, S. P. (1987). The social control of impersonal trust. *American Journal of Sociology 93*(3), 623–658.

Short, J., Williams, E. and Christie, B. (1976). *The social psychology of telecommunications.* London: John Wiley and Sons.

Sillence, E., Briggs, P., Fishwick, L. and Harris, P. (2004). Trust and mistrust of on-line health sites. In Proceedings of CHI 2004 (pp. 663–670), April 24–29, Vienna, Austria. New York: ACM Press.

Steinbrueck, U., Schaumburg, H., Duda, S. and Krueger, T. (2002). A picture says more than a thousand words – photographs as trust builders in e-commerce websites. In *CHI2002 Extended Abstracts* (pp. 748–749) New York: ACM Press.

Tan, Y. and Thoen, W. (2000). Toward a generic model of trust for electronic commerce. *International Journal of Electronics Commerce 5*, 61–74.

Walther, J. B., Slovacek, C. and Tidwell, L. C. (2001). Is a picture worth a thousand words? Photographic images in long term and short term virtual teams. *Communication Research 28*, 105–134.

Yamagishi, T. and Yamagishi, M. (1994). Trust and commitment in the United States and Japan. *Motivation and Emotion 18*, 129–166.

CHAPTER 6

Assessing interactivity in computer-mediated research

Sheizaf Rafaeli and Yaron Ariel

Introduction

Almost every scholarly examination of the concept of interactivity to date has mentioned conceptualization difficulties (Rafaeli 1988; Moore 1989; Heeter 2000; Schultz 2000; McMillan 2002). This chapter is an attempt to proceed beyond complaints about ambiguity and overuse of the interactivity concept. Both theory and practice require a well-defined, clear and measurable definition for interactivity. Interactivity shows up in a very large number of titles and publications and is very often cited in technical and marketing discourse. Despite both scientific and popular interest, the literature to date has provided too little focus on why interactivity matters and a surprising dearth of empirical reports on outcomes of interactivity. A basic common understanding of the concept is required, one that has enough openness to enable multidisciplinary examination of interactivity from different perspectives.

Interactivity has been a matter of debate and interest for almost three decades now. It is located at the confluence of mass and interpersonal communication and perhaps serves as one of the bridges of these two. Similarly, interactivity is poised between traditional and innovative media,

as an explaining construct. An important theoretical contribution would be to understand how interactivity can be used to traverse the transition between mass, interpersonal and intrapersonal (psychological), as well as the connection between old and new. In both cases, the advantage is in preserving the links to all sides, not in assigning the construct exclusively to one side. One of the interesting features of the concept of interactivity is its continued prominence in scholarly thought despite technological changes.

In this chapter, we argue that interactivity is not unique to computers or networks and cannot be reserved solely for the discussion of so-called 'New Media'. Restricting analysis of interactivity to the domain of computerized and new technology alone problematizes comparisons with traditional media as well as with further developments of the new media. If we study only 'new media', we are constrained in our ability to build a cumulative theory based on evidence, because the domain of 'New Media' itself changes rapidly. The term 'New Media' is old and misleading, since any latest technology is always new (Marvin 1988): furthermore, it does not necessarily create new concepts, though it can highlight some.

We begin by reviewing some of the leading definitions and then highlight the primary conceptual development of interactivity. We discuss the correlates of interactivity and the different ways studies have measured it and look into some of the effects of interactivity by surveying empirical findings. This chapter will also suggest treating interactivity as a unidimensional variable rather than a multidimensional construct. We claim expected, actual and perceived interactivity are the relevant frameworks when examining the variable. Finally, we highlight the importance of information, meaning and value and their relation to interactivity.

Definitions (etymology, use and misuse) of interactivity

Interactivity has been defined in various fields from different perspectives. Over the years, different definitions seem to have touched on a rich array of related concepts and it appears that studies have covered almost every possible aspect of new media characteristics. Among the more popular conceptualizations of interactivity we find synchronicity (Van Dijk 1999; Kiousis 1999; Liu and Shrum 2002; Mundorf and Bryant 2002), control (Neuman 1991; Rogers 1995; Jensen 1998; Lieb 1998; Shin 1998; Steuer 1992; Lombard and Snyder-Dutch 2001; Coyle and Thorson 2001; Stromer-Galley and Foot 2002), rapidity and speed (Lombard and Ditton 1997; Zeltzer 1992; Novak *et al.* 2000), participation (Dyson 1993), choice variety (Ha and James 1998; Liu 2003), directionality (Markus 1990; Van Dijk 1999; Downes and McMillan 2000), hypertextuality (Sundar *et al.* 2003; Amichai-Hamburger *et al.* 2004) connectedness (Ha and James 1998), experience (Burgoon *et al.* 2000; Wu 2000; Bucy 2004, a) and finally responsiveness (Rafaeli 1988; Heeter 2000; Miles 1992; Alba *et al.* 1997; Rafaeli and Sudweeks 1997; Wu 1999; Stewart and Pavlov 2002; Sundar *et al.* 2003).

In surveying the concepts used to describe interactivity, we can identify a rough distinction between a focus on functions of features and a focus on users. A focus on users splits into users' activities and users' behaviour. Let us examine each of these in its turn.

A focus on function leads to claims that interactivity is an attribute of technology (Steuer 1992; Kayany *et al.* 1996; Sundar 2004). Steuer

(1992) is a leading proponent of the conception of interactivity as situated within the medium and defines interactivity as 'the extent to which users can participate in modifying the form and content of a mediated environment in real time' (1992: 84). Note that while Steuer's definition ostensibly addresses the users, he is actually talking about the system, looking at interactivity as a feature of the medium, one that can be measured through three components: speed, range and mapping. While the feature of speed is obvious, range refers to the number of possible actions at a given time and mapping 'refers to the way in which human actions are connected to actions within a mediated environment' (Steuer 1992: 86). In light of these definitions, Steuer argues in favour of classifying media along a continuum, based on their level of interactivity. Thus, traditional media are low on his proposed interactive continuum and new media would be ranked as high on the interactive continuum. Likewise, Markus (1990) suggests that interactivity is a characteristic of technologies that enable multidirectional communication.

As a leader in the *focus on users*, Rogers defines interactivity as users' control: 'the degree to which participants in a communication process can exchange roles and have control over their mutual discourse' (Rogers 1995: 314). In the same vein, Shin (1998) suggests the users' ability to control the flow of information is the one that determines the degree of interactivity. Williams *et al.* (1988) defined interactivity as 'the degree to which participants in a communication possess control and exchange roles in mutual discourse'. In their view interactivity is a three-dimensional construct comprising control, exchange of roles and mutual discourse. Discourse was also at the centre of Rafaeli's (1998) definition: however he abandons the notion of control in the interest of clarity.

Rafaeli defined interactivity as

> a variable characteristic of communication
> settings . . . an expression of the extent that in
> a given series of communication exchanges, any
> third (or later) transmission (or message) is
> related to the degree to which previous exchanges
> referred to even earlier transmissions.

> (Rafaeli 1988: 111)

Therefore, Rafaeli examined interactivity as a process-related variable. In his definition, interactivity is predicated on the relatedness of sequential messages. A broader definition of interactivity was offered by Rafaeli (1990) and Rafaeli and Sudweeks (1997): 'The extent to which messages in a sequence relate to each other and especially the extent to which later messages recount the relatedness of earlier messages.' Rafaeli and Sudweeks emphasize that these exchanges are simultaneous, continuous and carry a social, binding force.

Some, like Ha and James (1998) use a combined definition. They consider interactivity as consisting of playfulness, choice, connectedness, information collection and reciprocal communication. Ha and James examined the interactivity of 110 business websites, testing their assumption that interactivity – as they define it using the above listed features – engages potential consumers and builds a relationship between a company and these consumers. Another hybrid, multidimensional definition is offered Liu and Shrum (2002), who defined interactivity as 'the degree to which two or more communication parties can act on each other, on the communication medium and on the messages and the degree to which such influences are synchronized'. In other words, their proposed definition merges three dimensions: active control, two-way communication and synchronicity.

In summary, we described some of the common definitions of interactivity and highlighted the differences between some of the conceptions. Definitions vary in focus (feature or user), scope (unidimensional or multidimensional) and temporal orientation (is interactivity a snapshot quality, or a process?). We subscribe to the user-oriented, unidimensional and process-based position.

Problematizing the definition

The above discussion reveals the complexity of establishing a clear definition for interactivity. Obviously, interactivity cannot be simultaneously defined in such diverse ways and still be useful to be studied. Some of the suggested keywords for interactivity can be considered as synonyms. Thus, instead of talking about website interactivity we can relate to website responsiveness or Internet application speed. Others considered these keywords when defining 'interactivity as –'. Many consider interactivity to be a multidimensional construct and therefore define it in an

even more blurred manner. We argue that these conceptual shortcuts, based as they are in technological developments (high synchronicity, broad bandwidth, multimedia capabilities, multitasking) or on the psychological assumptions that new media creates new mental abilities (control, involvement, choice availability, ease of use) could be misleading.

A relevant notion to our discussion is the concept of affordances (Gibson 1979; Norman 1988). '*Affordance* refers to the perceived and actual properties of the thing, primarily those fundamental properties that determine just how the thing could possibly be used' (Norman 1988: 9). For example, studies tried to compare email affordances in comparison with face-to-face communication (e.g. Sproull and Kiesler 1986). Most of the findings of this line of research tend to produce somewhat problematic results. Only an overly simplistic technological determinism approach will assume that technologies create or reshape the basic aspects of our human behaviour. This approach has been questioned increasingly in recent years (Rafaeli 2004). Although we support the idea that technology enable its users to perform activities, caution is called for when speaking about the inherent capabilities of the technology.

More generally, a conceptual definition should be considered more broadly than just a single situation, determined by specific environment and tools. When speed is affected by broader bandwidth, does interactivity – defined by speed – also disappear? Can we really talk about environments and telepresence in the same manner at the beginning of the twenty-first century as before? Hyperlinks are rapidly being woven into graphics, animation and other forms of expression and are no longer textual artefacts alone. Does this change their relation to interaction?

A basic and useful definition of interactivity is one that can be implemented on any medium, regardless of its characteristics, its actors or the specific situation. This is not to argue that interactivity always performs in the same way. Nevertheless, we do hope for a definition that holds the meaning constant. The definitions based on the elements of responsiveness emphasize the process and only assume media, actors and situation, rather than hang the definitions on them. As a process-related variable, the concept of interactivity is similar to the characteristics of other conceptual definitions. For example, when scholars examine the concept of 'Need for Cognition' they do not constrain themselves to particular situations. Instead, they try to examine whether and how the concept 'works' in different situations. So, a generalizable nomenclature should be used whether one embraces the responsiveness definition or not.

Concept development

We find consistently divergent approaches in explicating interactivity. It would be helpful to identify and discuss separately three qualitatively distinct literature-based frameworks of definition:

1. Interactivity as a process related variable,

2. Interactivity as an invariable medium characteristic, and

3. Interactivity as a perception-related variable.

The scholarly divergence on conceptualizations of interactivity is related directly to the choice of framework: studies that consider interactivity as a process-related variable focus on the ways that two (or more) participants transferred information between each other (e.g. Rafaeli 1985; Rogers 1995; Rafaeli and Sudweeks 1997; Stewart and Pavlou 2002). Studies that consider interactivity as a medium characteristic focus on the technological features and the ability to generate activity (e.g. Markus 1990; Rust and Varki 1996; Sundar 2004). Yet a third strand of studies considers interactivity as a perception related variable and focuses on users' experiences and self-reports (e.g. Wu 1999; Newhagen 2004).

There have been several attempts to divide interactivity into categories or classify its components (Hoffman and Novak 1996; Haeckel 1998; Jensen 1998; Stromer-Galley 2000; McMillan 2002). Hoffman and Novak (1996) contrasted person interactivity and machine interactivity. Stromer-Galley (2000) points to the distinction between human to human and human to media interaction. In a similar manner, Schultz (2000) offers two categories of interactivity when considering journalistic websites: reader to reader and journalist to reader interactivity. Many others have also considered

the interactivity that occurs between the user and the text (Bezjian-Avery *et al.* 1998; Steuer 1992; Williams, Rice and Rogers 1988). Furthermore, these categories seem to influence various fields studying interactivity, for example in relation to distance learning, Moore (1989) acknowledged three types of interactivity: learner–content, learner–instructor and learner–learner interactions. Hillman, Willis and Gunawardena (1994) added another type: learner–interface. These categories are an echo of the same classifications mentioned earlier.

For parsimony, we can think about interactivity literature as being present in one or more of the following categories: user to user, user to medium; user to content; medium or agent to medium or agent.

We turn first to the user to users/person to person/ human to human category. Prime examples of this approach include Rafaeli's (1988) definition of interactivity. The second category is user to medium/human to machine/ user to system. This category includes much of the work about para-social interaction (e.g. Horton and Whol 1956; Rafaeli 1990; Hoerner 1999; Cohen 2002) as well as scholars such as Jensen, who defined interactivity as 'A measure of a media's potential ability to let the user exert an influence on . . . the mediated communication' (Jensen 1998: 201). The third category is user to content/user to document/user to message. Here, for example, is Rice's (1984) seminal study. Rice was among the first to define new media as facilitating 'interactivity among users or between users and information' (1984: 35). Lastly, the fourth category is medium to medium/ agent to agent. For example, Pavlik (1998) defined interactivity as compatible and conducive for non-human actors. Interactivity, according to Pavlik is a 'two-way communication between source and receiver, or, more broadly, multidirectional communication between any number of sources and receivers' (1998: 137).

We suggest an alternative to this four-category approach. Although the who-to-whom dimensions in this categorization may be useful to describe various possible aspects of interactivity, we posit that a more significant theoretical contribution will be to explicate the generalizable antecedents and consequences of interactivity, going beyond specific nature of actor. For instance, when reviewing the conceptualization of interactivity Kiousis (2002) suggests differentiating between the information-technological structure of the medium, the context of communication settings and the users' perception. Although we find this more comprehensive than the previous frameworks of typology, it still raises some problems. In this chapter, we choose to deal with correlates and consequences, leaving the issue of antecedents (uses' personal psychological factors) of interactivity for a separate investigation.

Consider the following vignette, for example. In response to the use of offensive language by a participant in online synchronous discussion group, the participant is rebuked via a message from management. The user is told not to use such words in this application. Psychologically and motivationally, does it matter to the user (or to a bystander or anyone else) whether the rebuking message originated from a human entity or a machine-generated automatic response? Essentially, we claim that the 'real' origin, especially on CMC, is virtually unknowable and largely irrelevant for the analysis of the process. We can easily imagine an artificial intelligence participant mimicking a human response (see Reeves and Nass 1996). Of course, the dynamics of response and response to response are intriguing, hence the importance of the interactivity construct. However, does the identity or humanity of the rebuking person or agent necessarily affect the interactivity involved? If we examine the meaning of interactivity for the participants, we have to examine its consequences. Of course, the consequences vary across human and non-human participants. When dealing with human actors (fully or partly) we search for the cognitive and emotional effects. When dealing with synthetic actors we focus on functional effects.

Interactivity as a characteristic of the medium

Some scholars regard interactivity as the functional features of the medium (Durlak 1987; Heeter 2000; Sundar *et al.* 1998; Massey and Levy 1999; Ahern and Stromer-Galley 2000). For those scholars, functional features of the Internet include hyperlinks, chats, downloads and the like. For example, Massey and Levy (1999)

operationalized websites' interactivity by examining functional features such as email links, feedback forms and chat rooms. Similarly, McMillan (1998) examined bulletin boards, search engines, registration forms and online ordering.

Heeter (2000) suggested six dimensions to assess the measure of interactivity for a medium:

1. Complexity of choice available
2. Amount of effort users must exert to access information
3. Responsiveness of the medium
4. Monitoring information use
5. Ease of adding information and
6. Facilitation of interpersonal communication.

Heeter applied these dimensions to 53 different media, interpersonal through mass, assigning values to each dimension in order to obtain an interactivity measure for each medium.

Quite a few scholars have taken the position that interactivity is a characteristic of the medium (e.g. Markus 1990; Hoffman and Novak 1996). Note that identifying interactivity as a characteristic of the medium is not the same as describing interactivity as a feature of the medium. Often, characteristics and variability are confused needlessly. Those who claim that the Internet is by definition an interactive medium (Rust and Varki 1996) are actually suggesting a continuum of interactivity (Steur 1992). This approach divides media into 'low' and 'high' interactivity according to technological features and falls clearly on the side of treating interactivity as a variable, not a trait.

There is a continuum of interactivity only in the sense that interactivity is enabled by or through technological features and or their procedures. Enabling interactivity means that the actual process and its perceptions are optional. Nevertheless, even those who prefer to categorize media by their level of interactivity should realize that the convergence process that media, networks and computers have been undergoing makes it more difficult to differentiate media by their levels of interactivity. For example, consider a study measuring or manipulating website interactivity levels. Remember that a web page is a digital document that can contain various features of content, presented in different forms such as text, picture, audio, video etc.

Remember, too, that a page may be uniquely customized at the users' end, via variable interfaces (for example browser, resolution, size). So that which seems one way to the producer, may (and often does) display and behave quite differently to different surfers. Another important definition relating to websites should acknowledge that defining a web page as a medium constructed by HTML is to ignore the other various platforms that are enclosed by websites.

Technological features may not be interactive or non-interactive for themselves, but as the presence of our voice, hands and eyes have the potential to facilitate interactivity in face-to-face interaction so are various features other than HTML. HTML can offer the users the function of hypertext. However, dynamic applications such as Java scripts, ASP and Flash can prompt interactivity between the medium and the users or between the users themselves: for example, using dialog scripts on a website can enable elicitation and response to user's questions. Since websites tend to be a mixture of both static information and dynamic applications, one should be careful to examine or simulate the communication processes that use websites in a fashion that expresses the entire range of expressive and communicative potential.

Sundar, Kalyanaraman and Brown (2003) studied website interactivity by means of manipulating hyperlinks. They found that user's perceptions of interactivity in websites were positively associated with the amount of hyperlinks a website embedded. Similarly, Amichai-Hamburger *et al.* (2004) offer that interactivity increased as a result of more clickable hyperlinks available to the users. A critique of this approach might suggest that the use of hyperlinks may indicate user's control rather than actual interactivity. A more moderate definition linking interactivity and hypertextuality can be traced in Snyder-Dutch's (1996) work that suggests that hypertext is a non-linear feature that enhances interactivity.

Interactivity continuum is yet another misconception of interactivity:

> Generally, any new communication technology will be dubbed interactive if it allows some degree of user response. Traditional media (e.g. television, radio and newspapers) rank low because their capacity for feedback is limited.

> Among the various new media, interactivity is highly connected to the following: computers, cellular communications, digital communications, video-conferencing, software, virtual reality, the world wide web, etc.

(Kiousis 2002: 370)

We propose that interactivity is not merely a medium characteristic. Recent technological developments have simplified this argument. Presumably, we can agree that the notion of interactivity continuum based on the technology (print, audiovisual, digital) or continuum based on the medium (books–television–computer) are not useful anymore when considering new media such as a website, since it can perform in many different ways.

In the marketing literature, advertising effectiveness is associated with interactivity (Cho 1999; Leckenby and Li 2000, Macias 2000; Lombard and Snyder-Duch 2001) and examination of marketing communication interactivity places consumers at the centre of the study (Stewart and Pavlou 2002). Ghose and Dou (1998) suggest that interactivity improves businesses website quality and attract customers: 'We expect that the attractiveness of sites would increase with the increase in the number of interactive functions' (1998: 30). By 'interactive functions', they refer to features such as feedback, site surveys, key word search, software downloading, multimedia shows etc. Liu and Shrum (2002) examined online marketing web features alongside three dimensions of interactivity – active control, synchronicity and two-way communication. While most of the studies find relatively positive effects of interactivity on consumers' attitude and response toward websites' ads (Cho and Leckenby 1999; Yoo and Stout 2001), several studies find no effects or actual negative effects of interactivity (Sundar *et al.* 1998; Coyle and Thorson 2001).

Technological developments of new media may improve users' ability to perform exchanges of messages and engage in a communication process. Features that help improve the synchronicity, speed, presence and control can create a better environment that enables interactivity. Nevertheless, these features cannot be considered as the single determinant of interactivity.

Correlates of interactivity

Correlates of interactivity have been studied from a variety of perspectives. Table 6.1 presents some examples of studies that defined various variables as correlates of interactivity. Let us look at some psychological variables that were studied as associated with interactivity.

For example, Amichai-Hamburger, Fine and Goldstein (2004) concentrate on the concept of Need for Closure (NFC). Using Webster and Kruglanski's (1994) scale they examined the correlations between users with high vs. low NFC and the level of websites' interactivity. They found that low NFC users prefer a higher level of interactivity than high NFC users. This study uses hypertextual links as the operationalization for interactivity. As explained above, we question this operationalization, of interactivity as hypertextual links alone.

Sohn and Leckenby (2002) examined the correlations between users' internal vs. external 'locus of control' and perceived interactivity relative to Web surfing. They found internally controlled users more likely to perceive a higher level of interactivity than those oriented to external 'locus of control'. 'Locus of control' refers to 'the

extent to which persons perceive contingency relationships between their actions and their outcomes' (MacDonald 1973: 169). In a sense, this finding hints at perceived interactivity as a form of leverage. When people are more likely to act on the world (rather than expect the world to act on them), they are more likely to perceive interactivity in communication situations.

Interestingly, many studies mention various further correlates without providing empirical evidence to validate these claims. Among the more intriguing additional constructs still awaiting empirical verification are the postulated strong relation of 'ostensible sense of fun' to interactivity (Rafaeli 1988) and the subjective sense of telepresence – a user's perception of 'being in' the mediated environment (Steuer 1992). The notion that 'interactivity is out there' or is 'being out there' is rather vague. With this concept, perhaps more than with others, there is a danger of falling into a tautological trap. This ambiguity of causality, combined with the difficulties in achieving consensus on the very definition of interactivity and the effort required to operationalize interactivity properly, result in a multitude of studies that still lack construct validity and unified focus.

Table 6.1 Correlates of interactivity

Correlates of interactivity	References
Time flexibility	Lombard and Ditton 1997; Downes and McMillan 2000
Telepresence	Steuer 1992
Mimic interpersonal communication	Leary 1990
Social presence, transparency, user friendliness	Durlak 1987
User awareness of mediated environments	Murray 1997
Need for closure	Amichai-Hamburger, Fine and Goldstein 2004
Involvement	Rafaeli and Sudweeks 1997; Cho and Leckenby 1999
Sense of fun, cognition, learning, frankness, openness and sociability	Rafaeli 1988
Locus of control	Sohn and Leckenby (2002)
Need for cognition	Sohn, Leckenby and Jee 2003; Jee and Lee 2002

Measurements of interactivity

We presented some of the difficulties in describing interactivity. Table 6.2 offers some examples of approaches to operationalizing and measuring interactivity. As can be seen, the ontological divides are echoed in epistemology.

Methods of examining interactivity span a wide range of approaches. Scholars have used content analysis using human or automatic rating procedures (Schultz, 2000); self-reports (Cho and Leckenby 1999) and carried out a few experimental and quasi experimental studies. While some (e.g. Schultz, 2000) suggested coding interactivity by examining the availability of feedback tools in online journals, others (e.g. Lee 2000) suggested it should not be measured by counting medium features, rather by examining users' experience and perceive interactivity.

Massey and Levy (1999) content analysed Asian newspapers using five dimensions of interactivity: complexity of choice available, responsiveness to the user, the ease of adding information, facilitation of interpersonal communication and immediacy. Teo *et al.* (2003) studied the correlations between the level of website interactivity and factors such as users' efficiency. To test these relations they used a controlled laboratory experiment of undergraduates' students. In a qualitative, interview-based study, Downes and McMillan (2000) found that the direction of communication and control over the communication process influences the dimensions of the perceptions of interactivity.

To summarize, methodological choices do not necessarily resolve the conceptual fog. Rather, different methods follow, naturally, in the footsteps of divergent definitions.

We claimed earlier that a sound definition of interactivity is one that can be generalized beyond single situations, individual media or specific actors. When operationalizing interactivity, the main concern should be the unit of measurement. If the chosen unit of measurement is a technological feature of the medium, it could not by itself indicate user-related effects.

Table 6.2 Examples of scales and measures of interactivity

Measures/scale of interactivity	Unit of measurement	References
The degree to which a person actively engages in message (advertising) processing by interacting with (advertising) messages and advertisers using 7-item facet scales, 5-point Likert-type scales	The user	Cho and Leckenby 1999
Websites designed to have different degrees of interactive features and opportunities for interactive exchanges	Websites' feature	McMillan and Hwang 2002; Teo *et al.* 2003
The presence or absence of features (onsite poll, a 'contact us' email link etc.) enabling or facilitating user contact with a political candidate and/or campaign.	Websites' feature	Warnick, Xenos, Endres and Gastil (2005)
Perceived interactivity scale contained five items from respondents answers about the responsiveness of website and the easy of navigation in it	The user	Wu 1999
Number of choices in a website and whether there was a clickable image	Websites' feature	Coyle and Thorson 2001
Interactive websites that includes internal links relating to a software and a flat websites without links	Websites' feature	Amichai-Hamburger *et al.* 2004

A variable conceptualized at the medium level and measured at that level, will likely have its effects moderated by individual psychological filters. In such a case, to claim that interactive feature impacts individuals, evidence needs to rule out alternative, individual-level explanations. This is yet another reason to think about interactivity at the level of the participant perceptions or through the prism of process, that measures the actual performance of participants.

Empirical findings: interactivity impact/effects

In the preceding sections, we followed the conceptual development of interactivity, presented some of its definitions and discussed problems in defining interactivity as an internal feature of the medium. We presented a few of the correlates assigned to interactivity and surveyed the methods used to measure it. We turn now to empirical evidence regarding outcomes of interactivity. Table 6.3 presents some examples of interactivity consequences.

As can be seen in Table 6.3, many of these studies speak to the advantages offered by interactivity to the relations of individuals with the political process, institutes and figures. For example, Stromer-Galley's (2000) study highlights the effect of interactivity as a way to facilitate the citizen political involvement. Similarly, Ha and James (1998) and Sundar and Kim (2004) address users' involvement as an effect of interactivity in the marketing field. Many others (e.g, Hackman and Walker 1990; Liaw and Huang 2000) investigated several effects of interactivity in distance learning environments and find that higher interactivity leads learners to increase and refine their evaluation of the learning process.

Table 6.3 Consequences of interactivity

Effects of interactivity	Study
Increased interactivity leads to increased citizen participation in political process	Stromer-Galley 2000
Interactivity plays a role in creating the attraction of networks and in generating their growth	Rafaeli and Sudweeks 1997
Interactivity fosters engagement and relationship building between a company and its customers	Ha and James 1998
Interactive advertising has a positive influence on consumers' perceptions of brands and advertising	Macias 2003
The level of website interactivity influenced participants' perceptions of the political candidate as well as their levels of agreement with his policy positions	Sundar et al. 2003
Commercial advertising interactivity enhances user involvement with product by providing more product information hence leads to more positive evaluations	Sundar and Kim 2004
Interactivity provides an opportunity for organizations to build relationships with publics, through two-way symmetrical interactive applications	Samsup and Yungwook 2003
Higher degrees of interactivity yield better advertising effects (favourable attitude toward the target ad, favourable attitude toward the brand and high purchase intention)	Cho and Leckenby 1999
Interactivity led to a heightened sense of telepresence	Coyle and Thorson 2001
Interactivity leads to the social construction of meaning as students share knowledge and participatein collaborative and cooperative activities in the online environment	Maddux et al. 1997

Continued

Table 6.3 Consequences of interactivity *cont.*

Higher web site interactivity leads to a higher level of trust that brings about a positive effect on customers intention to purchase	Sukpanich and Chen 2000
Increased levels of interaction result in increased positive attitudes toward learning	Hackman and Walker 1990
Higher interactivity correlates with higher communication-processing load	Jones *et al.* 2004
Interactivity enhances student satisfaction	Liaw and Huang 2000
Increased interactivity on a website has positive effects on users' perceived satisfaction, effectiveness, efficiency, value and overall attitude towards a website	Teo *et al.* 2003

The preponderance of field empirical evidence regarding consequences of interactivity leans toward positive outcomes. Interactivity has been shown to correlate positively with citizen participation in political process, learning satisfaction, positive assessment of the website etc. It should be noted that there have been some indications that interactivity may have other than positive outcomes. However, only very few negative or problematic outcomes of interactivity have been given empirical documentation. Possible negative or problematic consequences include for example the contribution of interactivity to communication processing loads (Jones *et al.* 2004). Bucy (2004b) described the 'interactivity paradox' as another possible problematic consequence of interactivity: 'subjects evidently enjoyed news site interactivity and the active involvement it entailed more than reading electronic text, but this form of online participation produced a certain amount of disorientation, exacting a cognitive and emotional cost' (p. 65). Interactivity's effects are curvilinear. At a certain point saturation sets in.

Clearly, interactivity taxes the individuals involved, places demands on cognitive processing and weighs down on social processes. These complicating outcomes of interactivity ought to have a price. Serious research into interactivity must resist the temptation and enamour of interactivity long enough to view it critically and examine its costs as well.

In surveying some of the empirical evidence that studies found as consequences of interactivity, we call attention to one recurrent motif. It seems that regardless of the conceptual definition of interactivity postulated by these papers and regardless of their unit of analysis and the way they choose to operationalize it – the consequences of interactivity constantly lead to some attributes about the users. This is curious, in light of the advocacy in earlier interactivity literature for a differentiation of interactivity categories along user to user, user to medium; user to content; medium or agent to medium or agent. As we will further discuss later, interactivity is not confined to humans. Thus, we argue once again that it is essential to go beyond the nature of actor and try to explicate the generalizable antecedents, process and consequences of interactivity.

Following the investigation of interactivity as a concept, let us turn now to a further discussion of the constructs of interactivity as a variable.

Interactivity as a multidimensional variable

Several scholars examine interactivity as a multidimensional construct (e.g. Ha and James 1998; Heeter 2000; Massey and Levy 1999). A multidimensional approach is comforting and, indeed, expresses well the richness of online phenomena. Nevertheless, we argue for a unidimensional definition of interactivity instead. In our view interactivity would become a useful intellectual construct only if it is focused and its definition clarified. Variety and richness can be found in multiple and widespread applications rather than in internal ambiguity. Interactivity can and should be applied to the study of a long list of settings. However, for it to make sense and be helpful it should mean as few as possible things. In the same way other concepts from many fields (for example: 'need for cognition' or 'political involvement') can perform in various fields of our human life, with various scales and methods to study them – but they all refer to the same psychological/social meaning. One might change the unit of analysis, the vehicles through which to study the phenomena, but not its basic meaning.

Although we intuitively tend to describe and discuss interactivity as a human-related process, a generalizable conception should allow for interactivity involving non-human actors. We turn now to discuss interactivity as a human behaviour, in contrast (or not?) to non-human actors.

Interactivity as human behaviour

Does interactivity require humans? Some systems are intended purely for person-to-person interaction. Increasingly, though, systems are becoming hybrid, with portions of communication sequences and sometimes entire communication sequences carried out between humans and machines, or even between machines without human involvement at all. How does interactivity fit into this cyborgian landscape? When the actors are human, there is reason to focus on cognitive and emotional effects. With systems that contain only synthetic actors, the search is mostly for functional effects.

Our discussion regarding the importance of information in the process of interactivity has clear implications for human responsiveness. However, considering interactivity as a process involving transmissions/exchanges of messages is a general notion, because we refer to a rich spectrum of information types transmitted between communicants. This spectrum could contain data, gestures, spoken words, or any other symbols or content. In that sense, we can measure interactivity between users, between users and media and even amongst media. However, the differences are not that clear, since technological developments such as agents can perform in many similar attributes of human responsiveness. Agents are programmes that have self-presence in creation of content can mimic interpersonal behaviours. In addition, humans use their social rules in their interactions with computers (Reeves and Nass 1996).

The conceptions of medium richness (Daft and Lengel 1986) and reduced cues (Sproull and Kiesler 1986, 1991) postulated that media varied along a continuum defined by its information richness. These conceptions gained much popularity and some empirical evidence in the early (and old) years of new media studies. However, it is now apparent that the real question involves social presence (Short *et al.* 1976; Rice 1984) or virtual presence that engages with actors' sense of intimacy and immediacy and, not the more mechanical and simplistic channel bandwidth.

Rafaeli and Noy (2005) found virtual presence significantly affecting the bidding behaviour in online auction, resulting from the transmission of social cues during an auction. Thus, they note that even simple agents that can imitate face-to-face or human-like interaction and generate the interactivity effects. These laboratory results should impact the debate regarding medium richness, weighing against the medium traits approach.

Interactivity with the medium and through the medium

Because of the importance of perception in mediated interactivity, we can focus on the psychological aspects of user–content interaction. Interpersonal processing of information meaning might generate interactivity with evidently a static messaging. There exists a tradition of research into para-social interaction (Horton and Wohl 1956) which occurs when an individual interacts with figures or representations of content in a medium. In their seminal research, Horton and Wohl wrote, 'We propose to call this seeming face-to-face relationship between spectator and performer a para-social relationship' (1956: 215). Researchers that used this framework such as Houlberg (1984) found empirical evidence of such para-social relationships between viewing audiences and local television newscasters. Perse (1990) found that that a high degree of para-social interaction with a television persona strengthens the viewer's cognitive and affective involvement with the programme. Rafaeli (1990) raised some concerns regarding para-social interaction, assuming it could serve as a manipulation designed to attain a larger and more loyal audience. Hoerner (1999) suggested studies have to broaden their para-social definition: 'A more contemporary conceptualization of para-social interaction has been described as the interpersonal involvement of the user with the media being consumed.' Hoerner found that some websites' elements other than personas, such as styles of textual and graphic presentations, could serve to create para-social relations through interaction with the website.

In para-social interaction, the individual perceives the interaction as real, even though in reality there may be no interaction at all. This evokes a parallel concept of *perceived interactivity*. Both para-social interaction and perceived interactivity are intrapersonal perceptions that occur at the psychological level. From the intrapersonal perspective, human–computer interaction could be articulated as a para-social interaction (Sundar and Nass 2000), as whether or not it actually happened matters less than whether it was perceived to have happened.

We turn now to focus on the fundamental dimensions of interactivity from the user's perspective. We describe these dimensions as a process that contains the expected interactivity, its actual realization and the perceived interactivity.

Expected, actual and perceived interactivity

By now, it should come as little surprise that some have decided to abandon the debate regarding the way we can 'capture' interactivity in the physical world and turn to consider interactivity as an experiential phenomenon. For example, several scholars consider interactivity as an experience and define it as perceived interactivity (Lee 2000; McMillan and Downes 2000; Newhagen *et al.* 1996; Kiousis 1999).

The paradox is that even when research defines interactivity in a particular setting as high or low, users can subjectively have different feelings, experiences, or perceptions of interactivity of different levels or intensity. Therefore, subjective and objective interactivity might diverge and could confound study. Obviously, an advanced Internet user who is more literate and experienced in using a specific Internet application might have a different interpretation and might perform differently with 'interactive features'.

In order for this subjective, experiential process we call interactivity to work, individuals must assess other participants of communication exchanges as acting similarly. A 'theory of interaction' must form in the mind of the interactant for interactivity to take place. Thus, we can acknowledge the existence of indirect series of information exchanges between participants in which one should not expect his transmission to be returned by the previous exchanges. Interactivity may still exist when a response occurs at delayed time or physically removed location.

On the other hand, we can also articulate a concept of *expected interactivity*. Sohn and Leckenby (2002) defined expected interactivity as 'the extent of interactivity that a person expects to experience during a prospective interaction with the medium'. We argue this definition should have border limits, one that can contain the evaluation of interactivity as a process, not just interaction with the medium. For example, users of an Instant Messaging application have some expectations regarding the interactivity involved in an interaction with other users or with the application itself. Thus, defining expectations towards interactivity further highlights our notion on interactivity. The expected interactivity of any individual would be based on their unique personal characteristics, different psychological variances and mostly based on subjective experience with interactivity. This is essentially the reverse of perceived interactivity.

Newhagen (2004) argues that interactivity is an information-based process, embedding meaning in symbols, that takes place within the individual. In contrast, Sundar (2004: 386) argues that 'Interactivity is a message (or medium) attribute, not a user attribute'. According to Sundar, defining interactivity as a perceptual variable is inaccurate because it situates interactivity within the user, which further obscures the concept of interactivity. Thus, he argues that perceived interactivity could confound perceived usability. Although we agree with Newhagen that interactivity is an information-based process, we suggest that the process of attributing meanings be considered as perceived interactivity rather than interactivity itself. Moreover, although we agree with Sundar that perception or experience cannot be regard as interactivity itself, we cannot agree with his position in this debate, as he situates interactivity as a medium attribute. We prefer viewing interactivity as a process. In summary, we posit a definition that is at a midpoint between Newhagen and Sundar, though sufficiently divergent from either position.

We support the differentiation of expected interactivity, actual (realization of) interactivity and perceived or experienced interactivity. While the first and the last are subjective perceptions, the realization of interactivity is process related and real. Emphasizing subjectivity in the consideration of expected and perceived interactivity and considering interactivity as a process of information exchanges puts forward the notion of information meaning (Newhagen 2004). We turn, therefore, to a short discussion of the role of information in interactivity and ties to information theory.

The importance of information: meaning, value and its relations to interactivity

Following Rafaeli's (1988) definition we emphasize that interactivity is rooted in the realm of mediated interaction. A medium is involved. Although this definition is driven from interpersonal communication models of conversation, it has various wider applications. While this model states that transmission of information is in the centre of the process, it does not relate to the antecedents or implications of that process. While interactions can be studied in various areas from different perspectives, when we study the media information is obviously in the centre of the interaction. This conceptualization of interactivity situates the medium as an essential part of our inquiry.

The basic models of the communication process offered by Wiener (1948), Shannon and Weaver (1947), Osgood (1954), Schramm (1954) and others, also considered communication as an exchange of information/messages between sender and receiver. These exchanges depend on the channel of transmission and the process of coding and decoding these messages. While most of these early theoreticians hail from a technological background, the application of

their models to human behaviour is quiet obvious. Considering the responsiveness-based definition again, we can relate it to these models of information/messages transmission. While the information theory and transmission approach successfully maps the structure of the process, interactivity (defined as responsiveness) addresses the inner process. Thus, interactivity is offered as the concept that captures the substance of the communication process.

Conclusion

A sizeable number of fresh and mostly yet-unpublished dissertations about this subject from recent years (2000 and afterwards) investigate the various aspects of interactivity. Many of these studies examine interactivity in distance learning environments (e.g. Brady 2004; Dozier 2004; MacLean 2004). For example, Brady (2004) studies the effect of degrees of interactivity within an educational website on students and finds that interactivity positively influenced learning outcomes, website satisfaction and perception of flow and student time on task. Dozier (2004) examined the relationships of interactivity, social constructivism and satisfaction with distance learning among US Army Infantry soldiers participating in college distance learning courses. Findings support the use of highly interactive social constructivist instructional approaches in computer-mediated and other learning environments. MacLean (2004) also explores the role of interactivity in the learning environment. His study analysed archived online discussions forums to determine the factors contributing to asynchronous learning networks' interactivity. Among others, he found correlations between the motivation students had to post messages and the levels of interactivity displayed by the messages.

Categorizations of interactivity continue to serve as a framework of many studies. For example, Sukpanich (2004) used the results of an online survey to test two dimensions of interactivity – machine interactivity and person interactivity – in order to predict consumers' intentions to purchase online. Results indicate machine interactivity is positively associated with online purchase intentions through its influence on physical telepresence, attitudes, perceived behavioural control and trust. Person interactivity was positively associated with online purchase intentions through its influence on social telepresence, subjective norms, perceived behavioural control and trust. Users–agents interactivity is in the center of Huang's (2003) exploration. Huang studied emotional displays and interactive responses playing a key role in evoking social response from users to agent interactivity. Findings indicate interactive media users felt higher levels of mutual awareness with the animated characters presented.

Similar, to Sukpanich (2004), several studies (Johnson 2002; Yin 2002; Yu 2004) focused on the relations of interactivity and marketing/consumer behaviour. For example, Yin (2002) examined interactivity and its effect on some key consumer variables Yu (2004) surveyed video games' players to examine their perceived interactivity. The results showed respondents' buying behaviour was significantly influenced by the characteristics of interactivity and vividness.

Interactivity effects are still enigmatic. For example, Wang (2000) followed the effects of interactivity of web campaigns in Taiwan's 2000 presidential election. Contrary to the theory-based hypothesis, moderate interactivity seemed to produce the most positive online communication effects. Moderate interactivity yielded more effects than either high or low interactivity, suggesting a curvilinear relationship reminiscent of other communication variables. In the same manner, Hong (2003) studied the impacts of the levels of interactivity role, among other variables, in creating an experience of telepresence and the intention to revisit a website. Although interactivity had a strong effect on telepresence, it did not show the same significant effect on website revisiting intentions.

Thinking about the various conceptualizations of interactivity, we suggest that future research should be specific about articulating the part of the model chosen for focus. Figure 6.1 proposes a generic perspective of interactivity as a process of media expectations, realizations and perceptions.

Looking at this model, we can place interactivity studies along its phases. One can focus on the *exogenous* antecedents of interactivity, examining the external factors that influence the individual such as situations' place, norms, social restrictions, group pressures etc. or study the *internal* factors that consist of individuals' physiological and psychological needs. However, some studies could pass over this level and consider the various *expectations* users have towards interactivity. Although these expectations result from the internal and external factors, they can be considered as a user subjective attribute. Decision processes involve the assessments of prior expectations into frameworks of either rational or subjective decisions that result in the actual uses of the users. Actual uses are the *realizations* of interactivity, the traceable activities of the users (or artificial players) that researches can measure (e.g. posting a message in a forum). The results of these activities are measurable objective outcomes. Nevertheless, we can focus on the *perceived* outcomes as experienced by the users.

This chapter began with conceptualization difficulties of the construct of interactivity. We suggested forging and embracing a common definition. We propose viewing interactivity in a broader perspective than just that limited to new media, computers or networks. We support defining interactivity as a *process-related variable* concerning *responsiveness*. A generic model is offered that examines the interactivity process over time by considering expectations, realizations and perceptions sequentially. It appears that the concept of interactivity and the empirical studies moved from being medium-focused through a process focus, arriving at the perception focus

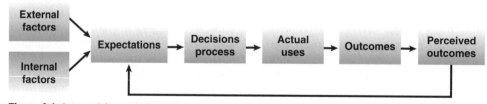

Figure 6.1 Interactivity analysis model.

proposed here. While the antecedents of interactivity are subject to further research and have not been covered here, this chapter offered a review of the correlates and consequences of the interactivity construct. The chapter takes one more step toward the formation of a theory of the interactivity process, the expectations, uses and perceptions of it and the role these play in understanding communication processes, including those that occur online.

References

Ahern, R. K. and Stromer-Galley, J. (2000). The interaction effect: an experimental study of high and low interactivity political websites. Paper presented at the 50th Annual Conference of the International Communication Association, Acapulco, Mexico.

Alba, J., Lynch, J., Weitz, B., Janiszewski, C., Lutz, R., Sawyer, A. and Wood, S. (1997). Interactive home shopping: consumer, retailer and manufacturer incentives to participate in electronic marketplaces. *Journal of Marketing 61*(3), 38–53.

Amichai-Hamburger, Y., Fine, A. and Goldstein, A. (2004). The impact of Internet interactivity and need for closure on consumer preference. *Computers in Human Behavior 20*(1), 103–117.

Brady, L. (2004). The role of interactivity on the effectiveness of an educational science website for middle school students. Unpublished dissertation. Wichita State University.

Bezjian-Avery, A., Calder, B. and Iacobucci, D. (1998). New media interactive advertising vs. traditional advertising. *Journal of Advertising Research 38*(4), 23–32.

Bucy, E. P. (2004a). Interactivity in society: locating an elusive concept. *Information Society 20*(5), 373–383.

Bucy, E. P. (2004b). The interactivity paradox: closer to the news but confused. In E. P. Bucy and J. E. Newhagen (eds), *Media access: Social and psychological dimensions of new technology use* (pp. 47–72). Mahwah, NJ: Erlbaum.

Burgoon, J. K., Bonito, J. A. *et al.* (2000). Interactivity in human-computer interaction: a study of credibility, understanding and influence. *Computers in Human Behavior 16*(6), 553–574.

Cacioppo, J. T. and Petty, R. E. (1982). The need for cognition. *Journal of Personality and Social Psychology 42*, 116–131.

Cohen, J. (2002). Deconstructing Ally: explaining viewers' different interpretations of popular television. *Media Psychology 4*, 253–277.

Cho, C-H. (1999). How advertising works on the WWW: modified elaboration likelihood model. *Journal of Current Issues and Research in Advertising 21*(1), 33–50.

Cho, C-H. and Leckenby, J. D. (1999). Interactivity as a measure of advertising effectiveness. In M. S. Roberts (ed.) *Proceedings of the American Academy of Advertising* (pp. 162–179). Gainesville, FL: University of Florida.

Coyle, J. R. and Thorson, E. (2001). The effects of progressive levels of interactivity and vividness in Web marketing sites. *Journal of Advertising 30*(3), 65–79.

Daft, R. L. and Lengel, R. H. (1986). Organizational information requirements, media richness and structural design. *Management Science 32*(5), 554–570.

Dozier, D. C. (2004). Interactivity, social constructivism and satisfaction with distance learning among infantry soldiers. Unpublished dissertation. Auburn University.

Downes, E. J. and McMillan, S. J. (2000). Defining interactivity: a qualitative identification of key dimensions. *New Media and Society 2*(2), 157–179.

Durlak, J. T. (1987). A typology for interactive media. In M. L. McLaughlin (ed.), *Communication yearbook 10* (pp. 743–757). Newbury Park, CA: Sage.

Dyson, E. (1993). Interactivity means 'active' participation. *Computerworld 27*(50), 33–34.

Ghose, S. and Dou, W. Y. (1998). Interactive functions and their impacts on the appeal of Internet presence sites. *Journal of Advertising Research 38*(2), 29–43.

Gibson, J. J. (1979). *The ecological approach to visual perception.* Boston, MA: Houghton Mifflin.

Ha, L. and James, E. L. (1998). Interactivity reexamined: a baseline analysis of early business Web sites. *Journal of Broadcasting and Electronic Media 42*(4), 457–474.

Haeckel, S. H. (1998). About the nature and future of interactive marketing. *Journal of Interactive Marketing 12*(1), 63–71.

Hackman, M. Z. and Walker, K. B. (1990). Instructional communication in the televised classroom: the effects of system design and teacher immediacy on student learning and satisfaction. *Communication Education 39*, 196–206.

Heeter, C. (2000). Interactivity in the context of designed experiences. *Journal of Interactive Advertising 1*(1). URL (Retrieved June 2005): http://www.jiad.org/vol1/no1/heeter

Hillman, D. C., Willis, D. J. and Gunawardena, C. N. (1994). Learner–interface interaction in distance education: an extension of contemporary models and strategies for practitioners. *The American Journal of Distance Education 8*(2), 30–42.

Hoffman, D. L. and Novak, T. P. (1996). Marketing in hypermedia computer-mediated environments: conceptual foundations. *Journal of Marketing* July, 50–68.

Hoerner, J. (1999). Scaling the web: a parasocial interaction scale for World Wide Web sites. In D. W. Schumann and E. Thorson (eds), *Advertising and the World Wide Web* (pp. 135–147). Mahwah, NJ: Lawrence Erlbaum.

Horton D. and Wohl, RR. (1956). Mass communication and para-social interaction; observations on intimacy at a distance. *Psychiatry 19*(3), 215–229.

Hong, S. (2003). The impacts of the levels of interactivity, vividness and motivation on telepresence and revisiting intention in the new media. Unpublished dissertation. The University of Texas at Austin.

Houlberg, R. (1984). Local television news audience and the para-social interaction. *Journal of Broadcasting 28*, 423–429.

Huang, H-Y. (2003). Effects of interactivity and expressiveness on perceived social presence, memory and persuasion in interactive health communications. Unpublished dissertation. The University of North Carolina at Chapel Hill.

Jensen, J. F. (1998). Interactivity: tracing a new concept in media and communication studies. *Nordicom Review* 19(1), 185–204.

Jee, J. and Lee, W. N. (2002). Antecedents and consequences of perceived interactivity: an exploratory study. *Journal of Interactive Advertising* 3(1). URL (Retrieved June 2005): http://jiad.org/vol3/no1/jee/index.htm

Jones, Q., Ravid, G. and Rafaeli, S. (2004). Information overload and the message dynamics of online interaction spaces: a theoretical model and empirical exploration. *Information Systems Research* 15(2), 194–210.

Kayany, J. M., Wotring, C. E. and Forrest, E. J. (1996). Relational control and interactive media choice in technology-mediated communication situations. *Human Communication Research* 22(3), 399–421.

Kiousis, S. (1999). Broadening the boundaries of interactivity: a concept explication. Paper read at Association for Education in Journalism and Mass Communication Annual Conference, August, at New Orleans, LA.

Kiousis, S. (2002). Interactivity: a concept explication. *New Media and Society* 4(3), 355–383.

Leary, T. (1990). The interpersonal, interactive, interdimensional interface. In B. Laurel (ed.), *The art of human–computer interface design*. Menlo Park, CA: Addison Wesley.

Leckenby, J. D. and Li, H. (2000). From the Editors: why we need the Journal of Interactive Advertising. *Journal of Interactive Advertising* 1(1). URL (Retrieved June 2005): http://www.jiad.org/vol1/no1/editors/index.html

Lee, J. Lee, W. N. (2002). Antecedents and consequences of perceived interactivity: an exploratory study. *Journal of Interactive Adevertising* 3(1). URL (Retrieved June 2005): http://Jiad.org/vol3/no1/jee/index.htm

Lee, J-S. (2000). Interactivity: a new approach paper presented at the Association for Education in Journalism and Mass Communication, Phoenix, AZ.

Liaw, S-S. and Huang, H-M. (2000). Enhancing interactivity in web-based instruction: a review of the literature. *Educational Technology* 40(3), 41–45.

Lieb, T. (1998). Inactivity on interactivity. *Journal of Electronic Publishing* 3(3). URL (Retrieved June 2005): http://www.press.umich.edu/jep/03-03/lieb0303.html

Liu, Y. P. (2003). Developing a scale to measure the interactivity of websites. *Journal of Advertising Research* 43(2), 207–216.

Liu, Y. P. and Shrum, L. J. (2002). What is interactivity and is it always such a good thing? Implications of definition, person and situation for the influence of interactivity on advertising effectiveness. *Journal of Advertising* 31(4), 53–64.

Lombard, M. and Ditton, T. B. (1997). At the heart of it all: the concept of presence. *Journal of Computer-Mediated Communication* 3(2). URL (Retrieved June 2005): http://jcmc.indiana.edu/vol3/issue2/lombard.html

Lombard, M. and Snyder-Dutch, J. (2001). Interactive advertising and presence: a framework. *Journal of Interactive Advertising* 1(2). URL (Retrieved June 2005): http://www.jiad.org/vol1/no2/lombard/index.htm

Macias, W. (2000). The effects of interactivity on comprehension and persuasion of interactive advertising. Unpublished doctoral dissertation, Department of Advertising, The University of Texas at Austin.

Macias, W. (2003). A preliminary structural equation model of comprehension and persuasion of interactive advertising brand web sites. *Journal of Interactive Advertising* 3(2). URL (Retrieved June 2005): http://www.jiad.org/vol3/no2/macias/index.htm

MacLean, R. L. (2004). Measuring and improving interactivity in an asynchronous learning network. Unpublished dissertation. The Claremont Graduate University.

Maddux, C. D., Johnson, D. L. and Willis, J. W. (1997). *Educational computing: Learning with tomorrow's technologies*, 2nd edn). Needham Heights, MA: Allyn and Bacon.

Markus, M. L. (1990). Toward a 'critical mass' theory of interactive media. In J. Fulk and C. Steinfeld (eds), *Organization and communication technology* (pp. 194–218). Newbury Park, CA: Sage.

Marvin, C. (1988). *When old technologies were new: Thinking about electric communication in the late nineteenth century*. New York: Oxford University Press.

Massey, B. L. and Levy, M. R. (1999). Interactivity, online journalism and English-language web newspapers in Asia. *Journalism and Mass Communication Quarterly* 76(1), 138–151.

McMillan, S. J. (1998). Who pays for content? Funding in interactive media. *Journal of Computer Mediated Communication* 4(1). URL (Retrieved June 2005): http://jcmc.indiana.edu/vol4/issue1/mcmillan.html

McMillan, S. J. (2002). Exploring models of interactivity from multiple research traditions: users, documents, systems. In S. J. McMillan and L. Lievrouw, *The handbook of new media: Social shaping and consequences of ICTs* (pp. 163–182). London: Sage.

McMillan, S. J. and Downes, E. J. (2000). Defining interactivity: a qualitative identification of key dimensions. *New Media and Society* 2(2), 157–179.

McMillan, S. J. and Hwang J-S. (2002). Measures of perceived interactivity: an exploration of the role of direction of communication, user control and time in shaping perceptions of interactivity. *Journal of Advertising* 31(3), 14–29.

Miles, Ian (1992). When mediation is the message: how suppliers envisage new markets. In M. Lea (ed.), *Contexts of computer-mediated communication* (pp. 145–167). New York: Harvester-Wheatsheaf.

Moore, M. (1989). Editorial: Three types of interaction. *The American Journal of Distance Education* 3(2), 1–7.

Mundorf, N. and Bryant, J. (2002). Realizing the social and commercial potential of interactive technologies. *Journal of Business Research* 55, 665–670.

Murray, J. (1997). *Hamlet on the holodeck: The future of narrative in cyberspace*. New York: The Free Press.

Newhagen, J. E. (2004). Interactivity, dynamic symbol processing and the emergence of content in human communication. *Information Society* 20(5), 395–400.

Newhagen, J. E., Cordes, J. W. and Levy, M. R. (1996). Nightly@Nbc.Com: audience scope and the perception of interactivity in viewer mail on the internet. *Journal of Communication, 45*(3), 164–175.

Neuman, W. R. (1991). *The future of the mass audience.* Cambridge, MA: Cambridge University Press.

Norman, D. A. (1988). *The psychology of everyday things.* New York: Basic Books.

Novak, T. P., Hoffman, D. L. and Yung, Y. F. (2000). Measuring the customer experience in online environments: a structural modeling approach. *Marketing Science 19*(1), 22–42.

Osgood, C. E. (1954). Psycholinguists: a survey of theory and research problems. *Journal of Abnormal and Social Psychology 49.* Morton Prince Memorial Supplemental.

Pavlik, J. V. (1998). *New media technology: Cultural and commercial perspectives*, 2nd edn. Boston, MA: Allyn and Bacon.

Perse, E. M. (1990). Media involvement and local news effects. *Journal of Broadcasting and Electronic Media 34*, 17–36.

Rafaeli, S. (1985). Interacting with media: Para-social interaction and real interaction. Unpublished doctoral dissertation, Stanford University.

Rafaeli, S. (1988). Interactivity: from new media to communication. In R. P. Hawkins, J. M. Wiemann and S. Pingree (eds), *Advancing communication science: Merging mass and interpersonal process* (pp. 110–134). Newbury Park, CA: Sage.

Rafaeli, S. (1990). Interacting with media: para-social interaction and real interaction. In B. D. Ruben and L. A. Lievrouw (eds), *Mediation, information and communication: Information and behavior*, vol. 3 (pp. 125–181). New Brunswick, NJ: Transaction Press.

Rafaeli, S. (2004). Constructs in the storm. In M. Consalvo, N. Baym, J. Hunsinger, K. B. Jensen, J. Logie, M. Murero and L. R. Shade (eds), *Internet research annual, volume 1* (pp. 55–65). New York: Peter Lang Publishers.

Rafaeli, S. and Sudweeks, F. (1997). Networked interactivity. *Journal of Computer-Mediated Communication 2*(4). URL (Retrieved June 2005): http://jcmc.indiana.edu/vol2/issue4/rafaeli.sudweeks.html

Reeves, B. and Nass, C. (1996). *The media equation: How people treat computers, television and new media like real people and places.* New York: Cambridge University Press.

Rice, R. E. (1984). New media technology: growth and integration. In R. E. Rice (ed.), *The new media: Communication, research and technology* (pp. 33–54). Beverly Hills, CA: Sage.

Rogers, E. M. (1995). *Diffusion of innovations*, 4th edn. New York: Free Press.

Rust, R. T. and Varki, S. (1996). Rising from the ashes of advertising. *Journal of Business Research 37*, 173–181.

Samsup, J. and Yungwook, K. (2003). The effect of web characteristics on relationship building. *Journal of Public Relations Research 15*(3), 199.

Schultz, T. (2000). Mass media and the concept of interactivity: an exploratory study of online forums and reader email. *Media, Culture and Society 22*(2), 205–221.

Schramm, W. (1954). How communication works. In W. Schramm (ed.), *The process and effects of mass communiction* (pp. 3–26). Urbana, IL: University of Illinois Press.

Shannon, C. and Weaver, W. (1947). *The mathematical theory of communication.* Urbana, IL: University of Illinois Press.

Shin, M. (1998). Promoting student's self-regulation ability: guidelines for instructional design. *Educational Technology 38*(1), 38–44.

Short, J., Williams, E. and Christie, B. (1976). *The social psychology of telecommunications.* London: John Wiley and Sons.

Sproull, L. and Kiesler, S. (1986). Reducing social context cues: electronic mail in organizational communication. *Management Science 32*(11), 1492–1512.

Sproull, L. and Kiesler, S. (1991). *Connections: New ways of working in a network organization.* Cambridge, MA: MIT Press.

Sohn, D. and Leckenby, J. D. (2002). Social dimensions of interactive advertising. *Proceedings of the Annual Conference of the American Academy of Advertising*, Jacksonville, Florida, March.

Sohn, D., Leckenby, J. D. and Jee, J. (2003). Expected interactivity the role of expected interactivity in interactive ad processing. Annual Conference American Academy of Advertising, Denver-Broomfield, Colorado.

Steuer, J. (1992). Defining virtual reality: Dimensions determining telepresence. *Journal of Communication, 42*(4), 73–93.

Stromer-Galley, J. (2000). Online interaction and why candidates avoid it. *Journal of Communication 50*(4), 111–132.

Stromer-Galley, J. and Foot, K. A. (2000). Citizens, campaigns and online interactivity. Paper presented at the International Communication Association, Acapulco, Mexico.

Stewart, D. W. and Pavlou, P. A. (2002). From consumer response to active consumer: measuring the effectiveness of interactive media. *Journal of the Academy of Marketing Science 30*(Fall), 376–396.

Sukpanich, N. and Chen, L. (2000). Interactivity as the driving force behind e-commerce. Proceedings of the American Conference on Information Systems (pp. 834–836), California.

Sukpanich, N. (2004). Machine interactivity and person interactivity: the driving forces behind influences on consumers willingness to purchase online. Unpublished dissertation. The University of Memphis.

Sundar, S. S. (2004). Theorizing interactivity's effects. *Information Society 20*(5): 385–389.

Sundar, S. S. and Kim, J. (2004). Interactivity and persuasion: influencing attitudes with information and involvement. *Paper presented to the Communication and Technology division at the 54th annual convention of the International Communication Association*, New Orleans, LA.

Sundar, S. S., Kalyanaraman, S. and Brown J. (2003). Explicating web site interactivity-impression formation effects in political campaign sites. *Communication Research 30*(1), 30–59.

Teo, H. H., Oh, L. B., *et al.* (2003). An empirical study of the effects of interactivity on web user attitude. *International Journal of Human-Computer Studies 58*(3), 281–305.

Van Dijk, J. (1999). *The network society: Social aspects of new media*, L. Spoorenberg (Trans.). Thousand Oaks: Sage.

Wang, T-L. (2000). The effects of interactivity on Web campaigning in Taiwan's 2000 presidential election. Unpublished dissertation. The University of Texas at Austin.

Warnick, B., Xenos, M., Endres, D. and Gastil, J. (2005). Effects of campaign-to-user and text-based interactivity in political candidate campaign web sites. *Journal of Computer-Mediated Communication 10*(3). URL (Retrieved June 2005): http://jcmc.indiana.edu/vol10/issue3/warnick.html

Webster, D. M. and Kruglanski, A. W. (1994). Individual differences in need for cognitive closure. *Journal of Personality and Social Psychology 67*, 261–271.

Wiener, N. (1948). *Cybernetics, or, control and communication in the animal and the machine*. Cambridge, MA: Technology Press.

Williams, F., Rice, R. and Rogers, E. M. (1988). *Research methods and the new media*. New York: Free Press.

Wu, G. (1999). Perceived interactivity and attitude toward website. Paper presented at the American Academy of Advertising annual conference, Albuquerque, NM.

Wu, G. (2000). The role of perceived interactivity in interactive ad processing. Unpublished dissertation. The University of Texas at Austin.

Yin, J. (2002). Interactivity of Internet-based communications: impacts on e-business consumer decisions. Unpublished dissertation. Georgia State University.

Yoo, C. Y. and Stout, P. A. (2001). Factors affecting users' interactivity with the web site and the consequences of users' interactivity. In C. R. Taylor (ed.), *Proceedings of the 2001 Conference of the American Academy of Advertising* (pp. 53–60). Villanova, PA: Villanova University.

Yu, Y-L. (2004). The impact of perceived interactivity and vividness of video games on customer buying behavior. Unpublished dissertation. Lynn University.

Zeltzer, D. (1992). Autonomy, interaction and presence. *Teleoperators and Virtual Environments 1*(1), 127–132.

CHAPTER 7

Social psychology of interactivity in human– website interaction

S. Shyam Sundar

Interactivity is arguably the single most important feature that distinguishes mass communication via the Web from traditional mass media. Unlike newspapers and television, the Web offers unlimited potential for interacting with information instead of simply transmitting it. Indeed, almost all computer-based media encourage audience activity, by requiring users to constantly specify their preferences via the mouse, touchpad, keyboard, joystick and other input devices. Users are active participants rather than passive recipients of communication. The flow of information is decidedly two-way, in stark contrast to the unidirectional transmission epitomized by traditional mass media. As a result, psychologically speaking, the computer is no longer seen as a mere medium of communication but as a source of interaction (Sundar and Nass 2000). That is, users orient toward computers as autonomous beings instead of as conduits for delivery of pre-programmed content. This explains the somewhat curious finding across many studies that computer users mindlessly apply rules of human–human communication

to their interactions with computers (Nass and Moon 2000). They indeed are polite to computers, apply gender stereotypes and generally behave socially in front of the computer (Reeves and Nass 1996). Furthermore, they tend to form long-term affiliations with particular computer terminals, showing anthropomorphic loyalty toward specific terminals (Sundar 2004a). Nass and colleagues have always maintained that the heightened level of interactivity afforded by computers is among the primary reasons for this 'media equation' of users exhibiting social tendencies toward such communication technologies (Nass and Steuer 1993; Nass and Moon 2000). However, they have not spelled out the theoretical mechanisms by which interactivity influences such source orientation.

What exactly does interactivity do? It can, at optimal levels, facilitate a seamless transaction between the user and the system, thereby enhancing telepresence (Steuer 1992) and encouraging a sense of oneness with the technology. But this notion is related to the speed of interaction (which has its own psychological effects – see

Sundar and Wagner [2002]) rather than the nature of interaction. Several classic explications of the nature of interactivity (e.g., Rafaeli 1988) have tended to focus on computer-mediated communication such as email and other forms of messaging between people, but these interactions closely parallel interpersonal interaction in their dynamic of message exchange, with the debate centring around the extent to which the social effects of such communication deviate from the face-to-face norm (for a quick summary, see Lievrouw *et al.* [2000]). What happens when interactivity is taken out of the interpersonal context and applied to mediated mass communication? The message exchange is no longer dependent on spontaneous activity by the various interactants involved. In fact, most, if not all, of the activity behind interactivity in such a situation would have to come from the user, given that the system supplying mass communication is programmed to serve prepared content, such as existing news stories that have been written and edited prior to the user's interaction. However, the system is not simply a stone tablet or a newspaper for the user to find his or her own way around in an already established layout. Instead, it is a complex multilayered system that is often searchable, offering not only the possibility for idiosyncratic navigation within the site but also opportunities to engage the medium in myriad ways. That is, each and every reader is able to interact with the website as a whole, calling up stories on a desired topic or area of interest, choosing particular stories over others, clicking on some embedded hyperlinks in the stories but not others, choosing to attend to animations of technical details in some stories, downloading an audio or video clip of certain news items, and so on. The news reader is in effect interacting with the mode, source and content of mediated communication.

Interactivity as a modality feature

One of the simplest ways to conceptualize interactivity is as a feature of the medium, specifically the variety of modalities that it offers for the user to experience the various parts of a website, from simple text to graphics, animation, audio and video. Different modalites lead to different perceptual representations, which means the use of different senses in transmitting and processing messages (Marmolin 1991; Hoogeveen 1997). As Sundar (2000) points out, the term 'multimedia' (which is often applied to internet-based media) is a misnomer because it is typically used to refer to multiple modalities (not media) within a single medium. The key difference between traditional media and the Web is that the latter offers the users (1) a number of different modalities at the same time, and (2) the seamless ability to switch back and forth between modalities (Sundar *et al.* 2000). Furthermore, with the arrival of multimodal interfaces which allow multiple input modes such as speech, touch, text, gaze and gestures (Oviatt 2003), the range of possibilities for interaction with the system becomes numerous as well as richly variegated. Together, they enhance the speed, range, and mapping of information – the three defining elements of interactivity, according to Steuer (1992). Or, as Reeves and Nass (2000) put it, they serve to increase 'perceptual bandwidth' by extending the type and number of sensory channels involved in interacting with users. In sum, the greater the number of input as well as output modalities offered by an interface, the greater its interactivity, under this conceptualization.

It should be kept in mind, however, that different modalities differ not simply in the senses they engage but also the functionality they bring to the interface. As McLuhan (1964) observed, each modality carries its own distinctive message. Likewise, in the Web medium, text conveys one kind of message whereas an animated graphic conveys another. Often, these different modalities are used to serve different purposes or functions. For example, on a news website, clicking on a link to open a form function for us to send email to the reporter serves a completely different function than clicking on a link that downloads an audio version of the news story. These two links represent not only different modalities but also different functions.

Sundar *et al.* (2003) call this the functional view of interactivity, whereby the greater the capacity for interaction offered by a website, the greater its level of interactivity. The more bells and whistles there are on the site, the greater its interactivity. This conceptualization obviously relies on technological aspects of the medium

(Heeter 1989), with sites offering more forms, downloads, chat facilities and so on being deemed more interactive. Several studies in communication have operationalized interactivity in terms of the availability (or lack thereof) of such functional features (e.g., Massey and Levy 1999; Ahern and Stromer-Galley 2000; Bucy 2003). The higher the number of such features on the site, the greater its interactivity. That is, it relies simply on a headcount of interaction-generating functions. How much or how effectively these features are put to use are not relevant to this definition of interactivity, given its focus on the sheer presence (or absence) of functions that go beyond a basic textual site.

In one experiment, Sundar *et al.* (1998) created three ordinal levels of interactivity in a political candidate website, with the low-interactivity version featuring no hyperlinks whatsoever, the medium condition offering a link to access additional information, and the high-interactivity site featuring a form function allowing users to send an email to the candidate directly. Results showed that greater site interactivity fostered more positive impressions of the candidate, with the politically apathetic participants feeling greater affinity toward him as a direct monotonic function of interactivity and the politically savvy participants showing an inverted V-pattern on perceived affinity, i.e., medium interactivity was associated with higher reported closeness in feeling to the candidate than the other two conditions. Interpreting this result with the lens of the Elaboration Likelihood Model (Petty and Cacioppo 1986), we may conclude that interactivity is seen as more of a peripheral cue than as a central message argument.

This kind of bells and whistles approach to interactivity was directly tested in an experiment varying modality availability on a news website (Sundar 2000). Study participants were exposed to news stories that were either text-only or text with pictures, or text with audio, or text with both pictures and audio, or text with pictures and video. They singled out audio and video downloads as being the best part of the site, yet their evaluations of the site and news content (as well as their memory for story content) were not as positive as when the site simply contained text and pictures. Bucy (2003) calls this the 'interactivity paradox' owing the negative effects

(despite their desirability) to navigational load and the resultant cognitive disorientation. In explaining the superiority of the text-only and text + picture conditions, Sundar (2000) suggests that audiovisual modalities trigger automatic processing (because they are perceptually equivalent to real-world experience, requiring little or no decoding of symbol systems) while textual processing is necessarily controlled. All of this indicates a deterministic orientation toward technological features wherein psychological processing is dictated by the structure or modality of mediated information. The most dramatic demonstration of such a phenomenon is the human tendency to adapt to voice-recognition systems by attempting to speak slowly and clearly (Oviatt *et al.* 1998).

Not only the modality used but also the manner in which the modality is deployed can have cognitive consequences. In a study of interactive news features, Sundar and Constantin (2004) found that the type of interactive device used in a story can make a difference to the manner in which the content is processed. In this experiment, drags were associated with stronger orienting responses compared to tabs and mouse-overs, perhaps because drag usage requires greater ongoing allocation of attention, interest, and effort. The authors speculated that drags may therefore command controlled processing, unlike tabs and mouse-overs which are likely to be processed automatically, especially by college students. Overall, the study found that the volume of user navigation (i.e., clicking activity) was positively correlated with the diversity of interactive elements (drags, tabs, mouse-overs) used in a news story. However, although greater navigation led to better encoding of news information, it resulted in poorer ratings of the structure of the news article.

Ultimately, navigational problems appear to cloud the perceived effectiveness of interactivity as a modality feature. While newer modalities offer newer perceptual representations of content and result in novel ways of engaging users with mediated content, they also carry a cognitive burden arising from a continual need for navigation and orientation. Beyond a point, the calls for interaction issued by the presence of multiple modalities or functions on a website can be so taxing that the user has no choice but to treat interactivity as a peripheral cue, given the natural human tendency to economize on the expenditure of cognitive resources. Therefore, while the addition of modalities or functional features to a website enhances its interaction potential and may lead to positive appraisals of the site itself, the actual experience of these features may result in negative cognitive as well as attitudinal outcomes.

Interactivity as a source feature

The source or sender of a message is the starting point in any chain of communication and has therefore been accorded primacy in the literature on media effects (e.g., Hass 1988). The vast social psychological literature on source credibility is essentially about the powerful effect of communication sources in shaping audience perceptions (e.g., Wilson and Sherrell 1993).

While most traditional media do not allow you to choose freely between sources, interactive media make it possible for users to constantly make decisions about their sources of information. Indeed, one may conceptualize interactivity as the ability of the user to manipulate the source of their information. After all, the fundamental goal of interactivity is to allow the user enough idiosyncratic choice to be able to receive a highly personalized end result. That is, interactivity is the degree to which the user is able to serve as a source or gatekeeper of information. Sites that allow users to customize their daily menu of information, particularly portals such as myYahoo.com, would then stack up on the high end of the interactivity continuum whereas static websites, particularly shovelware sites (i.e., traditional media organizations simply dumping their newspaper or broadcast content onto their website), would be considered low on interactivity because they do not allow for much customization by the user. In fact, Sundar and Nass (2001) created an experimental competition between just such a site and one where interactive technology was ostensibly used to allow for different types of sourcing.

Proceeding from a new typology of online sources, Sundar and Nass (2001) created four between-subjects conditions in which study participants ($N = 48$) read the same set of six stories.

One-quarter of the subjects were told that the stories were selected by news editors while another quarter was told that they were selected by the computer terminal on which they were accessing the stories. In the third condition, they were told that other users of the online service chose the stories. Respondents in the last condition were led to believe that they themselves were serving as the selecting source of the stories. Only the perceived source of the news stories was manipulated. The actual text of the stories was identical across all four conditions.

These four source manipulations operationalize different nominal categorizations of sourcing patterns in online information services. For example, the news editors' condition is a straightforward reflection of most news websites, especially those run by news organizations putting out traditional media products such as newspapers (e.g., NewYorkTimes.com) and audiovisual broadcasts (e.g., BBC.com). This is quite common on the Web and is often representative of the shovelware approach – generally low on interactivity, but still providing an important online venue for traditional-media news vendors.

The computer as a source is found in algorithm-based automated news platforms such as GoogleNews. In a novel way, this type of sourcing bypasses the traditional methods of gatekeeping, which invariably involved professional human intervention. In the link to 'About Google News' on the http://www.news.google.com/ site, the following statement is telling:

> Google News presents information culled from approximately 4,500 news sources worldwide and automatically arranged to present the most relevant news first. Topics are updated continuously throughout the day, so you will see new stories each time you check the page. Google has developed an automated grouping process for Google News that pulls together related headlines and photos from thousands of sources worldwide—enabling you to see how different news organizations are reporting the same story. You pick the item that interests you, then go directly to the site which published the account you wish to read. Google News is highly unusual in that it offers a news service compiled solely by computer algorithms without human intervention. While the sources of the news vary in perspective and editorial approach, their selection

for inclusion is done without regard to political viewpoint or ideology. While this may lead to some occasionally unusual and contradictory groupings, it is exactly this variety that makes Google News a valuable source of information on the important issues of the day.

This kind of sourcing is somewhat more interactive in that it allows the online news reader some choice in dictating the particular news sources from which they would like to receive their news information.

The third condition, wherein other users choose the stories for the readers' consumption, is now a fairly common occurrence, especially in sites that purvey technical information (e.g., cnet.com) and commercial sites that offer a wide range of a product or many different kinds of products (e.g., amazon.com). In general, how other netizens view a particular product or what they bought along with the product you purchased, or which news stories they e-mailed the most during a particular period (and so on) are all outcomes of interactive technological features that allow anyone and everyone in the online population to serve as a source of information – sometimes by proactively opining on issues, but oftentimes through their browsing and purchasing behaviours. This method of sourcing is even more interactive than the computer algorithm acting as a source because it allows each and every user to provide direct and seemingly influential input.

The self-as-source condition epitomizes the function of customized portals such as mylycos.com (which allow each user to specify their menu of information, i.e., selection of gates) on the one hand, and the increasingly ubiquitous offers of personalization (whereby you can have your own 'space' or account or domain in most commercial websites) on the other hand. Customization is a key outcome of interactivity in that it offers unlimited potential for the communication receiver to assume the role of the communication source, forcing a truly profound reconceptualization of traditional flow models. Blogging therefore represents the ultimate form of the self acting as a source.

While each of the four different types of sourcing reviewed above have somewhat different operational and commercial manifestations

on the Web, the experiment conducted by Sundar and Nass (2001) controlled for such variation by operationalizing all four sources in the context of online news delivery. In every condition, study participants received the same news content, and after reading each story, they filled out a questionnaire indicating their liking for the story as a whole, as well as evaluating its quality, credibility, and representativeness (i.e., newsworthiness).

In general, statistically significant differences in content evaluation were found as a function of sourcing. They summarize the findings as follows:

> When other users or audience members are perceived to be the source of online news, the stories are liked more and perceived to be higher in quality than when news editors or receivers themselves are perceived as the source. Furthermore, when other users are perceived to be the source of online news, the stories are considered more representative of news than when the receivers themselves are perceived as the source. When the computer terminal is perceived as the source of online news, the news stories are rated by receivers as being higher in quality than when news editors or receivers themselves are perceived to be the news source.

(Sundar and Nass 2001: 65)

In keeping with the aforementioned cognitive tendency to treat interactivity as a peripheral cue, different attributed sources appear to trigger different cognitive heuristics (Chaiken 1987). Perhaps the computer-as-source manipulation cued the 'machine heuristic' implying that if a mere machine chose the story, then it must be truly random and free of any professional judgements about the story's newsworthiness. This could lower a receiver's expectations for the story, resulting in more positive evaluations for an otherwise ordinary piece of journalism. More generally, interactivity as a source feature persuades the user to factor in the source while evaluating the interaction and communication resulting from it.

That is why it is somewhat surprising to note the relatively poor ratings given to content attributed to oneself in the Sundar and Nass (2001) study, especially given the primacy of self as source (Sundar, in press) and the natural human tendency for egocentrism. If the highest form of interactivity is the ability to customize one's own communication, then why is the outcome not so positive? Perhaps customization comes with high expectations for content that are seldom realized with average news stories, especially of the kind used in the experiment being discussed. Or perhaps the self-as-source condition is so devoid of contextual cues that we prefer the seemingly democratic selection procedure of the others-as-source condition, or even the bandwagon heuristic that it cues ('if everyone thinks it's a good story, then it must be good').

Alternatively, the self could be considered too subjective a source for selection of news, but this level of customization may be better received in other, non-news domains of communication. Kalyanaraman and Sundar (2006) studied the psychological effects of customization in the context of Web portals as a whole instead of simply news stories. In an innovative design, individuals ($N = 60$) in a between-participants experiment were randomly assigned to one of three experimental conditions. Using the customization feature of the Yahoo! portal, three different versions of the MyYahoo website were created to reflect low, medium, and high levels of customization. These sites were created based on participants' responses to a pre-questionnaire. Participants browsed through the site, and then indicated their perceptions of the portal on a questionnaire.

The results of this study indicated a significantly positive linear relationship between customization level and positive attitudes toward the portal. Perhaps more important for the current discussion, perceived interactivity of the site was found to be a significant mediator of the relationship between customization and attitude toward the portal. Clearly, interactivity was linked by study participants to the notion of customization – a major psychological verification of the idea behind considering interactivity as a source feature – with the attitudinal results overwhelmingly implying that perceptions of websites are generally positively influenced by the degree to which they build in interactivity. However, when reconciled with the Sundar and Nass (2001) experiment, these findings suggest that while user attitudes may be positive toward the site's ability to customize, they may not necessarily translate

over to user perceptions of content that is communicated. It appears as though users express a preference for customization without adequately thinking through its consequences on content selection. At least for content domains such as news, their evaluations appear to be based on the bandwagon heuristic and other contextual cues that represent external consensus, rather than personal taste, in gatekeeping. Content perceptions appear to be most positive under conditions of moderate interactivity (as represented by the other-users condition in the Sundar and Nass 2001 experiment), rather than high interactivity (self-as-source condition), even though the latter is preferred, particularly as a global characteristic of a website.

Interactivity as a message feature

Not only does interactivity allow us the ability to choose our sources of information (including the privilege of ourselves serving as gatekeepers of information), it also operates at the level of messages, most notably in the form of hyperlinks and buttons embedded in most website content. These hyperlinks are an invitation for the user to interact with the content or message. By clicking on them, the user is making decisions about which parts of the document to read and which to ignore. Furthermore, as the user navigates their way through various layers of a website, it is likely to be a unique path, characterized by a series of interlinked messages that reflect the user's idiosyncratic choices while perusing the message. When the user engages the message in this manner, they are interacting with the message.

This kind of message-based interactivity is best captured by the contingency principle – the idea that a given message is contingent upon reception of the previous message and the ones preceding that. In fact, Rafaeli (1988) defined interactivity as 'an expression of the extent that in a given series of communication exchanges, any third (or later) transmission (or message) is related to the degree to which previous exchanges referred to even earlier transmissions' (1988: 111). He identifies three ordinal levels: non-interactive, reactive, and responsive (or fully interactive) based on the degree to which later messages cohere with those preceding them. For example, in a chat room, if two people post messages without acknowledging each other's messages, then it is non-interactive; if one interactant posts a message that is a direct response to another's posting, then it is considered reactive. If the latter interactant then responds to this posting in a manner that takes into account not only the latest posting but also those before them, then it is considered responsive. For a message exchange to be fully interactive, the messages should have a flow or coherence, i.e., they can be threaded together in sequence. This kind of message-based interactivity is somewhat easier to conceptualize in the context of computer-mediated interpersonal communication where multiple human interactants exchange messages, either in real time or asynchronously.

In Web-based mass communication, however, messages are already embedded in site content, and, as a result, contingency-based interactivity can only be realized in the manner in which messages are transmitted to the user. Therefore, the emphasis here is on information organization. The extent to which a website is designed to promote contingent interaction would be a reflection of its interactive potential. Following this logic, Sundar et al. (2003) created three different versions of a political candidate's website that were identical in their content, but differed in the degree to which they afforded contingent interaction. In the low-interactivity version, all of the site's content appeared on one scrollable page, neatly organized under headings and subheadings, appearing one after the other. The medium-interactive site offered an extra layer of information such that users would have to click on hyperlinked headings to access more information about a particular platform issue. In the high-interactive condition, the information was further fragmented such that once the user entered a particular page by clicking on a heading, they were faced with a further set of clickable options by way of subheadings, and so on. One could argue that interactivity may be confounded with other factors, most notably navigability. We could also make the case that the medium and high versions are simply better organized (not necessarily more interactive) versions of the low-interactive site. These are

conceptual issues, but Sundar et al. demonstrated the construct validity of this operationalization by showing that study participants' ratings of perceived interactivity differed significantly across all three conditions in the intended direction.

However, the effect of these sites upon users' perception of the political candidate featured on the site was not so clearly linear. Study participants liked the candidate more – and indicated greater agreement with his policy positions – when the site had medium interactivity rather than low or high levels of interactivity. In general, an inverted V pattern was noticed on all impression-formation measures. The moderately interactive site led to the most positive perceptions, while the perceptual effects of low and high interactivity conditions were statistically indistinguishable. It appears that greater interactivity engenders greater navigational – and hence, cognitive – load on users (Sundar 2000). It must be noted that no differences were found on the perceived informativeness – and also actual memory – of content, implying that participants in the high-interactivity condition did process the content instead of simply ignoring it, but they were not too thrilled about working so hard to unearth the information in the site.

There were also no differences as a function of the participants' prior level of interest in politics. This was somewhat surprising because, in a previous study that also used a political website, clear differences were found between politically apathetic and politically involved participants (Sundar et al. 1998). The former, in general, tended to rate the candidate as a positive monotonic function of site interactivity whereas the involved voters showed the inverted V pattern found in this experiment.

The central difference between the two studies lies in the conceptualization of interactivity. The Sundar et al. (1998) study operationalized interactivity by way of bells and whistles on the interface, i.e., functional features such as email links, feedback forms, chat rooms, and audio and video downloads. The sheer presence of these features appears to promote a positive perception of the site, especially among the uninitiated, as would be expected with any peripheral cue.

The fact that we found no differences between apathetic and involved voters when interactivity was based on the contingency principle implies that this kind of interactivity triggers central, rather than peripheral, processing of interactivity as a stimulus attribute. This kind of information organization appears to force even the apathetic users to engage with the message because greater interactivity is associated with greater clicking activity and more exploration of message content and less emphasis on simple heuristic processing. The profound implication here is that interactivity has the real potential to involve even the uninvolved, especially in important public domains such as politics.

Several testable generalizations emerge from these studies. For example:

1. The greater the contingent interactivity, the more positive the perceptions of the site as a whole (positive influence on perception of interactivity), even though this may not translate over directly to perceptions of the content (inverted V pattern with impression-formation measures).

2. If anything, greater interactivity breeds more involvement, focusing more user attention on content, thus setting the stage for a more considered rating of content perception (this is perhaps where content effects take over from medium effects). This not only implies that user scrutiny of content would be higher under conditions of high interactivity, but also that interactivity is processed centrally, quite unlike other formal features of Web media, such as animation.

3. Greater contingency in a website is likely to trigger greater navigational activity thus promoting the perception of higher levels of knowledge acquisition from the site. ('If I worked so hard at navigating through the site, then I must have learned more.')

We sought to examine these propositions in the context of interactive advertisements, which provide a more focused domain compared to whole websites. Advertisements also afford us the opportunity to assess user attitudes toward the interactive feature, something that could not be assessed in site-based studies given that we do not have established scales of attitudes toward websites in the literature. So, if we were to discover that higher the interactivity in the ad, the more positive the attitudes toward the ad (Aad), we can say that the interactivity effects found

with political websites are not a direct reflection of users' attitude toward the site, but rather their considered opinion of the content found while reading through the site. That is, higher contingent interactivity would promote positive perception of the interactive feature itself without necessarily leading to positive content perceptions. It would however breed greater engagement with the content (given the navigational load) and lead to greater perception of acquired knowledge. Furthermore, this kind of central processing will stand in stark contrast to the nature of processing triggered by peripheral cues such as animation and ad shape.

Participants ($N = 48$) in a 3 (low, medium and high interactivity) $\times$ 2 (animated, static) $\times$ 2 (banner, square) fully crossed-factorial within-subjects experiment were exposed to 12 news-article Web pages, with one ad in each of them. Ads were obtained from various sources on the Web and extensively pretested to meet the requirements of a given cell in the factorial design. In order to minimize incidental confounds, we employed stimulus sampling such that we eventually had 3 ads for each of the 12 conditions. Interactivity in the ads was evaluated based on the contingency principle (Rafaeli 1988) discussed earlier, and operationalized in terms of the number of hierarchically hyperlinked layers or levels (Sundar *et al.* 2003) using Interactive Messaging Units (IMUs). While low-interactivity ads did not have any hyperlinks and therefore just one layer, medium ones had two layers that could be explored by clicking on hyperlinks, and high-interactivity ones featured three or more layers (see Figure 7.1 for an example of multiple layers in a high-interactive ad). In any given layer, there may be multiple parallel (not hierarchical) hyperlinks accessible via tabs. In some cases, the final layer consisted of a link to the advertiser's own site which would pop up over the stimulus page. Half the ads had animation in them while the other half did not. Half the ads were banner ads placed near the top of the page while the other half were square ads placed in the middle of the web page (see Sundar and Kim 2005 for more technical details of the experiment).

The experiment was administered to participants individually on a laptop in a laboratory setting. Participants were told that the study

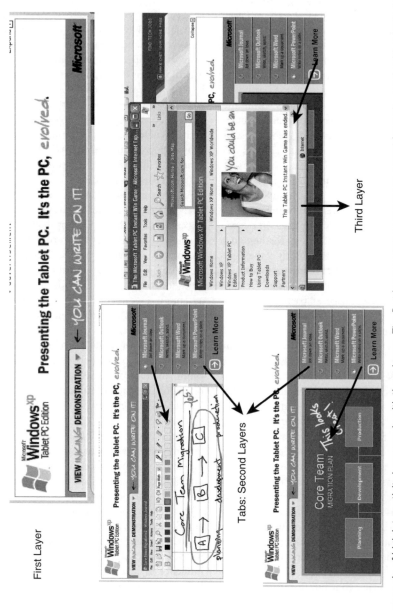

Figure 7.1 An example of high-interactivity banner ads with three layers. The first layer on top opens out to reveal four tabs, each with a radio button. Clicking on one of them refreshes the content on the left-hand side of the ad. The next layer is a web page that appears as a pop-up on top of this layer when the user clicks on the 'Learn More' link.

in which they were about to participate concerned browsing 12 different web pages including 12 main advertisements, and that they would be given a maximum of 90 seconds to browse through each page, following which they would fill out a questionnaire before going onto the next web page. They were told to view each web page as they would normally view a page on the internet, but that we were more interested in their reactions to the main advertisement in each page. Written instructions requested them to 'quickly take in the whole page at the beginning (without clicking on any of the links within the article text) and then proceed to explore the main advertisement on the page and spend most of your 90 seconds finding out as much as you can about the product or service that is advertised.' Participants were asked to feel free to click on the ads themselves and/or the links, if any, featured within those ads. In the event that a link in the ad transported them to a new web page on a separate window, they were told not go further. That is, they were asked to just look quickly at the page, then close the new window and return to the web page with the article and the ad. Before viewing the first experimental page, all participants practiced the procedure with a test page.

Analyses with the manipulation check items for interactivity and animation showed that the manipulations were very successful, with the conditions clearly differentiated by conservative post-hoc tests. Moreover, on a three-item index of perceived interactivity derived from Liu and Shrum (2002), participants distinguished clearly between the three levels of interactivity, and, interestingly, perceived animated ads as more interactive than static ones. In addition, participants' Aad was shown in the analysis to be positively linearly related to level of ad interactivity. This supports the first of the three propositions regarding the contingent model of interactivity – that indeed interactivity promotes positive perceptions of the interactive feature (the whole ad in this case).

Given this, we may conclude that the inverted V pattern found with impression-formation measures was a result of greater message scrutiny caused by high interactivity rather than a negative evaluation of the interactive design itself, especially considering the fact that interactivity was linearly related to perceived interactivity, which is generally considered a positive trait. Therefore, the new insight emerging from this analysis appears to be that interactivity does not, by itself, generate negative evaluations but simply focuses greater user attention upon content (and depending on the quality of content, the evaluations could be positive or negative). As Sundar and Constantin (2004) found, high levels of interactivity command conscious processing, thus bringing the user in closer contact with content. The flipside of this argument is that under low levels of interactivity, message scrutiny is lower, so evaluations of poorly argued content are likely to be less negative compared to high interactive situations. This leads us to the second proposition about interactivity's role in encouraging user involvement with content – the product advertised, in this case.

Analyses revealed that interactivity was positively related to product involvement, thus lending credence to the hypothesis that interactivity encourages involvement with content. On Aad, a significant interaction between interactivity and animation revealed that animation helps promote attitudes toward low- and medium-interactive ads, but it does not affect attitudes toward high-interactive ads. This is telling in that a peripheral cue such as animation ceases to have a positive impression under conditions of high interactivity (and, by extension, high involvement). By implication, we may conclude that interactivity, when conceptualized in terms of contingency, behaves less like a peripheral cue and more like a message argument.

Finally, in confirmation of our third proposition, respondents showed a statistically significant difference, in the expected direction, in their ratings of perceived product knowledge as a function of the three levels of interactivity. An analysis of covariance was performed as a follow-up, by entering perceived product involvement as a covariate. The F value for interactivity shrunk from 75.09 to 12.37, thus suggesting a mediating influence of involvement. That is, interactivity influences involvement, which in turn impacts perceived product knowledge, again, quite unlike peripheral cues which tend to be cosmetically, rather than informationally, significant.

A significant Ad Shape X Animation X interactivity three-way interaction effect was observed for perceived product knowledge. Participants did not show any major differences in perceived product knowledge as a function of animation in the low and medium interactivity condition. In the high-interactive condition, however, static ads were associated with higher levels of perceived product knowledge for banner ads than for square ads while animated ads did not lead to differential perception of product knowledge for banner versus square ads. That is, the difference between static and animated ads was pronounced only in high-interactive banners. This suggests that under conditions of high interactivity (which is characterized by high involvement), users tend to view peripheral cues like animation as distractions rather than as desirable ad features. Indeed, closer scrutiny of content, coupled with invulnerability to peripheral cues, could well be the reason for the so-called interactivity paradox.

Conclusion

In conclusion, whether conceptualized as a modality feature (perceptual bandwidth), source feature (customization) or message feature (contingency), the primary role of interactivity appears to be to generate greater involvement or engagement with content. When the object of user evaluation is the website itself or the interactive ad per se, then the message argument is the interactive design of the site or the ad, the manner in which it is constructed to effectively create a responsive system or flow between information points in the site or the ad. In this respect, interactivity is not only more involving, but also more persuasive. That is why user attitudes were found to be a direct positive function in the customization study (Kalyanaraman and Sundar 2006) and the IMU study (Sundar and Kim 2005). When the object of user evaluation is the message content in the site or the ad, then the role of interactivity appears to be more structural. Interactivity assures greater involvement with content, but the effects ensuing from such communication are dependent on the construction of the message content itself and not simply on the cleverness of the interactive design. This explains why Sundar and Nass (2001) did not find the most positive ratings for their most customized (self as source) condition. The mediocrity of the 'average' news stories used in that experiment became more apparent under

careful scrutiny by study participants. It also explains why the highest-interactivity condition in the Sundar et al. (2003) experiment with political websites failed to show the most positive impression-formation effects, and why modality enhancements in Sundar (2000) and Sundar et al. (1998) exposed the navigational burden imposed by increased interactivity and hence failed to positively persuade the actively engaged users.

Ultimately, the effect of interactivity does not lie so much in its function as a peripheral cue in the message context, but as a technological feature that boosts social–psychological effects of content by creating greater user engagement with it. Interactivity can manifest itself by extending the range and functionality of all three basic elements of mediated communication – source, modality, message – and, through theoretical mechanisms involving concepts such as perceptual bandwidth, customization and contingency, it can determine the manner in which content is psychologically processed by users. Each particular instantiation of modality-based, source-based, and message-based interactivity (e.g., text + audio, other users as source, nature of hyperlink) is rich with cues that lend themselves to heuristic processing of content attributes, especially when systematic processing is inhibited. In addition, the content itself is rife with cues (e.g., Sundar et al. in press) that suggest shortcuts in favor of more effortful processing of message details. When particular manifestations of interactivity such as blogging or use of drags on a Web-based map result in high levels of user engagement with content, peripheral cues become less important in decision-making and serve more as distractive influences (e.g., Sundar and Kim 2005). Ultimately, theorizing about interactivity's effects on user cognitions, attitudes and behaviour will need to involve other technological variables such as navigability (Sundar 2004b), but a simple model would begin by specifying key mechanisms through which interactivity generates user involvement with content, given the understanding that content characteristics as well as contextual cues (both technology-related and content-based) predict the nature and level of heuristic processing (see Figure 7.2). The ensuing style and depth of cognitive processing will in turn dictate how users receive, respond, and react to mediated content on the Web.

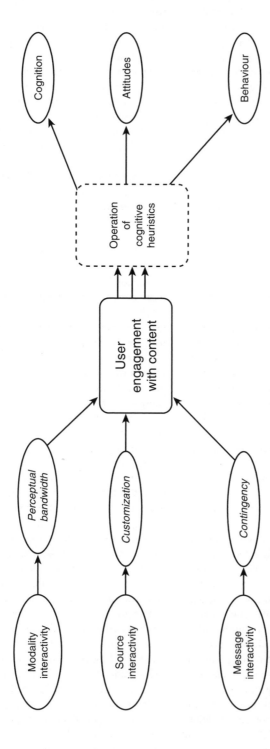

Figure 7.2 A model of interactivity effects. Modality, source, and message-based interactivity influence user engagement through the mediation of perceptual bandwidth use, customization level and contingency in message exchange, respectively. They also carry peripheral cues that, along with cues embedded in content, determine the nature and level of message processing, which in turn affects user cognitions, attitudes and behaviour.

References

Ahern, R. K., and Stromer-Galley, J. (2000, June). The interaction effect: An experimental study of high and low interactivity political Websites. Paper presented at the 50th annual conference of the International Communication Association, Acapulco, Mexico.

Bucy, E. P. (2003). The interactivity paradox: closer to the news but confused. In E. P. Bucy and J. E. Newhagen (eds), *Media access: Social and psychological dimensions of new technology use* (pp. 47-72). Mahwah, NJ: Erlbaum.

Chaiken, S. (1987). The heuristic model of persuasion. In M. P. Zanna, J. M. Olson, and C. P. Herman (eds), *Social influence: The Ontario symposium, vol. 5* (pp. 3–39). Hillsdale, NJ: Erlbaum.

Hass, R. G. (1988). Effects of source characteristics on cognitive responses and persuasion. In R. E. Petty, T. M. Ostrom, and T. C. Brock (eds), *Cognitive responses in persuasion* (pp. 141–175). Hillsdale, NJ: Lawrence Erlbaum Associates.

Heeter, C. (1989). Implications of new interactive technologies for conceptualizing communication. In J. Salvaggio and J. Bryant (eds), *Media in the information age: Emerging patterns of adoption and consumer use* (pp. 217–235). Hillsdale, NJ: Lawrence Erlbaum Associates.

Hoogeveen, M. (1997). Toward a theory of the effectiveness of multimedia systems. *International Journal of Human–Computer Interaction 9* (2), 151–168.

Kalyanaraman, S., and Sundar, S. S. (2006). The psychological appeal of personalized online content in web portals: Does customization affect attitudes and behaviors? *Journal of Communication, 56*, 110–132.

Lievrouw, L. A., Bucy, E., Finn, T. A., Frindte, W., Gershon, R., Haythornthwaite, C., Köhler, T., Metz, J. M., and Sundar, S. S. (2000). Building the subdisciplines: an overview of communication and technology research. *Communication Yearbook 24*, 271–295.

Liu, Y., and Shrum, L. J. (2002). What is interactivity and is it always such a good thing? Implications of definition, person, and situation for the influence of interactivity on advertising effectiveness. *Journal of Advertising 31*(4), 53–64.

Marmolin, H. (1991). Multimedia from the perspectives of psychology. In L. Kjelldahl (ed.), *Multimedia: Systems, interactions and applications. First Eurographics workshop, Stockholm, Sweden April 18-19 1991*. Berlin, Germany: Springer-Verlag.

Massey, B. L., and Levy, M. R. (1999). Interactivity, online journalism, and English-language Web newspapers in Asia. *Journalism and Mass Communication Quarterly 76*(1), 138–151.

McLuhan, M. (1964). *Understanding media*. New York: Signet.

Nass, C. and Steuer, J. (1993). Voices, boxes, and sources of messages: computers and social actors. *Human Communication Research 19*, 504–527.

Nass, C., and Moon, Y. (2000). Machines and mindlessness: social responses to computers. *Journal of Social Issues 56*(1), 81–103.

Oviatt, S. (2003). Multimodal interfaces. In J. A. Jaco and A. Sears (eds), The human–computer interaction handbook (pp. 228–304). Mahwah, NJ: Lawrence Erlbaum Associates.

Oviatt, S., MacEachern, M., and Levow, G.-A. (1998). Predicting hyperarticulate speech during human–computer error resolution. *Speech Communication 24*(2), 87–110.

Petty, R. E., and Cacioppo, J. T. (1986). *Communication and persuasion: Central and peripheral routes to attitude change*. New York: Springer-Verlag.

Rafaeli, S. (1988). Interactivity: From new media to communication. In R. Hawkins, J. Weimann and S. Pingree (eds), *Advancing communication science: Merging mass and interpersonal processes* (pp 124–181). Newbury Park, CA: Sage.

Reeves, B. and Nass, C. (1996). *The media equation: How people treat computers, television, and new media like real people and places*. New York: Cambridge University Press/CSLI. (Chapter 22 reprinted in *Culture and electronic media* [1998], Houghton-Mifflin).

Reeves, B., and Nass, C. (2000). Perceptual bandwidth. *Communications of the ACM 43*(3), 65–70.

Steuer, J. (1992). Defining virtual reality: dimensions determining telepresence. *Journal of Communication, 42*, 73–93.

Sundar, S. S. (2000). Multimedia effects on processing and perception of online news: a study of picture, audio, and video downloads. *Journalism and Mass Communication Quarterly 77*(3), 480–499.

Sundar, S. S. (2004a). Loyalty to computer terminals: is it anthropomorphism or consistency? *Behaviour and Information Technology 23*(2), 107–118.

Sundar, S. S. (2004b). Theorizing interactivity's effects. *The Information Society 20*(5), 387–391.

Sundar, S. S. (in press). Self as source: Agency in interactive media. In E. Konijn, M. Tanis, S. Utz and A. Linden (eds), *Mediated interpersonal communication*. Mahwah, NJ: Lawrence Erlbaum Associates.

Sundar, S. S., and Constantin, C. (2004, May). Does interacting with media enhance news memory? Automatic vs. controlled processing of interactive news features. Paper presented at the 54th annual conference of the International Communication Association, New Orleans, LA.

Sundar, S. S., and Kim, J. (2005). Interactivity and persuasion: influencing attitudes with information and involvement. *Journal of Interactive Advertising 5*(2). Available at http://www.jiad.org/vol5/no2/sundar/.

Sundar, S. S., and Nass, C. (2000). Source orientation in human-computer interaction: programmer, networker, or independent social actor? *Communication Research 27*(6), 683–703.

Sundar, S. S., and Nass, C. (2001). Conceptualizing sources in online news. *Journal of Communication 51*(1), 52–72.

Sundar, S. S., and Wagner, C. B. (2002). The world wide wait: exploring physiological and behavioral effects of download speed. *Media Psychology 4*, 173–206.

Sundar, S. S., Hesser, K., Kalyanaraman, S., and Brown, J. (1998, July). The effect of Website interactivity on political persuasion. Paper presented at the 21st General Assembly and Scientific Conference of the International Association for Media and Communication Research, Glasgow, UK.

Sundar, S. S., Kalyanaraman, S., and Brown, J. (2003). Explicating website interactivity: impression-formation effects in political campaign sites. *Communication Research 30*, 30–59.

Sundar, S. S., Kalyanaraman, S., and Jones, E. (2000). Modality effects on memory for multimedia messages. Paper presented at the 22nd General Assembly and Scientific Conference of the International Association for Media and Communication Research, Singapore.

Sundar, S. S., Knobloch-Westerwick, S., and Hastall, M. R. (in press). News cues: information scent and cognitive heuristics. *Journal of the American Society of Information Science and Technology*.

Wilson, E. J., and Sherrell, D. L. (1993). Source effects in communication and persuasion research: a meta-analysis of effect size. *Journal of the Academy of Marketing Science 21*(2), 101–11.

PART 2
Groups and Communities

CHAPTER 8

Characterizing online groups

David P. Brandon and Andrea B. Hollingshead

Our collective notions of what constitutes a group have changed radically in the past 15 years. Traditional boardroom notions of groups interacting face-to-face and having size and membership constraints have yielded to perspectives that account for the varieties of groups made possible by new technologies. The now omnipresent miscellany of information and communication technologies (from hand-held devices to laptops to videoconference rooms) provide a variety of channels (audio, video, text and graphics) that allow groups to move away from the conventional 'same time, same place' model of face-to-face groups to being 'all the time, everywhere', if so desired. The lack of time, space and other accessibility constraints opens membership to geographically and culturally distributed participants. Internet-based newsgroups, such as the thousands of support groups in existence, for example, can have literally hundreds of participants interacting asynchronously (Alexander *et al.* 2003).

The growth of online groups has been explosive, in both social and work life. In 2001, 90 million Americans used the Internet to make contact with some type of online group (e.g., trade/professional groups, hobby/interest groups, community groups, support groups) and on average, each user made contact with four different online groups (Horrigan *et al.* 2001). In 2002, taking part in an online group was a daily activity for approximately 4.1 million Americans (Pew Internet Project 2004).

The presence of networked, group-based technologies at worksites is now commonplace. Nearly half of the managers surveyed reported working in a virtual team (Training Journal Staff 2003). Statistics on computer network utilization indicate that in the year 2000 75 per cent of manufacturing organizations provided access to the Internet and 40 per cent used an intranet (US Bureau of the Census 2002). These technologies and various organizational needs promote the formation of different kinds of distributed organizational groups (Harrison *et al.* 2004).

The growth in online groups is not just in sheer number, but also in variety. For example in local area network (LAN) parties, a group of friends may meet at a central location and connect their computers to form a network and play an online game; thus, members are co-present but interact virtually (Warner 2000). In flash mobs, members – who may otherwise be strangers – interact online until signalled to appear in person at a given location for some often ephemeral purpose, such as a rally for a political candidate (Dell 2004; McFedries 2003). And with 1.07 billion expected worldwide

Internet users in 2005, an estimated growth rate of 125 per cent from 2000–2004 alone, it is likely that the number, form and nature of online groups will continue to grow (ClickZ Stats 2004; Computer Industry Almanac 2004; Internet World Stats 2004).

In short, the proliferation of information and communication technologies has fostered dramatic growth in both the number and variety of online groups over the past 15 years. Such growth necessitates a more sophisticated language for describing and capturing the diversity of online groups that moves away from traditional conceptualizations of online groups. Thus, the goal of this chapter is to place within a theoretical framework a set of dimensions useful in describing, categorizing and comparing online groups. Toward that goal, we begin this chapter with a definition and a review of previous conceptualizations of online groups. We do not offer a new typology or taxonomy, since those forms tend to imply a static set of categories (cf. Bailey 1994). Instead, our description of online groups borrows from and expands on the locales framework (Fitzpatrick 2003).

Definition of online groups

As a starting point, we define a group as an entity comprised of people having interdependent goals, who are acquainted, interact with one another and have a sense of belonging associated with their membership (Hollingshead and Contractor 2002). The term 'online groups' refers to groups using information and communication technologies commonplace on the Internet, as well as other computer-mediated communication tools such as knowledge management systems used on local networks (e.g. Lotus Notes©). Generally, it is assumed that the technology used by online groups is primarily the Internet-based tools (e.g. email, chat tools, websites and newsgroups), with no to occasional use of other tools. Further, the term 'online' does not here imply constant connectivity from a particular location, but encompasses wireless connectivity from any location. Moreover, as will be discussed below, not all action by the group has to be online.

A number of useful dimensions and typologies descriptive of online groups are already available to researchers, ranging from a basic

distinction between social groups (Rheingold 1993), distributed workgroups (Lipnack and Stamps 1997; Townsend *et al.* 1998) and organizations to more specific categories defining the relations formed by group members interacting online (Norris 2002; Sassenberg 2002). In this chapter, we seek to review, integrate and expand on previous formulations by extending the locales framework as an overall theoretical architecture for describing online groups (Fitzpatrick 2003). We extend the locales framework by including three additional categories to describe and compare online groups: (1) the types of technology used to support such groups (2) the ways that technology can support group tasks and (3) the public and private uses of technology by online groups.

Perspectives on technology and online groups

Early research on technology and small groups was interested in how technology allowed groups to overcome the time and place constraints inherent in face-to-face groups (McGrath and Hollingshead 1994). The study of online groups is now a field itself, as this handbook indicates, encompassing a variety of disciplines, theoretical perspectives and methodologies (Dahlberg 2004). Characterizing the nature of a group in relation to the technologies it uses is an ongoing issue. Is it the case that technology inevitably defines the nature of an online group? Or is it the case that social interaction defines technology? And when is it appropriate to describe a group as 'virtual'?

Several broad perspectives describing how groups and individuals shape and are in turn shaped by technology can be discerned (e.g. Dahlberg 2004) One perspective is technological determinism – how the form of the technology influences its users (cf. Lea 1991). A second is social determinism – or how a particular social/ cultural system reshapes the technology to its own purposes (cf. Lea 1991). A third perspective is a 'uses and gratifications' approach to how individuals and groups interact with Internet technologies (Blumler and Katz 1974; cf. Song *et al.* 2004). Influence between technology and group phenomena may in fact be reciprocal, crossing all three of these perspectives with groups selecting and modifying a technology for a particular use, but in turn the technology shapes to some degree the character of the interaction (cf. Kling *et al.* 1998). The relative impact of technological attributes versus social influences is a point of contention across theories that describe relations between groups and technology (see Hollingshead and Contractor 2002 for review).

Some theories combine aspects of two or more of these perspectives. Adaptive Structuration Theory suggests that a technology may present a set of rules and operations to a group, but that the group ultimately decides how it will use features of a technology and, thus, socially constructs their meaning (Poole and DeSanctis 1990). The Groups as Knowledge Networks approach considers groups as comprised of a network of agents that includes both human and non-human agents (e.g., knowledge repositories, web bots), each representing nodes engaged in information allocation and retrieval (Hollingshead and Contractor 2002). Information and communication technologies provide the infrastructure that allows the nodes in the knowledge network to develop relations. From the Groups as Knowledge Networks Approach, technology plays both moderating and mediating roles, depending on the type of technology. These theoretical approaches highlight the importance of considering how a group relates to its technology.

Virtuality

Concurrent with the debate on whether technology defines the group or vice versa has been the debate on just what makes a group 'virtual' – essentially raising the question of whether the online vs. offline distinction is a useful one to make. Traditionally, researchers viewed groups as either virtual or face-to-face. Face-to-face groups were physically co-present; virtual groups were geographically and/or temporally distributed. As more and more social and organizational groups have embraced technologies such as email, blackberries and mobile phones, it is difficult to find a group that meets solely face-to-face. As a result, some contemporary researchers argue that virtuality is a matter of degree; some groups are more 'virtual' than others. Others suggest that comparing face-to-face groups to online groups leads researchers to ignore the unique qualities of online groups (Wilson and Peterson 2002).

Previous efforts to define virtuality highlight the important attributes of online groups and delineate some of the critical issues that an organizing theoretical framework must address. One framework proposes multiple dimensions for differentiating conventional teams from virtual teams (Bell and Kozlowski 2002). Spatial configuration and communication media differentiate conventional teams (proximal, face-to-face communication) from virtual teams (distributed, technology-mediated communication). The framework further distinguishes degrees of virtuality based on member roles (multiple vs. singular), lifecycle (discrete vs. continuous), boundaries (multiple vs. singular) and temporal distribution (distributed vs. real time). A second framework describes teams as more or less virtual based on three dimensions, level of technology support (low to high), percentage of time apart on task and physical distance (close to far) (Griffith *et al.* 2003). From these dimensions, three types of teams emerge: traditional (i.e. face-to-face), virtual (all time on task spent apart) and hybrid, which mixes traits of the two other types of teams. What these efforts suggest is that virtual groups are a product of a context in which communication and information technologies are most likely to be useful – that is, when group members are separated by time and/or space while trying to accomplish some goal(s). These two typologies provide useful distinctions regarding virtual groups, but do not necessarily describe the impact of technology on groups.

Two recent conceptualizations of virtual teams offer input–process–output models that address how much technology influences virtual teams. One conceptualization views technology as an input variable, based on the influence of a technology's media richness on a group's amount of communication, team member relationships, commitment, trust, decision-making and performance (Martins *et al.* 2004). A second conceptualization considers computer-mediated communication as an input variable, as defined by a set of media characteristics (channel capacities, message sequence and time traits) (Driskell *et al.* 2003). Additionally, the communication channel represents a moderating variable influencing input on process and on the output of team performance. Across these descriptions of virtuality is a sense that communication and information technology influences the group's ability to accomplish its task, particularly when the group is reliant on technology to support interaction.

In the next section, we place the dimensions common across these definitions of virtuality into a central theoretical framework based on the locales framework (Fitzpatrick 2003). The locales framework focuses on the purpose of groups, yet flexibly accounts for both face-to-face and online group settings. It provides concepts and a language that enables researchers to think more broadly about the forms and nature of online groups.

The locales framework and online groups

The locales framework borrows from Strauss' (1993) Theory of Action as well as Activity Theory (Engeström 1991; Engeström *et al*. 1999) and was intended to bridge the gap between theory and the design of electronic tools for groups, such as groupware meant to support online groups (Fitzpatrick *et al*. 1995, 1996; Fitzpatrick 2000, 2003; Greenberg *et al*. 2000).

Taken from Strauss (1993) is the central notion of social worlds, described as groups or individuals with a common goal or commitment to collective action. The goal or commitment may be implicit or explicit, well or poorly defined and may evolve, become refined and is the subject of ongoing negotiation. A social world may be comprised of multiple subworlds with even their own subworlds and social worlds may or may not parallel typical social or organizational boundaries. For example, the social worlds concept can include an organization's goal(s) and within that organization are the subworlds of departments, branches or divisions, within which exist the subworlds of workgroups. This emphasis on a common goal as a defining characteristic is stated or implied in many descriptions of online groups: for example, Lipnack and Stamps (1997) include a 'common purpose' as a defining element of virtual teams and even definitions of large online groups include purpose as a key attribute (Porter 2004).

In addition to hosting a defining purpose, social worlds provide a context within which collective actions and interactions towards a goal,

or work practices, have meaning (Strauss 1993; Fitzpatrick 2000). Work practices are mediated by the site and means (that is, the resources, including technology) that are part of and facilitate interactions in the social world (Fitzpatrick *et al*. 1995). That is, the location of a group and its tools and resources mediate how the group will progress towards accomplishing its defining purpose. A construction crew that wants to build a house, for example, will not get far without tools and lumber and they will need somewhere to build. When the tools at hand are information and communication technologies and the site is online, they too will influence how the group interacts towards its goals.

The term 'locales' is used to refer to the site in which action in the social world occurs, the means of communication used by members of the social world and the means by which work practices are achieved (Greenberg *et al*. 2000). A locale may be physical (e.g., a conference room with its artefacts, the interacting persons, the face-to-face interaction they use) or virtual (e.g., persons interacting via a videoconference, massive multiplayer online role-playing game, email, etc.) as both provide the site and means to allow work practices within the context of the social world (Greenberg *et al*. 2000). Technology can thus provide part of the setting, or a subset of the conditions of a social world. In this sense, information and communication technology represents a middle ground in the discussion of technological or social determinism, as it is part of the socially defined context, yet can mediate the connection to the social world.

Social worlds can further be described in terms of a 'centre' and related 'peripheries', a conception meant as a counterpoint to descriptions of groups as having fixed boundaries (Fitzpatrick *et al*. 1996; Fitzpatrick 2000). The shared purpose of the social world defines, structures and relates the entities used to achieve the collective purpose, including people, objects, tools and resources. Locales facilitate and support the relationship among these entities, in that locales are the site and means – i.e., the people, places and things – used for work practices in support of the purpose(s) of the social world. That is, the social world centre attracts and gives meanings to locales and the people who use them, due to their connection to the purpose(s). Conference rooms or online chat tools, for example, do not have a lot of meaning on their own merits or features: their value comes from using them towards the purpose of the social world.

From this social world centre, work practice relationships can be described in terms of their proximity relationships to the centre: instead of being either in or out of a group, phenomena range along a continuum of central–peripheral, with this position dynamic over time depending on practice. Peripherality is characterized in particular by multidimensional concepts of degree of commitment (intense to wavering), limits of communication (face-to-face to distributed over time; as well as other communication barriers such as language differences) and levels of participation (active in core activities to passive, marginal activities) (Fitzpatrick 2000). That is, someone who does not care much about the group's purpose, rarely communicates with other group members and whose contributions have little influence on achieving the group goal, is more distant from the centre of the social world compared to active and involved members who have considerable influence on movement toward the group goal.

The locale, centre and periphery concepts are very useful for describing and comparing online groups. Arguments about the 'virtuality' of a group, focused on group member distance in time or space (cf. Martins et al. 2004), are directed to focus on how the group goes about accomplishing its work via physical or virtual locales. A conclusion about a locale should reflect both site and means and how much that combination facilitates the work of the social world. After all, the geographically distributed members of even the most virtual of virtual teams have to sit in a physical location somewhere, yet they are not defined by their office space, i.e. their physical site. For example, consider co-workers within three feet of each other interacting with the rest of their group primarily via a chat tool. For that period, their locale is virtual. Should this continue to be the locale of their work practices, it would be reasonable to view them as an online group. Their site is virtual and their means of doing work are virtual, hence they are an online group.

Or, consider LAN parties and flash mobs. These groups as described have both physical and virtual locales, but most of the work that goes into organizing them likely took place in online locales. Hence despite their notable physical co-presence during an actual LAN party or flashmob, they fall under the umbrella of online groups. Essentially, the locales framework can incorporate much of the criteria used to define virtuality (Bell and Kozlowski 2002; Griffith et al. 2003) to define whether locales used are physical or virtual. The emphasis is on the extent to which technology is used to achieve the group's purpose, with less concern about distance in time and space, to allow for technologies used by groups in the same location (see discussion below). What this perspective encourages is a rich portrait of group action by acknowledging the likelihood of both physical and virtual locales for group action (though one or the other locale will likely come to typify the group, i.e. as primarily physical or virtual).

The notions of centre and periphery and the associated dimensions that describe place on the periphery allow for easier characterization of the relations members can have to online groups. Instead of viewing group members as in or out of the group, members are described in terms of their participation, commitment and communication limits – or more specifically, limits of their effective communication (Fitzpatrick 2000) – with regards to the centre of the social world. This language allows description of a group member's contribution to the purpose of the social world that does not focus on location. For example, some group members may be co-located, but only make minor contributions to the group's social world, versus remote members who participate regularly, are devoted to the group's work and can effectively communicate with group members.

Group members use technology to stay in touch with or otherwise feel close to their group, or in locales framework terminology maintain their closeness to the centre of the social world. Groups use a range of technologies to support their activities and the resulting sense of group belonging (Powell et al. 2004; Sillence and Baber 2004). Survey results suggest that many people use the Internet to increase their participation in groups in which they are members (40 per cent), sometimes contacting their group several times a week (43 per cent) for informational purposes (76 per cent), getting involved in or learning about group activities (71 per cent), discussing issues with others (68 per cent), or maintaining relationships (49 per cent) (Horrigan et al. 2001). There is also evidence that a sense of physical proximity to others who are in fact remote can develop via electronic channels (McKenna and Green 2002). Developing social capital in traditionally face-to-face groups, such as political action or religious groups, can be supported by developing an online tool for coordination or outreach (Wellman *et al.* 2001, 2002).

The dimensions of peripherality encompass qualities used in prior definitions of online groups. Degree of commitment, for example, can potentially host concepts such as sense of belonging to a group (cf. Fisher *et al.* 2002; Hollingshead and Contractor 2002; Blanchard and Markus 2004; Song *et al.* 2004) and interdependence (Covert and Thompson 2001; Bell and Kozlowski 2002). Communication channel affordances and limitations are relevant to the effective communication dimension of the locales framework, as they are attributes that can inhibit effective communication, the most critical bounding factor for a social world (Fitzpatrick 2000; Hollingshead and Contractor 2002). With regards to the degree of participation dimension, research on the participation equalization effect associated with computer-mediated communication is relevant, as is other research speaking to factors influencing how willing group members are to interact online (Bonito and Hollingshead 1997).

Membership in the locales framework borrows again from Strauss, who views membership in a social world as dynamic with regards to what defines membership (Fitzpatrick 2000). Numerous dimensions are usable to describe groups, including size, longevity, stability, formal membership processes and so on (Fitzpatrick 2003). In general, dimensions of formal and/or persistent to informal and/or transient are useful for describing membership (Fitzpatrick 2000). While not pursued in depth here, the notion of formal versus informal groups is apparent in much of the research on online groups, as in the distinction between formal groups as represented by virtual teams and organizations (Lipnack and Stamps 1997; Townsend *et al.* 1998; DeSanctis and Monge 1999), versus more informal social online groups and communities (Rheingold 1993; Alexander *et al.* 2003; Blanchard 2004; Porter 2004). The persistent versus transient aspect captures an oft-noted aspect of some virtual project teams, their short lifecycle (Bell and Kozlowski 2002), while also allowing for longer-term groups. Many online groups have strong core memberships, as well as many visits from people temporarily dropping by to ask a question or make a comment (cf. Ahuja and Galvin 2003; Papadakis 2003). The drop-ins might be included as members in some definitions of groups but are better thought of peripheral to the social world's purpose.

Table 8.1 depicts how the locales framework corresponds to the online groups literature – the locales framework reasonably accommodates

Table 8.1 Correspondence of locales framework to extant online groups literature

Locales framework	Online groups literature
Physical/virtual locales – site and means used define physical or virtual locales	Degree of virtuality – based on separation in time space during task
Central/peripheral – to shared goals of social world, based on participation, commitment and communication	Shared goals – with sense that remote members or completely online groups will face more barriers than face-to-face groups
Degree of communication (overall effectiveness)	Media richness, media selection theories, synchronous/asynchronous
Degree of participation (in central vs. marginal activities)	Remote members face more barriers to participation; participation equalization
Degree of commitment (intense to wavering)	Interdependence towards group goals, sense of belonging to a group
Membership – formal and informal groups; persistent vs. transient memberships	Social groups (recreational, family, etc.) and organizational groups (virtual teams); core groups versus short life cycle teams or members

the assertions made by the online groups literature within its architecture. In sum, the locales framework and associated concepts provide a useful language for describing online groups that emphasizes purpose as the defining aspect of an online group or social world; moves away from rigid boundaries discussions; and accommodates and organizes components of prior definitions. Below, we add concepts not detailed in the theory, but essential for describing online groups.

Extending the locales framework

Supporting technologies, technology and the group task and privacy/accessibility

In this section, we propose and describe three additional categorizations that relate to and expand the locales framework, yet provide relatively simple terms for describing particular aspects of online groups. The first grouping classifies the technology used by online groups, which provides the locales framework a more specific means of describing the 'site and means' of a locale. The second grouping classifies technology penetration into task, which again contributes to defining the virtuality of a locale. A final grouping describes online groups in terms of privacy and accessibility based on a locales framework notion of access to resources based on group membership.

Technologies to support group functions

The locales framework lacks terminology for describing the technologies that online groups might utilize, which presents a problem for describing locales as physical or virtual and generally characterizing a group's relation to technology. McGrath and Hollingshead (1993, 1994; Hollingshead 2001) classify technologies based on the functional role that a given technology plays in that group via four categories:

1. Technologies that provide or modify within-group communication (termed Group Communication Support Systems or GCSS);

2. Databases that supplement or provide information to group members (i.e., Group Information Support Systems or GISS);

3. Technologies that provide or modify external communication with those outside the group (labeled Group eXternal Support Systems of GXSS); and

4. Technologies that structure group task performance processes and task products (i.e. Group Performance Support Systems or GPSS).

Group Communication Support Systems (GCSS) come in a variety of modalities (i.e., visual, audio, text/graphics, Internet) and time frames, i.e., either synchronous (e.g., video and phone conferences) or asynchronous (e.g., email, fax) and range in the size, nature and ambiguity of interactive partners they allow (e.g. from large newsgroups of relative strangers to a small videoconference). In terms of popularity, a study of virtual communities found that forum/discussion boards were most popular, followed by message/bulletin boards, chat rooms, newsletters and email (Lee *et al.* 2003). Interactive video and audio had only rare use and seemed less practical as group size increased. Of course, many websites now incorporate many forms of GCSS, for example a MySpace© page may incorporate sound, video, links to instant messaging, a forum and bulletin board and so on.

Group Information Support Systems (GISS) include archived information found in quantitative databases, as well as information management programs useful for organizing schedules, files, contacts and other information, such as a calendar program connected to relevant group email lists. A Group External Support System (GXSS) is a special case of GCSS and GISS. While the modalities described under GCSS can have uses for communicating with external groups, such interaction might be combined with non-human GISS tools such as web bots to further facilitate contact with the external group. For example, groups may develop media such as extranets, tailored web pages for providing information to external customers.

Examples of technologies in the final category, Group Production Support Systems (GPSS), include group decision support systems that structure how groups make decisions (Jessup and Valacich 1993; McGrath and Hollingshead

1993, 1994; Zigurs and Buckland 1998; Shim *et al.* 2002), as well as workflow management and enterprise planning tools. Of course, members of online groups might use one or many of these tools. As for which software tools are most popular in the workplace, survey data from 2001 found that for people 18 years old or older using computers on the job, 72.2 per cent used email, 67.2 per cent used word processing/desktop publishing applications, 62.5 per cent used spreadsheets/databases, 53.2 per cent used calendar/scheduling tools, 28.9 per cent used graphics/design software and 15 per cent or less engaged in programming or used software for other purposes. Of course, many – 43 per cent – used four or more of these categories of software (National Center for Education Statistics 2003). There is also the possibility of tools within one group being used for another purpose, such as using email (GCSS) to organize a calendar (GPSS), requiring close attention from researchers not only to what software is being used, but also how it is being used.

Technology and the group task

The locales framework describes a social world based on purpose and locales as the site and means for work practices towards the purpose; information and communication technologies can be part of locales and have the ability to expand (or hinder) the limits of effective communication (Fitzpatrick *et al.* 1996; Fitzpatrick 2000). What the locales framework does not emphasize is a means of deciding just how much use of technology defines the locale, or its penetration into work practices within the locale. This is a rather critical issue given the body of theory and research indicating that technology intertwines with task to influence group outcomes, such as the key variables of communication, participation and commitment.

Media choice theories, for example, state that groups choose a particular information and communication technology based on the fit of the technology to the task at hand, while another perspective indicates that different tasks require different degrees of media richness (McGrath and Hollingshead 1993, 1994; Hollingshead and Contractor 2002). The influence of task, in terms of type or complexity and the resulting

interdependence, plus the interaction of these factors with technology are standard components of virtual team definitions. As task complexity increases, interdependencies increase as well and hence create a need for more real-time communication technologies to support the team's work (Bell and Kozlowski 2002).

Similarly, the type of task, the information or communication technology used and the temporal context in which the team operates impact the degree of technological mediation on team processes (Driskell *et al.* 2003). The general public may also have its own ideas about how technology interacts with tasks that in turn influences their communication and participation patterns, such as considering email useful for basic coordination and information exchange issues but inadequate for more urgent or sensitive tasks (Fallows 2002; Beise *et al.* 2004). In sum, centrality–periphery and the nature of the locales in the social world are shaped to some degree by actual or perceived task–technology relations.

Describing how technology penetrates into task and hence into the locales of the social world, requires moving from general terminology about purpose and collective activities to more specific language to describe what members of social worlds do. The locales framework uses the terms 'focus' to refer to activities related to a goal and indicates that there are primary and secondary tasks involved in goal achievement. Focus and task(s) are then part of actions within trajectories, or patterns of actions over time (Fitzpatrick 2003).

While this approach provides some sense of hierarchical task structure, a more descriptive notion of tasks is provided by McGrath (1991), who describes group activities in terms of projects (a set of activities serving a goal), tasks (activities required to complete a project) and steps (a part of a task). For example, the goals of a therapeutic community website might be to provide general information to visitors, solicit their input for response by others and direct them to health care providers. Projects reflected at the group's website in service of these goals may be an information center containing a series of web pages about symptoms and treatment, an anonymous forum and a searchable database of physicians. Associated tasks and steps are those associated with maintaining the technologies that provide these features, responding to posted inquiries and so forth.

McGrath's model provides a detailed breakdown of tasks that in turn makes it easier to describe how technology might penetrate into those tasks, specifically the breadth and frequency of use. One means of categorizing technology penetration into task is suggested by Brandon and Hollingshead (1999), who discuss integrating technology-based collaborative and cooperative tasks into traditional instruction in a complementary fashion (interwoven into an existing instructional task), a supplementary fashion (as an addition to an existing instructional task), or in substitutionary fashion (as wholly replacing an existing task). Consider a paper-based exam as an example: allowing students occasional use of an online reference would be complementary; having the students write their essays online in addition to answering a paper test would be supplementary; and completely placing the test online would be substitutionary.

Merging the description of group activities with concepts describing technology integration into task, suggests the dimensions and cells in Figure 8.1. We acknowledge that the extent and frequency of use of a technology will vary (cf. Borghoff and Schlicter 2000).

The categories in Figure 8.1 are general descriptions of how information and communication technologies can be part of group locales. Supplementary use refers to occasional use of a technology for a few projects related to the social world purpose, such as a community action group that meets locally on a weekly basis but occasionally posts items regarding its annual fund-raising event on a municipal website. Complementary use is more widespread than supplementary, such as a co-located group that regularly uses email for picking sites for its next face-to-face meeting but then accomplishes most of its projects and tasks face-to-face.

While all four categories can involve multiple forms of information and communication technologies, use of more than one tool is more likely in the spanning and plenary categories, as use of technology across multiple projects is more likely to involve more than one type of tool. Spanning groups are those that use information or communication technologies across multiple projects, but not on a consistent or regular basis. An example would be a workgroup that updates its workflow software after significant milestones, occasionally updates a database and enters a group decision-making facility with a facilitator when projects reach a true impasse. In short, while locales occasionally involve technology, this is the exception more than the rule. Plenary use of technology is pervasive and frequent, maybe even defining, across all projects and associated group goals and is the category descriptive of technology use by prototypical virtual teams and technology-dependent social phenomena such as multiplayer gaming (Nielsen 2004).

Naturally, in light of the vast number of online groups in existence, there will be groups in which multiple categories of technology penetration apply, for example, a work group that uses email in a plenary fashion but makes supplementary use of a database it has developed. Such patterns are expected and it is not the purpose of the categories to force online group locales into one category or another, but rather to provide terms that are generally descriptive of how groups may use technology across task(s) to support a social world's purpose. One would anticipate, however, that an online group would have a majority of its locales typified by complementary or plenary uses of technology. Of course, the most thorough documentation of

Frequency of use of technology

Use of technology across project(s)		Occasional	Frequent
	Single/few projects	Supplementary	Complementary
	Most/multi-project	Spanning	Plenary

Figure 8.1 Technology penetration into group locales.

technology penetration will come from combining the aforementioned descriptions of types of technology provided by McGrath and Hollingshead with the concepts in Figure 8.1.

Identity and accessibility

If the influence of computer-mediated communication channels on the information group members have about one another is an issue of debate (Hollingshead 2001), there is little doubt that technology provides a means for groups to control membership based on what they know of others. Technology further allows people to attempt to control information about who they are and others to attempt to control such information as well, raising concerns about privacy, power and anonymity in a world now ubiquitous with information technology (Zuboff 1984; Mason 1986; Spears and Lea 1994). While avoiding standard conceptions of boundaries, the locales framework does allow for privacy via restriction of resources (Fitzpatrick *et al.* 1996). Specifically, locales may contain mechanisms that tie access to resources to different levels of membership, which in turn can promote privacy.

The online world, more so than the physical world, provides mechanisms to constrain such access to resources. Different levels of membership can promote privacy in a social world by granting or denying access to resources. Locales can provide mechanisms to control access to resources based on membership levels. The file permissions framework in the fundamental and ubiquitous UNIX operating system, for example, limits both access and behaviour; access can be limited to the individual, a group the individual belongs to, or the file can be 'world' accessible; once accessible, behaviour can be limited to reading, writing, or executing programs (Garfinkel and Spafford 1996).

A trait that sets some online groups apart from face-to-face groups is the ability to be wholly anonymous when interacting with others, or at least to feel more anonymous than when interacting in a face-to-face group (McKenna and Green 2002). Such anonymity may enhance participation in certain types of groups (cf. Alexander *et al.* 2003; McKenna and Bargh 1998). The need for anonymity will likely vary by person. For example, one typology describes unconcerned,

circumspect, wary and alarmed Internet user groups, based on concerns about online privacy (Sheehan 2002).

Scepticism about privacy in online interactions is widespread, particularly in commercial transactions, yet at the same time individuals often provide revealing information about themselves online (Fox *et al.* 2000; Metzger 2004). However, even modest amounts of social information can trigger group-related phenomena. Identifiability based on name and geographical location, for example, when available to ingroup members, can lead descriptions of outgroup members to become more stereotypical, as well as triggering other group phenomena related to perceptions of a shared social identity (Postmes *et al.* 1998; Douglas and McGarty 2002).

Interactions in online groups reflect both group-controlled access and individually controlled personal information. This suggests one useful means of categorizing online groups: to assess the degree to which people seeking to participate can assume and maintain a relatively anonymous identity, or must divulge their identity to participate in the group. Here, we define anonymity as the degree to which the individual must divulge one's personal identity to join or continue in an online group and includes personally identifying information (e.g. name, physical or electronic address, telephone number) demographic information, or preference information (e.g. hobbies, interests). Certainly, the degree to which individuals willfully provide information about their personal identity will vary (see Chapter 16 this volume).

For the purposes of simple classification, we categorize identity demands as either public (high amount of personal identity information required) or private (low amount of personal identity information required). Working via a corporate intranet as part of a virtual work team likely involves a high amount of personal identity information (e.g., a posted biography) and would be an example of public identity demands. Posting to any one of the thousands of groups found in social networking sites such as MySpace© (Hansell 2006) may require little more than a pseudonym accompanied by perhaps a temporary and easily fictionalized email address, and would be an example of private identity demands.

Another related means of categorizing groups is accessibility, or the degree to which the individual has permission to access and interact with an online group. As categorized here, accessibility refers to whether the technology used by an online group is open to the public for interaction with group members, such as the foundation USENET newsgroups (cf. Alexander *et al.* 2003; Krikorian and Kiyomiya 2003), or a relatively private, closed system such as a virtual private network (Khanvilkar and Khokar 2004). In a broader sense, the difference between private and public accessibility is the degree to which access to the group's information and communication technology requires passing through either or both technological or policy barriers, such as firewalls and other security restrictions, registration forms and corporate policies (cf. Federal Trade Commission 1998). The popular Facebook© social networking site, for example, requires participants to have a valid university email address (Toomey 2005). Of course, identity and accessibility are as related in online groups as they are in any other group, i.e. one typically has to provide personal identity information in order to increase one's access to a group. For example, participants in social networking sites often publicly provide extensive and very detailed personal information about themselves – more than is required for simple membership and use of the technology – as a means of connecting with others (cf. Gross and Acquisti 2005). We present a classification of online groups based on identity and accessibility in Figure 8.2.

We fully acknowledge that identity and accessibility can be matters of degree, not simple dichotomies, and there can be distinctions even within an online group. For example, newsgroups, while open to the public, can also have a private core of moderators and/or system administrators, who might know more about the personal details of group members (cf. Papadakis 2003). Additionally, over time group members may decide to meet in person, making privacy issues nearly moot (McKenna and Green 2002). The intention here is to provide general descriptors only; more intense scrutiny may require another approach, such as specifying particular subgroups.

An example of a 'Fishbowl' online group would be a newsgroup with minimal membership requirements, where group members use their real names and provide other contact information, such as in a signature file or hyperlink in their messages. Under the term 'Demesne' falls a typical corporate intranet, where access is limited to organization members or even organizational subunits, the public is firewalled out, but group member identity information is easily accessible to all group members. Perhaps the most common newsgroup formation can be termed an 'Arena', where the public can easily lurk and post messages, but identities are typically private via use of pseudonyms. Lastly, under the term 'Sanctum' are placed online groups such as a firewalled corporate intranet where identity is kept anonymous for some specific purpose, for example the use of a group decision-making tool where member anonymity is part of the process (Hollingshead 2001). Other examples of sanctums are therapeutic or support groups using a non-public password-protected chat tool, with member identity perhaps known to site managers but concealed from other group members.

Discussion

In this chapter, we presented a language derived from the locales framework and several additional dimensions for describing and comparing online groups. An online presence might be one locale used by a group toward accomplishing the purpose of its social world. Within that

Accessibility

		Public	Private
Identity	*Public*	Fishbowl	Demesne
	Private	Arena	Sanctum

Figure 8.2 Identity by accessibility.

online locale, groups may use one of several types of technology (GCSS, GISS, GXSS, GPSS), that have various penetrations (supplementary, complementary, spanning, or plenary) into the projects that the group uses to operationalize its purpose. By restricting access to resources within a locale, online groups can create environments in which personal and social identities vary in their prominence and accessibility, producing categories described here as fishbowls, demesnes, arenas and sanctums.

The goal is that these categories, which emphasize the connections between an online group and the technology it uses rather than characteristics that may span all types of groups (e.g., norms), will be useful to researchers in describing the burgeoning forms of online groups.

Of course, the sets of categories presented here are not an exhaustive list of those potentially useful for describing online groups.

For example, descriptions of virtual communities may include dimensions applicable to smaller online groups, particularly as uses of technologies themselves increasingly blur the group–community distention. One scheme classifies virtual communities based on whether they are member-initiated or organization-sponsored (Porter 2004). Member-initiated communities can be further broken down into social or professional orientations, whereas organization-sponsored communities can be broken down into commercial, non-profit making and government orientations. The scheme further includes purpose, place (technological mediation), platform (synchronous/asynchronous communication) and profit model (revenue generation mechanism) as key attributes of virtual communities. Other researchers describe virtual communities in terms of the general purpose of the group, such as patient support, education and e-business communities (Preece and Maloney-Krichmar 2003), or in terms of minimum levels of interaction and sustained membership (Jones 1997).

Descriptive statistical data helpful in further characterizing online groups is increasingly available. For example, a study of Internet users contacting groups found that about half contacted a trade association/professional group or a hobby/interest group; many (around 20–30 per cent)

contacted fan groups for sports teams or entertainers, local associations or community groups, lifestyle groups, or medical/personal support groups; about a quarter contacted groups with whom they share political or religious beliefs (Horrigan et al. 2001). A survey of virtual community websites found that most groups (43 per cent) were devoted to relationships among persons with similar experiences, closely followed by groups interested in a specific topic (38 per cent), then fantasy/entertainment groups (12 per cent) and information exchange groups (7 per cent) (Lee et al. 2003). Such survey results suggest broad notions of the social worlds of many online groups, i.e. general descriptions of the purposes of online groups.

Typologies developed to describe traditional offline groups may also have useful descriptive concepts applicable to online groups. One general taxonomy of groups includes categories of family, work group, community and circle (social) groups (Back 1981). In the organizational arena, survey data indicate that organizations use both ad hoc and ongoing teams (Devine et al. 1999). An extensive review of attempts to categorize teams in organizations produced two clusters of team types (intellectual and physical work teams) based on seven underlying dimensions (work cycle, physical ability requirements, temporal duration, task structure, active resistance, hardware dependence and health risk) (Devine 2002). It may be the case that only a subset of the 14 teams develop as online groups, e.g. service and sports teams may be less likely to make plenary use of technology than executive, negotiation and design teams. Or, with regards to the prior taxonomy, it may be the case that very few family groups have online analogs.

Future research should seek to refine the terms and language used for characterizing online groups. The array and types of online groups have evolved much quicker than the terminology used to describe them – i.e., virtual, online, or distributed – which seems imprecise and obsolete. As we have stressed throughout this chapter, it is rare to find groups that interact purely face-to-face or purely virtually and many of the current technologies available to groups are wireless and enable members to collaborate without having to be 'online'.

Large-scale surveys need to document the new forms of online groups that are sprouting across the globe. One such example is 'Internet hunting', a phenomenon uncovered in China where anonymous Web users come together to investigate allegations of morality breaches (adultery, fraud and the like) and to administer punishment to violators (French 2006). Unfortunately, much of the theory and research on online groups is based on case studies and laboratory work rather than on large-scale surveys, so it is difficult for researchers to keep up with the rapid change and evolution in the forms of online groups (Maznevski and Chudoba 2000; Belanger et al. 2002). In addition, most research on online groups (including research on which we have developed the present framework) is representative of primarily individualistic, English-speaking countries, non-English-speaking collectivistic cultures need to be included more often in our studies so that we gain a more complete and up-to-date understanding of the nature, forms and variety of online groups.

References

Ahuja, M. K. and Galvin, J. E. (2003). Socialization in virtual groups. *Journal of Management 29*(2), 161–185.

Alexander, S. C., Peterson, J. L. and Hollingshead, A. B. (2003). Help is at your keyboard: support groups on the Internet. In L. R. Frey (ed.), *Group communication in context: Studies of bona fide groups*, 2nd edn, LEA's communication series (pp. 309–334). Mahwah, NJ: Lawrence Erlbaum Associates.

Back, K. W. (1981). Small groups. In M. Rosenberg and R. H. Turner (eds), *Social psychology: Sociological perspectives* (pp. 320–343). New York: Basic Books, Inc.

Bailey, K. D. (1994). *Typoligies and taxonomies: an introduction to classification techniques*. London: Sage.

Beise, C. M., Niederman, F. and Mattord, H. (2004). IT project managers' perceptions and use of virtual team technologies. *Information Resources Management Journal 17*(4), 73–88.

Belanger, F., Watson-Manheim, M. B. and Jordan, D. H. (2002). Aligning IS research and practice: a research agenda for virtual work. *Information Resources Management Journal 15*(3), 48–70.

Bell, B. S. and Kozlowski, S. W. (2002). A typology of virtual teams. *Group and Organization Management 27*(1), 14–49.

Blanchard, A. (2004). Virtual behavior settings: an application of behavior setting theories to virtual communities. *Journal of Computer-Mediated Communication 9*(2). Retrieved 16 October 2004 from http://jcmc.indiana.edu/vo19/issue2/blanchard.html.

Blanchard, A. and Markus, M. L. (2004). The experienced 'sense' of a virtual community: characteristics and processes. *Database for Advances in Information Systems 35*(1), 65–79.

Blumler, J. G. and Katz, E. (1974). *The uses of mass communication*. Newbury Park, CA: Sage.

Bonito, J. A. and Hollingshead, A. B. (1997). Participation in small groups. *Communication Yearbook 20*, 227–261.

Borghoff, U. and Schlicter, J. (2000). *Computer-supported cooperative work*. Berlin: Springer.

Brandon, D. P. and Hollingshead, A. B. (1999). Collaborative learning and computer-supported groups. *Communication Education 18*(2), 109–126.

ClickZ Stats. (2004). *Population explosion!* Retrieved 7 December 2004 from http://www.clickz.com/stats/sectors/geographics/article.php/5911_151151.

Computer Industry Almanac, I. (2004). *Worldwide Internet users will top 1 billion in 2005*. Retrieved 7 December 2004 from http://www.c-i-a.com/pr0904.htm.

Covert, M. D. and Thompson, L. F. (2001). *Computer-supported cooperative work: Issues and implications for workers, organizations and human resource management*. London: Sage.

Dahlberg, L. (2004). Internet research tracings: towards non-reductionist methodology. *Journal of Computer Mediated Communication 9*(3), 1–27.

Dell, S. (2004). Flash mobsters. *Telephony 245*, 30.

DeSanctis, G. and Monge, P. (1999). Communication processes for virtual organizations. *Organization Science 10*(6), 693–703.

Devine, D. J. (2002). A review and integration of classification systems relevant to teams in organizations. *Group Dynamics 6*(4), 291–310.

Devine, D. J., Clayton, L. D., Philips, J. L., Dunford, B. B. and Melner, S. B. (1999). Teams in organizations: prevalence, characteristics and effectiveness. *Small Group Research 30*(6), 678–711.

Douglas, K. M. and McGarty, C. (2002). Internet identifiability and beyond: a model of the effects of identifiability on communicative behavior. *Group Dynamics: Theory, Research and Practice 6*(1), 17–26.

Driskell, J. E., Radtke, P. H. and Salas, E. (2003). Virtual teams: effects of technological mediation on team performance. *Group Dynamics 7*(4), 297–323.

Engeström, Y. (1991). Developmental work research: reconstructing expertise through expansive learning. In M. Nurminen and G. Weir (eds), *Human jobs and computer interfaces* (pp. 265–290). Amsterdam: Elsevier.

Engeström, Y., Engeström, R. and Vähäaho, T. (1999). When the center does not hold: the importance of knotworking. In S. Chaiklin, M. Hedegaard and U. J. Jensen (eds), *Activity theory and social practice* (pp. 345–374). Oakville, CT: Aarhus University Press.

Fallows, D. (2002). *Email at Work*. Washington, DC: Pew Internet and American Life Project.

Federal Trade Commission. (1998). *Privacy online: A report to Congress*. Washington, DC: US Federal Trade Commission.

Fisher, A. T., Sonn, C. C. and Bishop, B. J. (eds) (2002). *Psychological sense of community: Research, applications and implications*. New York: Kluwer Academic/Plenum Publishers.

Fitzpatrick, G. (2000). Centres, peripheries and electronic communication: changing work practice boundaries. *Scandinavian Journal of Information Systems 12*, 115–148.

Fitzpatrick, G. (2003). *The locales framework. Understanding and designing for wicked problems*. London: Kluwer Academic Publishers.

Fitzpatrick, G., Mansfield, T. and Kaplan, S. (1996). *Locales framework: exploring foundations for collaboration support*. Paper presented at the IEEE Proceedings of Sixth Australian Conference on Computer-Human Interaction (OzCHI'96), Hamilton, NZ, November.

Fitzpatrick, G., Tolone, W. J. and Kaplan, S. M. (1995). *Work, locales and distributed social worlds*. Paper presented at the Fourth European Conference on Computer-Supported Cooperative Work, Stockholm, Sweden.

Fox, S., Rainee, L., Horrigan, J. B., Lenhart, A., Spooner, T. and Carter, C. (2000). *Trust and privacy online. The Internet life report*. Washington, DC: The Pew Internet and American Life Project.

French, H. W. (2006). Online throngs impose a stern morality in China. *New York Times*, 3 June.

Garfinkel, S. and Spafford, G. (1996). *Practical unix and internet security, 2nd edn*. Sebastopol, CA: O'Reilly and Associates.

Greenberg, S., Fitzpatrick, G., Gutwin, C. and Kaplan, S. (2000). Adapting the locales framework for heuristic evaluation of groupware. *Australian Journal of Information Systems 7*(2), 102–108.

Griffith, T. L., Sawyer, J. E. and Neale, M. A. (2003). Virtualness and knowledge in teams: managing the love triangle of organizations, individuals and information technology. *MIS Quarterly 27*(2), 265.

Gross, R. and Acquisti, A. (2005). *Information revelation and privacy in online social networks*. Paper presented at the ACM Workshop on Privacy in the Electronic Society, Alexandria, VA.

Hansell, S. (2006). For MySpace, making friends was easy, big profit is tougher. *New York Times*, 23 April, p. 1.

Harrison, A., Wheeler, P. and Whitehead, C. (2004). *The distributed workplace: Sustainable work environments*. London: Spon Press.

Hollingshead, A. B. (2001). Communication technologies, the Internet and group research. In M. A. Hogg and R. S. Tindale (eds), *Blackwell handbook of social psychology: Group processes* (pp. 557–573). Oxford: Blackwell Publishers.

Hollingshead, A. B. and Contractor, N. S. (2002). New media and organizing at the group level. In L. A. Lievrouw and S. Livingston (eds), *Handbook of new media. Social shaping and consequences of ICTs* (pp. 221–235). London: Sage Publications.

Horrigan, J. B., Rainee, L. and Fox, S. (2001). *Online communities: Networks that nurture long-distance relationships and local ties*. Washington, DC: Pew Internet and American Life Project.

Internet World Stats (2004). *Internet usage statistics – the big picture. World Internet users and population stats*. Bogota, Colombia: Miniwatts International, Inc. Retrieved 7 December 2004 from http://www.internetworldstats.com/stats.htm.

Jessup, L. M. and Valacich, J. E. (eds) (1993). *Group support systems: New perspectives*. New York: MacMillan.

Jones, Q. (1997). Virtual communities, virtual settlements and cyber-archaeology: a theoretical outline. *Journal of Computer-Mediated Communication 3*(3). Retrieved 10 October 2004 from http://jcmc.indiana.edu/vol3/issue3/jones.html.

Khanvilkar, S. and Khokar, A. (2004). Virtual private networks: an overview with performance evaluation. *IEEE Communications Magazine 42*(10), 146–154.

Kling, R., Rosenbaum, H. and Hert, C. (1998). Social informatics in information science: an introduction. *Journal of the American Society for Information Science 49*(12), 1047–1052.

Krikorian, D. and Kiyomiya, T. (2003). Bona fide groups as self-organizing systems: applications to electronic newsgroups. In L. R. Frey (ed.), *Group communication in context: Studies of bona fide groups*, 2nd edn, LEA's communication series (pp. 335–365). Mahwah, NJ: Lawrence Erlbaum Associates, Publishers.

Lea, M. (1991). Rationalist assumptions in cross media comparisons of computer-mediated communication. *Behavior and Information Technology 10*(2), 153–172.

Lee, F. S., Vogel, D. and Limayem, M. (2003). Virtual community informatics: a review and research agenda. *Journal of Information Technology and Application 5*(1), 47–61.

Lipnack, J. and Stamps, J. (1997). *Virtual teams: Reaching across space, time and organizational boundaries*. New York: John Wiley and Sons.

Martins, L. L., Gilson, L. L. and Maynard, M. T. (2004). Virtual teams: what do we know and where do we go from here? *Journal of Management 30*(6), 805–835.

Mason, R. O. (1986). Four ethical issues of the information age. *MIS Quarterly 10*, 4–12.

Maznevski, M. L. and Chudoba, K. M. (2000). Bridging space over time: global virtual team dynamics and effectiveness. *Organization Science 11*(5), 473–202.

McFedries, P. (2003). Mobs R Us. *IEEE Spectrum 40*(10), 56.

McGrath, J. E. (1991). Time, interaction and performance (TIP): a theory of groups. *Small Group Research 22*(2), 147–174.

McGrath, J. E. and Hollingshead, A. B. (1993). Putting the 'G' back in GSS: some theoretical issues about dynamic processes in groups with technological enhancements. In L. M. Jessup and J. E. Valacich (eds), *Group support systems: New perspectives* (pp. 78–96). New York: Macmillan.

McGrath, J. E. and Hollingshead, A. B. (1994). *Groups interacting with technology*. Newbury Park, CA: Sage.

McKenna, K. Y. A. and Bargh, J. A. (1998). Coming out in the age of the Internet: identity 'demarginalization' through virtual group participation. *Journal of Personality and Social Psychology 75*, 681–694.

McKenna, K. Y. A. and Green, A. S. (2002). Virtual group dynamics. *Group Dynamics* 6(1), 116–127.

Metzger, M. J. (2004). Privacy, trust and disclosure: exploring barriers to electronic commerce. *Journal of Computer Mediated Communication* 9(4). Retrieved 10 October 2004 from http://jcmc.indiana.edu/vol9/issue4/metzger.html.

National Center for Education Statistics. (2003). *Digest of Education Statistics 2003*. Washington, DC: US Department of Education.

Nielsen, R. (2004). Their own world. *Wall Street Journal*, 26 April, p. R12.

Norris, P. (2002). The bridging and bonding role of online communities. *Harvard International Journal of Press/Politics 7*, 3–13.

Papadakis, M. C. (2003). *Computer-mediated communities: The implications of information, communication and computational technologies for creating community online*. Arlington, VA: SRI International.

Pew Internet Project (2004). *Online activities – daily internet activities*. Washington, DC: Pew Internet and American Life Project. Retrieved 28 October 2004 from http://www.pewinternet.org/trends/Internet_Activities_4.23.04.htm.

Poole, M. S. and DeSanctis, G. (1990). Understanding the use of group decision support systems: the theory of adaptive structuration. In J. Fulk and C. Steinfeld (eds), *Organizations and communication technology* (pp. 175–195). Newbury Park, CA: Sage.

Porter, C. E. (2004). A typology of virtual communities: a multi-disciplinary foundation for future research. *Journal of Computer Mediated Communication* 10(1). Retrieved 7 January 2005 from http://jcmc.indiana.edu/vol10/issue1/porter.html.

Postmes, T., Spears, R. and Lea, M. (1998). Breaching or building social boundaries? SIDE-effects of computer-mediated communication. *Communication Research* 25(6), 689–715.

Powell, A., Piccoli, G. and Ives, B. (2004). Virtual teams: a review of current literature and directions for future research. *Database for Advances in Information Systems* 35(1), 6–36.

Preece, J. and Maloney-Krichmar, D. (2003). Online communities. In J. Jacko and A. Sears (eds), *The human–computer interaction handbook: Fundamentals, evolving technologies and emerging applications* (pp. 596–620). Mahwah, NJ: Lawrence Erlbaum.

Rheingold, H. (1993). *The virtual community: Homesteading on the electronic frontier*. Reading, MA: Addison-Wesley.

Sassenberg, K. (2002). Common bond and common identity groups on the Internet: attachment and normative behavior in on-topic and off-topic chats. *Group Dynamics: Theory, Research and Practice* 6(1), 27–37.

Sheehan, K. B. (2002). Toward a typology of Internet users and online privacy concerns. *The Information Society 18*, 21–32.

Shim, J. P., Warkentin, M., Courtney, J. F., Power, D. J., Sharda, R. and Carlsson, C. (2002). Past, present and future of decision support technology. *Decision Support Systems* 33(2), 111–126.

Sillence, E. and Baber, C. (2004). Integrated digital communities: combining web-based interaction with text messaging to develop a system for encouraging group communication and competition. *Interacting with Computers* 16(1), 93–113.

Song, I., Larose, R., Eastin, M. S. and Lin, C. A. (2004). Internet gratifications and Internet addiction: on the uses and abuses of new media. *CyberPsychology and Behavior* 7(4), 384–394.

Spears, R. and Lea, M. (1994). Panacea or panopticon? The hidden power in computer-mediated communication. *Communication Research* 21(4), 160–176.

Strauss, A. (1993). *Continual permutations of action*. New York: Aldine de Gruyter.

Toomey, S. (2005). Facebook is new who's who for students: 6 million use online networking services nationwide. *Chicago Sun-Times*, 14 November, p. 6.

Townsend, A. M., Demarie, S. M. and Hendrickson, A. R. (1998). Virtual teams: technology and the workplace of the future. *Academy of Management Executive 27*, 17–29.

Training Journal Staff (2003, May). Managing virtual teams is fraught with difficulty, says new report. *Training Journal*, p. 5.

US Bureau of the Census (2002). *E-Stats: Detailed tabulations of manufacturing e-business process use in 2000*. Washington, DC: US Bureau of the Census, Economics and Statistics Administration.

Warner, M. (2000). Instant party, just add ethernet cables. *Fortune 142*, 42–43.

Wellman, B., Boase, J. and Chen, W. (2002). The networked nature of community: online and offline. *It and Society* 1(1), 151–165.

Wellman, B., Hasse, A. Q., Witte, J. and Hampton, K. (2001). Does the Internet increase, decrease, or supplement social capital. *The American Behavioral Scientist* 45(3), 436–455.

Wilson, S. M. and Peterson, L. C. (2002). The anthropology of online communities. *Annual Review of Anthropology 31*, 449–467.

Zigurs, I. and Buckland, B. (1998). A theory of task/technology fit and group support systems effectiveness. *MIS Quarterly* 22(3), 313–334.

Zuboff, S. (1984). *In the age of the smart machine*. New York: Harper Collins Publishers, Inc.

CHAPTER 9

Social networks and online community

Caroline Haythornthwaite

Introduction

The very notion of community in an online context can begin a hot debate. Those who would keep the term 'community' for the imagined ideal of cooperation and joint sharing of land, resources and goals ask: How can community exist without physical co-location and a geographic touchstone? How can the leanness of computer-mediated communication (CMC) support the richness inherent in a community? Yet we find online community members reporting the kinds of strong emotional and social bonds associated with local community, sharing the resources of stories and information, enjoying their time together online and working toward common goals (Rheingold 1993; Baym 2000; Haythornthwaite *et al.* 2000; Kendall 2002). At the same time, the term has been adopted so rapidly and attached to so many collective endeavours, that its use is questioned even by those who accept online as a legitimate venue for community. They ask: How can a group working on development of a computing platform be called a community? How can the richness of community be reduced to the use of a work-based knowledge sharing system, the social and emotional connotations of community reduced to an association between web pages? Yet we do find community both useful and applicable in describing open source computing communities (Moon and

Sproull 2002), for communities of practice that manage knowledge sharing at a distance and through computer technologies (Wenger 1998) and for the discovery of epistemic or associational communities connected by co-citation or reciprocal web linking (Thelwall and Vaughn 2004).

This chapter revisits the debate about community and online community and offers a means of conceptualizing and investigating online community using a social network perspective that frees it from its former geographical constraints. The argument is that despite a common understanding of community as associated with a geographical base and neighbourly relations, community emerges where the cumulative impact of interactions among individuals adds value above the level of pairwise interactions. Interactions such as exchange of information and advice, social support, mutual help and provision and receipt of services can have the cumulative impact of creating trust among network members, shared history and language and known expectations about behaviours that support the community in its common goals. By looking for the basis of community in interaction rather than geography, it is possible to liberate community from its physical setting and see it as based on relations that can be maintained anywhere and via any technology that makes interaction possible. This *social network* view of community provides a means of examining communities whether maintained online or offline, for neighbourly support or professional practice.

This chapter begins with a look at the challenges to community that have fed into arguments against online community and a section on the discovery of community online. It then addresses the case for a network view of community, starting with how the social network approach has been applied to offline communities and how this lays the groundwork for unbundling community from face-to-face interaction and geographic co-location. Following a brief section on the basics of social network terminology, the paper returns to the main topic of community with a focus on the network level aspects of community, showing how patterns of interpersonal ties can build a network with outcomes greater than the sum of the pairwise connections. The final sections explore variants on the theme of community, first by revisiting the online and offline dichotomy and addressing the advantages, and indeed the inevitability, of considering community from both online and offline sides. In the last two sections, the specialized communities of practice and link-based communities are discussed: this provides a test of a network definition of community and the opportunity to consider what kinds of relations are necessary to accept the realization of community. The paper concludes with a brief summary of how community can exist without physical co-location and a geographic touchstone.

Community debates

Why does it matter what label is given to a collective and whether we maintain ties online or off? The debate over the location of community and use of the term continues a long-standing concern that the local community is challenged and indeed threatened by trends of industrialization and urbanization, leading to the decline of society, increased crime and decreased quality of life. Each new disruption in the (imagined) ideals of home and town is met with resistance and fear of the further degradation of our daily experiences. Tönnies (1887[1955]) captured the worry about community in his characterization of Gemeinschaft (community) and Gesellschaft (society). Gemeinschaft embodies much of what

is considered to define a community: a collective based on strong interpersonal ties, face-to-face interaction, a shared focus and common purpose, language and identity, all largely associated with an ideal of the pastoral village.

By contrast, Gesellschaft describes all we associate with a failed community: people living near each other yet not connected by any interpersonal commitment, lacking a shared purpose or concern with locality, all largely associated with the worst of an anonymous, urban setting. Recent writers such as James Beninger (cited in Jones 1995) have used the word pseudocommunity to continue the discussion of the alienation of modern society, drawing attention to the powerlessness felt by individuals regarding the ability to control or have input in society and the inauthentic nature of community contact predicated on impersonal mass-media communication (for a discussion, see Jones 1995). As Putnam (2000) has phrased it, these people are bowling alone, failing to participate in activities that support the wider community and their own quality of life.

Online communication is the latest change, bringing another threat to community and the ideals the term embodies. As individuals migrate online, these arenas of interaction are discussed in the same manner as past changes in the physical organization of societal interaction. The relevance of physical 'place' compared to cyber 'space' is debated, as are the merits of offline versus online interaction (Meyrowitz 1985; Erickson 1993; Wellman 2001). Particular attention is given to how being online affects individual wellbeing and community. Being online is described as taking us away from 'real' face-to-face interactions, with resulting individual alienation and depression (e.g., Kraut *et al.* 1998; Nie and Erbring 2000; Putnam 2000; Nie 2001). Involvement in online communities is seen as taking resources and attention away from local communities, reducing our civic engagement and thereby impoverishing overall quality of life (Putman 2000; Nie 2001). Children are spending time online chatting with peers instead of family and playing video games instead of engaging in more appropriate physical or social activity, with even so-called 'social' video games leading to declines in attitudes toward and connections with friends (Williams 2006). Online activity brings us and our children in contact with undesirable and criminal elements, pushing pornography and get rich quick schemes and encouraging illegal activities such as computer hacking.

Such dystopic views are as often matched by utopic views: online communication is the way to make connections with people of similar interest, freeing us from the constraints of geography (Sproull and Kiesler 1991); it increases our connectedness to others, including family (Jones 1995; Kazmer and Haythornthwaite 2001; Howard *et al.* 2002; Quan-Haase and Wellman 2002); and it compensates for dislocations associated with moving to a new home or going to college (Hampton and Wellman 2002; LaRose *et al.* 2001). Studies find that teenagers' use of the Internet does not take them away from the more socially acceptable activities of reading or playing sports; instead, 'computer kids' are less likely to engage in the less socially accepted activities of just hanging around or doing nothing (Wagner *et al.* 2002). Internet users show a more active lifestyle than non-users; they sleep less and have more social contact with friends and co-workers (although less time with their children) (Robinson *et al.* 2002). Even video games can increase the feeling of being part of a larger community and are neutral in terms of effect on sense of community with local neighbourhood and engagement with family (Williams in press).

Thus, despite arguments against the possibility of online community, there are many vibrant online environments that fit the community model. The next section looks at how researchers and participants discovered community online.

Discovering community online

It is probably fair to say that the emergence of community online is as much a surprise to online participants as it is to non-participants. Although contemporary, wired life appears to bear similarity to Tönnies' atomized *Gesellschaft* view: many online venues have been shown to provide just the shared purpose, common language, affective relations and group orientation characteristic of *Gemeinschaft*. Often these are spaces where individuals who would not otherwise know or commune with one other come together to discuss a common interest or work

together for a common purpose (Mickelson 1997; Baym 2000; Kendall 2002; Moon and Sproull 2002). These online spaces resemble the 'great good places' described by Oldenburg (1989), where people gather in non-work, non-home settings (see also Kling 1996). A prime example is the Well community first described by Rheingold in 1993 (second edition 2000) which is the first major account to portray online relationships with social and emotional meaning for participants and a genuine sense of community among members.

Other in-depth examinations of online community show how essential elements of community develop online. Baym (1995, 2000), for example, presents an extended examination of communication and community among participants in a Usenet discussion group about soap operas (http://www.rec.arts.tv.soaps). Baym's account makes the connection between the role of soap operas in the lives of audience members as they share a common base for discussion of plots and characters with friends, family and co-workers and its extension into online discussion. She describes how the rules and conventions that grow out of members' common interests begin to structure online communication and parallel aspects of community found offline. For example, discussion group members follow group conventions on using message headers to signal the discussion of plot elements – plot 'spoilers' – within the message text, signalling to others not only the danger of reading ahead in the story, but also their adherence to group conversational norms.

Because online communities depend so much on written text, language plays a particularly significant role in determining the actions and responses of members. Sproull and Kiesler (1991) first pointed this out for email groups with the example of the 'rowdies' among whom flamboyant language was accepted as a norm. Not only does community emerge through the language used, but it is also reinforces the way language continues to be used. As Cherny (1999) describes in depth, online communities are 'speech communities', defined and emergent from 'shared rules of speaking and interpretations of speech performance' (Cherny 1999: 23). For more on language and community including 'rhetorical' and 'discourse' communities, see Clark (1996) and Miller (1984, 1994): for discussion of the way text and conversation merge in the notion of 'persistent conversation', see Erickson (1999).

Language plays 'a significant role in marking the community's boundary' (Cherny 1999: 23). Newbies need to learn how to use language appropriately and not knowing how to 'talk' online can be a barrier to entry. For example, Bregman and Haythornthwaite (2003) found that for online distance learners the visibility of their postings and uncertainty about what and how to post, hampered their ability to join the community. Language signals and reinforces differences between insiders and outsiders and, consciously or unconsciously, speakers learn to accommodate their language to fit with others (see Giles *et al.,* 1991, reaccommodation theory). Difference in language use mark some as newbies who do not know the rules and some as disrupters or 'trolls' who, knowing the rules, choose to go against them as a way to upset community actions. As online communities grow, like offline communities, they establish rules of behaviour that establish insider behaviour and also enforce those rules through sanctioning inappropriate behaviours (e.g., see the discussion of transgressor behaviours and conduct control described by McLaughlin *et al.,* 1995).

Other studies show how members of predominantly or wholly online endeavours not only develop strong interpersonal ties, but also perceive community to exist. Haythornthwaite *et al.* (2000) interviewed Internet-based distance learners to see whether they felt they belonged to a community and what characterized the community. Students indicated that their social and work interactions with other students, sustained via email, synchronous chat, asynchronous bulletin board postings, co-working arrangements and on-campus reunions, played an important part in creating and sustaining their sense of community. Strong working relations with administrative and technical support staff also helped with their experience of community. A separate study showed that members of this distance programme build a communal history, grounded in an emergent folklore of the community as they share common experiences and stories (Hearne and Nielsen, 2004; see also Kendall, 2002, for the role of stories in an online community).

Overall, we find that members of online environments who stay together for interest, work or learning, display the same kinds of characteristics of community found offline, such as common language, rules of behaviour and their enforcement, support during crises and communal history. By these means, work, learning, social and recreational groups accomplish their tasks just as in offline settings (Haythornthwaite 2001; Kendall 2002; Moon and Sproull 2002). While many still argue that such online interaction does not create true community, online participants vigorously extol the virtues of their online experience for providing just those aspects of social support, membership and identity that are the hallmarks of community.

The case for a network view of community

Why, despite evidence from studies that characteristics of community exist in online environments and testimony from online participants, are we still faced with a debate over whether online collectives qualify as 'community'? Why is there continued concern that embracing online collectives under the definition of community undermines our ability to seek or achieve the *Gemeinschaft* ideal (Jones 1995; Etzioni and Etzioni 1999; Haythornthwaite and Wellman 2002)? In looking at these debates, one aspect that stands out is that those who challenge the widespread application of the word community come with a definition in hand and test new instantiations against existing – often idyllic – models of community, ones in which characteristics of community are bundled with other factors such as geographic co-location. Those who accept a more general use of the term look at what is happening with those involved, ask about interactions and perceptions and allow community to emerge from the sharing and identification perceived by participants. They are willing to re-evaluate what is needed for community and to unbundle interactivity from geographic co-location.

It is in this latter approach that we find the utility of a *social network perspective*. Social network analysis focuses on what is happening between people, within collectives and across boundaries, in order to find what kind of collective exists. Geography, co-location, face-to-face meetings and home bases can be unbundled from communication, information exchange, knowledge sharing and provision of advice, social support, goods and services. Interpersonal interactions and relationships can be examined for the way they build network level characteristics such as co-orientation to common goals and purposes and trust in the ability of the network to regulate behaviour (described further below in the section Communal ties, relations and capital). This opens up the possibility of finding community among co-located or distributed participants, maintained solely offline or online, or maintained through combinations of computer-media and face-to-face communication.

This network view of community is rooted in the work of sociologist Barry Wellman in the 1970s (Wellman 1979, 1999). At the time, prevailing views of community considered community to be lost as a result of increased industrialization, with this loss evident in the decline of urban areas. Sociologists then found pockets of community action within larger urban areas, generating a *community saved* view. Wellman's work revealed a third view – that of *community liberated*. While both the lost and saved views come from an outsiders' observation and assessment of the presence of community, the liberated view focuses on *personal communities*, those experienced by individuals. As Wellman and colleagues have found, individuals maintain their own personal network of contacts – family, friends, workmates, distance relatives and acquaintances – all of whom contribute to their personal experience of community (Wellman and Leighton 1979; Wellman *et al.* 1988; Wellman and Tindall 1993). Thus, an external view of lost, local community does not need to translate into an individual lacking in community. At the time of the early studies, contacts were found to be maintained across distance by telephone calls and visiting by car and plane. Means of contact now include the full range of CMC, as well as the ubiquitous cell phone and continued travel by car and plane. Indeed, community is now so liberated it can be reinforced nearly anywhere at anytime with mobile computing and phone communication (Rheingold 2003; Wellman *et al.* 1996; Wellman 1997, 2001).

Thus, a network view provides a way of examining community in terms of what connects people rather than what is seen from the outside to constitute a cohesive unit. This view lets us examine and accept that personal communities that support individuals in their lives exist, and to see the atomized individual as actually engaged in communities not dependent on close physical proximity. It also allows us to accept that the communities we engage in overlap. As we take on specific roles in our lives, as Merton (1957) has described – co-worker, parent, television fan – we also take on specific communities – of practice, kinship, audience membership. We identify with different and *plural* communities, networks and social worlds (Strauss 1978; Kazmer and Haythornthwaite 2001; Haythornthwaite and Hagar 2005; Kazmer, forthcoming;). As Wenger describes it, 'each person is a unique intersection of multimembership' (2004: 5); 'our identities reflect the fluidity of our membership in multiple communities, at the same time and over the course of our lives' (2004: 6). As Wellman, Boase and Chen (2002) state 'Rather than relating to one group, people live and work in multiple sets of overlapping relationships, cycling among different networks' (2002: 160).

Although Wellman's perspective emphasized personal communities, the network view also addresses group collectives. As will be described further below, not only are interactions between network members the basic building blocks of community, but it is at the network level that community emerges and is perceived to exist. Thus, two perspectives of community are addressed with a network view: individual *personal* community, which, until recently, has been strongly bound to geographic location and which can entail membership in a number of collectives – for example family, work, local community, professional community – and the *whole network* of any one of those collectives, involving a set of individuals interacting in such a way as to exhibit network level community effects. The argument here is that community emerges not from whether the individuals meet and mingle in the same physical setting, nor whether the relations maintained are those of neighbourliness, but from the way the underlying association related to family, work, friendship, interest and/or play exhibits network level community effects.

To discuss this further, it is necessary to briefly introduce social network concepts. What follows is by no means a detailed look at the now rapidly developing field of social network analysis. Further details on social network analysis and application can be obtained from a number of sources (Wasserman and Faust 1994; Scott 2000; for network studies and theories, see Wellman and Berkowitz 1997; Monge and Contractor 2003; Wellman 1999; for general explanations, see Barabasi 2003; Stohl 1995; Watson 2003; for online social networks, see Garton *et al.* 1997).

Social network concepts

Actors, relations, ties and networks

Social networks are built on the foundation of *actors* who are connected or *tied* by the maintenance of one or more *relations*. The set of ties among actors describes a *social network*. The pattern of actors, relations and ties reveals structures of relational exchange, e.g., from and to whom information flows, positions of individuals within the network (e.g., who is most central) and how resources are distributed and circulate across the network as a whole.

Actors are generally thought of as people, particularly when discussing community, but network analysis, with its basis in graph theory, does not require that actors be individuals. The methods, measures and vocabulary can as easily be applied to associations between events, business boards, organizations, reference works and web pages. Thus, we may look for connections between events by how much overlap there is in who attended, between boards by whether we find the same people on different boards and between organizations by associations between members of different organizations. Similarly, we may look at who is citing the same literature in academic papers as a way of finding co-citation networks. *Bibliometric analysis* (or *infometric analysis*) is a long-standing method for exploring properties of knowledge networks, with vocabulary to describe positions in these networks that is very similar to that used in network analysis (for a paper exploring the relation between bibliometric and social connections, see White *et al.* [2004]). Recent work has taken this kind of analysis to the web in the emerging field of

webometrics, which encompasses what might formerly have been called *hyperlink* or *link analysis* (Thelwall and Vaughn 2004; Björneborn and Ingwersen 2004; for more on social network and web links, see Park 2003).

Relations connect actors. The connection may be based on the exchange of intangibles such as information, social support, or advice, or of tangibles such as money, goods, or services. The direction of giving and receiving can be important because it shows who is the major recipient of resources, or the major provider. This in turn shows the influence and prestige of individuals in the network, whether individual actors in a network are positioned to regulate the flow of resources in the network and how resources circulate in a network.

A pair of actors is said to have a *tie* when they maintain such a relation. A tie is *strong* when actors maintain many relations, particularly when those relations include social and emotional support and intimacy or self-disclosure. Strong tie relations are likely to be reciprocal, e.g., self-disclosure by one actor is matched by self-disclosure by the other, small services are repaid with other services. Our strong ties are with people we refer to as friends, close friends, collaborators and colleagues. We tend to have stronger ties with those more like us, who operate in the same general social circles that we do. Among friends and co-workers, more frequent exchange is also associated with stronger ties. (Kinship also connects people, but frequency of interaction and types of relations can operate differently than for ties based on the obligations and rewards of work and friendship relations.)

Although physical proximity has been bound up with the kinds of communication that build and sustain strong ties, online communication also captures many of the features of strong tie communication and outcomes associated with community. For example, Rafaeli and Sudweeks (1997) find evidence of *interactivity* in online communication, pertaining to the way 'messages in a sequence relate to each other and especially the extent to which later messages recount the relatedness of earlier messages' (online) and associated with outcomes of engagement, acceptance, satisfaction, performance quality, motivation, fun, learning, openness and sociability.

A tie is *weak* when little is shared and interaction is infrequent. Weak ties are maintained with people we describe as acquaintances, or someone we know from work. Those with whom we have weaker ties tend to be different from us and operate in different social circles from us. As much literature has explored and described, the benefit of a strong tie is the willingness of the actors to share resources and provide what input and help they can to each other. Yet the fact that they are like us and interact with people like us, means they are less likely to have access to new information or resources. Our weak ties are less motivated to share information with us, but, since they operate in different social circles, the *strength of weak ties* is that they have access to different information (Granovetter 1973, 1982).

Patterns of ties among actors build into *social networks* that show overall connectivity within networks. Ties show the direction of resource flow, but networks show the overall effect of these interconnections on resource distribution, e.g., how many people information must go through to reach an actor at the periphery, whether one individual receives or allocates most resources (network stars) or sits strategically in a position between others in the network (as a broker or bridge between subgroups). Whole network views can show who gives money and who receives services, who supports whom financially, emotionally, or with the provision of small services; they show the extent to which the network of actors is densely or sparsely connected and whether the network is centralized around key actors.

The network level can show where resources are pooled rather than directly exchanged. Thus, members may give help to one person without receiving anything in return; instead the return may be in the way the actor who received help in turn gives others help. This *generalized reciprocity* is a network level effect, not observable in pairwise interaction and it may be read as an indicator of community. Effects such as this that operate at the whole network level add value to network relations and represent the *social capital* inherent in the network. Social capital is strongly indicated as a correlate of community (e.g., Putman 2000). This is discussed further below.

Asking network questions

Social network analysts explore what kinds of relations are maintained in any particular network, what kinds of people maintain these relations and how these show the structure of personal or egocentric networks and of whole networks. Analysts may ask questions about overall interaction (e.g., Who do you work with? Who have you communicated with in the last week?) or more specific questions about particular kinds of interactions. Here is a question asked on the 1985 US census (known as the General Social Survey, GSS): 'From time to time, most people discuss *important matters* with other people. Looking back over the last six months – who are the *people* with whom you discussed matters important to you?' (Burt 1985: 119).

Participants can then be asked about the characteristics of those with whom they discuss these matters, e.g., whether they are friends, family members, etc., to see what kinds of people receive ties about important matters. On the GSS, individuals were asked for details of the first five people they named and for how well each of those people knew each other. Such data provide a view of the egocentric networks of individuals.

Analysts may ask about one kind of relation, or about several. In the author's study of interactions in an online learning environment (Haythornthwaite 2001, 2002b) students were asked about four relations:

How often in the last month (e.g., daily, weekly, monthly) have you ...

- Collaborated on class work
- Received or given information or advice about class work
- Socialized
- Exchanged emotional support (described as support during a minor or major upset) ... with each member of the class.

The data show not only how members of the network were tied by these relations, but also what relations were held in common by pairs of actors. This kind of *relational multiplexity* indicates a stronger tie between pairs because of their more multi-threaded engagement with each other. The kinds of relations held in common also show what sustains stronger ties in specific kinds of communities. For example, studies of scholarly communities show that collaborative pairs commonly combine friendship and work activities (Haythornthwaite 2001; Koku and Wellman 2004). Haythornthwaite (2006) found nine kinds of relations in an analysis of three distributed scholarly communities: relations included exchange of factual knowledge as well as learning the process of doing something, finding out about research methods, working jointly on research, learning about how to use a technology, generating ideas, socialization into the profession and providing access to a network of contacts.

Some studies have also asked about what media are used to maintain ties and relations. Haythornthwaite and Wellman (1998) asked a series of 24 questions about who talked to whom, about what and via which media. This study was the first to indicate that along with relational multiplexity, stronger ties were also associated with *media multiplexity*, i.e., the stronger the tie, the more media used (see also Haythornthwaite 2001, 2002b; Koku and Wellman 2004).

With the basics of social networks in mind – actors, ties and relations, that create networks based on patterns of interaction – we can now continue to discuss how this helps understand community and its extension to online environments.

Using a social network perspective to examine community

A social network perspective differs from other approaches in examining what is exchanged, communicated and shared by pairs of individuals, rather than the aggregated behaviour for a group, community or location. For example, we could study community in an aggregate way, perhaps choosing what we believe is a community – a town, suburb, university, online group – and asking whether and how often members have donated money, goods or services to the community, whether they participate in organizations or events and whether they give or receive emotional and social support. This can be useful information for gauging the extent of engagement and support in the community: but we can go further to ask questions from a network perspective.

For any set of people we can ask what they do with each other and see how (and if) community emerges from the kinds of interactions that happen. For example, people living in a suburb may or may not interact with each other; it may or may not resemble the pastoral village. A network view does not assume a suburb is a community because it can be geographically bounded. Instead it is not declared a community until it becomes evident from patterns of interaction among suburb members that they are acting as a community. Thus, we may ask members of our fictional geographic suburb, or of an online collective, who they talk to, to whom they give or receive money, goods, services, or social support, with whom they have attended events? A distinguishing feature of a network approach is that it examines interconnections to *discover* where groups exist, rather than determining *a priori* that a group exists based on external criteria such as membership in a town, organization, class or online discussion. Moreover, by asking about multiple kinds of interaction, it is possible to see what kinds of interactions hold together a particular network, e.g., whether the basis of group cohesion is common interest, work, profession, etc., rather than defining *a priori* that the collective must be based on particular kinds of relations. The resulting patterns of interaction reveal the group structures that support and sustain the network under examination.

A caveat is that there is no predetermined set of relations that can be used to discover a 'community'. While network patterns can show what interaction happens between whom and how interconnected network members are, interpreting that as 'community'– rather than, for example, an alliance, a collaborative work group, a collective, a cohort – is a judgement made by the researcher and/or by reports from network members. However, as will be seen in the discussion below, there are many network attributes that lead a researcher to be fairly confident that particular patterns of interaction are highly likely to correlate with members' perception of a community.

Communal ties, relations and capital

Etzioni and Etzioni (1999) define community as comprised of two attributes:

> First, it is a web of affect-laden relationships that encompasses a group of individuals – relationships

that crisscross and reinforce one another, rather than simply a chain of one-on-one relationships. To save breath, this attribute will be referred to as bonding. Second, a community requires a measure of commitment to a set of shared values, mores, meanings and a shared historical identity – in short, a culture.

(Etzioni and Etzioni 1999: 241)

In this definition social network aspects are evident in the 'web' of affiliation, the 'bonding' and close knit association between people in the network. Wenger (1998) describes a similar list of three dimensions that form the basis of a community of practice: mutual engagement, a joint enterprise and a shared repertoire (i.e., shared routines, vocabulary and concepts). Thus, for either kind of collective, these authors identify strong bonds (ties), co-orientation to a common viewpoint and engagement in a common purpose as essential for the definition and presence of community.

Community ties are maintained with people we feel are similar to us (at least in relation to the community focus), who we expect to understand and concur with our experience and viewpoint and with whom we share commitment to the common culture or enterprise. A benefit to the individual is that the work of getting to know others and negotiating common ground is reduced because the knowledge and practices of the community provide a given similarity in perspective – for example, consider how professions create common knowledge through education and acculturation before novices join the ranks of experts.

Another benefit of membership in a community is the way this facilitates asking for and receiving help or information. Online communication can make that even easier, as the lack of social exposure makes it easier to ask relative strangers for information (Constant et al. 1996). Help is also more likely to be sought from community members than from outside because insiders will understand their 'different kind of world' (Haythornthwaite et al. 2000). Explaining what you need can be easier when all members of the community share similar backgrounds.

Online discussion groups often take some time to build the ground rules for discussion as they develop their norms about question asking and answering and on- versus off-topic questions. FAQs (frequently asked questions) depositories establish ground rules and senior members sanction newbies who ask overly simplistic questions or post off-topic messages. For these forums and communities to work it must be possible to ask for help, but help must also be given. Because of continued orientation to the community, members may take up roles of community maintenance, spending their energy responding to others in the community, giving help without requiring an immediate payback or even any payback. This kind of generalized reciprocity and altruistic behaviour is important for initiating and sustaining the overall community (Markus 1990). It is a cultural attribute embedded in the whole network.

Both the structure of a network and the composition of ties within the network contribute to its perception and designation as a community. Strong tie behaviours of reciprocal interaction, shared understanding and mutual influence provide the basis on which work can get done, friendships deepen and persist and networks become stable. Because strong ties are associated with frequent communication and a higher motivation to share information, actors in networks with many strong ties are likely to have access to the same information at the same time. They are also aware of actions within the network and more able to monitor and manage the behaviour of other network members. These outcomes are possible only when sufficient network members are strongly tied. Note that the outcomes appear at the network level: the ability to monitor group member behaviour is not something possessed by an individual, but is instead a result of the overall network configuration. The network, then, possesses value above the benefits accruing to individual pairs in the network.

This added value is referred to as *social capital*, it is a social resource embedded in and constituted by social network ties (Burt 2000; Putman 2000; Lin 2001, forthcoming). It is an attribute of stable networks which makes it possible for individuals to gain access to resources through their connections with others. In terms of community, social capital makes the difference between individual connectivity and community connectivity. Social capital benefits include the ability to trust network members, to have a common language and to depend on network-based mechanisms to manage behaviours.

Dense, strong, *bonding* ties create a community level framework for trust. By knowing what is expected and seeing expectations met (for example as individuals follow and are reinforced for following group norms and as transgressions are sanctioned), network members can trust that the community will take care of certain aspects of behaviour. This relieves the individual of the responsibility of managing all aspects of every tie they maintain (albeit also exacting conformity to norms). For example, laws and their enforcement provide the back-up that allows individuals and businesses to enter into contracts and commercial arrangements. As Burt (2000) describes, where dense connections among network members afford oversight of everyone's behaviours, the risk associated with making ties with others is reduced (e.g., the risk of embarking on joint work). Risk is reduced because group sanctioning of offensive behaviour is facilitated and/or because the way in which individuals are constantly visible to each other increases their exposure and thus also their fear of sanction and loss of reputation (see Burt 2000).

Although a community needs strong ties, these are not all that comprise a community. Communities also include ties with people who are strangers, yet who can be expected to share the same outlook and can be called on to share resources. Thus, community also depends on *bridging* ties that connect subgroups and aid in the search for new resources, information and opportunities. Communities need the input of new ideas associated with transient, weak tie connections (Granovetter 1973; Putnam 2000). One drawback of much of the discussion and development of online environments has been an overwhelming emphasis on strong ties and the design of systems to support close working relations (e.g., development of computer-supported cooperative work tools and collaboratory environments). Yet our offline communities are not restricted to strong ties alone. Indeed, many communities fail precisely because their inward focus fails to recognize outside change, leading to groupthink and a failure to be aware of new technologies and innovations (Rogers 1995).

Overall, communities are – and need to be – composites of strong relations for internal management of trust and norms, combined with contact with weak ties for exposure to new information, opportunities and awareness. Online connections are becoming increasingly important for maintaining interpersonal communication at the foundation of communal ties. Moreover, the reach of online communication can also serve another function – as a low-level connector among community members, particularly among those who might not otherwise come in contact. Elsewhere I have suggested that group-wide media provide a foundation, a *latent tie* network (Haythornthwaite 2002a, 2005), on which ties may be initiated and can (potentially) grow into strong ties. Thus, we find a synergy between online and offline communication that relates to the way ties are initiated and maintained. These emerging synergies are discussed next.

Online/offline realities and synergies

What is rarely considered in debates about community is how online and offline may be used to advantage to leverage communities. Yet facing the reality of interpersonal ties and communities maintained online becomes necessary as online contact increasingly becomes part of everyday life, integrated into work, home, school and local community (e.g., Kraut *et al.* 1998, 2002; Kiesler *et al.* 2000; Wellman 2001; Kendall 2002; Wellman and Haythornthwaite 2002; Turow and Kavanaugh 2003). One reason we continue to find stark contrasts in views of online community is an adherence to simplistic dichotomies: *Gemeinschaft* versus *Gesellschaft*, offline versus online, face-to-face versus mediated, strong ties versus weak ties (see also Haythornthwaite and Nielsen, 2006). This trend goes hand in hand with overly simplistic approaches to identification of community, particularly by outsiders applying the label and by research that examines means of communication one at a time, e.g., looking at face-to-face, email, chat, instant messaging, or blogs only. These dichotomies and simplifications fail to capture the multiplexity of personal roles, relations, ties and means of communication that form our social environment. Again, a network view, with its emphasis on following interactions rather than means of communication becomes a way of discovering how online and offline interaction are synergistic in maintaining relations and thus of communities.

Etzioni and Etzioni (1999) emphasize how support via multiple modes is likely to have the best community outcomes. Building their argument from earlier research in learning, they suggest that 'communities that combine both f2f and CMC systems would be able to bond better and share values more effectively than communities that rely upon only one or the other mode of communication' (Etzioni and Etzioni 1999: 247, italics in original).

A study by Koku and Wellman (2004) provides an example of how the use of on- and offline communication fits with network relationships for scholarly members of 'TechNet' (a pseudonym). Face-to-face group meetings (seminars, conferences, grant preparation meetings, administrative meetings) were important for the visibility and availability of central scholars. At such meetings central scholars were seen to be present, thereby reinforcing the importance of the venue, as well as signalling that they felt the group to be of importance. They were also then available informally for advice-seekers. Central scholars found benefit in meeting advice-seekers in face-to-face meetings because the latter's presence at the meeting signalled the seriousness of their interest, making it worthwhile for central scholars to invest time in giving them advice. For TechNet, email served peripheral members by giving them remote access to the group even though they did not regularly attend meetings. In a similar way, Matzat (2004) found that activity in online discussion groups created visibility for researchers (although it did not provide egalitarian status for list members).

Similarly, as noted above, the discovery that more strongly tied pairs use more media to communicate than weakly tied pairs (media multiplexity) indicates the way online communications extend rather than replace face-to-face communications. Among co-located members of a research group, strongly tied pairs added email communications to scheduled and unscheduled face-to-face meetings (Haythornthwaite and Wellman 1998). Interestingly, face-to-face communication can also supplement and extend online communication. Distance learners whose main means of communication are online chat, bulletin boards and email, supplement these means with getting

together to socialize face-to-face during on-campus sessions (Haythornthwaite et al. 2000).

The drive to exploit online/offline synergies is also found in association with traditional, geographically based communities. Local, geo-communities find they need to create a presence online as well as support their constituents with online facilities. Community networking initiatives and community information systems use online initiatives to promote local community involvement and development (e.g., Bishop 2000; Cohill and Kavanaugh 2000; Gurstein 2000; Keeble and Loader 2001; Day and Schuler 2004; Foth 2006). Thus we can no longer separate local concerns from the use of online resources. Online distribution of information and online discussion of events of importance to local community and society (e.g., in the ideas of e-democracy and online town halls) become added modes for communication and interaction supporting the community.

Online interaction has also been found to correlate positively with geo-community activity, increasing the relevance and significance of community in individuals' lives. Matei and Ball-Rokeach (2002), for example, found that those who were online in the Los Angeles, California ethnic communities they studied were also more apt to interact offline and participate in local community. Similarly, Kavanaugh and Patterson (2002) found greater involvement in the local community among participants in the community networking initiative of the Blacksburg Village in Virginia. Although Kavanaugh and Patterson caution that this online engagement may reflect an active, more engaged, offline community in Blacksburg, the evidence from both of these studies is that online provides another useful and viable outlet from geo-community related interactions.

Specialized definitions of communities

Before we leave the discussion of community, it is worth taking a look at two ways the term community is used that are really quite different from traditional notions of neighbourly, locally based ties. In a way, these are tests of our acceptance of the term community for collectives identifiable from network connections. The first is communities of practice, predicated on relations of common professional or work-based interest: the second is communities 'found' through common online links.

Communities of practice

There has been a lot of recent attention to the potential for online interaction to support knowledge building and the development of shared understanding among professionals, co-workers and scholars. The term most often used is *community of practice*, but earlier and concurrent discussions include the terms knowledge or epistemic communities (Knorr-Cetina 1999), invisible colleges (Crane 1972), asynchronous learning networks (Harasim *et al.* 1995), scholarly networks (Koku *et al.* 2001; Koku and Wellman 2004) and learning communities (Haythornthwaite 2003; Riel and Polin 2004). Because exchanges in such communities are largely informational and because experts are likely to be distributed geographically, they have been perceived as ideal candidates for online maintenance.

The term *community of practice* was originated by Lave and Wenger (1991) to describe a community that supports 'participation in an activity system about which participants share understandings concerning what they are doing and what that means in their lives and for their communities' (1991: 98). The learning perspective brought by these authors connects with early comments about CMC: that online connection would overcome distance, bring people together based on shared interest, cross organizational lines and support invisible colleges of scholars, professionals and distributed workers (Sproull and Kiesler 1991; Jones 1995). More recently this is repeated in discussion of knowledge communities and the creation of collaboratories and knowledge management systems (e.g., Finholt 2002; Wenger *et al.* 2002).

Lave and Wenger particularly note that a community of practice does *not* imply 'co-presence, a well-defined, identifiable group, or socially visible boundaries' (1991: 98). Instead and in keeping with the network perspective advocated here, they state: 'A community of practice is a set of relations among persons, activity and world, over time and in relation with other tangential and overlapping communities of practice' (1991: 98).

The key community aspect is the development of joint knowledge and practice and socialization of newcomers into the norms and practices of the community of practice – the 'shared repertoire' (Wenger 1998). As such, it shares much with the ideal of *Gemeinschaft*, even if not co-located or geographically bound.

Is it a 'community'? From a network perspective, a well-working community of practice shows a set of actors interacting in such a way as to create social capital. The benefits to individuals in terms of participation, quality of life, access to help and support and network level outcomes such as common language, generalized reciprocity, etc., all look like they add up to a community. However, it is apt that these collectives are given a hybrid name, because their two-part naming signifies the underlying relations that create this community – here the relations are those of *practice* – about knowledge base, techniques, work routines, etc. Communities of practice are excellent examples of communities liberated from geography, well supported by online interaction, that can be verified by looking at network ties, relations and capital.

Link-based communities

The last kind of online community to be discussed is that uncovered by link relations between websites. As noted above, another way to collect network data is to look at connections between entities rather than people, e.g., looking at who cites who in research papers, or what websites link to what others. This approach finds associations around domains of knowledge exploration, political activism, organizational affiliation, product use and interest (for a study of how links regarding the Zapatista movement connect non-governmental organizations, see Garrido and Halavais [2003]). A caveat with this work is the way it has appropriated the word community. The computational ease with which large numbers of links between web pages can be assessed for interconnectivity has led some to use this technique to claim the discovery of communities. However, as Montfort (2004) points out:

> For the most part, these [web link analyses] studies, even the most mathematically impressive ones, stop short of considering whether the 'communities' they discover really align with social realities. . . .

Community and *friends* are defined in some of these studies purely with reference to the properties of subgraphs. Although a true, extrinsic meaning for these concepts is never established, researchers expect that their discovery of communities and their prediction of whether or not people are friends will correspond to the sociological meanings, or at least to some intuitive meanings, of these terms.

(Montfort 2004: 9)

It is important to bear in mind what kind of definition of community is being applied to these associations. Etzioni and Etzioni's (1999) definition of community, as well as that of many others, includes the notion of affect. It is difficult to argue that affect can be found in the web of linkages between Internet sites. Thus, to accept this configuration as a community, an argument needs to be made for the indirect connection between the programmed link and a person or persons with feeling. However, common citation and web linking do suggest a co-orientation to common knowledge and shared interest that is part of what constitutes definitions of human community. It has been argued here that a community should offer some kind of net benefit and itself contain some kind of social capital. The questions then are: What is the added value of such a network? And who draws a benefit from this kind of community? Again, it is here that the researcher is challenged to consider what is acceptable to them as a 'community' and to find evidence of those attributes in this kind of network.

This example also brings up another possibility. Perhaps we could approach these links between entities as suggesting that the affect-laden definition of community is too strict. Perhaps we want to accept an association among entities – websites, scholarly references, events – as indicating a community of a different sort. Perhaps community is that which is represented by a critical mass of interconnection, existing in a universe of more sparsely enacted connections, regardless of the relation(s) connecting actors or of the human-ness of the actor. Communities might be discovered from the network configurations rather than the relational bases. This takes us full circle to consider again whether we want to privilege 'community' for only those associations that resemble the pastoral, *Gemeinschaft*

ideal, or whether we can usefully borrow and expand it into new realms of inquiry. This is a question we leave open for further debate.

Conclusion

This paper started with the questions: How can community exist without physical co-location and a geographic touchstone? How can the leanness of computer-mediated communication support the richness inherent in a community? It has been argued that the answer lies in the network relations that connect actors and the cumulative effect of patterns of interaction that add value to the network above the level of pairwise interconnection. From research and writing on community and from examples of collectives, it is possible to say that not all networks constitute community because community is seen to require relations of emotional and social support, provision of small and large services and adherence to and policing of common norms exhibited through shared language, common purpose and shared history. However, it is also possible to say that these relations do not require physical co-location; they can be as evident among online soap opera fans as they can be absent in a suburb or urban enclave. The argument has also been that collectives that are communities show network level social capital that provides benefits to members beyond those obtained from pairwise interactions. Social capital is seen in network actions such as generalized reciprocity and group sanctioning of behaviour, and received by community members in reduced risk of engagement with others, reliance on the network to monitor behaviour and decreased overhead in social practices due to common language and norms. Again, these are effects as likely to emerge online as offline regardless of the leanness of mediated communications.

The paper ended with a few examples that challenge the researcher to grapple with their acceptance of the term community. Overall, it is still a judgement call on whether the kind of collective that is examined fits with a researcher's or participant's perception of the word. Yet when one hears so often from online participants that they feel they belong to a community, it is hard to continue to hold to an older image of a pastoral village. Instead, it is important to consider what relations and network-level outcomes make that image an ideal and then see if our newly constituted offline, online or hybrid collectives reproduce that ideal or whether they deserve new names and definitions for their collaborative, cooperative and group-oriented connections.

References

Barabasi, A. (2003). *Linked: How everything is connected to everything else and what it means for business, science and everyday life*. New York: Plume.

Baym, N. K. (1995). The emergence of community in computer-mediated communication. In S. Jones (ed.), *Cybersociety: Computer-mediated community and communication* (pp. 138–163). Thousand Oaks, CA: Sage.

Baym, N. K. (2000). *Tune in, log on: Soaps, fandom and online community*. Thousand Oaks, CA: Sage.

Bishop, A. (2000). Communities for the new century. *Journal of Adolescent and Adult Literacy*. Available at http://www.readingonline.org/electronic/jaal/2–00_Column.html.

Björneborn, L. and Ingwersen, P. (2004). Toward a basic framework for webometrics. *Journal of the American Society for Information Science and Technology 55*(14), 1216–1227.

Bregman, A. and Haythornthwaite, C. (2003). Radicals of presentation: visibility, relation and co-presence in persistent conversation. *New Media and Society 5*(1), 117–140.

Burt, R. S. (1985). General social survey network items. *Connections 8*, 119–23.

Burt, R. S. (2000). The network structure of social capital. *Research in Organizational Behavior 22*, 345–423.

Cherny, L. (1999). *Conversation and community: Chat in a virtual world*. Stanford, CA: CSLI Publications.

Clark, H. H. (1996). *Using language*. Cambridge, UK: Cambridge University Press.

Cohill, A. M. and Kavanaugh, A. L. (2000). *Community networks: Lessons from Blacksburg, Virginia*, 2nd edn. Boston, MA: Artech House.

Constant, D., Kiesler, S. B. and Sproull, L. S. (1996). The kindness of strangers: the usefulness of electronic weak ties for technical advice. *Organization Science 7*(2), 119–135.

Crane, D. (1972). *Invisible colleges: Diffusion of knowledge in scientific communities*. Chicago, IL: University of Chicago Press.

Day, P. and Schuler, D. (eds) (2004). *Community practice in the network society: Local action/global interaction*. London: Routledge.

Erickson, T. (1993). From interface to interplace: the spatial environment as a medium for interaction. Proceedings of the conference on spatial information theory. Available at http://www.pliant.org/personal/Tom_Erickson/Interplace.html.

Erickson, T. (1999). Persistent conversation: an introduction. *JCMC 4*(4), Available at http://www.ascusc.org/jcmc/vo14/issue4/ericksonintro.html.

Etzioni, A. and Etzioni, O. (1999). Face-to-face and computer-mediated communities, a comparative analysis. *The Information Society 15*(4), 241–248.

Finholt, T. (2002). Collaboratories. *Annual Review of Information Science and Technology 36*, 73–107.

Foth, M. (2006). Analysing the factors influencing the successful design and uptake of interactive systems to support social networks in urban neighbourhoods. *International Journal of Technology and Human Interaction 2*(2), 65–82.

Garrido, M. and Halavais, A. (2003). Mapping networks of support for the Zapatista movement: applying social-network analysis to study contemporary social movements. In M. McCaughey and M. D. Ayers (eds), *Cyberactivism: Online activism in theory and practice*. New York: Routledge.

Garton, L., Haythornthwaite, C. and Wellman, B. (1997). Studying online social networks. *Journal of Computer-Mediated Communication 3*(1). Available at: http://www.ascusc.org/jcmc/vo13/issue1/garton.html.

Giles, H., Coupland, N. and Coupland, J. (1991). Accommodation theory: communication, context and consequence. In H. Giles and J. Coupland (eds), *Contexts of accommodation: Developments in applied sociolinguistics* (pp. 1–68). New York: Cambridge University Press.

Granovetter, M. S. (1973). The strength of weak ties. *American Journal of Sociology 78*, 1360–1380.

Granovetter, M. S. (1982). The strength of weak ties: a network theory revisited. In P. V. Marsden and N. Lin (eds), *Social structure and network analysis* (pp. 105–130). Beverly Hills, CA: Sage.

Gurstein, M. (2000). *Community informatics: Enabling communities with information and communications technologies*. Hershey, PA: Idea Group Publishing.

Hampton, K., and Wellman, B. (2002). The not so global village of Netville. In B. Wellman and C. Haythornthwaite (eds), *The Internet in everyday life* (pp. 345-371). Oxford, UK: Blackwell.

Harasim, L., Hiltz, S. R., Teles, L. and Turoff, M. (1995). *Learning networks: A field guide to teaching and learning online*. Cambridge, MA: The MIT Press.

Haythornthwaite, C. and Wellman, B. (1998). Work, friendship and media use for information exchange in a networked organization. *Journal of the American Society for Information Science, 49*(12), 1101-1114.

Haythornthwaite, C. and Hagar, C. (2005). The social worlds of the web. *Annual Review of Information Science and Technology 39*, 311–346.

Haythornthwaite, C. and Wellman, B. (2002). Introduction: Internet in everyday life. In B. Wellman and C. Haythornthwaite (eds), *The Internet in everyday life* (pp. 3–44). Oxford, UK: Blackwell.

Haythornthwaite, C. (2001). Exploring multiplexity: social network structures in a computer-supported distance learning class. *The Information Society 17*(3), 211–226.

Haythornthwaite, C. (2002a). Building social networks via computer networks: creating and sustaining distributed learning communities. In K. A. Renninger and W. Shumar, *Building virtual communities: Learning and change in cyberspace* (pp. 159–190). Cambridge: Cambridge University Press.

Haythornthwaite, C. (2002b). Strong, weak and latent ties and the impact of new media. *The Information Society* 18(5), 385–401.

Haythornthwaite, C. (2003). Online communities of learners. In K. Christensen and D. Levinson (eds), *The encyclopedia of community* (pp. 1033–1039). Thousand Oaks, CA: Sage.

Haythornthwaite, C. (2005). Social networks and Internet connectivity effects. *Information, Communication and Society* 8(2), 125–147.

Haythornthwaite, C. (2006). Learning and knowledge exchanges in interdisciplinary teams. *Journal of the American Society for Information Science and Technology*. [in press]

Haythornthwaite, C. and Nielsen, A. (forthcoming). CMC: revisiting conflicting results. In J. Gackenbach (ed.), *Psychology and the Internet*, 2nd edn. San Diego, CA: Academic Press.

Haythornthwaite, C., Kazmer, M. M., Robins, J. and Shoemaker, S. (2000). Community development among distance learners: temporal and technological dimensions. *Journal of Computer-Mediated Communication* 6(1). Available at http://www.ascusc.org/jcmc/vol6/issue1/haythornthwaite.html.

Hearne, B. and Nielsen, A. (2004). Catch a cyber by the tale: Online orality and the lore of a distributed learning community. In Haythornthwaite, C. and Kazmer, M. M. (eds). *Learning, culture and community in online education: Research and practice* (pp. 59-87). NY: Peter Lang.

Howard, P., Rainie, L. and Jones, S. (2002). Days and Nights on the Internet. In B. Wellman and C. Haythornthwaite (eds), *The Internet in everyday life* (pp. 45-73). Oxford, UK: Blackwell.

Jones, S. G. (1995). Understanding community in the information age. In S. G. Jones (ed.), *CyberSociety: Computer-mediated communication and community* (pp. 10–35). Thousand Oaks, CA: Sage.

Kavanaugh, A. and Patterson, S. (2002).The impact of computer networks on social capital and community involvement in Blacksburg. In B. Wellman and C. Haythornthwaite (eds), *The Internet in everyday life* (pp. 325–344). Oxford, UK: Blackwell.

Kazmer, M. M. and Haythornthwaite, C. (2001). Juggling multiple social worlds: distance students on and offline. *American Behavioral Scientist* 45(3), 510–529.

Kazmer, M. M. (forthcoming). Beyond C U L8R: Disengaging from online social worlds. *New Media and Society*.

Keeble, L. and Loader, B. D. (2001). (eds), *Community informatics: shaping computer-mediated social relations*. New York: Routledge.

Kendall, L. (2002). *Hanging out in the virtual pub: Masculinities and relationships online*. University of California Press.

Kiesler, S., Lundmark, V., Zdaniuk, B., and Kraut, R. E. (2000). Troubles with the Internet: the dynamics of help at home. *Human Computer Interaction* 15, 323–351.

Kling, R. (1996). Social relationships in electronic forums: hangouts, salons, workplaces and communities. In R Kling (ed.), *Computerization and controversy*, 2nd edn (pp. 426–454). San Diego, CA: Academic Press.

Knorr-Cetina, K. (1999). *Epistemic cultures: how the sciences make knowledge*. Cambridge, MA: Harvard University Press.

Koku, E. F. and Wellman, B. (2002). Scholarly networks as learning communities: the case of TechNet. In S. A. Barab, R. Kling and J. H. Gray (eds), *Designing for virtual communities in the service of learning* (pp. 299–337). Cambridge: Cambridge University Press.

Koku, E. F., Nazer, N. and Wellman. B (2001). Netting scholars: online and offline. *American Behavioral Scientist* 44(10), 1752–1774.

Koku, E. F. and Wellman, B. (2004). Scholarly networks as learning communities: The case of TechNet. In S. A. Barab, R. Kling and J. H. Gray (eds). *Designing for virtual communities in the service of learning* (pp. 299-337). Cambridge UK: Cambridge University Press.

Kraut, R., Kiesler, S., Boneva, B., Cummings, J., Helgeson, V. and Crawford, A. (2002). Internet paradox revisited. *Journal of Social Issues* 58(1), 49–74.

Kraut, R., Patterson, V. L., Kiesler, S., Mukhopadhyay, T. and Scherilis, W. (1998). Internet paradox: a social technology that reduces social involvement and psychological well-being? *American Psychologist* 53(9), 1017–1031.

LaRose, R., Eastin, M. S. and Gregg, J. (2001). Reformulating the Internet paradox: social cognitive explanations of Internet use and depression. *Journal of Online Behavior* 1(2). Available at http://www.behavior.net/JOB/v1n2/paradox.html.

Lave, J. and Wenger, E. (1991). *Situated Learning: Legitimate Peripheral Participation*. Cambridge, UK: Cambridge University Press.

Lin, N. (2001). *Social capital: A theory of social structure and action*. Cambridge: Cambridge University Press.

Lin, N. (forthcoming). A network theory of social capital. In Castigline, van Deth and Wolleb, *Handbook of social capital*. Oxford: Oxford University Press.

Markus, M. L. (1990). Toward a 'critical mass' theory of interactive media. In J. Fulk and C. W. Steinfield (eds), *Organizations and communication technology* (pp. 194–218). Newbury Park, CA: Sage.

Matei, S. and Ball-Rokeach, S. (2002). Belonging in Geographic, Ethnic and Internet Spaces. In B. Wellman and C. Haythornthwaite (eds), *The Internet in everyday life* (pp. 404-427). Oxford, UK: Blackwell.

Matzat, U. (2004). Academic communication and Internet discussion groups: transfer of information or creation of social contacts? *Social Networks* 26(3), 221–255.

McLaughlin, M. L., Osborne, K. K. and Smith, C. B. (1995). Standards of conduct on usenet. In S. G. Jones (ed.), *CyberSociety: Computer-mediated communication and community* (pp. 90–111). Thousand Oaks, CA: Sage.

Merton, R. K. (1957). *Social theory and social structure*. New York: Free Press.

Meyrowitz, J. (1985). *No sense of place: The impact of electronic media on social behaviour*. Oxford University Press, Oxford.

Mickelson, K. D. (1997). Seeking social support: parents in electronic support groups. In Kiesler, S. (ed.), *Culture of the Internet* (pp. 157–178). Mahwah, NJ: Lawrence Erlbaum.

Miller, C. (1984). Genre as social action. *Quarterly Journal of Speech 70*(2), 151–167.

Miller, C. (1994). Rhetorical community: the cultural basis of genre. In A. Freedman and P. Medway (eds), *Genre and the new rhetoric*, pp. 67–78. Basingstoke, UK: Taylor and Francis.

Monge, P. R. and Contractor, N. S. (2003). *Theories of communication networks*. Oxford: Oxford University Press.

Montfort, N. (2004). *Discovering communities through information structure and dynamics: A review of recent research*. Technical Reports MS-CIS-04–18, Department of Computer and Information Science, University of Pennsylvania.

Moon, J. Y. and Sproull, L. (2002). Essence of distributed work: the case of the LINUX Kernel. In P. J. Hinds and S. Kiesler (eds), *Distributed work* (pp. 381–404). Cambridge, MA: MIT Press.

Nie, N. H. (2001). Sociability, interpersonal relations and the Internet: reconciling conflicting findings. *American Behavioral Scientist 45*(3), 420–435.

Nie, N. H. and Erbring, L. (2000). *Internet and society: A preliminary report*. Stanford Institute for the Quantitative Study of Society (SIQSS), Stanford University and InterSurvey Inc. Available at http://www.stanford.edu/group/siqss/

Oldenburg, R. (1989). *The great good place: cafés, coffee shops, community centers, beauty parlors, general stores, bars, hangouts and how they get you through the day*. New York: Paragon House.

Park, H. W. (2003). What is hyperlink network analysis? A new method for the study of social structure on the web. *Connections 25*(1), 49–61.

Putnam, R. D. (2000). *Bowling alone: The collapse and revival of american community*. NY: Simon & Schuster.

Quan-Haase, A. and Wellman, B. (2002).Capitalizing on the net: Social contact, civic engagement and sense of community. In B. Wellman and C. Haythornthwaite (eds), *The Internet in everyday life* (pp. 291–324). Oxford: Blackwell.

Rafaeli, S. and Sudweeks, F. (1997). Networked interactivity. *Journal of Computer-Mediated Communication 2*(4). Available at http://www.ascusc.org/jcmc/vo12/issue4/rafaeli.sudweeks.html.

Rheingold, H. (1993). *The virtual community: Homesteading on the electronic frontier*, Reading, MA: Addison-Wesley.

Rheingold, H. (2000). *The virtual community: Homesteading on the electronic frontier* (revised edition)., Cambridge, MA: MIT Press.

Riel, M. and Polin, L. (2004). Online learning communities: common ground and critical differences in designing technical environments. In S. A. Barab, R. Kling and J. H. Gray (eds), *Designing for virtual communities in the service of learning* (pp. 16–50). Cambridge: Cambridge University Press.

Robinson, J., Kestnbaum, M., Neustadtl, A. and Alvarez, A. (2002).The Internet and other uses of time. In B. Wellman and C. Haythornthwaite (eds), *The Internet in everyday life* (pp. 244–262). Oxford: Blackwell.

Rogers, E. M. (1995). *Diffusion of innovations*, 4th edn. New York: The Free Press.

Scott, J. (2000). *Social network analysis: A handbook*, 2nd edn. London: Sage.

Sproull, L. and Kiesler, S. (1991). *Connections: New ways of working in the networked organization*. Cambridge, MA: MIT Press.

Stohl, C. (1995). *Organizational communication: Connectedness in action*. Newbury Park, CA: Sage.

Strauss, A. L. (1978). A social world perspective. *Studies in Symbolic Interactions 1*, 119–128.

Thelwall, M. and Vaughn, L. (2004). Webometrics. *JASIST 55*(14), whole issue.

Tönnies, F. (1887 [1955]). *Community and organization*. London: Routledge and Kegan Paul.

Turow, J. and Kavanaugh, A. L. (2003). *The wired homestead: An MIT sourcebook on the Internet and the family*. Cambridge, MA: MIT Press.

Wagner, G., Pischner, R. and Haisken-DeNew, J. (2002). The changing digital divide in Germany. In B. Wellman and C. Haythornthwaite (eds), *The Internet in everyday life* (pp. 164–185). Oxford: Blackwell.

Wasserman, S. and Faust, K. (1994). *Social network analysis*. Cambridge, MA: Cambridge University Press.

Watson, D. J. (2003). *Six degrees: The science of a connected age*. New York: W. W. Norton.

Wellman, B. and Leighton, B. (1979). Networks, neighborhoods and communities. *Urban Affairs Quarterly 14*, 363–390.

Wellman, B. (1979). The community question. *American Journal of Sociology 84*, 1201–1231.

Wellman, B. (1997). An electronic group is a social network. In S. Kiesler (ed.), *Cultures of the Internet* (pp. 179–205). Mahwah, NJ: Lawrence Erlbaum.

Wellman, B. and Tindall, D. (1993). Reach out and touch some bodies: How social networks connect telephone networks. In W. Richards, Jr. and G. Barnett (eds), *Progress in Communication Sciences Vol. 12*, (pp. 63-93). Norwood, NJ. : Ablex.

Wellman, B. (2001). Physical place and cyber place: the rise of personal networking. *International Journal of Urban and Regional Planning 25*(2), 227–252.

Wellman, B. and Haythornthwaite, C. (eds) (2002). *The Internet in Everyday Life*. Oxford, UK: Blackwell.

Wellman, B., Boase, J. and Chen, W. (2002). The networked nature of community: Online and offline. *IT & Society, 1*(1), 151-165. Available online at: http://www.stanford.edu/group/siqss/itandsociety/v01i01/v01i01a10.pdf

Wellman, B. (ed.)(1999). *Networks in the global village*. Boulder, CO: Westview Press.

Wellman, B. and Berkowitz, S. D. (eds) (1997). *Social structures: A network approach*, updated edn. Greenwich, CT: JAI Press.

Wellman, B., Carrington, P. and Hall, A. (1988). Networks as personal communities. In B. Wellman and S. D. Berkowitz (eds), *Social structures: A network approach* (pp. 130–184). Cambridge: Cambridge University Press.

Wellman, B., Salaff, J., Dimitrova, D., Garton, L., Gulia, M. and Haythornthwaite, C. (1996). Computer networks as social networks: collaborative work, telework and virtual community. *Annual Review of Sociology 22*, 213–238.

Wenger, E. (1998). *Communities of practice: Learning, meaning and identity.* Cambridge: Cambridge University Press.

Wenger, E. (2004). *Learning for a small planet: A research agenda.* Retrieved 14 January 2005 from http://www.ewenger.com/theory/index.htm.

Wenger, E., McDermott, R. and Snyder, W. M. (2002). *Cultivating communities of practice.* Cambridge, MA: Harvard Business School Press.

White, H. D., Wellman, B. and Nazer, N. (2004). Does citation reflect social structure? Longitudinal evidence from the 'Globenet' interdisciplinary research group. *Journal of the American Society for Information Science and Technology 55*(2), 111–126.

Williams, D. (in press). Groups and goblins: the social and civic impact of online gaming. *Journal of Broadcasting and Electronic Media.*

CHAPTER 10

Online social support groups

Martin Tanis

To give and receive social support is an important aspect of social interaction, and since the Internet has become more and more integrated with everyday life, it is no surprise that much social support is exchanged online. Features of computer-mediated communication (CMC) offer possibilities for social support in a manner that would be less easy or even impossible in a face-to-face context. This chapter focuses on three key elements that are often mentioned when social consequences of CMC are discussed: the possibility to communicate relatively anonymously, the text-based character, and the opportunities it provides for expanding social networks without being hindered by time and space barriers, and it addresses how these may affect support-seeking. Conclusions are that interacting in online social support groups holds great potential for people that seek support but may also contain some potential hazards. However, even though the body of research is growing, we still know fairly little about how online social support groups affect the well-being of people that are in need of support. More research is required that not only investigates motives of users, but provides us with more insights in what the consequences of online social support are for the mental and physical health of individuals and groups.

In the last thirty years, numerous studies have shown that social support plays a vital role in everyday life and contributes to the mental as well as physical well-being of people (Burleson et al. 1994; Heany and Israel 1995; Uchino et al. 1996; Albrecht and Goldsmith 2003). A lot of attention in this area has been devoted to how social support may benefit individuals who suffer from a mental or physical disorder (such as depression, anxiety, obesity, cancer, HIV, etc., see Cohen and Syme [1985]), go through a period of uncertainty or anxiety caused by a traumatic experience (Pennebaker and Harber 1993; Leffler and Dembert 1998), or feel lonely or isolated because of a stigmatized personal characteristic (such as a deviant sexual preference, an extreme political or religious opinion, a history of imprisonment, etc., see McKenna and Bargh [1998]; Davison et al. [2000]). Social support consists of a whole range of ways in which people can tacitly or explicitly help one another to improve the quality of their lives (House and Kahn 1985; Thoits 1995; Colvin et al. 2004), and is found to be beneficial for reducing stress, decreasing feelings of loneliness and isolation, getting hold of knowledge and information and learning strategies to cope with the situation people are facing (Albrecht and Adelman 1987; Cohen and Wills 1985; Buunk and Hoorens 1992; Thoits 1995).

Given the booming use of the Internet and the wide range of people who have access to it, people are increasingly presented with an online alternative to the support from professionals, therapeutic groups organized by healthcare institutions, or from significant others (such as family, friends and colleagues): they can go online to seek help from people that face a similar situation, which has resulted in an exponential growth of online social support groups (Burleson *et al.* 1994; McKenna and Bargh 1998; Wright and Bell 2003). These online social support groups or *communities* have a number of features that potentially make them an appealing supplement or alternative for people who seek support (Rheingold 1993; Weinberg *et al.* 1995; Madara 1997; Braithwaite *et al.* 1999; Albrecht and Goldsmith 2003; Wright and Bell 2003).

What are online social support groups?

Online social support groups can take many forms. In its most simple form, such a group is organized around a list of email addresses that can be used to send messages to all the members on the list (sometimes automated by *listserver software*). In a more centralized form, people can subscribe to an electronic newsletter that contains information about a specific topic. However, the most common form in which people meet each other in order to exchange support online is via so-called *bulletin boards* or *discussion forums*. In these usenet or web-based discussion forums, members can contribute by posting messages that others can read, and if desired, respond to. So, the discussions have the form of *threads* that consist of reactions to previous postings, and members are free to start a new thread whenever they feel the need to do so. Contributions are stocked for a period of time and most forums offer the possibility to search through the list for a specific topic of interest. On these forums, active participation is not required and people can visit the forums without contributing to the discussion (people who do not contribute but only read postings are called *lurkers*) and on some forums newcomers are even advised not to contribute right away, and first get acquainted with the mode of conduct of the group. Web-forums are generally not under the supervision of healthcare professionals and are accessible to all visitors (even though registration is often required). Some forums are not moderated at all, and others have members (or administrators) that monitor the contributions and take action when inappropriate or irrelevant messages are posted.

All this makes these web-forums easy accessible locations where people can give and receive support and where people that are interested in the topic of the group can browse through the postings in an attempt to find the information they need. So these forums also provide the opportunity for people that do not need social support themselves but are close relatives or caregivers: for this group it is very easy to visit the web forum and read postings that can increase their level of understanding and knowledge about the specific situation the other is facing.

What is social support, and what is it good for?

Social support is a very broad concept that that comprises many qualitatively different kinds of support such as instrumental, informational or emotional assistance (House and Kahn 1985). It is impossible to find a generally accepted definition, but for the purpose of this article social support will be defined as the 'communication between recipients and providers that reduces uncertainty about the situation, the self, the other or the relationship and functions to enhance a perception of personal control in one's life experience' (Albrecht and Adelman 1987: 19). Thus, social support can be seen as a communication process that can help people manage and cope with uncertainty and thereby contribute to the wellbeing of (groups of) individuals. *Instrumental support* consists of providing goods or services and giving practical assistance with daily living, such as helping people out of bed, running errands, etc. Because of its *physical* character, this type of support will be less often come across in online social support groups. Therefore, the focus in this chapter will be mainly on how online support groups can provide informational and emotional support – forms of support that are found to be most common in online communities (Braithwaite *et al.* 1999; Finn 1999; Preece and Ghozati 2001).

Informational support concerns the exchange of practical information such as tips on new types of medication, relevant addresses of institutes, knowledge about medical or psychological treatments, legal issues, but also stories of first-hand or second-hand experiences by members. The primary function of this type of support is to expand one's knowledge-base (Reeves 2000). This type of support is important because it gives people more control over the situation and can reduce uncertainty about the self in such a way that better decisions can be made (Albrecht and Adelman 1987; Wright 2002).

Emotional support, on the other hand, refers to the display of understanding what the other person goes through and involves showing compassion and commitment (Albrecht and Adelman 1987; Albrecht and Goldsmith 2003). Thus, in emotional support, empathy plays a vital role: the ability of knowing what the other feels, feeling what the other feels, and responding to these feelings in an appropriate manner is what makes emotional support possible (Levenson and Ruef 1992: 234). This more affective form of support is characterized by comforting and encouraging interactions and can be highly important for the self-esteem of people (Reeves 2000). Emotional support is found to be especially relevant in situations where people feel they cannot change the situation they are in, but have to adapt to it (Albrecht and Adelman 1987; Wright 2000a). Providing emotional support can also imply giving people the opportunity to tell their story. Talking about painful or traumatic experiences, or disclosing personal information can have a therapeutic effect (Pennebaker 1997), and therefore to simply offer to listen to someone's story is a relatively passive, but nonetheless important form of social support. In particular in times of stress or distress, it can be comforting to be accompanied by others who are in the same or a similar situation (Davison *et al.* 2000), because part of the social and emotional problems that people endure stem from feelings of being misunderstood or cut off from society. Such perceptions can ultimately result in depression, loneliness, or alienation (Braithwaite *et al.* 1999).

Both of these forms of social support can contribute to the well-being of individuals. Social support is important for people who find themselves confronted with distress, (inter)personal problems or unwanted life situations

(Wills 1985; Taylor *et al.* 1986; House *et al.* 1988; Pennebaker and Harber 1993; Thoits 1995; Wright and Bell 2003). Research has shown that social support can reduce stress (e.g., Dean and Lin 1977; Cohen and Wills 1985; Buunk and Hoorens 1992; Thoits 1995), decrease depression (Cohen and Wills 1985), increase self-esteem (Metts and Manns 1996), increase internal control (Sullivan and Reardon 1985), and help people to more effectively cope with the situation (Sullivan and Reardon 1985; Kohn 1996). In addition, people who receive social support take better care of themselves than people who are socially isolated, and social support is positively correlated to an improved immune system, a reduced risk of particular illnesses (Cohen 1988), and longer life expectations (Cohen 1988; House *et al.* 1988).

There are generally two hypotheses of how social support may benefit the receiver. The first one posits that social support has a *direct effect* on well-being. This means that interpersonal contacts and being part of a larger social network have a straightforward effect on the welfare of others because it gives individuals the perception that they are appreciated by the community. Supportive interactions can contribute to general well-being because they clarify one's role in the community and provide a sense of predictability and stability in one's life situation (Cohen and Wills 1985; Thoits 1995; Wright 2000a). The second hypothesis posits that social support does not necessarily have a direct effect on well-being, but can mitigate the effect of stressful situations. In other words, social support can *buffer* the negative effects of stress and uncertainty that may arise from a multitude of causes, thereby reducing their impact on the physical and mental well-being of individuals (Dean and Lin 1977; Cohen and Wills 1985; House and Kahn 1985; Thoits 1995). Increasingly, both of these functions are met online, as will become apparent in the rest of this chapter.

Why social support via the Internet?

Given that the Internet has become integrated in everyday live (Bargh and McKenna 2004) and the communication of social support is an important part of interpersonal interaction, it is not surprising that much support is provided and received online. People can get in touch with others who are facing the same or a similar situation and can exchange informational or emotional support as they would like to do in an *offline* situation. Even though relationships are acquired in a different manner, in time some of them can become just as broad and deep as relationships that are formed offline (Walther 1992; Lea and Spears 1995; Parks and Floyd 1996). Nevertheless, interacting via the Internet has a number of characteristics that makes it fundamentally different from face-to-face communication (Rice and Gattiker 2001). The features of CMC can affect how people compose messages (Bordia 1997; Kiesler et al. 1984; Hancock and Dunham 2001), how they acquire and maintain relationships (Walther et al. 1994; Lea and Spears 1995; Parks and Floyd 1996; McKenna et al. 2002), and how groups are organized and structured (Hiltz and Turoff 1978; Fulk et al. 1996; Postmes et al. 1998; Spears, Lea, and Postmes 2001). Online support groups may therefore offer some unique characteristics compared to offline groups in that they allow anonymous participation, are text-based, and facilitate place and time independent interactions that offer possibilities to expand social networks. The potential consequences of each of these factors will be elaborated on in the next section.

Online support groups allow anonymous participation

CMC gives communicators the opportunity to remain anonymous if they wish to do so (Sproull and Kiesler 1991; Bordia 1997; Rice and Gattiker 2001). In most forums or chat rooms, people do not have to reveal their name or other personal information, and visitors are free to make use of pseudonyms or nicknames (Finn 1999). Not only do people not have to disclose their names, but the absence of cues that reveal information about one's identity (such as gender, age, appearance) is believed to enhance feelings of anonymity (Sproull and Kiesler 1986; Wallace 1999). The reduction of these cues can cause de-individuation (Sproull and Kiesler

1986), which is a state in which people lose their individuality because 'group members do not feel they stand out as individuals' and individuals act as if they are 'submerged in the group' (Postmes *et al.* [1998] for a review of relevant literature on effects of de-individuation). As stated by McKenna and Bargh (2000)

> when an individual posts an article in a newsgroup or enters a chat room full of strangers, he or she may well feel that his or her actions will be submerged in the hundreds (or thousands) of other actions taking place there.

> (2000: 60)

This perception of anonymity can have some consequences for the way people express themselves, and could partly be the explanation why online groups are characterized by such high levels of self-disclosure (Rheingold 1993; Parks and Floyd 1996; Wallace 1999; Wright 2000b; Joinson 2001; Swickert *et al.* 2002): 'Under the protective cloak of anonymity users can express the way they truly feel and think' (McKenna and Bargh 2000: 62).

Joinson (2001) found that people disclose more information about themselves in CMC compared to FtF interactions. A possible explanation for this is that the anonymity causes a reduction of public self-awareness and lowered feelings of accountability (Joinson 2001). This, combined with the private and safe location from which people engage in online interactions (sitting in front of a personal computer in the familiar environment of one's house) could be why people feel freer to express emotions and ask questions. The anonymity can provide the freedom to express oneself with less shame and without the feeling that one's privacy is violated, and affords people the means and power to ask intimate or potentially embarrassing questions they would not as easily ask in an offline context (Braithwaite *et al.* 1999; Wallace 1999).

Online support groups are text-based

Online support differs from offline support in that it is mainly text-based. Even though the visual and auditory options of the Internet increase (a number of forums offer the possibilities for webcams and audio), the lion's share of online interactions is in written form. Much of the early theorizing on mediated communication has predicted that this form of communication would be relatively cold, impersonal, and primarily task-focused because it is not capable of conveying non-verbal, social cues. This would make all forms of mediated communication inherently less suited for intimate interactions when compared to FtF communication (Kiesler *et al.* 1984; Hiltz *et al.* 1986; Connolly *et al.* 1990). However, this does not sit comfortably with the large number of individuals that voluntarily choose to open their heart, or engage in highly personal interactions by means of written text (a form of intimacy found in old-fashioned written correspondence as well as in personal disclosures on the Internet, and that is sustained even by the technically more limited means of text-messaging).

A possible answer to why people may choose to socially interact via a medium that is limited in its possibilities to convey non-verbal and social cues is provided by Walther's Social Information Processing (SIP) perspective (Walther 1992, 1996). According to SIP, people will adapt their linguistic and textual behaviours in an attempt to overcome the non-verbal limitations of CMC in such a way that the presentation of socially revealing and relational signals that may normally be conveyed through a variety of channels will now be communicated via text only. SIP thereby implies that CMC relationships can be as personal as FtF relations, given sufficient time. The reduction of non-verbal cues may even provide communicators with the possibility to present themselves in a more friendly, knowledgeable, emphatic way, because it gives them the opportunity to carefully shape their appearance, and enables selective self-presentation – a form of interaction that is referred to as *hyperpersonal* interaction (for detailed discussion of hyperpersonal interaction see Walther [1996] and Walther and Boyd [2002]). However, even though some work on hyperpersonality and social support exists (Walther and Boyd 2002; Wright and Bell 2003), more research is needed as to how this might affect the process of social support and the perceptions that are formed of support seekers and providers.

The text-based character of online social support may also have consequences on a completely different level: research by Pennebaker and colleagues has shown that writing about personal or emotional issues can positively affect mental and physical health (Pennebaker and Harber 1993; Pennebaker 1997; Pennebaker *et al.* 1997). Their findings suggest that the act of writing down feelings or experiences can be therapeutic in itself, because it causes cognitive changes: When disclosing personal feelings or traumatic experiences to others, individuals must narrate an understandable account of the situation. By doing so, they have to formulate a coherent and insightful explanation of the situation and their feelings, which provides them with more understanding of the situation they are in (Pennebaker *et al.* 1997). Furthermore, translating emotional experiences (such as traumas) in language seems more effective for the healing process than to express it in a different manner (Pennebaker and Harber 1993; Pennebaker 1997; Pennebaker *et al.* 1997; Miller and Gergen 1998).

Text-based interactions also afford people the opportunity to carefully compose and formulate their messages without having to worry about interruptions or immediate responses by others. This gives people the chance to reflect on messages before sending them to the group, which can be especially valuable when the topic of discussion is one that concerns highly sensitive or emotional issues (Weinberg *et al.* 1995; Walther 1996; Braithwaite *et al.* 1999). As a consequence the quality of interaction in online support groups might be higher than in their offline equivalents.

A more *practical* advantage of the text-based character is that people are valued for their contribution instead of on the basis of their physical appearance (Weinberg *et al.* 1995). This can be liberating, especially for people that see themselves confronted with prejudices based on age, sex or ethnicity in their offline life, but also for people that suffer from stigmatized physical characteristics such as obesity, a physical malformation, skin problems, etc. (Wallace 1999; Erwin *et al.* 2004). More directly, for people whose ability to speak or hear is affected or who have cognitive disabilities or other handicaps that cause them difficulty expressing themselves, text-based interactions can be highly liberating and empowering: compared with FtF interactions their potential to engage in social interaction is much greater online. Text-based online interaction enables them to participate in the same manner as the other members, and it provides them with equal opportunities to partake in the discussion (Nelson 1995; Braithwaite *et al.* 1999).

Online support groups offer possibilities to expand social networks

Probably the most prevalent reason why people participate in online communities is because it enables them to get into contact with others. Sitting in front of the computer, individuals can engage in social interactions with people all over the world who they may share some similarities with, or who potentially have understanding of their specific situation. Thereby, online communities can provide individual members with support and advice from a forum of 'experiential experts', unrestricted by geographical distance or time constraints (Finn and Lavitt 1994; Braithwaite *et al.* 1999; Rice and Katz 2001). The time- and space-independency provides members with the flexibility to post and read messages at times that suit them best and interact with others who live in other neighbourhoods, regions or even countries. In this way, online communities technically allow people to meet others who they would not be able to without the Internet. This might be especially helpful for people who have difficulties meeting others *in real life* because they live in geographically isolated parts of the world, are homebound because of disabilities that restrict their mobility, or because they have anxieties that cause them not to dare to leave their homes (Braithwaite *et al.* 1999; Finn 1999). Also for people who live in a social environment in which the needed support is not easily found, or feel ashamed, lonely, unique or misunderstood in the situation they are facing, participating in a virtual community can provide them with the opportunity to engage in social interaction in a manner less easily found offline.

It is, however, important to realize that online social support groups are not merely a palliative for people who are deprived of other social contacts. People who find themselves embedded in a close-knit social network may also benefit from online communities because online groups can provide them with forms of support that can be different from the support available in their offline network. The reason for this is that online communities are often structured around a central theme, and in these groups people will find others that are at least to a certain extent familiar with the topic to a higher degree then most likely encountered offline. As a consequence, there will be more perceived similarity in these groups, compared to one's offline network. At the same time however, there can be more variety in relations on a different dimension: one's offline social network exists to a large extent of kin, friends and colleagues, and these will also be the people one has to rely on when it comes to giving social support. So, offline social support will be predominantly provided by people with whom strong and long lasting relationships exist. Notwithstanding the fact that the online context allows for the development of relations as deep and valuable as offline relationships (Bargh *et al.* 2002; McKenna *et al.* 2002), at least part of the supportive interactions online will be with others with whom a more shallow and less strong contact exists, or even with total strangers. These contacts may show a large diversity in social, cultural or geographical background. As a side-effect of looking for others who are similar to the extent that they share an interest, online groups may very well show a larger diversity in the nature of relations, and the members of online groups may vary more in their background compared to most offline networks. In the following sections, the consequences of this perceived similarity on the one hand and variety of contacts on the other will be discussed.

Communities of perceived similar others

In online social support groups, people tend to meet others who find themselves in a similar situation, are faced by the same mental or physical deficiency, have gone through a similar traumatic experience, or at least share an interest in the topic of the group. So, in these groups people are among others who are to a certain extent alike. This perceived similarity, in combination with the ease of access to a large number of individuals that online communication affords, can provide a sense of universality and communality in online support communities that is not likely to be found offline (Madara 1997; Braithwaite *et al.* 1999; Wright 2000b; Preece and Ghozati 2001; Wright and Bell 2003). People who find themselves in a similar situation tend to be more empathic and show more understanding: 'the more similar we are the less we have to go outside of ourselves to gather cues and the more we can respond as we ourselves would naturally to the circumstances' (Hodger and Wegner 1997 in Preece and Ghozati 2001). As a consequence, research shows that in online support groups there is relatively little suspicion, and interactions are characterized by containing a low level of negative emotional remarks and a high level of emphatic communication (Finn 1999; Wallace 1999; Preece and Ghozati 2001). Finding similar others can be an important motivation for joining an online community because perceived similarity, and the feeling that one is part of a larger group, is part of the basic need *to belong*, which can be especially relevant for people who are lonely or isolated in their offline environment because they feel unique (Brewer 1991; Deaux 1993; McKenna and Bargh 1998).

The perceived similarity of other members of the online social group can even be increased by the anonymity of the online interactions. The absence of cues that give away information about the personal identity of the individuals who partake in the group can increase the attention to what binds the group together (i.e., a common interest or goal) and thereby engender strong feelings of 'groupiness' or cohesion (Postmes *et al.* 1998; Lea *et al.* 2001; Postmes *et al.* 2001; Tanis and Postmes, 2007). Based on the Social Identity model of Deindividuation Effects, or SIDE model (Spears and Lea 1992; Reicher *et al.* 1995) it can be argued that in online support communities where people recognize themselves and the others as sharing similarities on the basis of the situation they are facing, the absence of cues that might draw the attention to potential differences (such as age, gender, appearance, etc.) may even increase perceptions of similarity.

So, the less one knows about idiosyncratic characteristics of others in the group (i.e. the more anonymous the individual group members are), the less attention can be drawn to the (possible) interpersonal differences, and the more to the similarity based on the shared group membership (cf. Sassenberg and Postmes 2002). As a consequence, for online support groups that focus on a specific topic of concern, the inability to individuate its members may result in more perceived similarity (Sassenberg and Postmes 2002), more interpersonal trust (Tanis and Postmes 2005) and a stronger focus on the social norms of the group (Postmes *et al.* 2001). These groups can therefore have a vital function in learning people how to cope with the situation they are facing (Davison *et al.* 2000), and membership of groups like this can become an important part of one's self concept and self-definition (Bargh and McKenna 2004) as will be elaborated on below.

Social comparison

To participate in an online group can provide people with a sense of *belongingness* and helps people to realize they are not unique (Brewer 1991; Deaux 1993; McKenna and Bargh 1998). There is however a more instrumental function of being among similar others. People may use these groups to learn about how to behave and cope with the situation they are in. This assumption is supported by the research of Davison *et al.* (2000), which shows that people use online support communities for social comparison. Social comparison theory (Festinger 1954) posits that people will compare themselves with others in times of uncertainty or anxiety, especially in situations in which it is not possible to derive this from the direct environmental context. The need for social comparison is inherent to a physical or mental health setting, because of its high level of ambiguity and anxiety (Davison *et al.* 2000) and people may use the group to glean information on how to cope and behave. Social comparison is part and parcel of the process of social validation in which people use relevant groups they are part of to establish meaning, values and identity (see also Turner 1991). Importantly, social validation is best achieved when people can compare themselves with others that are relatively similar to them (and whose experiences are therefore diagnostic to the self). The availability of similar others makes online support groups a good stage for social comparison purposes.

There is however another reason why participating in this type of groups may benefit social comparison, which has to do with its online character. Research has shown that when the situation is humiliating or embarrassing, people do not want to be in the presence of others out of shame or loss of self-esteem (Sarnoff and Zimbardo 1961, as cited in Davison *et al.* 2000). Davison *et al.* (2000) show that people with conditions that they perceive as embarrassing, socially stigmatized, or disfiguring, do feel the need to seek support with similar others, but prefer to do this online. A tentative conclusion would be that because of the anonymity and the perception of privacy that online communities afford, joining online communities can be helpful for social comparison, especially when the situation is embarrassing or socially stigmatized.

De-marginalization and self-esteem

To be amongst others who face a similar situation, or at least have understanding of what someone is going through, can provide a sense of community and safety and make people feel less lonely and unique (King and Moreggi 1998). This can be especially relevant for people who suffer from a stigmatized physical or mental condition (such as obesity, stuttering, schizophrenia or manic depression) or who feel that an important part of their identity is not accepted by society (such as deviant sexual preferences, kleptomania, or extreme religious/political beliefs) because these people in particular run the risk of feeling lonely, not accepted, and cut off from society (Frable 1993; McKenna and Bargh 1998; Braithwaite *et al.* 1999; Davison *et al.* 2000). People who perceive themselves as outsiders or outliers because they differ from others on an important dimension of their identity – i.e., who have a *marginalized identity* (Frable 1993) – can have difficulties because they feel that they are deviant from the people in their social circle. For them, online social support groups can be an important place for meeting similar others, and to feel accepted and included in a social group.

Frable (1993) distinguishes between two forms of marginal identities: those that are conspicuous for others, and those that are concealable. People with visible or *conspicuous* marginal identities (for example people who suffer from obesity, skin conditions, mutilation, malformation or physical disabilities) can have a feeling that the first thing others notice about them is the part that is deviant from 'normal'. As a result, people can get the feeling that their social environment acts with uncertainty or awkwardly when they are present, which can ultimately lead to feelings of isolation and social exclusion (see Braithwaite *et al.* 1999). In online interaction (i.e. in the absence of visual cues) people can feel liberated from this burden, and feel valued on the basis of their written contributions and not on the basis of their extraordinary physical appearance (Weinberg *et al.* 1995).

The feeling of being unique can even be more acute for people who have *concealable* marginal identities (Frable 1993; McKenna and Bargh 1998). For them (who may have a venereal disease, multiple personality syndrome, deviant sexual preferences, extreme political beliefs, or a history as a prison inmate, for example) the chance of recognizing someone with a similar predicament is very small: 'those with hidden conditions are not able to see similar others in their environment, so there is no visible sign of others who share the stigmatized feature' (McKenna and Bargh 1998: 682). Especially when it concerns a stigmatized identity, it can be difficult to find support or understanding: it is not easy to take the first step in revealing stigmatized information about an important part of your identity, without knowing whether you can count on recognition or understanding. Because of the anonymity of interaction, online forums can make it easier to reveal hidden parts of one's personality, and the context increases the chance of meeting others that understand your situation.

Through participation in online social support communities, people with concealed as well as conspicuous marginal identities can attain more self-esteem and gain confidence with respect to their identity. According to McKenna and Bargh (1998), this can reduce the inner conflict between the marginalized part of the identity and the socially accepted standards, and eventually result in more openness to discuss this aspect of identity with significant others such as friends and family.

Heterogeneous networks

So, on the one hand online social support communities can be perceived of as more similar than most offline groups because the focus on a specific topic in combination with the lesser ability to *individuate* the members of online groups (at least compared to face-to-face groups) may lead to higher perceived similarity of its members. However, at the same time these groups consist of people who may very much differ in background (geographically, socially and culturally). Online networks are accessible for people who have different social or cultural backgrounds, come from different cities, regions or even countries, and may show great variations in age and education because they are not restricted by time or space boundaries and people can log in from any place at times that suit them best. So paradoxically, the fact that people select and join these groups because of the specific interest they share may result in a larger diversity in other personal characteristics than is typically encountered offline.

On a different dimension, online communities can also be more varied than one's offline group. This has to do with the *stability* of the relations within the network, and thereby with the composition of the network as a whole: individuals become a member of an online group out of their own accord, and visit the community because of its topic for as long as it is relevant to them. Thus, the only thing that binds the individuals together is topic of discussion and when someone's personal situation (and the reason for attending the group) changes, the online community may lose its relevance, and people will most likely stop attending the group. As a consequence, at least part of the network will exist of people who come and leave, making the online community more *fluid* compared to most offline networks who largely consist of more stable relationships such as relatives, friends and colleagues.

As opposed to one's offline social network that largely consists of people with whom strong and in general persisting relationships exist, part of the relations in online communities will be with people to whom one is not necessarily close (Adelman, Parks, and Albrecht 1987; Wright and Bell 2003). This can have an effect on the support that is provided in these groups. Whereas parents, partners, family, friends, and colleagues, or other close-by relatives predominantly provide support in the offline environment (Wills 1985), the chances are that in online support groups people will find useful support from relative strangers as well.

These so-called *weak ties* (Granovetter 1973) can play an important role in social support for a number of reasons. Even though strong ties with relevant others are very important for social support (Wills 1985; House *et al.* 1988; Thoits 1995; Cummings *et al.* 2002), research has shown that not only the quality of relations is important for people who face stressful situations, but also the size of one's social network (e.g., Dean and Lin 1977; Cohen and Wills 1985; Buunk and Hoorens 1992; Thoits 1995; Wright 2000a). Weak ties can play an important part in the well-being of people who seek support because an extended network may offer a large diversity of information (Granovetter 1973; Wellman 1997; Rice and Katz 2001), and weak ties may be able to provide support that strong ties can not (Granovetter 1973; Adelman *et al.* 1987; Albrecht and Adelman 1987; Thoits 1995; Wright and Bell 2003).

Varied information

Social networks that (partly) consist of weak ties can provide diverse information because they have the potential to be more heterogeneous sources of information than networks that consist of close ties only: weak tie relationships with members that are themselves embedded in other social communities can open up completely different sources of knowledge and information, and thereby offer more variety to the community (Wellman 1997). Therefore, one of the advantages of these online groups is that through these relations, information can be gathered that would otherwise not be available.

Social distance to partners

Another reason why weak ties might be beneficial is that they provide an opportunity for members to seek support and to talk about their situation without the risks that sometimes accompany talking to people who are close by (Thoits 1995; Wright and Bell 2003). In an offline situation, support is most often provided by significant others who are close to the individual (Wills 1985), and even though these people have an important function in supporting (House and Kahn 1985; Thoits 1995), these more or less obligatory relations can have negative consequences in that they may lead to expectations and demands that can cause stress by themselves (Thoits 1995).

People who are very close can push too hard, or anticipate seeing unrealistically swift improvements in the situation. These others can also be overprotective causing the individual to suffer under his or her perception of complete dependency. Another potential downside of receiving support from significant others may be that they can be inclined to give a verdict about the behaviour that is responsible for causing the situation: even though friends and family are close and bonds are strong, and despite their good intentions, they can sometimes be the first to judge (Wright and Bell 2003), especially when people find themselves in a situation for which they can be held responsible (for example HIV in relation to unsafe sex or intravenous use of drugs, cardiac disease in relation to not being able to give up smoking or drinking, financial problems in relation to a gambling addiction, etc.). Additionally, friends and family can have stronger role obligations that can result in listening to the problems not because they necessarily want to, but because they feel it is their duty to do so, which can be felt as a burden by the support seeker (Albrecht and Adelman 1987).

So it can be a relief to tell one's story to a relative stranger on the Internet where relations tend to be looser, chosen voluntarily and without strong reciprocal expectations (Thoits 1995), just as it can be comforting to open one's heart to a stranger on a train (Bargh and McKenna 2004). Another advantage of gaining support through weak ties has to do with the low risk in asking potentially embarrassing questions. According to Adelman et al. (1987) weak ties 'allow people to seek information and support without having to deal with the uncertainty of how those in primary [strong tie] relationships

might respond' (1987: 131), thereby facilitating 'low risk discussions about high-risk topics' (1987: 133).

What are the downsides of online social support groups?

As outlined, the relative anonymity, the text-based character and the possibility to expand one's social network holds potential benefits for people that seek support. At the same time we have to realize that exactly the features that may aid support seekers can cause for a number of negative outcomes as well.

It has often been argued that the relative anonymity that online communities afford their members may be responsible for the display of negative and anti-normative behaviour because of the reduced social control that online social support groups can exert over its members (Kiesler et al. 1984; Sproull and Kiesler 1986; Finn and Banach 2000). Even though meta-analyses and literature reviews suggest that it is probably not as prevalent as often assumed (Lea et al. 1992; Walther et al. 1994; Postmes and Spears 1998), disinhibited and hostile behaviour – often referred to as *flaming* – does seem to exist to a greater extent in online interactions compared to offline (Hiltz et al. 1986; Wallace 1999). If such messages do occur, or if ambiguous messages are interpreted as abusive in intent, people may feel offended or even emotionally abused, especially when they had presumed they were in a helping and supportive context (Finn and Banach 2000). The decreased *identifiability* of other participants may also lead to an increased risk of people sending intimidating messages, use someone's online identity to subscribe him or her to multiple online groups, or to gather various information that someone may have posted in forums in order to harass, threaten or intimidate a person online as well as offline (Finn and Banach 2000).

Even though little is known about the extent to which this so-called *cyberstalking* is taking place, it does present a potential concern for people who seek support in online communities, in particular when people find themselves in vulnerable or potentially embarrassing positions (Finn and Banach 2000). In the anonymous context of the online community, people might feel very comfortable in disclosing personal information without realizing that their contributions will be stored for an unknown period of time, and are easily accessible for everyone. People thereby run the risk of exposing more information than they actually planned to, and leave a *virtual trail* of information they might not want to be remembered of at a later stage or which others can misuse.

The quality and reliability of information that can be retrieved from online forums is also a potential point of concern. There is some limited empirical research that shows that the exchange of misinformation does occur in online social support groups, but in most instances other group members correct the misinformation (Finn and Lavitt 1994; Braithwaite *et al.* 1999). However, members may not read these corrections in time, and especially when people are in desperate need for a solution to their problems, the quality of information that is contributed to the group has to be taken seriously, particularly in groups that are not monitored by professionals or experts.

Another potential hazard that is often mentioned in literature concerns the risk that people become too dependent on their online community, and by doing so, neglect their offline network or delay to seek more traditional forms of support from family, friends or health-professionals (Madara 1997; Barak 1999; Bargh and McKenna 2004). Even though family and friends can be too demanding and overly protective (see Thoits 1995) they might be very important in providing assistance with adhering to health regimes (for instance 'forcing' people to take medication, to do their daily exercises, or refrain from taking drugs or alcohol) compared to the people one meets online who might have less control over such behaviour (Albrecht and Goldsmith 2003).

A final potential negative side-effect of spending much time among others who face a similar situation is that people can be reinforced in their belief that the situation they are in is hopeless, and that one has to come to terms with the situation instead of trying to improve it. Instead of finding ways of improving their situation, people can be reinforced in their beliefs that they are abnormal, that they have no prospect of improvement or emancipation, and because of that get caught in a vicious circle of feeling different from the people in their offline environment. Rather than using the online forum as a way of escaping their affliction or improving their situation, they may acquiesce and resign themselves to their fate. So, to be amongst like-minded others can lead to a less broad perspective on the situation, and close-mindedness or maybe even fatalism as a result.

It is, however, interesting to note that up until now, these negative outcomes are only rarely reported in empirical studies, even though these potential dangers are almost always addressed in introductions or discussions. There is no definite explanation for this. One of the reasons could be that most empirical studies make use of surveys or in-depth interviews and that people who experience negative effects stop participating in the group and therefore are not included in the sample (Eysenbach *et al.* 2004). Another reason could be that there is a publication bias, and research is more likely to be published when effects are positive due to a utopian belief among researchers or the publication outlet that technology is a force for good. It could even be the case that there are no wide-ranging negative consequences of participating in online support groups at all. This could be especially the case if people in general use the online communities as a supplement to their offline network, and not as a substitute. However, all this remains very speculative, and more research is necessary that specifically focuses these potentially negative consequences of online social support groups.

Conclusion

When looking at the literature on computer-mediated communication in general, and online social support groups specifically, conclusions are that online social support groups can form a valuable supplement to one's social network, and may be beneficial in providing people with the social support they seek. The anonymity that these groups provide offers opportunities for self-disclosure (Parks and Floyd 1996; Joinson 2001) and allows the asking of potentially embarrassing questions (Braithwaite *et al.* 1999; Wallace 1999) in a way that would be less easy in an offline context. The text-based type of interaction can work therapeutically in itself because it forces individuals to formulate a coherent story of their situation that can improve their understanding of it (Pennebaker *et al.* 1997; Miller and Gergen 1998). The written form also gives people the opportunity to carefully reflect on messages and compose reactions without having to worry about interruptions by others. Finally, online interactions are not restricted by geographical or time restraints and thereby enable people to get into contact with others that would otherwise never have been reached (Finn and Lavitt 1994; Braithwaite *et al.* 1999; Rice and Katz 2001). The online community can be a source of diverse information because they can partly consist of weak ties (Granovetter 1973; Wellman 1997), and these weak tie relationships can also offer support in a freer and less obligatory manner (Albrecht and Adelman 1987; Thoits 1995). The communities that emerge on the Internet can thereby provide its members the opportunity for social comparison (Davison *et al.* 2000) and help individuals to cope with their situation by increasing self-esteem and self-identity (McKenna and Bargh 1998).

In general, online support groups have a number of features that can make them a fruitful supplement for people who seek social support. Obviously, many of the capacities and strengths of online groups can also be associated with negative outcomes, and indeed with negative forms of support. Anonymity can potentially lead to hostile behaviour and abuse of trust, there is no guarantee with regard to the quality of the information, and to be amongst others that are in a similar situation might result in tunnel vision and a narrow-minded perspective on the situation at hand. However, more research is needed that focuses on these potentially negative consequences of online social support groups.

Another area that urgently requires more research is related to the physical and mental consequences of participation in these online groups. From the general literature on CMC we do know a fair amount about how the typical characteristics of CMC may affect interpersonal and group processes. We also know that characteristics such as perceived anonymity, the text-based type of interaction, and the possibilities it offers to get into contact with others are reasons why people may be drawn to online communities. But we know almost nothing about the health-related consequences of partaking in online social support communities in specific. A meta-analysis by Eysenbach *et al.* (2004) investigating the health benefits failed to find robust evidence that online support groups increase health. However, this analysis was based on too few studies to draw definite conclusions (Eysenbach *et al.* 2004: 1168), and future research must focus in more detail on how these groups affect people mentally as well as physically.

In order to be able to increase our knowledge about the actual impact of online social support groups on the mental and physical well-being of their users, it is time to go beyond speculating about their potential benefits and perils, and look more specifically at how the different types of support that can be found in online support groups affect the wellbeing of its members, and what variables affect this relationship. In order to answer this question, we have to understand what place online social support groups take in the lives of the people who make use of them and how they evaluate the support they encounter in these communities in relation to the support found offline. This will tell us more about the impact of online support on individuals, groups and the community as a whole and may provide us with some well-founded insights in the effects of these groups within the total array of (health related) support.

References

Adelman, M. B., Parks, M. R. and Albrecht, T. L. (1987). Beyond close relationships: support in weak ties. In T. L. Albrecht and M. B. Adelman (eds), *Communicating social support* (pp. 136-147). Newbury Park, CA: Sage.

Albrecht, T. L. and Adelman, M. B. (1987). Communicating social support: A theoretical perspective. In T. L. Albrecht and M. B. Adelman (eds), *Communicating social support* (pp. 18–39). Newbury Park, CA: Sage.

Albrecht, T. L. and Goldsmith, D. J. (2003). Social support, social networks and health. In T. L. Thompson, A. M. Dorsey, K. I. Miller and R. Parrott (eds), *Handbook of health communication* (pp. 263–284). Hillsdale, NJ: Erlbaum.

Barak, A. (1999). Psychological applications on the Internet: a discipline on the threshold of a new millennium. *Applied and Preventive Psychology* 8(4), 231–245.

Bargh, J. A. and McKenna, K. Y. A. (2004). The internet and social life. *Annual Review of Psychology 55*, 573–590.

Bargh, J. A., McKenna, K. Y. A. and Fitzsimons, G. M. (2002). Can you see the real me? Activation and expression of the 'true self' on the Internet. *Journal of Social Issues 58*(1), 33–48.

Bordia, P. (1997). Face-to-face versus computer-mediated communication: a synthesis of the experimental literature. *Journal of Business Communication 34*(1), 99–120.

Braithwaite, D. O., Waldron, V. R. and Finn, J. (1999). Communication of social support in computer-mediated groups for people with disabilities. *Health Communication 11*(2), 123–151.

Brewer, M. B. (1991). The social self: on being the same and different at the same time. *Personality and Social Psychology Bulletin 17*(5), 475–482.

Burleson, B. R., Albrecht, T. L. and Sarason, I. (1994). *Communication of social support: Messages, interactions, relationships and community.* Newbury Park, CA: Sage.

Buunk, B. P. and Hoorens, V. (1992). Social support and stress: the role of social comparison and social exchange processes. *British Journal of Clinical Psychology 31*(4), 445–457.

Cohen, S. (1988). Psychological models of the role of social support in the etiology of physical disease. *Health Psychology 7,* 269–297.

Cohen, S. and Syme, S. L. (1985). *Social support and health.* Orlando, FL: Academic Press, inc.

Cohen, S. and Wills, T. A. (1985). Stress, social support and the buffering hypothesis. *Psychological Bulletin 98*(2), 310–357.

Colvin, J., Chenoweth, L., Bold, M. and Harding, C. (2004). Caregivers of older adults: advantages and disadvantages of Internet-based social support. *Family Relations 53*(1), 49–57.

Connolly, T., Jessup, L. M. and Valacich, J. S. (1990). Effects of anonymity and evaluative tone on idea generation in computer-mediated groups. *Managemen Science 36*(6), 689–703.

Cummings, J. N., Sproull, L. and Kiesler, S. B. (2002). Beyond hearing: where real-world and online support meet. *Group Dynamics – Theory Research and Practice 6*(1), 78–88.

Davison, K. P., Pennebaker, J. W. and Dickerson, S. S. (2000). Who talks: the social psychology of illness support groups. *American Psychologist 55*(2), 205–217.

Dean, A. and Lin, N. (1977). The stress buffering role of social support: problems and prospects for systematic investigation. *Journal of Nervous and Mental Disease 165*(6), 403–417.

Deaux, K. (1993). Reconstructing social identity. *Personality and Social Psychology Bulletin 19*(1), 4–12.

Erwin, B. A., Turk, C. L., Heimberg, R. G., Fresco, D. M. and Hantula, D. A. (2004). The Internet: home to a severe population of individuals with social anxiety disorder? *Journal of Anxiety Disorders 18*(5), 629–646.

Eysenbach, G., Powell, J., Englesakis, M., Rizo, C. and Stern, A. (2004). Health-related virtual communities and electronic support groups: systematic review of the effects of online peer to peer interactions. *British Medical Journal 328*(7449), 1166–1170A.

Festinger, L. A. (1954). A theory of social comparison processes. *Human Relations 7,* 117–140.

Finn, J. (1999). An exploration of helping processes in an online self-help group focusing on issues of disability. *Health and Social Work 24*(3), 220–231.

Finn, J. and Banach, M. (2000). Victimization online: the down side of seeking human services for women on the Internet. *Cyberpsychology and Behavior 3*(2), 243–254.

Finn, J. and Lavitt, M. (1994). Computer-based self-help groups for sexual abuse survivors. *Social Work With Groups 24,* 220–240.

Frable, D. E. S. (1993). Being and feeling unique: statistical deviance and psychological marginality. *Journal of Personality 61*(1), 85–110.

Fulk, J., Flanagin, A. J., Kalman, M. E., Monge, P. R. and Ryan, T. (1996). Connective and communal public goods in interactive communication systems. *Communication Theory 6*(1), 60–87.

Granovetter, M. (1973). The strength of weak ties. *American Journal of Sociology 78,* 1360–1380.

Hancock, J. T. and Dunham, P. J. (2001). Impression formation in computer mediated communication revisited: an analysis of the breadth and intensity of impressions. *Communication Research 28*(3), 325–347.

Heany, C. A. and Israel, B. A. (1995). Social networks and social support. In K. Glanz, F. M. Lewis and B. K. Rimer (eds), *Health behavior and health education: Theory, research and practice,* 2nd edn (pp. 179–205). San Francisco, CA: Jossey-Bass.

Hiltz, R. S., Johnson, K. and Turoff, M. (1986). Experiments in group decision-making: communication process and outcome in face-to-face versus computerized conferences. *Human Communication Research 13,* 225–252.

Hiltz, S. R. and Turoff, M. (1978). *The network nation.* Cambridge, MA: MIT Press.

House, J. S. and Kahn, R. L. (1985). Measures and concepts of social support. In S. Cohen and S. L. Syme (eds), *Social support and health* (pp. 83–108). Orlando, FL: Academic Press.

House, J. S., Landis, K. R. and Umberson, D. (1988). Social relationships and health. *Science 241*(4865), 540–545.

Joinson, A. N. (2001). Self-disclosure in computer-mediated communication: the role of self-awareness and visual anonymity. *European Journal of Social Psychology 31,* 177–192.

Kiesler, S., Siegel, J. and McGuire, T. W. (1984). Social psychological aspects of computer-mediated communication. *American Psychologist 39,* 1123–1134.

King, S. A. and Moreggi, D. (1998). Internet therapy and self help groups – the pros and cons. In J. Gackenbach (ed.), *Psychology and the Internet. Intrapersonal, interpersonal and transpersonal implications* (pp. 77–106). San Diego, CA: Academic Press.

Kohn, P. M. (1996). On coping with daily hassles. In M. Zeidner and N. S. Endler (eds), *Handbook of coping* (pp. 181–201). New York: John Wiley and Sons, Inc.

Lea, M., O'Shea, T., Fung, P. and Spears, R. (1992). 'Flaming' in computer-mediated communication: observations, explanations, implications. In M. Lea (ed.), *Contexts of computer-mediated communication* (pp. 30–65). Hemel Hempstead, England: Harvester Wheatsheaf.

Lea, M. and Spears, R. (1995). Love at first byte? Building personal relationship over computer networks. In J. T. Wood and S. Duck (eds), *Under-studied relationships: Off the beaten track.* (pp. 197–233). Thousand Oaks, CA: Sage.

Lea, M., Spears, R. and de Groot, D. (2001). Knowing me, knowing you: anonymity effects on social identity processes within groups. *Personality and Social Psychology Bulletin 27*(5), 526–537.

Leffler, C. and Dembert, M. (1998). Posttraumatic stress symptoms among U. S. Navy divers recovering TWA flight 800. *Journal of Nervous and Mental Disorders 186,* 574–577.

Levenson, R. W. and Ruef, A. M. (1992). Empathy: a physiological substrate. *Journal of Personality and Social Psychology 63*(2), 234–246.

Madara, E. J. (1997). The mutual-aid self-help online revolution. *Social Policy 97*(3), 20–26.

McKenna, K. Y. A. and Bargh, J. A. (1998). Coming out in the age of the Internet: identity 'demarginalization' through virtual group participation. *Journal of Personality and Social Psychology 75*(3), 681–694.

McKenna, K. Y. A. and Bargh, J. A. (2000). Plan 9 from cyberspace: the implications of the internet for personality and social psychology. *Personality and Social Psychology Review 4,* 57–75.

McKenna, K. Y. A., Green, A. S. and Gleason, M. E. J. (2002). Relationship formation on the internet: what's the big attraction. *Journal of Social Issues 58*(1), 9–31.

Metts, S. and Manns, H. (1996). Coping with HIV and AIDS: the social and personal challenges. In E. B. Ray (ed.), *Communication and disenfranchisement: Social issues and implications* (pp. 347–364). Mahwah, NJ: Lawrence Erlbaum Associates.

Miller, J. K. and Gergen, K. J. (1998). Life on the line: the therapeutic potentials of computer-mediated conversation. *Journal of Marital and Family Therapy 24*(2), 189–202.

Nelson, J. A. (1995). The internet, the virtual community and those with disabilities. *Disability Quarterly 15*(2), 15–20.

Parks, M. R. and Floyd, K. (1996). Making friends in cyberspace. *Journal of Communication 46*(1), 80–97.

Pennebaker, J. W. (1997). Writing about emotional experiences as a therapeutic process. *Psychological Science 8*(3), 162–166.

Pennebaker, J. W. and Harber, K. D. (1993). A social stage model of collective coping: the Loma Prieta earthquake and the Persian Gulf War. *Journal of Social Issues 49*(4), 125–145.

Pennebaker, J. W., Mayne, T. J. and Francis, M. E. (1997). Linguistic predictors of adaptive bereavement. *Journal of Personality and Social Psychology 72*(4), 863–871.

Postmes, T. and Spears, R. (1998). Deindividuation and antinormative behavior: a meta-analysis. *Psychological Bulletin 123*(3), 238–259.

Postmes, T., Spears, R. and Lea, M. (1998). Breaching or building social boundaries? SIDE-effect of computer-mediated communication. *Communication Research 25*(6), 689–715.

Postmes, T., Spears, R., Sakhel, K. and de Groot, D. (2001). Social influence in computer-mediated communication: the effects of anonymity on group behavior. *Personality and Social Psychology Bulletin 27,* 1243–1254.

Preece, J. J. and Ghozati, K. (2001). Experiencing empathy online. In R. E. Rice and J. E. Katz (eds), *The internet and health communication* (pp. 237–260). Thousand Oaks, CA: Sage.

Reeves, P. M. (2000). Coping in cyberspace: the impact of Internet use on the ability of HIV-positive individuals to deal with their illness. *Journal of Health Communication 5,* 47–59.

Reicher, S., Spears, R. and Postmes, T. (1995). A social identity model of deindividuation phenomena. In W. Stroebe and M. Hewstone (eds), *European Review of Social Psychology*, vol. 6 (pp. 161-198). Chichester, England: Wiley.

Rheingold, H. (1993). *The virtual community: Homesteading on the electronic frontier.* Reading, MA: Addison-Wesley.

Rice, R. E. and Gattiker, U. E. (2001). New media and organizational structuring. In F. M. Jablin and L. L. Putnam (eds), *The new handbook of organizational communication* (pp. 544–581). Thousand Oaks, CA: Sage.

Rice, R. E. and Katz, J. E. (2001). *The internet and health communication: Experiences and expectations.* Thousand Oaks, CA: Sage.

Sassenberg, K. and Postmes, T. (2002). Cognitive and strategic processes in small groups: effects of anonymity of the self and anonymity of the group on social influence. *British Journal of Social Psychology 41,* 463–480.

Spears, R. and Lea, M. (1992). Social influence and the influence of the 'social' in computer-mediated communication. In M. Lea (ed.), *Contexts of computer-mediated communication* (pp. 30–65). Hemel Hempstead: Harvester Wheatsheaf.

Spears, R., Lea, M. and Postmes, T. (2001). Social psychological theories of computer-mediated communication: social gain or social pain? In H. Giles and P. Robinson (eds), *New handbook of language and social psychology* (pp. 601–624). New York: Wiley.

Sproull, L. and Kiesler, S. (1986). Reducing social context cues: electronic mail in organizational communication. *Management Science 32*(11), 1492–1512.

Sproull, L. and Kiesler, S. (1991). *Connections: New ways of working in the networked organization.* Cambridge, MA: The MIT Press.

Sullivan, C. F. and Reardon, K. K. (1985). Social support satisfaction and health locus of control: discriminators of breast cancer patients' style of coping. In M. L. McLaughlin (ed.), *Communication yearbook,* vol. 9 (pp. 707–722). Beverly Hills, CA: Sage.

Swickert, R. J., Hittner, J. B., Harris, J. L. and Herring, J. A. (2002). Relationships among Internet use, personality and social support. *Computers in Human Behavior 18*(4), 437–451.

Tanis, M. and Postmes, T. (2005). A social identity approach to trust: interpersonal perception, group membership and trusting behaviour. *European Journal of Social Psychology 35,* 413–424.

Tanis, M. and Postmes, T. (2007). Two faces of anonymity: paradoxical effects of cues to identity in CMC. *Computers in Human Behavior*, 23, 955–970.

Taylor, S. E., Falke, R. L., Shoptaw, S. J. and Lichtman, R. R. (1986). Social support, support groups and the cancer patient. *Journal of Consulting and Clinical Psychology* 54(5), 608–615.

Thoits, P. A. (1995). Stress, coping and social support: where are we? What next. *Journal of Health and Social Behavior 35*, 53–79.

Turner, J. C. (1991). *Social influence*. Milton Keynes: Open University Press.

Uchino, B. N., Cacioppo, J. T. and Kiecolt-Glaser, J. K. (1996). The relationship between social support and psychological processes: a review with emphasis on underlying mechanisms and implications for health. *Psychological Bulletin 119*(3), 488–531.

Wallace, P. (1999). *The psychology of the internet*. Cambridge: Cambridge University Press.

Walther, J. B. (1992). Interpersonal effects in computer-mediated interaction: a relational perspective. *Communication Research 19*(1), 52–90.

Walther, J. B. (1996). Computer-mediated communication: Impersonal, interpersonal and hyperpersonal interaction. *Communication Research 23*(1), 3–43.

Walther, J. B., Anderson, J. F. and Park, D. W. (1994). Interpersonal effects in computer-mediated interaction: a meta-analysis of social and antisocial communication. *Communication Research 21*(4), 460–487.

Walther, J. B. and Boyd, S. (2002). Attraction to computer-mediated social support. In C. A. Lin and D. J. Atkin (eds), *Communication technology and society: Audience adoption and uses* (pp. 153–188). Cresskill, NJ: Hampton Press.

Weinberg, N., Schmale, J., Uken, J. and Wessel, K. (1995). Computer-mediated support groups. *Social Work With Groups 17*, 43–54.

Wellman, B. (1997). An electronic group is virtually a social network. In S. Kiesler (ed.), *Culture of the Internet* (pp. 179–205). Mahwah, NJ: Lawrence Erlbaum.

Wills, T. A. (1985). Supportive functions of interpersonal relationships. In S. Cohen and S. L. Syme (eds), *Social support and health* (pp. 61–82). New York: Academic Press.

Wright, K. B. (2000a). Computer-mediated social support, older adults and coping. *Journal of Communication 50*(3), 100–118.

Wright, K. B. (2000b). Perceptions of on-line support providers: an examination of perceived homophily, source credibility, communication and social support within on-line support groups. *Communication Quarterly 48*, 44–59.

Wright, K. B. (2002). Social support within an on-line cancer community: an assessment of emotional support, perceptions of advantages and disadvantages and motives for using the community from a communication perspective. *Journal of Applied Communication Research 30*(3), 195–209.

Wright, K. B. and Bell, S. B. (2003). Health-related support groups on the Internet: linking empirical findings to social support and computer-mediated communication theory. *Journal of Health Psychology 8*(1), 39–54.

CHAPTER 11

Psychology, discrimination and hate groups online

Karen M. Douglas

Hate – an emotion of extreme dislike or aversion; detestation, abhorrence, hatred.

(*Oxford English Dictionary*)

Love, friendship, respect do not unite people as much as common hatred for something.

(Anton Chekhov 1860–1904: *Notebooks*, 1921)

Introduction

When I began studying the social psychology of online behaviour for my Ph.D. back in 1996, I found only a handful of websites advocating hate towards groups on the basis of race, religious beliefs, ethnicity, gender or sexual orientation. Of those that did exist, most were racist hate sites. However, as a new user to the Internet, I was both shocked and fascinated by the sites I did find, and this interest largely provided me with the motivation for my research into the nature and purpose of online hate sites, and people's reactions and responses to this phenomenon called *cyberhate*. Several years on, I still remain shocked and surprised, but for other reasons in addition to the prejudiced content of these websites. First, I am amazed by their sheer number. An examination of *The Hate Directory* (http://www.bcpl.net/~rfrankli/hatedir.pdf) revealed that on 15 April 2006, there were over 2300 websites advocating hate towards a particular social group. This has increased from a figure of around 1500 listed in the

2005 version of the directory, and approximately 400 listed in the 1999 version of the directory.

Second, I am surprised by the diversity of online methods used by hate groups. *The Hate Directory* lists websites (WWW), file archives (FTP), web logs (blogs), mailing lists (LISTSERV), newsgroups (USENET), Internet relay chat (IRC), clubs and groups in various Internet communities (e.g., Yahoo and MSN) and web rings. Hate messages are extremely far-reaching across users and usage of the Internet. Given the ever-growing number of users, the Internet is therefore a powerful forum whereby hate groups can broadcast their views (Beckles 1997; Zickmund 1997; Leets 2001;). It is also fast, inexpensive and easy to use (Whine 1997; Perry 2000). In a medium where an email 'spam' message or joke can cross the world in a matter of hours, a posting to an Internet message board can reach thousands of users as soon as it is posted, and people can publish their own web pages which in principle can be accessed by anyone with Internet access, the Internet provides hate groups with a powerful means of reaching many more people than could ever be reached by other means. Indeed, before the advent of the Internet, many extremists worked in relative isolation and were forced to make a great effort to connect with others who shared their ideology (Anti-Defamation League 2005). This can now be achieved with the click of a button.

The proliferation of online hate groups over the past few years has brought two main issues into focus. First, legal and political scholars have questioned the extent to which such hate speech should be regulated (Zickmund 1997; Leets 2001; Levin 2002). According to the First Amendment to the Constitution of the USA, speech may not be penalized simply because its content is overtly prejudiced against a particular social group. However, laws relating to the policing of Internet crime in the USA are constantly changing. As such, it is unclear how current laws should apply to hate expressed online in the USA, and online hate groups presently have a substantial amount of freedom to express their views. Making matters much worse is the fact that the Internet is an international forum and no two countries' laws are exactly the same. For example, Leets (2001) observed that in France, Germany, Sweden and Canada, there are national laws criminalizing racist hate messages. Under these laws, hate sites are subject to prosecution and can be closed down. If hate sites are to be regulated worldwide, however, countries need first to be in agreement that this is appropriate. Then, nations would need to agree on the guidelines for doing so. All things being ideal, policing cyberhate would then still be very difficult. Indeed, Siegel (1999) argues that European and Canadian laws designed to combat cyberhate have been largely ineffectual. Many organizations based outside the USA use American-based websites to broadcast their views due to the more relaxed laws in the USA (Gerstenfeld *et al.* 2003). Prosecution of online hate speech is therefore extremely problematic.

Second, and perhaps more importantly, there is a great deal of concern about the *effects* of hate expressed online – specifically, if it incites violence and hostility between groups in the physical world. While violent actions against groups based on racial grounds, for example, are illegal, the speech to incite such actions may not necessarily be illegal and may remain protected as free speech. However, speech that advocates violence may encourage such actions. Therefore, theorists in the USA have argued that hate rhetoric and hate speech may lie at the border of protection by the First Amendment when its long-term and indirect effects are considered (Zickmund 1997; Leets 2001; Levin 2002).

Understanding cyberhate therefore provides an important challenge for psychologists. Specifically, it is important to understand why online hate is so widespread and the content of online hate sites often so insulting and aggressive given that the physical activities of hate groups are much more covert. In this chapter, I attempt to provide a psychological perspective on the nature and purpose of online hate groups and their underlying motivations, their strategies, psychological theories and research that provides insight into disinhibited online behaviour, the actions being taken to combat cyberhate, and some challenges for future research.

The nature and purpose of online hate groups

The general overarching feature of online extremist groups is that they express *hate* towards other groups. In words taken from *The Hate Directory*, they 'advocate violence against, separation from, defamation of, deception about or hostility towards others' (p. 2) based on one or more social group memberships. Online hate groups achieve this by presenting themselves in a variety of different ways. For example, many White-power and White-pride websites sell their merchandise (e.g., racially intolerant music and clothing with White-power symbols and other racist symbols such as swastikas, see Micetrap Distribution, http://www.micetrap.net); others include mission statements with information and religious and scientific statements supporting views on White superiority (e.g., White Camelia Knights http://www.wckkkk.com/index2.html). Others promote activities such as protests and action rallies in the real world (e.g., Knights of the Ku Klux Klan, http://www.kkk.bz), but fewer promote more extreme violent activities. A recent review of 43 White-power websites (Douglas *et al.* 2005) revealed that only 16 per cent of websites mentioned endorsement of violent activities, but 37, 21 and 11 per cent used divine, scientific and social scientific justifications, respectively, to argue for White superiority.

Other non-racially motivated hate websites are similar in their overall appearance and activities. For example, God Hates Fags (http://www.godhatesfags.com) is an extreme anti-gay website that uses excerpts from the bible and other arguably reputable sources to make arguments against legalization of gay sex and arguments against pro-gay laws in countries like Sweden. As another example, one anti-Semitic website (Jewish Conspiracies, http://www.adlusa.com/voteforusa/jewishconspiracies/) uses political arguments and reference to historical events to express hate against Jewish people in the United States. The overall appearance and activities of online hate groups are quite similar, despite a wide range of groups who are the targets of the prejudice.

Why do these sites exist? What is their purpose? The answer to this question depends largely on who the hate groups focus on as their target audience. One argument is that online hate sites allow individuals to seek solidarity with other like-minded individuals who would not otherwise take action against other groups (e.g., Lee and Leets 2002; Levin 2002; Gerstenfeld et al. 2003). Expressing strong nationalist views, for example, would ordinarily be difficult in everyday terms because of the social undesirability or political incorrectness of expressing such prejudiced views. In much in the same way as the Internet is said to be liberating for people who are members of marginalized groups, for example gays (McKenna and Bargh 1998) and for people with interests that society generally deems to be deviant (e.g., Back 2002), so too the Internet provides those who have socially undesirable views with an outlet for their opinions and frustrations. This argument is supported in research by Gerstenfeld et al. (2003), where a review of 157 extremist websites revealed that over 80 per cent of these sites contained links to other external sites espousing similar viewpoints, and over 50 per cent contained links to international organizations. There is some evidence, therefore, that extremist groups use the Internet as a way of linking people with similar views, often permitting small and diverse groups to link together to form larger groups with a collective identity and common purpose (see also Schafer 2002). Using the Internet, hate groups can let others know that they are not alone in holding their views, and convince them that their views are not extreme at all (Gerstenfeld, et al. 2003).

Along the same lines, the Internet allows people running online hate sites to recruit new members, some of whom may already be peripheral group members, 'into the fold' giving groups the opportunity to build and grow into a community (e.g., Levin 2002; Douglas et al. 2005). For example, some websites explicitly ask people to help their group grow by applying for membership, donating money and participating in activities such as demonstrations and protests (e.g., The Knights' Party, http://www.christianconcepts.net/informat.htm). Gerstenfeld et al.'s (2003) analysis revealed that over 30% of sites included membership forms and offered bulletin boards and mailing lists for interested people. Also, Douglas et al.'s (2005) review of White supremacist websites showed that, of the websites surveyed, 51% were of online communities that claimed to be active on the Internet and in other domains. So, over half of the websites surveyed in this analysis were the work of many people and not simply disgruntled, unaffiliated individuals. Gerstenfeld et al.'s (2003) analysis suggested that this percentage of supposed online communities may be even higher amongst general extremist websites. Of the websites sampled in this analysis, which included White-power, Holocaust denial, Christian identity and neo-Nazi websites, over 90% were purportedly the work of more than one individual.

Another view on the purpose of hate sites is that they are a public face to counteract negative views of real physical groups such as the Ku Klux Klan and to control their public image (Gerstenfeld et al. 2003). Many of the sites have impressively professional features and look attractive, making them more appealing to the visitor. Some websites have statements and 'frequently answered questions' sections devoted to 'educating' people about the history and ethos of their organization. For example, the website run by the Knights of the Ku Klux Klan states that 'those who want to associate with the Klan because they believe the Klan will be fertile ground to promote their hatred toward Negroes quickly learn the Klan is based on LOVE and not hate!' Again, this kind of statement may be part of a greater goal to recruit new members and expand the organization, but it is clear that the Internet also creates a platform for these groups to inform those who do not know much about the organization that they are not all bad. Using this global medium, online hate groups are able to promote a more positive image of themselves and other groups like themselves.

Interestingly, some websites contain pages providing information designed for children (for example one of the very first extremist websites called Stormfront, http://www.kids.stormfront.org/, and a Ku Klux Klan site, http://www.kkk.bz/just_for_kids.htm). Here, the groups provide information about themselves typically for the purpose of helping children with their school projects. Also, children who are members of these groups offer information and advice to other children, and often invite other children to get involved in the groups. Indeed, many sites argue that the main way for their organizations to grow is to recruit individuals while they are young. Research does show that many racist websites target their efforts at young people (Blazak 2001; Turpin-Petrosino 2002). Also, many nationalist websites have links to racially violent games, arguably targeted at younger individuals (Back 2002). The Internet provides a unique opportunity for hate groups to appeal to young people due to the appeal of the Internet to youths worldwide (Perry 2000).

In summary, the main objectives of online hate groups appear to be to link, educate and recruit. Many sites are aimed at the wider community, including children, while many appear to have like-minded individuals as their primary target. To broadcast their message, sell their merchandise and recruit new members, online hate groups need to be position themselves as effective champions of their cause. In the next section of this chapter, I outline *why* the Internet provides hate groups with the ideal opportunity to express their hate towards other groups. I also overview some social psychological research that explores *how* online hate groups achieve their aims.

The *whys* and *hows* of cyberhate

It is interesting to note that the Ku Klux Klan (KKK) is 'showing some revitalisation through the World Wide Web' (Leets 2001: 292). After periods of growth during times of social and economic discontent such as post-Civil War times and the Depression, but a steady loss of appeal in the KKK in the decades after WWII, there has been a resurgence in interest and appeal of the organization with the rise in popularity of the Internet. It is also interesting to note that Ku Klux Klan websites are considered amongst the most hateful on the Internet (Gerstenfeld *et al.* 2003). So what makes the Internet the ideal vehicle for such groups? One theory is that the ease of publishing one's views *anonymously* and without accountability makes the expression of cyberhate very easy for hate groups.

There is a wealth of social psychological literature examining the consequences of anonymity for online behaviour. Many studies of computer-mediated communication (CMC) have focused on the medium's anonymity and on the hypothesis that communication via computers is different than other modes of communication. This idea has been explored extensively in a variety of settings since the very beginnings of CMC, such as work-related behaviour (e.g., Siegel *et al.* 1986; Sproull and Kiesler 1986), the development of online relationships (e.g., van Gelder 1985; Lea and Spears 1995), and the high levels of hostile, disinhibited or *flaming* behaviour witnessed over computer networks (e.g., Kiesler *et al.* 1984; Lea, O'Shea, Fung and Spears 1992; Douglas and McGarty 2001, 2002). The general argument that communication over the Internet is disinhibited stems from the idea that anonymous behaviour releases people from constraints that would normally keep behaviour regulated and in line with societal norms and standards. This concept of deindividuation (Zimbardo 1969; Diener 1980) means that people are able to get away with bad behaviour because they do not need to answer for it. Although there is little support for the idea that anonymity on its own increases flaming or anti-normative behaviour (see Lea *et al.* 1992; Walther *et al.* 1994; Postmes and Spears 1998), the belief that anonymity has these effects is widespread. It is therefore unsurprising that the Internet is perceived to be the ideal medium for extremist groups (e.g., Back 2002). They can broadcast their views and promote themselves without the accountability that a face-to-face speech or campaign would entail.

However, there are potentially other reasons why the choice to be anonymous or identifiable on the Internet may encourage the proliferation of extremist groups. The social identity model of deindividuation effects (SIDE) (Spears and Lea 1994; Reicher, Spears and Postmes 1995) proposes that anonymity can facilitate the enactment of social identity. Rather than proposing that anonymity always leads to chaos and deregulated behaviour, Spears and Lea (1994) proposed that anonymity of the self to a powerful audience may be liberating in another way – anonymous communicators need not feel pressured to conform to the norms and expectations of the group (see also Reicher and Levine 1994a, b), but may enact other aspects of their identity that the group would normally deem unacceptable. There is therefore more purpose to anonymous behaviour than previous theories might suggest. Following this rationale, if extremist groups perceive their target audience as an outgroup, they would perhaps be likely to choose to express their views anonymously. However, the SIDE model also proposes that *identifiability* can facilitate the enactment of identity when the intended audience is an ingroup audience. In this case, the support provided by the presence of like-minded others can lead to heightened expression of ingroup normative views (see also Reicher *et al.* 1998; Douglas and McGarty 2001, 2002). Therefore, perhaps those extremists who perceive their audience to be other like-minded individuals and group members, would most effectively express their views having chosen to do so identifiably. Overall therefore, the Internet provides people with a choice to either identify themselves or not, wherever and whenever they feel this is opportune, and this freedom may facilitate the expression of their identity to both opponents and like-minded individuals and groups.

Now that we have some idea *why* the Internet is useful to extremist groups, it is important to know *how* these groups express their hate. What strategies do they use to promote themselves and recruit new members? McDonald (1999) content analysed 30 websites belonging to racist/nationalist hate groups. The websites were coded for the use of several persuasive techniques (i.e., warnings, disclaimers, objectives/purposes, social approaches, and more sophisticated counterargument strategies), and technical aspects such as global/local links and word counts. The analysis revealed that the most prevalent persuasive technique was the objective approach of stating the views of the group in a neutral manner, without insults or advocated violence. Thirty-seven per cent of the sites analysed employed this technique. This is interesting because this

strategy allows groups to appear rational and balanced. As McDonald notes, this sophisticated persuasive technique may not persuade many people to advocate the groups' viewpoints, or become racist themselves, but clearly does not dissuade people from their viewpoints. It is also another way of maintaining a good public image of the group.

A recent review by Douglas *et al.* (2005) examined the strategies that 43 online White-supremacist groups use to achieve their goals of self-promotion and recruitment. Drawing on social identity theory, this research started from the premise that White-power groups feel superior to other groups but also feel in an insecure position due to the threat posed by other groups (Green *et al.* 1999). As the self-defined high-status group, White-supremacists have a number of self-promotion and self-enhancement strategies available to them that enable them to sell their products, spread their views, and recruit new White-supremacists to continue their cause effectively. Douglas and colleagues (2005) drew on Haslam's (2001) interpretation of social identity theory (SIT) (Tajfel and Turner 1979) which states that groups can adopt different self-enhancement strategies depending on their status, the permeability of group boundaries (i.e., the extent to which people are able to move freely between groups) and the security of relations among groups. For White-power groups, the threat from outgroups (i.e., non-Whites) is the main reason for their very existence, and Haslam's reading of SIT would predict overt racism, advocated conflict and hostility under these conditions.

However, surprisingly, Douglas *et al.* (2005) did not find strong evidence of advocated conflict, and especially little advocacy of violence, in White-supremacist websites. Instead, these groups used more *socially creative* strategies that redefine or alter the elements of the comparative situation without being overtly conflictual or hostile. In other words, White-supremacist websites appear to attempt to get their messages across by using persuasive arguments in favour of White-superiority, and supremacist ideologizing that attempts to justify the position of Whites over non-Whites. They typically do not advocate violence. Of course, it is not surprising that White-supremacist websites advocated less violence than other forms of conflict and social creativity. However, the fact that very little violence was advocated over all, in what we call 'hate' sites, is quite surprising. This research suggests instead that legal, economic and social grounds for conflict, and socially creative arguments, are White-supremacists' main tools of persuasion.

It is important to consider the usefulness of social creativity strategies for hate groups in general. Social creativity may serve the function of helping to create conflict by making the ingroup (usually Whites) feel disadvantaged. An excellent example of this strategy in action is in Holocaust denial sites. These sites do not, in general, advocate violence against Jews. Instead, they challenge the accuracy of historical claims and suggest that Jews either invented these claims or even that they committed the violent acts themselves. The power of this tactic is that it serves to redefine Jews who survived the Holocaust from being victims worthy of sympathy to violent perpetrators of horrific crimes – or just plain liars.

Combatting cyberhate

So, what can people do about cyberhate? At least in the United States, options for shutting down hate sites are limited because of the protection of freedom of expression provided by the First Amendment. People are generally permitted to express their views openly, provided they do not explicitly encourage violence. However, many websites are rightly closed down because they explicitly incite violence towards groups and others are simply sabotaged by well-meaning individuals (Leets 2001). One has to question the usefulness of this latter strategy, however. Censorship of information on the Internet, while arguably positively intentioned, creates problems.

First, it contradicts the deeply entrenched view that the Internet is a medium where information can flow freely and any type of information is immediately accessible. This is a characteristic that many believe to be an essential feature of the medium that should not be violated. In other words, when well-intentioned individuals sabotage hate sites, it is appropriate that they are essentially determining what people can and cannot see? Also, even if it was deemed appropriate, out of the hundreds of hate websites on line at any given time, how would it possible to weed out the ones that are unacceptable? What would be the criteria for them to be deemed unacceptable? Of course, these are questions that are impossible to answer, but they highlight the problematic nature of censoring hate material on the Web.

Second, people may feel that they are doing so to protect vulnerable others from the influence of such material when this is in fact a misconception: people assume that others are more susceptible to persuasive media than themselves – the so-called 'third-person' effect (Davison 1983), but instead of over-estimating the influence it has on others, they simply underestimate the influence it has on themselves (Douglas and Sutton 2004). Censorship therefore, is probably not the answer and may indeed make hate groups more determined to expand their horizons.

As an alternative to censorship or bans, a handful of anti-hate activists are using the Internet to expose hate and discrimination online. In the same way that the Internet is a powerful tool for online hate groups to spread their views, sell their products and recruit new members, it can also be powerful in exposing the flaws behind racist, sexist or generally prejudiced attitudes. By monitoring the hate, it is also possible to 'know one's enemy' and keep an eye on their statements and activities. Most of these websites, such as Hatewatch (http://www.splcenter.org/intel/hatewatch/) and The Nizkor Project (http://www.nizkor.org) are primarily concerned with the actions of physical hate groups, some of which have a presence of the Internet, and others such as *The Hate Directory* itself are primarily concerned with exposing and increasing awareness of hate expressed online. However, it is interesting to note that in comparison to over 2300 sites advocating hate on the Internet as listed on *The Hate Directory* in 2006, there are only 25 similar sites listed with an explicit aim to combat hate.

Future research and conclusions

One very important question that remains relatively unanswered is the question of the direct consequences of online hate messages. That is, do these sites really meet their aims of self-promotion, linking with other groups, education and recruitment? One study by Turpin-Petrosino (2002) showed that the efficacy of extremist websites to recruit new, young members, was not clear. Out of 567 youths sampled, only 10 reported having Internet contacts with White-supremacist groups and only four reported supporting them. Instead, greater support was associated with more traditional media such as word-of-mouth and printed matter. However, Gerstenfeld *et al.* (2003) argued that youths may be visiting hate websites and may simply not be aware that they are extremist. As such, they may not realize that they are being influenced by the content of the sites. Again, people may generally be unaware of the influence that persuasive media have on themselves while predicting a substantial influence on others, so Internet hate sites may indeed be a more powerful influence on attitudes than self-report data may suggest (Douglas and Sutton 2004).

Lee and Leets (2002) examined the effectiveness of persuasive narrative techniques used by online hate groups. Adolescent participants were exposed to hate material with either high or low narrative content, and either explicit or implicit arguments. Measuring attitudes before and after exposure to these messages, Lee and Leets found that websites with high narrative content and implicit arguments were the most immediately persuasive. However, this persuasion did not stay stable, suggesting that the more sophisticated, 'sugar-coated' message is perhaps not as effective as is intentioned. Research in this area is clearly important but is rather limited. Assessing the direct effects of hate sites therefore provides an important challenge for future research.

Another important question relates to the nature of the people who visit hate sites. Because Internet users largely self-select which sites to visit, it may be that only existing extremists, monitors of hate sites or people conducting research (Back 2002) visit the sites. If this is the case, then the administrators of such sites may not be recruiting new members – instead they may just be signing on people who already agree with them. Further, Internet 'firewalls' and 'Net nannies' may prevent extremists from gaining the attention of young people and children, as many clearly aim to do. Examining the visitors to online hate sites would therefore provide a useful indication of the potential effectiveness of such sites.

Another issue for future research might be to examine the impact that world events have on extremist speech online (Gerstenfeld *et al.* 2003). For example, following the devastating Asian Tsunami in December 2004, the God Hates Fags website advocated the view that the disaster was 'God's wrath' against American and particularly European sex tourists to places such as Thailand. Following the 11 September attack on the World Trade Center, many hate sites contained reports of Jewish and/or Israeli conspiracies related to the event. What sort of impact does this type of discourse have? Are these forms of cyberhate merely old messages with a convenient new vehicle with which to express them? Does the content of cyberhate change with changing international relations and world events? Also, what effects do these changes have on the impact of hate websites, such as recruitment of new members? In the past, American society has seen fluctuations in activity of the Ku Klux Klan related to periods of societal tension (Leets 2001). Might this also be the case with relation to particular world events and the expansion of the World Wide Web?

Online prejudice and hate provide both an interesting and difficult challenge for researchers. It is clear that the Internet is a powerful tool for hate groups to express their views and attempt to recruit new members to their cause, and understanding why and how this is done is important in gaining an understanding of the groups themselves. In this chapter, I hope to have shed a light on some of these issues. As the Internet is constantly expanding and changing dramatically, perhaps the greatest challenge for researchers in understanding cyberhate will be to keep up with these changes.

References

Anti-Defamation League (2005). *Poisoning the Web: Hatred online.* Retrieved March 23 2005, from http://www.adl.org/poisoning_web/net_hate_tool.asp.

Back, L. (2002). Aryans reading Adorno: cyber-culture and twenty-first century racism. *Ethnic and Racial Studies 25,* 628–651.

Beckles, C. (1997). Black struggles in cyberspace: cyber-segregation and cyber-Nazis. *Western Journal of Black Studies 21,* 12–19.

Blazak, R. (2001). White boys to terrorist men: target recruitment of Nazi skinheads. *American Behavioral Scientist 44,* 982–1000.

Davison, W. P. (1983). The third-person effect in communication. *Public Opinion Quarterly, 47,* 1–15.

Deiner, E. (1980). Deindividuation: the absence of self-awareness and self regulation in group members. In P. Paulus (ed.), *The psychology of group influence.* (pp. 1160–1171) Hillsdale, NJ: Erlbaum.

Douglas, K. M. and McGarty, C. (2001). Identifiability and self-presentation: computer-mediated communication and intergroup interaction. *British Journal of Social Psychology 40,* 399–416.

Douglas, K. M. and McGarty, C. (2002). Internet identifiability and beyond: A model of the effects of identifiability on communicative behavior. *Group Dynamics 6,* 17–26.

Douglas, K. M., McGarty, C., Bliuc, A. M. and Lala, G. (2005). Understanding cyberhate: social competition and social creativity in online White supremacist groups. *Social Science Computer Review 23,* 68–76.

Douglas, K. M. and Sutton, R. M. (2004). Right about others, wrong about ourselves? Actual and perceived self-other differences in resistance to persuasion. *British Journal of Social Psychology 43,* 585–603.

Gerstenfeld, P. B., Grant, D. R. and Chiang, C. P. (2003). Hate online: a content analysis of extremist internet sites. *Analyses of Social Issues and Public Policy 3,* 29–44.

God Hates Fags (2005). Retrieved on 29 March 2005, from http://www.gothatesfags.com.

Green, D. P., Abelson, R. P. and Garnett, M. (1999). The distinctive political views of hate-crime perpetrators and white supremacists. In D. A. Prentice, D. T. Miller (eds), *Cultural divides: Understanding and overcoming group conflict.* (pp. 429–464). New York: Russell Sage Foundation.

Haslam, S. A. (2001). *Psychology in organizations: The social identity approach.* London: Sage.

Hatewatch (2005). Retrieved on 23 March 2005 from *http://www.splcenter.org/intel/hatewatch/.*

Jewish Conspiracies (2005). Retrieved on 20 March 2005 from http://www.adlusa.con/voteforusa/jewishconspiracies/.

Kiesler, S., Siegel, J. and McGuire, T. W. (1984). Social psychological aspects of computer-mediated communication. *American Psychologist 39,* 1123–1134.

Knights of the Ku Klux Klan (2005). Retrieved on 5 March 2005 from http://www.kkk.bz/ and *http://www.kkk.bz/just_for_kids.htm* .

Knights' Party (2005). Retrieved on 5 March 2005 from http://www.christianconcepts.net/informat.htm.

Lea, M., O'Shea, T., Fung, P. and Spears, R. (1992). 'Flaming' in computer-mediated communication. Observations, explanations, implications. In M. Lea (ed.), *Contexts of computer-mediated communication.* (pp. 89–112) New York: Harvester Wheatsheaf.

Lea, M. and Spears, R. (1995). Love at first byte? Building personal relationships over computer networks. In J. T. Wood and S. Duck (eds), *Under-studied relationships: off the beaten track. Understanding relationship processes,* vol. 6 (pp. 197–233). Thousand Oaks, CA: Sage.

Lee, E. and Leets, L. (2002). Persuasive storytelling by hate groups online: examining its effects on adolescents. *American Behavioral Scientist 45,* 927–957.

Leets, L. (2001). Response to Internet hate sites: is speech too free in cyberspace? *Communication and Law Policy 6,* 287–317.

Levin, B. (2002). Cyberhate: a legal and historical analysis of extremists' use of computer networks in America. *American Behavioral Scientist 45,* 958–988.

McDonald, M. (1999). Cyberhate: extending persuasive techniques of low credibility sources to the World Wide Web. In E. Thorson, D. W. Schumann (eds), *Advertising and the World Wide Web* (pp. 149–157). Mahwah, NJ: Lawrence Erlbaum Associates.

McKenna, K. Y. A. and Bargh, J. A. (1998). Coming out in the age of the Internet: identity 'demarginalization' through virtual group participation. *Journal of Personality and Social Psychology 75,* 681–694.

Micetrap Distribution (2005). Retrieved on 1 March 2005 from http://www.micetrap.net/.

Nizkor Project (2005). Retrieved on 23 March 2005 from http://www.nizkor.org/.

Perry, B. (2000). 'Button down terror': the metamorphosis of the hate movement. *Sociological Focus 33,* 113–131.

Postmes, T. and Spears, R. (1998). Deindividuation and anti-normative behavior: a meta-analysis. *Psychological Bulletin 123,* 238–259.

Reicher, S. and Levine, M. (1994a). Deindividuation, power relations between groups and the expression of social identity: the effects of visibility to the out-group. *British Journal of Social Psychology 33,* 145–163.

Reicher, S. and Levine, M. (1994b). On the consequences of deindividuation manipulations for the strategic communication of self: identifiability and the presentation of social identity. *European Journal of Social Psychology 24,* 511–542.

Reicher, S., Levine, R. M. and Gordijn, E. (1998). More on deindividuation, power relations between groups and the expression of social identity: three studies on the effects of visibility to the in-group. *British Journal of Social Psychology 37,* 15–40.

Reicher, S., Spears, R. and Postmes, T. (1995). A social identity model of deindividuation phenomena. *European Review of Social Psychology 6,* 161–197.

Schafer, J. A. (2002). Spinning the web of hate; Web-based hate propagation by extremist organizations. *Journal of Criminal Justice and Popular Culture 9,* 69–88.

Siegel, M. L. (1999). Hate speech, civil rights and the Internet: the jurisdictional and human rights nightmare. *Albany Journal of Science and Technology 9,* 375–398.

Siegel, J., Dubrovsky, V., Kiesler, S. and McGuire, T. W. (1986). Group processes in computer-mediated communication. *Organizational Behaviour and Human Decision Processes 37,* 157–187.

Spears, R. and Lea, M. (1994). Panacea or panopticon? The hidden power in computer-mediated communication. *Communication Research 21,* 427–459.

Sproull, L. and Kiesler, S. (1986). Reducing social context cues: electronic mail in organizational communication. *Management Science 32,* 1492–1512.

Stormfront (2005). Retrieved on 1 March 2005 from http://www.kids.stormfront.org/.

Tajfel, H. and Turner, J. C. (1979). An integrative theory of intergroup conflict. In W. G. Austin and S. Worchel (eds), *The social psychology of intergroup relations* (pp. 33–47). Monterey CA: Brooks/Cole.

The Hate Directory (2005). Retrieved 16 February 2005 from http://www.bcpl.net/~rfrankli/hatedir.pdf.

The Hate Directory (2006). Retrieved May 16 2006 from http://www.bcpl.net/~rfrankli/hatedir.pdf.

Turpin-Petrosino, C. (2002). Hateful sirens . . . who hears their song?: An examination of student attitudes towards hate groups and affiliation potential. *Journal of Social Issues 58*, 281–301.

van Gelder, L. (1985). 'The strange case of the electronic lover'. *Ms Magazine* October. Reprinted in C. Dunlop and R. Kling (eds). *Computerization and controversy: Value conflicts and social choices* (pp. 533–546). San Diego, CA: Academic Press (1996).

Walther, J. B., Anderson, J. F. and Park, D. (1994). Interpersonal effects in computer-mediated interaction: a meta-analysis of social and anti-social communication. *Communication Research 21*, 460–487.

Whine, M. (1997). The far right on the Internet. In B. D. Loader (ed.), *The governance of cyberspace: Politics, technology, and global restructuring.* (pp. 209–227). London: Routledge.

White Camelia Knights (2005). Retrieved on 26 February 2005 from http://www.wckkkk.com/index2.html.

Zickmund, S. (1997). Approaching the radical other: the discursive culture of cyberhate. In S. G. Jones (ed.), *Virtual culture: Identity and communication in cybersociety* (pp. 185–205). Thousand Oaks, CA: Sage Publications.

Zimbardo, P. G. (1969). The human choice: individuation, reason, and order versus deindividuation, impulse, and chaos. In W. J. Arnold and D. Levine (eds), *Nebraska Symposium on Motivation: vol. 17* (pp. 237–307) Lincoln NE: University of Nebraska Press.

CHAPTER 12

The psychological dimensions of collective action, online

Tom Postmes

Introduction

The study of collective action has been a long-standing concern in the social sciences, and for good reason. How is it possible for a group of individuals, each with their own individual objectives and purposes, to take on one and the same direction, often quite abruptly and sometimes with major consequences?

With the advent of modern communication technology and the Internet, the means of collective action have changed. The last decade has seen the emergence of a thriving literature on topics such as cyberactivism and online social movements (e.g., Rheingold 2002; McCaughey and Ayers 2003; Meikle 2003; Van de Donk *et al.* 2004b; Dartnell 2006). These publications usually take as their starting point an array of powerful and telling cases which speak to potential roles that technology can fulfil for the future organization of collective action. Among the oft-cited events are the 1994 Zapatista uprising (Ronfeldt *et al.* 1998), the 1999 'Battle of Seattle' (Smith 2001; DeLuca and Peeples 2002) and the toppling of Filipino president Estrada in 2001 (Tilly 2004).

Earlier forecasts were that the Internet would so profoundly innovate collective action that it would revolutionize politics and civil society,

introducing a 'paradigm shift' on dimensions illustrated in Table 12.1 (Kapor 1993; Rheingold 1993; Barlow 1995). Although echoes of these are still heard (Rheingold 2002; Dartnell 2006), the contemporary literature is notably more guarded and nuanced (e.g., Tilly 2004). Indeed, in contrast with what some forecasts would have us believe, the World Wide Web is bringing us at least as much progress in Western 'liberal' consumer culture as in progressive politics (Meikle 2003; Tilly 2004). The study of the social effects of technology is not, as a rule, helped by extrapolations of the *potential* that this technology affords the user. Key to understanding its social effects is also (if not more so) to analyse what the users of that technology may be motivated and influenced by.

The approach in this chapter is therefore to begin with a review of psychological aspects of collective action in general, considering potential impacts of the Internet only later. The chapter argues that despite the many technological advances and some social transformations we are witnessing today, the theoretical issues remain to a large extent unchanged. That may seem paradoxical and unlikely. Ostensibly, the collective action in particular of crowds could not appear to be more different from those on the Internet. In the crowd we find ourselves in the close proximity

Table 12.1 Paradigm shifts: predicted changes in the nature of collective action from the industrial age to the information age

	Industrial	Information age
Organization	Physically co-located	Global
Power	Social organizations	Individual
Means of conflict	Physical	Informational
Theatre of conflict	Physical space	'Hearts and minds'
Identity	Collective	Individual

of many others – their presence is almost overwhelming. In many ways the crowd is the ultimate collective experience. In contrast, for the isolated Internet user the presence of others is always mediated and therefore dependent on a good deal of imagination. The technology therefore appears to be, in some ways, psychologically individuating and atomizing. On a continuum of social contexts ranging from individualistic to collectivistic, the Internet and the crowd would be somewhere at the extremes. So, if collective action is increasingly taking place in online contexts, does this not render the classic analyses of such actions in terms of the dynamics in co-located crowds obsolete?

This chapter examines the consequences of the migration of collective action into the mediated sphere. It focuses on the impact of the Internet on key psychological factors which are involved in collective action. The structure of this review is as follows. First, we will consider the theoretical backdrop to the themes of this paper, focusing first on the classic literatures on crowds and on mediated communication, followed by more contemporary perspectives – identifying the underlying consistencies in the theoretical themes these literatures address. This section ends by identifying some key psychological factors that drive collective action. Then, we consider how the Internet changes the nature of collective action and the context in which it takes place. Subsequently, we elaborate how these changes might affect the key factors previously identified. Finally, we take a step back from all this and return to the question of whether this amounts to a revolution in the way collective actions take place.

Theories of collective action and online action

We will first review some classic perspectives on the crowd and on the Internet. For all the obvious differences between crowd and Internet, both contexts highlight one of the fundamental questions in the social sciences: What is the role of psychological processes in the social structuration of human society? Can human behaviour be explained entirely or sufficiently in terms of individual psychological processes, or can we safely ignore the individual and focus largely on the collective?

Classic perspectives on the crowd

The crowd has long been recognized to present psychology with a fundamental challenge. The 'model' crowd considered in most classic research is the violent mob. Here, actions of individual crowd members seem to fall well outside of the range of 'normal' individual functioning (Zimbardo 1969). More problematically for psychology, these actions are not random: crowd members act as if they are driven by a single purpose (Turner and Killian 1972). If, as some psychologists believe, all human behaviour is ultimately explained best at the individual (psychological) level, how can such behaviours arise?

The mainstream theories of social influence tend to suggest that social influence in groups is either due to rational individual information processing, or to conformity pressures, for example the classic distinction between informational and normative influence (Deutsch and Gerard 1955; see Sassenberg and Jonas, Chapter 18 in this volume, for more background to this literature). But according to the classic analysis, neither of these can account for crowd behaviour (Zimbardo 1969; Turner and Killian 1972): collective action in the crowd can arise in situations without a clear normative framework and without accountability. This rules out that conformity can sufficiently explain crowd actions. Moreover, the actions of some crowds appear far from rational, and it was thought the conditions in the crowd prevent its members from engaging in thorough and systematic information processing. The classic solution has been to suggest that crowds behave as they do because normal individual cognitive processing is suspended in them.

Thus, the stimuli found in the crowd strip away certain normal cognitive functions, making the crowd members revert back to instinctive behaviour or primary drives which motivate all our actions, but which are normally held in check (Allport 1924; see also Zimbardo 1969). The reason for the apparent uniformity of crowd actions is that, at heart, we all want more or less the same thing. The contemporary theory of deindividuation further elaborated how normal cognitive functions are suspended in the crowd (Postmes and Spears 1998, for a critical review). It proposed that certain features of the crowd reduce awareness of self, preventing the individual from monitoring and regulating their actions (Diener 1980; Prentice-Dunn and Rogers 1989).

The overriding impression is that crowds are exceptional circumstances, in which normal psychological functioning ceases. Reversing the reasoning, this theoretical intervention was only necessary because the crowd defied social psychology's understanding of social influence. In this respect, it has a lot in common with Internet research: both contexts challenge excessive individualism in explanations of social behaviour (Reicher et al. 1995).

Classic perspectives on the social effects of mediated communication

Although studies of the Internet are a recent phenomenon, there is a much longer tradition of research on the psychological consequences of mediated communication (e.g., Short et al. 1976; Hiltz and Turoff 1978). The ideas in this early work are surprisingly current, despite the enormous advances in technology. The challenge then, as now, was to account for the considerable influence of social processes in a context where mainstream theories would predict they should be absent or attenuated (for an early example see Short [1974]; reviews by Spears and Lea [1992]; Walther et al. [1994]).

When the literature on mediated communication emerged, it was common to characterize this medium as essentially individualistic and asocial (Postmes and Baym 2005). As several chapters in this volume have identified, these theories tended to argue that online interaction would weaken the social ties between individual communicators, thereby reducing their sensitivity to social influence (Short et al. 1976; Daft and Lengel 1984; Kiesler et al. 1984). Indeed, departing from the classic perspectives on social influence this prediction seemed to make a lot of sense, at the time.

As noted above, two kinds of social influence were widely documented and researched: conformity to norms/social pressure and informational influence. There is little disagreement that mediated communication provides greater freedom from social strictures and reduces social accountability. This is often attributed to the relative anonymity that users can create for themselves online (Kiesler et al. 1984; Jessup et al. 1990; Spears et al. 2002), but other factors that might contribute are the ability to strategically present the self (Reicher et al. 1995; Walther 1996) and the greater control over whether to 'tune in' or 'out' afforded by physical isolation. For all these reasons it follows that conformity is likely to be minimized online. As for informational influence, one of the key factors which decides whether others are seen as a valid source of information in the first place is one's relationship to them: informational influence is stronger to the extent that it is exerted by others who are perceived as similar to the self on key dimensions (Festinger 1954; Turner 1991). If the Internet weakens social ties, then informational social influence should also be reduced.

As is the case with the crowd, the realities of the Internet are less straightforward. In the interpersonal sphere, relationships on the Internet can vary from weak ties to relationships at the opposite end of the spectrum (Lea and Spears 1995; Walther 1996). At the level of the group, there is a large literature documenting the phenomenon that when interactions are anonymous and depersonalized, the social influence exerted by factors such as group norms and shared identity can indeed be reduced, but can also (under subtly different conditions) be much stronger (Sassenberg and Jonas, Chapter 18, this volume). At the macro level, the implication that the Internet would produce individualization, atomization and social alienation has not been confirmed either. Some scholars have argued that the Internet actually facilitates social relationships by overcoming limits of geographical isolation, isolation caused by stigma, illness, shyness, lack of mobility and so forth (McKenna and Bargh 2000; Katz *et al.* 2001) and have extolled the virtues and vibrancy of virtual communities (e.g., Rheingold 1993; see Haythornthwaite, Chapter 9, this volume, for a review).

In order to account for the unexpected occurrence of these (mixed) social effects, the response of psychologists has often been to suggest that online communication was somehow a special and exceptional case (i.e., implying that there is a need for a psychology of Internet and computer-mediated groups that was somehow distinct from the mainstream literatures). For example, observing an unexpected degree of attitude polarization in online discussions, Sara Kiesler and colleagues imported some elements of de-individuation theory into their perspective on computer-mediated communication (CMC), arguing that the anonymity in CMC reduces self-awareness and thereby produces disinhibited and extreme behaviour (Kiesler *et al.* 1984; McGuire *et al.* 1987).

This state of affairs once again points to the potential uses of the Internet for the development of social psychological theory. Online interaction is not really such an exceptional case: it is a fruitful testing ground for social psychological theory, highlighting the need for a social dimension to explanations of online behaviour, because in some cases the more individualistic explanations fail to make sense of it (Spears and Lea 1994; Postmes and Baym 2005). The not infrequent occurrence of genuine collective action online illustrates the point perfectly: the very existence of such phenomena should prompt us to reconsider the question of how social influence is exerted to make such actions possible in the first place.

Contemporary perspectives on the Internet

Although the influence of classic perspectives today should not be underestimated, it is probably fair to say that the majority of the literature has moved on. One reason is that, over time, the perspective on the nature of the question and the assumptions underlying it has changed dramatically. In the case of the crowd, the characterization of its actions as irrational and abnormal became increasingly untenable as researchers pointed out that it could also be patterned, restrained and orderly (e.g., Rudé 1964).

The introduction of the World Wide Web generated a similar reality check for the characterization of online interaction as asocial and disinhibited. On the contrary, researchers observed, in many ways the Internet was perhaps best characterized as a *social* medium, more than anything else (Kraut *et al.* 1999). Increasingly, the idea that technology had certain fixed effects on social and psychological outcomes (technological determinism) became problematic. Instead, scholars suggested that properties of the medium were a function of its social use rather the other way around (Fulk 1993). Thus, a major shift in emphasis took place in the 1990s, away from the assumption that it is the medium that transforms the individual, towards the view that we need to understand how users choose to use the medium (agency), undermining the very notion of 'social effects'.

This development is the prime reason why the analysis of collective action online is not to consider the 'special' features either of the Internet or of the collective. Rather that starting point should be the identification of key psychological and social processes which play a role in collective action per se.

Identifying key processes involved in collective action

In psychology, current work on collective action largely revolves around three distinct (but not necessarily independent) psychological states that are assumed to motivate collective action. These are (a) a sense of injustice, (b) a sense of efficacy and (c) a sense of shared social identity (Gamson 1992; Kelly and Breinlinger 1996; Klandermans 1997, 2004).

Injustice and collective action

In psychology, the emphasis on a sense of injustice as one key motivator of collective action was articulated in relative deprivation theory (RDT) (see Runciman 1966; Walker and Smith 2002). Despite early suggestions that 'objective' economic deprivation prompted collective action, there is little support for this across the board. If hardship does not propel people into action, then what does? According to RDT, it is the *subjective* psychological experience of deprivation (i.e., a sense of injustice) which is a key predictor of collective action.

The literature acknowledges a range of factors which play a role in whether perceptions of injustice arise and when they will be consequential. One is that people need to be prepared compare themselves to particular target others to perceive any inequality that may exist (cf. Festinger 1954). Moreover, perceptions of inequality will only lead to collective action if they are collectively anchored, that is if they are grounded in comparisons between groups – fraternal deprivation – rather than comparisons between individuals – egotistical deprivation (see Runciman 1966; Guimond and Dubé-Simard 1983; H. J. Smith and Ortiz 2002).

There are actually two aspects to this issue. One is that one needs groups (not individuals) to arrive at a *shared* perception of inequality: only if there is (implicit) consensus can collective action begin to be possible. The second is that for this to develop into actual feelings of relative deprivation one needs to achieve a shared view that this is *inequity*. Although this probably does not require actual consensus, it certainly requires a shared frame of reference (see the section on social identity below) which leads a sizeable part of the ingroup to interpret the inequality as unjust. Ultimately, this depends on a fair amount of intragroup interaction (Postmes *et al.* 2005).

Finally, research has shown that relative deprivation can be broken down into two related aspects. One is the knowledge that inequity exists (a cognitive component), the second the feelings of injustice associated with it (an affective component). The affective component is a much stronger predictor of collective action (Smith and Ortiz 2002). The importance of affect and emotions as motivators is again something that is relevant to online collective action and which we will return to below.

Efficacy

One basic problem facing the collective action literature is to explain that, despite the large social inequalities that are commonly found, collective action is such an infrequent occurrence. One reason for this, it has been argued, is the difficulty of eliciting support for social movements (McCarthy and Zald 1977). This support depends on decisions by individual, rational actors who aim to minimize personal losses and maximize personal gains (Olson 1968).

Against this background Klandermans (1984) proposed that individual motivations for collective action were a function of subjective expectancy-value products. In his model, participation in social movements is partly dependent on the value of the intended outcomes of collective action, but it is also and crucially dependent on the expectation of whether collective action would be possible and whether it would be effective. In the wake of this proposal, efficacy has become one of the key explanations of collective action (Simon and Klandermans 2001). Relatedly, collective actions have been associated with feelings of collective power (Reicher 1996, 2001; Drury and Reicher 2005). In all this work, the central psychological construct is the feeling that existing social realities can be changed – a feeling that, once again, depends on social consensus among in-group members.

Social identity and identification

As noted, efficacy and justice are not mere individual perceptions and feelings. They are grounded in assessments of collective history and future expectations in which the individual is strongly dependent on opinions and consensus within their *psychological* in-group. Moreover, as social identity theory (Tajfel and Turner 1979) argues, those assessments are also influenced by the nature of the intergroup relations.

Social identity theory is unique among theories of collective action because it elaborates the various processes that lead to collective inaction. It notes two key reasons why low status groups cease to strive for improvement of their position: individual mobility and social creativity (which occurs when people collectively explain away their disadvantages). Only when group boundaries are impermeable (i.e., individuals can't abandon it), the status differential is perceived as illegitimate (i.e., there is a sense of injustice) and when status relations are insecure (i.e., there is a sense of efficacy) does collective action become likely. Under these very specific conditions, collective action becomes possible to the extent that group members are prepared to mobilize on behalf of their group. One key factor involved in this is group members' identification with the group – and particularly its politicized ideology (Simon 1998; Simon and Klandermans 2001; Stürmer and Simon 2004).

Recent advances in the social identity literature have noted that, in addition to these factors, there are important dynamics both within and between groups that play a role in the emergence of collective action. Reicher (1996) noted that the conditions for collective action are created not just by the in-group, but also (and often more so) by an outgroup whose actions can unite and focus the in-group (i.e., heighten social identification, clarifying the categorical distinction between in- and out-group and inviting particular responses). As an example of this, coercion can disastrously backfire because it invites resistance (Turner 2005). But there are dynamics within groups, too, which can not be ignored. Recent work has begun to examine the intragroup negotiation and consensualization which plays a part in this focusing of minds (Haslam 1997; Drury and Reicher 2000; Stott and Drury 2004) and in the accompanied development of a sense of in-group identity (Postmes *et al.* 2005). The latter development is especially important, because it broadens the focus of the social identity approach to consider interactions within groups as much as between them: and intragroup interactions are especially relevant to collective actions online.

The possibilities and limitations of the Internet

Having considered the key factors involved in motivating collective action, we can now turn to the question of how they interact with features of the Internet. In order to do this, it is useful to consider characteristics of the Internet and other contemporary forms of technology. This is not intended to be an exhaustive overview of the objective 'properties of technology', nor does it mean that these properties exist solely by virtue of the technology itself, but the Internet does offer a range of *perceived* choices and possibilities to users which are likely to be relevant to guiding behaviour. Moreover, the increasing reliance on Internet and (mobile) communication technology also introduces certain limitations, for example by preventing or distracting users from engaging in other social activities. Finally, the Internet draws on a range of (perceived or actual) capacities which may limit non-users as well as users. This selection process is likely to have (unintended) social consequences in its own right.

Perceived possibilities

The (perceived) possibilities of the Internet play a large role in explaining its psychological impact, and it is here that most of the excitement about online collective action originates. Many who witnessed the successive waves of interactive technology that flourished on the Internet since the late 1980s were grasped by a sense of limitless opportunity – the metaphors were of pioneers on the electronic frontier, colonizing cyberspace (Meikle 2003; Kapor 2004). Even those not infected by the technological utopianism of early visionaries such as Negroponte and Rheingold were struck by the potential, and for many the advent of world-wide Web technology generated a palpable sense of excitement and empowerment.

Adopting a more clinical approach to this, one might say that essentially, these possibilities are derived from three features of technology. The first is that, through technology, users can contact other users (i.e., links are established, data can be transferred). The second is that the technology can be programmed (configured) to fulfil a range of communication forms (interpersonal, group-based, or mass communication; written, vocal, or videoed; synchronous, quasi-synchronous and asynchronous). The third is that all non-verbal forms of mediated communication leave a record. It should be noted that although some of these features are shared by many communication media (certainly since the printing press extended the uses of paper),

CMC is unique in the flexibility it allows – being able to program the medium has given rise to extensive experimenting with innovative forms of interaction and collaborative work, involving multiple 'media' in the traditional sense (Postmes *et al.* 1998).

According to such a clinical analysis, the Internet could be said to give rise to a number of qualitative shifts (e.g., in terms of new possibilities for interacting, for organizing work, etc.), but according to the statistics of Internet use, the pervasive changes introduced are not in this qualitative corner of dramatic innovations (see e.g., the Pew Internet and American Life's statistics on net usage at http://www.pewinternet.org). A minority of users might do genuinely innovative things with it, but the majority of communicative uses of the Internet is comparable to offline equivalents (letter-writing, newsletters, newspapers, mail catalogue ordering, car boot sales, etc.). Moreover, the communication potential of the Internet appears to integrate seamlessly with, rather than radically revolutionize, existing means of interaction (Boase *et al.* 2006; also Brandon and Hollingshead, Chapter 8 this volume). Indeed, the excitement of the Internet appears to be more with the revolutionary new things which the package promises, than with what comes out of the box.

First and foremost, the Internet unlocked a wealth of access to social and informational resources: connectivity is a large part of the attraction. The informational aspect of this is becoming increasingly obvious, with the Internet gradually replacing the functions of library and newsstand (not least because these migrate towards online equivalents). Coupled with a pervasive perception that, in the modern economy, information has become a means of production, this generates a real sense of excitement among some.

A similar case can be made for social resources – the 'social capital' that networks could supposedly unlock (e.g., Kavanaugh *et al.* 2005). In 2006, more than 50 per cent of the population of western industrialized nations are estimated to have ready access to the Internet (UN Statistics Division, http://www.millenniumindicators.un. org/). Such access to a vast *social* network (if only virtual and imagined) forms a large part of the attraction of the Internet and has done so from its early days. The psychological breakdown

of barriers of place is only part of this. Another factor is the realization among a sizeable proportion of users that they have ready access to means of mass communication through websites, blogs, newsgroups and so on. Although contributors to these are a relative minority (e.g., only 9 per cent of Internet users had ever blogged in 2005, http://www.pewinternet.org) the success of various other online activities requiring some form of participation (e.g., as on Ebay) does suggest that users are generally welcoming a varied range of opportunities for engaging in 'collective' social activities online.

A further factor is the considerable freedom of choice. The fact that the Internet allows users to decide whether and how to participate in a variety of social activities endows users with a feeling of autonomy and freedom – 'networked individualism' (Boase *et al.* 2006). This aspect of the Internet has been extensively researched, in particular with regard to the consequences of users' choices to remain anonymous or to adopt pseudonymous alternative identities. Although doubts have been cast over the (f)actual ability to achieve anonymity (e.g., Joinson 2003) as well as users' willingness to resort to it, there can be no doubt that the psychological perception of all these options may have far-reaching consequences for how users engage with technology and how it affects their social lives.

Standing back from these opportunities and possibilities, it is apparent that a great many of them revolve around the individual (Streeter 2003). Even to the extent that great social changes are predicted to result from communication technology, this process is mediated by factors at the individual psychological level. A good example of this is the assertion that the Internet would inevitably make organizations less hierarchical, more horizontal and self-directed (Malone and Rockart 1991). Ignoring that most of these observations are based on what organizations do, without necessarily being able to conclusively attribute these developments to networks or information/communication technology (e.g., Micklethwait and Wooldridge 1996), at the centre of the analysis is the assumption that power in the 'modern' organization is grasped by the (technology-savvy) individual employee. The idea is that the ability to harvest online information and set up personal networks gives them 'social capital' and transforms them into the organization's informal leaders (Adler and Kwon 2002). Such an analysis assumes a remarkable degree of agency. Elsewhere we argued that this implicit individualism is a consistent theme in most analyses and theories of usages of the Internet and a major limitation to our ability of understanding of its (more complex) social effects (Postmes and Baym 2005).

Limitations

The utopian visions of technologies' empowering, democratizing and progressive potential may have been blind to some sober realities, but there are similar myopic properties of the early dystopian visions, which focused too exclusively on (imagined) limitations. Early critics compared CMC not with technology such as the telephone (which in many ways would have been the appropriate comparison or 'control condition') but almost invariably with face-to-face interaction. In this comparison, face-to-face comparison became the 'rich' standard that CMC fell short of.

They were also mainly concerned with the question what *groups* and *organizations* could achieve with CMC. Looking at the micro level in particular, there did not appear to be much that CMC would allow collaborative teams to do better or more efficiently. Online collaborations tend to be, by and large, rather clunky and cumbersome. Factors contributing to this are the isolation of collaborators for each other (reducing flexibility in their interactions), the relative anonymity of their contributions, the fact that typing introduces a number of delays and restrictions and so on. More recently, literatures (e.g., on virtual communities and virtual teams) have claimed that CMC radically transforms groups and social networks, but the evidence for this remains far from conclusive (Kraut *et al.* 1999; Breu and Hemingway 2004). A recent review noted inconsistent outcomes across the board, with some pointedly negative exceptions such as a general tendency for virtual groups to need more time to complete tasks and members of those teams being less satisfied (Martins *et al.* 2004). However, irrespective of the virtues and vices of virtual teams, the fact is that the usage of the Internet is not concentrated in teamwork, but in interpersonal and mass communication.

When we focus on these interpersonal and mass communication domains we can identify some relatively undisputed limitations. One obvious area is that the Internet (like all communication media) favours particular forms of information and knowledge (written text, static images and to a much lesser degree voice and low-resolution video), encourages particular uses of this information (e.g., Deuze 2003; Cassidy 2005) and encourages a focus on particular topics (Van de Donk *et al.* 2004a: 8).

A second limitation of online interaction means that users are (in practice) physically isolated from each other. This is the converse of the decreasing relevance of barriers of space and may have some negative side-effects (see also Sassenberg and Jonas, Chapter 18 this volume). Isolation may foster the dissociation and fragmentation of social movements, for example (Bennett 2004; Wright 2004). Although we are lacking systematic research into the micro-level consequences of such effects, more macro-level research suggests that fears that this would produce social atomization are likely to be exaggerated (Katz *et al.* 2001; Kraut *et al.* 2002; Boase *et al.* 2006).

A third issue is that online interaction limits the ability to individually identify *others*. This may be restrictive as much as liberating. The key issue here is that anonymity of others reduces one's ability to individuate them. Although this may have positive consequences (see Spears, Lea and Postmes, Chapter 17 this volume), the literature emphasizes the negative consequences of this. In collaborations with 'outsiders' for example, uncertainties over others' identity may diminish trust and disrupt co-action (Tanis and Postmes 2005). An inability to identify others within one's group may restrict one's ability to offer in-group support and express social solidarity (Spears, Lea *et al.* 2002). A lack of identifiability of out-group members decreases the likelihood of engagement with them and may increase chances of stereotyping (Postmes and Spears 2002; Postmes *et al.* 2002).

A final limitation of the Internet is that the much-trumpeted virtues of networking (and the powers associated with them) are, by necessity, restricted to those who have access. Access was a key issue in the research literature of the early 1990s, with digital divides of gender and race attracting considerable concern. However, with the disappearance of in particular gender inequality in the USA, interest in digital divides has waned somewhat. This is not justified, however (DiMaggio *et al.* 2001; Rice and Katz 2003). In most organizations, several classes of employees (cleaners, porters) are systematically excluded from organizational communication because they have no workstations to access email and intranets from. In Western societies, class, ethnic and generational differences are more resistant to change than gender has proven to be, these affect political participation (Jennings and Zeitner 2003). Language on the Internet is also throwing up considerable barriers.

Perhaps the most dramatic divide concerns divides between developed and developing nations. As shown in Figure 12.1, certain developing countries are lagging a long way behind (including rapidly industrializing nations with a considerable IT presence such as India, of whose population no more than 1.75 per cent were estimated to have Internet access in 2003, which in turn is considerably better than most African countries such as Uganda, with only 0.49 per cent). More surprising perhaps is the number of highly developed nations (such as Spain) that have markedly slow adoption. The most concerning feature of these statistics is that the traditional pattern of adoption (Rogers 2003) is not met in certain developing nations at all. The figure illustrates how in countries such as South Africa, India and Russia Internet adoption rates are faltering or slowing down.

The digital divides in organizations and within and between societies are limitations of the Internet in several regards. To the extent that the 'social capital' residing in online networks excludes some social strata, those parties are disempowered and the value of the network as a whole is diminished. Persistent divides also mean that the Internet is appropriated by those who do have access, capacities, skills and resources that allow them to take ownership. To a large extent, this favours existing power holders (Zuboff 1988). It could also empower a technology-savvy segment (the archetypal teenage nerds, young academics, etc.) with relatively limited power in the traditional sense, but to the extent that these parties mostly subscribe to Western and middle-class values, they are unlikely to challenge existing power holders (cf. George 2005) and are more

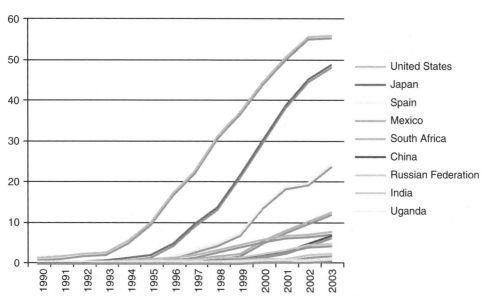

Figure 12.1 Percentage of population with access to Internet for a selection of developed and developing nations. Source: UN Statistics Division, millennium indicators.

likely to join ranks, either immediately or in due course (e.g., the former 'hacktivist' turned Internet security expert).

This trend towards *disempowerment* of the individual user is very much in evidence on the Internet today, where the progressive counter-culture of the early days of the Internet (which espoused a version of 'freedom' with a distinctly Californian flavour, see also Dahlberg [2001]) has not entirely vanished, but is increasingly trumped by commercialization, Westernization and liberal individualism (Meikle 2003). Napster may have sown the seeds, but iTunes is picking the fruits. Against this backdrop, the potential for collective action online is unlikely to be a straightforward story.

Modern activism

During the 1990s, online equivalents emerged for most forms of direct collective action that we are familiar with offline. Online letter writing, lobbying and petitioning are commonplace now. The Internet has also become a platform for civil disobedience, sabotage, blockades and black-mail. Although a relatively fringe activity, this can be highly effective. 'Hacktivism' can take the form of defacements, denial of service attacks, site hijacking and so on. Web defacements in par-ticular have become very frequent. Defacement statistics (archived by the now discontinued alldas.org) suggested about 1,775 website deface-ments took place per month in 2001 (Postmes and Brunsting 2002). Current statistics (collected from http://www.zone-h.org) suggest that for the year from 1/4/2005 to 1/4/2006, an average of about 1,400 successful attacks took place *per day*. Moreover, the motivations for these attacks according to statistics collected by zone-h.org suggest that although many defacements are just 'for fun' 11.8 per cent of attacks were conducted for political reasons, while 9.6 per cent were motivated by 'patriotism'.

Good examples are the 'defacement war' between Palestinian and Israeli hackers during the 2001 Intifadah, a wave of anti-war defacements around the start of the war on Iraq in March 2003 and Peruvian hackers' targeting of Chilean govern-ment websites and vice versa in 2005. Many defacements target global corporations, govern-ment agencies and NGOs under a broad banner of activism for freedom of information access and exchange and opposing regulation and commercialization of the Internet (see also Eschenfelder *et al.* 2005).

The predominant use of Internet and modern communication technologies is not as a vehicle for direct action; it is to support and organize offline actions (Horton 2004) and to form (new) movements and organizations (Adams and Roscigno 2005). The first occurs when established movements integrate the mass communication potential of the Internet into their established repertoire of devices to influence established media or to establish alternative sources of news (e.g., indymedia), with the purpose of raising awareness about their agenda and activities, with an eye to mobilizing political pressure to further their cause. The second is a more indi-rect phenomenon where the Internet diverts the nature and purpose of movements themselves (Bennett 2004). There is abundant commentary about these trends, perched on a somewhat nar-rower empirical basis. Nonetheless, we can infer quite a lot from existing research (mainly on online groups and social movements) about how the Internet affects the key psychological processes underlying collective action: injustice, efficacy and social identity.

Injustice

Feelings of injustice are fed, among others, by particular understandings of social reality. In inter-group relations, for example, a sense of injustice may arise when there is a discrepancy between what those social relations ought to be like and the observed relationship. The Internet potentially impacts on this in two ways. One is by affecting the existing patterns of inequality and their visibility. The second is by affecting how inequalities give rise to socially shared feel-ings of injustice.

Inequality and its visibility

Ignoring for the moment the digital divides noted above, communication technology is often heralded as a social leveller in its own right. There is a lively literature to support this. A consistent and robust finding in the group decision support systems (GDSS) literature, is that electronic brainstorming is more equal using such systems

(Chun and Park 1998; Rains 2005). In face-to-face groups, certain group members may dominate a brainstorming session, not so in GDSS. A key factor in producing this effect may be that GDSS systems are designed to extract as many ideas as possible. To achieve this, they encourage users to generate ideas in a procedure reminiscent of a production line – contributions are essentially entirely individually generated, with some comparison of ideas generated by others (Munkes and Diehl 2003; Dugosh and Paulus 2005). This is markedly different from face-to-face groups on a number of dimensions, not least because in conversations we take turns, which 'blocks productivity' for those who are doing the listening (Stroebe and Diehl 1994).

For several reasons, generalization of such findings of equalization to other online contexts may be premature. The equality in GDSS may not be a consequence of online interactions, so much as of the particular way in which these have been configured (Barki and Pinsonneault 2001). Comparisons with results of other (more controlled) studies of discussion groups suggest that electronic communications are not necessarily more equalizing per se (e.g., as argued by Dubrovsky et al. [1991]), but may also exacerbate existing status differences and foster greater inequality (Weisband 1994; Weisband, Schneider and Connolly 1995) and increased stereotyping (Postmes and Spears 2002). Adding to this, the number of non-contributing 'lurkers' in most online fora (typically a large majority) suggests that equal participation is not all that evident in natural online groups either (Preece, Nonnecke and Andrews 2004). Finally, there is a lot of evidence to suggest that the Internet encourages self-segregation into similarly minded groups (Adams and Roscigno 2005, see also Douglas, Chapter 11 this volume), thereby exacerbating *inter-group inequalities*.

There is a further factor to consider here. The literature consistently emphasizes the freedoms of the *individual*, discounting the relevance or very existence of social groups (Postmes and Baym 2005). The persistent belief that the Internet and organizational intranets give all individuals an equal chance to participate may itself stifle the ability to recognize and counteract inequalities between groups where they do occur. The promise of individual mobility opportunities is a most

effective way to undermine collective action (Tajfel and Turner 1979; Wright and Taylor 1998). Furthermore, claims of universal democratization and empowerment (e.g., Rheingold 1993) undermine the notion that there are any social groups and social classes in society at all. Instead, we are left with a highly individualized perception of Internet users who are liberated from any restrictions (e.g., Turkle 1995). This individualized perception of Internet users may, because it is so widely shared, undermine the capacity for users to perceive inequalities along group and class lines that persist or *are newly introduced* through electronic media.

Social sharing of social understandings

As noted above, analyses of injustice and deprivation implicitly acknowledge the importance of a shared frame of reference and a certain form of (implicit) consensus. A sense of injustice is part and parcel of the formation of an opinion – but because the subject of this opinion is in the realm of inter-group relationships and their explanation, this opinion ultimately must rely on certain collectively shared understandings too.

There is no doubt that the Internet enhances the capabilities and versatility for intra-group debate and interaction (see also Flanagin et al. 2006). As noted above, the Internet has been able to foster increased discussion on political topics in web-based discussion fora, to increase targeted mass-communication of social movements to provide their perspective on specific events or issues and to provide more continuous streams of 'alternative' perspectives on news. Although offline metaphors could be applied to these (the café, the newsletter, etc.), there is nonetheless a reasonable case that the Internet introduces both quantitative and qualitative changes to what activists can achieve and who can join them (Bennett 2004).

Through these means, social movements and interested parties may create awareness of their cause, may engage others in debate about inter-group relations and the nature of inequality and how to address it. Involvement in such debates mobilizes (Scheufele et al. 2004). The classic (widely documented) case of how modern communication technologies may play a role is the Zapatista movement (Castells 1997; Ronfeldt et al. 1998). This illustrates how local concerns in

Chiapas, Mexico, gained 'worldwide' attention through a highly effective campaign in which the Zapatistas harnessed the support of various movements and organizations, mainly in the USA. The pressure exerted by the coordinated effort of these movements was so considerable that it greatly enhanced the success of the Zapatistas in its struggle with the Mexican government. The underlying process is largely one of persuasion, facilitated by electronic means of communication. Other good examples are anti-corporate 'pressure groups' (sometimes just one person, often only a handful) who seek to change corporate practices by documenting and exposing malpractices (Rosenkrands 2004).

The persuasive messages and propaganda may take a variety of forms and on the Internet, affective and emotional processes are no less relevant than informational processing is. Although there is little work on the transmission of online emotions and affect, there is no consistent support for early assumptions that online interactions would induce a shift towards greater task-orientation and less socio-emotional involvement (e.g., Walther *et al.* 1994). Also in online collective actions, passions remain a prominent motivator. This is partly because of the increasing possibilities to provide uncensored news and views. Due to the anonymity and perceived lack of (legal) control, the Internet and modern communication technology are excellent vehicles for rumour and the leaking of sensitive and confidential information. In 2000, the Philippine Government complained about the rude jokes and false rumours circulating via text messages: they were destabilizing president Estrada, who was already accused of corruption and impeached at the time (BBC news online 17 November 2000, Estrada crisis fuels mobile mania, http://news.bbc.co.uk/1/hi/world/asia-pacific/1027992.stm) and instrumental in fuelling the mass protests that eventually brought him down (cf. Tilly 2004).

Frequent though the cases of grassroots movements developing and gaining power may be, the more common pattern is for established movements to use the Internet to garner support for their issues and actions, inviting participation at all levels from letter-writing to direct action on the ground. This, too, can be highly emotive and effective, but there is widespread scepticism in the social movement literature whether these organizations' use of modern media is anything else than an extension of their current activities to include different means of (mass) communication (Tilly 2004).

Potentially more influential is how Internet changes those organizations and gives rise to new movements (e.g., Schussman and Earl 2004). There is a large literature documenting the way in which social movement organizations rely on modern communication technologies for the organization of their activities (e.g., Van de Donk *et al.* 2004b). The Internet enables multiple organizations to synchronize their activities and agendas and to subscribe to united causes: the anti-globalization movement is a good illustration of this phenomenon (Clark and Themudo 2006). Researchers have argued that the Internet has played a role in the 'globalization' of certain concerns and the unification of these concerns under a common banner – ironically of anti-globalization (Rosenkrands 2004). Case studies also demonstrate how the movement organizations involved in this interfaced with local organizations to transform local protests (e.g., of farmers against world trade agreements) into protests that are (perceived to be) under this common banner (Fisher *et al.* 2005).

A final consideration is that the Internet can be the forum for the development of online communities which can mobilize collective action for their own concerns. Looking at the nature of activities in online communities, however, with the exception of those communities which are formed around a collective interest in politics and/or activism, their concerns appear to be mainly relational, personal and/or restricted to the topic on which they focus. Although collective action is not exceptional in online communities, most of it is concerned either with issues that overlap with the nucleus of that community's concerns, or it is concerned with the regulation of the community's own online activities (e.g., when its rules are violated).

Efficacy

When considering the impact of the Internet on efficacy perceptions, it is worthwhile to distinguish three aspects of this (Klandermans 1997). One is the assessment of the degree to which others are likely to join in – some actions may not be widely supported and hence may not ever become truly 'collective' actions. A second is the belief that the collective action, if carried through, would be efficacious and result in the desired outcome. The third is the belief that the own contribution to the action will make a difference to its success. It is typical for the social movement literature to assume that relatively individualistic and 'rational' cost–benefit analyses take into account these aspects of efficacy when individuals decide to join actions or movements (see also Simon and Klandermans 2001).

The influence of the Internet on these beliefs could be considerable when one takes into consideration the hype surrounding the Internet itself. There is some evidence that the Internet increases political participation. Jennings and Zeitner (2003) showed that Internet access had a positive impact on political engagement, but also that it deepens digital divides. Research in one specific online community network suggests that those who were previously active are particularly likely to become more involved in community activities by going online (Kavanaugh et al. 2005). Putting both together, one could infer that the Internet amplifies existing trends and efficacy beliefs may play a role here. To the extent that users are inclined to believe that this medium empowers the user and to the extent that they believe in its ability to affect change in others, their actions may become self-fulfilling.

A belief in the power of Internet (cf. Sallot, Porter and Acosta-Alzuru 2004) would directly informing efficacy beliefs. Thus, to true believers in the Internet's virtues it would appear self-evident that it increases communal involvement and therefore support for collective action (cf. Rheingold 1993). Moreover, there are no reasons why online actions could not be equally efficacious (and plenty of reasons why they could be more so). Finally, for true believers the Internet would markedly increase their sense of self-efficacy. After all, if the Internet radically extends (rather than supplants or replaces) the means of social engagement and the informational power base, then these users should perceive this as empowering and be convinced that they can make a difference.

There is some evidence which speaks to these issues. Brunsting and Postmes (2002) targeted a large sample of environmental activists (some of whom were deeply involved in direct actions in the traditional 'bricks and mortars' sense), sympathizers and a non-activist control group, asking them to compare their experiences with online and offline actions. Efficacy was one of the key variables in the survey. On the whole, results showed that the perceived efficacy of online actions was remarkably high. The strongest effect was found for the anticipated participation of others, which was expected to be much higher for online actions, but the perceived efficaciousness of the actual actions was more ambiguous. Although the effectiveness of 'soft' (persuasive) actions was somewhat similar for online and offline forms, 'hard' (confrontational) actions offline were believed to be more effective when they were conducted offline (e.g., actual blockades and sit-ins were deemed more effective than their virtual equivalents). Importantly, however, the perceived *self-efficacy* was lower for online actions. That is, across the whole range of online collective actions considered, people felt that their participation mattered less to the success of the action than if it were online. It should be noted that this effect was not for the simple reason that they expected others to have a bigger impact: all three forms of efficacy were *positively* related.

Thus, the psychological impact of the Internet on efficacy appears to be somewhat two-sided. On the one hand, the surveyed activists and sympathizers shared the high hopes, but this did not coincide with the subjective sense that their own actions would also be empowered and more efficacious. This may be contrasted with the way that some professionals feel empowered by the Internet (Sallot et al. 2004). It is also unlikely to hold true for cases where collective action is itself concerned with online issues and debates (as for the Electronic Frontier Foundation, see for example Kapor [1993]). Nonetheless, precisely because of the fact that this study sampled the 'traditional' environmental movement members and its sympathizers, results are unlikely to be atypical of the more general pattern, which is that the Internet does not necessarily increase activist engagement.

This ambiguous influence of the Internet should also be considered in light of the alternative consequences it purportedly has. There is a large literature on the 'weak ties' networks that the Internet supposedly encourages (Pickering and King 1995, see Haythornthwaite, Chapter 9 this volume for a review; Wellman *et al.* 1996). Its association with particular strands of individualism has also been observed (Dahlberg 2001; Meikle 2003; Streeter 2003; Boase *et al.* 2006). And finally we noted some of the strategic possibilities that Internet offers in the relational sphere (see also McKenna and Bargh 1998). All these factors together may account for the fact that users sometimes feel less personally responsible for online actions, despite the fact that they may more easily tune in. Thus, while it may be true that in certain cases the Internet subjectively empowers the individual, this may not necessarily coincide with a greater willingness of the individual to use those powers for the collective good.

Social identity and identification

Social identity online has been extensively researched and summaries of the research on this topic are provided in Chapter 13 in this volume, among others. This research provides a useful counterpoint to assertions that the Internet is an individualizing force. In line with the trends for increased individualism and personal autonomy online, many have declared that the Internet would hasten the demise of traditional social identities of race, class, gender, culture, religion and so on. Evidence from a wide range of sources suggests this to be a misdiagnosis of societal trends more generally (e.g., ignoring growing social inequalities both nationally and internationally, increasing influence of religions, political polarization etc.). Research on the Internet confirms that despite the undoubted potential for Internet users to be more individualistic, a remarkable degree of social embeddedness in 'real life' social contacts and social identities persists (Bargh and McKenna 2004; Boase *et al.* 2006). That social identities, among others, continue to be a major social influence on the Internet is particularly powerful because it suggests that, despite the freedom to 'play' with identities, people are inclined to use these freedoms also to explore and deploy existing and new social identities more fully.

A proper understanding of this continued reliance on established identities should not just take into account the relative continuity in the individual's idiosyncratic self-perceptions and motivations, for example in terms of 'personality' (Chapter 13 this volume), but take on board the full implications of the now largely uncontested understanding that self and identity are, in many ways, constituted *socially* (Mead 1934; Sedikides and Brewer, 2001). Online identities are not markedly different from offline identities in this respect, nor can they be. The underlying psychological process is one, after all, whereby the individual self is defined largely by affiliations with myriad social in-groups (social identities) and (under different conditions) by myriad contrasts to those in-groups as well (personal identities). This is not just due to mere conservatism or a lack of imagination. Social identities are part of what makes interactions meaningful in the first place (Turner 1991; Postmes 2003; Swaab *et al.* in press;), hence users engage in processes of social identification, self-categorization and social identity formation, because this is the way that they can make sense of the world 'out there' and the position of the self within it. An extreme example of this phenomenon is provided in a GDSS implementation for decision support among EU diplomats (Lyytinen *et al.* 1993). GDSS systems tend to rely on anonymity to ensure high quality of contributions (Valacich *et al.* 1991), but when EU diplomats were given the opinion to contribute anonymously they objected because their national identity was an inalienable part of the message. Without their national identity, they neither knew what to say, nor did they know how to understand others. The underlying process here is of course much more general: awareness of social identities involved has huge implications for how we understand others and for our own behaviour in relation to them.

In keeping with this, there is a lot of evidence that speaks to the myriad ways in which social identities are influential online (Spears *et al.* 2002). For instance, despite the opportunities for dissimulation and deceit online, evidence suggests that most users strive to present the same persona online and off (Spears *et al.* 2000). A key component of the argument that the Internet liberates users to display their 'real self', for example, is in the observation that users display their stigmatized *social identities* and bond with others in online social groups such as gays, disabled people, racists, religious people, etc.

(McKenna and Bargh 1998). Far from individualizing them, the Internet enables them to 'socialize' more and self-segregate. In parallel with this, there is a large experimental literature which has examined the degree to which Internet users are susceptible to social influences exerted by their social identity. By and large this work shows that, despite the greater freedom (and perhaps to compensate for the essentially indeterminate nature of an environment without any boundaries) people are very likely to self-stereotype and apply group characteristics to themselves online (Chapter 17 this volume). Effects of this extend to a range of social influences in online groups (Chapter 18 this volume). Social identities, far from going out the window with the freedoms that the Internet provides, are very much a feature of online social life.

As elaborated in the Social Identity model of Deindividuation Effects (SIDE), there are two dimensions to the influence of social identity in mediated contexts. Both of these are relevant to collective action. On the one hand, CMC has the ability to make certain aspects of identity (personal or social) more or less salient (Spears and Lea 1992; Reicher et al. 1995). One extensively researched aspect of this is the possibility that, under particular conditions of relative individual anonymity, group members in online groups can become depersonalized in a fashion which, in some sense, echoes ideas found in the classic crowd literature. Importantly, however, SIDE replaces the idea that online anonymity de-individuates people (rendering them less responsive to social norms) with the idea that online anonymity can enhance the salience of their social identity and consequently their social identification with the group (rendering them more responsive to in-group norms, e.g., Lea et al. 2001). The implications of this for collective action are that established identities, far from losing impact and relevance, may also gain prominence and support online.

Perhaps more importantly to collective action, SIDE also elaborates the consequences of the strategic opportunities provided by the programmable flexibility and the relative anonymity of the Internet (Spears and Lea 1994; Reicher et al. 1995; Spears, Lea et al. 2002). This allows groups to configure their interactions in such a way that they empower themselves relative to their out-group(s). There are a number of factors which play a role here. One is the relative anonymity from out-group members, which enhances the strategic freedom among in-group members to engage in actions which would otherwise be punishable (Reicher and Levine 1994). Another factor is the ability for in-group members to provide each other with meaningful support (Spears et al. 2002), which enhances their capacity for joint action (in parallel to their capacity to arrive at socially shared perceptions of injustice, as noted above). This capacity is enhanced by intra-group identifiability and the capacity to freely exchange information and views. Once again, however, the important point is that people are not just inclined to use these strategic opportunities to 'go solo' and rid themselves of the social restrictions imposed on them by group memberships. Of course there are some conditions under which this will happen – for example among low identifiers (Barretto and Ellemers 2001) or when personal identities are salient – but there are also many conditions under which the opposite may occur, with people seizing the strategic opportunities of the Internet to support the collective actions of their group. The point is that anonymity and isolation are seized upon not merely as instruments for individual liberation, but that (the social being an intrinsic part of the individual, too) they can equally be mobilized for social ends.

Conclusion

The Internet has myriad consequences, even if we concentrate on the psychological level. The contradictory evidence for predicted 'social effects' may prevent us from drawing any obvious and firm conclusions about 'the nature of the Internet' – but it does support the characterization of the Internet as malleable (Castells 2001). In line with this characterization, it is more fruitful to consider how characteristics of technology interact with (and are produced by) social and psychological factors. One way of understanding the Internet's influence is as a function of the interplay between the various limitations and opportunities that a communication medium provides, as seen through the lens of the individual user as a social actor. This means that a psychological perspective on the social implications of technology should depart from a theoretically informed understanding of the motives of active users in their social contexts, before it can understand how the online environment interacts with it. These processes are not markedly different from those in online collective action.

In this chapter, the points of departure therefore were some key psychological factors (injustice, efficacy and social identity) that impact on collective action. We then looked at various properties of communication technology and how they interact with these factors. Using such an approach, one may conclude that apparent empirical contradictions may be accounted for by a limited set of (parsimonious) theoretical assumptions. In these, the concept of identity is likely to play a key role. Essentially, the questions of the Internet revolve around the issue of how and why the isolated and autonomous individual engages in some very social and apparently selfless behaviours. One solution to this may could be that self is also social, which resolves part of the apparent contradiction.

Having come this far, can we now return to the question of what the Internet 'means' for collective action? Is it a 'paradigm shift', a radical transformation of collective action as we know it? The analysis above certainly leads one to conclude that the Internet allows things to change, but the overall pattern is far from evident. Collective action today is different in terms of its organization, but not perhaps as different as some have argued or anticipated it would be (e.g., Table 12.1). To all intents and purposes, there is only limited evidence that the purported decreasing relevance of nation states is due to this technology, or that hierarchy has lost its relevance and that networks, communities, self-directed teams have come in its place. Although some organizations have lost powers, others (such as the global corporation) appear more powerful and menacing than ever before and, at least in the West, the individuals' much-touted freedom of choice is increasingly restricted to a narrow range of options that fit with a liberal-individualist and capitalist ideology. There are also limits to the extent that the Internet makes us increasingly global and connected – this is more likely to be true for elites in certain parts of the world. The means of engagement seem to have shifted remarkably little. The importance

of the 'battle for hearts and minds' is nothing new, and physical battlefields are still the key political and public concerns. Finally, the charge that in the age of the Internet our social interactions would be increasingly individualist has been thoroughly challenged by the rediscovered relevance of religion and other social identities. There is no doubt that some changes are occurring, but it is not always obvious how instrumental the Internet is in producing these, nor is it obvious how these changes will play out. In sum, although a variety of communication technologies are influencing collective action and protest, it remains a moot point whether this amounts to a 'paradigm shift' or radical change.

This chapter considered how virtual interaction, with all its ephemeral qualities, can give rise to sustained collective actions in which individuals sacrifice valued resources in the pursuit of some common goal. The very fact that this occurs makes it a most interesting case against which theories of self and social influence can be tested. The challenge of online collective action is not so much to understand it as a 'special' case, but to see why it fits the normal pattern of why and how humans are compelled to act for social change.

References

Adams, J. and Roscigno, V. J. (2005). White supremacsts, oppositional culture and the world wide web. *Social Forces 84*, 759–778.

Adler, P. S. and Kwon, S. W. (2002). Social capital: prospects for a new concept. *Academy Of Management Review 27*, 17–40.

Allport, F. H. (1924). *Social Psycology*. New York: Houghton Mifflin.

Bargh, J. A. and McKenna, K. Y. A. (2004). The Internet and social life. *Annual Review Of Psychology 55*, 573–590.

Barki, H. and Pinsonneault, A. (2001). Small group brainstorming and idea quality – is electronic brainstorming the most effective approach? *Small Group Research 32*, 158–205.

Barlow, J. P. (1995). Property and speech: who owns what you say in cyberspace? *Communications of the ACM 38*, 19–22.

Barreto, M. and Ellemers, N. (2000). You can't always do what you want: social identity and self-presentational determinants of the choice to work for a low-status group. *Personality and Social Psychology Bulletin 26*, 891–906.

Bennett, W. L. (2004). Communicating global activism: strengths and vulnerabilities of networked politics. In W. Van de Donk, B. D. Loader, P. G. Nixon and D. Rucht (eds), *Cyberprotest: New media, citizens and social movements* (pp. 123–146). London: Routledge.

Boase, J., Horrigan, J., Wellman, B. and Rainie, L. (2006). *The strength of internet ties: The internet and email aid users in maintaining their social networks and provide pathways to help when people face big decisions.* Pew Internet and American Life project, http://www.pewinternet.org/PPF/r/172/report_display.asp.

Breu, K. and Hemingway, C. J. (2004). Making organisations virtual: the hidden cost of distributed teams. *Journal Of Information Technology 19*, 191–202.

Brunsting, S. and Postmes, T. (2002). Social movement partcipation in the digital age–predicting offline and online collective action. *Small Group Research, 33*, 525–554.

Cassidy, W. P. (2005). Variations on a theme: the professional role conceptions of print and online newspaper journalists. *Journalism and Mass Communication Quarterly 82*, 264–280.

Castells, M. (1997). *The information age: Economy society and culture, vol. 2: The power of identity.* Oxford, UK: Blackwell.

Castells, M. (2001). *The internet galaxy: Reflections on internet, business and society.* London: Oxford University Press.

Chun, K. J. and Park, H. K. (1998). Examining the conflicting results of GDSS research. *Information and Management 33*, 313–325.

Clark, J. D. and Themudo, N. S. (2006). Linking the web and the street: Internet-based 'dotcauses' and the 'anti-globalization' movement. *World Development 34*, 50–74.

Daft, R. L. and Lengel, R. H. (1984). Information richness: a new approach to managerial behavior and organizational design. *Research in Organizational Behavior 6*, 191–233.

Dahlberg, L. (2001). Democracy via cyberspace – mapping the rhetorics and practices of three prominent camps. *New Media and Society 3*, 157–177.

Dartnell, M. (2006). *Insurgency online: Web activism and global conflict.* Toronto: University of Toronto Press.

DeLuca, K. M. and Peeples, J. (2002). From public sphere to public screen: democracy, activism and the 'violence' of Seattle. *Critical Studies In Media Communication 19*, 125–151.

Deutsch, M. and Gerard, H. B. (1955). A study of normative and informational social influences upon individual judgement. *Journal of Personality and Social Psychology 51*, 629–636.

Deuze, M. (2003). The web and its journalisms: considering the consequences of different types of newsmedia online. *New Media and Society 5*, 203–230.

Diener, E. (1980). Deindividuation: the absence of self-awareness and self-regulation in group members. In P. B. Paulus (ed.), *The psychology of group influence* (pp. 209–242). Hillsdale, NJ: Lawrence Erlbaum.

DiMaggio, P., Hargittai, E., Neuman, W. R. and Robinson, J. P. (2001). Social implications of the Internet. *Annual Review Of Sociology 27*, 307–336.

Drury, J. and Reicher, S. (2000). Collective action and psychological change: the emergence of new social identities. *British Journal of Social Psychology 39*, 579–604.

Drury, J. and Reicher, S. (2005). Explaining enduring empowerment: a comparative study of collective action and psychological outcomes. *European Journal Of Social Psychology 35*, 35–58.

Dubrovsky, V.J., Kiesler, S. and Sethna, B. N. (1991). The equalization phenomenon: status effects in computer-mediated and face-to-face decision-making groups. *Human Computer Interaction, 6*, 119–146.

Dugosh, K. L. and Paulus, P. B. (2005). Cognitive and social comparison processes in brainstorming. *Journal Of Experimental Social Psychology 41*, 313–320.

Eschenfelder, K. R., Howard, R. G. and Desai, A. C. (2005). Who posts DeCSS and why? A content analysis of Web sites posting DVD circumvention software. *Journal Of The American Society For Information Science And Technology 56*, 1405–1418.

Festinger, L. (1954). A theory of social comparison processes. *Human Relations 7*, 117–140.

Fisher, D. R., Stanley, K., Berman, D. and Neff, G. (2005). How do organizations matter? Mobilization and support for participants at five globalization protests. *Social Problems 52*, 102–121.

Flanagin, A. J., Stohl, C. and Bimber, B. (2006). Modeling the structure of collective action. *Communication Monographs 73*, 29–54.

Fulk, J. (1993). Social construction of communication technology. *Academy of Management Journal 36*, 921–950.

Gamson, W. A. (1992). The social psychology of collective action. In A. D. Morris and C. M. Müller (eds), *Frontiers in social movement theory* (pp. 53–76). New Haven, CT: Yale University Press.

George, C. (2005). The internet's political impact and the penetration/participation paradox in Malaysia and Singapore. *Media Culture and Society 27*, 903–920.

Guimond, S. and Dubé-Simard, L. (1983). Relative deprivation theory and the Quebec nationalist movement: the cognition-emotion distinction and the personal-group deprivation issue. *Journal of Personality and Social Psychology 44*, 526–535.

Haslam, S. A. (1997). Stereotyping and social influence: foundations of stereotype concensus. In R. Spears, P. J. Oakes, N. Ellemers and S. A. Haslam (eds), *The social psychology of stereotyping and group life* (pp. 119–143). Oxford, England: Blackwell.

Hiltz, S. R. and Turoff, M. (1978). *The network nation.* Cambridge, MA: MIT Press.

Horton, D. (2004). Local environmentalism and the Internet. *Environmental Politics 13*, 734–753.

Jennings, M. K. and Zeitner, V. (2003). Internet use and civic engagement – a longitudinal analysis. *Public Opinion Quarterly 67*, 311–334.

Jessup, L. M., Connolly, T. and Galegher, J. (1990). The effects of anonymity on GDSS group processes with an idea-generating task. *MIS Quarterly 14*, 313–321.

Joinson, A. N. (2003). *Understanding the psychology of Internet behaviour; Virtual worlds, real lives.* Basingstoke: Palgrave.

Kapor, M. (1993). Where is the digital highway really heading? *Wired* 1.03, available at http://www.wired.com/wired/archive/1.03/kapor.on.nii.html.

Kapor, M. (2004). Power to the (wired) people. *San Francisco Chronicle*, 17 October.

Katz, J. E., Rice, R. E. and Aspden, P. (2001). The Internet 1995–2000 – access, civic involvement and social interaction. *American Behavioral Scientist 45*, 405–419.

Kavanaugh, A., Carroll, J. M., Rosson, M. B., Reese, D. D. and Zin, T. T. (2005). Participating in civil society: the case of networked communities. *Interacting With Computers 17*, 9–33.

Kavanaugh, A., Reese, D. D., Carroll, J. M. and Rosson, M. B. (2005). Weak ties in networked communities. *Information Society 21*, 119–131.

Kelly, C. and Breinlinger, S. (1996). *The social psychology of collective action: Identity, injustice and gender.* Washington, DC: Taylor and Francis.

Kiesler, S., Siegel, J. and McGuire, T. W. (1984). Social psychological aspects of computer-mediated communication. *American Psychologist 39*, 1123–1134.

Klandermans, B. (1997). *The social psychology of protest.* Oxford, UK: Blackwell.

Klandermans, B. (2004). The demand and supply of participation: social-psychological correlates of participation in social movements. In D. A. Snow, S. A. Saule and H. Kriesi (eds), *The Blackwell companion to social movements* (pp. 360–379). Oxford: Blackwell.

Kraut, R., Kiesler, S., Boneva, B., Cummings, J., Helgeson, V. and Crawford, A. (2002). Internet paradox revisited. *Journal of Social Issues 58*, 49–74.

Kraut, R., Mukhopadhyay, T., Szczypula, J., Kiesler, S. and Scherlis, B. (1999). Information and communication: alternative uses of the Internet in households. *Information Systems Research 10*, 287–303.

Kraut, R., Patterson, M., Lundmark, V., Kiesler, S., Mukopadhyay, T. and Scherlis, W. (1998). Internet paradox – a social technology that reduces social involvement and psychological well-being? *American Psychologist 53*, 1017–1031.

Kraut, R., Steinfield, C., Chan, A. P., Butler, B. and Hoag, A. (1999). Coordination and virtualization: the role of electronic networks and personal relationships. *Organization Science 10*, 722–740.

Lea, M. and Spears, R. (1995). Love at first Byte? Building personal relationships over computer networks. In J. T. Wood and S. Duck (eds), *Understudied relationships: Off the beaten track.* (pp. 197–233). Beverly Hills, CA: Sage.

Lea, M., Spears, R. and de Groot, D. (2001). Knowing me, knowing you: anonymity effects on social identity processes within groups. *Personality and Social Psychology Bulletin 27*, 526–537.

Lyytinen, K., Maaranen, P. and Knuuttila, J. (1993). Unusual business or business as usual: an investigation of meeting support requirements in multilateral diplomacy. *Accounting, Management and Information Technologies 4*, 97–119.

Malone, T. W. and Rockart, J. F. (1991). Computers, networks and the corporation. *Scientific American 265*(3), 92–95.

Martins, L. L., Gilson, L. L. and Maynard, M. T. (2004). Virtual teams: what do we know and where do we go from here? *Journal Of Management 30*, 805–835.

McCarthy, J. D. and Zald, M. N. (1977). Resource mobilization and social movements: a partial theory. *American Journal of Sociology 82*, 1212–1241.

McCaughey, M. and Ayers, M. D. (2003). *Cyberactivism: Online activism in theory and practice.* New York: Routledge.

McGuire, T. W., Kiesler, S. and Siegel, J. (1987). Group and computer-mediated discussion effects in risk decision making. *Journal of Personality and Social Psychology 1987*, 917–930.

McKenna, K. Y. A. and Bargh, J. A. (1998). Coming out in the age of the Internet: identity 'demarginalization' through virtual group participation. *Journal of Personality and Social Psychology 75*, 681–694.

McKenna, K. Y. A. and Bargh, J. A. (2000). Plan 9 from cyberspace: the implications of the internet for personality and social psychology. *Personality and Social Psychology Review 4*, 57–75.

Mead, G. H. (1934). *Mind, self and society.* Chicago, IL: University of Chicago Press.

Meikle, G. (2003). *Future active: Media activism and the Internet.* New York: Routledge.

Micklethwait, J. and Wooldridge, A. (1996). *The witch doctors: Making sense of the management gurus.* New York: Random House.

Munkes, J. and Diehl, M. (2003). Matching or competition? Performance comparison processes in an idea generation task. *Group Processes and Intergroup Relations 6*, 305–320.

Olson, M. (1968). *The logic of collective action: Public goods and the theory of groups.* Cambridge, MA: Harvard University Press.

Pickering, J. M. and King, J. L. (1995). Hardwiring weak ties – interorganizational computer-mediated communication, occupational communities and organizational-change. *Organization Science 6*, 479–486.

Postmes, T. (2003). A social identity approach to communication in organizations. In S. A. Haslam, D. van Knippenberg, M. J. Platow and N. Ellemers (eds), *Social identity at work: Developing theory for organizational practice* (pp. 81–98). Philadelphia, PA: Psychology Press.

Postmes, T. and Baym, N. (2005). Intergroup dimensions of Internet. In J. Harwood and H. Giles (eds), *Intergroup communication: Multiple perspectives* (pp. 213–238). New York: Peter Lang Publishers.

Postmes, T. and Brunsting, S. (2002). Collective action in the age of internet: mass communication and online mobilization. *Social Science Computer Review, 20*, 290–301.

Postmes, T., Haslam, S. A. and Swaab, R. (2005). Social influence in small groups: an interactive model of social identity formation. *European Review of Social Psychology 16*, 1–42.

Postmes, T. and Spears, R. (1998). Deindividuation and anti-normative behavior: a meta-analysis. *Psychological Bulletin 123*, 238–259.

Postmes, T. and Spears, R. (2002). Contextual moderators of gender differences and stereotyping in computer-mediated group discussions. *Personality and Social Psychology Bulletin 28*, 1073–1083.

Postmes, T., Spears, R. and Lea, M. (1998). Breaching or building social boundaries? SIDE-effects of computer-mediated communication. *Communication Research 25*, 689–715.

Postmes, T., Spears, R. and Lea, M. (2002). Intergroup differentiation in computer-mediated communication: effects of depersonalization. *Group Dynamics 6*, 3–16.

Preece, J., Nonnecke, B. and Andrews, D. (2004). The top five reasons for lurking: improving community experiences for everyone. *Computers In Human Behavior 20*, 201–223.

Prentice-Dunn, S. and Rogers, R. W. (1989). Deindividuation and the self-regulation of behavior. In P. B. Paulus (ed.), *The psychology of group influence*, 2nd edn (pp. 86–109). Hillsdale, NJ: Lawrence Erlbaum.

Rains, S. A. (2005). Leveling the organizational playing field – virtually – a meta-analysis of experimental research assessing the impact of group support system use on member influence behaviors. *Communication Research 32*, 193–234.

Reicher, S. (1996). 'The Battle of Westminster:' developing the social identity model of crowd behaviour in order to explain the initiation and development of collective conflict. *European Journal of Social Psychology 26*, 115–134.

Reicher, S. (2001). Social identity definition and enactment: a broad SIDE against irrationalism and relativism. In T. Postmes, R. Spears, M. Lea and S. Reicher (eds), *SIDE effects centre stage: Recent developments in studies of de-individuation in groups* (pp. 175–190). Amsterdam, the Netherlands: Elsevier.

Reicher, S. and Levine, M. (1994). Deindividuation, power relations between groups and the expression of social identity: the effects of visibility to the out-group. *British Journal of Social Psychology 33*, 145–164.

Reicher, S., Spears, R. and Postmes, T. (1995). A social identity model of deindividuation phenomena. In W. Stroebe and M. Hewstone (eds), *European Review of Social Psychology*, vol. 6 (pp. 161–198). Chichester: Wiley.

Rheingold, H. (1993). *The virtual community: Homesteading on the electronic frontier*. Reading, MA: Addison-Wesley.

Rheingold, H. (2002). *Smart mobs: The next social revolution*. Cambridge, MA: Perseus.

Rice, R. E. and Katz, J. E. (2003). Comparing internet and mobile phone usage: digital divides of usage, adoption and dropouts. *Telecommunications Policy 27*, 597–623.

Rogers, E. (2003). *Diffusion of innovations*, 5th edn. New York: Simon and Schuster.

Ronfeldt, D., Arquilla, J., Fuller, G. and Fuller, M. (1998). *The Zapatista social netwar in Mexico: RAND corporation*. Available at http://www.rand.org/pubs/monograph_reports/MR994/index.html.

Rosenkrands, J. (2004). Politicizing homo economicus: analysis of anti-corporate websites. In W. Van de Donk, B. D. Loader, P. G. Nixon and D. Rucht (eds), *Cyberprotest: New media, citizens and social movements* (pp. 57–76). London: Routledge.

Rudé, G. (1964). *The crowd in history: A study of popular disturbances in France and England 1730–1848*. New York: Wiley.

Runciman, W. G. (1966). *Relative deprivation and social justice: A study of attitudes to social inequality in twentieth-century England*. Berkeley, CA: University of California Press.

Sallot, L. M., Porter, L. V. and Acosta-Alzuru, C. (2004). Practitioners' web use and perceptions of their own roles and power: a qualitative study. *Public Relations Review 30*, 269–278.

Scheufele, D. A., Nisbet, M. C., Brossard, D. and Nisbet, E. C. (2004). Social structure and citizenship: examining the impacts of social setting, network heterogeneity and informational variables on political participation. *Political Communication 21*, 315–338.

Schussman, A. and Earl, J. (2004). From barricades to firewalls? Strategic voting and social movement leadership in the Internet age. *Sociological Inquiry 74*, 439–463.

Sedikides, C. B. and Brewer, M. (ed.). (2001). *Individual self, relational self, collective self*. Philadelphia, PA: Psychology Press.

Short, J. A. (1974). Effects of medium of communication on experimental negotiation. *Human Relations 27*, 225–234.

Short, J. A., Williams, E. and Christie, B. (1976). *The social psychology of telecommunications*. Chichester: John Wiley.

Simon, B. (1998). Individuals, groups and social change: on the relationship between individual and collective self-interpretations and collective action. In C. Sedikides, J. Schopler and C. A. Insko (eds), *Intergroup cognition and intergroup behavior* (pp. 257–282). Mahwah, NJ: Erlbaum.

Simon, B. and Klandermans, B. (2001). Politicized collective identity – a social psychological analysis. *American Psychologist 56*, 319–331.

Smith, H. J. and Ortiz, D. J. (2002). Is it just me? The different consequences of personal and group relative deprivation. In I. Walker and H. J. Smith (eds), *Relative deprivation: Specification, development and integration* (pp. 91–115). Cambridge: Cambridge University Press.

Smith, J. (2001). Globalizing resistance: The Battle of Seattle and the future of social movements. *Mobilization 6*, 1–20.

Spears, R. and Lea, M. (1992). Social influence and the influence of the 'social' in computer-mediated communication. In M. Lea (ed.), *Contexts of computer-mediated communication* (pp. 30–65). Hemel Hempstead, England: Harvester Wheatsheaf.

Spears, R. and Lea, M. (1994). Panacea or panopticon? The hidden power in computer-mediated communication. *Communication Research 21*, 427–459.

Spears, R., Lea, M., Corneliussen, R. A., Postmes, T. and Ter Haar, W. (2002). Computer-mediated communication as a channel for social resistance – the strategic side of SIDE. *Small Group Research 33*, 555–574.

Spears, R., Postmes, T., Lea, M. and Wolbert, A. (2002). The power of influence and the influence of power in virtual groups: A SIDE look at CMC and the Internet. *The Journal of Social Issues. Special Issue: Social impact of the Internet 58*, 91–108.

Spears, R., Postmes, T., Wolbert, A., Lea, M. and Rogers, P. (2000). *Social psychological influence of ICT's on society and their policy implications* (Scientific survey). Amsterdam, the Netherlands: Infodrome.

Stoll, C. (1995). *Silicon snake oil: Second thoughts on the information highway.* New York: Doubleday.

Stott, C. and Drury, J. (2004). The importance of social structure and social interaction in stereotype consensus and content: is the whole greater than the sum of its parts? *European Journal of Social Psychology 34,* 11–23.

Streeter, T. (2003). The romantic self and the politics of Internet commercialization. *Cultural Studies 17,* 648–668.

Stroebe, W. and Diehl, M. (1994). Why groups are less effective than their members: on productivity losses in idea-generating groups. In W. Stroebe and M. Hewstone (eds), *European review of social psychology,* vol. 5, (pp. 271–303). Chichester, England: Wiley.

Stürmer, S. and Simon, B. (2004). Collective action: Towards a dual-pathway model. *European Review of Social Psychology, 25,* 59–99.

Swaab, R. I., Postmes, T., Spears, R. and Van Beest, I. (in press). Shared cognition as a product of and precursor to, shared social identity: The role of communication in negotiations. *Personality and Social Psychology Bulletin.*

Tanis, M. and Postmes, T. (2005). A social identity approach to trust: interpersonal perception, group membership and trusting behavior. *European Journal of Social Psychology, 35,* 413–424.

Tajfel, H. and Turner, J. C. (1979). An integrative theory of intergroup conflict. In S. Worchel and W. G. Austin (eds), *The psychology of intergroup relations* (pp. 33–47). Monterey, CA: Brooks-Cole.

Tilly, C. (2004). *Social movements 1768–2004.* Boulder, CO: Paradigm.

Turkle, S. (1995). *Life on the screen: Identity in the age of the internet.* New York: Simon and Schuster.

Turner, J. C. (1991). *Social influence.* Milton Keynes, UK: Open University Press.

Turner, J. C. (2005). Explaining the nature of power: A three-process theory. *European Journal Of Social Psychology 35,* 1–22.

Turner, R. H. and Killian, L. M. (1972). *Collective behavior,* 2nd edn. Englewood Cliffs, NJ: Prentice-Hall.

Valacich, J. S., Dennis, A. R. and Nunamaker, J. F., Jr. (1991). Electronic meeting support: the groupsystems concept. Special issue: Computer-supported cooperative work and groupware: I. *International Journal of Man Machine Studies 34,* 261–282.

Van de Donk, W., Loader, B. D., Nixon, P. G. and Rucht, D. (2004a). Introduction: Social movements and ICTs. In W. Van de Donk, B. D. Loader, P. G. Nixon and D. Rucht (eds), *Cyberprotest: New media, citizens and social movements* (pp. 1–25). London: Routledge.

Van de Donk, W., Loader, B. D., Nixon, P. G. and Rucht, D. (eds). (2004b). *Cyberprotest: New media, Citizens and social movements.* London: Routledge.

Walker, I. and Smith, H. J. (2002). *Relative deprivation: Specification, development and integration.* Cambridge: Cambridge University Press.

Walther, J. B. (1996). Computer-mediated communication: impersonal, interpersonal and hyperpersonal interaction. *Communication Research 23,* 1–43.

Walther, J. B., Anderson, J. F. and Park, D. W. (1994). Interpersonal effects in computer-mediated interaction: a meta-analysis of social and anti-social communication. *Communication Research 21,* 460–487.

Weisband, S. P. (1994). Overcoming social awareness in computer-supported groups: Does anonymity really help? *Computer-Supported Cooperative Work 2,* 285–297.

Weisband, S. P., Schneider, S. K. and Connolly, T. (1995). Computer-mediated communication and social information: status salience and status differences. *Academy of Management Journal 38,* 1124–1151.

Wellman, B., Salaff, J., Dimitrova, D., Garton, L., Gulia, M. and Haythornthwaite, C. (1996). Computer networks as social networks: collaborative work, telework and virtual community. *Annual Review Of Sociology 22,* 213–238.

Wright, S. (2004). Informing, communicating and ICTs in contemporary anti-capitalist movements. In W. Van de Donk, B. D. Loader, P. G. Nixon and D. Rucht (eds), *Cyberprotest: New media, citizens and social movements* (pp. 77–93). London: Routledge.

Wright, S. C. and Taylor, D. M. (1998). Responding to tokenism: individual action in the face of collective injustice. *European Journal of Social Psychology 28,* 647–667.

Zimbardo, P. G. (1969). The human choice: individuation, reason and order vs. deindividuation, impulse and chaos. In W. J. Arnold and D. Levine (eds), *Nebraska Symposium on Motivation,* vol. 17 (pp. 237–307). Lincoln, NE: University of Nebraska Press.

Zuboff, S. (1988). *In the age of the smart machine.* New York: Basic Books.

PART 3

Personality, Self and Identity

CHAPTER 13

Personality, individual differences and Internet use

Yair Amichai-Hamburger

Personality represents 'those characteristics of the person that account for his consistent pattern of behaviour' (Pervin 1993: 3). The key to understanding regularities in the thoughts, feelings and overt behaviours of people is knowledge of their personality. Whereas most areas of psychology explore specific aspects of human behaviour, such as perception or memory, the psychology of personality sees the individual as one integrative unit.

The study of personality has always been an integral part of the study of psychology; however, the study of the psychology of the Internet may be seen as a new addition to a traditional practice. Nevertheless, what at first sight may seem to be the marrying of opposites, the 'hard' technology of the Internet against the 'soft' field of studying human beings, is not really so (see also Buchanan, Chapter 28 this volume). For although the Internet is obviously a technological entity, it is actually brought into being by the hundreds of millions of people who surf the net. It is, therefore, a mutual need of psychologists and Internet designers to cooperate together to enhance the understanding of human-Internet interactions, so that both may better understand the requirements of Internet users. At present, Internet designers and psychologists hold mutually

exclusive attitudes towards the Internet and its users. Net designers have a tendency to view users as a single entity, ignoring personality differences, while psychologists tend to stereotype the Internet as one unit, ignoring its variety and richness (Amichai-Hamburger 2002).

This chapter seeks to enhance our understanding of human Internet interaction from three different angles. First, we discuss those unique features of the Internet that are relevant to personality. The second angle is an analysis of the work of personality theorists and its application to the Internet. The final part discusses specific personality characteristics and their interaction with the Internet.

Internet psychological context

Internet use involves special factors which together create a unique psychological environment for the user. McKenna et al. (2002) suggest four major factors that differentiate between Internet interaction and face-to-face interaction:

1. Greater anonymity;
2. The diminution of the importance of physical appearance;

3. Greater control over the time and pace of interactions;

4. The ease of finding similar others.

It is interesting to learn how these differences interact with our personality.

Greater anonymity

On the Internet, people can easily maintain their anonymity. They can choose a false name and falsify or hide other personal and identifying details. This secrecy around their identity encourages people to express themselves more freely and sincerely than they would in a face-to-face interaction, since they are not subject to the usual social rules and norms (Turkle 1995). In fact, the opportunity provided by the Internet to hide or falsify one's identity and remain undetected may well encourage people to do so. However, when a common social identity is available in the net interaction, for example through email address, it is likely to enhance intergroup differentiation (Postmes *et al.* 2000, 2002).

In our daily lives, it is only in brief temporary interactions, for example when ordering coffee, that we do not disclose our identity. We will only give our name if we want to give greater significance to the encounter. We are unlikely to give false details unless we have a particular motive and/or are unlikely to be discovered. Sometimes, however, the opposite is true. Two strangers meeting on the train might actually feel safe to open up to one another and reveal very intimate secrets, since they are strangers and unlikely to meet again. Rubin (1975) termed this process the 'strangers-on-a-train phenomenon': in Alfred Hitchcock's 1950 movie *Strangers on a Train*, two men, Guy and Robert, meet on a train and reveal confidences to one another. This later leads to some interesting scenes. A similar process leading to self-disclosure is likely to occur on the web. Joinson (2001) found that a pair of students working on an academic task over the Internet revealed more personal information in the encounter than did students performing the same task offline. Tidwell and Walther (2002) found that people who interacted with one another through email demonstrated a more direct and intimate relationship and perceived the interaction as more effective as compared with those who interacted face-to-face.

Anonymity is also likely to give people the courage to join web communities when they belong to a group with a negative social stigma (McKenna and Bargh 1998; McKenna *et al.* 2002). This is particularly true of people belonging to a group, such as one with marginalized sexual interests, where members conceal their stigma in daily life. When they become members of a group of similar others, their self-esteem is likely to rise, leading to a greater possibility that they will eventually choose to 'come out' to the offline world (McKenna and Bargh 1998).

Anonymity may also encourage people to explore different aspects of their identity in a way that is not possible or sanctioned according to traditional social rules and norms (Turkle 1995). In the same way, the fact that people are 'faceless' on the Internet may give them the confidence to acquire goods and services that they would refrain from purchasing if they were concerned that they might be identified (Hamburger and Fox 2000). This paradox is discussed in greater detail by Joinson and Paine in Chapter 16, Self-disclosure, privacy and the Internet.

Diminution of physical appearance

Physical appearance is one of the focal determinants of the way in which we are perceived by others. Cialdini (1984) suggested that attractive people have an enormous social advantage in our culture; they are better liked, more frequently helped and seen as possessing better personality traits and intellectual capabilities. This advantage is bestowed due to what is termed the halo effect. This occurs when one positive characteristic of a person, such as attractiveness, dominates the way a person is viewed by others. Just as the halo effect plays in favour of the physically attractive, the reverse is true for people who are physically unappealing. The first physical impression is likely to set the course for the rest of the interaction (Fiske and Taylor 1991), and will play a large part in determining the outcome of any kind of association, be it a working relationship or a romantic one (Hatfield and Sprecher 1986). Since a typical Internet social interaction is solely text-based, the physical characteristics of the participants remain undisclosed. This will be particularly significant for people with unsightly or unattractive physical characteristics who are likely to suffer from discrimination in a face-to-face interaction. On the Internet they have an opportunity to present themselves in any way they choose. They may hope that if and when the interaction progresses to a face-to-face one, any negative physical presence will not be relevant. This process is not that simple, firstly, because in many cases the negative perception of those people by others gets accepted and internalized by them into their self-esteem and so the negative responses to their physical appearance create a self-fulfilling prophecy. Secondly, the person with negative physical characteristics might avoid face-to-face interaction and may choose to have online interactions only. Interestingly, Ben-Ze'ev (2005) points out that the anonymity of the Internet encounter may also be enjoyed by people who are very physically attractive and who are concerned that their appearance is the only reason that others wish to get to know them. For such people, the obscurity provided by cyberspace interactions brings freedom and a release.

Greater control

People who are socially inhibited, very shy, or have not mastered significant social skills may often feel a lack of control and even fear during a typical face-to-face encounter. Those same individuals will probably experience greater control when they communicate through the Internet. This is due to several factors: first, the timing of the encounter is in the hands of each of the participants. Each one decides when he or she will write a message and when he or she will reply. Moreover, there is an opportunity to review the communication before it is sent and it will only be sent, if at all, when the writer is sufficiently satisfied with the content. This thought and review process is obviously non-existent in face-to-face encounters. This progression of writing an email and then reviewing it on the screen creates the potential for high self-awareness, since the writer observes themself as an object and so is likely to write the message in terms which will create the impression they hope to achieve (Duval and Wicklund 1972). This impression may contrast with the persona they hold in everyday life.

The unique facet of Internet communication is that for the participant, the whole encounter is taking place in an environment of their choosing and this may well be a source of security and comfort. Thus, the Internet user is able to 'go out to meet the world,' from their own living room. You, the user, may encounter strangers, but you remain in your own room, wearing your slippers, holding your cup of coffee. The flexibility of the Internet interactions fits very well with the demands of the modern man and woman. For many people, kin and friendship networks are spread throughout the world. The ability to send and answer emails at a time of their choosing, in the knowledge that the recipient is able to receive the message almost instantaneously, enables people to support and maintain their social contacts. Should the Internet discussion or partner not be to your liking, you have the ability to terminate the interaction at the press of a button and then disappear into oblivion with no social consequences – something that remains in the realm of fantasy in a face-to-face interaction. Paradoxically, the power awarded to an Internet user by the Internet to sever a connection with such ease actually creates a platform for intense romantic relationships. This is because the knowledge that they have the ability to cut off the exchange and vanish at any given moment gives users a feeling of tremendous control and so invites significant self-disclosure (Ben Ze'ev 2005). The resources offered by the Internet may significantly assist certain groups in society, for example those with special needs, to lead independent lives. This help is given in ways that traditional services are unable to provide. For example, a person with such handicaps may now carry out certain tasks independently or with greater ease, such as shopping and paying fees to local authorities or banking over the Internet. This clearly has a great impact and tremendous potential for the self-efficacy of previously socially excluded and marginalized communities.

Finding similar others

The Internet is accessed every day by many millions of users, all of whom have various interests. This, together with the ease of finding details of the different interests and services offered by the net, makes it exceptionally easy to discover like-minded others visiting the same site. This fact has opened up opportunities for people belonging to hidden stigmatized groups.

These individuals are likely to suffer two major psychological implications arising from their membership of such groups:

1. They will be able to hide their group identity, but may experience difficulties in detecting similar others and this may create feelings of loneliness.

2. Since they are not known to belong to one of these stigmatized groups, members of such groups are likely to be present in situations where other people express their negative stereotypes about their group, which in turn will lower their self-esteem (Frable 1993).

On the Internet, many thousands of different groups exist and it is fairly straightforward to find a group of similar others without having to risk publicly revealing your identity as belonging to a stigmatized group. Visiting websites of similar others may make people feel that their group is much larger than they had imagined, and this may lead them to feel confident. In a series of studies, McKenna and Bargh (1998) tested the implications of belonging to a newsgroup (an Internet-based discussion about a particular topic) of similar others. They concentrated their research on hidden stigmatized groups, such as those whose members had marginalized sexual interests or marginal political views and ideology. They found that people belonging to a stigmatized identity group were more likely to be involved in a newsgroup of similar others, and considered their belonging to the group as being more important to their identity as compared with those who identified with a non-stigmatized interest newsgroup. For those posting to the newsgroup, this involvement elevated their self-esteem, self-acceptance and reduced feelings of social loneliness. In addition, they were highly motivated to make their identity a social reality by telling their close circle of family and friends that they belonged to a stigmatized group. This is in comparison to those people who did not become deeply involved in the newsgroup (lurkers).

The Internet creates a unique setting which has no equivalent in the offline world. This highly protected environment affects people in different ways. In some cases, it releases the individual from the 'normative persona mask' they wear in face-to-face interactions and so may help them to explore themselves and experiment with different aspects of their identity (Turkle 1995). A highly supportive net environment might also help people to reach their deepest level of personality, also called the 'true self' (McKenna and Bargh 2000). Some people might exploit the feeling of protection they receive from the Internet, and express different forms of aggression against others on the net. Others may feel that the protected environment allows them the opportunity to help others on the net, while still determining their own limits. For others, it will speed the process of getting from the first phase of a romantic relationship to an intimacy and closeness stage (Cooper and Sportolari 1997; McKenna and Bargh 2000).

The sheltered environment provided by the Internet also assists people in the selection and buying of products. Many people feel uncomfortable browsing or asking for information in a regular store. They may feel that this creates an obligation to buy, with the result that they may not buy a product at all or feel that they have bought under pressure and may be unsure of their purchase. Shopping on the Internet alleviates much of this stress. The consumer may request as much information and take as much time as he or she chooses. In addition, surfers may examine as many different products as they wish, without the embarrassment of an obligation to buy (Hamburger and Fox 2000). For those people who are unhappy about their size or appearance, the ability to order clothes over the Internet and try them on in the privacy of their own home brings immense relief and may lead to an improvement in self-esteem.

The ease with which a consumer may ask questions and obtain products at a commercial site may be of particular help to people suffering from social inhibitions; for not only are they able to receive the knowledge and goods they require, but, in addition, they have the opportunity to practice interacting with others in a 'safe' environment. For example, people with social anxiety may suffer severe unease during a face-to-face interaction. On the Internet they will not experience this anxiety. People are much more likely to cope well with rejection on the net, since the environment is a game-like or virtual reality and so the negative experience can be disassociated and easily suppressed (Suler 2004). This can help people build their confidence and self-esteem.

Other advantages of the Internet for the socially inhibited and others may include group learning in an e-learning protected environment. These are only some of the implications and advantages of the highly protected Internet environment.

We will now move on to learn how some of the major classical psychological theories contribute to the understanding of human behaviour on the net.

Leading personality theories and how they relate to Internet use

Many different psychologists have sought to explain the human personality. In this section, we will examine aspects of those theories that have particular relevance to the interaction between human beings and Internet technology. In this way we hope to reach a greater understanding of the phenomenon.

Sigmund Freud

Some relevant aspects of his theories

Freud saw all human behaviour as motivated by natural drives or instincts which, in turn, are the neurological representations of physical needs. According to him (1915a, b), the personality is divided into three substructures: id, ego and superego. The id is the uninhibited primitive sexual and destructive impulses (also called the libidinal energy). These have a strong desire to be expressed. The ego is the mechanism helping the id to express itself in ways that are socially acceptable. The superego is made up of the moral values that society has assimilated into the individual. The ego has to create a balance between the aspiration of the id to express itself fully and that of the superego to suppress the id. Freud suggested that our personality crystallizes early in our childhood. Moreover, he believed that throughout our lives, the disputes between these three areas of our personality are conducted in an unconscious area where our suppressed wishes and desires reside.

Is the Internet an id environment?

The Internet is a protected environment, where an individual can behave as they wish without identifying themself. It is also a place that does not allow society an opportunity to pass judgement on the activities held there. When people are granted this complete freedom away from the mores of society, are they likely to freely express their id, since the constraints imposed by their superego are largely irrelevant? In other words, does the Internet arena encourage people to expose their uninhibited id explicitly?

Fenichel (2004) pointed out that the Internet enables free association, transference and projection and that there are many places on the net where the libido may be expressed. Turkle (1995) studied identity swapping on the Internet through the multi-user dimension (MUD). At a MUD session, users build the roles of social interaction as they go along and construct their self through interaction with others using text only. Turkle found that people who play frequently on the MUD take on the persona of the individual they are impersonating. This is consistent with Fine (1983) who argued that in fantasy games, when a person plays a character for a long time, they become more and more identified with that character and begin to mutually experience the emotions and feelings of that character. But do these fantasy games actually build a character that is a free expression of the id? It seems that, in general, the answer is no. First of all, according to Freudian theory, our personality is determined quite early in life and, therefore, it does not seem that the Internet environment will create a strong enough counter-force to free the id. This conclusion is reinforced when we examine the behaviour of a newcomer to a website or forum. When an individual enters a website or forum for the first time, they will attempt to learn the established norms of the environment and adapt themself to them (Amichai-Hamburger 2005). People take it upon themselves to learn the rules of the website and know that if they break them, they are likely to be expelled. Even the identity games, in which people take on different roles at different MUD sessions, demonstrate the power of the ego, rather than the id, since the user is actually obeying the norms of the MUD-specific environment. The identity chosen by the user might be a reflection of a personal desire, but this is, in all likelihood, a reflection of a conscious rather than an unconscious wish. It appears that what the

Internet has actually created is a context for people to express the desires and wishes of which they are already aware.

The Internet demonstrates the strength of the ego through its capacity to deal with contradictions. This power of the ego is closer to post-Freudian theories, rather than those of Freud himself. For example, Klein (1961) suggested that, in addition to the traditional understanding of the ego's role of allowing the id to be expressed in a socially acceptable manner, the ego also initiates stimulating situations in order to experience and master them. A feeling of mastery is achieved by improving the control and synthesis functions (see also Black and Black 1974; Kohut 1977). What might seem as a regression in the MUD is actually a reflection of a mechanism of regression controlled by the ego. People may express their fantasies on the MUD or any other relevant Internet service, but they leave them whenever they choose.

The danger of the net

Basing our knowledge on Freudian theory, we suggest that surfing parts of the Internet may have serious consequences for people who have suffered a severe trauma and have not received treatment for it. Trauma is likely to occur to an individual who 'experienced, witnessed or was confronted with an event or events that involved actual or threatened death or serious injury, or a threat to the physical integrity of self or others' (DSM-IV) (American Psychiatric Association 1994: 427). As a consequence of the trauma, the individual holds in their memory many experiences and fears. Without treatment, these are likely to remain suppressed (Freud 1915a, b). For such people, the Internet experience may be like opening Pandora's box and release previously suppressed memories. This, in turn, is likely to lead to an experience of extreme anxiety, helplessness and horror and for those people who have experienced extreme trauma, it is likely to result in strong feelings of learned helplessness. Even without the Internet, the suppressed thoughts strive to be expressed and surface in different forms of dreams and thoughts: the individual is always on the alert, feeling that a catastrophe is going to occur. The safe and unstructured environment provided by the Internet in the form of fantasy games may allow

these suppressed traumatic experiences to appear in the conscious mind. Since the traumatic experience is constantly on the surface of the conscious mind, what at first may appear as a controlled release of psychological pressure may actually result in a flood to the conscious of the unbearable past experience. Unable to cope with this return to the traumatic experience, the mental health of the individual may be severely harmed.

Freudian psychoanalysis meetings over the Internet

Internet therapy is a controversial topic (Maheu and Gordon 2000; Ragusea and Vandecreek 2003). One of the main criticisms levelled against e-therapy is that the Internet session lacks the component of non-verbal communication between the patient and the psychologist. This may lead to poor interpretation and diagnosis. However, when we examine the classical Freudian setting for a psychoanalysis therapy session, we learn that the therapist and the patient do not see one another during therapy (for the therapist, this is optional). In a typical Freudian session, the patient lies on the couch and the therapist sits in a chair writing comments. It seems, therefore, that even in the classical setting, there is a lack of non-verbal communication. Freud himself treated some patients from a distance, exclusively through written text, rather than in person. It can also be argued that Freud's psychoanalytic techniques were designed to foster the very reduction of inhibition which naturally occurs on the Internet (Fenichel *et al.* 2002). Freud believed that the therapeutic process is based on the narrative of the client. This, by its very nature, is a virtual object existing only in the minds of the patient and therapist. It is the feelings of security felt by the participants that play a major part in transforming this narrative into a therapeutic process. In this sense the Internet is able to provide similar feelings of security which enable a therapeutic process to take place (Green 2004).

Carl Jung

Some relevant aspects of his theory

Jung was a follower of Freud, but added and changed several components in Freud's psychoanalytical theory. One of Jung's unique contributions was the understanding that our personality consists of opposites which can create a significant whole. The concept of opposites is common in Eastern philosophy as, for example, is demonstrated in the Taoist symbol of Yin and Yang, which stands for a complex of inexorable opposites. According to Jung, opposites produce a tension that creates the psychic energy that enables life to exist. Jung believed that the danger lies on one side expressing itself so strongly that the contradictory side is prevented from expressing itself in a satisfactory way. One of the specific illustrations of the idea of complementary opposites is extroversion vs. introversion orientations (Jung 1939; Campbell 1971). The extrovert is a friendly person who seeks company, desires excitement, takes risks and acts on impulse, whereas the introvert is a quiet, reflective person who prefers his or her own company and does not enjoy large social events; introverts do not crave excitement and may be seen by some as distant and remote. Most scholars using these definitions have considered these personality components to be two extremes of the same continuum (see, for example, Eysenck and Eysenck 1975). Jung himself, however, believed that they coexist simultaneously within the same personality; while one may dominate, the other is also present, although it may be unconscious and undeveloped.

The extroversion–introversion coexistence

This coexistence of extroversion–introversion is particularly relevant to Internet use. This is because the unique components of the Internet may assist introverted individuals to express themselves more freely on the net than they feel able to in an offline relationship. This hypothesis was confirmed with regard to women (Hamburger and Ben-Artzi 2000). Amichai-Hamburger (2005) suggests that, in time, introverted males will also come to realize that the Internet social services may answer their social needs, since the protected net environment allows them to express themselves freely.

Maldonado *et al.* (2001) evaluated computer-mediated messages and found that introverted subjects send messages with an extroverted tone. Their messages contained more information than those sent by extroverted subjects. It seems that on the net, introverts do not behave in accordance with their usual behaviour patterns, but, due to

the secure environment, conduct themselves in ways associated with extroverts in offline relationships (see also Amichai-Hamburger *et al.* 2002). This uncharacteristic online behaviour by introverts accords with the teachings of Jung. Since human beings are made up of opposing sets of characteristics, an extroverted person will also be an unexpressed introvert, the introversion lying mainly in the unconscious. The opposite is true for the introvert. Well-being is the result of a successful creation of a balance between these two opposing forces. The Internet may be able to assist in the construction of such an equilibrium, by allowing individuals to express the undeveloped part of their personalities. Thus, introverts may express their extroversion in online relationships.

Erik Erikson

A few relevant aspects of his theory

Erik Erikson was also a follower of Freud, though he, too, changed some important elements in Freud's theory. Erikson (1968) and Freud viewed the early stages of childhood in a similar way, but, in addition to focusing on libidinal tension, Erikson also emphasized the rational or ego processes involved. As a result, his theory places a greater emphasis on societal and cultural influences. Erikson argued that our personality starts to form from earliest infancy and continues to develop throughout our lives. According to Erikson, the ability to give and receive mature adult love is based on intimacy, the ability to reflect your identity on your partner. To be able to do so, an individual needs a sense of coherent identity during their adolescence. Those who fail to develop a sense of identity are likely to experience isolation. One of Erikson's suggestions for adolescents in our society is the psychosocial moratorium, a little 'time out': namely, to have a change in your life, go abroad ... leave school ... get a job ....

How the Internet can help to develop a sense of coherent identity

Erikson believed that the main challenge of the adolescent stage of development was to find the answer to the all-pervasive question 'Who am I?' The Internet's secure environment may help young people to solve this dilemma. Erikson (1968) believed that a game may serve as a means through which experience is formulated. Turkle (1995) took up this idea and suggested that participation in Internet identity games is similar to participation in psychodrama. During their developmental years, individuals experiment with different identities until they adopt one. According to Turkle, the Internet identity game helps to bring about psychological maturity. This is achieved by being able to discover different aspects of the self and experiencing flexible transitions between different identities. Turkle believes that the Internet supplies an individual with space, warmth, safety and understanding. This is, in fact, a similar setting to that provided by psychotherapy, so that both the Internet and the psychotherapy room will often create a safe environment in which to rework elements from the past and try out different alternatives for the present and the future. The ability to experience different parts of our identity through the Internet may help an individual to come to a satisfactory answer to the question 'Who am I?' In addition, the Internet supplies an environment that helps to create a 'time out' for the individual and so it can serve as a moratorium as was recommended by Erikson for adolescents in our society (Turkle 2004).

Albert Bandura

A few words on his theory

Albert Bandura is a post-behaviourist psychologist who became the leader of the cognitive movement. Behaviourist theory argued that the understanding of personality lies in learning the impact of an individual's environment on their behaviour. Bandura (1977) believed this to be too simplistic an approach to explain the aggressive behaviour he was observing in adolescents. He began to see personality as the result of an interaction between the environment, behaviour and the individual's psychological processes. Bandura defined this interaction as reciprocal determination. He called his theory Social Learning Theory. His emphasis on the importance of the intermediation of cognitive variables led him to become a leader of the cognitive movement.

Aggression and the Internet

Malamuth *et al.* (2005) argue that the unique components of the net prompt displays of violent behaviour that are not exhibited in other communication channels. They suggest that Internet aggression may be explained by a general framework advocated by Social Learning Theory (Bandura 1977), which focuses on the causes of aggressive behaviours – motivational, disinhibitory and opportunity aspects. The *motivational aspect* of the net relies on the fact that it is continually open and, therefore, creates an aggressive message that is available all the time and at little cost (if any) to the millions of people who surf the net. In addition, the net surfer experiences no restrictions in this interactive and very engaging medium. The Internet's *disinhibitory aspects* maintain aggression since the content of the net is unregulated and many participants remain anonymous and therefore do not feel accountable. Participation is unmonitored by society and therefore there is no social cost to aggressive behaviour. Conversely, other participants are likely to endorse and encourage hostile behaviour. The *opportunity aspects* for violence are very common on the net, since it is very easy to find targets. Moreover, not only are you, the aggressor, anonymous, but the targets of your aggression are unknown, maybe faceless, dehumanized and will not retaliate.

Prosocial behaviour on the net

The social learning theory can explain a whole range of behaviours on the net from aggression to prosocial behaviour. Sproull *et al.* (2005) use social learning theory (Bandura 1977) to explain prosocial behaviour on the Internet. They suggest that in a collaborative work group positive reinforcement is given to prosocial behaviour and positive social role models are much in evidence. In addition, help may be given to others over the net at very low cost, both in terms of time and effort. These components, according to Social Learning Theory, are likely to explain prosocial behaviour on the Internet.

It is interesting to note that aggressive behaviour and prosocial behaviour are explained by the same psychological mechanism, which might indicate that the Internet only creates an escalation of the tendencies existing before. Since it is extremely easy on the net to find similar others, people are likely to find communities that reinforce their natural tendencies. This is especially powerful with tendencies that are unlikely to find reinforcement in the offline world (as is the case with aggression).

Carl Rogers

A few relevant aspects of his theory

Carl Rogers saw his movement as an alternative to those of psychoanalysis and behaviourism. His Human Potential Movement believed that contemporary life had led people to abandon their innate character traits, in favour of the development of a new personality that they believed would assure them the devotion of others. These actions were ultimately inadequate, for despite all their pretense and effort to gratify others, their recipients remained dissatisfied. Rogers (1980) suggested that, for healthy people, there is no tension between the self and the experience because they are not so self-protective as to be unable to experience new phenomena. Rogers believes that children who experience unconditional love from their parents are those who achieve the self-awareness gained from their ability to be open to new experiences and to give their own interpretation to the world around them.

The structure of the Rogerian personality (Rogers 1961) contains three different selves: *The self-concept* (the phenomenological self) – the subjective perception of the self. This includes both the parts that are expressed and conscious beliefs about the self, as influenced by culture and education. *The true self* – or the organismic valuing process, represents the real self, for most people as yet unfulfilled. It is the deepest part of our personality which knows what is good or bad for the individual. *The ideal self* – what the person would like to be. This is not necessarily the same as the true self, since the person can have an ideal self that is totally at odds with that to which they should aspire.

The true self and the net

McKenna *et al.* (2002) believe that the secure protective environment found on the Internet is likely to have a positive effect on net relationships. They argue that the unique atmosphere created by cyberspace allows people to share self-relevant information in a way that they would be unwilling to in the offline world. McKenna and her colleagues use the concept of

the 'real me' to refer to a version of the self that someone believes is the truth, but that they find difficulty in expressing. They derive their concept from the 'true self' concept used by Rogers (1961) for the feelings of patients after successful therapy, when they manage to become more truly themselves.

McKenna *et al.* (2002) differentiate between people who locate their real me on the Internet – that is, reveal their real self over the net – and those who locate their real me in face-to-face relationships – they prefer to reveal their real self in traditional offline relationships. They suggest that the location of the real me defines where people will have their more significant relationships, online or offline. When a person locates their 'real me' on the Internet, it is expected that they will have a more significant relationship over the net than when a person locates their 'real me' in offline relationships. In addition, based on the work of Gollwitzer (1986), they suggest that these people will strive to move those significant relationships outside of the net, so as to make them a social reality. In a series of three experiments, they demonstrated that people who found it easier to express their 'real me' over the net reported a rapid formation of cyberspace relationships and that those relationships endured over time. They also found that people who are socially anxious and lonely can better express themselves on the Internet than in offline relationships. Social anxiety and loneliness are linked to relationship intimacy by mediation of the location of the self. There is no direct relationship between social anxiety and loneliness on one hand and intimacy and closeness on the other. In addition, they found that in order to create a social reality, people strive to move their significant Internet relationships to their non-Internet social life.

Amichai-Hamburger *et al.* (2002) attempted to relate the Internet 'real me' concept (see McKenna *et al.* 2002) to the Extroversion and Neuroticism personality theory (Eysenck and Eysenck 1975). They found that among participants who were regular users of chat rooms, introverted and neurotic people locate their 'real me' on the Internet, while extroverts and non-neurotic people locate their 'real me' through traditional social interaction. The social services, (for example, newsgroups, forums, communities) found on the Internet provide an excellent solution for people who experience great difficulty in forming social contacts due to their introverted neurotic personality. The main reasons for this are the special properties of such services when they are provided on the Internet: for example, anonymity, lack of the need to reveal physical appearance, ability to control the degree of information revealed in the interaction; and also the ease with which it is possible to find like-minded people. These results are reinforced by the fact that the social anxiety and loneliness variables that McKenna *et al.* (2002) found as relating to the location of the 'real me' on the Internet are highly related to introversion and neuroticism. As Norton *et al.* (1997) reported, there is a positive relationship between social anxiety and neuroticism and a negative one between loneliness and extroversion.

The concept of the 'real me' enables us to understand the importance of the Internet for certain types of people; for example, those people who find that they express themselves more effectively on the Internet than through the more traditional channels of communication. This implies that for a significant number of people, such as introverts, neurotics, lonely people and people with social anxiety, the Internet may become a very significant part of their lives and perhaps the only one in which they truly express themselves. We suggest, however, that the Rogerian (1961) concept of the 'true self' be treated with caution. This concept refers to the existence of a self that is largely unknown to its host, while the phenomenon found on the Internet is largely related to people who feel that it is safe to reveal their intimate secrets to a stranger. It is possible that, should the well-protected Internet environment be utilized only by surfers who are sensitive and warm, the resulting interaction would create optimal conditions, as specified by Rogers, for the building of a therapeutic environment. This, in turn, may allow a surfer to discover their true self.

Much of the discussion so far has concentrated on the Internet as a compensatory tool for people with personality tendencies that create a social deficit. It is, however, important to mention a different opinion, that expressed by Kraut *et al.* (2002), who found that, although both extroverts and introverts benefit from their increased Internet use by enlarging their social circles, introverts report a higher loneliness level. Kraut and his colleagues explained their results by 'the rich get richer' phenomenon, namely, that people who have many friends anyway will make more friends on the net, whereas people who suffer from social problems are likely to gain less from Internet interaction. That said, many other scholars hold that the Internet creates opportunities for the 'poor to get rich', i.e., the protected environment created by the Internet produces a situation in which people who cannot express themselves through the more traditional channels of communication find themselves able to do so on the net (e.g., Hamburger and Ben-Artzi 2000; Maldonado *et al.* 2001; McKenna *et al.* 2002).

Erich Fromm

A few relevant aspects from his theory

Fromm was a romantic humanistic psychologist who argued that human beings strive for freedom and autonomy, but at the same time have a need to relate to significant others. The way that this tension is resolved will depend on the particular society. In a capitalist system that values individual freedom and power, people are more likely to feel loneliness and isolation, whereas in a collectivist society, which stresses the human need to belong to a group, members may have to make sacrifices in terms of their individuality and personal fulfillment for the greater good of the collective.

According to Fromm, the human conflict between striving for freedom and striving for security is a result of five basic human needs:

1. A need to relate to others – to have someone to care for, share with and be responsible for;

2. A need for transcendence – a need to rise above our animal nature, to be creative;

3. A need to be rooted – to replace our separation from nature with feelings of kinship with others;

4. A need for identity – to achieve distinctiveness through one's efforts or through identification with another person or group;

5. A need for a frame of reference – to have a stable structure or framework that will aid in organizing and understanding one's experience.

A similar hypothesis dealing with the contradictions in human instincts was offered by the optimal distinctiveness theory of Brewer (1991). According to this theory, people are motivated by two contradicting motives: the need to express individuality and the need to belong to a large, significant group. Brewer differentiated between collective identity – the belonging to large groups and the interpersonal identity – the relating to others on an individual basis. In both, the individual defines themself as an identity related to others, either as part of a large group or as individuals. These needs contradict one another: satisfying one means evoking the need for satisfying the other. People strive to belong to a group that satisfies both needs in the most optimal way (see also Brewer and Gardner 1996).

Bettencourt and Sheldon (2001) attempted to resolve the dichotomy of Brewer's (1991) motive contradiction by introducing the social role. According to Biddle (1979), the social role refers to 'a behavioural repertoire, characteristic of a person or a position; a set of standards, descriptions, norms, or concepts held for the behaviours of a person or social position' (1979: 9). Social roles 'by definition' involve an interaction with group members. As role holders contribute to group goals through the fulfillment of their role, they become more connected to the group. This is especially true when they fit their roles well. When their social role is consistent with their core skills, they are likely to feel autonomy and self-expression as well. It means that the seemingly contradicting motives of autonomy and relatedness may be mutually achieved when the individual performs social roles that fit their ability and characteristics. This argument was proved in a series of studies.

Can the Internet help with the human conflict between freedom and striving for security?

When these needs are considered in terms of constituents of the Internet, it is clear that the net has the ability to answer the high need to belong and relate to others. This is achieved, for example, through the ease with which it is possible to find similar others and groups of mutual interest. In this way, the Internet can compensate for the isolation and loneliness found in our culture. Fromm's (1941) list of basic human needs, especially relatedness, identity and frame of reference, may be answered by the various services offered on the net.

Despite the seemingly optimistic approach of Bettencourt and Sheldon (2001), it is important to stress that, in many cases, offline groups demand that individuals take on roles not necessarily of their choosing. Those responsible for allocating these roles will inevitably not take into account the skills, abilities and motives of the individual, but will rather look to the needs of the group. In addition, roles are frequently allocated according to the social role to which the group is aspiring. In such a case, an individual may be chosen to perform a certain role according to the general perception that is held of them. This perception may not be in keeping with who they really are, or may be outdated and, therefore, the fit between personality and social roles in many cases will not be accurate. This may be the case even when the group attempts to choose the best person for the role.

In the Internet arena, it may be easier to find social roles that allow individuals their self-expression and even their self-actualization, since the net provides more freedom to choose the groups and the social roles that suit them. It is also the case that the number and variety of groups and the ease with which it is possible to find them online is far greater than in the offline world. The act of compelling someone to take on a role does not exist on the Internet, since any attempt to do so will lead the person to: (a) disagree or (b) express alternatives and, should this not be acceptable, they can (c) leave without any social consequences. It seems that the Internet creates an environment where the conflict between the need to relate and the need for autonomy is very limited and, in fact, the Internet is able to sustain situations in which both needs are mutually fulfilled. In this case, there are positive implications to be considered that pertain to individual well-being.

The present discussion has focused on the relevance of the main personality theories to Internet use. We will now move on to discuss specific personality characteristics that we suggest are relevant to our understanding of differentiated Internet use.

Personality characteristics and Internet use

Many personality characteristics will impact on the way an individual surfer behaves on the Internet.

Need for closure

People who have a high need for closure are motivated to avoid uncertainties. They tend to 'freeze' the epistemic process (Kruglanski and Freund 1983), and to reach conclusions speedily. They tend to get locked into conceptions and ignore contradicting information. People with a low need for closure are predisposed to unfreeze many alternative hypotheses and to test as many implications of their own hypothesis as possible. Amichai-Hamburger *et al.* (2004) found that in the case of commercial websites, people with a low need for closure preferred a website with many hyperlinks over one that was relatively flat: people with a high need for closure preferred the flat website over the one with many hyperlinks. This was found to be the case only when the participants were surfing without a time limit. When they were under time pressure the results were reversed, namely, people with a high need for closure preferred a website with many hyperlinks over one that was relatively flat. People with a low need for closure preferred the flat website over the one with many hyperlinks. It would appear that when there is no time pressure, subjects choose their preferred alternative; thus, it may be assumed that they express their natural preferences. Participants with a low need for closure prefer the interactive site. This provides a perceived legitimacy to pressing repeatedly on different hyperlinks. In addition, the interactive site causes those who visit it to feel that they have chosen to receive additional information, by pressing the links, as opposed to information being given to them. Apparently, these characteristics fulfil the need of participants with a low need for closure to receive further information before they make a decision. The interactive site thus provides the tools necessary to achieve 'epistemic melting' and so serves the need to avoid closure. Conversely, participants with a high need for closure, who have a need to reach 'epistemic freezing' in a relatively short span of time, prefer a flat site.

However, when they surf under time pressure, participants are unable to choose their preferred alternatives with ease. In this condition, those with a low need for closure prefer the flat site. According to Kruglanski and Webster (1996), people with a high need for closure experience its absence as aversive. The same may be said to be true for people with a low need for closure. They perceive the necessity of deciding quickly, having no opportunity to receive further information and so running the risk of making mistakes, as aversive. Therefore, it would seem that to find themselves at an interactive site, in which each hyperlink provides potentially relevant information, without being able to 'check' them as they would wish, is frustrating and undesirable. Therefore, participants with a low need for closure who operate under time pressure prefer a flat site.

Participants with a high need for closure prefer the interactive site under time pressure, but their motivation may be different from that of participants with a low need for closure operating with no time pressure. It may be assumed that participants with a high need for closure strive to reach a certain decision as soon as possible; the tendency for urgency is more dominant than the one for permanence. When participants with a high need for closure are required to make a decision under time pressure, their desire to achieve a final answer, mediated by the urgency tendency, is activated more intensively. Therefore, they are willing to filter information and make a decision based on relatively few parameters. The hyperlinks on the interactive site enable them to filter information and choose only those hyperlinks that will assist them directly in their decision-making. In this way, the hyperlinks serve the urgency tendency and allow participants to reach 'epistemic closure'. Therefore, those with a high need for closure who operate under time pressure prefer the interactive site over the flat site.

When it comes to the social aspect of the Internet, it seems likely that people with a low need for closure will be willing to explore their identity on the net and are open to finding new relationships there, while those with a high need for closure will be more inhibited about exploring their identity or starting new Internet relationships.

Need for cognition

People vary in how they treat information. The best-known effort to define and measure this tendency was performed by Cacioppo and Petty (1982), who created the 'Need for Cognition' variable. This refers to an individual's tendency to engage in and enjoy effortful cognitive endeavours. It is considered a stable trait that may be influenced by certain situational factors (Cacioppo *et al.* 1996). The differences in this tendency range from individuals described as having a 'low need for cognition' to those described as having a 'high need for cognition'. Those with a low need for cognition do not enjoy cognitive efforts and when dealing with complicated issues will prefer to rely on the opinion of others, preferably experts, while individuals with a 'high need for cognition' are those who possess a natural motivation to seek knowledge and so will acquire more information and engage with it (Verplanken *et al.* 1992). Amichai-Hamburger *et al.* (in press) studied the behaviour of surfers on commercial websites. They found a clear difference in the willingness of individuals with a low need for cognition to return to the site in favour of an interactive site (a site with many hyperlinks). This preference was not found among individuals with a high need for cognition. It appears that the need for cognition determines one's susceptibility to peripheral cues, such as the site's appearance. This finding is consistent with previous research on the influence of need for cognition on responsiveness to peripheral cues, as presented in Petty and Cacioppo's (1981) elaboration likelihood model (ELM). According to the ELM, people seek to hold correct and reality-tuned attitudes. However, when people lack motivation or ability, they may engage in an easier and more superficial processing of the message. The ELM proposes two routes to attitude change. The central route involves carefully thinking about the real merits of a message. In this case, people are sensitive to the quality of the argument and respond differentially to strong and weak arguments. The second route is a peripheral one, which includes any kind of attitude change that occurs without cognitive elaboration. In this case, people are not sensitive to the argument's quality and could be influenced by persuasion heuristics (e.g., attractive people), the quantity of arguments (regardless to their strength), the arousal of positive affect and other factors that are unrelated to the validity of the message. Individuals with a low need for cognition appear to be more attracted to the interactive aspect of the website representing the peripheral aspect of the site. Those with a high need for cognition, i.e. with a tendency to engage in and enjoy effortful cognitive endeavours, appear to concentrate more on the core message.

Das *et al.* (2003) found that people who enjoy cognitively demanding processing tasks are more likely to use the Internet information search tools since they enjoy this activity in a similar way.

Locus of control

People with an external locus of control believe that life events are the result of external factors, like chance or luck. People with an internal locus of control believe in their own ability to control their life events (Rotter 1966, 1982). People with an internal locus of control expect that their efforts will lead to success and therefore are highly motivated to master their environment (Phares 1976). People with an external locus of control use the Internet more for inclusion, as compared with people with an internal locus of control (Flaherty *et al.* 1998). People with a high internal locus of control use the Internet as a supplement to other activities and in a more goal-directed manner, for example, as a tool to search for information to complete a task, or to reduce purchase uncertainties, whereas people with an external locus of control tend to use the Internet more experimentally as a substitute for other activities, such as spending time with friends. They tend to spend greater amounts of time surfing the net than surfers with an internal locus of control. However, they are less likely to engage in goal-directed behaviours such as shopping, making purchases and gathering product information (Hoffman et al. 2002). It was also found that people with an internal locus of control felt higher control over the web interaction process and procedures and had a higher trust in online transaction safety as compared with those with an external locus of control (Sohn and Leckenby 2001).

Sensation-seeking and risk-taking

These are two highly related personality dimensions. Sensation-seeking focuses on the need for new and varied experiences through uninhibited behaviour: these include dangerous activities, a non-conventional lifestyle and a rejection of monotony (Zuckerman 1971). Risk-taking is a personality dimension; people vary as to the degree to which they are ready to take an action that involves a significant degree of risk (Levenson 1990). Alonzo and Aiken (2004) found that sensation-seeking predicted flaming (posting hostile and insulting messages) on the net. There was a stronger prediction for males than for females. They suggest that anonymity on the net encourages people to act without inhibitions and to engage in taking risks in flaming activity for entertainment and to pass the time.

It also seems very possible that people who are high on sensation-seeking and risk-taking will be more open to new experiences on the net. They will, therefore, be more likely to use the Internet to explore different aspects of their personality. Should a net relationship develop, it is this type of person who is most likely to take the initiative and suggest a meeting. People who are low on sensation-seeking and risk-taking will conversely behave more cautiously on the net and will be less open to identity experiments.

Extroversion and neuroticism (as measured by Eysenck's Personality Inventory EPI)

The extrovert is outward oriented, whereas the introvert is inward oriented. The neurotic person is an anxious, worried individual who is overly emotional and reacts too strongly to all types of stimuli (Eysenck and Eysenck 1975).

Hamburger and Ben-Artzi (2000) analysed levels of extroversion and neuroticism and Internet use and found that these showed different patterns for men and women in their interactions with the Internet services scale. For men, extroversion was positively linked to the use of leisure services and neuroticism was negatively related to information services, whereas for women, extroversion was negatively related and neuroticism positively related to the use of social sites. The latter results are particularly interesting because they confirm earlier studies showing

that women have higher self-awareness and are more likely to use their social network for support. The differences found in the extra-neurotic personalities in their Internet behaviour are consistent with those found in the main personality theories. These results on the net can actually be partly supported by the gender pattern for television use. Weaver (2001) found similar gender motived interactions. He found that males watched TV for information and stimulation, while females watched television for companionship and to pass the time. However, Amichai-Hamburger (2005) discusses gender differences and their impact on Internet use and suggests that this gender difference will eventually disappear as more people enter the net and the awareness of web services grows. He suggests that in the future, male and female introverts and neurotics will gradually understand the compensating factor of Internet social services and will start to use them more extensively.

Extroversion, neuroticism and psychoticism (as measured by Eysenck's Personality Questionnaire Revised-EPQ-R)

The EPQ-R questionnaire includes psychoticism, in addition to extroversion and neuroticism. Psychotics show disregard for authority, social norms and rules. They are unlikely to feel sensitivity to the feelings of others (Eysenck *et al.* 1985). Hamburger and Ben-Artzi (2000) were among the first to examine the interaction between personality and Internet use. Amiel and Sargent (2004) continued this work, branching out into three main areas:

1. Using the EPQ-R questionnaire, they extended the Hamburger and Ben-Artzi (2000) study of extroverted and neurotic personality types to include the psychotic personality type.

2. They increased the number and distribution of the subjects.

3. They increased the number of possible motives for Internet use.

They found that gender differences disappeared. When it comes to neuroticism, people who scored high on the neuroticism scale reported that they used the net for the feeling of belonging to a group. Extroverts, on the other hand, 'rejected the social communal aspects of the Internet and were negatively correlated to statements like I use the Internet "because I feel more comfortable talking to people on line".' They were interested in voicing their opinion, but not in listening to that of others.

Amiel and Sargent (2004) found that those scoring high on the neuroticism scale expressed a high interest in alternative news and the need to learn about potential threats. Extroverts rejected the use of the net for information, but surfed for alternative news. In contrast to Hamburger and Ben-Artzi (2000) who found a negative link for neurotics and information services, Amiel and Sargent (2004) found that people scoring high on neuroticism expressed a high motive for the need to acquire information. They suggest that Hamburger and Ben-Artzi (2000) encompassed within the term 'Information services' work- and study-related information, rather than only concentrating on news which, in terms of Internet use, is less likely to be related information for use at work or for studies.

In contrast to Hamburger and Ben-Artzi's (2000) findings, Amiel and Sargent (2004) found no link between extrovert personalities and random surfing or sex website use. The authors explain these differences by stating that this use is much more in line with psychoticism which Hamburger and Ben-Artzi (2000) did not measure.

They also found that neuroticism demonstrated a need for information and belonging, a preference for alternative news (as opposed to mainstream or interactive news) and the need to be informed of possible dangers.

Neurotics did announce a social communal motive, but practically all were negatively related to some of the social services as text messaging tools (interpersonal/group communication) or willingness to engage in discussion.

Amiel and Sargent (2004) found that people high on psychoticism showed a lack of interest in the social communal aspects of the net. However, they demonstrated an interest in more sophisticated and deviant aspects of the net. In addition, they showed a great interest in using file-sharing services (distribution of pirated materials) and pornography. They were interested in learning what could happen to them, but not what could happen to others.

The NEO-PI-R

The NEO-PI-R questionnaire (McCrae and Costa 1997) includes five broad personality domains, also called the Five-Factor Model. In addition to extroversion and neuroticism (previously mentioned), it includes agreeableness, conscientiousness and openness to experience. Agreeableness refers to individual differences in cooperation and the ability to build social harmony with others. Agreeable individuals have an optimistic approach to the world. They are friendly, helpful and willing to compromise in favour of others. Disagreeable individuals put their own needs ahead of the need to get along with others. They do not trust others and therefore express more hostility and less cooperativeness than agreeable individuals. Conscientiousness refers to the way in which we control, regulate and direct our impulses. People with a level of conscientiousness are well organized, governed by their task. In contrast, low conscientious people are impulsive. Openness to experience describes a dimension of cognitive style that distinguishes imaginative, creative people from down to earth, conventional people. Open people are intellectually curious and appreciative of art. They tend to be more aware of their feelings and to think and act in individualistic and nonconforming ways, as compared to more closed people. Swickert *et al.* (2002) used the big five questionnaire and found a negative relationship between neuroticism and leisure activity.

Heinström (2005) examined the link between personality and information-seeking. She found three general patterns for information-seeking:

1. Fast surfing: people who skim are disorganized, not task oriented and have a low need for achievement. For these people, the depth and quality of information is a minor consideration, as against the need for speed.

2. Broad scanning – people who tend to be flexible in their information-seeking, utilizing a wide range of sources. Their broad scanning searches are developed gradually rather than being planned.

3. Deep diving – people who are hard workers, desire quality rather than quantity. They put much effort into information seeking, but do not necessarily search for information in a broad manner.

She found that the broad scanning style, which is typical of the extrovert personality, combined with openness to experience and competitiveness, was related to using the net as a tool for information-seeking. Other styles were not found to be related to the use of the Internet for information-seeking.

Final word

The study of personality and Internet use is growing in importance as the Internet takes on an ever-increasing significance in our lives. The adults among us can still remember the days before the Internet; for our children, the Internet is a natural part of life. The profile of the population of Internet users is becoming ever closer to that of the general population. In addition, the variety of services is constantly growing and is gradually encompassing almost every aspect of our existence. Both in terms of our work and our leisure activities, the net is becoming an essential part of our functioning.

This chapter emphasized three main points:

1. The Internet is a unique psychological environment;

2. The theories of leading psychologists in the field of personality are particularly relevant to the understanding of people's behaviour on the net. This demonstrates that, although the Internet is a unique environment, its users behave in accordance with findings of the main personality theories;

3. Personality-specific characteristics can explain differential behaviour of people on the net.

These three pillars create a stage for understanding the field of personality and the Internet. The chapter opened by describing the seemingly large gap between the fields of personality and the Internet and closed by demonstrating a clear understanding of how these two fields relate powerfully to one another.

The chapter described the interaction between personality characteristics and Internet use. However, it is important to stress that research on the Internet and personality is only at its initial stage. It is the responsibility of psychologists to rise to the challenges raised by this paper and to continue to examine in greater detail human personality characteristics and the way in which they interact with the Internet. The best method to do this, we believe, is through long-term studies, examining how the complex personality structures of the surfers, together with their behaviour on the net, impact their well-being.

Future studies are likely to increase our knowledge as to the impact of the Internet on the surfer's well-being. This chapter illustrated how significant the Internet can be for people with social deficiencies: for some of them, the Internet may become their preferred social environment, where they can express their real self. This is an indication of the potential of the Internet in affecting psychological well-being. There is no doubt that the impact of the Internet on our lives will increase in the coming years. In the future, an Internet website might even ask for the personality profile of the user and shape the environment in accordance with their answers. In this way, the Internet will not only become a more significant tool in our lives, but also one that enhances our well-being.

References

Alonzo, M. and Aiken, M. (2004). Flaming in electronic communication. *Decision Support Systems 36*, 205–213.

American Psychiatric Association (1994). *Diagnostic and statistical manual of mental disorders*, 4th edn. Washington, DC: American Psychiatric Association.

Amichai-Hamburger, Y. (2002). Internet and personality. *Computers in Human Behavior 18*, 1–10.

Amichai-Hamburger, Y. (2005). Personality and Internet. In Y. Amichai-Hamburger (ed.), *The social net: Understanding human behavior in cyberspace* (pp. 27–55). New York: Oxford University Press.

Amichai-Hamburger, Y., Fine, A. and Goldstein, A. (2004). The impact of Internet interactivity and need for closure on consumer preference. *Computers in Human Behavior 20*, 103–117.

Amichai-Hamburger, Y., Kinar, O. and Fine, A. (2006). The effects of need for cognition on Internet use. *Computers in Human Behavior 23*, 880–891.

Amichai-Hamburger, Y., Wainapel, G. and Fox, S. (2002). 'On the internet no one knows I'm an introvert': extroversion, neuroticism and internet interaction. *Cyberpsychology and Behavior 2*, 125–128.

Amiel, T. and Sargent, S. L. (2004). Individual differences in Internet usage motives. Computers in Human Behavior, *20*, 711–726.

Bandura, A. (1977). *Social learning theory*. Oxford, England: Prentice-Hall.

Ben-Ze'ev, A. (2005). 'Detattachment': the unique nature of online romantic relationships. In Y. Amichai-Hamburger (ed.), *The social net: Understanding human behavior in cyberspace* (pp. 115–138). New York: Oxford University Press.

Bettencourt, B. A. and Sheldon, K. (2001). Social roles as a vehicle for psychological need satisfaction within groups. *Journal of Personality and Social Psychology 81*, 1131–1143.

Biddle, B. J. (1979). *Role theory: Expectations, identities and behaviors*. New York: Academic Press.

Black, R. and Black, G. (1974). *Beyond ego psychology*. New York: Columbia University Press.

Brewer, B. M. (1991). The social self: on being the same and different at the same time. *Personality and Social Psychology Bulletin 17*, 475–482.

Brewer, B. M. and Gardner, W. L. (1996). Who is this 'we'? Levels of collective identity and self-representations. *Journal of Personality and Social Psychology 71*, 83–93.

Cacioppo, J. T. and Petty, R. E. (1982). The need for cognition. *Journal of Personality and Social Psychology 42*, 116–131.

Cacioppo, J. T., Petty, R. E., Feinstein, J. A. and Jarvis, W. B. G. (1996). Dispositional differences in cognitive motivation: the life and times of individuals varying in need for cognition. *Psychological Bulletin 119*, 197–253.

Campbell, J. (1971). *The portable Jung*. New York: Viking.

Cialdini, R. (1984). *Influence: The new psychology of modern persuasion*. New York: Quill Publishing.

Cooper, A. and Sportolari, L. (1997). Romance in cyber-space: understanding online attraction. *Journal of Sex Education and Therapy 22*, 7–14.

Das, S., Echambadi, R., McCardle, M. and Luckett, M. (2003). The effect of interpersonal trust, need for cognition and social loneliness on shopping, information seeking and surfing on the web. *Marketing Letter 14*, 185–202.

Duval, S. and Wicklund, R. A. (1972). *A theory of objective self-awareness*. New York: Academic Press.

Erikson, E. H. (1968). *Identity: Youth and crisis*. New York: Norton.

Eysenck, H. J. and Eysenck, S. E. G. (1975). *Manual: Eysenck Personality Inventory*. San Diego, CA: Educational and Industrial Testing Service.

Eysenck, S. G. B., Eysenck, H. J. and Barrett, P. (1985). A revised version of the psychoticism scale. *Personality and Individual Differences 6*, 21–29.

Fenichel, M. A. (2004). Online behavior, communication and experience. In R. Kraus., J. Zack and G. Stricker (eds), *Online counseling* (pp. 3–18). Oxford: Elsevier.

Fenichel, M., Suler, J., Barak, A., Zelvin, E., Jones, G., Munro, K., Meunier, V. and Walker-Schmucker, W. (2002). Myths and realities of online clinical work. *CyberPsychology and Behavior 5*, 481–497.

Fine, G. A. (1983). *Shared fantasy: Role-playing games as social worlds*. Chicago, IL: The University of Chicago Press

Fiske, S. T. and Taylor, S. E. (1991). *Social cognition*. New York: McGraw-Hill.

Flaherty, L., Pearce, K. and Rubin, R. (1998). Internet and face-to-face communication: not functional alternatives. *Communication Quarterly 46*, 250–268.

Frable, D. E. S. (1993). Being and feeling unique: Statistical deviance and psychological marginality. *Journal of Personality 61*, 85–110.

Freud, S. (1915a). Repression. In J. Strachey (ed.) *The standard edition of the complete psychological works of Sigmund Freud*, vol. 14, edited by J. Strachey, translated by C. M. Baines and J. Strachey (pp. 143–158). London: Hogarth Press, 1957.

Freud, S. (1915b). The unconscious. *The standard edition of the complete psychological works of Sigmund Freud*, vol. 14, edited by J. Strachey, translated by C. M. Baines and J. Strachey (pp. 161–204). London: Hogarth Press, 1957.

Fromm, E. (1941). *Escape from freedom*. New York: Rinehart.

Gollwitzer, P. M. (1986). Striving for specific identities: the social reality of self-symbolizing. In R. Baumeister (ed.), *Public self and private self* (pp. 143–159). New York: Springer-Verlag.

Green, D. (2004). Freud and mental treatment on the Internet. *Nefesh, Psychological Quarterly 5*, 87–92.

Hamburger, Y. A. and Ben-Artzi, E. (2000). The relationship between extraversion and neuroticism and the different uses of the Internet. *Computers in Human Behavior 16*, 441–449.

Hamburger, Y. and Fox, S. (2000). Virtual organizations on the Internet. *Megamot 40*, 512–530.

Hatfield, E. and Sprecher, S. (1986). *Mirror, mirror: The importance of looks in everyday life*. New York: SUNY Press.

Heinström, J. (2005). Fast surfers, broad scanners and deep divers as users of information technology – relating information preferences to personality traits. *Proceedings of the American Society for Information Science and Technology 40*, 247–254.

Hoffman, D. L., Novak, T. P. and Schlosser, A. (2002). Locus of control, web use and consumer attitudes towards interent regulations. *Journal of Public Policy and Marketing 22*, 41–57.

Joinson, A. N. (2001). Self-disclosure in computer-mediated communication: the role of self-awareness and visual anonymity. *European Journal of Social Psychology 31*, 177–192.

Jung, C. G. (1939). *The integration of the personality*. New York: Farrar and Rinehart.

Klein, M. (1961). *Narrative of a child analysis*. London: Hogarth Press.

Kohut, H. (1977). *The restoration of the self*. New York: International Universities Press.

Kraut, R., Kiesler, S., Boneva, B., Cummings, J. N., Helgeson, V. and Crawford, A. M. (2002). Internet paradox revisited. *Journal of Social Issues 58*, 49–74.

Kruglanski, A. W. and Freund, T. (1983). The freezing and unfreezing of lay inferences: effects on impressional primacy, ethnic stereotyping and numerical anchoring. *Journal of Experimental Social Psychology 19*, 448–468.

Kruglanski, A. W. and Webster, D. M. (1996). Motivated closing of the mind: 'seizing' and 'freezing'. *Psychological Review 103*, 263–283.

Levenson, M. R. (1990). Risk taking and personality. *Journal of Personality and Social Psychology 58,* 1073–1080.

Maheu, M. M. and Gordon, B. L. (2000). Counseling and therapy on the Internet. *Professional Psychology: Research and Practice 31,* 484–489.

Malamuth, N., Linz, D. and Yao, M. (2005). The Internet and aggression: motivation, disinhibitory and opportunity aspects. In Y. Amichai-Hamburger (ed.), *The social net: Understanding human behavior in cyberspace* (pp. 163–190). New York: Oxford University Press.

Maldonado, G. J., Mora, M., Garcia, S. and Edipo, P. (2001). Personality, sex and computer communication mediated through the Internet. *Anuario de Psicologia 32,* 51–62.

McCrae, R. R. and Costa, P. T. (1997). Personality trait structure as a human universal. *American Psychologist 52,* 509–516.

McKenna, K. Y. A. and Bargh, J. A. (1998). Coming out in the age of the Internet: identity 'de-marginalization' through virtual group participation. *Journal of Personality and Social Psychology 75,* 681–694.

McKenna, K. and Bargh, J. (2000). Plan 9 from cyber-space: the implications of the Internet for personality and social psychology. *Personality and Social Psychology Review 4,* 57–75.

McKenna, K. Y. A., Green, A. S. and Gleason, M. J. (2002). Relationship formation on the Internet: what's the big attraction? *Journal of Social Issues 58,* 9–32.

Norton, G. R., Hewitt, P. L., McLeod, L. and Cox, B. J. (1997). Personality factors associated with generalized and circumscribed social anxiety. *Personality and Individual Differences 21,* 655–700.

Pervin, L. A. (1993). *Personality: Theory and research.* New York: John Wiley and Sons.

Petty, R. E. and Cacioppo, J. T. (1981). *Attitudes and persuasion: Classic and contemporary approach.* Dubuque, IA: William C. Brown.

Phares, E. J. (1976). *Locus of control in personality.* Morristown, NJ: General Learning Press.

Postmes, T., Spears, R. and Lea, M. (2000). The emergence and development of group norms in computer-mediated communication. *Human Communication Research 26,* 341–371.

Postmes, T., Spears, R. and Lea, M. (2002). Intergroup differentiation in computer- mediated communication: effects of depersonalization. *Group Dynamics 6,* 3–16.

Ragusea, A. S. and Vandecreek, L. (2003). Suggestions for the ethical practice of online psychotherapy. *Psychotherapy: Theory, Research, Practice, Training 40,* 94–102.

Rogers, C. (1961). *On becoming a person.* Boston, MA: Houghton Mifflin.

Rogers, C. (1980). *A way of being.* Boston, MA: Houghton Mifflin.

Rotter, J. (1966). Generalized expectancies for internal versus external control of reinforcements. *Psychological Monographs 80,* Whole No. 609.

Rotter, J. B. (1982). *The development and applications of social learning theory: Selected papers.* New York: Praeger.

Rubin, Z. (1975). Disclosing oneself to a stranger: reciprocity and its limits. *Journal of Experimental Social Psychology 11,* 233–260.

Sohn, D. and Leckenby, J. D. (2001). Locus of control and interactive advertising. Paper presented at the 2001 Annual Conference of the American Academy of Advertising, Salt Lake City, Utah.

Sproull, L., Conley, C. A. and Moon, J. Y. (2005) Prosocial behavior on the net. In Y. Amichai-Hamburger (ed.), *The social net: Understanding human behavior in cyberspace* (pp. 139–161). New York: Oxford University Press.

Suler, J. R. (2004). The online disinhibition effect. In *The Psychology of Cyberspace.* Retrieved 7 April 2005 from http://www.rider.edu/~suler/psycyber/psycyber.html (article originally published 2002).

Swickert, R. J., Hittner, J. B., Harris, J. L. and Herring, J. A. (2002). Relationships among internet use, personality and social support. *Computers in Human Behavior 18,* 437–451.

Tidwell, L. C. and Walther, J. B. (2002). Computer-mediated communication effects on disclosure, impressions and interpersonal evaluations: getting to know one another a bit at a time. *Human Communication Research 28,* 317–348.

Turkle, S. (1995). *Life on the screen: Identity in the age of the internet.* New York: Simon and Schuster.

Turkle, S. (2004). Whither psychoanalysis in computer culture? *Psychoanalytic-Psychology 21,* 16–30.

Verplanken, B., Hazenberg, P. T. and Palenéwen, G. R. (1992). Need for cognition and external information search. *Journal of Research in Personality 26,* 128–136.

Weaver, J.S. (2001). Individual differences in television viewing motives. Paper presented at the meeting of the International Communication Association, Washington, DC.

Zuckerman, M. (1971). Dimensions of sensation seeking. *Journal of Consulting and Clinical Psychology 36,* 45–52.

CHAPTER 14

Through the Internet looking glass

Expressing and validating the true self

Katelyn Y. A. McKenna

When Alice steps through the looking glass, she finds herself in a world that closely resembles her own – but with some subtle (and some not so subtle) differences. Similarly, social interactions that take place on the Internet, through the computer monitor glass, do resemble those that take place face-to-face (Tyler 2002). But, as in the looking-glass world, it is the differences that open the door to new possibilities as to how one sees oneself, as well as how one views and is viewed by others.

On the Internet, people are often able to interact with others under conditions of relative anonymity and in the absence of the physical presence of the other person. These conditions facilitate the sharing of important inner or 'true' aspects of self that are often difficult to express in 'real life'. Thus, one may present the self somewhat differently to online acquaintances than to those in one's non-Internet social circle. One may also be perceived somewhat differently by one's online acquaintances than by those one gets to know 'in person', not only because of the possible differences in self-presentation, but also because of critical differences in the communication modalities that affect the bases for impression formation. Thus, a different self may be reflected back through the computer monitor than is generally reflected back from one's real life family and friends. I will suggest here that expressing and gaining validation and acceptance for these aspects of self often has important implications for one's sense of self, as well as for one's close relationships.

One important issue is the degree to which people are conscious of and intend these self-presentational effects; whether the person is aware of and intending to present the self in these ways, or is not aware of the effects that Internet versus face-to-face communication modes influence and affect their self-presentation and their perceptions of interaction partners. One of the themes of this article will be to consider each of the various self-presentational and social-perceptual effects in terms of its 'conscious' versus 'automatic' nature. Conscious or controlled processes have been defined as those of which the person intends (i.e., strategic), is aware of (i.e., can accurately self-report), are attention-demanding and effortful, and are controllable (i.e., can be stopped if so desired); automatic processes are characterized by the diametrically opposed qualities: unintentional, the person is not aware of the effect, efficient and minimally demanding of limited attentional resources, and are not controllable (see Bargh 1994). Because these qualities do not really occur in such an all or none fashion, but often instead in mixtures of some conscious and some automatic qualities (Bargh 1989), I will consider each of the central phenomena of this article separately as to its intentionality, the person's degree of awareness of it, and its naturalness or efficiency of operation.

The article begins with a brief overview of conceptions of self. It then focuses upon a version of self that is current and private, but also which the individual would very much like to be made public and known to others. It is most similar to what Carl Rogers (1951) called the 'true self'. First I will examine the nature of the true self, next the reasons why it may go unexpressed in everyday life, and conclude by describing the evidence suggesting that the Internet has become a prime venue for the expression and validation of the true self – in fact, perhaps the best venue there ever was.

Mirror, mirror on the wall, which one am I of them all?

The reflected self

It was Cooley (1902) who, a century ago, first introduced the idea of a reflected or looking glass self. Cooley argued that the self we create for ourselves is a reflection of how we perceive that others view us. That is, we look to others to see how we are perceived and then incorporate those views or perceptions into our self-concept. In Cooley's view, changes in one's self-concept occur when there are changes in the way others perceive oneself. Mead (1932) built on Cooley's theory by suggesting that the self-concept is also affected by the way a person believes wider society views them, based on cultural norms and standards.

However, as Tice (1992) has noted, the social interactionist idea of a looking glass self may be too simplistic. A growing body of empirical evidence shows that while people are indeed adept at knowing how others in general view them, they are not very good at discerning how they are viewed by specific others (e.g., Ichiyama 1993; Kenny and DePaulo 1993). Further, as Shrauger and Schoeneman (1979) argue, people often see 'through the glass darkly', meaning that they often have certain a priori conceptions of self that they then believe (wrongly) others believe true of them as well (see also Kenny and DePaulo 1993).

In addition, we may tend to 'be' and to be perceived by others quite differently across different social domains. For instance, a person may have a cool and radical image among friends, while with co-workers she is hardworking and conscientious. Sensitive and caring qualities of self may predominate with her spouse, and to her parents she is respectful and successful. But, although she may feel that she is indeed all of these things she outwardly manifests to others, she may also feel there are additional true self-defining qualities that she has difficulty expressing to any of the others in her life. We would expect that she is conscious of these discrepancies, and also desires to express them if she only could.

Multiple selves, multiple identities

The idea that individuals possess multiple senses of self and identity has long been discussed in psychology and sociology. William James noted, 'A man has as many social selves as there are individuals who recognize him' (1892: 179). One important historical version of the multiple self notion is the distinction between the public and private self (e.g., Baumeister 1986). Both Goffman (1959) and Jung (1953) focused on this distinction. Goffman used the metaphor of the theatre to describe the multiplicity of self and identity. He argued that people wear different masks for their various social interactions, playing at the role(s) best suited for a particular situation and audience, and only going maskless when in private. For Jung, one's conscious ego (the self that is presented to others) is less authentic than is the unconscious ego – in other words, according to Jung, one's real individuality resides in one's private self.

More recently, further distinctions have been made in the idea of multiple selves. The tendency for people to have potential senses of self that they have not yet realized and, indeed, may never realize, has been examined. Markus and Nurius (1986) first broached this concept of possible selves. Possible selves are those selves that we possibly might become in the future. They include versions of self that we would like to become as well as those we hope to avoid becoming (i.e., the 'dreaded self'). Along similar lines is the conception of the 'ideal self', which contains those attributes of self-hood that we would ideally like to possess and which we strive to become. Although possible and ideal selves are not selves currently possessed by the individual, they do not exist only in the abstract. Rather, they serve as important guides to actual behaviour in the present (Higgins 1987).

Thus, an individual's self-concept includes not only the public and private versions of self, but also future and current versions of self.

The true self

Current versions of self are certainly shaped to some extent by the aspects one expresses and has reflected back through the eyes of others. Cultural norms and standards exert additional influences on one's sense of 'me-ness'. Further adding to an individual's sense of 'who am I now?' are the traits he believes others see in him – even if he feels that he doesn't really possess them. All of these external factors help the individual to define who he really is. But this definition of the current self remains incomplete because it does not take into account the conceptions of self that one does not express socially. Rogers (1951) and Horney (1946), among others, have argued that aspects of self that go unexpressed and are not acknowledged by others nonetheless remain a fundamental part of an individual's sense of self. Indeed, these unexpressed aspects may often be more crucially defining for the individual than are those he expresses freely. These self-defining yet unexpressed aspects of self make up what Rogers (1951) called the 'true self'.

The true self is said to be comprised of identity-important aspects of self that an individual currently possesses, yet is generally unable to readily express to others in most situations, despite very much wishing to do so. Rogers likened the experience of those who are unable to express these hidden aspects of self to a prisoner in a dungeon, 'tapping out day after day a Morse code message, Does anybody hear me?' (1980: 10). The answer to that question, as we'll see, is often 'no'.

Rogers' (1951) conception of the true self was informed by Jung's (1953) distinction between the *unconscious self* and the *persona*, or the public, enacted version(s) of self. Rogers proposed that much of what occurs in therapy is related to the individual feeling that 'he was not being his real self, often he did not know what his real self was, and felt satisfaction when he had become more truly himself' (1951: 136). Thus, for Rogers, an important part of the therapy process was working toward the discovery of the true self, in order for the client to be able to express it more freely in their interactions with others. The focus here, however, will be upon those true self-qualities an individual has already discovered within themselves and about which they are consciously aware.

The true self differs conceptually from the ideal self and from possible selves in that it actually exists psychologically; it is a current rather than a future version of self. It also differs from other current versions of self, such as the *ought* self and the *actual* self (see Higgins 1987). The ought self, for instance, contains those qualities an individual feels obligated to possess and express and the actual self those they embrace themselves and actually, readily express to others in their everyday lives. In other words, these are the public versions of self that we generally share with others. The true self, on the other hand, is said to be comprised of those qualities a person feels they do indeed possess at present but that are not fully expressed in social life.

Like other versions of self, the characteristics of the true self are idiosyncratic, differing from individual to individual, and can include both positive and negative qualities. For instance, a male who feels he must behave in a stereotypically macho manner may also feel that he has a sensitive, unexpressed side to his personality, or a woman may feel that she has a selfish nature others do not perceive. One might assume that true self attributes tend to be along the lines of ideal self attributes. That is, that people believe they have many wonderful self-qualities that for some reason they can't express well and that others do not perceive and validate – a kind of 'nobody seems to know what a great person I really am' phenomenon. However, research has shown that not to be the case. Indeed, laboratory studies comparing the positivity of the content of participants' actual versus true self descriptions indicate that, while the qualities generated by participants for both the actual and the true self were generally positive in valence, true self attributes were actually significantly *less* positive than those of the actual self (Bargh *et al.* 2002).

Labeling the inner and unexpressed aspects of self the true self may be something of a misnomer in that it may give the (misleading) impression that only those aspects of self that go unexpressed are authentic and valid aspects of self. Further, one might conclude that, should a person begin to express these true self-aspects – thereby making them part of the actual self – the true self would then diminish. Such is not the case. Rather, when an individual is able to express both those authentic aspects of self that come easily to the fore and those that are more difficult to bring out in one's social interactions, then they are more likely to feel that the 'real me' is being expressed.

The relational self

Recent research into the relational nature of the self (e.g., Baldwin 1997; Andersen and Chen 2002) has shown that conceptions of self do not exist in a vacuum. Rather, one also tends to incorporate one's important relationships – along with one's important group identities (Tajfel and Turner 1986; Deaux 1996) into one's sense of self. Considerable research has shown the strong, even automatic associations between representations of these significant others and of the self. By unobtrusive and sometimes subliminal priming techniques, activation of the significant other representation causes activation of those aspects of the self related to the type of person one is when with that other person (see Andersen and Chen 2002). Importantly, only relationships of high personal significance tend to be incorporated into the self in this way: in these studies, control stimuli related to another experimental participant's significant other produce no such activation-of-self effects.

One might expect then that should an individual form a relationship in which they are able to express important inner aspects of self that go unexpressed within other, existing relationships, this new relationship would become highly important to the individual. This new relationship, with its relational association to aspects of the inner or true self, should also tend to be incorporated into one's sense of self. Indeed, this does appear to be the case, as is discussed in more detail later.

Why does the true self often go unexpressed?

There are many reasons why an individual may not express true self aspects to others, or, if they do express them, is not accorded validation of these self-qualities by others. For instance, when society marginalizes an identity (e.g., homosexuality, fringe ideologies) individuals who possess those identities may be motivated to conceal them in order to avoid censure. Clearly people are aware of the way society devalues this aspect and are consciously and effortfully trying to hide it from others. Of course, not all marginalized aspects of identity can be easily concealed: socially devalued characteristics such as obesity or stuttering are readily identifiable by others and so concealment is not an option. However, when devalued identity aspects are not conspicuous and can be concealed, many choose to do so (e.g., Jones *et al.* 1984; Frable 1993). Given the strong social disapproval of stigmatized identities, a person's desire for concealment is understandable, but true self aspects are not necessarily aspects that are marginalized or censured by society. So why then are normative aspects of the true self not expressed?

Role expectancies and constraints

One reason may be that the social roles a person fills preclude the expression of some self-aspects. People define themselves and are defined by others to a great extent by their social roles and obligations (Burke and Tully 1977; Burke 1980; Stryker and Statham 1985). An individual may consider many roles important for their identity – for instance, those of daughter, wife, mother, businesswoman, gardener, and animal rescuer – or they may focus their self-definition on only one or two of these (Deaux 1996). Research has shown that those who have a larger number of self-defining identities tend to be better prepared to deal with life changes and stress (Sarbin and Allen 1968). They also tend to experience better health (Linville 1985; Verbrugge 1986), and to feel more satisfied with their lives (Spreitzer *et al.* 1979) than do those who have only a few defining identities.

The identities and self-qualities an individual is able to express may also be constrained by that person's existing relationships and current roles (Stryker and Statham 1985). That is, based upon the roles we are perceived to fill, the others around us have certain expectations about how we should behave, the opinions, attitudes, and qualities we should express, and the other kinds of identities we should claim for ourselves. If an individual expresses self-qualities or identities that run counter to those expectations, their peers and family members may be unwilling to accept or acknowledge them. One's significant social circle may even respond quite negatively. Expecting and fearing such a rejecting response, an individual may not even attempt to express these aspects of self with those in their social circle (Pennebaker 1989; Derlega *et al.* 1993), as part of their conscious and strategic management of others opinion of them.

Conditional acceptance

One may also be thwarted in expressing the true self when faced with high levels of conditional acceptance or conditional support. In other words, when love, approval, or acceptance from important others is not based upon whom one is, but rather is contingent upon one's living up to their externally imposed standards, the true self may be suppressed. For instance, children – particularly adolescents – who experience higher levels of conditional support from parents and conditional acceptance by peers are more likely to hide the true self from others (Harter 1997). Instead, these adolescents often engage in what Harter terms 'false self' behaviour. Harter's conception of the false self differs markedly from both the true and the actual self in that, while an individual may be expressing false self aspects, they do not feel that these are

aspects they actually possesses. That is, they are consciously aware of and intend to express opinions they do not really hold and engage in behaviours that are at odds with their own sense of who they are, in order to gain approval and acceptance from important others. Indeed, the degree to which the child feels hopeless about being able to please important others is an important mediator between parental and peer conditionality and the child's suppression of the true self (Harter *et al.* 1998). Thus, those garnering low levels of approval from parents or peers and who feel the least capable of meeting the expectations others have for them are more likely to hide their true selves in an attempt to elicit greater levels of approval.

Social anxiety and loneliness

Forging relationships with others that would allow one to express important self-qualities, particularly true self aspects, may be quite difficult for those who experience high levels of social anxiety when meeting new people, taking part in social group activities, or talking with someone whom they find attractive (e.g., Leary and Atherton 1986). Thus they may be barred from the benefits (e.g., feelings of belonging, acceptance; increases in self-esteem) that close relationships and group memberships often bring, including the opportunity to reveal and have validated identity-important aspects of the self (e.g., Deaux 1996; McKenna and Bargh 1998). Similarly, those who are lonely and without a satisfactory social circle may also lack the chance to 'be' their true self with others.

The need for containment vs. the need for expression

On the one hand, people have a strong motivation to express important aspects of identity to others (Gollwitzer 1986; Swann 1990), but there is often a simultaneous need to contain and protect information about the self (Rubin 1975; Pennebaker 1989). Because the opinions that the significant others hold of oneself are so vitally important to one's self-esteem, anxiety levels, and happiness (e.g., Baumeister and Leary 1995), both of these motives are likely to be chronic over the life-term, and thus well-practiced and highly efficient – potentially automatic or implicit in their operation as a result (see Bargh 1990). Tice *et al.* (1995) have shown, for example, that different self-presentational strategies (modesty vs. self-promotion) are more natural or automatic in different social contexts (interacting with a friend vs. new acquaintance). Thus in most face-to-face situations the two well-ingrained motivations may oppose each other and tend to cancel each other out, but under conditions when the one is not operating (such as under conditions of anonymity where the need to contain or protect is much lower), the other motivation may emerge untethered and drive behaviour without the person realizing it. In this way the relative anonymity of the Internet may produce strong tendencies towards self-disclosure without the person being aware of or necessarily intending it.

Considerable research on intimate relationships has shown that both self-disclosure and partner disclosure increase the experience of intimacy in interactions (e.g., Reis and Shaver 1988; Laurenceau *et al.* 1998). With these two considerations in mind, people do not usually disclose intimate information right off the bat. Instead, intimate disclosures generally begin only after liking and trust have been established within a relationship. People usually wait until they are confident that they have formed a 'dyadic boundary', insuring that intimate information disclosed by one is not disseminated by the other to mutual acquaintances (Derlega and Chaikin 1977).

However, there are real risks in disclosing personal information (e.g., the risk of ridicule, outright rejection by one's family and friends, penalties within the workplace), as Pennebaker (1989) and others (e.g., Derlega, *et al.* 1993) have shown. Even socially acceptable opinions and behaviours may produce disapproval from one's group or close relationship partners if they deviate from one's usual repertoire (Cooley 1902; Rogers 1951; Goffman 1959). When embarking upon an intimate self-revelation, there is no guarantee that the dyadic boundary will not be violated or that the other member will respond positively and supportively to the disclosure. The motivation to contain the information may overcome the motivation to disclose in the face of such uncertainty as to the outcome of self-disclosure. However, the suppression of important self-aspects may have unintended consequences.

The consequences of suppression

If the motivation to disclose is a strong one and a person is blocked from disclosing to those within their social circle, that person may look for other, safe, avenues in which to disclose. Thus, they may find themself engaging in what Rubin (1975) calls the 'strangers on a train' phenomenon, sharing quite intimate information with an anonymous seatmate – or anyone else whom they never expect to see again. As Derlega and Chaikin (1977) note, people often engage in greater self-disclosure with strangers because the stranger does not have access to that person's social circle and thus the dyadic boundary cannot be violated.

Attempts at suppression may also not be wholly successful. Much research has shown that self-regulation often requires a great deal of mental and physical exertion and also depletes cognitive capacity (e.g., Pennebaker and Chew 1985; Gilbert *et al.* 1988). People tend to be more susceptible to self-regulatory break-downs – i.e., inappropriate emotional outbursts (Baumeister *et al.* 1994) – when tired and under stress. Further, when a person engages in self-regulation in one domain they then experience diminished capacity on subsequent (and unrelated) self-regulatory tasks (e.g., Muraven *et al.* 1986). And, as Wegner and colleagues have shown, suppression efforts are only partly successful and are often followed by a rebound effect (e.g., Wegner *et al.* 1987; Wegner 1994). That is, ironically, when an individual attempts to not think about white bears, for instance, once the suppression exercise is over they often experiences a resurgence of the forbidden thought, making the thought of white bears more salient and accessible (Wegner 1989). Thus, if a person is attempting to suppress and hide aspects of self from others, the unintended consequence would be that not only are those aspects of self likely to become more strongly salient but the discrepancy between one's public self and private self may also become more salient and more conflicted.

Horney (1946) argued that such conflicts between the public persona and the private self are the major cause of unhappiness and the development of neuroses. Hiding important self-aspects for fear of social sanctions creates tension and conflict for the individual because, at the same time, people have a real need to have others share their view of themselves (e.g., Gollwitzer 1986; Swann 1990). These tensions and conflicts may result in impaired functioning for the individual.

An analogy: the 'true jaw'

I liken the negative effects that the constraint and suppression of the true self can create to an experience I've had with my jaw. I went through seven years of orthodontic treatment as a child, having teeth pulled and wearing braces to correct an overcrowded set of teeth. At the end of that time, I was six teeth fewer and showing off a perfectly even smile. Unfortunately, the process of moving my teeth into alignment had also moved my jaw out of alignment. After a few years I began to experience headaches and muscles aches, my jaw began to make loud popping sounds, and eventually it became too painful to eat. Recently a new specialist hooked me up to a computer, watched on a state of the art graphics display my jaw and jaw muscles functioning, and came to the conclusion that my jaw was not being allowed to be its true self. That is, to create a perfect smile my bite had been rearranged so that my jaw muscles and joints could not function naturally. To remedy the situation, Dr Redface attached electrodes to my face which sent electric shocks through the jaw muscles, causing them to move as they naturally would. Then, based on this information as to the muscles' natural patterns of movement, he fashioned a device to retrain my bite to return it to where it naturally wanted to go. This device has allowed my jaw to be its true self and consequently, eating and speaking for me are now free of pain.

In an analogous way, the tensions between the self a person really feels themselves to be, and the self they feel they must appear to be to others can result in both mental and physical distress. The reduction of those discrepancies should result in increased happiness and mental health (e.g., Horney 1946; Rogers 1951; Higgins 1987) and perhaps even enhanced immunological functioning (e.g., Pennebaker 1989). And, as is discussed in the next section, some surprising consequences for one's self and one's relationships may result when a person is able to 'be' the true self with others.

The Internet and the true self

The Internet – with its relative anonymity and multiple venues for social interaction – can be, as Sherry Turkle (1995) noted, a kind of virtual laboratory where an individual can express and experiment with different versions of self. Several unique aspects of the Internet enable people to take on various personae, to express hidden facets of themselves without fear of disapproval or sanctions from those in their real life social circle, and to bypass many of the other barriers to self-expression that exist in face-to-face and telephone interactions (see McKenna and Bargh 2000). What are these special features and how do they facilitate greater self-expression and disclosure?

Qualities of online communication that facilitate self expression

There are several unique features of the Internet that foster self-expression. First and foremost is the ability for one to be relatively anonymous or non-identifiable in individual or group interactions on the Internet. When interacting with others in this way, one is free from the expectations and constraints placed on us by those we know. Further, the cost and risk of incurring social sanctions for the things said in that anonymous environment are greatly reduced. As with the stranger on a train to whom we might disclose quite intimate information, there is little fear that the information we disclose will get back to members of our offline social circle. Yet, unlike with the stranger on a train, we may have repeated interactions with the stranger at the other computer. Thus our Internet self-disclosures may end up laying the foundation for an ongoing, close relationship.

A second way in which the Internet facilitates self-expression is that it provides people the opportunity to easily find others who share important aspects of identity – hobbies, political views, sexual preferences – and who may not be readily identifiable in one's community. Topical newsgroups, electronic community groups, blogs and listservs number in the hundreds of thousands on the Internet and there are website bulletin boards, chat rooms, etc., that cater to every topic and interest imaginable. Membership and participation in such identity-relevant groups provides the opportunity to share these important parts of self with similar others and to have them socially validated (McKenna and Bargh 1998, Howard *et al.* 2001; Joinson 2001, Joinson and Paine, Chapter 16 this volume).

For those who experience social anxiety when interacting with others in person and for those who, because of physical attributes (e.g., obesity, stuttering), find it difficult to get beyond others' stereotyped images of them, there is a third way in which online communication may facilitate self-expression. Interacting in the absence of physical cues and features on the Internet may enable these people to develop relationships that otherwise would not have started in the first place (McKenna and Bargh 1999). For the socially anxious, interacting in the physical absence of the other removes many of the situational factors that spark anxiety (e.g., Leary 1983). Research has shown that in Internet interactions socially anxious individuals feel more comfortable and confident than when interacting face-to-face (McKenna *et al.* 2005, 2006). Social anxiety has also proven to be a more reliable predictor of who will be more likely to feel that they can better express the true self on the Internet rather than in traditional face-to-face venues (McKenna *et al.* 2002).

Similarly, physical appearance has been shown to have a strong impact not only upon first impressions but also in determining whether a friendship will begin between two people (e.g. Hatfield and Sprecher 1986). We have a tendency to immediately and unconsciously categorize others based on physically available features – their ethnicity, attractiveness, age (Bargh 1989). Research on zero-acquaintance studies have shown that there is extremely high consensus in impression formation across a wide variety of measurements and based solely on physical appearance (e.g., Allbright *et al.* 1988). These studies demonstrate that people automatically form impressions of others based upon physical appearance alone. We then integrate information others provide about themselves into our understanding of the category in which

we've placed them (Bruner 1957; Olsen *et al.* 1996). In other words, we make assumptions that go beyond the information that is actually out there. So for instance, if an overweight man tells us that he has just recently run a marathon, we might find ourselves thinking 'and he probably crossed the finish line sometime around midnight', thereby resolving the inconsistency with our beliefs about overweight people if we hold that stereotype. On the Internet a person's physical characteristics are often not in evidence, at least initially. Thus, impressions are formed based on the opinions expressed and the information about the self that is revealed, rather than on more superficial physical features. Interestingly, this represents the removal over the Internet of a usually operating automatic effect on first impressions and initial liking in face-to-face interactions – the categorization and evaluation of a person based on easily perceived physical characteristics – so that impression formation can then proceed in the absence of this initial biasing influence.

A further way in which online interactions can differ from those which occur in person, is the degree of control an individual has over the way they present the self. Because online interactions are at the minimum slightly asynchronous (as in instant messaging) and at the maximum wholly asynchronous (as in email) an individual has more time to formulate, and even edit, what they wish to say than usually is the case when one engages in synchronous, spoken interactions. In the absence of one's physical presence, there is no 'leakage' of non-verbal cues accompanying one's stated information. In other words, one is able to consciously engage in more strategic self-presentation online.

For these reasons, the Internet is a potentially powerful means by which people can express their true selves and meet important social and psychological needs that are not being met in real life. In what follows, I delineate the evidence that suggests that the Internet does indeed facilitate the expression of the true self for many people, and the consequences that may result.

Activation and expression of the true self online

If it is the case that the unique qualities of online communication facilitate the expression of the true self, then one would expect an individual's true self concept to be cognitively more accessible during an Internet interaction with a *new* acquaintance than in a traditional, face-to-face interaction. Conversely, if a person typically expresses the actual self in the face-to-face environment, then the actual-self concept should be cognitively more accessible during face-to-face than during Internet interactions. Several studies were conducted to test these predictions.

Bargh *et al.* (2002, Study 1) conducted two laboratory experiments in order to assess the degree to which the true self, as opposed to the person's actual self concept, was more accessible and activated while interacting on the Internet versus face-to-face. In Study 1, participants were asked to list the characteristics of their actual self and those of their true self. Each participant listed five traits or other characteristics that they believed they actually possess and readily express to others in social settings (the *actual self* measure) and, separately, five traits that they believe they possess and would like to be able to express but are not usually able to in most social settings (the *true self* measure). Participants then interacted with a new acquaintance either in an Internet chat room or face-to-face. Following the interaction, participants individually engaged in a speeded self-judgement task, responding as quickly as possible with either the 'me' or 'not me' key on each trial, according to whether they considered the adjective presented on the computer screen to be self-descriptive or not (see Markus 1977). The actual and true self characteristics the participant provided were embedded in a larger list of positive and negative adjectives. In line with the predictions, participants were faster to respond to content related to the actual self following a face-to-face interaction than following an Internet interaction. Conversely, content related to the participants' true self was more accessible following an Internet interaction than following a face-to-face interaction.

Additional conditions showed that it did not matter for the obtained differential accessibility effects whether the interaction lasted for 5 minutes or for 15 minutes. Thus the effect was not an artefact of differences in the amount of information that can be conveyed in a face-to-face versus an Internet encounter (see Walther 1996). Given that the true self becomes more

activated than the actual self after just five minutes of online interaction suggests that qualities of Internet communication very quickly bring out a person's true self.

A second study showed that the true self did not become more accessible when participants merely anticipated but did not actually engage in an Internet versus a face-to-face interaction. This argues again for the naturalness or automaticity of true-self concept activation as a consequence of Internet communication conditions, because if its activation and use were part of a deliberate and conscious strategy on the part of the individual, the anticipation of Internet-level communication should have caused it to become active in preparation for the interaction.

Thus the self-concept accessibility effects seem to be a consequence of the Internet interaction experience itself. Indeed, the default or baseline state seems to be for the actual self to generally be more accessible for use than the true self-concept. In this experiment, in the absence of any actual Internet interaction, all participants showed greater accessibility of their actual self than their true self concept.

The true self reflected

These two experiments indicate that an individual's true self concept will become more accessible and ready to use in Internet interactions than in face-to-face interactions – but does that mean that true self-aspects are actually expressed in online interactions and, if so, are they perceived by one's online interaction partner?

Bargh *et al.* (2002, Study 3) conducted a further experiment to find out if people are more successful at getting the true self across to others in online versus face-to-face interactions. In this study participants again listed actual and true self characteristics prior to interacting with a randomly assigned partner in an Internet chat room or face-to-face. Following the interaction, participants then privately gave a free response description of their partner. We coded these descriptions of one's partner for matches with the partner's own description of their actual self and true self. An analysis of variance on the numbers of these matches showed that participants successfully conveyed more true self than actual self features in Internet interactions.

In contrast, in the face-to-face condition there were significantly more actual self than true self matches with the partner's spontaneous description of the person. Thus, on the Internet – as assessed by their partner's own candid and spontaneous descriptions of them – participants were better able to convey their true selves.

The Bargh et al. (2002) studies demonstrated that (a) true self characteristics become more activated and accessible in online vs. face-to-face interactions, (b) that this greater activation does not appear to be the result of a conscious, self-presentational strategy, and (c) that people are, indeed, expressing and effectively conveying these true-self characteristics more so in their online vs. offline interactions. Are they, however, aware that they are doing so? McKenna et al.(2006) conducted a study replicating the Bargh et al. (Study 1) findings of greater activation of true self characteristics in online vs. face-to-face interactions. This study also included explicit measures assessing the degree to which participants were able to report having expressed actual and true self characteristics during their interactions. Results showed that online and face-to-face participants looked identical as to the degree to which they felt they had expressed these aspects of self. As is frequently found in studies containing implicit and explicit measures, for both the online and the face-to-face interactions, the implicit and explicit measures were wholly uncorrelated. Thus it appears to be the case that, while people are indeed expressing more true self aspects in their online interactions, they are often unaware of doing so.

As previously mentioned, true self characteristics were found to be, on average, significantly less positive than the actual self characteristics. (However, it is important to note that both true and actual selves tended to be positive in valence.) Thus, over the Internet, participants were expressing and conveying aspects of self that were less positive than the self-aspects that were being conveyed by those who interacted face-to-face. One might therefore think that partners would like one another more in the face-to-face condition, given that these participants were expressing and conveying more positive self-aspects. However, this was not the case. Partners who interacted on the Internet liked one another significantly more so than did those

who interacted face-to-face, despite – or perhaps even because of – sharing less positive aspects of self with one another. Why might that be?

I believe that the greater self-disclosure which results naturally and which is an unintended (and probably unaware) effect of Internet communication is responsible. First, we know that self-disclosure and partner disclosure tend to increase the intimacy in interactions (e.g., Reis and Shaver 1988; Laurenceau et al. 1998). We tend to like those to whom we make disclosures and, in turn, to like those who disclose to us (Collins and Miller 1994). The fact that the Internet participants were expressing aspects of the true self with one another – aspects they are generally unable to express with others – may well have increased the bonds of empathy and understanding between them. As Derlega and Chaikin note, 'a major function of friendships and love relationships may be to validate one's self-concept by obtaining the support and understanding of the other person' (1977: 110). Moreover, it must be kept in mind that these were randomly paired college undergraduates participating in a psychology experiment – not intentionally seeking a friend or romantic partner during the study; yet the effects of Internet communication on greater liking still applied. This also supports the conclusion that the effects of the Internet communication situation are unintended and nonstrategic. Secondly, research has shown that when people meet new acquaintances (face-to-face) in contexts where no other friends or acquaintances are present, they tend to present themselves less modestly than they do if one of their friends is also present (Tice et al. 1995). The presence of a friend tends to moderate the qualities, attributes and accomplishments one claims. It may be that when we meet new others we implicitly (or even explicitly) assume that they are giving us a polished-up version of themselves – just as we are attempting to present ourselves in the best light to them. Presenting a more modest version of self to a new acquaintance on the Internet may feel more similar to the way an individual presents himself among friends, and thus have associations to and accentuate feelings of friendship. It is also possible that if, while presenting the more positive aspects of self, a person also reveals a few less positive aspects to the new acquaintance, she may be perceived as being more 'authentic' by the other person and thus more likable. Again, these effects appear to be unintended consequences of the ability of Internet communication to draw forth one's true self for expression.

Same old friends, same old self

In contrast to interactions with new acquaintances, online or face-to-face we generally express the same aspects of self to members of our *existing* social circle. In line with the findings of Andersen and Chen (2002), results from a recent survey and laboratory studies reveal that the average person generally continues to express the 'actual self' to those whom he or she initially met in person, whether the interaction takes place online or not (McKenna *et al.* 2005, 2006). For instance, in one study participants were asked to bring along a close friend to the laboratory. These participants then interacted either face-to-face or through instant messaging with the friend they brought along or with a stranger (the other half of another friendship pair). Following the interaction participants immediately engaged in the reaction time task used by Bargh and colleagues (Bargh *et al.* 2002). Again, when stranger pairs interacted online vs. face-to-face the participants were significantly faster to respond to true self descriptions. Not so for those who interacted with a friend: indeed, there was no difference in the activation of the true self online vs. offline.

Results from a survey study conducted with nearly 500 participants are consistent with this finding. The average participant in this study reported expressing their true self to existing friends online no more than they did with those friends face-to-face. Even those participants who reported being able to present and express the true self more online with strangers than they can in their face-to-face lives reported that they did not do so online with their face-to-face friends.

There was one exception to this general finding, and that occurred in the case of those who reported experiencing higher levels of social anxiety in their face-to-face lives. These socially anxious participants reported being better able to express the true self when interacting online both with their online-initiated relationships and with their friends and family members (albeit to a greater extent even so with online-initiated relationships).

In addition to conscious self-regulatory processes that are likely to be at work (e.g., the need for consistency in one's self presentation to family and friends), non-conscious processes may also be at work to inhibit the expression of the true, or inner, self with existing friends while interacting online. Recent research (e.g., Fitzsimmons and Bargh 2003; Shah 2003) suggests that when important mental representations of others become activated, so too do the self-goals and motivations that are associated with that relationship become activated. These goals then operate, outside of the individual's conscious awareness, to affect the individual's behaviour, even in quite unrelated situations. This suggests that when one is interacting online with a friend or family member the mental associations that one has with that person are likely to be activated, and strongly so. Thus the same self-qualities that one generally presents when with the friend in person, along with the same goals and motivations, are also likely to be activated and expressed during the online interaction.

Results from a recent laboratory study (McKenna *et al.* 2006, Study 3), suggests that this is indeed the case. Research by Tice *et al.* (1995) found that when two strangers meet (face-to-face) for the first time and the meeting takes place in the absence of any friends or acquaintances, they tend to behave with less modesty. That is, they tend to present more of their ideal self-qualities to strangers than they do to friends. The presence of a friend at the meeting provoked more modest self-presentation. In a replication and extension of this study, including two additional and comparable online conditions, McKenna and colleagues (2006, Study 3) found that individuals are indeed more likely to present a significantly less modest version of self when interacting face-to-face with a stranger alone than if a friend is also present. The results become quite interesting when it comes to the online conditions, however. When a friend was a present (although passive) participant in the chat room, the participant presented a version of self in line with that of the stranger–friend face-to-face condition – more modestly than when two strangers interact alone face-to-face. When two strangers interacted online and alone, however, the *most* modest version of self was elicited. Thus it does seem that individuals are motivated to present themselves in the same, relatively modest, way in the presence of friends, regardless of interaction venue. Further, they tend to be even more modest in their self-presentation when they interact online solely with a stranger. Modesty goes out the window, however, when one meets a new person face-to-face and in the absence of any known acquaintances.

From the studies above it is obvious that the qualities of online communication can elicit different qualities of self than the standard ones generally activated and presented in face-to-face life if the interaction involves a potential new acquaintance. An individual's 'default' aspects of self and accompanying goals become activated and expressed with existing friends, however, just as occurs in one's non-Internet interactions with those same people. We turn now to an examination of the consequences that may stem from expressing the true self on the Internet.

The consequences of expressing the true self for the self-concept

If an individual does begin to express their true self with others on the Internet, what effects might this have on their self-concept? Research conducted with people who have socially marginalized aspects of the true self may provide some insight. McKenna and Bargh (1998) studied Internet users involved in electronic newsgroups catering to marginalized aspects of identity. One study focused on those who have marginalized sexual proclivities (e.g., homosexuality, bondage) and a replication focused on stigmatized ideologies (e.g., believers in government conspiracies). The assumption was that active participation in identity-relevant electronic groups would lead to the same benefits for individuals as has been found for group membership and identification in traditional face-to-face groups (e.g., Ethier and Deaux 1994; Deaux 1996). Specifically, to the extent that participation in these groups leads to stronger group identification, the individual should come to accept the marginalized identity as part of, rather than distinct from, their self-concept.

Results indicated that active participation in the online groups did allow these individuals to reap the self-related benefits of joining a group of similar others. Moreover, because these groups dealt with stigmatized identities, for most participants this was the first time and the only way possible for them to find similarly minded others. Participation in the groups allowed these individuals to disclose, in a social context, a long-secret yet important part of their identity, and in return gain emotional and motivational support from their fellow group members (see Derlega *et al.* 1993; Jones *et al.* 1984). Participation in the online group resulted in increased feelings of self-acceptance of one's marginalized identity, and also caused the person to feel less isolated from society in general.

Again, it would appear that people are not aware of and do not intend the effects of Internet newsgroup participation on one's identity and self-acceptance – otherwise, the non-participants (those who merely read the newsgroup but did not contribute to its postings), who presumably also would want the benefits of greater self-acceptance participation brings, would have participated as well.

Moreover, not only did these individuals reveal having this marginalized identity to their fellow electronic group members, but also – and as a direct result of their group participation – more than 40 per cent of the participants across both studies brought the concealed identity into the open, telling family and friends about it for the first time. Given that sexual preferences are often formed early in life, the findings of the first study seem particularly remarkable. The mean age of that sample was 37 years, and thus involvement in the electronic groups caused these people to reveal something to close family members and friends that many had kept hidden well into their adult years.

Simply finding others who shared the marginalized aspect of self was not enough to bring about these self-changes, however. Those who only read others' contributions to the online forum, but who did not themselves participate in the group, did not reap these benefits. Those who became actively involved in the group, revealing to fellow members that they too shared this secret aspect of self, garnered the acceptance and validation needed to replace a negative view of self with a more positive one (e.g., Gollwitzer 1986; Harter 1993; Heatherton and Nichols 1994). They acquired a positive group identity where before there were only feelings of being isolated and different, and often shame as well.

Consequences for relationships

Expressing the true self with others on the Internet should also have consequences for one's close relationships. We hypothesized that people who feel they better express the true self on the Internet than in face-to-face settings would be more likely to form close relationships with others online. If a person is expressing and disclosing their true self with others online, we would expect these relationships to become important to his identity, for two main reasons. First, as discussed above, mental representations of external social entities, such as groups, through which a person defines their identity tend to become incorporated into one's self-concept. Secondly, because the self is relational in nature, one's self becomes 'entangled' or defined in large part in terms of those important relationships (e.g., Baldwin 1997).

It is known that people are highly motivated to make important aspects of their identity a 'social reality' (e.g., Gollwitzer 1986), through making them known to their friends and family members – as we saw above in the case of the marginalized group members. If important online relationships also become incorporated as aspects of one's identity, then we should expect people to be motivated to make them a social reality as well, by making them public and face-to-face – that is, bringing them into their real life social circle.

To test these hypotheses, McKenna et al. (2002) conducted a study of nearly 600 randomly selected Internet newsgroup users with normative, mainstream interests – gardening, history, animal care. As predicted, people who felt that they were better able to express or 'locate' their true self on the Internet than in face-to-face settings were more likely to have fashioned close online relationships. Those who felt that their true self resides on the Internet, compared to those who didn't, were significantly more likely to have become engaged to, or have an affair with, someone they met on the

Internet. They were also more likely than others to have brought their online relationships into their everyday, non-Internet life. Just as many of those with marginalized identities were not content to consign the true self to the online world, so too were these Internet relationship partners not content to relegate the people to whom they expressed the true self to only the virtual realm. As Gollwitzer (1986) and Swann (1983) have shown, people are motivated to make important aspects of identity a social reality by making them known to their face-to-face social circles.

Online relationships developed intimacy more quickly than do face-to-face relationships for those who express the true self online. It may well be the faster disclosure of one's true self in these online interactions that drives these relationships to form more quickly. Along these lines, laboratory studies (Bargh et al. 2002; McKenna et al. 2002) have shown that people tend to like one another more if they first become acquainted through the Internet than if they first meet in person.

These relationships are also likely to prove to be stable over time. First, because these relationships become incorporated into one's identity, one should be motivated to maintain them. This should be particularly so if these relationships do, indeed, become entangled with one's true self, as this part of oneself is generally not expressed in one's other relationships.

Secondly, a stronger base for the relationship may occur if these relationships form because of mutual self-disclosure and shared interests, rather than on more superficial physical attributes. If a positive impression of the other person is formed on these stronger premises, the good impression may last even if less positive information later comes to light. Research has shown that initial impressions are difficult to overcome (e.g., Fiske and Taylor 1991). In subsequent interactions, people tend to selectively focus on information that confirms rather than disconfirms one's initial judgement (e.g., Higgins and Bargh 1987). If such is the case, these relationships should be better able to weather the move from online to offline interactions. That is, features such as the person's physical appearance may not carry as much weight in determining whether the relationship will go forward, once participants do meet in person, because liking, intimacy, and a positive impression have already been established.

Supporting this supposition are the results of a laboratory study that found, first of all, that people tend to like the same person more if they initially meet on the Internet than if they meet in person (McKenna *et al.* 2002, Study 3). Participants were told that they would be meeting with two different people, one of whom they would talk with on the Internet, and the other in person. In actuality, they interacted with the same person both times, although neither partner was aware of that fact. Following each interaction, participants were asked to assess the degree to which they liked the other person and to evaluate the quality of the interaction. Not only was there greater liking for the same person when the meeting took place online rather than face-to-face, but, in the Internet condition, the degree of liking was significantly correlated with the quality of the interaction. In particular, participants felt that they knew their online partner better than their face-to-face partner (again, it was the same person on both occasions), and were more likely to have told the other person specifically what they liked about them on the Internet.

Bearing directly on whether Internet relationships can survive a face-to-face meeting is a second finding of this study. Two conditions were included in which participants knowingly interacted with the same person on two occasions. Participants were randomly paired to interact either first in an Internet chat room and then in a subsequent face-to-face meeting, or the pairs engaged in two face-to-face meetings. After each meeting, liking for partner and the quality of the interaction was assessed. Results showed that, for those who initially met in person, additional face-to-face interaction did not alter their original feelings of liking for the other. In other words, their initial impressions did not change following additional interaction. In contrast, impressions did change, and positively so, for those who started out online and then moved the interaction to a face-to-face setting. For those who first met online, liking significantly increased following a further face-to-face interaction. Indeed, those who started out online and then moved to a face-to-face interaction liked one another significantly more so than did those who only interacted face-to-face.

Relationships that begin online can also be long-lasting. A follow-up study was conducted to see how the relationships reported by the 600 newsgroup users had fared after two years. McKenna *et al.* (2002) found that the majority of these participants' online relationships were enduring two years later. Indeed, 75 per cent of the relationships were ongoing, with the majority being characterized as having grown closer and stronger over the intervening years. The stability of these relationships compares favourably to relationships that form and develop in traditional face-to-face settings. For instance, a longitudinal study by Hill *et al.* (1976) found that slightly more than 50 per cent of the dating couples in their study were still together after two years.

It is not the Internet *per se* that drives these effects

It is the unique qualities of Internet communication that drive the effects discussed in this article, rather than the Internet per se. Different forms of communication have different qualities or combinations of qualities and are thus likely to produce differential – and often quite powerful – effects. For instance, with interactions that take place face-to-face the participants are identifiable (even if their names are not known), and available visual and aural cues have a strong impact on impression formation, the future development (or not) of friendship, and so forth. The telephone allows individuals to interact in real time and with aural but not visual cues present. Voicemail shares some qualities in common with the telephone and some with the Internet. As with the telephone, we can hear the other person's voice speaking as if in real time when they leave their message, but, as with electronic mail (or letter by the post), a real time give and take conversation does not take place. Whitty (Chapter 3 this volume) provides many examples of historical precursors to the Internet that shared some of the same qualities and produced many of the same effects – whether it be through Victorian love letters or relationships that blossomed between telegraph operators.

Conclusion

The unique features of the Internet can indeed foster the expression of important self-aspects that are otherwise barred from expression in one's life. Not only can one more easily express aspects of the true self with others on the Internet, but there is a greater likelihood that these important self-aspects will be perceived by others online. This acknowledgement and validation by others may well result in changes in the individual's conception of self. Expressing one's true self on the Internet can lead to greater self-acceptance and to heightened feelings of belonging and connectedness with others. Actively participating in identity-relevant groups and sharing one's 'inner self' within dyadic relationships online, can result in the development of close and intimate relationships – relationships that may not have formed were the partners to have first met face-to-face instead. Because these relationships encompass and help to define important aspects of self, they are likely to be brought into one's everyday, non-Internet life, and they are likely to survive such a transposition, becoming durable additions to one's existing social circle.

Just as occurs in the face-to-face environment, both conscious and non-conscious processes are at work to influence a wide range of online phenomena – from impression formation, judgements, intimacy, and perhaps most importantly the expression of aspects of the self – and to produce differential outcomes. The unique qualities of online communication can interact with these processes, however, and produce quite different effects than what occurs in face-to-face life. Research on the role of non-conscious processes in online interactions is just beginning and should prove to be a rich area for further research.

References

Allbright, L., Kenny, D. A. and Malloy, T. E. (1988). Consensus in personality judgments at zero acquaintance. *Journal of Personality and Social Psychology 55*, 387–395.

Andersen, S. M. and Chen, S. (2002). The relational self: an interpersonal social-cognitive theory. *Psychological Review 109*, 619–645.

Baldwin, M. W. (1997). Relational schemas as a source of if–then self-inference procedures. *Review of General Psychology 1*, 326–335.

Bargh, J. A. (1989). Conditional automaticity: varieties of automatic influence in social perception and cognition. In J. S. Uleman and J. A. Bargh (eds), *Unintended thought* (pp. 3–51). New York: Guilford.

Bargh, J. A. (1994). The Four Horsemen of automaticity: awareness, efficiency, intention and control in social cognition. In R. S. Wyer, Jr. and T. K. Srull (eds), *Handbook of social cognition*, 2nd edn (pp. 1–40). Hillsdale, NJ: Erlbaum.

Bargh, J. A., McKenna, K. Y. A. and Fitzsimons, G. M. (2002). Can you see the real me? Activation and expression of the 'true self' on the Internet. *Journal of Social Issues 58*, 33–48.

Baumeister, R. F. (1986) (Editor) *Public Self and Private Self*. New York: Springer-Verlag.

Baumeister, R. F. and Leary, M. R. (1995). The need to belong: desire for interpersonal attachments as a fundamental human motivation. *Psychological Bulletin 117*, 497–529.

Baumeister, R. F., Heatherton, T. F. and Tice, D. M. (1994). *Losing control: How and why people fail to self-regulate*. San Diego, CA: Academic Press.

Bruner, J. S. (1957). Going beyond the information given. In J. S. Bruner, E. Brunswik, L. Festinger, F. Heider, K. F. Muenzinger, C. E. Osgood and D. Rapaport (eds), *Contemporary approaches to cognition* (pp. 41–69). Cambridge, MA: Harvard University Press.

Burke, P. J. (1980). The self: measurement implications from a symbolic interactionist perspective. *Social Psychology Quarterly 43*, 18–29.

Burke, P. J. and Tully, J. (1977). The measurement of role/identity. *Social Forces 55*, 881–897.

Collins, N. L., & Miller, L. C. (1994). Self-disclosure and liking: a meta-analytic review. *Psychological Bulletin, 116*, 457–475.

Cooley, C. H. (1902). *Human nature and the social order*. New York: Scribners.

Deaux, K. (1996). Social identification. In E. T. Higgins and A. W. Kruglanski (eds), *Social psychology: Handbook of basic principles* (pp. 777–798). New York: Guilford Press.

Derlega, V. L. and Chaikin, A. L. (1977). Privacy and self-disclosure in social relationships. *Journal of Social Issues 33*, 102–115.

Derlega, V. L., Metts, S., Petronio, S. and Margulis, S. T. (1993). *Self-disclosure*. London: Sage.

Ethier, K. A. & Deaux, K. (1994). Negotiating social identity when contexts change: maintaining identification and responding to threat. *Journal of Personality and Social Psychology, 67*, 243–251.

Fiske, S. T. and Taylor, S. E. (1991). *Social cognition*, 2nd edn. New York: Scott, Foresman.

Fitzsimons, G. M. & Bargh, J. A. (2003). Thinking of you: nonconscious pursuit of interpersonal goals associated with relationship partners. *Journal of Personality and Social Psychology, 84*, 148–164.

Frable, D. E. S. (1993). Being and feeling unique: statistical deviance and psychological marginality. *Journal of Personality 61*, 85–110.

Gilbert, D. T., Krull, D. S. and Pelham, B. W. (1988). Of thoughts unspoken: social inference and the self-regulation of behavior. *Journal of Personality and Social Psychology 55*, 685–694.

Goffman, E. (1959). *The presentation of self in everyday life*. New York: Doubleday Press.

Gollwitzer, P. M. (1986). Striving for specific identities: the social reality of self-symbolizing. In R. Baumeister (ed.), *Public self and private self* (pp. 143–159). New York: Springer.

Harter, S. (1993). Causes and consequences of low self-esteem in children and adolescents. In R. F. Baumeister (Ed.), Self-esteem: the puzzle of low self-regard (pp. 87–116). New York: Plenum Press.

Harter, S. (1997). The personal self in social context: barriers to authenticity. In R. D. Ashmore and L. Jussim (eds), *Self and identity: Fundamental issues*, vol. 1 (pp. 81–105).

Harter, S., Waters, P. L., Whitesell, N. R. and Kastelic, D. (1998). Level of voice among female and male high school students: relational context, support and gender orientation. *Developmental Psychology 34*, 892–901.

Hatfield, E. and Sprecher, S. (1986). *Mirror, mirror: The importance of looks in everyday life*. Albany, NY: State University of New York Press.

Heatherton, T. F. and Nichols, P. A. (1994). Personal accounts of successful versus failed attempts at life change. *Personality and Social Psychology Bulletin 20*, 664–675.

Higgins, E. T. (1987). Self-discrepancy theory. *Psychological Review 94*, 1120–1134.

Higgins, E. T., & Bargh, J. A. (1987). Social cognition and social perception. *Annual Review of Psychology*, *38*, 369–425.

Hill, C. T., Rubin, Z., & Peplau, L. A. (1976). Breakups before marriage: The end of 103 affairs. *Journal of Social Issues*, *32*(1), 147–168.

Horney, K. (1946). *Our inner conflicts: A constructive theory of neurosis*. London: Routledge and Kegan Paul.

Howard, P. E. N., Rainie, L. and Jones, S. (2001). Days and nights on the Internet. *American Behavorial Scientist 45*, 383–404.

Ichiyama, M. A. (1993). The reflected appraisal process in small-group interaction. *Social Psychology Quarterly 56*, 87–99.

James, W. (1892). Psychology: the briefer course. In *William James: Writings 1879–1899*. New York: Library of America.

Joinson, A. N. (2001). Knowing me, knowing you: reciprocal self-disclosure in internet-based surveys. *Cyberpsychology and Behaviour 4*, 587–591.

Jones, E. E., Farina, A., Hastorf, A. H., Markus, H., Miller, D. T. and Scott, R. A. (1984). *Social stigma: The psychology of marked relationships*. San Francisco, CA: WH Freeman.

Jourard, S. M. (1964). *The transparent self*. New York: Van Nostrand.

Jung, C. G. (1953). *Two essays in analytical psychology* (trans. R. F. Hull). New York: Pantheon.

Kenny, D. A. and DePaulo, B. M. (1993). Do people know how others view them? An empirical and theoretical account. *Psychological Bulletin 21*, 1161–1166.

Laurenceau, J. P., Barrett, L. F. and Pietromonaco, P. R. (1998). Intimacy as an interpersonal process: the importance of self-disclosure, partner disclosure and perceived partner responsiveness in interpersonal exchanges. *Journal of Personality and Social Psychology 74*, 1238–1251.

Leary, M. (1983). Social Anxiousness: The Construct and its Measurement. *Journal of Personality Assessment, 47*, 66–75.

Leary, M. R. and Atherton, S. (1986). Self-efficacy, anxiety and inhibition in interpersonal encounters. *Journal of Social and Clinical Psychology 4*, 256–267.

Linville, P. W. (1985). Self-complexity and affective extremity: don't put all of your eggs in one cognitive basket. *Social Cognition 3*, 94–120.

Markus, H. (1977). Self-schemata and processing information about the self. Self-schemata and processing information about the self. *Journal of personality and Social Psychology 35*, 63–78.

Markus, H. and Nurius, P. (1986). Possible selves. *American Psychologist 41*, 954–969.

McKenna, K. Y. A. and Bargh, J. A. (1998). Coming out in the age of the Internet: identity demarginalization through virtual group participation. *Journal of Personality and Social Psychology 75*, 681–694.

McKenna, K. Y. A., & Bargh, J. A. (1999). Causes and consequences of social interaction on the Internet: A conceptual framework. *Media Psychology, 1*, 249–269.

McKenna, K. Y. A. and Bargh, J. A. (2000). Plan 9 from cyberspace: the implications of the Internet for personality and social psychology. *Personality and Social Psychology Review 4*, 57–75.

McKenna, K. Y. A., Buffardi, L. and Seidman, G. (2005). Self presentation to friends and strangers online. In Karl-Heinz Renner, Astrid Schutz, and Franz Machilek (eds) *Internet and Personality* (pp. 175–188): Hogrefe and Huber Publishers.

McKenna, K. Y. A., Buffardi, L. and Seidman, G. (2006). Strange but true: differential activation of the 'true-self' to friends and strangers online and in person. Manuscript under review.

McKenna, K. Y. A., Green, A. S. and Gleason, M. E. J. (2002). Relationship formation on the Internet: What's the big attraction? *Journal of Social Issues 58*, 9–31.

Mead, G. H. (1932) *Mind self and society from the standpoint of a social behaviorist*. Chicago, IL: University of Chicago.

Muraven, M., Tice, D. M. and Baumeister, R. F. (1998). Self-control as limited resource: regulatory depletion patterns. *Journal of Personality and Social Psychology 74*, 774–789.

Olson, J. M., Roese, N. J. and Zanna, M. P. (1996). Expectancies. In E. T. Higgins and A. W. Kruglanski (eds), *Social psychology: Handbook of basic principles* (pp. 341–352). New York: Guilford.

Pennebaker, J. W. (1989). Confession, inhibition and disease. In L. Berkowitz (ed.), *Advances in experimental social psychology*, vol. 22, (pp. 211–244). New York: Academic Press.

Pennebaker, J. W. and Chew, C. H. (1985). Behavioral inhibition and electrodermal activity during deception. *Journal of Personality and Social Psychology 49*, 1427–1433.

Reis, H. T. and Shaver, P. (1988). Intimacy as an interpersonal process. In S. Duck, D. Hay, S. E. Hobfoll, W. Ickes and B. M. Montgomery (eds), *Handbook of personal relationships: Theory, research and interventions* (pp. 367–389). Chichester, England: John Wiley and Sons.

Rogers, C. (1951). *Client-centered therapy*. Boston, MA: Houghton-Mifflin.

Rogers, C. (1980). *A way of being*. Boston, MA: Houghton-Mifflin.

Rubin, Z. (1975). Disclosing oneself to a stranger: reciprocity and its limits. *Journal of Experimental Social Psychology 11*, 233–260.

Sarbin, T. R. and Allen, V. L. (1968). Role theory. In G. Lindzey and E. Aronson (eds), *The Handbook of social psychology*, 2nd edn (pp. 488–567). Reading, MA: Addison-Wesley.

Shah, J. Y. (2003). The motivational looking glass: how significant others implicitly affect goal appraisals. *Journal of Personality and Social Psychology, 85*, 424–439.

Shrauger, J. S. and Schoeneman, T. J. (1979). Symbolic interactionist view of self-concept: through the glass darkly. *Psychological Bulletin 86*, 549–573.

Spreitzer, E., Snyder, E. and Larson, D. (1979). Multiple roles and psychological well-being. *Sociological Focus 12*, 141–148.

Stryker, S. and Statham, A. (1985). Symbolic interaction and role theory. In G. Lindzey and E. Aronson (eds), *Handbook of social psychology*, vol. I (pp. 311–378). New York: Random House.

Swann, W. B., Jr. (1983). Self verification: bringing social reality into harmony with the self. In J. Suls & A. G. Greenwald (Eds.), *Social psychological perspectives on the self (Vol. 2, pp. 33–66)*. Hillsdalel, NJ: Erlbaum.

Swann, W. B., Jr. (1990). To be known or to be adored? The interplay of self-enhancement and self-verification. In E. T. Higgins and R. M. Sorrentino (eds), *Handbook of motivation and cognition*, vol. 2, (pp. 408–448). New York: Guilford.

Tajfel, H. and Turner, J. C. (1986). The social identity theory of intergroup behavior. In S. Worchel and W. G. Austin (eds), *Psychology of intergroup relations* (pp. 7–24). Chicago, IL: Nelson-Hall.

Tice, D. M. (1992). Self-presentation and self-concept change: the looking-glass self is also a magnifying glass. *Journal of Personality and Social Psychology 63*, 435–451.

Tice, D. M., Butler, J. L., Muraven, M. B. and Stillwell, A. M. (1995). When modesty prevails: differential favorability of self-presentation to friends and strangers. *Journal of Personality and Social Psychology 69*, 1120–1138.

Turkle, S. (1995). *Life on the screen: Identity in the age of the Internet*. New York: Simon and Schuster.

Tyler, TR (2002). Is the Internet changing social life? It seems the more things change, the more they stay the same. *Journal of Social Issues 58*, 195–205.

Verbrugge, L. M. (1986). Role burdens and physical health of women and men. *Women and Health 11*, 47–77.

Walther, J. B. (1996). Computer-mediated-communication: impersonal, interpersonal, and hyperpersonal interaction. *Communication Research, 23*, 3–43.

Wegner, D. M. (1989). *White bears and other unwanted thoughts*. New York: Vintage.

Wegner, D. M. (1994). Ironic processes of mental control. *Psychological Review 94*, 34–52.

Wegner, D. M., Schneider, D. J., Carter, S. R. and White, T. L. (1987). Paradoxical effects of thought suppression. *Journal of Personality and Social Psychology 53*, 5–13.

CHAPTER 15

Impression management and identity online

Andrea Chester and Di Bretherton

When an individual appears in presence of others, there will usually be some reason for him to mobilize his interests to activity so that it will convey an impression to others which it is in his interests to convey.

Erving Goffman (1959: 15–16)

In her study of an online community, Jennifer Mnookin (1996) concluded that online impressions 'need not in any way correspond to a person's real life identity; people can make and remake themselves, choosing their gender and the details of their online presentation' (1996: para. 5). This comment came to represent the way the Internet was portrayed both in the popular media and within academic writing in the 1990s. Online communication was seen to hold the potential for unique opportunities to present the self: no longer constrained by corporeal reality, users could invent and reinvent themselves. They could manage impressions in ways never before possible. The Internet was described as the quintessential playground for postmodern plurality, fragmentation, and contextual construction of self (Bruckman 1993; Reid 1994; Turkle 1995).

This chapter examines the process of impression management online and considers whether these conceptualizations of identity experimentation still accurately describe 'life on the screen'.

Impression management: an introduction

Impression management is the process of controlling the impressions that other people form. Although it is possible to manage impressions of just about anything, from objects and events, to ideas and even other people, impression management typically refers to the process of influencing the impressions an audience forms about oneself. The term 'impression management' is therefore often used synonymously with 'self-presentation'.[1]

Other people's perceptions of us play an important role in our lives; they impact on our interactions, shaping the rewards we receive. Children in Western cultures are often taught that other people's impressions are not as important as the way one perceives oneself: however, for most people, the two are intricately linked, with others' impressions influencing self-perception and validating our sense of self. Most of us do appear to care what other people think of us. As Mark Leary (1995) notes, 'virtually everyone

[1] For a discussion of the wider use of the term impression management, as it refers to the management of any impressions, see Schlenker (2003).

thinks about other people's impressions of him or her from time to time and some people worry a great deal about how others regard them' (1995: 1). Even when our primary goal is not impression management, we rarely intentionally behave in ways that will create disadvantageous impressions (Leary 1995). Our daily behaviour is therefore often influenced by impression management concerns.

This chapter examines the extent to which these same impression management concerns operate online. In the first half of the chapter two components of impression management are introduced: impression motivation and impression construction, and the effect of online media on these two processes is considered. In the second half some contemporary empirical work is explored and compared with the picture that was drawn in the mid 1990s. The chapter begins, however, by considering one of the best-known stories of impression management online.

Impression management online: the case of Alex/Joan

The story of Alex/Joan was first documented by van Gelder (1991), a journalist with *Ms Magazine*. The article, entitled 'The case of the electronic lover', detailed the story of Alex, a middle-aged American psychiatrist who, in the 1980s, joined a chat room using the screen name 'Shrink Inc'. Although used to dealing with personal issues in his professional practice, Alex was reportedly surprised by the vulnerability and intimacy of his interactions with women online. He realized that his gender-neutral handle had been misinterpreted; these women had assumed he was female. According to van Gelder, Alex was excited by this new potential for helping people as a woman and he established a female character, Joan Greene.

Joan emerged on chat with a carefully wrought self-presentation, providing the perfect excuse for avoiding face-to-face meetings: Her boyfriend had been killed in a car accident in which she herself was paralysed, disfigured, and had lost her ability to speak. Not only did she find it difficult to get around, but the facial disfigurement caused by the accident also left her embarrassed. Face-to-face meetings were therefore physically

and emotionally difficult. Online, however, Joan Greene flourished. Over the course of several years Alex managed the impressions created, transforming Joan from suicidal recluse to socially confident woman with a wide circle of online friends. Indeed when, after three years, Alex attempted to kill Joan off by inventing a terminal illness, he was met with an outpouring of grief and distress.

Few of us have probably ever engaged in impression management to the same extent as Alex, but anyone who has ever visited a chat room or sent a message to a newsgroup has no doubt been aware of the self-presentational freedoms afforded online; in the virtual world it is possible to construct impressions in ways that are difficult or even impossible offline. Users can, as Alex did, swap gender. They can alter their age, change physical characteristics, construct different personality traits. Impression management includes a wide spectrum of behaviour from outright deception, such as pretending to be someone one is not, through to more subtle selective disclosure, such as concealing certain information. (See Chapter 19 in this book for a more detailed discussion of deception online.) What are the features of online contexts that permit such impression management behaviour?

The unique characteristics of online communication that impact on impression management

Online interactions are characterized by a range of features that distinguish them from offline interactions – the most obvious of these is anonymity. The anonymity of online communication is best described along a continuum. At one end of this continuum is identifiability, where users may be traced by the use of their real name or through features of their email address. At the other end of the continuum is the potential to be completely untraceable online. It is possible, for example, to lurk on a discussion board, reading the contributions without anyone, except the system administrators, knowing you have been there (Suler 2003). In this case one is invisible, or almost, creating no impression.

Most text-based online communication, however, falls somewhere between these extremes, in a state of visual anonymity, where those who are communicating do not see each other, but have access to some identifying data (Joinson 2003). The case of Alex/Joan illustrates this middle ground, a kind of *managed anonymity* in which the user chooses a screen name, which generally has meaning to the individual. This pseudonymity is common to many online interactions, including chat and multi-user domains (MUDs).

In this state of managed anonymity, aspects of impression management that are normally outside one's control in face-to-face interactions, such as one's gender, age and ethnicity, become negotiable. Impressions can therefore be managed in unique ways online. Unconstrained by the limitations that operate in the offline world, users are free to self-select traits. As Joinson (2003: 78) notes, 'it is difficult to misrepresent yourself to someone sitting opposite you'. Online, however, certain deceptions, including those about the physical self, are much less likely to be detected. Joinson refers to the impression management opportunities afforded by the visual anonymity of the medium as the 'degrees of freedom' inherent in visually anonymous online interaction.

As well as visual anonymity, many online contexts explicitly call attention to impression management by inviting and often requiring users to choose a screen name, select a gender and write a description of themselves. In each of these tasks users can make decisions about how to present themselves online. Researchers have examined each of these three acts as processes of impression management, including the choice of screen name (Bechar-Israeli 1996; Chester 2004), gender selection (Turkle 1995; Roberts and Parks 1999; Chester 2004), and the role of the character description (Turkle 1995; Chester 2004).

Impression management is a concept with wide application, and many variables have been hypothesized to impact on it. Synthesizing these influences, Mark Leary (1995) conceptualized a three-stage model explaining how and why people manage their public presentations. According to this model, impression management involves at least two discrete but interrelated processes: impression motivation and impression construction. In the following sections we consider evidence for these processes online.

Impression motivation online

Impression management in the offline world is driven by the desire to achieve certain goals. The motivation to create a particular impression is determined by three factors: the extent to which the desired impression will contribute to the attainment of a goal, the value of that goal and the discrepancy that exists between the image the actor wishes others to hold and the image the audience already holds (Leary 1995). Goals for impression management include social and material gains, such as securing a job at an interview or attracting someone enough to get a date. Other goals include the development of identity and maintenance of self-esteem.

In the case of Alex/Joan, one could speculate about the source of motivation for the impression management behaviour. Alex's motivation, at least according to van Gelder (1991), was initially altruistic and therapeutic. He wanted to help women in ways he'd been unable to in his psychiatric practice. As time went on, however, his motivation grew more self-serving and, according to van Gelder, more conscious. Joan 'was by my own recollection and by the accounts of everyone interviewed, an exquisitely wrought character' (van Gelder 1991: 367). Alex also began to engage in 'lesbian' netsex with women he met online and ultimately used the character of Joan to introduce women to the offline Alex: the sexual rewards were considerable. It is unclear, however, from van Gelder's account whether Alex derived pleasure from the deception itself, a motive that Turkle (1995) discusses in her work.

Qualitative researchers, like Turkle (1995), have studied the motivation for impression management online extensively. Drawing on data gathered from face-to-face interviews with MUD players, Turkle describes the complex motives that propel people to manage impressions online. Although these include a desire to establish relationships and the power associated with deception, a strong theme to emerge was also a desire to express unexplored parts of identity or aspects that are inhibited in face-to-face interactions.

According to Turkle, people are driven more by this desire to develop identity than a wish to deceive or manipulate. The goal of much online impression management appears therefore to be self-knowledge.

The degrees of freedom that characterize many online contexts permit users to step outside their customary impression management behaviours and experiment with alternative presentations. Many writers support this view. Wallace (1999), for example, describes the Internet as 'an identity laboratory, overflowing with props, audiences, and players for our personal experiments' (1999: 48). Danet (1996) agrees, describing the playful manipulation of personae by online users whose own identity and existence is 'for all intents and purposes irrelevant' as 'verbal puppetry'.

Qualitative research has highlighted self-exploration as a motive for impression management online, but this is clearly not the only reason users engage in this practice. Just as in the offline world, people seek to attract others and reap the rewards of establishing new relationships when online. Cornwell and Lundgren (2001) examined how chat users' motivation to attract other people impacted on their impression management behaviour. Participants were asked about the areas in which they had misrepresented themselves in order to increase someone's interest in them, either in online relationships or in offline relationships. Participants were also asked to rate their involvement in their relationships in terms of seriousness, commitment, potential for emotional growth and satisfaction on 10-point scales.

Overall, reported misrepresentations were low in both types of relationships. However, misrepresentations were more likely online than offline and were most often related to physical appearance and age. Although these areas of misrepresentation reflect the 'degrees of freedom' afforded by the visual anonymity of the medium (Joinson 2003), the authors note that they were not a direct product of the media. Rather, misrepresentation was related to the perceived level of involvement in the relationship; on the single item measures, participants rated 'real space' romantic relationships as more serious and more committed than online relationships. Regression analyses suggested that the communication context predicted level of relationship involvement and involvement, in turn, predicted degree of misrepresentation. This finding is consistent with offline research suggesting that deceptive impression management is more likely to occur when the actor believes the relationship will be short-lived rather than long-term (DePaulo and Kashy 1998). Although there is little doubt that online relationships can lead to long-term, intimate relationships, this research suggests that those involved in online romantic relationships typically rate their online relationships as less serious and committed – although interestingly, no less satisfying – than their offline relationships.

Impression management online is therefore different to the offline process: compared to the offline context, the visual anonymity (degrees of freedom) and the reported lower level of commitment to romantic relationships enable the creation of impressions that might be difficult to create in the offline world: At least according to Cornwell and Lundgren (2001), users are more likely to misrepresent their age or physical characteristics to attract another person online than they are offline.

Impression construction online

Where did Alex's character of Joan come from? Was Alex's online gender swapping the acting out of aspects he found difficult to express in face-to-face interaction? Was she a manifestation of a well-developed feminine component of Alex's self-concept or did she represent a desired identity, a supportive, nurturing hoped-for self? Much of the writing on online impression management has focused on impression construction, examining the content of impressions that are created.

Early work on impression construction online concluded that many impressions were directly related to users' hoped-for selves. Several writers noted that impression management online offered opportunities to present highly desirable self-images and provided a chance for wish-fulfilment (Reid 1994; Curtis 1997; Romano 1999). Turkle (1995), for example, used a series of case studies to show how desired identity images feature in players' self-exploration online. The normative processes that operate online to encourage this kind of impression management have also been documented (Reid 1994). This emphasis in the early literature on idealized self-presentation is consistent with the focus, found in the same work, on self-exploration motivation.

Issues of impression management online were examined by Chester (2004) using a two-stage mixed-method design, focusing on MOOs. MOOs are a form of MUD with an Object Orientation (meaning players use commands to interact with and add to the environment). They are network-accessible virtual environments that allow both private one-to-one interactions as well as many-to-many synchronous communication. MOO users, or players as they are typically called, operate within and navigate their way around a virtual environment usually described entirely in text.

It is estimated that MOOs and MUDs are played by about 30 per cent of Internet users, far fewer than, for example, log on to the Internet to read and send email (90 per cent) (UCLA Center of Communication Policy (CCP) 2003). Nevertheless, MOOs offer an interesting forum for exploration of impression management processes. Like many forms of online communication, MOOs are characterized by managed anonymity. Added to this, however, MOOs are inherently playful places; many MOOs actively encourage users to construct virtual identities and role-play (Butler and Chester, 2005). Of all the places one might find idealized and exploratory impression management online, MOOs seem to offer one of the most likely sites.

In the first quantitative study participants' private self-concept and desired selves were compared with their first impression management behaviour in a MOO. A second qualitative study with a smaller group of MOO participants then examined the process of impression construction over a 12-week period. The following sections describe these two studies and their outcomes.

Developing an impression online

Participants in this first study were 75 undergraduate Australasian university students (54 females and 21 males). Ages ranged from 18 to 54 years ($M = 21.35$, $SD = 5.32$), nearly all participants (95 per cent) spoke English as a first language.

Participants completed a series of offline measures, including a description of their self-concept, together with a measure of desired identity. Online, participants entered a MOO, called The Place, which was described as an online community for social interaction. Upon entering the MOO, participants were invited to construct an impression by choosing a screen name, selecting their gender (female, male, neuter, or plural), and writing a character description. In addition, participants were asked, in an open-ended question, how they would like to be perceived by others online. After completing the data collection tasks participants logged off; participants did not interact with each other in the MOO. To control for order effects, participants were randomly assigned to receive either the offline or online measures first.

Self-presentational research from offline contexts suggests that much impression construction involves attempts to present ourselves as we really think we are (DePaulo 1992; Leary 1995). In face-to-face contexts we therefore often want others to see and validate us as we see ourselves. Results from the first study indicate this motivation can be generalized to online contexts. Online self-presentations were influenced more by participants' current perceptions of themselves than desirable future selves, Z (65) = −4.54, $p = 0.000$, $d = 0.85$. In addition, items considered central to identity were more likely to be presented online than items rated of lesser importance, χ^2 (3, N=65) = 55.21, $p = 0.000$. Schlenker (1986) hypothesized that important aspects of identity are thought about more often, are salient in a range of contexts and thus are likely to be presented to others. The results of this study support the application of this assumption online. Together, these results suggest that MOO impression construction is fundamentally similar to impression construction in offline contexts.

Although the presentation of a desired identity image was infrequent, its occurrence was particularly predominant amongst those with low levels of Internet experience, χ^2 (2, N=65) = 11.41, $p = 0.003$. This finding is consistent with other work that has found self-presentations become more 'truthful' as online experience increases (e.g., Roberts et al. 1996).

As well as examining the extent to which self-concept influenced the impression constructed

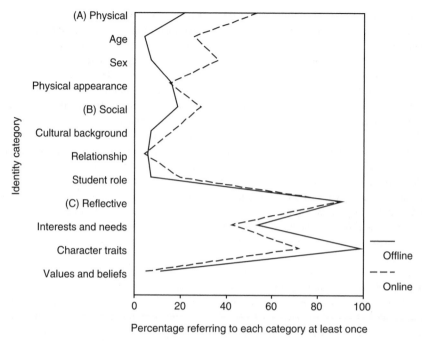

Figure 15.1 Identity referential frame profiles for offline self-concept and online MOO description.

online, a content analysis of the MOO character descriptions was carried out, using a coding scheme adapted from work by Gordon (1968) and Rees and Nicholson (1994) (see Figure 15.1).

More than half the MOO character descriptions (52 per cent) included reference to age, sex, or physical appearance. This emphasis on the physical body online complements anecdotal evidence that users routinely seek information about 'asl' (age, sex, location) in initial interactions. Online users want to situate themselves and others with physical information. In the offline world age, sex and ethnicity are often communicated without conscious intention. These facets of identity are fundamental to the ways we categorize ourselves as well as others (O'Brien 1999). Onscreen, if we want to be sure others know this information, we have to consciously give it. The emphasis on these characteristics in participants' MOO descriptions suggests an awareness of the importance of these features in online interactions. The results replicate previous findings in MOOs (Reid 1994) as well as other online domains (Rutter and Smith 2000).

Most important in the online impression construction process, however, were personality traits. Outgoing descriptions were the most common type of self-presentation. Friendliness and sense of humour were frequently occurring themes in this subcategory; 'fun-loving' presentations were common. For example,

Loves to chat and meet new people as well as having fun.

(22-year old, Australian male)

I have a good sense of humour and am quite witty ...

(19-year old, Australian male)

Also of interest were those offline personality characteristics concealed online. These primarily related to confidence, caring, well-being, emotional stability and reliability. Each of these was reported as characteristic of self by nearly 50 per cent of participants offline, but presented far less frequently online. Of particular note are the characteristics of caring and intelligence. Although nearly two-thirds of participants described themselves as caring offline, very few explicitly stated this in their MOO description. Intelligence was also referred to less often in the MOO descriptions than in offline measures of self-concept. It is not the case, however, that participants didn't care how they were perceived on these dimensions; on the contrary, both caring and intelligence figured in ideal impressions. Participants wanted to be seen as both caring and intelligent, but they did not explicitly present these attributes.

There are a number of ways to explain the use of concealment in impression management online. Concealment is an obvious self-presentation strategy to use online; the visual anonymity of the medium affords opportunities to selectively disclose aspects of identity normally given off in face-to-face interaction. While it is not true that players maintain perfect control over the impressions that others form of them, they do, nevertheless, have the chance to hide some aspects of identity. Concealing specific aspects of identity online may also be an unconscious response to the dilemma of presenting a complex self in a limited amount of words, a natural part of the editing process. Information is omitted simply because we cannot present everything about ourselves in any interaction.

Not disclosing aspects of identity online can also protect against social anxiety. Social anxiety arises when we seek to make a good impression but do not think we will be able to do so (Schlenker 2003). One tactic used in such situations is to say as little as possible. Although this does not necessarily create a good impression, neither does it make a poor impression. The approach is known as protective self-presentation (Leary 1995) and may explain the motivation for the sizable group of individuals (32 per cent) whose MOO description bore little relationship to their self-concept or desired identity image statements.

The absence of caring and intelligent self-presentations online can also be explained by the impression management dilemma known as the likeability–competence trade-off. Describing oneself to others as caring or intelligent creates a paradox for the actor. Any form of self-promotion runs the risk of alienating others. That is, likeability decreases with increases in presented competence. In addition, truly caring and intelligent people don't need to tell others that they are and

so specifically alluding to these traits might be perceived as evidence of their lack. Perhaps the participants intended to show others they had these traits. Despite unique opportunities afforded by online communication to explicitly state the impression one seeks to create, some offline norms of impression management appear to operate online, regulating behaviour.

Although the images presented online were not idealized, they were nonetheless self-promoting, with positive images frequently presented. The process of online impression management in MOOs is therefore best described as a subtle process of putting one's best foot forward rather than more overtly playful wish-fulfilment.

Personality attributes were presented in a particularly positive way. According to offline research by Leary (1995), the most desirable impressions, at least for American university students, are friendly, intelligent, attractive, fun, outgoing, sincere, funny, caring and easy to talk to. More than half of these were common personality themes in the MOO self-presentations: participants described themselves as friendly, outgoing, confident, fun-loving and having a good sense of humour. The results of this study therefore suggest that we seek to create desirable impressions online that are similar to those that are considered desirable in the offline world.

Participants' ideal impressions were also examined. These descriptions of how they wanted to be perceived by others in the online community were also positively skewed; the most frequently occurring adjectives were fun, friendly, approachable, caring and intelligent, mirroring those attributes generated by the students in Leary's (1995) offline study. Correspondence between desired impressions and actual self-presentation was, however, only moderate (see Figure 15.2). Nearly half of the MOO descriptions made no reference to the specific ideal impressions and more than 70 per cent of statements about ideal impressions included information that was not presented online. The impression management dilemma detailed above may explain this discrepancy.

No sex differences were noted in the impression construction process online, suggesting that women are no more likely than men to disclose personal information in their initial self-presentational statements online. This is

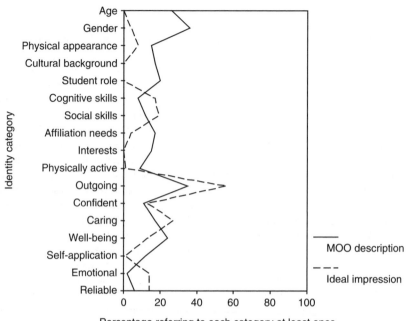

Figure 15.2 Identity referential frame profiles for MOO description and ideal online impression.

consistent with offline research that has indicated sex differences in self-disclosure are small (Dindia 2002). One finding qualified this general conclusion: women were more likely than men to disclose negative information online. The numbers of participants who engaged in this practice were small, however, and any conclusions are necessarily tentative.

The results of this first study suggested that impressions constructed in online social contexts are primarily accurate reflections of how self is perceived offline, but with a positive spin. This picture is different to those originally posed by writers such as Turkle (1995) and Curtis (1997), who emphasized the wish-fulfilling nature of impression management online. This first study offers a snapshot of the impression construction process online and raises questions about how these impressions are maintained over time in ongoing communities. The second study was designed to address these questions.

Maintaining an impression online

The second qualitative study followed a smaller group of 20 undergraduate students (12 females

and 8 males) enrolled in an online course on the psychology of cyberspace, as they interacted in a MOO over a 12-week period (Chester 2004). The aim was to explore the ways impressions are constructed in an ongoing group and how they are played out over time, using student journals and transcripts from the MOO. The ages of these students ranged from 19 to 26 years ($M = 22.27$, $SD = 1.77$). Nearly all participants (95 per cent) spoke English as a first language.

At the start of the course about half the participants described in their journals the potential of the medium for impression management.

One of the aspects that I find most interesting and exciting about the internet and chat rooms is that you can be anyone you want to be.

(Material_Girl)[2]

So I could write whatever I wanted other people to see me as, even become someone I am not.

(Tinkerbell)

Despite this potential, however, there was a widespread desire for authentic self-presentation.

[2] In an effort to protect the confidentiality of participants, real screen names have not been used.

Players reported in their journals that they intended, for the most part, to manage impressions that were consistent with their offline identity.

> The description I gave BritChick in MOO is the same as the real life me. After chatting online for a while, I have found that it's best and easier to tell people the truth .... Basically the 'virtual' me, is me!
>
> (BritChick)

> From the start, my character was supposed to just be a vessel to hold the real me. I was not trying to be something other than I am in real life ...
>
> (Andromeda1978)

In reflection, at the end of the course they believed they did this, both intentionally and unintentionally.

> During my time in the MOO I feel I acted like my normal everyday self.
>
> (Weevil)

> I feel that my character online was no different to my character in real life.
>
> (Aquarius)

The intention to present one's 'real' self was a strong theme in participants' journals. They described a desire for connection with others and indicated that authentic communication was the best way to achieve this. Creating an impression of anything other than one's 'real' self was viewed as dishonest, difficult to achieve, and motivated by dissatisfaction with oneself. And besides, even if one isn't authentic in one's self-presentation eventually, as one participant cautioned, 'your true self will seep through'. Another participant agreed:

> Of course, people will eventually be able to see the real me ... I know I'll inadvertently give the game away.
>
> (The_Umpire6)

Despite the emphasis on authentic and accurate self-presentation, the intention to play with impressions was nevertheless widespread in the sample. For example, several participants began the semester taking on fantasy characters, often with highly idealized characteristics: wizards, fairies and robots. These characters often proved effective vehicles for initiating interaction with others: however, over time, all found themselves reverting to a presentation of their offline self. One participant described this as a natural, but unconscious progression in wanting to develop deeper relationships with others. Intimacy called for more 'normal' rather than 'playful' communication. Her experience fits well with the self-disclosure literature that suggests self-disclosure increases with liking (Collins and Miller 1994). Although not conscious of her motivation at the time, in retrospect the player observed that the props which had been useful in facilitating communication early on were not only redundant as the semester progressed, but got in the way of more meaningful communication.

Overtly idealized and fantastical character play were not, however, the only forms of impression management observed online. Other more subtle techniques included the presentation of socially desirable information and the use of concealment, both of which are illustrated in the following comment made by a participant about his character description.

> The real me is interesting enough so I don't really have to add too much to it. I have taken the liberty of slightly (open to interpretation really) enhancing my good points and not mentioning the bad.
>
> (Andromeda1978)

Although few participants discussed their intention to present desired identity images, analysis of the character descriptions revealed presentation of socially desirable, if not idealized, characteristics. Characters tended to be friendly and caring and when physical descriptions were included they were almost all tall and slim.

> A girl who likes to smile and get to know people...
>
> (Jogirl)

> Green_Day waves hello with a large furry paw.
>
> (Green_Day Char)

> A tall and slim man with broad shoulders smiles back at you.
>
> (Andromeda1978)

Undercutting these idealized presentations, however, was the disclosure of more commonplace or vulnerable descriptions. For example, the 'girl who likes to smile and get to know people' was also 'a little frustrated by all of this'.

Other players, males and females, used the same strategy, incorporating socially desirable and less desirable, but nevertheless endearing characteristics.

> If only he wasn't wearing such daggy clothes... Faded black jeans and a target shirt...
>
> (Andromeda1978)

> I'm very passionate with things that I like such as making friends, chatting on the Internet and trying to figure out other people's personalities. At the same time I'm a bit shy.
>
> (Faithful)

Despite the emphasis on presentation of the 'real' me, the character descriptions that were written for the MOO revealed relatively little personal information. Most of the character descriptions were short, generally only one or two sentences. The descriptions focused on sociable traits and physical appearance. Other information, such as gender and online experience was often given off, rather than expressly given in the descriptions. The descriptions were crafted so as to honestly provide just enough information to attract others.

Several participants were aware of editing their impressions, concealing aspects of self.

> I wanted to be myself, but with a little mystery.
>
> (Tinkerbell)

As Tinkerbell's comment suggests, the concealment of information was perceived as alluring and described as a short-term strategy, designed to intrigue and engage others, and accordingly its value diminished as the semester progressed. Selective self-disclosure is an important protective strategy adopted in the development of relationships, allowing partners to manage vulnerability (Dindia 2002). None of the participants, however, described the strategy as motivated by this desire, although the type of information that was concealed suggests this protective motivation may have been operating, albeit unconsciously. One participant, for example, reflected that she preferred not to describe her physical appearance online so that her relationships might be based on her ideas rather than her looks. To describe one's looks is to risk being rejected on those grounds.

One rich source of data in the impression management process was found in the dorm rooms that participants created in the MOO. These rooms, created and decorated by the students as they learned the skills of MOOing, ranged from plausible to fantastic, from messy student rooms with bed, TV, computer, books and clothes piled on the floor, to elaborately decorated rooms replete with murals and obscure, prized objects. The dorm room descriptions were designed to entertain with their humorous, retro geekishness, welcome with their comfy couches and mood lighting, or dazzle with their intricate and exotic detail. All gave off information about their creator.

The dorm rooms functioned as a stage for identity management, with a set designed specifically to contextualize the impression presented in the character description. For example, the fairy had a four-poster bed with a spare set of wings lying on white linen; the flame-haired mage displayed jewel-encrusted staffs on her wall and an ancient chalice on a table. Less fantastical, but nevertheless idealized objects were prominent, such as large screen TVs, enormous beds, minibars and huge windows. Participants who emphasized relationships with others created rooms that were warm and inviting.

Participants with previous online experience demonstrated their knowledge and skill in their dorm room, creating humorous exit messages (the message that appears on one's screen when one leaves a room) and constructing objects for visitors to interact with. One participant filled his cupboard with five folded and numbered pink sheets. When worn as a cape this sheet enabled the wearer to jump from the window unhurt. Without the sheet the unsuspecting visitor plummeted to their death and found themselves in a coffin, complete with helpful instructions for resurrection. Details like these added to impressions of technical proficiency.

At the end of the course participants reflected on the impressions they thought they had created. The process surprised several participants. One participant, for example, was taken aback by the impressions others formed on the basis of the way she wrote, rather than what she actually said.

> I have noticed that many people have picked upon the style in which I have written my description and

asked whether my interests include book and role-playing games. I have answered yes to both and found it fascinating how much unconscious information can be conveyed by a few simple sentences.

(Oracle)

Primarily focused on crafting the given information, she had not considered that the style of her writing might also create impressions.

Signification is the recognition and validation of impression management behaviour (Leary 1995). The ultimate signification occurred for participants who attended a face-to-face meeting held in the last week of semester.[3] Not surprisingly, the knowledge of this meeting shaped impression management intentions at the start of the course.

I describe myself how I actually am. Especially when we are all going to meet up at the end of the course, it is best not to create a false impression of myself.

(BritChick)

Knowing that I was going to meet these people made me be more natural.

(Jogirl)

At the end of the course the face-to-face meeting was viewed as a test of how accurately they had presented themselves over the previous 12 weeks.

Misperceptions did occur; that is, players thought they had been incorrectly perceived. Although participants were surprised that they had been misperceived in fundamental ways, such as in terms of gender or ethnicity, these tended to be seen as anomalies and participants did not dwell on them. These misperceptions did not therefore alter individuals' basic beliefs in their authentic impression construction.

One of the most intriguing misperceptions concerned two Anglo-Australian participants,

Andromeda1978 and Ice_Maiden, who spent considerable time interacting in the MOO and nevertheless perceived each other as Asian. This fundamental misperception challenged the often cited belief that impression management online is a perfectly controllable process: 'When interacting via computer, only one type of information is provided: information a person wishes to give, whether factual or fiction' (Bechar-Israeli 1996: para. 5). Although it is true that self-presentations in MOOs are entirely textual which permits considerable control over impression management, participants in the present study also reflected on ways they had less consciously created impressions. Identity is therefore presented both intentionally and unintentionally and, as Andromeda1978 and Ice_Maiden discovered, one does not have control over how others interpret either type of information.

The types of misperceptions that occurred point to a desire to classify people on the same categories that are fundamental in face-to-face interaction, even when information in the MOO is scarce or ambiguous. The finding challenges Howard Rheingold's (1995) optimistic assumption that online communities enable people to be treated as they 'always wanted to be treated – as thinkers and transmitters of ideas and feeling beings' (1995: 26). Although MOO players may be better able to focus on the thoughts and feelings, the present study suggested that thinkers and feelers are perceived nevertheless in embodied ways.

Conclusions

Despite the use of different methodologies, both studies by Chester (2004) produced strikingly similar findings. Although online contexts provide unique opportunities to manage impressions, for the most part these impressions were based on socially desirable aspects of offline personality and a desire to present an authentic impression.

In the first study a range of offline identity measures were examined as potential predictors of online impression construction. Contrary to early writing, results indicated that although participants in social MOOs do present some idealized or hoped for images, they more commonly put a positive spin on existing personality traits.

[3] Members of online communities often meet offline. For example Rutter and Smith (2000) supplemented their analysis of messages posted to the discussion board RumCom.local, with observations of regular face-to-face weekend meetings of the group. Kendall (2002), who studied a MUD, also noted that geographically close members often developed offline relationships. Although the presence of the online meeting in the present study is likely to have affected the kinds of impressions that were constructed, it also mirrors the way educational MOOs often operate.

In the second study, users reflected on the processes that operated as they constructed and maintained impressions online over a 12-week period. Results suggested that users were motivated by a strong desire to present the 'real' self, but nevertheless used strategies to attract others such as putting one's best foot forward and concealing information.

The results stand in contrast to earlier work, which had conceptualized online contexts as 'identity laboratories'. This view of the Internet as a site for playful impression construction has been widely assumed (e.g., Bruckman 1993; Reid 1994; Turkle 1995). Given the chance, it was argued, people would remake themselves, choosing highly desirable, unfulfilled, or fantasy images. As Turkle argued, 'when we live through our electronic self-representations we have unlimited possibilities to be many. People become masters of self-presentation and self-creation. The very notion of an inner, 'true self' is called into question (1994: 164).

More recent research, however, has provided only limited support for this position. Both Lori Kendall (2002), who conducted a three-year ethnographic study of a social MOO, and Ellen Bewersdorff (2001), who interviewed players in LambdaMOO, concluded that online impression management is used to present and explore accountable and core aspects of identity. Both researchers rejected the highly fragmented, fantastical self-presentations proposed by previous writers. According to Bewersdorff, 'Individuals do not experience fluidity and multiplicity of self posited by postmodern theorists' (2001: 2). The research presented in this chapter confirms this position, suggesting a strong connection with a real self.

Research on other forms on online communication is beginning to emerge to support this view of authentic online self-presentation. Research on email communication provides an interesting counterpoint to the studies by Chester (2004) in which participants did not know each other offline, as much email communication operates between people who also interact offline. One might expect that, given the limited degrees of freedom in such relationships, idealized and deceptive impression management would be relatively low. Research by Hancock et al. (2004) on deception in everyday life supports this and goes even further, demonstrating that email is associated with less deception than phone and face-to-face interactions. The asynchronous nature of email, together with the record that is generated, is hypothesized to reduce lying and hence increase authenticity online.

Other researchers, exploring chat, have also suggested that the online medium increases authentic self-presentation. Bargh et al. (2002) note that the accessibility and expression of the 'true self' (those characteristics the individual believes they possess and would like to present, but generally does not) is enhanced during chat compared to face-to-face interactions, even when the online experience lasts only five minutes.

The picture of identity play online described in the literature in the early 1990s is therefore beginning to shift, from idealized and plural experimentation to more consistent, accurate impression management. The current picture is therefore one quite close to the type of impression management that often transpires in the offline world, in which individuals seek to 'reflect a slight polished and glorified conception of self, but one that is genuinely believed by the actor to be true' (Schlenker 2003: 493). Some research goes further to suggest that online self-presentation may be an even more accurate portrayal of the self than is offered in face-to-face interactions.

This changing perception of how users manage impressions online begs the question why such a change might have occurred. Early research in the 1980s emerged when there were fewer than 1000 Internet hosts, when email was just beginning to take off as a communication tool, and as the first MUD was developed. Research in these early days was cautious about the benefits of online communication. Online interaction was viewed as a diminished version of face-to-face communication. Sensationalistic reports focused on socially undesirable visions of the Internet, emphasizing disinhibition, identity deception and manipulation.

By the early 1990s the World Wide Web was released and the number of Internet hosts had increased to more than two million. Coinciding with the hyperbole surrounding the dot.com boom and postmodern ideas about the self, writing began to emerge that described the rich, self-presentational and relational possibilities of 'life on the screen'. The Internet, and in particular

MOOs, were viewed as unique places for identity experimentation and seen by many writers as a frontier land, a place quite different to the face-to-face world.

At the beginning of the new century that picture has begun to change and a middle ground has begun to emerge more strongly. In their book *The Internet in Everyday Life*, Barry Wellman and Caroline Haythornthwaite (2002) pronounced a new way of thinking about cyberspace, not as a different and separate world, but rather as a transactional space embedded in everyday life. Now more than 20 years on, the Internet is simply a part of life for hundreds of millions of people. Most Western students entering university in 2006 have grown up with the Internet; to them it is as commonplace as mobile phones and TV, embedded in their daily interactions. The research presented in this chapter confirms Wellman and Haythornthwaite's conclusion: online users no longer perceive the Internet as a different world, but rather as one of a range of communication tools, albeit with some unique facilities.

Within this context, it is not surprising that psychological theories, like impression management, originally developed to explain social behaviour before the advent of the Internet was even imagined, are able to provide valuable explanations of online behaviour. Cyberspace is not a virtual world without connection to the rest of people's lives. What we do and who we are online are shaped consciously and unconsciously by who we are offline. The Internet is, after all, a part of our real life.

References

Bargh, J. A., McKenna, K. Y. A. and Fitzsimons, G. M. (2002). Can you see the real me? Activation and expression of the 'true self' on the Internet. *Journal of Social Issues 58*(1), 11–48.

Bechar-Israeli, H. (1996). From <Bonehead> to <cLoNehEAd>: Nicknames, play and identity on internet relay chat. *Journal of Computer-Mediated Communication 1* (2). Retrieved 10 August 1998 from http://www.usc.edu/dept/annenberg/vol1/issue2/bechar.html.

Bewersdorff, E. (2001). Virtuality and its discontents: an examination of self in cyberspace. *Dissertation Abstracts International 62*(3-B), 1638.

Bruckman, A. (1993). *Gender swapping on the Internet*. Retrieved 6 September 1998 from ftp://ftp.media.mit.edu/pub/asb/papers/gender swapping.txt.

Butler, M. and Chester, A. (2005). Spheres of influence: MOOs, identity and learning communities. In G. Latham and G. Morris (eds), *Virtual classrooms: Changing pedagogy, changing identities* (pp. 38–55). Melbourne: RMIT University Press.

Chester, A. (2004). Presenting the self in cyberspace: Identity play online. Doctoral dissertation, University of Melbourne, 2004. Retrieved 14 February 2005 from http://eprints.unimelb.edu.au/archive/00000534/.

Collins, N. L. and Miller, L. C. (1994). The disclosure-liking link: from meta-analysis towards a dynamic reconceptualization. *Psychological Bulletin 116*, 457–475.

Cornwell, B. and Lundgren, D. C. (2001). Love on the internet: involvement and misrepresentation in romantic relationships in cyberspace vs. real space. *Computers in Human Behavior 17*, 197–211.

Curtis, P. (1997) Mudding: social phenomena in text-based virtual reality. In S. Keisler (ed.), *Culture of the Internet* (pp.121–142). Mahwah, NJ: Erlbaum.

Danet, B. (1996). Text as mask: Gender and identity on the Internet. Paper presented at the Masquerade and Gendered Identity conference, Venice, Italy. Retrieved 12 July 2003 from http://atar.mscc.huji.ac.il/~msdanet/mask.html.

DePaulo, B. M. (1992). Nonverbal behavior and self-presentation. *Psychological Bulletin 111*(2), 203–243.

DePaulo, B. M. and Kashy, D. A. (1998). Everyday lies in close and casual relationships. *Journal of Personality and Social Psychology 74*, 63–79.

Dindia, K. (2002). Self-disclosure research: knowledge through meta-analysis. In M. Allen, R. W. Preiss, B. M. Gayle and N. A. Burrell (eds), *Interpersonal communication research: Advances through meta-analysis* (pp. 169–185). Mahwah, NJ: Erlbaum.

Goffman, E. (1959). *The presentation of self in everyday life*. Harmondsworth: Penguin.

Gordon, C. (1968). Self-conceptions: configurations of content. In C. Gordon and K. J. Gergen (eds), *The self in social interaction* (pp. 115–136). New York: John Wiley and Sons.

Hancock, J. T., Thom-Santelli, J. and Ritchie, T. (2004). Deception and design: the impact of communication technologies on lying behavior. In E. Dykstra- Erickson and M. Tscheligi (eds), Conference on Computer Human Interaction (pp. 29–134). New York: ACM Press.

Joinson, A. (2003). *Understanding the psychology of internet behaviour: Virtual worlds, real lives*. Basingstoke: Palgrave Macmillan.

Kendall, L. (2002). *Hanging out in the virtual pub: Masculinities and relationships online*. Berkeley, CA: University of California Press.

Leary, M. R. (1995). *Self-presentation: Impression management and interpersonal behaviour*. Madison, Wisconsin: Brown and Benchmark.

Mnookin, J. L. (1996). Virtual(ly) law: the emergence of law in LambdaMOO. *Journal of Computer-Mediated Communication 2* (1), Part 1. Retrieved 2 August 2003 from http://jcmc.juji.ac.il/vol2/issue1/.

O'Brien, J. (1999). Writing in the body: gender (re)production in online interaction. In M. A. Smith and P. Kollock (eds), *Communities in cyberspace* (pp. 76–104). London: Routledge.

Rees, A. and Nicholson, N. (1994). The twenty statements test. In C. Cassell and G. Symon (eds), *Qualitative methods in organiszatioanl research: A practical guide* (pp. 37–54). London: Sage.

Reid, E. (1994). Cultural formations in text-based virtual realities. Unpublished master's thesis, University of Melbourne, Australia. Retrieved 4 January 1998 from http://www.ee.mu.oz.au/papers/emr/cult-form.html#Pubs.

Rheingold, H. (1995). *The virtual community: Finding connection in a computerized world*. London: Minerva.

Roberts, L. D. and Parks, M. R. (1999). The social geography of gender-switching in virtual environments on the Internet. *Information, Communication and Society 2*(4), 521–540.

Roberts, L. D., Smith, L. M. and Pollock, C. M. (1996). Exploring virtuality: telepresence in text-based virtual environments. Paper presented at the Cybermind Conference. Retrieved 13 July 2003 from http://web.archive. org/web/200010629220330/psych.curtin.edu.au/people/roberts.

Romano, S. (1999). On becoming a woman: pedagogies of the self. In G. E. Hawisher and C. Selfe (eds), *Passions, pedagogies and the 21st Century Technologies* (pp. 249–267). Logan, UT: Utah State University Press.

Rutter, J. and Smith, G. (2000). Presenting the of-line self in an everyday, online environment. Paper presented at Virtual Society? Oxford, UK. Retrieved 22 July 2003 from http://les.man.ac.uk/cric/Jason_Rutter.

Schlenker, B. R. (1986). Self-identification: towards an integration of the private and public self. In R. F. Baumeister (ed.), *Public self and private self* (pp. 21–62). New York: Springer-Verlag.

Schlenker, B. R. (2003). Self-presentation. In M. R. Leary and J. P. Tangey (eds), *Handbook of self and identity* (pp. 492–518). New York: Guilford Press.

Suler, J. (2003). The psychology of cyberspace. Retrieved 2 June 2003 from http://www.ascusc.org/jcmc/.

Turkle, S. (1995). *Life on the screen: Identity in the age of the Internet*. London: Weidenfeld and Nicolson.

UCLA Center for Communication Policy (2003). *The UCLA Internet report: surveying the digital future*. Retrieved 22 July 2003 from http://www.ccp.ucal.edu.

Van Gelder, L. (1991). The strange case of the electronic lover. In C. Dunlop and R. Kling (eds), *Computerization and controversy: Value conflicts and social choices* (pp. 364–375). New York: Boston Academic Press.

Wallace, Patricia. (1999). *The psychology of the Internet*. Cambridge: Cambridge University Press.

Wellman, B. and Haythornthwaite, C. (2002). *The Internet in everyday life*. Oxford: Blackwell.

CHAPTER 16

Self-disclosure, privacy and the Internet

Adam N. Joinson and Carina B. Paine

I n this chapter, we examine the extant research literature on self-disclosure and the Internet, in particular by focusing on disclosure in computer-mediated communication (CMC) and web-based forms – both to surveys and in e-commerce applications. We also consider the links between privacy and self-disclosure, and the unique challenges (and opportunities) that the Internet poses for the protection of privacy. Finally, we propose three critical issues that unite the ways in which we can best understand the links between privacy, self-disclosure and new technology: trust and vulnerability, costs and benefits and control over personal information.

Central to the chapter is the notion that self-disclosure is not simply the outcome of a communication encounter: rather, it is both a product and process of interaction, as well as a way for regulating interaction dynamically. We propose that by adopting a privacy approach to understanding disclosure online, it becomes possible to consider not only media effects that encourage disclosure, but also the wider context and implications of such communicative behaviours.

What is self-disclosure?

Self-disclosure is the telling of the previously unknown so that it becomes shared knowledge, the 'process of making the self known to others'

(Jourard and Lasakow 1958: 91). This shared knowledge might exist between pairs of people, within groups, or between an individual and an organization. It has a variety of purposes, in part dependent on the context in which disclosure occurs. For instance, within dyads, particularly romantic relationships, it serves to increase mutual understanding (Laurenceau et al. 1998), and builds trust by making the discloser increasingly vulnerable (emotionally or otherwise) to the other person (Rubin 1975). Since self-disclosure is often reciprocated it frequently serves to strengthen the ties that bind people in romantic or friendship-based relationships (Jourard 1971).

Disclosure within groups can serve to enhance the bonds of trust between group members, but it can also serve to legitimize group membership and strengthen group identity. For instance, the admission of a negative identity (e.g. 'I am an alcoholic') within a shared identity group serves both to increase trust by revealing a stigmatized identity and acts as a membership card for a particular group (Galegher et al. 1998). Personal growth may also be an outcome of honest self-disclosure (Jourard 1971). In a study reported by Pennebaker et al. (1988), participants assigned to a trauma-writing condition (where they wrote about a traumatic and upsetting experience for four days) showed immune system benefits, compared to a non-trauma writing group. Disclosure in this form has also been associated with reduced visits to medical centres and psychological benefits in the form of improved affective states (Smyth 1998). For people using the Internet to talk about their problems (or to publish weblogs), their activities may well have unforeseen, positive, health and psychological benefits.

Finally, disclosure between an individual and an organization can serve authentication purposes – for instance, to establish identity, allow authentication of a claim to identity and to enable an organization to recognize you in the future in order to personalize its offerings to you. Organizations might also ask for personal information for marketing purposes – for instance, when registering to access a website or joining an online community. Of course, organizations, in the form of researchers, might also ask for personal information in the name of academic research.

New technology, and in particular the Internet, might well change the demands upon people to disclose personal information, as well as the possible implications of such disclosure. For instance, disclosing personal information to another person online might not involve the increased vulnerability that usually follows self-disclosure of personal information offline (Ben-Ze'ev 2003). Organizations might also demand more information in the name of authentication (although this need not always be personal information). Furthermore, new technology changes the scope of personal information that can be disclosed or collected. For instance, the development of ambient and ubiquitous devices, such as smart mobile phones and Radio Frequency Identification (RFID) tags, makes it likely that information about location, movements and social interactions are likely to be collected in the future in some form. How we negotiate the disclosure of such information is a critical issue, equally as important as how systems are designed to minimize privacy violations while also providing adequate levels of functionality.

Measuring self-disclosure

Within person-to-person and person-to-group interactions, self-disclosure has tended to be studied using either content analysis or self-report.

In the case of content analysis, the issue of what constitutes self-disclosure, and how it is scored, is particularly important. One option would be to count the number of instances within a conversation in which a person discloses information about themselves. However, there are a number of problems with this approach. First, it is not always clear what constitutes an act of self-disclosure – for instance, to express an opinion may well be classified in some contexts, but not in others. Second, self-disclosure can only be properly understood in terms of the ongoing interaction. For instance, does one count answers to a specific question – 'How old are you?' – as self-disclosure, or only spontaneous occurrences of disclosure (see Antaki et al. [2005] for a recent discussion of this issue). Moreover, given the dynamics of reciprocity, it may not even be possible to count occurrences of spontaneous disclosure as independent of the conversational dynamic. For these reasons, it is usual to treat discussions between people as a single unit of analysis (Kenny and Judd 1986).

Finally, not all self-disclosure is equal – disclosing your season of birth is not the same as disclosing your age, which is not the same as disclosing your sexual fantasies. One option is to use a three-layer categorization scheme proposed by Altman and Taylor (1973) to guide the content analysis of depth. Altman and Taylor suggest that disclosure can be categorized into either peripheral, intermediate, or core layers. The peripheral layer is concerned with biographic data (e.g. age), the intermediate layer with attitudes, values and opinions and the core layer with personal beliefs, needs, fears, and values. Joinson (2001b) instead used a 7-point Likert scale with which two scorers allocated the degree to which an utterance 'revealed vulnerability'. However, Antaki et al. (2005) argue that the act of disclosure needs to take into account the interactional context rather than simply being scored on a checklist. For instance, the phrase 'I'm the world's worst cook' could be disclosure, a plea for help or self-deprecation. Without the context, they argue, it is not possible to be certain.

Alternatively, lists of topics can be used to score intimacy – although again there are a number of problems with their application in practise to communication research (see Tidwell and Walther 2002).

Self-report measures of disclosure have been used successfully, for instance to compare levels of disclosure in face-to-face (FtF) and online relationships, or to link marital satisfaction with disclosure within the relationship. For instance, Parks and Floyd (1996) asked their participants to report the level of self-disclosure in their Internet relationships using self-report (e.g. high scores on 'I usually tell this person exactly how I feel' and low scores on 'I would never tell this person anything intimate or personal about myself'). However, the same problem – a lack of context – arise for such self-report measures too.

Measures of dispositional self-disclosure can also be used. For instance, within the International Personality Item Pool (IPIP) the subscale of items 'similar to the Temperament and Character Inventory (TCI)' has 10 items such as 'Am open about myself to others' (positive coding) and, 'Reveal little about myself' (negative coding) to measure general self-disclosure. However, it is not currently clear how such personality type measures might interact with different media, or indeed with people's behaviour within a specific interaction.

Self-disclosure outside of person-to-person and group interactions can also be measured in a number of different ways. One system is to count the number of words typed into text boxes in response to a personal or sensitive question, and to rate those responses by their intimacy or depth (e.g. Joinson 2001b; Moon 2000). Joinson (2005) also describes the use of non-response as a measure of self-disclosure in studies. There are two main ways in which non-response can be operationalized in survey methodology and e-commerce. The first is non-response – either submitting a default selection, or where there is no default option, submitting no response. A second is to add an option that allows participants to select 'I prefer not to answer' (Buchanan et al. 2002; Knapp and Kirk 2003). The use of 'I prefer not to answer' as a response option to a sensitive question is methodologically similar to the provision of a 'no opinion' response in attitudinal surveys. While it has been argued that the provision of 'no opinion' choices may increase satisficing in attitude surveys (Holbrook et al. 2003), there is little reason to assume that a similar process would operate in the use of 'I prefer not to answer' responses to sensitive

personal questions. Indeed, Joinson et al. (2007) report that the provision of 'I prefer not to answer' options in a salary question may improve data quality by reducing the number of non-responses or default selections. In our own research (in preparation) we established that people are more likely to use an 'I prefer not to say' option when faced with a sensitive rather than non-sensitive question, and that priming participants for online privacy (by asking them about their privacy concerns and behaviours) significantly increases the use of 'I prefer not say' as an option to sensitive questions.

Finally, self-disclosure can be measured using statistical techniques, for example the randomized response technique (Musch et al. 2001). In the randomized response technique, participants are asked to answer a sensitive question either truthfully or with a prespecified answer, depending on the result of a random event such as a coin toss. So, for instance, the question might be, 'do you lie to your partner about anything important?' Participants are asked to toss a coin, and if it is heads, they tell the truth, if it is tails they say 'yes' regardless of the truthful answer. Using statistical probabilities, a population estimate for a behaviour can be found, without knowing if any one individual told the truth or simply followed the instructions for 'tails'.

As noted earlier, self-disclosure in the age of ubiquitous computing poses novel challenges. For instance, it is likely that people will disclose information without full awareness or control (e.g. their location via a cell phone) – instead they may need to rely on privacy profiles or preferences to negotiate the disclosure on their behalf. In these circumstances, discussion or measurement of a single instance of disclosure is meaningless without full consideration of the context in which disclosure occurred.

Self-disclosure and the Internet

A rapidly increasing body of experimental and anecdotal evidence suggests that CMC and general Internet-based behaviour can be characterized as containing high levels of self-disclosure. For instance, Rheingold (1993) claims that new, meaningful relationships can be formed in cyberspace because of, not despite, its limitations. He further argues that 'the medium will, by its nature . . . be a place where people often end up revealing themselves far more intimately than they would be inclined to do without the intermediation of screens and pseudonyms'. Similarly, Wallace (1999) argues that 'The tendency to disclose more to a computer . . . is an important ingredient of what seems to be happening on the Internet' (151). Self-disclosure has been studied in a number of different settings using computers. For instance, Parks and Floyd (1996) studied the relationships formed by Internet users. They found that people report disclosing significantly more in their Internet relationships compared to their real life relationships. Similarly, in their study of 'coming out on the Internet', McKenna and Bargh (1998) argue that participation in online newsgroups gives people the benefit of 'disclosing a long secret part of one's self' (682). Chesney (2005), in a small-scale study of online diaries, reported high levels of disclosure of sensitive information, with half of his participants claiming to never withhold information from their diaries.

In the series of studies reported by Joinson (2001a), the level of self-disclosure measured using content analysis of transcripts of FtF and synchronous CMC discussions (Study one), and in conditions of visual anonymity and video links during CMC (Study two). In keeping with the predicted effect, self-disclosure was significantly higher when participants discussed using a CMC system as opposed to FtF.

In the second study, incorporating a video link while the participants discussed using the CMC program led to levels of self-disclosure similar to the FtF levels, while the comparison condition (no video link) led to significantly higher levels of self-disclosure.

These two studies together provide empirical confirmation that visually anonymous CMC tends to lead to higher levels of self-disclosure. The results of these studies also suggest that high levels of self-disclosure can effectively be designed out of an Internet interaction (e.g. through the use of a video link or accountability cues (Joinson 2001a, Study 3), as well as encouraged.

Further empirical confirmation of increased self-disclosure during CMC comes from the work of Tidwell and Walther (2002). They proposed that heightened self-disclosure during CMC may be due to people's motivation to reduce uncertainty. According to Uncertainty Reduction Theory (URT) (Berger and Calabrese 1975), people are motivated to reduce uncertainty in an interaction to increase predictability. In FtF interaction, uncertainty can be reduced through both verbal and non-verbal communication and cues. Tidwell and Walther hypothesize that during CMC, uncertainty reducing behaviours are text-based only, including increased levels of self-disclosure and question asking. To test this, Tidwell and Walther recruited 158 students to discuss in opposite sex pairs with an unknown partner using a CMC system or FtF. The subsequent conversations were content-analysed for disclosure using the breadth and depth indices developed by Altman and Taylor (1973; see above for a description).

Tidwell and Walther found that those in the CMC condition displayed higher levels of both question asking and self-disclosure compared the FtF condition. The questions asked by CMC discussants were also more probing and intimate than those asked by those talking FtF, while both the questions and disclosure by FtF interactants tended to be more peripheral than those in the CMC condition. Tidwell and Walther conclude that the limitations of CMC encourage people to adapt their uncertainty-reducing behaviours – they skip the usual asking of peripheral questions and minor disclosure, and instead opt for more direct, intimate questioning and self-disclosure.

Surveys and research administered via the Internet, rather than using paper methodologies, have also been associated with reductions in socially desirable responding (Joinson 1999; Frick et al. 2001), higher levels of self-disclosure (Weisband and Kiesler 1996) and an increased willingness to answer sensitive questions (see Tourangeau 2004).

In a similar vein, survey methodology techniques that tend to reduce human involvement in question administration also increase responses to sensitive personal questions. For instance, compared to other research methods, when data collection is conducted via computer-aided self-interviews (where participants type their answers on to a laptop) people report more health-related problems (Epstein et al. 2001), more HIV risk behaviours (Des Jarlais *et al.* 1999), more drug use (Lessler *et al.* 2000), and men report less sexual partners, and women more (Tourangeau and Smith 1996). Medical patients tend to report more symptoms and undesirable behaviours when interviewed by computer rather than FtF (Greist *et al.* 1973). Clients at a STD clinic report more sexual partners, more previous visits and more symptoms to a computer than to a doctor (Robinson and West 1992). Ferriter (1993) found that pre-clinical psychiatric interviews conducted using CMC compared to FtF yielded more honest, candid answers. Similarly, automated or computerized telephone interviews, compared to other forms of telephone interviewing, lead to higher levels of reporting of sensitive information (see Lau *et al.* 2003; Tourangeau 2004).

Conversely, methods that increase the social presence of the surveyor (e.g. by using photographs of the researcher) have been predicted to lead to a reduced willingness to answer sensitive questions (Tourangeau *et al.* 2003), although the findings of Tourangeau *et al.* were equivocal. However, Sproull *et al.* (1996) found that participants 'present themselves in a more positive light to the talking-face displays' (116) than to text-only interfaces. Joinson *et al.* (2007) report that although personalizing the research experience leads to higher response rates to a self-administered survey, it also reduces self-disclosure.

Within the Human–Computer Interaction (HCI) literature, the assumption seems to be that people will avoid disclosing information to commercial web services (Metzger 2004) due to their privacy concerns (Jupiter Research 2002). An online survey stated that the three biggest consumer concerns in the area of online personal information security were: companies trading personal data without permission, the consequences of insecure transactions, and theft of personal data (Harris Interactive 2002). For example, Hoffman *et al.* (1999) report that almost 95% of Internet users declined to provide personal information when requested to do so by a website, and over 40% provided false demographic information when requested. Quittner (1997) reports that 41% of survey respondents would rather exit a web page than reveal personal information. Clearly then, open self-disclosure is not a universal experience on the

Internet: for commercial organizations, consumers are often less than forthcoming, usually because of a combination of privacy concerns, lack of trust and concern about how personal information will be used (Hoffman *et al.* 1999; Metzger 2004). For instance, Olivero (2001) studied the willingness to disclose information about the self to a commercial organization, and manipulated the level of trustworthiness of the organization, whether a financial reward was offered for disclosure and the level of intrusiveness of the questions. She found that the level of trust was associated with participants' willingness to disclose to highly intrusive questions, but that an awareness of data mining/privacy concerns moderated this effect of trust. Andrade *et al.* (2002) conducted a similar study by examining three approaches to encourage self-disclosure of personal information online – the completeness of a privacy policy, the reputation of a company and the offer of a reward. They found that the completeness of privacy policy and reputation of the company reduce the level of concern over self-disclosure while the offer of a reward heightens concern.

However, there are a number of 'counter surveys' and much empirical evidence suggesting that there is a significant discrepancy between privacy principles and privacy practices. Very few individuals actually take any action to protect their personal information, even when doing so involves limited costs (Berendt *et al.* 2005; Jenson *et al.* 2005) i.e. there is a dichotomy between stated attitudes and actual behaviours of people in terms of their protection of personal information.

Models of self-disclosure online

Explanations for high levels of self-disclosure in person-to-person CMC have tended to focus on the psychological effects of anonymity: 'This anonymity allows the persecuted, the controversial, and the simply embarrassed to seek information – and disseminate it – while maintaining their privacy and reputations in both cyberspace and the material world' (Sobel 2000: 1522).

Theoretically, it has been argued that anonymity in CMC works by replicating a 'strangers on the train' experience (Bargh *et al.* 2002), promoting private self-awareness and reducing accountability concerns (Joinson 2001a), creating a need for uncertainty reduction (Tidwell and Walther 2002) or a combination of the media and the process of interaction itself (Walther 1996).

Similarly, explanations for increased self-disclosure to online surveys and web forms have also tended to stress anonymity (Joinson 1999), alongside the reduced social presence (and judgement) of the researcher (Tourangeau 2004), reduced vulnerability (Moon 1998) and increased privacy of the research environment (Tourangeau 2004). Once privacy is reduced, or social presence increased, self-disclosure also tends to be reduced (Joinson *et al.* 2007).

However, explanations for people's unwillingness to disclose personal information to e-commerce services invariably stress people's privacy concerns (e.g. Hoffman *et al.* 1999), in particular, issues surrounding the level and type of information collected, and people's lack of knowledge about how it may be used in the future, or control over that use (Metzger 2004).

These differing approaches to understanding disclosure and non-disclosure of personal information illustrate the paradox of self-disclosure on the Internet. On the one hand, the Internet provides an environment in which people can express themselves with relative immunity via pseudonyms, but in order to access these services and sites they often need to disclose high levels of personal information during the registration process.

Within the privacy literature, this paradox is relatively easy to solve – the provision of information about the self is treated quite separately from the use of privacy or pseudonymity to express one's inner desires. However, it is rare for CMC self-disclosure research to explicitly consider privacy, in particular the multifactor approaches to privacy discussed in the socio-legal literature.

Within e-commerce, there are further paradoxes which may be solved by looking at both the literature on interactional person-to-person disclosure and the privacy literature concurrently. For instance, there are occasions when you need to disclose a lot of personal information (e.g. purchasing online), but other factors (e.g. lack of social presence) make such privacy concerns less pressing. The answer to this paradox

is that it is the author to whom one is disclosing that is critical – if one trusts the recipient of the personal information, then one can act with relative freedom in the pseudonymous world such disclosure purchases. Only by considering the wider context can such seemingly paradoxical impacts of new technology on personal disclosure be fully understood.

This interpretation also strongly suggests that any explanation of self-disclosure online that relies solely on media effects (i.e. visual anonymity) is mistaken. Disclosure, while often 'given away' is also something that is carefully considered within the context of an ongoing interaction and wider environment – regardless of whether that interaction is interpersonal or human–computer. We would suggest that a wider theoretical scope is needed – not only is it important to consider the particular context of an interaction, but also how the person accessed that environment in the first place. For instance, while the use of pseudonyms may enable expressive freedom on a discussion board, we would also ask how access was gained to the board, what registration process was in place, what records of postings are kept remotely and locally and so on? Without this knowledge, one is forced to assume that people somehow dropped into an online environment out of the sky, rather than as a motivated act (see Joinson 2003).

While concern about the privacy implications of new technology are nothing new (Home Office 1972), the development and linking of databases with biometrics, and the tension between the need for identification, protection of privacy and full participation in the e-society (Raab *et al.* 1996) makes an understanding of the relations between privacy and the disclosure and use of personal information critical. In the next section of this chapter, we consider what privacy is, how the Internet and new technologies threaten privacy, and the implications of privacy for understanding self-disclosure within an interaction.

What is privacy?

There have been many attempts at definitions of privacy. In a legal context, privacy is largely synonymous with a 'right to be let alone' (Warren and Brandeis 1890). However, others have argued that privacy is only the right to prevent the disclosure of personal information. Many researchers have referred to the difficulties involved in trying to produce a definition (e.g. Burgoon *et al.* 1989) and despite various attempts to create a synthesis of existing literature (e.g. Parent 1983; Schoeman 1984) a unified and simple account of privacy has yet to emerge. Despite there being no unitary concept of privacy it is clear that both individuals, and society, attach a level of importance to privacy. For example, Ingham states that 'man, we are repeatedly told is a social animal, and yet he constantly seeks to achieve a state of privacy' (1978: 45).

Within psychological literature both Westin's and Altman's theories figure prominently in the major reviews of privacy in the 1970s. Westin provides a link between secrecy and privacy and defines privacy as 'the claim of individuals, groups, or institutions to determine for themselves when, how and to what extent information about them is communicated to others' (1967: 7). At the psychological level, Westin states that privacy provides opportunities for self-assessment and experimentation and therefore the development of individuality. Specifically, Westin (1967) proposes four main functions of privacy:

1. *Personal autonomy* applies to the need for the development of individuality and the avoidance of manipulation by others;

2. *Emotional release* refers to the need for opportunities to relax and escape from the tensions of everyday life in order to support healthy functioning;

3. *Self-evaluation* is the application of individuality onto events and the integration of experience into meaningful patterns, and

4. *Limited and protected communication* refers to both the sharing of personal information with trusted others and the setting of interpersonal boundaries.

Altman (1975) incorporates both social and environmental psychology in understanding the nature of privacy. He defines privacy as 'the selective control of access to the self' (p. 24) and believes privacy is achieved through the regulation of social interaction, which can in turn provide us with feedback on our ability to deal with the world, and ultimately affect our definition of self. Although Westin and Altman emphasize

different aspects of privacy, there are many similarities between the theories. For example, both theories are examples of 'limited-access' approaches to privacy in that they both emphasize controlling or regulating access to the self. Such commonalties between these theories suggest that 'their ideas provide a reasonable foundation for understanding the fundamentals of privacy as a psychological concept' (Margulis 2003: 424). A large amount of work has supported and extended both Westin's (e.g. Marshall 1974; Pederson 1979) and Altman's work (e.g. Kupritz 2000) and as such both of their theories have stimulated much of the research and theory development of privacy.

Since these earlier definitions, the highly complex nature of privacy has resulted in an alternative way of defining it – through its various dimensions. Burgoon *et al.* (1989) distinguish four dimensions of privacy and define it using these dimensions as 'the ability to control and limit physical, interactional, psychological and informational access to the self or one's group' (Burgoon *et al.* 1989: 132). Each of the dimensions they distinguish is briefly described below with some examples.

1. *The physical dimension* Physical privacy is the degree to which a person is physically accessible to others. This dimension is grounded within the human biological need for personal space. Examples of violations to physical privacy include: surveillance, entry into personal space and physical contact.

2. *The interactional dimension* Interactional (or social/communicational) privacy is an individual's ability and effort to control social contacts (Altman 1975). Burgoon *et al.* (1989) summarize the elements of this dimension as control of the participants of, the frequency of, the length of and the content of an interaction. Non-verbal examples of violations to social privacy include close conversational distance and public displays of affection. Verbal examples include violations of conversational norms (e.g. commenting on mood or appearance) and initiating unwanted conversation.

3. *The psychological dimension* Psychological privacy concerns the ability of human beings to control cognitive and affective inputs and outputs, to form values, and the right to

determine with whom and under what circumstances thoughts will be shared or intimate information revealed. As such, psychological privacy can either develop or limit human growth. Examples of violations to psychological privacy include psychological assaults through name-calling and persuasion.

4. *The informational dimension* Informational privacy relates to an individual's right to determine how, when, and to what extent information about the self will be released to another person (Westin 1967) or to an organization. According to Burgoon *et al.* (1989), this dimension is closely related to *psychological privacy*: however, the control differs from the individual self-disclosure associated with psychological privacy because it is partly governed by law/custom and as it often extends beyond personal control. Examples of violations to informational privacy include going through another person's mail and sharing personal information with others.

DeCew (1997) also reflects the multidimensional nature of privacy in her definition: however, she distinguishes only three dimensions:

1. *The informational dimension* Informational privacy covers personal information such as finances, medical details and so on that an individual can decide who has access to and for what purposes. If disclosed, this information should be protected by any recipients of it. By protecting informational privacy individuals avoid invasions (or potential invasions) to their privacy.

2. *The accessibility dimension* Accessibility privacy refers to physical or sensory access to a person. It 'allows individuals to control decisions about who has physical access to their persons through sense perception, observation, or bodily contact' (DeCew 1997: 76–7).

3. *The expressive dimension* Expressive privacy 'protects a realm for expressing one's self-identity or personhood through speech or activity. It protects the ability to decide to continue or to modify ones behaviour when the activity in question helps define oneself as a person, shielded from interference, pressure and coercion from government or from other individuals' (DeCew 1997: 77). As such, internal control over self-expression and

the ability to build interpersonal relationships improves, while external social control over lifestyle choices and so on are restricted (Schoeman 1992).

Using these multidimensional approaches to define privacy results in some overlap of the features between each dimension. For example, within Burgoon *et al.*'s dimensions some features of informational privacy overlap with psychological privacy, and some features of social privacy overlap with physical privacy. Within DeCew's dimensions there is some overlap between accessibility and informational privacy, and expressive privacy is conceptually linked with both of these dimensions. In addition, there is also some overlap between Burgoon *et al.*'s and DeCew's dimensions. For example, the informational dimension appears in both definitions and Burgoon *et al.*'s physical and social dimensions appear to map onto DeCew's accessibility and expressive dimensions respectively.

Of direct relevance to this chapter are the dimensions of informational and expressive privacy. Central to these dimensions are the desire to keep personal information out of the hands of others, or in other words *privacy concern* (Westin 1967), and the ability to connect with others without interference. In a systematic discussion of the different notions of privacy, Introna and Pouloudi (1999) developed a framework of principles that explored the interrelations of interests and values for various stakeholders where privacy concerns have risen. In this context, concern for privacy is a subjective measure – one that varies from individual to individual based on that person's own perceptions and values. In other words, different people have different levels of concern about their own privacy.

One scheme for categorizing the different levels of privacy concerns is the Westin privacy segmentation (Harris and Associates Inc. and Westin 1998). The Harris Poll is a privacy survey conducted by telephone across the United States among approximately 1,000 people. This survey has been conducted regularly since 1995 and divides respondents into one of three categories depending on their answers to three statements. The three categories of respondents are: *Privacy Fundamentalists* who view privacy as an especially high value which they feel very strongly about.

Currently about a quarter (35%) of all adults are privacy fundamentalists (Computerworld 2005); *Privacy Pragmatists* also have strong feelings about privacy. They weigh the value to them and society of providing their personal information. Currently around approximately 55% of all adults are privacy pragmatists (Computerworld 2005); *Privacy Unconcerned* who have no real concerns about privacy. Approximately 10% of all adults are privacy unconcerned (Computerworld 2005).

Although levels of concern may differ between people, a failure to achieve any level of privacy will result in 'costs'. For example, by not obtaining privacy a person will not benefit from the opportunities that the functions of privacy provide – which could results in stress or negative feedback about the self. There are also costs of losing privacy either through privacy invasion – when conditions for privacy are not achieved, for example being overheard – or privacy violation when recipients of personal information, intentionally provided by the discloser or gained through a privacy invasion, pass it on to others – for example, gossip). In the early privacy research described, invasions and violations were not emphasized. Ingham (1978) states that 'In everyday social life most individuals are only rarely confronted with an invasion of their privacy, although the number of potential threats is very large' (40). However, more recently, technology has fuelled debate and controversy about potential invasions and violations to privacy (Dinev and Hart 2004), as will be described below.

Privacy and the Internet

Since the concept of privacy has been applied to technology (e.g. Agre and Rotenberg 1997; Austin 2003) there have been numerous cases reported of the clash between privacy and new technology – how these technologies allow intrusions into private, enclosed spaces, eroding the distinction between public and private space and therefore compromising the very idea of private space. For example, at the end of last year, a body scanning machine was introduced in an airport in the UK. This x-ray machine produces 'naked' images of passengers enabling any hidden weapons or explosives to be discovered.

However, this introduction of this technology raised concerns about privacy both among travellers and aviation authorities (*The Sunday Times* 2004).

The concept of privacy has also been applied to the Internet (e.g. Cranor 1999). The increased use of computers and of the Internet now fills many parts of people's lives including online shopping, the sharing of documents and various forms of online communication. It is this increased use of the Internet which raises concerns about privacy, in particular, those described above under informational privacy. There are concerns that the Internet seems to erode privacy (Rust *et al.* 2002) and that offline privacy concerns are magnified online (Privacy Knowledge Base 2005). Indeed, the subject of online privacy has been appearing in newspaper articles regularly over the last few years (e.g. *The Times* 2001; The *Guardian* 2004).

Personal information is fast becoming one of the most important ethical issues of our information age (Milberg *et al.* 1995): personal information has become a basic commodity and users' online actions are no longer simply actions but rather data that can be owned and used by others. Advances in technology and the increased use of the Internet have changed the ways in which information is gathered and used. A wide variety of information data is now collected with increasing frequency and in different contexts, making individuals become ever more transparent. The costs of obtaining and analysing this are also decreasing with the advances in technology. However, the value of the users' information which is collected is increasing.

> At no time have privacy issues taken on greater significance than in recent years, as technological developments have led to the emergence of an 'information society' capable of gathering, storing and disseminating increasing amounts of data about individuals.
>
> (Schatz Byford 1996: 1)

There are a number of specific threats to online privacy. For example, the impact of 'ubiquitous' computing (Weiser 1988) means that we leave data footprints in many areas of our lives that were previously considered 'offline'. The extremely rapid development of computing power, in terms of greater processing speed, increased storage capacity, wider communication connectivity and lower machine size all impact on privacy (Sparck-Jones 2003). These rapid advances mean that information can be efficiently and cheaply collected, stored and exchanged – even data which may be deemed sensitive by the individuals concerned. Information that is drawn from the physical world is harboured in electronic databases, which give these records permanence, malleability and transportability that has become the trademark of technology. As such, massive databases and Internet records of information about individual financial and credit history, medical records, purchases and so on exist.

Sparck-Jones (2003) labels a number of specific properties of the information collected which have consequences for privacy:

- *Permanence* – once recorded, information rarely disappears. As such, fine-grained, searchable, persistent data exists on individuals and there are sophisticated, cheap, data-mining devices can also be used to analyse this information;

- *Volume* – the ease with which information is now recorded using technology results in huge data sets. Furthermore, storage is cheap, therefore large volumes of information sets can exist indefinitely;

- *Invisibility* – all information collected seems to exist within an opaque system and so any information collected may not be 'visible' to whom it relates. Even if information collected is available to a person they may not be able to interpret it due to the use of incomprehensible coding;

- *Neutrality* – the ease with which information can be collected means that any qualifying information may be lost. So information may be absorbed regardless of its metadata. i.e. there are no distinctions between intimate, sensitive information and non-sensitive information;

- *Accessibility* – there are a number of tools for accessing information meaning that any information collected can possibly be read by any number of people. The ease with which information can be copied, transferred,

integrated and multiplied electronically further increases this accessibility;

- *Assembly* – there are many effective tools for searching for and assembling and reorganizing information from many quite separate sources;

- *Remoteness* – information collected is usually both physically and logically away from the users to whom it refers. However, this information can be accessed and used by people who the user does not know.

Each of the above features affects privacy and their effect in combination is even greater. Although massive data collection and storage is possible in many environments, the online privacy problem is further exacerbated by the very structure of the Internet and its additional feature of *connectivity*. The Internet allows for interactive two-way communication and is woven into people's lives in a more intimate way than some other media as it connects people with places and people with people. Accordingly it poses unique information privacy threats that differ from issues previously addressed by research (e.g. Smith *et al.* 1996) therefore, making information collection, sharing and so on even easier.

There are also *benefits* to the technological advances described, such as personalized services, convenience and efficiency. In this way, the collection of personal information can be considered a 'double-edged sword' (Malhotra *et al.* 2004). Users can trade off providing valuable information about themselves to take advantage of benefits – for example, providing personal details and credit card information in order to have the convenience of completing an online transaction. Jupiter Research (2002) have found evidence that even privacy concerned individuals are willing to trade privacy for convenience or to bargain the release of very personal information in exchange of relatively small rewards. However, consumer concern over disclosing personal information is growing as they realize that data about their Internet behaviours is being collected without their knowledge and agreement. These privacy concerns can ultimately reduce the personalization benefits that companies can deliver to consumers. The question is whether the benefits of the advances in technology and the use of the Internet are diminished by endangering privacy.

Linking models of privacy and CMC

According to Berscheid (1977), privacy is the 'hidden variable' in many social psychological studies. In the years since her article was published, there have been relatively few attempts to expose this hidden variable to scrutiny in the psychological literature. Privacy is particularly important for understanding self-disclosure, since the relationship between privacy and self-disclosure is somewhat paradoxical. Privacy is a prerequisite for disclosure, and yet, the process of disclosure serves to reduce privacy. The Internet may, in some instances, serve to solve this paradox – disclosure and intimacy can be achieved without concurrent increases in vulnerability or losses of privacy (see Ben-Ze'ev 2003). But this introduces a further paradox – the Internet, and new media in general, have tended to erode privacy through, amongst others, the processes we outline above. Often the impression of privacy is a mirage – high levels of personal information are held by a number of gatekeepers – whether it is through the process of registration, caches and logs kept on various servers or even locally based records. It therefore becomes critical to understand the role of these gatekeepers to understand fully disclosure of personal information online. We propose that as well as looking at the micro-level impacts of the media environment on disclosure, one also needs to look at the macro-level – the wider context in which the micro-level behaviour is enacted.

Trust and disclosure

Trust is a critical issue in both FtF and online disclosure of personal information. By disclosing information, we are making ourselves vulnerable – one reason it is often easier to disclose to strangers than to close friends and family (Rubin 1975). This applies equally to disclosure to web-based forms – for instance, Moon (1998) found that people are more willing to disclose personal information to geographically distant servers – presumably because the vulnerability of doing so is reduced. In e-commerce, the issue of trust is also critical – people will generally not disclose personal information to a web service that they do not trust (Hoffman *et al.* 1999).

However, many attempts to establish trust between people and within groups rely on methods that increase the media richness of the interaction – for instance, by introducing video, audio or photographs (see Olsen *et al.* 2002; Chapter 5 this volume). Quite apart from the substantial problems with media richness approaches to understanding online behaviour (see Walther 1996), introducing cues that are supposed to improve trust may well serve to reduce privacy in an interpersonal context.

However, in some instances trust will be critical. For instance, if you register to a discussion board, dating site or other web-based service, you will commonly be required to disclose to the owner of the site your real name, age, location/ZIP or postal code, and email address. It is not uncommon to also be asked questions about salary, occupation, marital status and other marketing-related queries. In the cases of discussion boards and dating sites, this disclosure of personal information purchases access to a pseudonymous interactive environment in which participants can seek help, be intimate or just play, with little concern for the repercussions in their offline lives. In this situation, expressive privacy has been obtained through the loss of informational privacy to a third party. Critically, we would argue that it is this separation between the location of the expressive environment, and the third party, that is important. Obviously too, one would also expect that for this bargain to work, the third party must be trustworthy.

For trust to be established, it is not always necessary for privacy to be reduced. For instance, reputation systems (as used on eBay, the auction site) allow trust to be established through the use of peer-ratings of pseudonyms (Utz 2004). However trust is established, it is clearly critical to understanding online behaviour, and is likely to become more important as we leave our personal data at the door of pseudonymous environments.

Cost and benefits

In the example above, access to an environment in which expressive privacy is enabled has been effectively purchased with personal information. This commodification of personal information is nothing new – witness the growth in customer cashback or 'loyalty' cards provided by grocery shops – but what is interesting is that one form of privacy is lost to gain another form. Andrade *et al.* (2002) adopt a social exchange framework to study consumers' willingness to disclose personal information, although their results suggest that considering people's decision-making within this framework alone does not explain the results of the study. For instance, while manipulations that seemed to reduce the cost of personal disclosure (e.g. privacy policy) did indeed have the desired effect, the offer of a reward worked to reduce disclosure. Presumably this may be because offering financial rewards opened questions of trust.

There are many other occasions when decisions about whether or not to disclose personal information can be interpreted from a social exchange approach. For instance, in many cases a loss of privacy provides benefits in terms of convenience rather than financial gain. Within person-to-person interaction, self-disclosure can also be understood in terms of costs and benefits. As Antaki *et al.* (2005) note, disclosure needs to be 'brought off' – it does not occur without repercussions for both interactants. By disclosing personal information, the cost to a person is increased vulnerability and a loss of privacy. However, in many cases, the benefits – a building of trust, rapport, and reciprocation – will outweigh the costs. However, this is not to say that disclosure is not without risks. For instance, a teenager agonizing about whether to confess to a romantic crush is likely to be acutely aware that disclosure to the object of their desire is a potentially risky business that will lead to either a joyful reciprocation of feelings, or rejection.

In terms of e-commerce, there are also clear cost–benefit issues regarding privacy and disclosure. For instance, imagine the same teenager has successfully arranged their date, and they now wish to purchase prophylactics. They have two options: the first, to pay in their local town with cash, is reasonably high in privacy – there is no data trail, and unless the server behind the counter knows them, they have high information privacy. The alternative is to use a credit card to purchase the desired products online,

and to have them delivered at their home address in a plain envelope. In this second case, the level of information privacy is low – they will need to disclose their name, address and credit card details, but expressive or social privacy is high. The method chosen will illustrate the relative costs and benefits our fictional teenager attaches to information and expressive/social privacy.

A critical issue in applying such an economic model to understanding privacy and disclosure is the value placed upon personal information by the individual, and their interpretation of the likely costs of disclosure. As such, people's privacy concerns and the level of trust they have in the recipient of the disclosure will determine the outcome of any cost–benefit analysis.

Control

A further context issue that we believe is important to understanding self-disclosure online is control – that is, control over what information is collected, and how and with whom information is shared.

Information is often collected online with or without the user's knowledge or consent. From a technical standpoint, some types of information are easier to obtain than others. Information can be gathered unobtrusively, which requires little cooperation on the part of the person supplying the information. For example, information may be collected by means of cookies and other software designed to track users' movements over the Internet. Other types of information are less accessible, forcing companies to rely on more intrusive means to obtain important data. This typically involves asking people to engage in some type of self-disclosure.

Individual control over personal information is more difficult than ever before. Even when personal information is voluntarily provided, privacy may still be compromised due to the inability of an individual to control the use of the information. For example, privacy may be comprised on two dimensions (Culnan and Armstrong 1999):

1. *Environmental control* – if personal information is accessed by unauthorized means (e.g. through a security breach or an absence of appropriate internal controls);

2. *Control over secondary use of information* – if information provided for one purpose is used for unrelated purposes, without the individual's knowledge or consent. (e.g. through the duplication and sharing of computerized information).

The secondary use of information and the fact that information may be logged and preserved for future access mean that threats to privacy on the Internet can be immediate as well as future threats.

Most people do not know what information is stored about them or who has access to it. However, there is now a growing awareness, as well as resentment, of the routine practice of collecting and analysing personal information (Nissenbaum 1998). This is partly due to reports in newspapers and on online news sites. For example the 'extent of UK snooping revealed' story reported that 'officials in the UK are routinely demanding huge quantities of information about what people do online and who they call, say privacy experts' (BBC News 2003a). Also the 'Top UK sites 'fail privacy test'' story reported '98% do not give enough information about the text files which track user movements, or provide a single-click opt-out option' (BBC News 2003b).

Within the context of person-to-person interaction, clearly control is also a critical issue. Walther (1996) argues that hyperpersonal social interaction online occurs, at least in part, because of the increased control afforded by synchronous, visually anonymous CMC. For instance, we can control what information we choose to disclose, in what manner, and how we disclose it. If privacy and self-disclosure are viewed as dynamic processes, then the removal of control affects the ability of people to effectively regulate their social interactions. We may wish to control the flow of personal information for a number of reasons – for instance, to maintain a desired level of intimacy and privacy, or to maintain social harmony by not disclosing specific information – but without control over what is disclosed and to whom, this is not possible.

Conclusions

Self-disclosure is one of the few widely replicated and noted media effects of online interaction. However, despite the evidence that self-disclosure

occurs in a number of different contexts online, including CMC, weblogs and submission of web forms, most approaches to understanding the phenomenon confine themselves to considering the impact of a single factor – anonymity. We argue that by focusing solely on this micro-level media effect, the wider context in which disclosure is given, or required, is ignored – and that ignoring this context limits how we can conceptualize online behaviour. By considering the wider context, and in particular its implications for privacy, it is possible to develop a more nuanced picture of online behaviour across situations.

Acknowledgements

The writing of this chapter was supported by a grant from the Economic and Social Research Council (RES-341–25–0011).

References

Agre, P. E. and Rotenberg, M. (eds) (1997). *Technology and privacy: The new landscape.* Cambridge, MA: MIT Press.

Altman, I. (1975). *The environment and social behavior.* Monterey, CA: Brooks/Cole.

Altman, I. and Taylor, D. (1973). *Social penetration: The development of interpersonal relationships.* New York: Holt, Rinehart and Winston.

Andrade, E. B., Kaltcheva, V. and Weitz, B. (2002). Self-disclosure on the web: the impact of privacy policy, reward, and company reputation. *Advances in Consumer Research 29,* 350–353.

Antaki, C., Barnes, R. and Leudar, I. (2005). Self-disclosure as a situated interactional practice. *British Journal of Social Psychology 44,* 181–200.

Austin, L. (2003). Privacy and the question of technology. *Law and Philosophy 22,* 119–166.

Bargh, J. A., McKenna, K. Y. A. and Fitzsimons, G. M. (2002). Can you see the real me? Activation and expression of the true self on the Internet. *Journal of Social Issues 58,* 33–48.

BBC News (2003a). Extent of UK snooping revealed. 16 May. Available at http://news.bbc.co.uk/1/hi/technology/3030851.stm. Accessed 20 June 2005.

BBC News (2003b). Top UK sites 'fail privacy test'. 11 December. Available at: http://news.bbc.co.uk/1/hi/technology/3307705.stm. Accessed 20 June 2005.

Ben-Ze'ev, A. (2003). Privacy, emotional closeness, and openness in Cyberspace. *Computers in Human Behavior 19,* 451–467.

Berendt, B., Gunther, O. and Spiekerman, S. (2005). Privacy in E-commerce: stated behaviour versus actual behaviour. *Communications of the ACM 48,* 101–106.

Berger, C. R. and Calabrese, R. J. (1975). Some explorations in initial interaction and beyond: toward a developmental theory of interpersonal communication. *Human Communication Theory 1*, 99–112.

Buchanan, T., Joinson, A. N. and Ali, T. (2002). Development of a behavioural measure of self-disclosure for use in online research. Paper presented at German Online Research 2002, Hohenheim, Germany.

Burgoon, J. K., Parrott, R., LePoire, B. A., Kelley, D. L., Walther, J. B. and Perry, D. (1989). Maintaining and restoring privacy through communication in different types of relationship. *Journal of Social and Personal Relationships 6*, 131–158.

Chesney, T. (2005). Online self disclosure in diaries and its implications for knowledge managers. In *UK Academy for Information Systems Conference proceedings*, 22–24 March, Northumbria University, UK.

Computerworld (2005). Global CRM Requires Different Privacy Approaches. Available at http://www.computerworld.com/printthis/2005/0,4814,101766,00.html. Accessed 20 June 2005.

Cranor, L. F. (1999). Internet privacy. *Communications of the ACM 42*, 29–31.

Culnan, M. J. and Armstrong, P. K. (1999). Information privacy concerns, procedural fairness, and impersonal trust: an empirical investigation. *Organization Science 10*, 104–115.

DeCew, J. (1997). *In pursuit of privacy: Law, ethics, and the rise of technology*. Ithaca, NY: Cornell University Press.

Des Jarlais, D. C., Paone, D., Milliken, J., Turner, C. F., Miller, H., Gribble, J., Shi, Q., Hagan, H. and Friedman, S. (1999). Audio-computer interviewing to measure risk behaviour for HIV among injecting drug users: a quasi-randomised trial. *The Lancet 353*(9165), 1657–1661.

Dinev, T. and Hart, P. (2004). Internet privacy concerns and their antecedents – measurement validity and a regression model. *Behaviour and Information Technology 23*, 413–423.

Epstein, J. F., Barker, P. R. and Kroutil, L. A. (2001). Mode effects in self-reported mental health data. *Public Opinion Quarterly 65*, 529–550.

Ferriter, M. (1993). Computer-aided interviewing and the psychiatric social history. *Social Work and Social Sciences Review 4*, 255–263.

Frick, A., Bächtiger, M. T. and Reips, U.-D. (2001). Financial incentives, personal information and drop-out in online studies. In Reips, U.-D. and Bosnjak, M. (eds), *Dimensions of internet science* (pp. 209–219). Lengerich: Pabst.

Galegher, J. Sproull, L. and Kiesler, S. (1998). Legitimacy, authority and community in electronic support groups. *Written Communication 15*, 493–530.

Greist, J. H., Klein, M. H. and VanCura, L. J. (1973). A computer interview by psychiatric patient target symptoms. *Archives of General Psychiatry 29*, 247–253.

Guardian, The (2004). The privacy debate: this time it's personal. 26 April.

Harris and Associates Inc. and Westin, A. (1998). E-commerce and privacy: what net users want. Privacy and American Business and Pricewaterhouse Coopers LLP. Available at http://www.pandan.org/ecommercesurvey.html. Accessed 20 June 2005.

Harris Interactive (2002). First major post-9/11 privacy survey finds consumers demanding companies do more to protect privacy; public wants company privacy policies to be independently verified. Available at http://www.harrisinteractive.com/news/allnewsbydate.asp?NewsID=429. Accessed 20 June 2005.

Hoffman, D. L., Novak, T. P. and Peralta, M. (1999). Building consumer trust online. *Communications of the ACM 42*, 80–85.

Holbrook, A. L., Green, M. C. and Krosnick, J. A. (2003). Telephone vs. face-to-face interviewing of national probability samples with long questionnaires: comparisons of respondent satisficing and social desirability response bias. *Public Opinion Quarterly 67*, 79–125.

Home Office (1972). *Report of the Committee on Privacy*. Rt. Hon. Kenneth Younger, Chairman. London: HMSO.

Ingham, R. (1978). Privacy and psychology. In Young, J. B. (ed.) *Privacy* (pp. 35–59). Chichester: Wiley.

Introna, L. D. and Pouloudi, A. (1999). Privacy in the information age: stakeholders, interests and values. *Journal of Business Ethics 22*, 27–38.

Jensen, C., Potts, C. and Jensen, C. (2005). Privacy practices of internet users: self-reports versus observed behaviour. *International Journal of Human Computer Studies*. Special issue on HCI Research in Privacy and Security *63*, 203–227.

Joinson, A. N. (1999). Anonymity, disinhibition and social desirability on the Internet. *Behaviour Research Methods, Instruments and Computers 31*, 433–438.

Joinson, A. N. (2001a). Self-disclosure in computer-mediated communication: the role of self-awareness and visual anonymity. *European Journal of Social Psychology 31*, 177–192.

Joinson, A. N. (2001b). Knowing me, knowing you: reciprocal self-disclosure on the internet. *Cyberpsychology and Behavior 4*, 587–591.

Joinson, A. N. (2003). *Understanding the psychology of internet behaviour: Virtual worlds, real lives*. Basingstoke and New York: Palgrave Macmillan.

Joinson, A. N. (2005). Internet behaviour and the design of virtual methods. In C. Hine (ed.), *Virtual methods: Issues in social research on the internet* (pp. 32–44). Oxford: Berg.

Joinson, A. N., Woodley, A. and Reips, U-R. (2007). Personalization, authentication and self-disclosure in self-administered Internet surveys. *Computers in Human Behavior 23*(1), 275–285.

Jourard, S. M. (1971). *Self-disclosure: An experimental analysis of the transparent self*. New York: Krieger.

Jourard, S. M. and Lasakow, P. (1958). Some factors in self-disclosure. *Journal of Abnormal and Social Psychology 56*(1), 91–98.

Jupiter Research (2002). Security and privacy data. Presentation to the Federal Trade Commission Consumer Information Security Workshop. Available at http://www.ftc.gov/bcp/workshops/security/0205201leathern.pdf. Accessed 20 June 2005.

Kenny, D. A. and Judd, C. M. (1986). Consequences of violating the independence assumption in the analysis of variance. *Psychological Bulletin 99*, 422–431.

Knapp, H. and Kirk, S. A. (2003). Using pencil and paper, Internet and touch-tone phones for self-administered surveys: does methodology matter? *Computers in Human Behaviour 19*, 117–134.

Kupritz, V. W. (2000). The role of the physical environment in maximising opportunities for the aging workforce. *Journal of the Industrial Teacher Education 37*, 66–88.

Lau, J. T. F., Tsui, H. Y. and Wang, Q. S. (2003). Effects of two telephone survey methods on the level of reported risk behaviours. *Sexually Transmitted Infections 79*, 325–331.

Laurenceau, J. P., Barrett, L. F. and Pietromonaco, P. R. (1998). Intimacy as an interpersonal process: the importance of self-disclosure, partner disclosure, and perceived partner responsiveness in interpersonal exchanges. *Journal of Personality and Social Psychology 74*, 1238–1251.

Lessler, J. T., Caspar, R. A., Penne, M. A. and Barker, P. R. (2000). Developing computer-assisted interviewing (CAI) for the National Household Survey on Drug Abuse. *Journal of Drug Issues 30*, 19–34.

Malhotra, N. K., Kim, S. S. and Agarwal, J. (2004). Internet users' information privacy concerns (IUIPC): the construct, the scale and a causal model. *Information Systems Research 15*, 336–355.

Margulis, S. T. (2003). On the status and contribution of Westin's and Altman's theories of privacy. *Journal of Social Issues 59*, 411–429.

Marshall, N. J. (1974). Dimensions of privacy preferences. *Multivariate Behavior Research 9*, 255–272.

McKenna, K. Y. A and Bargh, J. (1998). Coming out in the age of the Internet: identity demarginalization through virtual group participation. *Journal of Personality and Social Psychology 75*, 681–694.

Metzger, M. J. (2004). Privacy, trust and disclosure: exploring barriers to electronic commerce. Available at http://www.jcmc.indiana.edu/vo19/issue4/metzger.html. Accessed 20 June 2005.

Milberg, S. J., Burke, S. J. and Smith, H. J. (1995). Values, personal information privacy, and regulatory approaches. *Communications of the ACM 38*, 65–74.

Moon, Y. (1998). Impression management in computer-based interviews: the effects of input modality, output modality, and distance. *Public Opinion Quarterly 62*, 610–22.

Moon, Y. (2000). Intimate exchanges: using computers to elicit self-disclosure from consumers. *Journal of Consumer Research 27*, 323–339.

Musch, J., Broder, A. and Klauer, K. C. (2001). Improving survey research on the World-Wide Web using the randomized response technique. In U. D. Reips and M. Bosnjak (eds), *Dimensions of Internet science* (pp. 179–192). Lengerich, Germany: Pabst Science Publishers.

Nissenbaum, H. (1998). Protecting privacy in an information age: the problem of privacy in public. *Law and Philosophy 17*, 559–596.

Olivero, N. (2001). Self-disclosure in e-commerce exchanges: relationships among trust, reward and awareness. Paper presented at the Psychology and the Internet: A European Perspective conference, DERA, Farnborough, UK.

Olson, J. S., Zheng, J., Bos, N., Olson, G. M. and Veinott, E. (2002). Trust without touch: jumpstarting long-distance trust with initial social activities. In *CHI2002 Conference Proceedings* (pp. 141–146). New York: ACM Press.

Parent, W. (1983). Privacy, morality and the law. *Philosophy and Public Affairs 12*, 269–288.

Parks, M. R. and Floyd, K. (1996). Making friends in cyberspace. *Journal of Communication 46*, 80–97.

Pederson, D. M. (1979). Dimensions of privacy. *Perceptual and Motor Skills 48*, 1291–1297.

Pennebaker, J. W., Kiecolt-Glaser, J. K. and Glaser, R. (1988). Disclosure of traumas and immune function: health implications for psychotherapy. *Journal of Consulting and Clinical Psychology 56*, 239–245.

Privacy Knowledge Base (2005). Available at http://privacyknowledgebase.com. Accessed 20 June 2005.

Quittner, J. (1997). Invasion of privacy. *Time Magazine*, 25 August, pp. 30–31.

Raab, C. Bellamy, C., Staylor, J., Dutton, W. H. and Peltu, M (1996). The information polity: electronic democracy, privacy and surveillance. In Dutton, W. H. (ed.) *Information and communication technologies: Visions and realities*. Oxford: Oxford University Press.

Rheingold, H. (1993). *The virtual community*, revised edn. London: MIT Press.

Robinson, R. and West, R. (1992). A comparison of computer and questionnaire methods of history-taking in a genito-urinary clinic. *Psychology and Health 6*, 77–84.

Rubin, Z. (1975). Disclosing oneself to a stranger: reciprocity and its limits. *Journal of Experimental Social Psychology 11*, 233–260.

Rust, R. T., Kannan, P. K. and Peng, N. (2002). The customer economics of internet privacy. *Journal of the Academy of Marketing Science 30*, 455–464.

Schatz Byford, K. (1996). Privacy in cyberspace: constructing a model of privacy for the electronic communications environment. *Rutgers Computer and Technology Law Journal 24*, 1–74.

Schoeman, F. (1984). Privacy and intimate information. In Schoeman, F. (ed.) *Philosophical dimensions of privacy* (pp. 403–417). Cambridge: Cambridge University Press.

Smith, H. J., Milberg, S. J. and Burke, S. J. (1996). Information privacy: measuring individuals' concerns about organizational practices. *MIS Quarterly 20*, 167–196.

Smyth, J. M. (1998). Written emotional expression: effect sizes, outcome, types, and moderating variables. *Journal of Consulting and Clinical Psychology 66*, 174–184.

Sobel, D. L. (2000). The process that 'John Doe' is due: addressing the legal challenge to Internet anonymity. *Virginia Journal of Law and Technology 5*.

Sparck-Jones, K. (2003). Privacy: what's different now? *Interdisciplinary Science Reviews 28*, 287–292.

Sproull, L., Subramani, M., Kiesler, S., Walker, J. H. and Waters, K. (1996). When the interface is a face. *Human–Computer Interaction 11*, 97–124.

Tidwell, L. C. and Walther, J. B. (2002). Computer-mediated communication effects on disclosure, impressions, and interpersonal evaluations: getting to know one another a bit at a time. *Human Communication Research 28*, 317–348.

Times, The (2001). Governments seem determined to overthrow online privacy – even if they have to behave like hackers to do so. Technobabble, 3 December.

Times, The (2001). Junk e-mails cost £6.4bn. 3 February.

Times, The (2004). Plane passengers shocked by their x-ray scans. 7 November.

Tourangeau, R. (2004). Survey research and societal change. *Annual Review of Psychology 55*, 775–801.

Tourangeau, R. and Smith, T. W. (1996). Asking sensitive questions: the impact of data collection mode, question format, and question context. *Public Opinion Quarterly 60*, 275–304.

Tourangeau, R., Couper, M. P. and Steiger, D. M. (2003). Humanizing self adminstered surveys: experiments on social presence in web and IVR surveys. *Computers in Human Behaviour 19*, 1–24.

Utz, S. (2004). Trust at eBay – influenced by the reputation of the seller or the description of the product? Paper presented at German Online Research 2004, University of Duisburg-Essen, Germany.

Wallace, P. (1999). *The psychology of the internet.* Cambridge: Cambridge University Press

Walther, J. B. (1996). Computer-mediated communication: impersonal, interpersonal, and hyperpersonal interaction. *Communication Research 23*, 3–43.

Warren, S. and Brandeis, L. D. (1890). The right to privacy. *Harvard Law Review 4*, 193–220.

Weisband, S. and Kiesler, S. (1996). Self-disclosure on computer forms: meta-analysis and implications. *Proceedings of CHI96.* Available at http://www.acm.org/sigchi/chi96/proceedings/papers/Weisband/sw_txt.htm. Accessed 20 June 2005.

Weiser, M. (1988) Ubiquitous Computing. Available online at http://www.ubiq.com/hypertext/weiser/UbiHome.html. Accessed on June 20th 2005.

Westin, A. (1967). Privacy and Freedom, New York: Atheneum.

CHAPTER 17

Computer-mediated communication and social identity

Russell Spears, Martin Lea and Tom Postmes

Introduction

The reader is asked to tolerate a degree of egocentrism if this chapter appears to be written from an 'in-group' point of view, particularly with an emphasis on our own theoretical slant, and to some extent research. Our excuse is that this is difficult to avoid to some extent given the focus on social identity, computer-mediated communication (CMC) and the Internet. When we started working in this area in the mid-1980s there was very little research on the role of social identities in CMC (and of course the Internet did not exist back then). The research in those early days seemed to present CMC as an ideal medium for escaping from the restrictions of social categories and identities that bind us to them (e.g., Kiesler *et al.* 1984). Although these early approaches to CMC did not deny that social constraints could sometimes be good, when they were presented in a more positive light (by providing social standards), once again CMC was construed as subverting them. In both cases social identity (and perhaps the social dimension more broadly) seemed to be excommunicated from the realm of CMC.

The other dominant image of cyberspace in the early approaches was a new site of liberation where we could (re)invent the self and escape the strictures and stigma of embodiment and social categories (e.g., Haraway 1990; Turkle 1995). Here social identities could be seen as part of the potential paintbox of how we present ourselves, but potentially something as much to be escaped, manipulated or dissimulated rather than truly represented (see also Walther 1996). Even those who have advocated CMC as a medium to present the true and authentic self (Bargh *et al.* 2002) by implication see social identities as a barrier, something that is blinding others to appreciating unique individuals in terms of their authentic self. In all these accounts the implication has been that social reality, and social categories and identities, were something that could best be transcended through CMC and cyberspace. We are not claiming this can never occur; the point is rather that this does not provide a fertile basis for viewing social identity as central to CMC and the Internet.

It was against this backdrop that we tried to argue that, paradoxically perhaps, social identities could find *especial* expression in CMC, and moreover, that this might not necessarily always be a bad thing. For this reason we hope the reader will indulge a little egocentrism in structuring this overview around our own approach, although empirical work in this area has multiplied well beyond our own research network. There are other approaches that also point to the influence of social identities in CMC, many from outside of social psychology, and we also give these credit. However, we start with an elaboration of the Social Identity model of De-individuation Effects – SIDE for short (Spears and Lea 1994; Reicher *et al.* 1995) because this provides an early explanation of why social identities can become even more powerful and consequential in media such as CMC and the Internet.

The roots of the SIDE model: collectivist behaviour and CMC

The SIDE model has its roots in the social identity approach (social identity theory [SIT] and self-categorization theory [SCT]), but more specifically in two lines of research grounded in this approach: research on collective behaviour in crowds, and research on computer-mediated communication. Although applicable to a range of other contexts these are the two field settings in which the model was developed, notably because of the importance of anonymity, accountability and surveillance in these contexts. Because the work on crowd behaviour preceded that on CMC, we present this first. However, the work on CMC was just as critical in developing the model, not only in showing its applicability to different domains (providing a critique of earlier work on CMC in the process), but also in explicitly formulating and formalizing the theoretical principles. In this sense it is probably true to say that the SIDE model as such only became explicit with the addition of the work on CMC.

SIDE is not the only social identity approach to CMC, but it is perhaps the only or main one tailored to the distinctive properties of these communication media, focusing on the effects of anonymity and isolation in particular. SIDE builds on and develops social identity theory and self-categorization theory and so incorporates these theories into its analysis of the effect of the new media. It goes without saying, but deserves statement nevertheless, that these theoretical traditions can explain many of the patterns of behaviour within CMC just as behaviour outside.

A related theoretical tradition deserves mention here that also has its roots firmly in the social identity tradition: organizational identity theory (OIT) (Ashforth and Maehl 1989). This approach applies the principles of social identity theory to the realm of organizations, and particularly examines the importance of social identification qua organizational commitment as a crucial factor in explaining organizational behaviour. Given the importance of the new communications media in organizational and commercial contexts, both within and between organizations, this application of SIT is particularly relevant (see also Lea, Spears and Rogers [2003] for a discussion of CMC in organizations from a SIT/SIDE perspective). A second area where developments of social identity theory are relevant is in the use of CMC and the Internet for mobilizing social support in collective action and through virtual communities. Once again a range of social identity concepts and approaches are relevant here (see e.g. Brunsting and Postmes 2002).

Having said this, it is worth noting that SIDE is perhaps the social identity framework most specifically attuned to the differences between CMC and face-to-face (ftf) communication, and is designed to explain these. In particular SIDE developed to explain and to anticipate the idea that these media could be more social, in various ways, in their nature and effects than ftf communication. For these reasons SIDE is at the forefront of our theoretical focus here. We now consider in more detail how SIDE grew out of the social identity approach, as applied to collective behaviour and CMC in particular.

The roots of SIDE in the social identity approach

Being grounded in social identity and self-categorization theories, the SIDE model shares their meta-theory and assumptions. According to social identity theory, contexts can implicate us as individuals (interpersonal contexts) or as group members (intergroup contexts). In intergroup contexts social identity becomes salient, and is defined as that part of the self-concept corresponding to group memberships (Tajfel 1978). Self-categorization theory made even more explicit the distinction between personal and social identities as distinct elements of the self, with group self-categorizations implying an inter-group comparative context in which social identity as an in-group member is contrasted to some outgroup (Turner 1985). Both theories make it clear that social identities (and the social groups and categories from which they derive) are potentially no less important or self-defining than the person defined at an individual or personal level (and indeed just as we have diverse social identities that vary with context, so may this be true of personal identities, plural). Rather than seeing social identities as a source of problems, these theories see them as appropriate forms of situational self-definition, where it makes sense to self-categorize at the group level. It then becomes clear why social identities from this perspective are not seen as a source of bias, or a barrier to (individual) freedom: they define who we are and (combined with identification) who we *want to be* in group contexts.

A central proposition of both social identity and self-categorization theories is that perception and behaviour becomes transformed in intergroup contexts such that people come to see themselves and others in terms of the group membership, accentuating intergroup difference and intragroup similarities along group defining dimensions. In self-categorization terms this process is defined as 'depersonalization', which can be contrasted with the personalization or individuation characteristic of more interpersonal contexts. Depersonalization occurs when group identity is rendered salient, because the context is defined in intergroup terms, perhaps because of intergroup conflict (SIT) or because of the presence of clear differences between groups and readiness to perceive the context in group terms (fit and accessibility: SCT)(see Oakes 1987). The process of depersonalization is central to the SIDE model.

The roots of SIDE in research on collective behaviour

One of the roots of the SIDE model is grounded in the critique of de-individuation theory provided by Reicher in his analysis of collective behaviour (e.g. Reicher 1987). De-individuation theory has a long and rich history that can be traced back to the ideas of Le Bon (1895) on crowd behaviour. Le Bon proposed that people immersed in the crowd lose their sense of self (or self-awareness) and become taken over by the collective unconscious, regressing to a primeval state. Although criticized at the time, and in the earliest developments of social psychology (Allport 1924), for being unfounded and unscientific, these ideas were picked up from the early 1950s onwards and reproduced in de-individuation theory. Thus Festinger *et al.* (1952) argued that group immersion would lead to more uninhibited behaviour and reduced accountability. Subsequent researchers tried to show that group immersion led to reduced self-awareness that would result in antisocial behaviour in the mass (Zimbardo 1969; Diener 1980; Prentice-Dunn and Rogers 1989).

However, evidence for a de-individuated state remained elusive. Attempts to show that de-individuation (resulting from factors such as group immersion and arousal) was associated with reduced private self-awareness met with limited success and are open to alternative explanations (Postmes and Spears 1998). Moreover it became clear that some of the de-individuation effects could simply be explained by a more conscious process of being able to avoid sanction or punishment under the cover of anonymity (Prentice-Dunn and Rogers 1989).

It was against this background that Reicher (1984, 1987) proposed a social identity-based reinterpretation of de-individuation effects; rather than losing one's identity in the crowd (or experiencing reduced self-awareness), crowd behaviour reflects a switch from personal to social identity (depersonalization) and this helps to explain the spontaneity and uniformity of crowd behaviour. Most important for our purposes he argued that the classic de-individuation conditions of anonymity and group immersion could explain the group-based behaviour in terms of group conformity rather than rejection of social norms and standards.

This was demonstrated in an early experiment (Reicher 1984) in which students who were made aware of their group identity (e.g. as a science student rather than as an individual), who were also divided clearly into two groups (science vs. social science students), and rendered anonymous by means of mask and overalls (the classic de-individuation manipulation), were more likely to observe group normative behaviour (in this case endorsing pro-vivisection attitudes). In short this study was the first to show that what was proposed to be a mindless and unregulated process by de-individuation theory might actually be the product of a mindful and self-regulated group process.

Some years later we provided further substance to this critique by performing a meta-analysis of the de-individuation literature (Postmes and Spears 1998) in which we confirmed that most of the de-individuation effects studied in the literature could better be explained by conformity to a local group norms or situational demands, rather than in terms of some generic anti-social or anti-normative behaviour as de-individuation theory proposed. In other words, the classic de-individuation conditions of anonymity, group size and reduced self-awareness (see Zimbardo 1969) actually produced greater conformity to these norms rather than less, suggesting a far a more rational and self-regulated process.

The roots of SIDE in CMC

Although it may not be immediately apparent how this work on crowd behaviour relates to the more refined and rational world of CMC, its relevance is due to the fact that the body of research on de-individuation is the first in social psychology to systematically examine the effects of anonymity on social behaviour. This prompted the earliest theories in this domain to address a link between the observation of disinhibited behaviour within the relatively anonymous CMC systems – for example 'flaming' and de-individuation (Kiesler et al. 1984; Siegel et al. 1986). This has persisted in more recent reviews (McKenna and Bargh 2000). For our own part, the social identity critique of the role of anonymity in the crowd could also be used to understand the impact and effects of social identity in CMC.

A second important input into this process was a critique of the rationalist and technologically determinist accounts of CMC that were prevalent until the 1990s (Lea 1991). Tracing these accounts back to their roots in the bandwidth model of information theory, Lea and colleagues contributed to a 're-socializing' of approaches to CMC (Lea 1991; Lea and Giordano 1997; Spears

et al. 2001). This critique was applied to the reduced social cues approaches to group decision-making and group polarization that were grounded implicitly or explicitly in this metatheory (Lea and Spears 1991; Spears and Lea 1992). The SIDE critique was extended to understanding interpersonal relationships using CMC (Lea and Spears 1995) and also to a critique of understanding social process in the uses of Group Decision Support Systems (GDSSs). Within this context, the SIDE model was developed to fill a clear theoretical gap and furnish the missing social dimension in CMC.

Two sides of anonymity, two sides to SIDE

One feature that crowds and CMC have in common is relative anonymity. However, anonymity in the crowd is much more contingent than the original de-individuation theorists proposed, applying more to anonymity of oneself to an out-group than generic anonymity within the crowd itself. This raises a basic distinction about anonymity that is also fundamental to the SIDE model. There are at least two sides to anonymity: anonymity *of* others to oneself – the perceiver – and anonymity – of oneself – *to* others (see Reicher et al. 1995). These two sides of anonymity correspond broadly to two sides of the SIDE model, the cognitive and strategic dimensions respectively. The cognitive dimension is concerned with the salience of social (and personal) identity and is more affected by the salience of others to oneself, primarily by accentuating depersonalization. Anonymity to others feeds more into the strategic component of the model because this will affect how accountable one is for one's behaviour, especially to powerful outgroups or authorities. There will often be constraints on behaviour, especially where others disapprove of and can sanction this behaviour. The strategic component thus builds on the salience of any given identity (the cognitive SIDE) and asks to what extent the free expression of this identity is possible in the context. This theme is related to the accountability route addressed by Prentice-Dunn and Rogers (1989): however their model lacks an analysis of the different levels of self and this is what the SIDE model adds to an analysis of accountability effects (see also Klein *et al. in press*). As we shall see the strategic component is not confined to the effects of anonymity but may also be influenced by isolation and co-presence of others (see further below). We now review evidence for the cognitive and strategic effects of the model before proceeding to deal with some refinements and caveats.

Cognitive SIDE effects

The cognitive dimension of the SIDE model (Spears and Lea 1992, 1994; Reicher *et al.* 1995) develops the theme that the anonymity *of* group members will depersonalize social perception, if that group identity is salient. If personal identity is salient however anonymity may reinforce that identity also, either by emphasizing isolation (and freedom) from the group and its norms, or by enhanced self-awareness of the individual self.[1]

Although the SIDE analysis follows the self-categorization analysis of identity salience and depersonalization, the early statements of SIDE did consider the role of self-awareness. Indeed self-awareness plays a role in the social identity/self-categorization account of self-regulation in the group (see e.g., Abrams and Brown 1989). However, SIDE addresses self-awareness issues somewhat differently than do de-individuation and other approaches (cf. Joinson 2003; Matheson and Zanna 1989). The first point to note here is that the reduced social cues approach suggested, along the lines of de-individuation theory, that people might become less self-aware when using CMC (e.g., Kiesler *et al.* 1984; Siegel *et al.* 1986). In contrast with this proposal, early evidence from Matheson and colleagues (e.g., Matheson and Zanna 1989) showed that people actually become more (privately) self-aware in CMC.

This theme has been developed by Joinson in his self-awareness analysis of CMC effects where he builds on the private–public self-awareness distinction introduced by Fenigstein *et al.* (1975), and adopted and adapted by Prentice-Dunn and Rogers to de-individuation effects. More recently, it has been extended yet further by Sassenberg and colleagues (Sassenberg *et al.* 2005 and Chapter 18 this volume).

In our earliest writings on the cognitive SIDE (Spears *et al.* 1990; Lea and Spears 1991; Spears and Lea 1992) we did not rule out a role for self-awareness, and indeed the whole analysis in terms of salience and depersonalization is one grounded in attentional focus (see Postmes *et al.* [2002] for illustrative empirical data). However, self-awareness theories have tended to remain individualistic, and even the public–private distinction tends to associate private self-awareness with the individual self (awareness of inner states and feelings, etc.), whereas if the group is acknowledged, it is as an external audience to whom the individual is accountable as in public self-awareness. What is missing in this conceptualization is the internalized group self (or indeed audience) corresponding to a social identity. In other words the private–public dualism seems to reinforce the notion of a group as an external source of group pressure or normative influence, rather than as intrinsic to group self-definition (see Turner 1991). In short we are not denying a role for self-awareness processes here, but this awareness of self should vary with the level of self-categorization.

Although we have generally measured self-awareness we have found few if any effects (see e.g., Lea *et al.* 2001; Postmes *et al.* 2002). In theoretical terms this is not so surprising, because the crucial factor for our approach is not the degree of self-awareness, but for the cognitive component of SIDE at least, the question to which aspect of self this attention is directed (see Joinson [2003] and Sassenberg *et al.* [2005] for further elaborations of the effects of self-awareness). Regarding the effects of public self-awareness we would argue that the audience question (which public? In-group or out-group? Which out-group?) is crucial and highly relevant for the strategic component of SIDE (considered below).

[1] This is why we refer to the SIDE model as the social identity model of *de-individuation* effects, not *depersonalization* effects; it also refers to identity effects not covered by depersonalization. The term 'de-individuation effects' should also not be read as implying any commitment to de-individuation theory which SIDE directly critiques: this is just used as a convenient collective term to cover the effects of anonymity and group immersion studied by this literature.

The basic model describing the cognitive component of SIDE can be summarized in three steps (see Figure 17.1):

1. which identity is salient?

2. the influence of anonymity, and

3. the (psychological and behavioural) outcomes.

When group identity is salient the depersonalizing effects of anonymity are likely to lead to a range of group-related outcomes including heightened group salience, self-stereotyping in group terms, group cohesiveness and conformity to group norms (i.e., group-based social influence). In intergroup contexts, classic correlates of intergroup behaviours are also likely to manifest themselves (differentiation, competition, in-group bias and so forth).

Intragroup contexts

Perhaps the most widespread application of these ideas to CMC to date has been to the realm of social influence. Because this theme is covered directly in another chapter in this handbook (see Chapter 18) we will only deal sketchily with this theme here, and more to illustrate the theoretical argument and processes. Our first idea was to transport some of the themes examined by Reicher (1984) into the group polarization paradigm using CMC (Spears *et al.* 1990). From a self-categorization theory viewpoint, group polarization is a case of conformity, in which the group norm (or its prototypical position), is shifted to the pole of the scale where most group members are located. One way to think of this is that conformity involves not just convergence on the mean of the in-group, but also differentiation from potential out-groups, in this case represented by the positions on the other side of the response scale.

In this study we reinforced the progressive norm present in our undergraduate psychology students by providing them with feedback about the general distribution of student views on a series of discussion topics. We then manipulated the salience of group identity by telling them in the group identity condition that we were only interested in them as psychology students and would be looking at group means, whereas in the individual identity conditions we informed them that we were interested in individual personality differences in communication style.

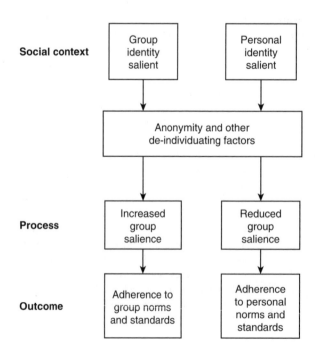

Figure 17.1 The Social Identity Model of De-individuation Effects (SIDE): the cognitive dimension.

Finally, orthogonal to this, we also manipulated anonymity: participants were seated at computers in the same room so that they were visually identifiable, or they were in separate rooms and thus anonymous. In line with the SIDE model we found that group polarization in the normative direction was greatest in the anonymous-group identity condition (depersonalization). In the anonymous individual identity condition we actually found evidence of reliable depolarization. This can be explained as people defining their individuality in contrast to the group norm. Additional measures and analyses also ruled out a range of alternative explanations for group polarization (Lea and Spears 1991).

A possible criticism of this first study is that group norms were (experimentally) imposed, raising the question of whether norm-based social influence follows the same patterns in naturally occurring groups. This issue was addressed by Postmes et al. (2000) who used network analysis to show how group norms emerged in interaction of ad hoc groups.

Further research has provided more insight into the social influence process, its normative bases, and the mediating mechanisms. For example, Postmes et al. (2001, Study 1) used a subtle priming procedure to manipulate the group norm. A scrambled sentence task, ostensibly linked to another study was used to make salient either efficiency-oriented or more prosocial concepts. Anonymity, in this case, was manipulated by displaying photos of participants on the screen in the identifiable conditions. Groups then discussed a dilemma about a hospital in which the priority of patient care versus management efficiency were debated in order to determine the best policy for the hospital. In line with SIDE, groups tended to conform to the primed norm, and this effect grew stronger over time, but only in the anonymous condition.

In a follow-up study we wanted to establish that this effect was caused by true intragroup influence and was not just an individually based cognitive priming effect. To do this we primed two group members from groups of four with one of the primes (the efficiency prime) but primed the other two group members with a neutral prime that had nothing to do with the discussion topic. Once again we found that the impact of the norm was stronger in the anonymous condition, and

most importantly the effect transferred just as strongly from the efficiency-primed to the neutrally primed group members. This research also provided evidence that influence was mediated by group identification, a proxy for group salience. Other studies also provide evidence of anonymity enhancing group-based influence confirming that the salience of group identity and a group norm are important preconditions for this pattern (see Sassenberg and Boos 2003).

This analysis is not just applicable to the content of group norm but also to the style of group interaction. For example the well-known phenomenon or flaming, or evidence of disinhibited behaviour in CMC, can be explained by this norm-based analysis (Lea et al. 1992; Postmes et al. Lea 2000; Lea and Spears 1992). Importantly an analysis grounded in group norms can explain the variations found in flaming behaviour, and explain why it does not always occur, and indeed is much less frequent than was originally mooted (Lea et al. 1992). Although some have claimed that being able to explain both the presence and absence of flaming is a problem for SIDE (Joinson 2003), we argue that the very explanatory power depends on the (variability in the) content of the norm. Of course, these cannot always be specified beforehand, and may emerge or be socially constructed in interaction (Postmes et al. 2000). However normative explanations are of course empirically testable. As well as varying with the salience of group identity and anonymity as specified by SIDE, disinhibited behaviour based on local norms should also be moderated by group identification (Spears 2001). In short, behaviour such as flaming is predictable (and explicable) so long as the key theoretical parameters are known. The more important point here, however, is to correct the misnomer that CMC reduces the conformity to normative cues, which has deflected researchers from the power of this explanation for behaviour within CMC and the Internet.

It is useful to back up at this stage, and consider some perhaps more basic group and social identity effects that derive from similar depersonalization mechanisms. For example, following self-categorization principles we would expect social attraction (attraction to the group or its prototype) and group cohesiveness to be enhanced under conditions of anonymity. This is what was found in a study by Lea *et al.* (2001). This study also measured some of the intervening variables thought to play a role in depersonalization, namely self-categorization and the stereotyping of other group members. As predicted, anonymous discussion conditions led to greater group attraction and cohesiveness and these were mediated by self-categorization as a group member and also stereotyping of other group members. More recently Lea *et al.* (in press) have also shown that self-categorization processes mediate anonymity effects on group attraction under high (but not low) group salience (see further below).

Similar effects of have now also been demonstrated in a range of contexts, and with a range of outcomes. Cress (2005) manipulated the anonymity of contributors to a knowledge database by means of portrait pictures. She found that anonymity increases knowledge sharing within groups, but only for those whose social identity is salient. Tanis and Postmes (2005) found a comparable effect of anonymity on trust in an otherwise very different study of sharing in dyads. Students first performed a collaborative task with an in-group member (a student at the same university) or an out-group member (student at a rival university). After this task, participants were told that if they transferred their participant reward to their collaboration partner, the total reward would be tripled in value. Their partner would then have the option of returning some of the proceeds back to them. The question was if they would invest trust in their partner. When participants were anonymous, trusting behaviour was based entirely on expectations of reciprocity inferred from group membership, with out-group members receiving very little money, and in-group members a lot more. In contrast, when participants were identifiable, trusting behaviour was entirely dependent on the interpersonal impression that participants had formed of the other's trustworthiness. In both these studies, participants are comfortable sharing valued goods with in-group members when anonymous, as predicted by SIDE.

Further research demonstrates that these effects of depersonalization can have apparently opposite effects at the levels of individual and group. Lea and Spears (1992) found that recipients' evaluations of paralanguage use (typographic tricks such as emoticons) in text messages were negative between anonymous individuals, but positive if they shared a group identity with the anonymous sender. Tanis and Postmes (2003; in press) demonstrated in a series of five studies of dyadic (intragroup) interaction that anonymous in-group members leave more negative impressions and are considered more ambiguous characters as *individuals*, but they are nonetheless preferred in collaboration. Recent studies have linked the latter effect to the enhanced perception of a shared identity in anonymous dyads (Postmes and Tanis 2006).

Intergroup contexts

So far we have primarily considered intragroup effects within CMC.[2] We now move to consider the intergroup context of CMC and the role of social identity process here more explicitly. One process associated with salient social identities is the accentuation of intergroup differences as well as intragroup similarities (Tajfel 1978). In line with depersonalization principle in the SIDE model we propose that these processes will be enhanced by anonymity, so long as the group boundaries remain distinct and group identities salient (Reicher 1984). We investigated this hypothesis in two studies (Postmes *et al.* 2002). In Study 1 we used groups in Manchester and Amsterdam that were anonymous with respect to each other but not themselves. Discussion topics were chosen on the basis of piloting such that differences might be expected between these student groups. In the depersonalized conditions participants were identified by initials and a name tag (A or M) whereas in the individuated conditions they were identified by first name and by the display of photos (all saw a standard set of photos and believed that their photos were displayed to the outgroup). As predicted, the depersonalized groups tended to diverge as a result of discussion whereas individuated groups actually converged (depolarization).

---

[2] Although it should be remembered that from a self-categorization perspective there is always at least an implicit intergroup context that renders group identity salient. Indeed ostensibly intragroup phenomena such as group polarization are also premised on an intergroup dimension (a differentiation process).

In Study 2, psychology students were led to believe that they were communicating with an in-group of three psychology students and an out-group of three business or sociology students. As in the previous study, groups tended to converge in the individuated conditions but this effect was attenuated (rather than showing actual differentiation) in the depersonalized conditions. However, other depersonalization effects consistent with SIDE predictions emerged: in the depersonalized conditions participants identified more with the in-group, saw the out-group as more homogeneous, held more negative stereotypes of the out-group, and were more likely to see group members as interchangeable by making more within than between group recall errors. In sum there is clear evidence for both differentiation and depersonalization being fostered by anonymity in line with SIDE principles.

Research by Lee (2004, Study 1) also revealed evidence of the cognitive SIDE using a different means to depersonalize participants in group discussion. Specifically she either used uniform avatars to represent group members that were either all the same (depersonalized in our terms) or different (indicating more individuation). Results showed greater conformity under depersonalized representations but only in intergroup conditions, in other words conditions that naturally render group identity salient.

In a more recent study by Lea et al. (in press) related effects were also found for intergroup discussion involving groups from different nationalities in terms of attraction and group cohesiveness. This study also employed a Dutch (Amsterdam) and British (Manchester) intergroup discussion, but in this case focused on attraction (interpersonal and group-based) and group cohesiveness as measures. In line with predictions from the SIDE model we found that when national identity was salient (namely when discussing topics which pre-testing showed to reveal systematic differences between Dutch and British), anonymity produced stronger depersonalization (measured by prototypicality of self and self-categorization), which in turn produced greater group attraction and group cohesiveness. Visibility, on the other hand, increased (interpersonal) attraction, and group cohesiveness under conditions of low salience, a more

interpersonal route to group formation and solidarity (see also Postmes et al.; see below).

Effects of status and power

The other classic dimension on which we might expect intergroup effects is in terms of status or power differences between groups. This is important because some theorists have championed CMC as the medium par excellence of status equalization and minimized power differentials (e.g., Dubrovsky et al. 1991; see also Kiesler and Sproull 1992). From the perspective of the SIDE model we have questioned and contested this proposition, arguing that so long as social category cues penetrate the medium – as they often do (see e.g., Thomson and Murachver 2001) then differentiation along status and power lines may persist and even be accentuated by the depersonalizing effects of anonymity (Spears and Lea 1994; Postmes et al. 1998). To be sure there are opportunities to resist power differences in CMC precisely for reasons of anonymity and isolation, and we consider these in detail where we address the strategic component of SIDE. However, where status and power are considered in terms of the cognitive component (i.e. in relation to identity salience) then we expect that making salient the social categories bearing status and power relations will also accentuate these relations.

Proponents of the reduced social cues approach have argued that status differences are played down in CMC. However, in some of their demonstrations of this principle, status has been conceived in rather individualistic terms, showing simply that discussion time is more equalized within CMC compared to FTF groups. Matters become somewhat less clear when the status (and power) is clearly tied to social categories and group identities that provide a basis of intergroup differentiation. A study which satisfies this criterion and appears to support the status equalization idea was performed by Dubrovsky et al. (1991). Here discussion groups comprised one (post)graduate student (high status) and three undergraduates (low status). Dubrovsky et al. found, in line with status equalization, that the high status group member had less impact in the CMC than in the ftf conditions.

However, this study has been criticized on methodological grounds (Spears and Lea 1994;

Weisband *et al.* 1995). In particular, in this design there appears to be a confound between (sub)group size and power/status such that the high status subgroup is in a minority. Weisband *et al.* replicated this study with an amended design in which there were now two (post)graduate students to one undergraduate. In this case the effect reversed and status differences were accentuated in the CMC condition in line with SIDE principles.

A similar argument was applied to the analysis of gender and CMC by Postmes and Spears (2002, Study 2). Gender can be considered a status characteristic (Ridgeway and Smith-Lovin 1999) and men may often dominate discussion, although this effect is likely to be moderated by discussion topic, being less true of female stereotypic topics. The question here was whether anonymous CMC might accentuate any status differences (following SIDE) or reduce them (status equalization). In this study all participants used visually anonymous CMC but we either individuated participants by means of detailed personal profiles (biographies) or not. This allowed us to keep all individuals' gender concealed (i.e., by providing gender-neutral profiles to all participants). Rather than varying visible gender differences (which we did not want to do here for reasons elaborated below), we subtly manipulated the accessibility of gender stereotypes using a scrambled sentence test. Finally, we also varied the discussion topic to suit men or women.

The prediction that men would dominate when stereotypes were activated and group members depersonalized was borne out on 'male' topics. Although the pattern was mirrored for women on 'female' topics this effect was not as strong, suggesting a stronger male dominance overall (albeit moderated by topic). These findings provide further support for the SIDE principle that anonymous CMC will tend to reinforce group norms and accentuate intergroup differences. However it should be noted that in this study there was no ftf condition; individuation was achieved in this case by means of written profiles. This raises the questions of what the effects of visibility might be in the case of gender, and we turn to this in the next section, where we consider refinements to the SIDE model.

Refinements to the cognitive SIDE

In this section we consider refinements and caveats to the SIDE model that address the relations between social identities and CMC. As with all theoretical frameworks there is a danger that we essentialize and reify the nature of social identity and regard the effects of anonymity in CMC as inevitably producing the effects we have considered so far. However, this would be to fall into the trap of technological determinism that the SIDE model was developed to counter within the CMC literature (Lea and Spears 1992; Spears and Lea 1994; Spears *et al.* 2002a). Although SIDE is explicit about key features of technology (e.g. visual anonymity in CMC) interacting with social identity, to assume these will always result in the same patterns would surely constitute a mild form of technological determinism. This would be to ignore the possibility of variability in the nature of the technology (there are likely to be varying degrees and forms of anonymity in the new communications media, and indeed absolute visual anonymity may not exist at all) but also variability in the nature of social categories and identities, and their contents. If these components vary, their interaction is likely to vary also and it is important to be wise to this possibility to guard against determinism of both technological and social forms. We now discuss some important lessons of this nature, which remind us to guard against these oversimplifying and essentializing tendencies. This is also important in order to ensure the theoretical development that keeps pace with social and technological changes.

Gender is a particularly interesting case for the SIDE model, raising questions about the prediction that anonymity will necessarily always lead to greater category salience and depersonalization. Although visual anonymity deflects attention from the individual differences that can provoke interpersonal comparison and cue personal identity, gender is an interesting case because it is one social category that is clearly visually cued. Men and women look different from each other physically, also in terms of how they dress. To use the language of self-categorization theory, there is high comparative and normative fit (Oakes 1987). This is less true of some of the other categories we have considered thus far (e.g., study majors, British vs. Dutch nationals) where identity might be less visually cued. However gender is by no means a special case. Many other important social categories such as ethnicity and age have clear visual markers associated with them. Indeed some researchers have referred to gender, age, and ethnicity as the 'big three' social categories (e.g., Brewer and Liu 1989). It has been argued that these categories are activated almost automatically, presumably helped by these strong visual cues (e.g., Fiske and Neuberg 1990).

With regard to such visually cued categories, a clear tension within the SIDE model opens up regarding the idea that visual anonymity will enhance depersonalization. Visual cues associated with gender (and some other categories) may be sufficiently strong to overpower the depersonalizing anonymity effect, by making clear, or clearer than was the case, the gendered identity of the interlocutors.

We investigated this idea in a study that has already been partially described earlier (Lea et al. in press). Recall that in that study we had groups of four people comprising two Dutch and two British group members. There were also two males and two female students, cross-cutting the nationality categorization. Although the nationality categorization produced the 'classic' SIDE pattern of greater depersonalization, group attraction and cohesion under conditions of anonymity, we were open to the possibility that this would not be the case for gender for the very reasons identified here. For gender, *visibility* was indeed associated with greater depersonalization and group-level attraction and cohesiveness under conditions of high group salience (i.e. where gender-relevant topics produced high gender fit in the group discussions). Low salience also produced enhanced interpersonal attraction and cohesiveness under conditions of visibility just as it had for the nationality category (a more interpersonal process).

We used this research to provide a perspective on a particular group typology that has appeared in the group dynamics literature, and specifically the distinction between so-called 'common-bond' and 'common-identity' groups (Prentice et al. 1994). Common-bond groups

are groups grounded in personal bonds and interpersonal attraction between group members, whereas common identity groups share a common identity and can be attracted to this identity (group attraction) without this being grounded in interpersonal relations. In other words this corresponds to Tajfel's conception of a social identity (1978), and Turner's cognitive redefinition of the group (1982). Sassenberg (2002) found some support for both types of groups in their use of the Internet and validated this distinction by showing that common-bond groups show greater interpersonal attraction but common identity groups greater conformity to group norms and greater identification.

Lea et al. (in press) argued against viewing groups as falling neatly into this typology, and showed that essentially the same underlying depersonalization process (albeit by a somewhat different route), underlies the effects of anonymity and visibility on group cohesion and attraction, depending on the availability of particular group features (specifically whether category identity is visually cued; see also Spears et al. 2002b). Rogers and Lea (2005) have also recently argued that in CMC 'social presence' is more a function of the relation to the group in terms of shared identity (i.e. closer to common identity) than the interpersonal bonds that might prosper in ftf communication.

In a similar vein Postmes et al. (2005) argued that it is possible to contrast groups and group identities that form 'deductively' from a shared social identity, versus those that emerge more inductively though interpersonal interaction. Although this distinction looks similar to the common-bond/common-identity distinction our focus is on process and group history, rather than emphasizing qualitatively different kinds of group, because the outcome in terms of group measures such as group identification may well be similar. However, this formation process does have important consequences in relation to key features of CMC such as anonymity. Specifically, Postmes et al. (2005) argued that whereas groups that are self-defined deductively are likely to reveal the depersonalizing effects of anonymity in line with the classic predictions of the cognitive SIDE, groups that emerge inductively through interpersonal interaction are likely to be strengthened by visibility as this is likely to foster these interpersonal links. This is what we found. Using direct (Study 1) and more subtle and naturalistic means (Study 2) to manipulate the inductive and deductive bases of group formation, we consistently found two-way interactions on measures of group commitment and conformity such that anonymity enhanced this effect for deductively formed groups (à la 'classic SIDE') with the a reversal of this pattern for inductively formed groups.

The findings discussed and developed in this section therefore caution against treating the SIDE model as a static prescription. Rather, like any good theory, it is approximate, provisional, and has to develop, along with the theories on which it builds (SIT, SCT) along with our understanding of group processes and the effects of technological features. These caveats and 'exceptions' should therefore be used to develop and extend the model rather than being seen as criteria for falsification, which would throw the baby out with the bathwater, and discard the useful insights this approach has generated.

Strategic SIDE effects

The SIDE model has a second dimension that corresponds to the freedom to express identities once salient (Spears and Lea 1994; Reicher *et al.* 1995). However it is true to say that this dimension, although explored in the context of collective behaviour more generally, has received much less attention within the realm of CMC. It should also be noted that many effects relating to social identity in CMC may have a strategic dimension and can be interpreted using this framework. There is therefore much still to be done by applying the strategic SIDE to CMC. In the meantime we focus on what little research there is.

Because the strategic SIDE is concerned with potential constraints on free identity expression, it follows that it primarily concerns contexts where there is a power relation, especially in intergroup contexts (e.g. gender) although this is not the only case (see Klein *et al.* in press, for a recent review of the strategic SIDE). How do features of CMC relate to factors that might affect power, or the resistance to power? We briefly consider these in terms of three typical features

of CMC: anonymity, isolation (vs. co-presence) and communication. We consider how these relate to two key dimensions of power and empowerment, namely surveillance and sanctions (and how to avoid them), and social support (and how to recruit it).

We first briefly consider these two key power dimensions in terms of the three characteristic CMC features. Anonymity is typically thought of as a protection against sanction by removing accountability to an audience (see the de-individuation studies discussed earlier). Recall that whereas the cognitive dimension of SIDE is generally concerned with anonymity *of* others (enhancing depersonalization) here the issue is of anonymity *to* (powerful) others (see also Sassenberg and Postmes 2002, for evidence relating to this distinction). CMC may often be characterized by 'anonymity to', although there is also a flip side to this. CMC is a medium in which interactions are registered and recorded in text, and whose message logs become widely distributed and impossible to destroy once sent. It is therefore also the ultimate medium of surveillance, a 'panopticon' if you will (Spears and Lea 1994) at least for those who control the system and are able to trace identities.

The isolation associated with CMC is similarly double-edged. CMC may provide isolation from the source of power and its sanctions. However it may also cut people off from the social support of others because, unlike ftf communication, these are unlikely to be co-present (isolation is another feature of the panopticon). However, one important factor that undermines the panopticon metaphor in its most extreme form is clearly the ability to communicate using CMC. Indeed this is the *raison d'être* of CMC. This allows for the communication of social support and information about the willingness to resist power, and provides a medium through which to coordinate this resistance. It is well known, for example, that email (and mobile telephone technology) have formed a vital means of communication in coordinating disruption of world summits in the anti-globalization movement (Postmes and Brunsting 2002; Tilly 2004).

We now consider some experimental evidence of these features in terms of this analysis of the strategic dimension. Reicher and Levine (1994a, b; Reicher *et al.* 1998) developed a paradigm to research the resistance to authority, which pitted the relatively powerless group of undergraduate students against (powerful) lecturing staff. They showed that students were more likely to endorse behaviour corresponding to an in-group student norm that was, however, punishable by the staff (e.g., not attending lectures) if they were anonymous with respect to the staff, and could count on social support from fellow students (Reicher and Levine 1994a, b). We adapted this paradigm to the realm of CMC (Spears *et al.* 2002b).

In the first study we tried to separate out two key features of CMC, namely visual anonymity and the ability to communicate via email, while keeping a third constant (isolation: all participants were in the same room). Anonymity was manipulated by dividing co-present group members by means of screens. In line with the cognitive dimension of SIDE we found that the anonymity manipulation enhanced conformity to *non*-punishable in-group norms. However in line with the strategic dimension, the availability of email increased endorsements of potentially *punishable* in-group normative behaviour (i.e. challenging lecturers' authority), presumably by channelling support for resistance. In a follow-up experiment we manipulated the social support for punishable normative behaviour directly to confirm the causal role of this factor (Spears *et al.* 2002b, Study 2).

In the previous experiments the effects of anonymity were still of the cognitive kind, but anonymity can also be used to escape the effects of powerful outgroups. We present two recent examples relating to gender (Flanagin *et al.* 2002; Spears *et al.* 2002a). In an attempt to integrate research on status equalization and the SIDE model critique thereof, Flanagin *et al.* (2002) argued that the strategic dimension of SIDE might be a case where low power groups are more likely to use (and maintain) their anonymity within CMC in order to annul the power differential. This is indeed in keeping with our analysis of the strategic effect (see also Spears and Lea 1994). In a series of experimental studies Flanagin *et al.* showed that women were more likely to maintain anonymity for this reason whereas men were much happier to identify their gender, presumably because of the status/power advantages this status characteristic endows (Ridgeway and Smith-Lovin 1999).

In conceptually related research Wolbert and colleagues (see Spears *et al.* 2002a; Spears *et al.* in preparation) argued that women were more likely to adopt neutral or male identities on the Internet (e.g., on discussion boards and in chat rooms) as a means of being taken seriously by predominantly male discussants, especially in male stereotypic domains. This is what we found: women were much more likely to shift to neutral and male identities (in terms of their choice of gendered avatars), especially when this matched the stereotypic nature of the topic, whereas men stuck to predominantly male identities. It should be noted that this was primarily an intellectual task, however. There is more evidence of men switching to female identities in more romantic or sex-related contexts on the Internet. However, even here there seems to be a power-based or even exploitative dimension: males may know they will be less likely engage women in conversation with male identities and this may be a way of preying on unsuspecting women (e.g., Van Gelder 1985).

Although gender dissimulation by women might seem one way to escape the power differential, the paradox is that this may serve to make women even less visible as a group on the internet, undermining the social support that these media might otherwise afford (Spears *et al.* 2002a). However, it is interesting that as soon as gender is made salient, simply by the experiment requiring participants to indicate their sex before choosing their gendered avatar identities, the topic-gender-matching pattern of dissimulation among women disappeared or even reversed. It seems that women resist the gender agenda when they become more aware of their own gender. Presumably, they do not want to be seen as expert on male gender topics, nor do they want to be stereotyped as experts on female topics (both of which could defer to the male 'gender agenda').

Overall there is considerable evidence that some of the characteristic features of CMC can be deployed strategically, both to resist and to reinforce power relations. The effects are complex and multifaceted, however, because of the different features of CMC and their multiple effects, and because of the sometimes interacting and opposing effects of the cognitive and strategic dimensions of SIDE (Sassenberg and

Postmes 2002, Spears *et al.* 2002b). It should also be noted that not all strategic effects reflect overt and conscious management of identities to powerful outgroups. There is also evidence of more subtle self-presentational effects when accountable to an *in-group* audience. For example, Douglas and McGarty (2001, 2002) showed that in-group members were more likely to describe out-groups in stereotypic ways (i.e. ways that would appeal to an in-group audience) on an implicit measure when they were identifiable to the in-group. They refer to this type of effect as duty or obligation to the in-group. It is not clear whether this belongs to the cognitive or to strategic realm and indeed whether it reflects power relations or is more internalized (or perhaps both: see Spears and Lea 1994).

Concluding comments

To conclude, rather than being less relevant in ftf communication than CMC we would argue that social identities not only populate CMC and the Internet, but they often thrive there, both by designation (of identity: the cognitive dimension) and by design (the strategic dimension in which identities and their agendas are contested). This means that far from being eliminated in CMC, the group and its effects often shine through in CMC (intragroup cohesiveness and conformity, intergroup contrast and competition).

In terms of status and power differentials this can mean that the power and status relations associated with categories are reinforced, both cognitively by being tied to the roles and relations associated with these identities, and strategically by the surveillance that CMC can sometimes bring. Indeed, the power of surveillance and the rise in webcam technology, have led at least one commentator to query whether the anonymity that plays such a central role in this review is not increasingly a thing of the past (Joinson 2005). We disagree. As research discussed above shows, some people will choose to maintain their anonymity for strategic reasons. Email does not seem to be disappearing any time soon, and anonymity characterizes how many people use the Internet, both in terms of their consumption and communication behaviour. At the cognitive level, visual anonymity should still have depersonalizing

effects even when the people are known to each other.

Moreover as the research by Lea *et al.* (in press) and Postmes *et al.* (2005) shows, the new technologies that do incorporate visibility (such as webcam, streaming video) do not eliminate depersonalizing processes or the utility of a SIDE-based analysis. Clearly depersonalization and individuation are achieved in various ways through various forms of CMC, both by visibility versus visual anonymity, but also through biographical information (Postmes and Spears 2002). So far SIDE has been up to the task of analysing these changing technological forms in terms of identity-based process, and clearly, further research needs to consider further the degrees and types of anonymity associated with CMC and other ICTs.

CMC and the Internet also provide the mobilizing potential for resisting power. The strategic battles between those on both sides of the power divide can be similar to power struggles in other domains. However, because of the different territory provided by the technology, the rules (by which to play) and resources (at one's disposal) may be different, and new possibilities therefore become available to both sides. Although we have somewhat neglected the constructionist theme in this review, the mobilizing potential of CMC and the Internet make it a technology that can help us to construct new identities and make new social connections. More often, however, and in keeping with our interactionist theme, it will allow people to exploit current identities and identity projects embedded in their everyday lives. Of course CMC, the Internet and other ICTs can also further identity projects that exploit others through surveillance and control. In short CMC provides a local and global technology to extend both the up and the down sides of social identity.

References

Abrams, D. and Brown, R. (1989). Self-consciousness and social identity – self-regulation as a group member. *Social Psychology Quarterly 52*, 311–318.

Allport, F. H. (1924). *Social psychology*. New York: Houghton Mifflin.

Ashorth, B. E. and Mael, F. (1989). Social identity theory and the organization. *Academy of Management Review 14*, 20–39.

Bargh, J. A., McKenna, K. Y. A. and Fitzsimons, G. M. (2002). Can you see the real me? Activation and expression of the 'true self' on the Internet. *The Journal of Social Issues 58*, 33–48.

Brewer, M. B. and Lui, L. N. (1989). The primacy of age and sex in the structure of person categories. *Social Cognition 7*, 262–274.

Brunsting, S. and Postmes, T. (2002). Social movement participation in the digital age – predicting offline and online collective action. *Small Group Research 33*, 525–554.

Cress, U. (2005). The ambivalent effect of member portraits in virtual groups. *Journal of Computer-Assisted Learning 21*, 281–291.

Diener, E. (1980). Deindividuation: the absence of self-awareness and self-regulation in group members. In P. Paulus (ed.), *The psychology of group influence* (pp. 000–000). Hillsdale, NJ: Erlbaum.

Douglas, K. M. and McGarty, C. (2001). Identifiability and self-presentation: computer-mediated communication and intergroup interaction. *British Journal of Social Psychology 40*, 399–416.

Douglas, K. M., McGarty, C. (2002). Internet identifiability and beyond: a model of the effects of identifiability on communicative behavior. *Group Dynamics – Theory Research and Practice 6*, 17–26.

Dubrovsky, V. J., Kiesler, S. and Sethna, B. N. (1991). The equalization phenomenon: status effects in computer-mediated and face-to-face decision-making groups. *Human Computer Interaction 6*, 119–146.

Fenigstein, A., Scheier, M. F. and Buss, A. H. (1975). Public and private self-consciousness – assessment and theory. *Journal of Consulting and Clinical Psychology 43*, 522–527.

Festinger, L., Pepitone, A. and Newcomb, T. (1952). Some consequences of de-individuation in a group. *Journal of Abnormal and Social Psychology 47*, 382–389.

Fiske, S. T. and Neuberg, S. L. (1990). A continuum of impression formation, from category-based to individuating processes: influences of information and motivation on attention and interpretation. In M. P. Zanna (ed.), *Advances in experimental social psychology*, vol. 2 (pp. 1–74). New York: Random House.

Flanagin, A. J., Tiyaamornwong, V., O'Connor J. and Seibold, D. R. (2002). Computer-mediated group work: the interaction of member sex and anonymity. *Communication Research 29*, 66–93.

Haraway, D. (1990). A manifesto for cyborgs: science technology, and socialist feminism in the 1980s. In L. Nicholson (ed.) *Feminism/postmodernism*, New York: Routledge.

Joinson, A. N. (2003). *Understanding the psychology of Internet behaviour; Virtual worlds, real lives.* Basingstoke: Palgrave, Macmillan.

Joinson, A. N. (2005). Who's watching you? Power, personalization and on-line compliance. Paper presented at Conference on Group processes in computer supported interaction: Technological and social determinism. Miami University, Oxford, Ohio.

Kiesler, S., Siegel, J. and McGuire, T. (1984). Social psychological aspects of computer-mediated communications. *American Psychologist 39*, 1123–1134.

Kiesler, S. and Sproull, L. (1992). Group decision making and communication technology. *Organizational Behavior and Human Decision Processes 52*, 96–123.

Klein, O., Spears, R. and Reicher, S. (in press). Identity performance: extending the strategic side of the SIDE model. *Personality and Social Psychology Review.*

Lea, M. (1991). Rationalist assumptions in cross-media comparisons of computer-mediated communication. *Behaviour and Information Technology 10*, 153–172.

Lea, M. and Giordano, R. (1997). Representations of the group and group processes in CSCW research: a case of premature closure? In G. C. Bowker, S. L. Star, W. Turner and L. Gasser, (eds). *Social science, technical systems and cooperative work: Beyond the great divide* (pp. 5–26). Mahwah, NJ: Lawrence Erlbaum Associates.

Lea, M., O'Shea, T., Fung, P. and Spears, R. (1992). 'Flaming' in computer-mediated communication: observations, explanations, implications. In M. Lea (ed.). *Contexts of computer-mediated communication* (pp. 89–112). Hemel Hempstead: Harvester-Wheatsheaf.

Lea, M. and Spears, R. (1992). Paralanguage and social perception in computer-mediated communication. *Journal of Organizational Computing 2*, 321–342.

Lea, M. and Spears, R. (1995). Love at first byte? Building personal relationships over computer networks. In J. T. Wood and S. Duck. (eds), *Understudied relationships: Off the beaten track* (pp. 197–233). Thousand Oaks, CA: Sage.

Lea, M. and Spears, R. (1991). Computer mediated communication, de-individuation, and group decision-making. *International Journal of Man-Machine Studies 34*, 283–301.

Lea, M., Spears, R. and De Groot, D. (2001). Knowing me, knowing you: effects of visual anonymity on self-categorization, stereotyping and attraction in computer-mediated groups. *Personality and Social Psychology Bulletin 27*, 526–537.

Lea, M., Spears, R. and Rogers, P. (2003). Social processes underlying effects of electronic team work in organizations: the central issue of identity. In S. A. Haslam, N. Ellemers, M. Platow and D. Van Knippenberg (eds), *Social identity in organizations* (pp. 99–115). Philadelphia, PA: Psychology Press.

Lea, M., Spears, R. and Watt, S. E. (in press). Visibility and anonymity effects on attraction and group cohesiveness. *European Journal of Social Psycology.*

Le Bon, G. (1995). *The crowd: A study of the popular mind.* London: Transaction Publishers. (Original work published in 1895).

Lee, E. J. (2004). Effects of visual representation on social influence in computer-mediated communication. *Human Communication Research 30*, 234–259.

Matheson, K. and Zanna, M. P. (1989). Persuasion as a function of self-awareness in computer-mediated communication. *Social Behaviour 4*, 99–111.

McKenna, K. Y. A. and Bargh, J. A. (2000). Plan 9 from cyberspace: the implications of the Internet for personality and social psychology. *Personality and Social Psychology Review 4*, 57–75.

Oakes, P. J. (1987). The salience of social categories. In J. C. Turner, M. A. Hogg, P. J. Oakes, S. D. Reicher and M. S. Wetherell, *Rediscovering the social group: A self-categorization theory* (pp. 117–141). Oxford: Basil Blackwell.

Postmes, T. and Brunsting, S. (2002). Collective action in the age of internet: mass communication and online mobilization. *Social Science Computer Review 20*, 290–301.

Postmes, T. and Spears, R. (1998). Deindividuation and anti-normative behavior: A meta-analysis. *Psychological Bulletin 123*, 238–259.

Postmes, T. and Spears, R. (2002). Behavior online: does anonymous computer communication reduce gender inequality? *Personality and Social Psychology Bulletin 28*, 1073–1083.

Postmes, T., Spears, R. and Lea, M. (1998). Breaching or building social boundaries? SIDE-effects of computer-mediated communication. *Communication Research 25*, 689–715.

Postmes, T., Spears, R. and Lea, M. (2002). Intergroup differentiation in computer-mediated communication: effects of depersonalization. *Group Dynamics: Theory, Research and Practice 6*, 3–16.

Postmes, T., Spears, R., Lea, A. T. and Novak, R. J. (2005). Individuality and social influence in groups: inductive and deductive routes to group identity. *Journal of Personality and Social Psychology 89*, 747–763.

Postmes, T., Spears, R., Sakhel, K. and De Groot, D. (2001). Social influence in computer-mediated groups: the effects of anonymity on social behavior. *Personality and Social Psychology Bulletin 27*, 1243–1254.

Prentice, D., Miller, D. and Lightdale, J. (1994). Asymmetries in attachments to groups and to their members: distinguishing between common identity and common-bond groups. *Personality and Social Psychology Bulletin 20*, 484–493.

Prentice-Dunn, S. and Rogers, R. W. (1989). Deindividuation and the self-regulation of behavior. In P. B. Paulus (ed.), *The psychology of group influence*, 2nd edn (pp. 86–109). Hillsdale, NJ: Lawrence Erlbaum.

Reicher, S. D. (1984). Social influence in the crowd: attitudinal and behavioural effects of de-individuation in conditions of high and low group salience. Special Issue: Intergroup processes. *British Journal of Social Psychology 23*, 341–350.

Reicher, S. D. (1987). Crowd behaviour as social action. In J. C. Turner, M. A. Hogg, P. J. Oakes, S. D. Reicher and M. S. Wetherell (eds), *Rediscovering the social group: A self-categorization theory* (pp. 171–202). Oxford: Basil Blackwell.

Reicher, S. D. and Levine, M. (1994a). Deindividuation, power relations between groups and the expression of social identity: the effects of visibility to the out-group. *British Journal of Social Psychology 33*, 145–163.

Reicher, S. D. and Levine, M. (1994b). On the consequences of deindividuation manipulations for the strategic considerations of self: identifiability and the presentation of social identity. *European Journal of Social Psychology 24*, 511–524.

Reicher, S. D., Levine, M.and Gordijn, E. (1998). More on deindividuation, power relations between groups and the expression of social identity: three studies on the effects of visibility to the in-group. *British Journal of Social Psychology 37*, 15–40.

Reicher, S. D., Spears, R. and Postmes, T. (1995). A social identity model of deindividuation phenomena. *European Review of Social Psychology 6*, 161–198.

Ridgeway, C. L. and Smith-Lovin, L. (1999). The gender system and interaction. *Annual Review of Sociology 25*, 191–216.

Rogers, P. and Lea, M. (2005). Social presence in distributed group environments: the role of social identity. *Behaviour and Information Technology 24*, 151–158.

Sassenberg, K. (2002). Common-bond and common-identity groups on the Internet: attachment and normative behavior in on-topic and off-topic chats. *Group Dynamics – Theory Research and Practice 6*, 27–37.

Sassenberg, K. and Boos, M. (2003). Attitude change in computer-mediated communication: effects of anonymity and category norms. *Group Processes and Intergroup Relations 6*, 405–422.

Sassenberg, K., Boos, M., & Rabung, S. (2005). Attitude change in face-to-face and computer-mediated communication: Private self-awareness as mediator and moderator. *European Journal of Social Psychology, 35*, 361–374.

Sassenberg, K. and Postmes, T. (2002). Cognitive and strategic processes in small groups: effects of anonymity of the self and anonymity of the group on social influence. *British Journal of Social Psychology 41*, 463–480.

Siegel, J., Dubrovsky, V., Kiesler, S. and McGuire, T. (1986). Group processes in computer-mediated communication. *Organizational Behaviour and Human Decision Processes 37*, 157–187.

Spears, R. and Lea, M. (1992). Social influence and the influence of the 'social' in computer-mediated communication. In M. Lea (ed.), *Contexts of computer-mediated communication.* (pp. 30–65). Hemel-Hempstead: Harvester-Wheatsheaf.

Spears, R. and Lea, M. (1994). Panacea or panopticon? The hidden power in computer-mediated communication. *Communication Research 21*, 427–459.

Spears, R., Lea, M., Corneliussen, R. A., Postmes, T. and Ter Haar, W. (2002b). Computer-mediated communication as a channel for social resistance: the strategic side of SIDE. *Small Group Research 33*, 555–574.

Spears, R., Lea, M. and Lee, S. (1990). De-individuation and group polarization in computer-mediated communication. *British Journal of Social Psychology 29*, 121–134.

Spears, R., Lea, M. and Postmes, T. (2001). Computer-mediated communication: social pain or social gain?. In P. Robinson and H. Giles (eds), *The handbook of language and social psychology* (pp. 601–623). Chichester: Wiley.

Spears, R., Postmes, T., Lea, M. and Wolbert, A. (2002a). When are net effects gross products? The power of influence and the influence of power in computer-mediated communication. *The Journal of Social Issues 58*, 91–107.

Spears, R., Wolbert, A. and De Wolf, M. (in prep). Girls will be boys? Gender dissimulation and the Internet. Unpublished ms, Cardiff University.

Spears, R, Scheepers, D., Jetten, J., Doosje, B., Ellemers, N. and Postmes, T. (2004). Entitativity, group distinctiveness and social identity: getting and using social structure. In V. Yzerbyt, C. M. Judd and O. Corneille (eds), *The psychology of group perception: Contributions to the study of homogeneity, entitativity and essentialism* (pp. 293–316). Philadelphia, PA: Psychology Press.

Tajfel, H. (ed.) (1978). *Differentiation between social groups: Studies in the social psychology of intergroup relations.* London: Academic Press.

Tajfel, H. and Turner J. C. (1986). The social identity theory of intergroup behavior. In S. Worchel and W. G. Austin (eds), *Psychology of intergroup relations* (pp. 7–24). Chicago, IL: Nelson Hall.

Tanis, M. and Postmes, T. (2003). Social cues and impression formation in CMC. *Journal of Communication 53,* 676–693.

Tanis, M. and Postmes, T. (2005). A social identity approach to trust: interpersonal perception, group membership and trusting behavior. *European Journal of Social Psychology 35,* 413–424.

Tanis, M. and Postmes, T. (2006). *Cues to identity in online collaboration.* Manuscript submitted for publication.

Tanis, M. and Postmes, T. (2007). Two faces of anonymity: paradoxical effects of cues to identity in CMC. *Computers in Human Behavior.*

Thomson, R. and Murachver, T. (2001). Predicting gender from electronic discourse. *British Journal of Social Psychology 40,* 193–208.

Tilly, C. (2004). *Social movements, 1768–2004.* Boulder, CO: Paradigm.

Turkle, S. (1995). *Life on the screen: Identity in the age of the internet.* Simon and Schuster: New York.

Turner, J. C. (1982). Towards a cognitive redefinition of the group. In H. Tajfel (ed.), *Social identity and intergroup relations* (pp. 15–40). Cambridge: Cambridge University Press.

Turner, J. C. (1991). *Social influence.* Milton Keynes: Open University Press.

van Gelder, L. (1991). The strange case of the electronic lover. In C. Dunlop & R. Kling (Eds.), *Computerization and controversy: Value conflicts and social choices* (pp.364-375). New York: Boston Academic Press.

Walther, J. B. (1996). Computer-mediated communication: impersonal, interpersonal and hyperpersonal interaction. *Communication Research 23,* 1–43.

Weisband, S. P., Schneider, S. K. and Connolly, T. (1995). Computer-mediated communication and social information: status salience and status differences. *Academy of Management Journal 38,* 1124–1151.

Zimbardo, P. G. (1969). The human choice: individuation, reason, and order vs. deindividuation, impulse and chaos. In W. J. Arnold and D. Levine (eds), *Nebraska Symposium on Motivation,* vol. 17 (pp. 237–307). Lincoln: University of Nebraska Press.

PART 4

Psychological Aspects of Internet Use

CHAPTER 18

Attitude change and social influence on the net

Kai Sassenberg and Kai J. Jonas

ommunication via messengers, email, chats, online-phone calls and online-videoconferes is one of the prime applications of the Internet (Greenspan 2004). Indeed, the use of these means, referred to as computer-mediated communication (CMC), predicts whether Internet newbies stay online or stop using the Internet (Kraut *et al.* 1999) and thus seems to be one of the Internet's key incentives. Any social interaction involves a substantial amount of social influence, as the person initiating communication aims to influence the counterparts the other communication partners to show a certain behaviour (e.g., to answer a question), to influence their attitude (e.g., that online interaction is useful), or simply to inform them (e.g., about a talk by an invited speaker). Social influence can be defined as the influence of a person or a group on an individual's thoughts, actions and physical states. Within this, attitude change is a particular type of social influence. As the Internet restricts the information available about communication partners compared to direct communication, a large body of research addresses social influence on the net.

This chapter summarizes how social influence can be exerted in CMC. Even though most computers are equipped for audio transmission and

beyond, text-based communication is still the most prevalent form of CMC on the Internet (e.g., Jackson *et al.* 2002). Therefore, the focus of research on social influence on the Internet and also of this summary will be on text-based CMC. In many of the studies reviewed here CMC was not studied directly on the Internet, but instead via LAN (a local area network, i.e., in a lab) for the sake of better experimental control. As the general features of CMC do not differ depending on whether it takes place on the Internet or in a LAN, results from research using LAN clearly speak to the topic of social influence on the net as well.

More specifically, this chapter outlines research on short-term effects of CMC on attitudes and behaviour, rather than on long-term effects of social influence (i.e., changes in users' identity, see Chapter 17 in this volume). This will be done by first presenting a model of three types of social influence that can be discerned in groups, representing the current state of research on social influence. Subsequently, the characteristics of CMC relevant to social influence are described and related to this model. Following this, classical and contemporary research is reviewed. The final section outlines a model summarizing the knowledge on social influence in CMC and identifies topics for further research.

Types of social influence

An in-depth analysis of the impact of CMC on social influence presupposes a clear-cut idea of what social influence is. In research on social influence, a classic distinction between two types of social influence is being made (for an overview see Wood 1999). Deutsch and Gerard (1955) suggested distinguishing social influence resulting from 'normative' needs from social influence resulting from 'informational' needs. When the influence is based on normative needs, individuals comply with the influence to conform with other people's expectations. People who are influenced for informational reasons are motivated by validity concerns. There is a long tradition of modifications concerning this dual distinction (e.g., Moscovici 1985), and as many authors have pointed out, Deutsch and Gerard's (1955) concept of normative influence actually refers to *compliance* (e.g., Allen 1965).

Deutsch and Gerard's (1955) definition of informational influence has also been questioned. Importantly, some informational influence is based on group-normative processes, and some have argued this needs to be considered as a separate form of influence. This perspective has been advanced in social identity theory (Tajfel and Turner 1979) and self-categorization theory (Turner *et al.* 1987). These theories suggest that the self-concept consists of a personal identity and (many different) social identities. Personal identity refers to those aspects of individuals' self-concepts which define them as idiosyncratic individuals. Social identities are those elements of individuals' self-concepts which they derive from membership in social groups. By means of their social identities individuals internalize characteristics of the groups to which they belong (i.e., their norms), and are in turn influenced by those groups and their norms in their behaviour and thinking. Such norm-based influence however is not due to conformity to social pressure from the group, but a result of self-determined action undertaken by individuals as members of their group. According to the social identity approach, these normative processes related to social identity affect all our interactions with in- and out-group members: Opinions and arguments in line with in-group norms are seen as more valid than those differing from them (Turner 1991).

In other words: other in-group members' attitudes serve as standards for validity judgments (i.e., they are considered more seriously) and can therefore elicit informational influence. Sassenberg *et al.* (2005) labelled this type of social influence *norm-based influence*.

However, social influence also takes place for purely informational reasons. This is likely to occur when personal identity is salient (i.e., people perceive themselves as distinct individuals and not as members of a group). It has been argued that individuals influence each other more strongly the closer their interpersonal bonds are (Postmes and Spears 2000; Sassenberg and Boos 2003) and that social influence is also driven by individuals' striving for distinctiveness from the communication partners and by their attempt to fulfil other personal needs when personal identity is salient (Spears *et al.* 1990). To summarize, when personal identity is salient, personal needs channel how relevant others are used as sources of social validation of information. This kind of (informational) social influence under a salient personal identity can be labelled *interpersonal influence*.

In sum, three forms of social influence can be distinguished: compliance, norm-based influence, and interpersonal influence. The distinction between these three types of social influence provides the basis for understanding *social influence* in CMC, but what are the special properties of the medium that have made the study of social influence in CMC into a research domain in its own right? The next section will discuss these properties as relevant to social influence.

Characteristics of CMC

To understand the effects of CMC on social influence, it is essential to first of all identify the characteristics of this communication mode that might alter the way in which influence is exerted in the first place. There are three contextual features that differ between CMC and face-to-face (ftf) communication and that are especially relevant concerning social influence (Spears and Lea 1994):

◆ *Anonymity*: Messages received in CMC are, at least to some extent, more anonymous than they are in ftf communication. Even though names, email addresses, or nicknames reveal a lot about the identity of the sender, many sources of information about the communication partners that we might (unconsciously or consciously) use in our interpretation and processing of their messages remain unknown in CMC. One of the main sources of information that we rely on a lot in ftf interaction is non-verbal communication (language use, facial expressions, posture, gesture, etc.) and appearance. The hyperpersonal communication model (Walther 1996) as well as the social identity model of deindividuation effects (SIDE) (Spears and Lea 1992, 1994; Reicher et al. 1995; Postmes et al. 1998) suggest that, due to anonymity, users of CMC typically have less access to information about their communication partners. In turn, each of the remaining social cues has a stronger impact.

◆ *Identifiability*: The reduced transfer of information is not restricted to messages that are received, but it also applies (in a potentially different way) to sent messages. In other words, in CMC people are less identifiable than in ftf communication. If they become aware of this fact, they will also feel less identifiable and as a result fear the consequences of their actions less (Reicher and Levine 1994 a, b). This in turn cannot only lead to uninhibited presentations of the actual self, but also to strategic and unrealistic presentations of the self (Walther 1996).

◆ *Physical isolation*: A feature that CMC shares with all other media is that it allows communicators to be physically isolated – from each other, but also from other people. Above and beyond anonymity and low identifiability, which are outcomes of the physical isolation, physical isolation can also have direct and independent effects on the psychological state. In physical isolation, for example, attention can be directed freely towards the self or any object of interest, relatively independently of others' efforts to attract or retain that attention. As a result, in CMC attention is more likely to be directed to the self. Research has indeed shown that private self-awareness – i.e., a focus on thoughts, feelings, and perceptions (Prentice-Dunn and Rogers 1982) increases in CMC compared to ftf communication

(Franke 1997; Matheson and Zanna 1998, 1999; Joinson 2001; Sassenberg et al. 2005).

All these contextual features are present in different forms of text-based CMC and to a certain extent they are also shared by other forms of CMC, even though these characteristics become less important the more communication channels are included in the media. In what follows, the impact of these features (especially anonymity and identifiability) will be discussed in a relative and not in an absolute sense (e.g. more vs. less anonymous instead of anonymous vs. non-anonymous). Thereby we refer to communication as being 'anonymous' when communication in one situation is comparatively more anonymous than in another. Thus, this terminology is not intended to convey absolute anonymity, if only because we take for granted that this does not exist. We now give a short summary of the classic theoretical perspectives on social influence in CMC, before reviewing the research that has examined these characteristics of CMC.

Classic approaches to social influence in CMC

The classic theories of CMC and mediated communication neither differentiated between the types of social influence, nor did they discuss the role of specific features of CMC. These approaches share the overarching assumption that media have straightforward effects on social influence: The restrictions a medium imposes on the information exchange will impair users' abilities in one way or the other (e.g., by undermining interpersonal relations).

The first influential and systematic programme of research that studied how mediated communication (in this case via telephone or intercom) affected social influence led to the formulation of the *social presence model* (Short et al. 1976), according to which the critical factor that determines the social impact of mediated compared to direct communication is 'social presence'. Social presence was defined as the degree of acoustic, visual and physical contact that a medium allows. According to the social presence model, an increase in social presence will lead to increased social influence. In their research Short *et al.* (1976) found that ftf inter-actions are characterized by stronger perceived social presence compared to television, tele-phone and business letters. In line with these findings, CMC should be characterized by less perceived social presence than ftf communica-tion, and therefore be less conducive to social influence (Spears and Lea 1992). However, Short's own findings contradicted the social presence model (for a summary see Spears and Lea [1992]) as he found more social influence between people who communicated via intercom compared to ftf communication. This disconfirmation of the social presence model called for a re-start in the development of models about the impact of media use on social influence. Additionally, it provided a first indication that media character-istics do not have straightforward effects on social influence, as the overarching assumption of the early approaches suggest.

Subsequently, Rutter *et al.* (1987) criticized the social presence model not only based on Short's findings, but also for considering social presence to be an attribute of a medium, even though the assessment of this construct rather captured a psychological consequence. Nonetheless, his own *cuelessness model* (Rutter 1984, 1987) had much overlap with Short's approach. Cuelessness was originally defined as an information-based con-cept: The lower the number of social cues trans-mitted by the medium, the more *cueless* it was (Rutter *et al.* 1987). Rutter (1987) assumed that cuelessness does not simply reduce the amount of communication, but that it principally reduces aspects of communication that are socially ori-ented (cf. Bales 1950), and much less so those aspects that are task-oriented. Due to the greater transfer of task-oriented information resulting from the cuelessness of media, social influence in the task-domain was expected to increase during the media use. Comparing certain media (mostly intercom and ftf communication), the predic-tions of the cuelessness model about social influ-ence were supported by Short's and Rutter's work (for a summary see Rutter 1987). For CMC – being even more cueless than intercom commu-nication – the cuelessness model implies that, compared to ftf communication, it should lead to more social influence, and that this is because CMC is a less socio-emotional and even more task-oriented form of communication.

Although this was a powerful suggestion, picked up, amongst others, by media richness the-ory (Daft and Lengel 1984), there was not much support for it in CMC research. Contrary to cuelessness predictions, CMC has been found to sustain very high levels of socio-emotional communication, and to be not nearly as task-oriented as some expected (Myers 1987; Finholt and Sproull 1990; Wilkins 1991; Walther 1992, 1995, 1996; Lea and Spears 1995; Utz 2000, 2003; Joinson 2001. A meta-analysis indicated that compared to ftf communication CMC is neither task-oriented nor socio-emotional ori-ented per se (Walther *et al.* 1994). Hence, the dif-ferences in social influence between CMC and ftf communication cannot be explained from the cuelessness model, because the process lead-ing to social influence (i.e., less socio-emotional communication) does not map on to the effects of CMC on the communication content.

The most-cited classic theory of social influ-ence in CMC has become known as the *reduced social cues approach* (RSC) (Kiesler *et al.* 1984; Siegel *et al.* 1986; McGuire *et al.* 1987; Dubrovsky *et al.* 1991; Sproull and Kiesler 1991), which integrated many of the ideas of the approaches mentioned already (see Spears and Lea [1992] for a review). It assumed that CMC would lead to less self-awareness and, therefore, to more anti-normative, extreme, and disinhibited behaviour (Kiesler *et al.* 1984). Polarizing atti-tudes in computer-mediated discussions were considered one form of such extreme behaviour. Hence, RSC assumed that in CMC (compared to ftf communication) less social influence would occur in terms of societal norms, but also that more attitude change would occur. Some early studies supported this prediction (e.g., Kiesler *et al.* 1984; Siegel *et al.* 1986), but con-trary to RSC predictions others did not find support (e.g., Weisband 1992) or showed effects contrary to the predictions (McGuire *et al.* 1987).

More problematic for the assumptions of RSC is that there is no evidence that CMC reduces self-awareness. Actually, the physical isolation in CMC leads to increased levels of pri-vate self-awareness (see above). Moreover, there is no consistent evidence for more extreme behaviour in CMC (Lea *et al.* 1992). In sum, RSC does neither provide an adequate explanation of social influence in CMC, nor do its predictions hold. However, at a conceptual level it set the stage for a better understanding of media effects. One lasting contribution of RSC has been that it made researchers realize that to understand social effects of CMC, social influence is pivotal. Another has been its suggestion that CMC changes the relation between the self and the environment, which in turn results in changed perceptions of self and others. Finally, RSC has for the first time separated media characteristics and their psychological consequences as two distinct theoretical elements that are both essential ingredients of any explanation of the social impact of communication media. All in all, the specifics of the RSC may have been wrong, but it highlighted many of the important theoretical building blocks that were groundbreaking for more resent research, summarized in the current chapter.

In sum, classic approaches to social influence in CMC failed to conclusively identify the psychological processes that are triggered by CMC and that in turn foster or hamper social influence. Moreover, these early approaches did not build on a coherent and theoretically informed analysis of what social influence in groups entails. The remainder of this chapter will focus on more resent research and theorizing, which has increasingly included both the critical characteristics of CMC and the different forms of social influence in its analyses.

The state of the art in research on social influence in CMC

What can be predicted about the impact of anonymity, low identifiability, and physical isolation in CMC, on the three forms of social influence summarized above? As mentioned above, models such as SIDE and the hyperpersonal perspective propose that the relative anonymity (or lack of cues) in CMC increases the value attached to the remaining information (i.e., each bit of information receives more attention). These perspectives are very similar in many regards, but SIDE is concerned more with social influence, and indeed has become a dominant framework for the study of social influence in CMC. Therefore, this review largely

focuses on the body of research that has investigated its predictions.

SIDE (Spears and Lea 1992, 1994) considers not just what information is visible 'out there', but what information is cognitively attended to ('in here'). It suggests that the social categorization of the self and other group members as different individuals (i.e., when personal identities are salient) or as members of social groups (i.e., when social identities are salient) is a key factor guiding social influence processes. In communications in which personal identity is initially salient, individual needs and attitudes related to them are more important and will be accentuated in CMC compared with ftf communication. Conversely, when social identity is initially salient, the impact of social factors is amplified in CMC and thus attitudes will be oriented to a larger degree towards group norms. In other words: SIDE predicts that when personal identity is salient, CMC (compared with ftf interaction) will lead to less social influence, and that when social identity is salient, CMC will lead to an increase in normative social influence, understood as a form of autonomous self-expression. Hence, anonymity impacts on norm-based and interpersonal influence.

In 1995, SIDE was extended to consider the third kind of social influence discerned above, conformity (Reicher et al. 1995). In SIDE's analysis, conformity to another's expectations is not affected by anonymity (the ability of me to see them) but by identifiability (the ability of them to see me). The low identifiability in CMC will most likely lead to a decrease in conformity – offering the subject greater strategic freedoms for resistance of social pressure. Thus, identifiability is relevant for conformity but not for interpersonal or norm-based influence.

Regarding the third characteristic of CMC, physical isolation, SIDE has not distinguished its effects from identifiability and anonymity empirically, nor has it been a core concern theoretically. Spears and Lea (1994) suggested that isolation leads to heightened private self-awareness. Therefore, it might be relevant for those types of influence that are based on the self: interpersonal influence (because the personal self is especially relevant for this type of influence) and norm-based influence (because the social self is especially relevant for this type of influence).

We will therefore review the impact of physical isolation in relation to both of these types of social influence.

Norm-based influence

The impact of anonymity

Spears et al. (1990) were the first to address the impact of anonymity in CMC on norm-based influence. They developed a paradigm that was applied with slight alterations in most of the studies on norm-based influence in CMC. In this paradigm, before members of a joint social category discussed a set of political judgements in groups of three, they received feedback about the mean attitudes of the members of this social category (i.e., the norm of the joint social category). In one condition social identity was salient, whereas in the other condition personal identity was salient. The first condition is relevant here, because it studied norm-based influence (for a discussion of the second condition studying interpersonal influence see the next section). Independent of the social categorization the communication condition was varied: the groups either discussed in anonymous or in non-anonymous CMC. Participants' attitudes towards the political topics were measured before and after the discussion to assess attitude change. The results supported the predictions derived from SIDE: participants showed more attitude change towards the group norm in anonymous compared to non-anonymous CMC. This basic finding (i.e., higher levels of anonymity lead to more norm-based influence when social identity is salient) has been replicated several times using different manipulations of anonymity, various forms of CMC, and different measures of social influence (for overviews see Postmes et al. 1998; Spears et al. 2001, 2002).

Postmes et al. (2001), for example, used the same paradigm as Spears et al. (1990) in a social welfare context. They manipulated the group norm by activating different goals (efficient vs. pro-social) in an ostensibly unrelated task before the group discussions took place. In line with their predictions, participants in anonymous CMC more often came to a decision in line with the activated norm and used more words that were related to this norm (compared to participants in non-anonymous CMC). In a second study, the norm was only activated in half of the group members. Again more attitude change towards the group norm and more communication content consistent with this norm was found in the anonymous condition for both participants who had received a norm-activating treatment and also for those who did not receive this treatment. These findings demonstrate that group members in anonymous CMC adhere more strongly to the norm of an interacting group by means of their communication content and their attitudes, independent of whether they personally know about the norm before the discussion or not.

The underlying process

Postmes et al. (2001) found evidence for the processes that SIDE proposes underlie the impact of anonymity on norm-based influence (see also Lea et al. 2001): anonymity increased the salience of the social categorization and that in turn lead to more norm-based influence. In their studies, the impact of anonymity on norm adherence was indeed mediated by social identification with the ad hoc group (i.e., an indicator of social identity salience). This can be contrasted with private self-awareness, which does not appear to impact on norm-based influence. For example, private self-awareness could not be shown to explain influence effects in either comparisons of anonymous vs. identified CMC (Postmes et al. 2001) or in comparisons of ftf versus CMC discussions (Matheson and Zanna 1989). In sum, anonymity and the salience of social identity seem to be the most important factors for norm-based influence in CMC, consistent with predictions of the SIDE model. Physical isolation leading to heightened private self-awareness does not seem to be an important factor for norm-based influence in CMC.

Preconditions for norm-based influence

The importance of the a-priori existence of an unambiguous group norm has been demonstrated by Sassenberg and Boos (2003; see also Waldzus and Schubert 2000). In their studies, which also used an attitude change paradigm, more social influence was only found in anonymous CMC (compared to non-anonymous CMC and ftf communication) when social identity was salient *and* participants were informed about the norm attached to the social category providing the basis for this social identity. When no norm was provided, anonymity did not impact on social influence (compared to non-anonymous CMC) or even lead to less social influence (compared to ftf communication), despite social identity being salient. In sum, anonymity only increases social influence in CMC when the group norm is known (at least to a substantial part of the group) and the respective social identity is salient. Both are prerequisites for norm-based influence.

The extent of norm-based influence in CMC and the impact of anonymity on this type of influence not only depends on the existence of a group norm, but also on the type of group. Social identity theory and SIDE focus (as indicated by their names) on groups that are contributing to their members' social identity. Prentice *et al.* (1994) distinguished these so-called common identity groups from common bond groups. Common identity groups stick together because group members feel strong ties to the group as a whole, whereas common bond groups are held together because their members have strong interpersonal ties (e.g., as in peer groups). For members of common identity groups norms are very important because they are part of the self-image and therefore norm-based influence is very likely to occur. In contrast, for members of common bond groups the group and its norms are not a part of their identity. Hence, norm-based influence is not very likely to occur in these groups.

Sassenberg (2002) has shown that both types of groups exist on the Internet. Chats set up to discuss a certain topic (e.g., a specific software) fit the criteria for common identity groups (so-called on-topic chats), while chats serving as a forum to get to know other people fit the criteria for common bond groups (so-called off-topic chats). In on-topic chats the adherence to group norms (i.e., the use of similar smileys and acronyms by members of one group) is, as expected, higher than in off-topic chats. This difference is due to the higher social identification with on-topic compared to off-topic chats. To get an idea of how these norms might develop online see Graham (2003) and Postmes *et al.* (2000).

In line with the idea that norm-based influence is fostered by anonymity in CMC, Postmes

and Spears (2000) found that social influence in anonymous CMC (compared to non-anonymous CMC) was higher in common identity groups. However, in common bond groups anonymity led to a decrease in social influence. This decrease is most likely based on interpersonal influence and will therefore be discussed in the next section. In sum, norm-based influence and its increase due to conditions of anonymity is restricted to common identity groups and does not occur in common bond groups.

Intragroup uniformity and intergroup differentiation

The findings summarized so far suggest that anonymous CMC leads to more agreement (i.e., similar attitudes of group members) when social identity is salient. Other studies even suggest that statements indicating agreement by not expressing a deviant opinion and sticking to the topic are driving the norm-based influence in the group process (e.g., Sassenberg and Postmes 2002). At the same time, however, anonymity also increases the risk of intergroup conflict, as Postmes *et al.* (2002) have shown. They used an attitude change paradigm but allowed two groups to discuss the same topic at a time. They found more norm-based influence within each of the groups in anonymous discussions, but differences in attitudes between the two groups increased more due to anonymous than due to non-anonymous discussion settings. This effect results from the tendency of groups and their members to differentiate themselves from other groups (Haslam *et al.* 1998). Hence, anonymity increases the likelihood that members of a group stick to their norm and therefore show stronger agreement within the group during CMC discussions. Disagreement between groups, however, becomes more pronounced in anonymous than in non-anonymous discussions.

Most of the studies summarized in this section address norm-based influence in terms of attitude change. Exceptions are Postmes *et al.* (2001) and Sassenberg (2002), who also report differences in communication content and style resulting from norm-based influence. Additional evidence for norm-based influence on a behavioural levels stems from Lea and Spears (1991), who found stronger norm-based influence in anonymous CMC co-occurred with fewer messages and greater equality in participation, indicating that less disagreement occurred in these groups. Moreover, Postmes and Spears (2002) showed at the intergroup level (similar as Postmes *et al.* 2002 summarized above) that anonymity in CMC can also impact on the social influence target person's attempt to *exert* influence: when gender stereotypes (i.e., gender norms) are activated males tend to dominate in anonymous communication, but only if the communication is about stereotypic male topics. Here the males follow the group norms when the gender categorization is especially salient. Hence, they exert social influence by being dominant as a result of norm-based influence (i.e., in line with stereotypically male norms). Overall, these studies show that norm-based influence resulting from anonymity increases the display to attitudes and behaviour that are in line with group norms. Thus, within-groups assimilation and between-groups differentiation takes place.

Summary

Taken together, anonymous group discussions in CMC (compared to non-anonymous group discussions) lead to more norm-based influence when a shared social identity is salient and when group members share the same unambiguous perception of the group norm. As past research has demonstrated, this pattern of greater norm-based influence in anonymous CMC is not restricted to attitude change, but it also occurs for intragroup agreement, discussion content, and communication behaviour. The effect of anonymity on norm-based influence is mediated by social identity salience instead of by self-awareness. In intergroup discussions, however, the stronger norm-based influence in anonymous CMC (compared to non-anonymous CMC) leads to an accentuation of the disagreement between groups. So far, research has not directly addressed the impact of physical isolation on norm-based influence.

Interpersonal influence

The impact of anonymity

SIDE was not only very influential in the domain of norm-based influence; it also made predictions about interpersonal influence that inspired research in this domain. Research originally assumed that anonymous interaction in CMC will lead to less adherence to group norms when personal identity (compared to social identity) of the interaction partners is salient, because under this condition group members will seek to differentiate themselves as individuals from the collective (cf. Spears *et al.* 1990). Moreover, in anonymous CMC interaction partners with a salient personal identity tend to show less interpersonal influence then when personal identity is salient and the others are not anonymous. This is due to the fact that anonymity increases the salience of personal identity (just as it increases the salience of social identity) and in turn leads the interacting individuals to stick to their personal thoughts and individual needs (Spears and Lea 1992). It might be added to this prediction of SIDE that anonymous CMC also reduces interpersonal influence when personal identity is salient, because it is harder to establish and maintain interpersonal bonds in anonymous communication. Thus, the better the interpersonal relation is, the more interpersonal influence can be exerted.

In the study summarized above, Spears *et al.* (1990) found support for these predictions concerning social influence: less attitude change towards the group norm was found in anonymous CMC when personal identity was salient both compared to when social identity was salient and also when personal identity was salient in non-anonymous communication (for similar findings see Sassenberg and Boos [2003]). A closer analysis of the communication in this study supported the prediction that the processes underlying the impact of anonymity on interpersonal influence are in line with the assumptions of SIDE. Compared to non-anonymous groups participants in anonymous CMC insisted more on their personal views, which is indicated by a higher number of remarks, longer remarks and more equal participation within the group (Lea and Spears 1991). Overall these results confirm that interpersonal influence under conditions of anonymity is reduced, because individuals are more aware of their personal needs, and this appears to obstruct the ability to exert effective interpersonal influence.

A factor promoting interpersonal influence in CMC has been demonstrated by studies of the so-called 'foot-in-the-door' phenomenon: interpersonal relations. The number of people answering positively to an email request asking for participation in a long questionnaire was much higher when targets where first asked to complete a short questionnaire and the long questionnaire was presented in a second request, than when they were immediately requested to answer the long questionnaire (Guéguen and Jacob 2001, 2002; Guéguen 2002). Hence, the relationship which was established by means of the short questionnaire helped to exert more interpersonal influence. In a similar vein, Postmes and Spears (2000) found less attitude change in newly formed common bond groups (i.e., groups sticking together, because of interpersonal bonds) when the group members remained anonymous compared to when they were not anonymous. Members of common bond groups felt that they were more able to form an impression of non-anonymous group members (a prerequisite to form a relationship). Hence, more interpersonal influence co-occurs with the option to form or the existence of interpersonal relations (such as low anonymity or a foot in the door).

The impact of status differences

Another way to approach interpersonal influence in CMC is to study whether and how status differences within the interaction group, existing naturally beforehand or implemented prior to the communication, impact on the communication and its outcome. If status differences have less impact in CMC than in ftf communication this would indicate reduced influence based on personal characteristics (i.e., interpersonal influence). It has often been reported that status differences are equalized in CMC, at least in terms of the proportion of communication (e.g., Zigurs et al. 1988; Dubrovsky et al. 1991; Strauss 1996). Even individuals newly joining an existing CMC discussion do not appear to suffer in their ability to equally participate (Thompson and Coovert 2002). However, more recent research has found that interaction partners seen as experts in terms of task-relevant knowledge (i.e., high in status) are given more space during information exchange and are regarded as useful sources of information (Sassenberg et al. 2001). Taken together, status differences in CMC are equalized when they are considered irrelevant to the discussion topic. However, research also suggests that status can be *more* pronounced when it is relevant within the context

of the discussion (e.g., Weisband 1992; Postmes et al. 2002). These effects most likely are also an outcome of the scarce information available on the communication partners resulting from anonymity in CMC.

Most of the time the equalization of irrelevant status information as well as the 'hyper-accessibility' of relevant status information in CMC is advantageous because the reduction of task-irrelevant status effects in CMC allows interaction partners with a lower status a fair share in the discussion. Hence, their possibly valuable contributions are not hindered by irrelevant status differences. On the other hand, when status differences are relevant for the discussion, specific expert information particularly relevant for the correct decision will receive the necessary attention. Nonetheless, it should be noted that there is a risk that illegitimate but relevant (perceived) status differences can cause differences in individuals' impact on both group discussion and group products, potentially reducing the quality of group work.

Agreement in CMC

Additionally, the equalization and the scarce information about communication partners in CMC bears another risk: coming to an agreement has proven to be more difficult in CMC than in ftf interaction. Insufficient mutual representations of information and others opinions were originally held responsible for this (Hiltz et al. 1987). However, the focus on personal needs in an interpersonal context might also contribute to this effect. Solutions for this problem have been suggested mostly at a technical level, for example by allowing for many-to-many linkages and mutual representations through electronic voting (Whihworth et al. 2001). Negotiations are major field of application of research on interpersonal influence in CMC for which such technical solutions have proven to be helpful (Morris et al. 2002; for a review see Thompson and Nadler [2002]). Overall, it is harder to reach an agreement and to resolve conflicts of interest in CMC, but tools helping are available that help to solve this problem.

Physical isolation

The second media characteristic that might impact on interpersonal influence is physical isolation. Even though it is experimentally hard to disentangle from anonymity and identifiability, it can be inferred from the existing research that physical isolation has an impact on the psychological state of participants that is independent of anonymity: on the one hand, research has shown that CMC heightens private self-awareness compared to ftf communication (Matheson and Zanna 1988, 1989; Joinson 2001; Sassenberg *et al.* 2005). On the other hand, anonymity and identifiability do not impact on private self-awareness (Postmes and Spears 1998; Postmes *et al.* 2001). Physical isolation could be a prime candidate to account for this increase in private self-awareness (see also above).

We know from other research that such effects on private self-awareness are relevant to the effects of communication media on attitude change. Private self-awareness is known to hinder social influence (Scheier 1980; Froming and Carver 1981). Studies of interpersonal interaction in CMC (compared with ftf interaction) confirm that private self-awareness plays a role, too. Sassenberg *et al.* (2005) found a mediation by situational variations of private self-awareness and a moderating impact of trait private self-awareness: First, the impact of the communication medium on interpersonal influence (less attitude change in CMC than in ftf communication) was mediated by situational variations of private self-awareness. Secondly, interpersonal differences in private self-awareness moderated the impact of the communication medium on interpersonal influence: Interpersonal influence is only stronger in ftf compared to CMC for individuals high in trait private self-awareness. Taken together, physical isolation in CMC reduces interpersonal influence by increasing levels of private self-awareness that is situationally induced. Chronic differences in private self-awareness moderate the impact of the communication media on interpersonal influence.

Person-communication match

The relevance of individual differences for social influence in CMC is also apparent in research from another tradition. This research leads us back to the impact of anonymity and points simultaneously to the importance of several specific communication characteristics and to the context in which interpersonal influence is exerted. In a study on the moderating impact of gender on the influence of single persuasive messages on attitudes Guadagno and Cialdini (2002, Study 1) found that females show less attitude change from emails than from ftf communication, whereas males changed their attitudes to the same extent in both media. Similar gender differences also occurred for social influence on behaviour. Male subjects agreed more readily to a request asking them to participate in an online survey when the solicitor (i.e., an individual with a persuasive motive) was female and non-anonymous, whereas females did not show this heightened readiness to non-anonymous mail, regardless of the solicitors' gender (Guéguen and Jacob 2002).

More recent research suggests that not the interindividual differences per se but the match between an individual's attributes and the communication medium and style fosters attitude change. Messages in a communication style matching the target's gender (i.e., 'cooperative' for females and 'independent' for males) do not lead to media differences in attitude change. Males have been found to be influenced more in CMC than in ftf communication, because communication via CMC generally has an independent style (Guadagno and Cialdini 2002, Study 2).

Similarly, Luna *et al.* (2003) found that websites in a second language with simple messages exert more social influence than those with complex messages. In contrast, websites in a first language with complex messages elicit more influence than if they have messages. In other words: the match between the communication style on the one hand and the target of communication on the other hand is an important precondition for interpersonal influence. Higher levels of interpersonal influence will occur, the more there is a match between the communication style and the target of a message (e.g., high complexity fits high competence).

Summary

Taken together, anonymity and physical isolation both reduce interpersonal influence by heightening the focus on personal needs and private self-awareness; the communication–recipient match, good interpersonal relations, and relevant status differences facilitate interpersonal influence in CMC as in any other form of communication.

One might form the impression from all this that interpersonal influence is difficult to achieve in CMC, but we want to close this section by reporting a phenomenon demonstrating that despite some barriers to interpersonal influence, very strong social forces can be at work in CMC, too. A prime example is ostracism on the Web – the effects of being ignored during CMC interaction (Williams *et al.* 2000). The experimental paradigm is as follows: while playing a virtual tossing game, ostensibly with two other players, a target person suddenly does not receive the ball anymore. Participants undergoing this silent treatment online felt bad, had a feeling of loss of control, and a reduced sense of belonging (Study 1). Additionally, they showed more compliance in a subsequent task (Study 2). Hence, resulting from this minimal treatment a strong interpersonal influence can already be achieved.

Compliance

The characteristic of CMC that has been considered most relevant for compliance is the (low) identifiability of the self. According to SIDE, identifiability raises strategic concerns, while a lack of it creates strategic possibilities (Spears and Lea 1994; Reicher *et al.* 1995). If individuals are less identifiable, they are less likely to be held back by the judgement of others, and are less likely to adjust their opinions and/or behaviours to avoid sanctions. Conversely, greater identifiability to a person or group who have sanctioning power is likely to lead to conformity with their norms and expectations. Contrary to this overall trend, however, some research has shown that individuals not only show compliance to a larger extent, but they also compensate for this 'sell-out' by emphasizing those elements of their (personal or social) identity that they can not be sanctioned for (Reicher and Levine 1996).

Early studies showed that CMC reduces compliance to others (e.g., Smilowitz *et al.* 1988). The explanation for this phenomenon at the time was that the bad computer network quality in the early days of CMC reduced the social presence of interaction partners, but this work

did not examine issues of personal and social identity.

More recent research has demonstrated effects that are consistent with predictions derived from the (strategic) SIDE model, showing that the impact of identifiability on compliance occurs on several levels of self-categorization. In an interpersonal context, choices made in dilemmas more often followed the unanimous vote given by others when the responses were given in public compared to votes given in private (Lee and Nass 2002, Study 1). In an intergroup context group members used more stereotype-consistent language while describing members of an outgroup when they were identifiable to their own group than when they were not (Douglas and McGarty 2001, 2002, Study 1). Furthermore, Sassenberg and Kreutz (2002) showed that objects were more often evaluated in line with outgroup expectations under increasing identifiability to this group (Study 2). However, identifiability does not increase compliance when support from the own group is available (Spears *et al.* 2002). Finally, Sassenberg and Postmes (2002, Study 2) reported evidence for the strategic communication of one's personal identity in CMC. Their participants stressed their individual distinctiveness by switching the topic more often, when they were identifiable to the group compared to when they were not.

Taken together, research on compliance in CMC shows that recipients of social pressure are quite likely to give in to the demand and express their identity on dimensions that most likely do not lead to sanctions as compensation. This effect does not occur when social support is available.

Summary and future perspectives

CMC provides a specific setting for social influence because of its characteristics: anonymity of others, low identifiability of the self, and physical isolation. Each of these characteristics is evident to some extent in CMC, certainly when looking at its most-used forms (email, messaging, chat). Of course, there are huge differences between different forms of CMC, and correspondingly factors such as anonymity and identifiability can be present more or less depending on the CMC system under observation. Nonetheless, compared with ftf communication at least, all these characteristics remain an appropriate description of even the most life-like form of CMC. As reviewed above, anonymity, identifiability, and physical isolation have different psychological consequences, namely increased salience of self-categorization, heightened accountability and stronger private self-awareness, respectively. Therefore, they impact differently on the three main forms of social influence: norm-based influence exerted by the own group, interpersonal influence exerted by individual others and compliance to powerful others. Increasing anonymity fosters norm-based influence and hinders interpersonal influence. Identifiability leads to an increase in compliance (i.e., CMC leads to less compliance than ftf communication), and physical isolation also leads to less interpersonal influence (see also Table 18.1).

Even though the current state of the art in research on social influence in CMC allows for the predictions summarized above, evidence for some aspects of CMC's impact on social influence is more substantial than for others. Especially in the field of interpersonal influence, there is a lack of research that ties together loose ends of existing findings. On the one hand, it is known that anonymity and physical isolation in CMC make it hard to exert interpersonal influence. On the other hand, research has shown that relations can be built up online and, therefore,

very strong interpersonal influence can result from CMC. Hence, further research should study under which conditions interpersonal influence occurs in CMC and by doing so extend knowledge about restricting factors. Important classes of variables for such research endeavours are interindividual differences in needs (e.g., the need for affiliation) and other traits.

Another field in which additional research is necessary pertains to the distinction between anonymity, identifiability, and physical isolation that was already made by Spears and Lea as far back as 1994. In many cases (including in the research of Spears, Lea and their co-workers) these media characteristics have been assessed in a confounded manner – in particular, the effects of physical isolation have not been studied systematically, yet. Moreover, one might argue that anonymity and identifiability have different effects depending on whether they are currently given in a communication situation or have been present on a long-term basis.

The overview provided above demonstrates at least two limitations of this field of research. First, research is somewhat fragmented and mostly follows a static approach to studying social influence and attitude change. Therefore, dynamic and more integrated models of social influence that have been presented very recently (Postmes *et al.* 2005) should be applied to social influence on the net, too. Second, great effort has been made to study the three forms of social

Table 18.1 The impact of CMC compared to ftf communication on norm-based influence, interpersonal influence, and compliance for relevant media characteristics and psychological variables

	Source of influence	CMC (compared to ftf)	Media characteristic	Psychological mediator	Preconditions
Norm-based influence	Own group	More	Anonymity	Salience of social identity	Shared norm, social self-categorisation, common identity group
Interpersonal influence	Liked other(s)	Less	Anonymity (a) Physical Isolation (b)	Salience of personal identity (a) Private self-awareness (b)	Good relationship, personal identity salient
Compliance	Powerful other(s)	Less	Low identifiability	Accountability	No support from own group, risk of sanctioning

influence separately. However, in real world settings, they might all act simultaneously. Thus, it would be very valuable to learn more about their interplay.

Somewhat related, one might object that the current conclusions are mostly based on experimental work that was partly conducted in the lab. Certainly, replications of the findings in field studies would help to warrant generalization. Indeed, many of the findings reported here have been replicated (or originally found) in field settings. Moreover, the reported research (as all lab research) can only demonstrate relations between variables that exist. The questions that await empirical answers concern the topic of how important these phenomena are (i.e., in terms of the size of their effects) in specific field contexts, and relative to other factors. A research programme analysing the (change in) all three forms of social influence over a longer course of time including the use of different modes of communication (e.g., the change between text-based CMC and ftf communication) would provide valuable answers to these questions.

A final limitation to the research presented in this chapter might be that it cannot keep up with and reflect the latest trends in client and server software development. Indeed, psychological publications on a topic such as the Internet can never fully keep up with the speed of innovation in this domain, because of the time needed for the development of models and hypotheses, the conduction of studies, the writing up and finally the publication process. However, in our opinion the approach taken here allows us to circumvent this problem almost completely. Based on the set of dimensions presented here, on which each new form of CMC can be classified (anonymity, identifiability and physical isolation), predictions for the likelihood of the different forms of social influence in new forms of CMC can be derived. Hence, the strength of the current approach is to utilize the persistence of psychological processes tied to media characteristics to make predictions that are flexible enough to cope with rapid technological changes.

References

Allen, V. L. (1965). Situational factors in conformity. In L. Berkowitz (ed.), *Advances in experimental social psychology*, vol. 2 (pp. 133–175). New York: Academic Press.

Bales, R. F. (1950). *Interaction process analysis: A method for the study of small groups*. Chicago, IL: Chicago University Press.

Daft, R. L. and Lengel, R. H. (1984). Information richness: a new approach to managerial behavior and organization design. In B. Staw and L. L. Cummings (eds), *Research in organizational behavior*, vol. 6 (pp. 191–233). Greenwich, CT: JAI Press.

Deutsch, M. and Gerard, H. B. (1955). A study of normative and informational social influences upon individual judgement. *Journal of Personality and Social Psychology 51*, 629–636.

Douglas, K. M. and McGarty, C. (2001). Identifiability and self-presentation: computer-mediated communication and intergroup interaction. *British Journal of Social Psychology 40*, 399–416.

Douglas, K. M. and McGarty, C. (2002). Internet identifiability and beyond: a model of the effects of identifiability on communicative behavior. *Group Dynamics: Theory, Research and Practice 6*, 17–26.

Dubrovsky, V. J., Kiesler, S. and Sethna, B. N. (1991). The equalization phenomenon: status effects in computer-mediated and face-to-face decision-making groups. *Human Computer Interaction 6*, 119–146.

Finholt, T. and Sproull, L. S. (1990). Electronic groups at work. *Organization Science 1*, 41–64.

Franke, G. H. (1997). Über die Möglichkeiten der computerunterstützten Darbietung beim revidierten Freiburger Persönlichkeitsinventar. Zwei experimentelle Studien [Computer-based administration of the Freiburg Personality Inventory. Two experimental studies.]. *Zeitschrift für Experimentelle Psychologie 44*, 332–356.

Froming, W. J. and Carver, C. S. (1981). Divergent influences of private and public self-consciousness in a compliance paradigm. *Journal of Research in Personality 15*, 159–171.

Graham, C. R. (2003). A model of norm development for computer-mediated teamwork. *Small Group Research 34*, 322–352.

Greenspan, R. (2004). Users connect online with offline. Retrieved 1 April 2005 from http://www.clickz.com/stats/sectors/demographics/article.php/3398361.

Guadagno, R. E. and Cialdini, R. B. (2002). Online persuasion: an examination of gender differences in computer-mediated interpersonal influence. *Group Dynamics: Theory, Research and Practice 6*, 38–51.

Guéguen, N. (2002). Foot-in-the-door technique and computer-mediated communication. *Computers in Human Behavior 18*, 11–15.

Guéguen, N. and Jacob, C. (2001). Fund-raising on the web: the effect of an electronic foot-in-the-door on donation. *CyberPsychology and Behavior 4*, 705–709.

Guéguen, N. and Jacob, C. (2002). Social presence reinforcement and computer-mediated communication: the effect of the solicitor's photography on compliance to a survey request made by email. *CyberPsychology and Behavior 5*, 139–142.

Haslam, S. A., Turner, J. C., Oakes, P. J., McGarty, C. and Reynolds, K. J. (1998). The group as a basis for emergent stereotype consensus. *European Review of Social Psychology 8*, 203–239.

Hiltz, S. R., Johnson, K. and Turoff, M. (1986). Experiments in group decision making. Communication process and outcome in face-to-face versus computerized conferences. *Human Communication Research 13*, 225–252.

Jackson, L. A., Barbatsis, G., Biocca, F., Zhao, Y., von Eye, A. and Fitzgerald, H. E. (2002). Home Internet use in low-income families: frequency, nature and correlates of early Internet use in the HomeNetToo Project. *WWW2002 Alternate Paper Tracks Proceedings of the 11th International World Wide Web Conference in Honolulu, Hawaii*. Retrieved on 1 April from http://www2002.org/CDROM/alternate/649/.

Joinson, A. N. (2001). Self-disclosure in computer-mediated communication: the role of self-awareness and visual anonymity. *European Journal of Social Psychology 31*, 177–192.

Kiesler, S., Siegel, J. and McGuire, T. W. (1984). Social psychological aspects of computer-mediated communication. *American Psychologist 39*, 1123–1134.

Kraut, R., Mukhopadhyay, T., Szczypula, J., Kiesler, S. and Scherlis, B. (1999). Information and communication: alternative uses of the internet in households. *Information Systems Research 10*, 287–303.

Lea, M., O'Shea, T., Fung, P. and Spears, R. (1992). 'Flaming' in computer-mediated communication: observations, explanations, implications. In M. Lea (ed.), *Contexts of Computer-mediated Communication* (pp. 30–65). Hemel Hempstead: Harvester Wheatsheaf.

Lea, M. and Spears, R. (1991). Computer-mediated communication, de-individuation and group decision making. *International Journal of Man-Machine Studies 39*, 283–301.

Lea, M. and Spears, R. (1995). Love at first byte? Building personal relationships over computer networks. In J. T. Wood and S. Duck (eds), *Understudied relationships: Off the beaten track* (pp. 197–233). Thousand Oaks, CA: Sage.

Lea, M., Spears, R. and de Groot, D. (2001). Knowing me, knowing you: anonymity effects on social identity processes within groups. *Personality and Social Psychology Bulletin 27*, 526–537.

Lee, E.-J. and Nass, C. (2002). Experimental tests of normative group influence and representation effects in computer-mediated communication. *Human Communication Research 28*, 349–381.

Luna, D., Peracchio, L. A. and de Juan, M. D. (2003). The impact of language and congruity on persuasion in multicultural E-marketing. *Journal of Consumer Psychology 13*, 41–50.

Matheson, K. and Zanna, M. P. (1988). The impact of computer-mediated communication on self-awareness. *Computers in Human Behavior 4*, 221–233.

Matheson, K. and Zanna, M. P. (1989). Persuasion as a function of self-awareness in computer-mediated communication. *Social Behaviour 4*, 99–111.

McGuire, T. W., Kiesler, S. and Siegel, J. (1987). Group and computer-mediated discussion effects in risk decision making. *Journal of Personality and Social Psychology 52*, 917–930.

Morris, M., Nadler, J., Kurtzberg, T. and Thompson, L. (2002). Schmooze or lose: social friction and lubrication in email negotiations. *Group Dynamics: Theory, Research and Practice 6*, 89–100.

Moscovici, S. (1985) Innovation and minority influence. In S. Moscovici, G. Mugny and E. van Avermaet (eds), *Perspectives on minority influence* (pp. 9–51). Cambridge: Cambridge University Press.

Myers, D. (1987). 'Anonymity is part of the magic': individual manipulation of computer-mediated communication contexts. *Qualitative Sociology 10*, 251–266.

Postmes, T., Haslam, S. A. and Swaab, R. (2005). Social influence in small groups: an interactive model of social identity formation. *European Review of Social Psychology 16*, 1–42.

Postmes, T. and Spears, R. (1998). Deindividuation and anti-normative behaviour: A meta-analysis. *Psychological Bulletin 123*, 238–259.

Postmes, T. and Spears, R. (2000). Refining the cognitive redefinition of the group: deindividuation effects in common bond vs. common identity groups. In T. Postmes, R. Spears, M. Lea and S. Reicher (eds), *Side issues centre stage: Recent developments in studies of de-individuation in groups* (pp. 31–45). Amsterdam: KNAW.

Postmes, T. and Spears, R. (2002). Behavior online: does anonymous computer communication reduce gender inequality? *Personality and Social Psychology Bulletin 28*, 1073–1083.

Postmes, T., Spears, R. and Lea, M. (2000). The formation of group norms in computer-mediated communication. *Human Communication Research 26*, 341–371.

Postmes, T., Spears, R. and Lea, M. (1998). Breaching or building social boundaries? SIDE-effects of computer mediated communication. *Communication Research 25*, 689–715.

Postmes, T., Spears, R. and Lea, M. (2002). Intergroup differentiation in computer-mediated communication: effects of depersonalisation. *Group Dynamics 6*, 27–37.

Postmes, T., Spears, R., Sakhel, K. and de Groot, D. (2001). Social influence in computer-mediated communication: the effects of anonymity on group behavior. *Personality and Social Psychology Bulletin 27*, 1243–1254.

Prentice, D. A., Miller, D. T. and Lightdale, J. R. (1994). Asymmetries in attachments to groups and to their members: distinguishing between common-identity and common-bond groups. *Personality and Social Psychology Bulletin 20*, 484–493.

Prentice-Dunn, S. and Rogers, R. W. (1982). Effects of public and private self-awareness on deindividuation and aggression. *Journal of Personality and Social Psychology 43*, 503–513.

Reicher, S. and Levine, M. (1994 a). Deindividuation, power relations between groups and the expression of social identity: the effects of visibility to the out-group. *British Journal of Social Psychology 33*, 145–164.

Reicher, S. and Levine, M. (1994 b). On the consequences of deindividuation manipulations for the strategic communication of self: identifiability and the presentation of social identity. *European Journal of Social Psychology* 24, 511–524.

Reicher, S. D., Spears, R. and Postmes, T. (1995). A social identity model of deindividuation phenomena. *European Review of Social Psychology* 6, 161–198.

Rutter, D. R. (1984). *Looking and seeing: The role of visual communication in social interaction.* Chinester: Wiley.

Rutter, D. R. (1987). *Communicating by telefone.* Oxford: Pergamon.

Rutter, D. R., Stephenson, G. M. and Dewey, M. E. (1987). Visual communication and the content and style of conversation. *British Journal of Social Psychology* 20, 41–52.

Sassenberg, K. (2002). Common bond and common identity groups on the Internet: attachment and normative behavior in on-topic and off-topic chats. *Group Dynamics: Theory, Research and Practice* 6, 27–37.

Sassenberg, K. and Boos, M. (2003). Attitude change in computer-mediated communication: effects of anonymity and category norms. *Group Processes and Intergroup Relations* 6, 405–422.

Sassenberg, K., Boos, M. and Klapproth, F. (2001). Wissen und Problemlösekompetenz: Der Einfluss von Expertise auf den Informationsaustausch in computervermittelter Kommunikation [Knowledge and problem solving competence: The influence of expertise on information exchange in computer-mediated communication]. *Zeitschrift für Sozialpsychologie* 32, 45–56.

Sassenberg, K., Boos, M. and Rabung, S. (2005). Attitude change in face to face and computer-mediated communication: private self-awareness as mediator and moderator. *European Journal of Social Psychology* 35, 621–632.

Sassenberg, K. and Kreutz, S. (2002). Online research and anonymity. In B. Batinic, U.-D. Reips and M. Bosnjak (eds), *Online Social Sciences* (pp. 213–229). Seattle, WA: Hogrefe and Huber.

Sassenberg, K. and Postmes, T. (2002). Cognitive and strategic processes in small groups: effects of anonymity of the self and anonymity of the group on social influence. *British Journal of Social Psychology* 41, 463–480.

Scheier, M. F. (1980). Effects of public and private self-consciousness on the public expression of personal beliefs. *Journal of Personality and Social Psychology* 39, 514–521.

Short, J. A., Williams, E. and Christie, B. (1976). *The social psychology of telecommunications.* Chichester: Wiley.

Siegel, J., Dubrovsky, V., Kiesler, S. and McGuire, T. (1986). Group processes in computer-mediated communication. *Organizational Behaviour and Human Decision Processes* 37, 157–87.

Smilowitz, M., Compton, D. C. and Flint, L. (1988). The effects of computer-mediated communication on an individual's judgement: a study based on the methods of Asch's social influence experiment. *Computers in Human Behavior* 4, 311–321.

Spears, R. and Lea, M. (1992). Social influence and the influence of the 'social' in computer-mediated communication. In M. Lea (ed.), *Contexts of computer-mediated communication* (pp. 30–65). Hemel Hempstead: Harvester-Wheatsheaf.

Spears, R. and Lea, M. (1994). Panacea or panopticon? The hidden power in computer-mediated communication. *Communication Research* 21, 427–459.

Spears, R., Lea, M., Corneliussen, R. A., Postmes, T. and ten Haar, W. (2002). Computer-mediated communication as a channel for social resistance: the strategic side of SIDE. *Small Group Research* 33, 555–574.

Spears, R., Lea, M. and Lee S. (1990). De-individuation and group polarization in computer-mediated communications. *British Journal of Social Psychology* 29, 121–134.

Spears, R., Postmes, T., Lea, M. and Watt, S. E. (2001). A SIDE view of social influence. In J. P. Forgas and K. D. Williams (eds), *Social influence: Direct and indirect processes* (pp. 331–350). New York: Psychology Press.

Spears, R., Postmes, T., Lea, M. and Wolbert, A. (2002). When are net effects gross products? The power of influence and the influence of power in computer-mediated communication. *Journal of Social Issues* 58, 91–107.

Sproull, L. and Kiesler, S. (1991). *Connections: New ways of working in the networked organization.* Cambridge, MA: MIT Press.

Straus, S. G. (1996). Getting a clue. The effects of communication media and information distribution on participation and performance in computer-mediated and face-to-face groups. *Small Group Research* 27, 115–142.

Tajfel, H. and Turner, J. C. (1979). An integrative theory of intergroup conflict. In W. G. Austin and S. Worchel (eds), *The social psychology of intergroup relations* (pp. 33–47). Monterey, CA: Brooks/Cole.

Thompson, L. F. and Coovert, M. D. (2002). Stepping up to the challenge: a critical examination of face-to-face and computer-mediated team decision making. *Group Dynamics: Theory, Research and Practice* 6, 52–64.

Thompson, L. and Nadler, J. (2002). Negotiating via information technology: theory and application. *Journal of Social Issues* 58, 109–124.

Turner, J. C. (1991). *Social influence.* Milton Keynes: Open University Press.

Turner, J. C., Hogg, M. A., Oakes, P. J., Reicher, S. D. and Wetherell, M. S. (1987). *Rediscovering the social group: A self-categorization theory.* Oxford: Blackwell.

Utz, S. (2000). Social information processing in MUDs: the development of friendships in virtual worlds. *Journal of Online Behavior, 1.*

Utz, S. (2003) Social identification and interpersonal attraction in MUDs. *Swiss Journal of Psychology* 62, 91–101.

Waldzus, S. and Schubert, T. (2000). Group norm and category norm in anonymous situations: two sources of social influence. In T. Postmes, R. Spears, M. Lea and S. Reicher (eds), *Side issues centre stage: Recent developments in studies of de-individuation in groups* (pp. 31–45). Amsterdam: KNAW.

Walther, J. B. (1992). Interpersonal effects in computer-mediated interaction: a relational perspective. *Communication Research* 19, 52–90.

Walther, J. B. (1995). Relational aspects of computer-mediated communication: experimental observations over time. *Organization Science* 6, 186–203.

Walther, J. B. (1996). Computer-mediated communication: impersonal, interpersonal and hyperpersonal interaction. *Communication Research 23*, 1–43.

Walther, J., Anderson, J. F. and Park, D. W. (1994). Interpersonal effects in computer-mediated interaction: a meta-analysis of social and anti-social communication. *Communication Research 21*, 460–487.

Weisband, S. P. (1992). Group discussion and first-advocacy effects in computer-mediated and face-to-face decision making groups. *Organizational Behavior and Human Decision Processes 53*, 352–380.

Whitwoth, B., Gallupe, B. and McQueen, R. (2001). Generating agreement in computer-mediated groups. *Small Group Research 32*, 625–665.

Wilkins, H. (1991). Computer talk: long-distance conversations by computer. *Written Communication 8*, 56–78.

Williams, K. D., Cheung, C. K. T. and Choi, W. (2000). Cyberostracism: effects of being ignored over the Internet. *Journal of Personality and Social Psychology 79*, 748–762.

Wood, W. (1999). Motives and modes of processing in the social influence of groups. In S. Chaiken and Y. Trope (eds), *Dual-process theories in social psychology* (pp. 547–570). New York: Guilford.

Zigurs, M. I., Poole, S. and DeSanctis, G. L. (1988). A study of influence in computer-mediated group decision making. *MIS Quarterly 12*, 625–644.

CHAPTER 19

Digital deception

Why, when and how people lie online

Jeffrey T. Hancock

Deception is one of the most significant and pervasive social phenomena of our age (Miller and Stiff 1993). Some studies suggest that, on average, people tell one to two lies a day (DePaulo *et al.* 1996; Hancock *et al.* 2004a), and these lies range from the trivial to the more serious, including deception between friends and family, in the workplace and in power and politics. At the same time, information and communication technologies have pervaded almost all aspects of human communication and interaction, from everyday technologies that support interpersonal interactions, such as email and instant messaging, to more sophisticated systems that support organizational interactions.

Given the prevalence of both deception and communication technology in our personal and professional lives, an important set of questions has recently emerged at the intersection of deception and technology, or what we will refer to as '*digital deception*'. These questions include issues concerned with deception and self-presentation, such as how the Internet can facilitate deception through the manipulation of identity. A second set of questions is concerned with how we produce lies. For example, do we lie more in our everyday conversations in some media more than in others? Do we use different media to lie

about different types of things, to different types of people? Another type of question concerns our ability to *detect* deception across various media and in different online communication spaces. Are we worse at detecting lies in a text-based interaction than we are in face-to-face (ftf)? What factors interact with communication media to affect our ability to catch a liar?

In the present chapter I examine these questions by first elaborating on the notion of digital deception in the context of the literature on traditional forms of deception. The chapter is then divided into two main sections, one concerned with identity-based forms of deception online, and the other focusing on the lies that are a frequent part of our everyday communications.

Digital deception defined

Deception has been studied in a wide variety of contexts (Ekman 2001), including organizational settings (Grazioli and Jarvenpaa 2003a; Schein 2004), forensic and criminal settings (Vrij 2000; Granhag and Stromwall 2004), in power and politics (Ekman 1985; Galasinski 2000) and in everyday communication (DePaulo *et al.* 1996; DePaulo and Kashy 1998; Hancock *et al.* 2004a, b). In the present chapter, we consider deception in the context of information and communication technology, or what I will call *digital deception*, which refers to *the intentional control of information in a technologically mediated message to create a false belief in the receiver of the message*. While this definition is an adaptation of Buller and Burgoon's (1996) conceptualization of deception, i.e., 'a message knowingly transmitted by a sender to foster a false belief or conclusion by the receiver' (1996: 205), the characteristics of this definition are consistent with most definitions of deception (for review of the many issues associated with defining deception, see Bok 1978; Galasinski 2000). The first characteristic is that an act of deception must be intentional or deliberate. Messages that are unintentionally misleading are usually not considered deceptive, but instead are described as mistakes or errors (Burgoon and Buller 1994). Similarly, forms of speech in which the speaker does not mean what they say but intend for their addressee to detect this, such as irony, joking, etc, are not considered deceptive. The second characteristic is that deception is designed to mislead or create a false belief in some target. That is, the deceiver's goal is to convince someone else to believe something that the deceiver believes to be false. These characteristics can be observed, for example, in Ekman's (2001: 41) definition – 'deliberate choice to mislead a target without giving any notification of the intent to do so' – and in DePaulo *et al.*'s (2003: 74) – 'a deliberate attempt to mislead others.'

Digital deception requires an additional characteristic, namely that the control or manipulation of information in a deception is enacted in a *technologically mediated message*. That is, the message must be conveyed in a medium other than the basic ftf setting. As such, digital deception involves any form of deceit that is transmitted via communication technology, such as the telephone, email, instant messaging, chat rooms, newsgroups, weblogs, listservs, multiplayer online video games etc.

Although a number of different typologies have been proposed for categorizing deception – for example deception by omission vs. by commission, active vs. passive deception, etc. (see Robinson 1996; Galasinski 2000), for the purposes of discussing how the Internet and communication technologies may affect deception and its detection, I break digital deception down into two broad types: those based on a communicator's identity, and those based on the actual messages that comprise a communication. In particular, *identity-based digital deception* refers to deceit that flows from the false manipulation or display of a person or organization's identity. For example, an email designed to look like it originated from someone in Africa that needs a partner to extricate vast sums of money (in order to trick the recipient into providing their bank information) is a case of identity-based digital deception. *Message-based digital deception*, in contrast, refers to deception that takes place in the communication between two or more interlocutors or agents. In particular, it refers to deception in which the information in the messages exchanged between interlocutors is manipulated or controlled to be deceptive. For example, when one friend calls another on his mobile phone to say that he will be late to their meeting because the traffic is bad (when in fact he simply left the office late) is an example of message-based digital deception. The two friends' identities are known to one another, but the information provided by the first friend has been manipulated to create a false belief in the second friend.

Clearly these identity-based and message-based forms of digital deception are not mutually exclusive. Indeed, the messages in a communication may serve to enhance a deception about identity and, when identity-based digital deception is enacted, the messages that make up the communication are more than likely to also be deceptive. For instance, in the email example above, there are several possible relationships between identity- and message-based deceptions. For example, the identity of the sender may be deceptive (i.e., the person is not really someone in Africa), but the message truthful (e.g., the person really does have access to money). Or, the identity of the sender may be accurate (i.e., the person really is in Africa) but the message is deceptive (e.g., the person does not have access to money). Or, both the identity and message could be false. As such, the distinction between identity-based and message-based deception is not intended to be set in stone, but is intended only as a pragmatic distinction that may help us consider how communication technologies may or may not affect deception.

Finally, it should be noted that the definition of digital deception described above includes a number of issues that are beyond the scope of this chapter. For example, the advent of sophisticated and relatively inexpensive digital editing software makes image-based digital deception, such as misleading editing or selection, an important issue (Messaris 1997; Galasinski 2000). Also, the very broad topic of information security, such as attacks and vulnerabilities on information infrastructure (see Schneider 1999), hacking and deceptive intrusion of information networks (see Stolfo et al. 2001), will also not be discussed here. Instead, the focus will be on deception in our everyday mediated communication.

Identity-based digital deception

Perhaps the most obvious deception issue to consider is the affordances provided by information and communication technologies to manipulate or obscure our identity. As Turkle (1995) observed, the relative anonymity and multiple modes of social interaction provided by the many forms of online communication conducted via the Internet provide users with unique opportunities to play with their identity and explore their sense of self. As many have now noted (e.g., Walther 1996; Berman and Bruckman 2001; Bargh et al. 2002; Spears et al. 2002; Walther and Parks 2002), because online communication typically involves text-based interaction or virtual representations of self (e.g., avatars), people can self-present in ways that they can not in ftf encounters. Boys can be girls, the old can be young, ethnicity can be chosen, 15-year-olds can be stock analysts – and on the Internet no one knows you're a dog.

While this growing body of research has revealed some of the fascinating effects that the relative anonymity of the Internet can have on identity and social interaction, such as the enhancement of group effects (e.g., Postmes et al. 1999; Douglas and McGarty 2001) and the potential hyerpersonalization of interpersonal interactions (Walther 1996; Hancock and Dunham 2001a; Walther et al. 2001), the affordances of online communication for manipulating identity also have important implications

for deception. In one of the first systematic investigations of identity-based deception in online contexts, Donath (1998) observed how different aspects of Usenet newsgroups (asynchronous text-based message exchange systems supporting a wide range of topical discussions) affected participants sense of identity and their abilities to deceive or be deceived by their fellow community members.

Drawing on models of deception from biology (e.g., Zahavi 1993), Donath distinguished between assessment signals, which are costly displays directly related to an organism's characteristics (e.g., large horns on a stag), and conventional signals, which are low-cost displays that are only conventionally associated with a characteristic (e.g., a powerful-sounding mating call). In online communication, conventional signals include most of the information that is exchanged in messages, including what we say (e.g., that I'm very wealthy) and the nicknames we use to identify ourselves (e.g., 'richie-rich'). Assessment signals may be more difficult to come by online, but can include links to a person's 'real-world' identity, such as a phone number or an email address (e.g., emails ending in.ac.uk or .edu suggest that the person works at a university), or levels of knowledge that only an expert could display (e.g., highly technical information about a computer system).

Online, conventional signals are an easy target for deceptive identity manipulation, and Donath notes several types of deceptive identity manipulations in the Usenet communities, including trolling, category deception, and identity concealment. Trolling refers to an individual posing as a legitimate member of a community who posts messages intended to spark intense fights within the community. Category deception refers to deceptions that manipulate our perceptions of individuals as members of social groups, or categories, such as male vs. female, white vs. black, student vs. worker, hockey player vs. squash player. Online, gender deception is perhaps the most commonly discussed example of category deception (e.g., Turkle 1995; Berman and Bruckman 2001; Herring and Martinson 2004). Finally, identity concealment refers to hiding or omitting aspects of one's identity, such as using a pseudonym when posting, in order to shield one's identity.

Research by Whitty and her colleagues (Whitty and Gavin 2001; Whitty 2002) suggests that the notion of using deception to shield one's identity is important for many participants interacting in relatively anonymous online spaces, such as chat rooms. In particular, in one survey of chat room participants, women reported using deception to conceal their identity for safety reasons, such as avoiding harassment. Men, on the other hand, reported using identity deception in order to allow themselves, somewhat paradoxically, to be more expressive and to reveal secrets about themselves (Utz 2005). Indeed, a number of studies have suggested that self-disclosure and honesty tend to increase online when participants' identities are not manifest (e.g., Joinson 2001; Bargh *et al.* 2002).

More recently, however, the Internet has evolved from a virtual space for exchanging information, chatting with others and forming virtual communities into a massive venue for financial and business transactions, with estimates of revenue generated from online transactions in the billions, and an increasing number of businesses and individuals engaging in commerce online. As might be expected, more serious and criminal forms of deception are keeping pace with the increase in money flowing through the Internet (Grazioli and Jarvenpaa 2003b). Indeed, the Internet Fraud Complaint Center (IFCC 2003) reported almost fifty thousand incidences of fraud online, a threefold increase from the previous year, the majority of which involved fraudulent Internet auctions, but also included credit card fraud and identity theft, in which someone's personal information is stolen and used for the gain of another individual.

In their work on deception that takes place in business and consumer contexts, such as touting unsound investments for personal gain or making misleading claims about goods for sale at an auction site, Grazioli and Jarvenpaa (2003a, b) have identified seven common deception tactics. The first three tactics are concerned with obscuring the nature of the goods to be transacted, and include

1. *Masking* – eliminating critical information regarding an item (e.g., failing to disclose that the publisher of a newsletter receives advertisement money from stocks the newsletter recommends)

2. *Dazzling* – obscuring critical information regarding an item (e.g., free trials that lead to automatic enrolment without making that clear to consumers)

3. *Decoying* – distracting the victim's attention from the transaction (e.g., offers of free products that require the revealing of highly detailed personal information).

The four other types of deception tactics involve manipulating information about the transaction itself, and include:

1. *Mimicking* – assuming someone else's identity or modifying the transaction so that it appears legitimate (e.g., the creation of a 'mirror' bank site virtually identical to the legitimate site, inducing users to disclose personal information such as account information)

2. *Inventing* – making up information about the transaction (e.g., Internet auctioneers who advertise merchandise that they do not have)

3. *Relabelling* – describing a transaction expressly to mislead (e.g., selling questionable investments over the Internet as sound financial opportunities)

4. *Double play* – convincing a victim that they are taking advantage of the deceiver (e.g., emails designed to look like internal memos sent by mistake and which appear to contain insider information).

As Grazioli and Jarvenpaa (2000) note, the Internet offers a highly flexible environment for identity-based forms of deception that can make it difficult for even technologically savvy users to detect deception.

While the Internet certainly offers a number of advantages to the deceiver that may not be available face-to-face, an important question is whether one is more likely to encounter identity-based deception online or in more traditional face-to-face social exchanges. While this question is difficult to address for obvious reasons, a recent report comparing identity fraud that took place online or ftf suggests that identity fraud is still much more likely to take place ftf, and that when it does occur online it tends to be much less costly than when it occurs offline (Javelin Strategy and Research 2005).

While this is only one report, it does serve as a reminder that although Internet-based communication provides many features that may facilitate identity-based digital deception, and that this type of deception appears to be on the rise online, more traditional ftf forms of communication are certainly not immune to identity related deception. Nonetheless, identity-based digital deception is an important area for future research, especially given reports that criminal entities, such as organized crime and terrorist organizations, are increasingly relying on information technologies to communicate (Knight 2004).

Message-based digital deception

Although we typically associate Internet-based communication with relatively anonymous communication spaces, such as chat rooms, newsgroups, online games, etc., most people's everyday use of communication technologies tend to be with people that they know, such as an email to a colleague, an instant message with a friend, or text messaging on the phone with a spouse. In these instances, much like many of our ftf interactions, the identity of our interlocutors is known to us. How do communication technologies affect deception when identities are known? Let us consider first the production of digital deception.

Producing digital deception

Research suggests that deception in general is a fundamental and frequent part of everyday human communication, both in interpersonal settings as well as in work and organizational contexts (Camden et al. 1984; Lippard 1988; Metts 1989; DePaulo et al. 1996; Hancock et al. 2004a, b). Some research suggests that people tell an average of one to two lies a day (DePaulo et al. 1996; Hancock et al. 2004a, b), and these daily lies range from the trivial, such as a false opinion about someone's appearance, to the more serious matters, such as deception in business and legal negotiations, power and politics, and workplace issues. Indeed, as noted above, some have argued that deception is one of the most pervasive social phenomena of our age (Miller and Stiff 1993).

How do communication technologies affect the frequency with which we produce lies? In particular, are we more likely to lie in some media than in others? Some have speculated that Internet-based communication is rife with deception. For example, Keyes (2004: 198) argues that 'electronic mail is a godsend. With email we needn't worry about so much as a quiver in our voice or a tremor in our pinkie when telling a lie. Email is a first rate deception-enabler'. While this may reflect a popular view of how communication technology might affect deception, theoretical approaches to media effects suggest several possible ways that media may affect lying behaviour.

Media Richness Theory (Daft and Lengel 1986; Daft et al. 1987), for example, assumes that users will choose rich media, which have multiple cue systems, immediate feedback, natural language and message personalization, for more equivocal and complex communication activities. Because lying can be considered a complex type of communication, media richness theory predicts that users should chose to lie most frequently in rich media, such as ftf, and least frequently in less rich media, such as email. In contrast, DePaulo et al. (1996) argued that because lying makes people uncomfortable, users should choose less rich media in order to maintain social distance between the liar and the target, an argument I refer to as the social distance hypothesis. According to this hypothesis, users should choose email most frequently for lying, followed in order by instant messaging, telephone and finally ftf (see also, Bradner and Mark 2002).

Note that both of these approaches assume that communication technology varies along only a single underlying dimension (i.e., richness, distance) that will influence deception, and ignore other important differences in their design that may have important implications for deception. In our feature-based model of media and deception (Hancock et al. 2004a, b), we proposed that at least three features of media are important for the act of deception, including (1) the *synchronicity* of the medium (i.e., the degree to which messages are exchanged instantaneously and in real-time) (2) the *recordability* of the medium (i.e., the degree to which the interaction is automatically documented), and (3) whether or not the speaker and listener are *distributed* (i.e., they do not share the same physical space).

In particular, synchronous media should increase opportunities for deception because the majority of lies are unplanned and tend to emerge spontaneously from conversation (DePaulo *et al.* 1996). For example, if during a conversation a new friend says to another that his favorite movie is one that she hates, she is now presented with a decision to lie or not about her opinion of the movie. This type of emergent opportunity is less likely to arise when composing an email. Thus, media that are synchronous, such as ftf and telephone, and to a large degree instant messaging, should present more situations in which deception may be opportune.

The more recordable a medium, the less likely users should be willing to speak falsely. Email is perhaps the most recordable interpersonal medium we have ever developed, with copies being saved on multiple computers (including the targets). In contrast, ftf and telephone conversations are typically recordless. Although instant messaging (IM) conversations are logged for the duration of an exchange and can be easily saved, most people do not save their IM conversations. Of course, this may change as IM enters the workplace and companies begin automatically recording IM by employees. In order to avoid being caught, speakers may choose to lie more frequently in recordless media, such as ftf and the telephone, than in more recordable media, such as email and instant messaging.

Finally, media in which participants are not distributed (i.e., co-present) should constrain deception to some degree because they limit deception involving topics or issues that are contradicted by the physical setting (e.g., 'I'm working on the case report' when in fact the speaker is surfing news on the Web). In fact, software is now available that can be downloaded into a phone that plays ambient noise that may be consistent with your lie (e.g., playing the sounds of an office when in fact you are in a car). Because mediated interactions such as the phone, IM and email involve physically distributed participants, this constraint should be reduced relative to ftf interactions. Some support for this notion comes from a study by Bradner and Mark (2002), in which participants were more likely to deceive a partner when they believed their partner was in a distant city than if they were in the same city.

According to our feature-based model, the more synchronous and distributed but less recordable a medium is, the more frequently lying should occur. As such, if these design features of communication media affect deception, then lying should occur most frequently on the telephone, followed by ftf and instant messaging, and least frequently via email.

To test the predictions flowing from the theories described above, we (Hancock *et al.* 2004a) conducted a diary study adapted from DePaulo *et al.*'s (1996) procedures. After a training session on how to record and code their own social interactions and deceptions, participants recorded all of their lies and social interactions for seven days. For each interaction, they recorded in which medium the interaction took place, ftf, phone, IM, email, and whether or not they lied. The results suggested that participants lied most frequently on the telephone (37 per cent of social interactions), followed by ftf (27 per cent) and IM interactions (21 per cent), and that they lied least by email (14 per cent). These data are not consistent with either media richness theory or the social distance hypothesis, which predict that deception will vary linearly along a single dimension, such as richness or social distance. In contrast, the data are consistent with our feature-based model of deception, which predicted that deception production should be highest in synchronous, recordless and distributed media. The data also go against the conventional wisdom that the online world is rife with deception and subterfuge.

Although the features described in the feature-based model predicted overall rates of digital deception, lies are not homogenous (DePaulo *et al.* 1996; Feldman *et al.* 2002). Deception, for example, can be about one's actions – 'I'm in the library' when in fact the speaker is at the pub – feelings – 'I love your shirt' with regard to a friend's ugly shirt – facts – 'I'm an A student' – and explanations – 'I couldn't make it because my car broke down'. Do people select different types of media for different types of deception? The feature-based model of deception makes several predictions. First, lies about actions should be less likely to occur in non-distributed communicative settings, where the target of the lie can physically see the speaker. Because lies about feelings are most likely to arise in synchronous interactions (e.g., a friend asking whether you like their ugly shirt), lies about feelings were predicted to occur most frequently face-to-face and on the telephone. Lies about facts should be least likely to be told in recordable media that can later be reviewed, such as email. Finally, explanation type lies were predicted to take place most frequently in asynchronous media, such as email, which provides the liar with more time to construct and plan their explanation than synchronous media.

People also lie differently to different types of people. For example, because people report valuing authenticity and trust in close relationships, people tend to lie less to close relationship partners, such as spouses, family and friends, than to casual relationship partners, such as acquaintances, colleagues and strangers (Metts 1989; Millar and Millar 1995; DePaulo and Kashy 1998). Lies to close and casual relationship targets also seem to differ qualitatively. In particular, lies told in close relationships tend to be more altruistic, in which the lie is told primarily to benefit the target (e.g., false compliments, pretend agreement) than self-serving, in which the lie benefits the liar, while lies in casual relationships tend to be more self-serving than altruistic.

In order to examine whether people used different media to lie about different things or to different people, we conducted another diary-based study in which we also assessed the content and target of the lie (Hancock et al. 2004b). While we saw the same pattern of deception frequency across media (i.e., highest rate of deception on the phone, followed by ftf and IM, and least frequently email), the data provided only mixed support for our predictions regarding deception content and target relationship. As predicted, asynchronous interactions involved the least lies about feelings (i.e., email) but involved the most explanation-based lies, which involve explanations about why some event or action occurred – for example 'My dog ate my homework' as an explanation for why a student didn't complete the homework). Distributed media were predicted to involve more lies about actions, but this was only true for lies on the telephone. Finally, lies about facts did not differ across media. With respect to relationships, relative to ftf interactions, phone lies were most likely told to family and significant others. Instant messaging lies were most likely to be

told to family. Finally, email lies were most likely to involve lies to higher status individuals, such as a student's professor.

Carlson and George (2004; George and Carlson 2005) have taken a similar approach to examining how the features of a medium, including synchronicity, recordlessness and richness, may affect deception production. While synchronicity and recordlessness are also in the feature-based model described above, Carlson and George (2004) argue that synchronicity may be preferred by deceivers for a somewhat different and very good reason, namely because it increases the deceiver's ability to assess and react to the receiver's behaviour. Richness is considered a positive for deception for the same reason – increased richness should lead to enhanced control over how the receiver perceives the deceiver as truthful. In this approach, however, richness is determined not only be availability of cues and speed of feedback, but also by the participant's experience with that medium (Carlson and Zmud 1999).

In two studies, Carlson and George (2004; George and Carlson 2005) provided a variety of scenarios to business managers that described situations in which they would be required to lie. In general, the results suggested that participants were most likely to choose synchronous and recordless media when they needed to lie, regardless of the severity of the situation. Although these data are generally consistent with the feature-based model, the results in these studies suggested that ftf tended to be the most frequent choice for deception, not the telephone. One possible reason for this difference may be the method employed, which does not control for the different baseline frequencies with which we interact in different media. That is, despite the wide range of communication technologies available to us, the majority of our interactions tend to be ftf. As such, we might expect ftf to be the place that people imagine they will lie most frequently in absolute terms simply because that is where most of their interactions take place.

Regardless of this methodological difference, when considered together, the data from these studies and the ones described above suggest that contrary to some speculations (e.g., Keyes 2004), asynchronous and recordable media, such as email, are unlikely places for people to lie in during their everyday communication.

Instead, more synchronous and recordless forms of media, such as the telephone and ftf settings, appear to be where we lie most.

A final question concerned with how technology might affect deception is whether our language use is different when we lie compared to when we tell the truth online. In groundbreaking work in this area, Zhou and colleagues (Zhou *et al.* 2004a, b, Zhou and Zhang 2004) use computer-assisted, automated analysis of linguistic cues to classify deceptive and non-deceptive text-based communication. In this approach, the language of deceptive and truthful participants' communication are subjected to an automated analysis along a number of linguistic dimensions, including word count, pronoun usage, expressivity, affect and non-immediacy (i.e., less self-reference), among others. For example, in one study examining asynchronous text-based exchanges, Zhou *et al.* (2004) found that, compared to truth-tellers, liars used more words, were more expressive, non-immediate and informal and made more typographical errors. In one of our studies, we (Hancock *et al.* in press a) found similar patterns in synchronous online interaction (i.e., instant messaging), including increased word use and fewer self-references, during deception. Perhaps even more interestingly, we also found that the targets of lies, who were blind to the deception manipulation, also changed systematically depending on whether they were being lied to or told the truth. In particular, when being lied to targets used shorter sentences and asked more questions. These data suggest the fascinating possibility that targets had an implicit awareness or suspicion about the veracity of their partner, despite the fact that when asked whether they thought their partners were lying or not they performed at chance levels. While additional research is required for this novel line of research, these data suggest that how people use language online may change systematically according to whether or not they are being truthful. If this is the case, then the implications for deception detection online are substantial. We turn now to this issue, the detecting of digital deception.

Detecting digital deception

While an extensive literature has examined deception detection in ftf contexts (for review,

see Zuckerman and Driver 1985; Vrij 2000; DePaulo *et al.* 2003), the question of how communication technologies affects deception detection has only begun to be addressed. Are we worse at detecting a lie in a text-based interaction than we are in a face-to-face exchange? How do factors that affect deception detection in ftf contexts, such as motivation, suspicion and non-verbal cues, interact with the effects of communication technology?

Although the extensive literature on ftf deception detection suggests that our accuracy to detect deception tends to be around chance (Vrij 2000), there are a number of factors that appear to reliably influence an individual's ability to detect deceit, and these factors may have important implications in the context of digital deception. Perhaps the most intuitively obvious factor for digital deception is the reduction of non-verbal cues that are associated with deception in mediated communication. Previous research suggests that there are a small set of reliable verbal, non-verbal and vocal cues to deception (for review, see DePaulo *et al.* 2003). Perhaps the most important of these are 'leakage cues', which are non-strategic behaviours (usually non-verbal) that are assumed to betray the senders' deceptive intentions or feelings, such as a decrease in illustrators, body movements and higher pitch (Ekman 2001).

Given that these types of leakage cues are eliminated in text-based CMC interactions, one might suppose that deception detection would be less accurate in CMC than in ftf interactions (Hollingshead 2000). However, the relationship between communication media and deception appears to be much more complex than a simple reduction of cues. In perhaps the first theoretical framework to consider systematically the detection of message-based digital deception, Carlson *et al.* (2004) draw on Interpersonal Deception Theory (Buller and Burgoon 1996) to identify a number of variables that may interact with the communication medium in the context of deception detection. These factors include the (1) characteristics of the deceiver and receiver, and of their relationship, and (2) aspects of the communication event and the medium in which it takes place.

Characteristics of the deceiver and receiver that are considered relevant to success rates of deception detection include the motivation to lie or catch a lie, each individual's intrinsic abilities at deceiving or detecting deceit, aspects of the task and the various cognitions and affect that may arise from the discomfort associated with lying. Experience and familiarity are also assumed to play an important role in the model, including the relational experience between the deceiver and receiver, as well as both individuals' experience with the communication medium and context.

Aspects of the communication medium that are considered important include synchronicity, symbol variety (i.e., the number of different types of language elements and symbols available, including letters, basic symbols, fonts, etc.), cue multiplicity (i.e., number of simultaneous information channels supported), tailorability (i.e., ability to customize the message for the audience), reprocessability (i.e., the inverse of recordlessness described above) and rehearsability (i.e., the degree to which it gives participants time to plan, edit and rehearse messages). In this model, the relationships between these variables and deception detection is not assumed to be simple or one-to-one. Instead, the model assumes a 'deceptive potential' that is derived from constellations of these media variables. In particular, Carlson et al. propose that media with higher levels of symbol variety, tailorability, and rehearsability increase deceptive potential and reduce the likelihood of deception detection. In contrast, media that have higher levels of cue multiplicity and reprocessability decrease deceptive potential.

An important underlying assumption of this model, derived from the Interperonal Deception Theory, is that deception is a strategic act that is part of an ongoing, interactive communication process, and that all of the factors described above interact in important and predictable ways. A number of the factors described in the model have begun to be examined in several recent studies examining deception detection in online communication (Heinrich and Borkenau 1998; George and Carlson 1999; Hollingshead 2000; Horn 2001; Horn et al. 2002; Burgoon et al. 2003; George and Marrett 2004, Carlson and George 2004 Study 2; George et al. 2004; Hancock et al. in press b).

A survey of these studies suggests that, as Carlson et al. (2004) predict, the relationship between communication media and deception detection is not a simple one. Some studies, for example, have found more accurate deception detection in richer media (e.g., Heinrich and Borkenau 1998; Burgoon et al. 2003), others have found higher accuracy in less rich media (e.g., Horn et al. 2002), while still others have found no overall difference between media (Hollingshead 2000; George and Marrett 2004; Woodworth et al. 2005). Instead, it appears that a number of factors, such as those described above, interact with the communication medium to determine deception detection accuracy.

Hancock et al. (in press b), for example, examined the impact of motivation of the deceiver and the communication medium on deception detection. People who are highly motivated to get away with their deceptive behaviour tend to act differently than those who are less concerned with the outcome, and their non-verbal behaviour (e.g., increased behavioural rigidity) is more likely to give them away (DePaulo et al. 1983). The observation that highly motivated liars are more likely to be detected has been referred to as the *motivational impairment effect* (DePaulo and Kirkendol 1989).

Because CMC eliminates nonverbal cues, the motivation impairment effect should be attenuated for highly motivated liars interacting in CMC. In addition, Burgoon and her colleagues (Burgoon and Buller 1994; Buller and Burgoon 1996) argue that moderately motivated liars engage in strategic communication behaviors to enhance their credibility. If that is the case, then there are several aspects of the CMC environment that should be advantageous to a sufficiently motivated liar (Carlson et al. 2004): (1) CMC speakers have more time to plan and construct their utterances, and (2) CMC settings enable the sender to carefully edit their messages before transmitting them to their partner, even in synchronous CMC, which affords speakers greater control over message generation and transmission (Hancock and Dunham 2001b). As such, CMC may not only attenuate the motivational impairment effect, but actually reverse it.

To test this possibility, Hancock et al. (in press b) examined deceptive and truthful interactions in ftf and CMC environments. Half of the senders were motivated to lie by telling them that research has shown that successful liars tend to have better jobs, higher incomes and more success with finding a mate (see Forrest and Feldman 2000), while the other half were not. Deception detection accuracy did not differ across ftf and CMC conditions or across motivation levels. However, an interaction between communication environment and motivation was observed. Consistent with the motivation impairment effect, relative to unmotivated liars, motivated liars in the ftf condition were detected more accurately. In contrast, motivated liars in the CMC condition were detected *less* accurately than unmotivated liars. In fact, a comparison across the four conditions in the study reveals that the highly motivated CMC liars were the *most* successful in their ability to deceive their partner.

We refer to this observation as the *Motivation Enhancement Effect*, which has a number of important implications for digital deception. For example, investigators have warned of the increasing number of intrinsically highly motivated sexual offenders (particularly paedophiles) who have been using various online communication forums to lure potential victims (Mitchell *et al.* 2001). This is a particularly important development given the results of the present study, which suggest that highly motivated liars in CMC contexts are not detected very accurately.

As this study suggests, and the Carlson *et al.* (2004) model predicts, the effect of communication technologies on how humans detect deception is complex. Another interesting line of detection research, however, involves computer-assisted detection of deception (Burgoon *et al.* 2003; Burgoon and Nunamaker 2004). As described above, research on automated textual analysis suggests that there are detectable differences in linguistic patterns across deceptive and non-deceptive text-based communication (e.g., Zhou *et al.* 2004a; Hancock *et al.* in press a). Can a tool be developed that exploits these differences to detect digital deception in real time, as an interaction unfolds? While the prospect of creating this type of tool is appealing, the task of automating the detection of such a complex communication process as digital deception is a clearly daunting one (Burgoon and Nunamaker 2004). Nonetheless, the research findings from the studies described above, which suggest a high diagnostic value of text-based cues (e.g., word quantity, pronoun use, etc.) in digital

deception, and the tremendous advances in computing power and statistical classification techniques, lay a foundation for the development of such a tool.

Conclusions

Given the degree to which information and communication technologies pervade many aspects of our lives, it is perhaps difficult to overestimate the impact such technologies may have on one of the oldest aspects of human life, deception. The present chapter provides an overview of the state-of-the-art on the early stages of research on digital deception. Additional research is needed to examine systematically the wide variety of factors that the literature has identified as affecting deception face-to-face, including, among others, the motivation to detect deception, the relationship between deceiver and target, the type and magnitude of the deception, the role of suspicion (e.g., George and Marrett 2004) and experience with the medium.

Similarly, as new technologies are developed and employed, their features and affordances with respect to deception will need to be identified. For example, how do online dating sites, on which people post profiles of themselves, affect deception and its perception (Cornwell and Lundgren 2001; Ellison *et al.* 2004)? How frequently do people lie in their profiles, and what kinds of lies are considered acceptable?

While further studies are needed, the research to date suggests that the questions posed at the beginning of this chapter concerning the intersection of deception and technology have complex answers, but the research also suggests that communication technologies do indeed affect how frequently we lie, about what and to whom. The data also suggest that deception detection will be as complicated, if not more so, online as it is face-to-face, although the potential for computer-assisted deception detection may create new avenues for this age-old issue.

References

Bargh, J. A., McKenna, K. Y. A. and Fitzsimons, G. J. (2002). Can you see the real me? The activation and expression of the 'true self' on the Internet. *Journal of Social Issues* 58, 33–48.

Berman, J. and Bruckman, A. (2001). The Turing game: exploring identity in an online environment. *Convergence 7*, 83–102.

Bradner, E. and Mark, G. (2002). Why distance matters: effects on cooperation, persuasion and deception. *Proceedings of the 2002 ACM Conference on Computer Supported Cooperative Work* (pp. 226–235). ACM Press: New York.

Buller, D. B. and J. K. Burgoon. (1996). Interpersonal deception theory. *Communication Theory 6*, 203–242.

Burgoon, J. K. and Buller, D. B. (1994). Interpersonal deception: III. Effects of deceit on perceived communication and nonverbal behavior dynamics. *Journal of Nonverbal Behavior 18*, 155–184.

Burgoon, J. K. and Nunamaker, J. F. (2004). Toward computer-aided support for the detection of deception. *Group Decision and Negotiation 13*, 1–4.

Burgoon, J. K., Stoner, G. M., Bonito, J. A. and Dunbar, N. E. (2003). Trust and deception in mediated communication. *Proceedings of the 36th Annual Hawaii International Conference on System Sciences* (10 pages). IEEE Computer Society Press: Washington, D. C.

Burgoon, J. K., Stoner, G. M., Bonito, J. A. and Dunbar, N. E. (2003). Trust and deception in mediated communication. *Proceedings of the 36th Hawaii International Conference on Systems Sciences*, Maui, USA.

Bok, S. (1978). *Lying: Moral choice in public and private life.* New York: Pantheon.

Bradner, E. and Mark, G. (2002). Why distance matters: effects on cooperation, persuasion and deception. *Proceedings, Computer Supported Cooperative Work (CSCW 02)* (pp. 226–235). November, New Orleans, LI.

Camden, C., Motley, M. T. and Wilson, A. (1984). White lies in interpersonal communication: a taxonomy and preliminary investigation of social motivations. *Western Journal of Speech Communication 48*, 309–325.

Carlson, J. R. and George, J. F. (2004). Media appropriateness in the conduct and discovery of deceptive communication: the relative influence of richness and synchronicity. *Group Decision and Negotiation 13*, 191–210.

Carlson, J. R., George, J. F., Burgoon, J. K., Adkins, M. and White, C. H. (2004). Deception in computer-mediated communication. *Group Decision and Negotiation 13*, 5–28.

Carlson, J. R. and Zmud, R. W. (1999). Channel expansion theory and the experiential nature of media richness perceptions. *Academy of Management Journal 42*(2), 153–170.

Cornwell, B. and Lundgren, D. C. (2001). Love on the Internet: involvement and misrepresentation in romantic relationships in cyberspace vs. realspace. *Computers in Human Behavior 17*, 197–211.

Daft, R. L. and R. H. Lengel. (1986). organizational information requirements: media richness and structural design. *Management Science 32*(5), 554–571.

Daft, R. L., R. H. Lengel, and L. K. Trevino. (1987). Message equivocality, media selection, and manager performance: implications for information systems. *MIS Quarterly 11*(3), 355–366.

DePaulo, B. M. and Kashy, D. A. (1998). Everyday lies in close and casual relationships. *Journal of Personality and Social Psychology 74*, 63–79.

DePaulo, B. M. Kashy, D. A., Kirkendol, S. E., Wyer, M. M. and Epstein, J. A.(1996). Lying in everyday life. *Journal of Personality and Social Psychology 70*, 979–995.

DePaulo, B. M. and Kirkendol, S. E. (1989). The motivational impairment effect in the communication of deception. In J. C. Yuille (ed.), *Credibility assessment* (pp. 51–70). Dordrecht, Netherlands: Kluwer Academic.

DePaulo, B. M., Lanier, K. and Davis, T. (1983). Detecting the deceit of the motivated liar. *Journal of Personality and Social Psychology 45*, 1096–1103.

DePaulo, B. M., Lindsay, J. J., Malone, B. E., Muhlenbruck, L., Charlton, K. and Cooper, H. (2003). Cues to deception. *Psychological Bulletin 129*, 74–118.

Donath, J. S. (1998). Identity and deception in the virtual community. In M. A. Smith and P. Kollock (eds) *Communities in Cyberspace* (pp. 29–59). New York: Routledge.

Douglas, K. M. and McGarty, C. (2001). Identifiability and self-presentation: computer-mediated communication and intergroup interaction. British Journal of Social Psychology 40, 399–416.

Ekman, P. (2001). *Telling lies: Clues to deceit in the marketplace, politics and marriage.* New York: W. W. Norton.

Ellison, N. B., Heino, R. D. and Gibbs, J. L. (2004). Truth in advertising? An explanation of self-presentation and disclosure in online personals. Paper presented at the Annual Convention of the International Communication Association, New Orleans, LA.

Feldman, R. S., Forrest, J. A. and Happ, B. R. (2002). Self-presentation and verbal deception: do self-presenters lie more? *Basic and Applied Social Psychology 24*, 163–170.

Forrest, J. A. and Feldman, R. S. (2000). Detecting deception and judge's involvement: lower task involvement leads to better lie detection. *Personality and Social Psychology Bulletin 26*, 118–125.

Galasinski, D. (2000). *The language of deception. A discourse analytic study.* Thousand Oaks, CA: Sage.

George, J. F. and J. R. Carlson. (1999). Group support systems and deceptive communication. *Proceedings of the 32nd Hawaii International Conference on Systems Sciences*, Maui, HI.

George, J. F. and J. R. Carlson. (1999). Group support systems and deceptive communication. *Proceedings of the 32nd Annual Hawaii International Conference on System Sciences* (10 pages). IEEE Computer Society Press: Washington, D. C.

George, J. F. and Carlson, J. R. (2005). Media selection for deceptive communication. *Proceedings of the of the 38th Annual Hawaii International Conference on System Sciences* (10 pages). IEEE Computer Society Press: Washington, D. C.

George, J. F. and Carlson, J. R. (2005). Media selection for deceptive communication. *Proceedings of the 38th Hawaii International Conference on System Sciences.* Big Island, HI.

George, J. F. and Marrett, K. (2004). Inhibiting deception and its detection. *Proceedings of the 34th Hawaii International Conference on System Sciences.*

George, J. F. and Marrett, K. (2004). Inhibiting deception and its detection. *Proceedings of the 34th Annual Hawaii International Conference on System Sciences* (10 pages). IEEE Computer Society Press: Washington, D. C.

George, J. F., Marrett, K. and Tilley, P. (2004). Deception detection under varying electronic media and warning conditions. *Proceedings of the 34th Hawaii International Conference on System Sciences.*

George, J. F. and Marrett, K and Tilley, P. (2004). Deception detection under varying electronic media and warning conditions. *Proceedings of the 34th Annual Hawaii International Conference on System Sciences* (10 pages). IEEE Computer Society Press: Washington, D. C.

Grazioli, S. and Jarvenpaa, S. (2000). Perils of Internet fraud: an empirical investigation of deception and trust with experienced Internet consumers. *IEEE transactions on Systems, Man, and Cybernetics 3*, 395–410.

Grazioli, S. and Jarvenpaa, S. (2003a). Consumer and business deception on the Internet: content analysis of documentary evidence. *International Journal of Electronic Commerce 7*, 93–118.

Grazioli, S. and Jarvenpaa, S. (2003b). Deceived! Under target on line. *Communications of the ACM 46*, 196–205.

Hancock, J. T., Curry, L., Goorha, S., and Woodworth, M. (in press a). On Lying and Being Lied To: A Linguistic Analysis of Deception in Computer-Mediated Communication. *Discourse Processes.*

Hancock, J. T. and Dunham, P. J. (2001a). Impression formation in computer-mediated communication revisited: an analysis of the breadth and intensity of impressions. *Communication Research 28*, 325–347.

Hancock, J. T. and Dunham, P. J. (2001b). Language use in computer-mediated communication: the role of coordination devices. *Discourse Processes 31*, 91–110.

Hancock, J. T., Thom-Santelli, J. and Ritchie, T. (2004a). Deception and design: The impact of communication technologies on lying behavior. *Proceedings, Conference on Computer Human Interaction* (pp. 130–136). New York, ACM.

Hancock, J. T., Thom-Santelli, J. and Ritchie, T. (2004b). What lies beneath: the effect of the communication medium on the production of deception. Presented at the Annual Meeting of the *Society for Text and Discourse*, Chicago, IL.

Hancock, J. T., Woodworth, M., and Goorha, S. (in press b). See no evil: The effect of communication medium and motivation on deception detection. *Group Decision and Negotiation.*

Heinrich, C. U. and Borkenau, P. (1998). Deception and deception detection: the role of cross-modal inconsistency. *Journal of Personality 66*, 667–712.

Herring, S. C. and Martinson, A. (2004). Assessing gender authenticity in computer-mediated language use: evidence from an identity game. *Journal of Language and Social Psychology 23*, 424–446.

Hollingshead, A. (2000). Truth and lying in computer-mediated groups. In M. A. Neale, E. A. Mannix, and T. Griffith (eds), *Research in managing groups and teams, vol. 3: Technology and teams* (pp. 157–173). Greenwich, CT: JAI Press.

Horn, D. B. Is seeing believing? Detecting deception in technologically mediated communication. *Proceedings, Extended Abstracts of CHI'01.*

Horn, D. B., Olson, J. S. and Karasik, L. (2002). The effects of spatial and temporal video distortion on lie detection performance. *Proceedings, Extended Abstracts of CHI'02.*

Horn, D. B., Olson, J. S. and Karasik, L. (2002). The effects of spatial and temporal video distortion on lie detection performance. *Extended Abstracts of the CHI' 02 Conference on Human Factors in Computing Systems* (pp. 714–715). ACM: New York.

Internet Fraud Complaint Center (2003). *Internet Fraud Report*. The National White Collar Crime Center. Washington, D. C.

Joinson, A. N. (2001). Self-disclosure in computer-mediated communication: the role of self-awareness and visual anonymity. *European Journal of Social Psychology 31*, 177–192.

Keyes, R. (2004). The post-truth era: Dishonesty and deception in contemporary life. *New York:* St. Martin's Press.

Knight, J. (2004). The truth about lying. *Nature 428*, 692–694.

Messaris, P. (1997). *Visual persuasion*. Thousand Oaks, CA: Sage Publications, Inc.

Lippard, P. V. (1988). 'Ask me no questions, I'll tell you no lies': situational exigencies for interpersonal deception. *Western Journal of Speech Communication 52*, 91–103.

Metts, S. (1989). An exploratory investigation of deception in close relationships. *Journal of Social and Personal Relationships 6*, 159–179.

Millar, M. and Millar, K. (1995). Detection of deception in familiar and unfamiliar persons: the effects of information restriction. *Journal of Nonverbal Behavior 19*, 69–84.

Miller, G. R. and Stiff, J. B. (1993). *Deceptive communication: Sage series in interpersonal communication, vol. 14*. Thousand Oaks, CA: Sage Publications, Inc.

Mitchell, K. J., Finkelhor, D. and Wolak, J. (2001). Risk factors and impact of online solicitation of youth. *Journal of the American Medical Association 285*, 3011–3014.

Postmes, T., Spears, R. and Lea, M. (1999). Social identity, group norms, and 'deindividuation': lessons from computer-mediated communication for social influence in the group. In N. Ellemers, R. Spears and B. Doosje (eds), *Social identity: Context, commitment, content* (pp. 164–183). Oxford: Blackwell.

Robinson, W. P. (1996). *Deceit, delusion, and detection*. Thousand Oaks, CA: Sage Publications Inc.

Schein, E. H. (2004). Learning when and how to lie: a neglected aspect of organizational and occupational socialization. *Human Relations 57*, 259–273.

Schneider, F. B. (Ed.) (1999). *Trust in cyberspace.* Washington, DC: National Academy Press.

Spears, R., Postmes, T. and Lea, M. (2002). The power of influence and the influence of power in virtual groups: a SIDE look at CMC and the Internet. *The Journal of Social Issues. Special Issue: Social impact of the Internet 58,* 91–108.

Stolfo, S. J., Lee, W., Chan, P. K., Fan, W. and Eskin (2001). Data-mining based intrustion detectors: an overview of the Columbia IDS project. *SIGMOD Record 30,* 5–14.

Turkle, S. (1995). *Life on the screen: Identity in the age of the Internet.* New York: Simon and Schuster.

Utz, S. (2005). Types of deception and underlying motivation: what people think. Social *Science Computer Review 23,* 49–56.

Vrij, A. (2000). *Detecting lies and deceit: The psychology of lying and its implications for professional practice.* Chichester: John Wiley and Sons.

Walther, J. B. (1996). Computer-mediated communication: impersonal, interpersonal, and hyperpersonal interaction. *Communication Research 23,* 1–43.

Walther, J. B. and Parks, M. R. (2002). Cues filtered out, cues filtered in: computer-mediated communication and relationships. In M. L. Knapp and J. A. Daly (eds), *Handbook of interpersonal communication*, 3rd edn. (pp. 529–563). Thousand Oaks, CA: Sage.

Walther, J. B. and Slovacek, C. and Tidwell, L. C. (2001). Is a picture worth a thousand words? Photographic images in long term and short term virtual teams. *Communication Research 28,* 105–134.

Whitty, M. T. (2002). Liar, Liar! An examination of how open, supportive and honest people are in chat rooms. Computers in Human Behavior *18*(4), 343–352.

Whitty, M. and Gavin, J. (2001). Age/sex/location: uncovering the social cues in the development of online relationships. *CyberPsychology and Behavior 4*(5), 623–630.

Zahavi, A. (1993). The fallacy of conventional signaling. *The Royal Society Philosophical Transaction 340,* 227–230.

Zhou, L., Burgoon, J. K., Nunamaker, J. F. and Twitchell, D. (2004a). Automating linguistics-based cues for detecting deception in text-based asynchronous computer-mediated communication. *Group Decision and Negotiation 13,* 81–106.

Zhou, L., Burgoon, J. K., Twitchell, D., Qin, T. and Nunamaker, J. F. (2004b). A comparison of classification methods for predicting deception in computer-mediated communication. *Journal of Management Information Systems 20,* 139–165.

Zhou, L. and Zhang, D. (2004). Can online behavior unveil deceivers? An exploratory investigation of deception in instant messaging. *Proceedings of the 37th Hawaii International Conference on Systems Sciences,* Maui, USA.

Zhou, L. and Zhang, D. (2004). Can online behavior unveil deceivers? An exploratory investigation of deception in instant messaging. *Proceedings of the 37th Annual Hawaii International Conference on System Sciences* (10 pages). IEEE Computer Society Press: Washington, D. C.

Zuckerman, M. and Driver, R. E. (1985). Telling lies: verbal and nonverbal correlates of deception. In A. W. Siegman and S. Feldstein (eds), *Multichannel integrations of nonverbal behavior* (pp. 129–147). Hillsdale, NJ: Erlbaum.

CHAPTER 20

Phantom emotions

Psychological determinants of emotional experiences on the Internet

Azy Barak

Truth is a necessary phantom.

Mason Cooley

Introduction: old psychological concepts in an emerging social environment

This chapter refers to emotional experiences in cyberspace. Although at first thought this seems to be a simple topic, it is actually rather convoluted and perplexing, because emotion and affect are complicated psychological constructs (Ben-Ze'ev 2000; Russell 2003) and cyberspace is a very complicated concept (Strate *et al.* 2003). Theories relating to the generation of emotions underline the fundamental role of numerous cognitive-processing mechanisms and the dynamic interaction among these processes in contributing to the production of emotion (O'Rorke and Ortony 1994; Ortony *et al.* 1988). Special emphasis is frequently given to the appraisal of meaning processes (Smith and Kirby 2000) which, for example, call for an active,

perhaps conscious involvement in manufacturing emotion. On the other hand, approaches such as Prinz's (2004) argue that cognitive involvement is not imperative, as emotion can be caused by perceptions rather than higher level concepts. This latter view thus leaves room for an exogenous generation of emotions, which leads to Prinz's conceptualization of 'gut reactions'. Generally, however, the digestion and cultivation of external information by the senses in interaction with input from one's internal framework are considered to elicit a subjective mental experience. This general approach – in addition to the introduction less than two decades ago of the concept of Emotional Intelligence (Mayer and Salovey 1997), which called for a reconceptualization of the relationship between reason and emotion – made the understanding of emotional reactions even more complex. It is interesting to note that although we regularly and commonly experience emotions, this construct is apparently among the most complicated to conceptualize – which explains why more than 150 theories have been proposed in trying to understand the concept

(Strongman 2003). One of the basic characteristics common to most of these theories, however, is the fundamental place they regularly assign to the interaction of person (e.g., personality, perceptions, appraisals), on the one hand and environment and culture, on the other, in understanding emotions (Ben-Ze'ev 2000; Reeve 2005; Strongman 2003) – a point of central importance to the current discussion. However, it seems that we can commonly accept the notion that emotion is a multidimensional concept that is known to have four basic components: *subjective*, which refers to a phenomenological experience; *biological*, which refers to bodily arousal; *purposive*, which relates to motivational state toward action; and *social*, which refers to the communicative aspect (Reeve 2005).

Internet environments, or cyberspace, provide us with an interesting opportunity to observe and re-examine cognitive, social psychological and interpersonal communication models (McKenna and Bargh 2000; Riva 2002), as well as theoretical arguments referring to personality structure and dynamics (Amichai-Hamburger 2002) in the context of emotional experiences, interpersonal and group behaviour. The argument advanced in this chapter is that personal emotions experienced in Internet-based communication – especially text-based as most Internet communications are, in particular (but not only) between strangers – are based, in principle, on what later will be presented as *phantom sensations*. That is, although these emotions are subjectively experienced as authentic, well-founded and even rational, they frequently rely on erroneous information that the interacting parties – self and partner/s – supply simultaneously and actively, apparently out of a need to satisfy psychological needs, whether the motivation for doing so is malicious or innocent. Thus invalidated emotional accounts, of any type, experienced online – and regularly leading to certain behaviours and/or bodily reactions – are regarded as powerful, prime moderators in the attempt to understand, explain and control human phenomena in cyberspace.

Internet-based communication channels connect people. When these people then communicate with one another, the personal experience – in addition to the mere exchange of information – involves the eliciting of feelings and emotions

(Levine 1998; Mantovani 2001a; McKenna *et al.* 2002). This is no different from any other mode of communication between human beings, as the emotional dimension is considered to be inseparable from the interpersonal experience. Although much research, as well as personal introspection, has led researchers to understand the dynamics of the creation, development and flux of emotions in the 'real world', as noted earlier, much less is known and understood about this subject in the context of cyberspace. The reasons for this lack of knowledge have to do with the relatively new state of the Internet as an accepted, widespread communication vehicle, as well as with the paucity of scientific psychological investigations in this area to date. However, the subject has attracted a growing number of researchers in recent years and we seem to know significantly more now than a decade ago (Johns *et al.* 2004). That said, this body of knowledge, relative to other areas in social sciences, is still in a preliminary stage, as much of this information is based on speculations, non-objective data, unreplicated research and biased self-observations.

The conceptual proposition advanced in this chapter refers to Internet-based communication in general; however, it might be more relevant and more salient when employing this means of communication between strangers. Cyberspace – different from any other social environment – has made meetings between strangers more commonplace, even if virtual (Bargh and McKenna 2004). A variety of online communication tools, from personal homepages and blogs to email, chat rooms and forums, enable contact between people in a way that is affordable, convenient, efficient and relatively private and safe. Indeed, these virtual interactions have become almost standard among people in modern society (Bargh and McKenna 2004), constituting a customary usage among workers in an organization, as well as among family members, friends and students. Online interactions with *known* partners – for formal business as well as for casual interactions – complement face-to-face meetings: their utility might lie in their offering an additional channel of message delivery, often with unique and significant psychological value (Chan *et al.* 2004). However, the broad, rapid expansion of the use of online communication among people who are, in principle, strangers to one another has created a new, perhaps revolutionary, notion and perspective of interpersonal relationships. For example, according to the Pew Internet Project (2005), more than 33 million adult Americans regularly use virtual chat rooms. If we add to this figure the millions of teenagers, as well as the untold number of users of other online communication tools that are frequently employed to communicate with complete strangers (e.g., instant messaging, forums) and despite the fact that a proportion of these people use online means to communicate with people they are acquainted with, it is clear that a new, quite different social environment has emerged (Calvert 2002). The question of how relationships are established in cyberspace and what characterizes them has now attracted researchers to investigate a wide range of populations, online environments and psycho-social aspects (e.g., Chan *et al.* 2004; McKenna and Seidman 2005). Much effort has been invested in developing online social interaction technologies to allow those with more means and opportunities to communicate conveniently (Whittaker 2004). However, the dynamics of the affective dimension – one of the basic components of what comprises emotion (Reeve 2005) – in Internet-based interactions has largely remained untouched as a subject of investigation.

Internet-based interpersonal communication

Common Internet-based communication is characterized by several essential features that make it different from any other means of human communication. First, the partners to the communication are *invisible* to one another (except for the much less frequent use of video communication through a webcam). This situation creates two independent characteristics for online communication: one is that physical information is totally missing; this absence of the visible has a direct effect on the communicating parties that is related to important personal details, such as skin colour, weight, height and general looks, all of which are known to affect interpersonal perceptions (Kenny 1994). In online interaction, these details are practically

non-existent and, therefore, are not a direct part of an individual's awareness. As a result, common stereotypes and stigmatic attributions relating to ethnicity, age, disability and the like – all commonly influential, visible personal characteristics – are entirely absent in the complexity of interpersonal interaction online, obviously assuming they are unknown to the communicating parties (Spears *et al.* 2002). Consequently, emotional effects (i.e., affects, attitudes, behaviours) normally caused and elicited by these attributions and stereotypes (Blair 2002) – including on the Internet when such details are known (Postmes and Spears 2002) – are absent, too. For instance, in a virtual situation in which identifiability is absent, accelerated aggressive behaviours might be expected (Douglas and McGarty 2001), possibly because of the cognitive processes of attribution, unlike a similar interpersonal situation offline. Another characteristic, related to the absence of personal physical details, is that non-verbal communication cues – such as hand movements and gestures, facial expressions (smiles, tears, frowns, etc.) and body lean – do not take part in delivering messages as they do in common face-to-face communication (e.g., Knapp and Hall 2001). In consequence, online messages are transmitted and received mainly on the basis of verbal communication. The significant, essential, often critical role of non-verbal communication cues is missing.

Second, most Internet communication is based on *typed text* (Pew Internet Project 2003). This factor has several independent effects:

◆ Interpersonal verbal messages *do not include voice*, which is another major vehicle providing meta-communication features of human messages through such factors as loudness, intonation, pitch and breaks (e.g., Pickett 1998), as well as recognition of some personal traits, such as gender and age.

◆ Messages can easily be saved, retrieved, copied, forwarded, encrypted and backed-up – features that go beyond more conventional 'snail mail', or traditional handwriting communication. This characteristic opens up a wide range of opportunities that might directly affect people's experiences with interpersonal communication in a manner that they would ordinarily not experience in other modes of communication (Suler 2004a). For instance, unlike common interpersonal communication, an episode or a gesture from the past, if logged, can easily be revived in online communication and re-experienced at a later time for an authentic (positive or negative) present experience. Such experiences can easily be shared with others for possible additional excitement.

♦ When a person *writes*, they tend to express things that might not be expressed at all in other modes of communication or that might be expressed differently (Pennebaker *et al.* 2003; Barak and Miron 2005). This is perhaps due to the ability to plan, edit and organize written text better than spoken words, as well as to engage in personal reflection. Apparently, this feature also owes to the experience of *aloneness* in writing, or a sense of complete privacy (Ben-Ze'ev 2003; Viseu *et al.* 2004) that produces an as-if feeling of self-talk in stark contrast to actually speaking with a partner. Cumulative experimental and clinically oriented research has consistently provided evidence of the special psychological influence of writing in effecting emotions and consequent behaviours (see reviews by Esterling *et al.* 1999; Pennebaker *et al.* 2003). Clinical experience, as well as research, shows that *reading*, too, exerts a tremendous emotional effect, one that is perhaps stronger than other channels of communication (Cupchik *et al.* 1998). The textual relations created between partners in online communication contribute to augmented interpersonal openness and closeness, despite the physical distance and the mediation of complicated technology (Suler 2004a).

♦ There is absolutely *no eye contact* between the partners when communicating online. It should be noted, though, that the absence of eye contact is a different entity and has different effects from invisibility, as visibility does not automatically mean the existence of eye contact. Communicating by written correspondence, on the other hand, necessarily entails a total absence of eye contact between people who communicate. As eye contact directly refers to personal behaviours and feelings that have to do with comfortableness, self-disclosure, intimacy, openness, honesty and deception

(Kleinke 1986; Webbink 1986), this factor is of significant value in human communication and the elicitation of emotions. Lack of eye contact in online communication, therefore, presumably has essential affective and behavioural impacts on individuals communicating with each other electronically. It should be noted that emerging trends in integrating online voice communication (VoIP) and video communication (through webcam) over the net may have an impact on users' experience. These effects, however, which have hardly been investigated to date, are apparently uncommon in comparison with text-based online communication.

Third, Internet communication allows different degrees of *synchronicity* between parties. Communication might be entirely synchronous (e.g., chat room), entirely asynchronous (e.g., email), or under the user's control in regard to the degree of synchronicity (as in instant messaging). The flexible degree of synchronicity – also termed elasticity of synchronicity (Newhagen and Rafaeli 1996) or temporal fluidity (Suler 2004a) – allows better control of immediacy, as well as better reflection, than does a rigid type of interaction, such as in-person, non-mediated, face-to-face communication. This special characteristic is considered essential in enabling advanced friendship-development and relationship-formation as well as work-collaboration (Cho *et al.* 2005), since communicating partners can give attention simultaneously and alternatively to both their online and offline environments. The unique ability of online communication to control the level of synchronicity also enables a special method of human communication – *multi-conversing*, which allows people to communicate in parallel with different people on different subjects, sometimes on different communication channels and yet to engage in independent, confidential individual conversations. Users of chat and instant messaging exploit this capability to engage simultaneously with several partners, who may or may not know of the existence of the other conversations. The multi-conversing experience itself is usually a source of stimulation and excitement (Ben-Ze'ev 2004). The excitement is an addition to the psychological effects of the very *dynamic interactivity* that is inherent in online communication, far beyond what people experience in offline contacts (Sundar 2004; Sohn and Lee 2005). Online service providers, too – be they salespersons in online shops or counsellors who provide online therapy and support – take advantage of this ability to multi-converse, by communicating simultaneously and privately with more than one customer/client (Barak 2004; Suler 2004a) in order to promote business and better exploit time.

Fourth, Internet communication is in a way *richer* than face-to-face communication in that it can employ various add-ons to simple language, such as still pictures, animation and multimedia, as well as supply links to numerous websites (a capability termed hypertextuality). Such features not only contribute to the design and attraction of communication but also make it more efficient in terms of operating a multi-sensual channel of communication for the more effective delivery of messages and information. In addition, the common use of emoticons (i.e., small textual or graphic signs, such as a 'smiley', that users add to their textual messages) compensates, at least to some degree, for the lack of non-verbal cues and can enrich the colourfulness of communication (Walther and D'Addario 2001). Similarly, by using more advanced design technology, avatars (i.e., individually selected graphic representations of users) may be used to establish – or influence – perceptions related to mood, gender and credibility (Nowak and Rauh 2005), as well as to enhance the communication of emotions (Kamada *et al.* 2005).

Although interpersonal communication on the Internet – based on numerous tools, languages, cultures, subcultures and the special characteristics described above – is convenient, rich, colourful and exciting, it also seems to have the potential to produce massive miscommunication. This abuse of communication might include any of several forms of communication disturbances: offensive verbal conduct, known as flaming; listening without making your presence known, known as lurking; delivering a message to someone who would not otherwise choose to receive it, known as spamming or bombing; and identity deception, known as spoofing. However – as thoughtfully analysed and postulated by Riva (2001a) – these disturbances could be viewed as

a 'pared-down' communication network that actually operates according to and concurs with several psychologically based models, thus obeying certain social rules. Nonetheless, the special communication features cited above – though perhaps mainly the factors of anonymity, lack of eye contact and the mode of writing – create the psychological phenomenon known as the 'online disinhibition effect' (Joinson 1998, 1999, 2001, 2003; Suler 1996–2005, 2004b). This effect occurs when individuals tend to behave in ways they would not act in face-to-face interaction. As is clear from the term, 'online disinhibition' occurs because typical personal inhibitions diminish when communicating in cyberspace, thereby creating two phenomena: first, people reveal personal information about themselves that they would not regularly disclose, in terms of the *nature* of the content, *depth* of exposure and *time* required to disclose it (see Chapter 16, this volume). Attempting to explain this phenomenon, Tidwell and Walther (2002) argued that accelerated intimacy and disclosure in computer-mediated communication, in contrast to face-to-face communication, was a direct result of and perhaps compensation for, the lack of non-verbal communication cues that make people feel closer to one another, as suggested by the Uncertainty Reduction Theory (Berger and Calabrese 1975), which will be referred to later in the chapter. Tidwell and Walther (2002), too, referred to online disinhibition by stating that 'the absence of nonverbal cues, as well as editing capabilities, identity cues and temporal characteristics may prompt CMC users to engage in selective self-presentation and partner idealization, enacting exchanges more intimate than those of FtF counterparts' (pp. 319–320). This personal opening-up is characterized by the disclosure of a wide range of intimate contents and feelings as Internet surfers have experienced to a great extent (Joinson 2003). The second phenomenon, which is related to the previous one, is that many people tend to behave in the way of *acting out* when online. Offline, this behaviour is typically characteristic of problematic children: their reactions are impulsive and they exhibit disruptive, annoying and anti-social behaviours (Suler and Phillips 2000; Joinson 2003; Thompson 2003). On the Internet, because communication is text-based, such actions are considered destructive and harassing, though in different ways from offline communication (Ybarra and Mitchell 2004; Barak 2005).

Effects of presence and ambiguity

The special characteristics of Internet communication described above make cyberspace a unique environment, at least insofar as interpersonal communication is concerned. In addition, as in a movie, a person who stays in this environment – especially in a social interactive area – experiences immersion. That is, this person's senses become quite isolated or disconnected from the offline environment (often called the 'real world') and are completely (or at least predominantly) submerged in the wide-scope of information flowing out from the computer. It is an experience equated with the psychological state of *presence* (IJsselsteijn *et al.* 2001), a concept that has regularly been investigated in regard to human sensations in a Virtual Reality (VR) situation. In the context of text-based virtual environments, presence can be described as

> a feeling of getting lost or wrapped up in the representations of the text – of being involved, absorbed, engaged, or engrossed in or by them . . . Conceptualized as flow, presence refers to a merging of action and awareness, during which a person loses self-consciousness and a sense of time, focusing on the present and blocking out the past and the future . . . . Presence may also be said to entail an unselfconscious transparency in which a participant enters a virtual world, looking through rather than at the text that represents it.
>
> (Jacobson 2001: 654)

This subjective experience, which is clearly reflected through physiological and behavioural measures (Insko 2003), creates a sense of 'being there' (IJsselsteijn and Riva 2003). It is as though one is mentally present in an environment – an actual, physically real environment – other than one's own.

Not surprisingly, the personal state of 'being there' is clearly associated with the concept of empathy; that is, the ability to experience the 'as if' condition (and emotional state) of another. Indeed, an individual's empathic tendency was found to moderate personal experiences of presence (Nicovich *et al.* 2005). Furthermore, this 'as if', or virtual, experience of presence induces dramatic cognitive, affective and motivational effects in the participating individual (Gaggioli *et al.* 2003) and it apparently affects modes of thought, as well (Granic and Lamey 2000). Furthermore, as Grigorovici (2003) has shown, emotional arousal, information processing and cognitive awareness while experiencing presence in an immersive virtual environment have significant effects on gullibility, which subsequently increases one's vulnerability to persuasion. Experiences of presence on the one hand and emotions on the other, it is argued, are *conceptually* orthogonal to each other (Robillard *et al.* 2003); that is, the two states are considered distinct constructs. *Empirically*, however – for apparently casual interactions and procedures that are in need of further exploration, as is currently accepted among researchers (Bouchard 2004; Slater 2004) – they correlate. It seems that the complex construct of presence, including its antecedents and consequences, is far from having been thoroughly investigated and thus remains only partially understood, especially in regard to emotional effects (Alcañiz *et al.* 2003). It is clear, however, that 'presence' significantly reflects on one's subjective experiences in cyberspace.

As mentioned by Jacobson (2001), the construct of presence is closely related to the concept of 'flow' (Csikszentmihalyi 1975, 1982). In the VR environment, including cyberspace on the Web, people's minds flow, as it were, in the virtual space, a mental condition in which they tend to forget their mind states and problems and, instead, integrate themselves with keyboard and monitor into cyberspace (Chen *et al.* 2000; Chen 2006). As shown by Chen *et al.* (2000), Web users experience a fading away of their physical world and live through the present issues they are debating and the words and sentences they are typing and reading. Web users who experience flow feel as though there is no separate 'me', but a merging of human and machine occurring. During flow episodes, there is the loss of a sense of time and hours feel like minutes, mostly of enjoyable moments. This view is closely related to Strate's (2003) concept of 'cybertime', in which VR elicits a subjective sense of illusory virtual time.

Although, as noted, clear relationships between presence and flow and emotional experiences in cyberspace are still to be discovered, it is clear that personal, powerful experiences of presence and flow are typical of users of computer-mediated communication and considerably influence their physiological, affective, cognitive and behavioural reactions (Chen 2006). For example, to make the principle of presence and flow more realistic in terms of Web users' actual activities, we can refer to a typical, yet paradoxical experience that a person encounters in cyberspace: this is what Ben-Ze'ev (2005) termed 'detattachment'. This describes a person who – despite being detached because of distance, relatively lean communication, anonymity, common deception, discontinuity of contact and marginal physical investment – still feels intimately close and attached to another person. Although 'our emotional system is not yet structured to deal with such opposing features' (2005: 134), this unique phenomenon, experienced by most Internet users, is characteristic of the effects of presence and flow in the cyberspace/VR environment.

Moreover, because of the common and quite usual lack of known or clear information about the identity or descriptive characteristics of one's partner in online communication (with the exception of communication between acquaintances), or 'reduced cues' in the interpersonal situation (Walther 1996) – an element related to invisibility and anonymity – and because of the ambiguity of the whole experience, cyberspace leaves much room for individual dynamics to fill in the gaps (Mantovani 2002). In this situation, an individual often attempts to clarify absent or unclear details in their environment by *projecting* from their own personal repertoire (Fenichel 2004; Suler 1996–2005). Suler (1996–2005), for example, described a psychological analysis of a user of email communication that dealt with the person's non-replying to email. Calling this a 'black hole phenomenon', he suggested that multiple psychological processes come into play in generating personal dynamics in this ambiguous situation. In another example, Gabbard (2001) referred to powerful sexual desires induced by what he termed 'e-rotic transference' in communicating with unknown, ambiguous partners. In this context, transference refers to an unconscious process of projecting onto others in the present environment feelings and attitudes – from hate and hostility to love and affection – that possibly were originally linked with significant figures in one's early life. Similarly, Civin (2000) analysed romantic relationships initiated online as a result of individuals' projections onto one another that basically reflected needs for relatedness. Consistent with this view, Weinberg (2002) analysed transference and countertransference processes in online group (email list) dynamics that exist between group participants and moderator.

Walker *et al.* (2003) reported on an experiment that exemplified the existence of person-technology transference. Using participants' attributional ratings, they were able to show evaluative and emotional references that could explain pathological behaviours, such as phobia and addiction. This relational process, which in some ways is similar, though not necessarily identical, to the psychoanalytic concept of projection is perhaps *psychodynamic* in nature in that it involves the complicated operation of mental mechanisms and a broad range of origins, such as basic instincts, personality needs and values, memories and associations, wishes and daydreams, habituated responses and the various possible conflicts among them (Turkle 2004). Indeed, the process of projection entails the use of a person's personal dynamics of personality for perceptions, attributions and interpretations of others, on the one hand and the use of 'objects', on the other. Although objects might include anything in one's virtual (or real) environment, a person likely projects her or his own dynamics onto other people. As mentioned, Civin (2000), applying psychoanalytic views, showed how intergender relationships formed through email were reinforced and accelerated by mutual projections. Mantovani (2001a) and Ben-Ze'ev (2004) emphasized that cyber-attraction involved the idealization of virtual partners. In the same vein, Levine (2000) refers to ambiguous, unclear, incomplete and missing personal information in cyberspace encounters as a possible catalyst of online attraction.

Ambiguity is a central characteristic of an online communication environment. Mantovani (2002) referred to three aspects that contributed to the ambiguous nature of cyberspace: *user's self-presentation*, involving the fabrication of any appearance at will; *the social context*, which refers to the lack of visible social cues and the reliance on an assumptive social environment; and *estimation of the reality of the situation*, which is related to the subjective perception of the virtual reality of what is individually experienced in electronic environments. In all, these factors assign a major role to an individual's cognitive processes, referred to by Mantovani as 'the ubiquity of mediation' (2002: 319), by which he stresses the overwhelming and critical human experience in cyberspace over mere technology. Ambiguity, thus, is inherent in computer-mediated communication, resulting in dynamic personal processes that stem from the very subjectively perceived nature of the situation. Cyberspace ambiguity lays the grounds for what psychoanalysis considers optimal for generating highly active psychodynamic processes, such as projection and transference (Bordin 1955), which, in turn, elicit a person's strong emotions. Actually, advocates of psychoanalysis view cyberspace as a special environment in which natural human dynamic mechanisms go into action in a predictable way (Suler 1996–2005; Bird 2003; Turkle 2004; Zizek 2004; Whitty and Carr 2006). A non-psychoanalytical view of ambiguity in cyberspace is Walther's (1996) *hyperpersonal* model of interpersonal computer-mediated communication, which refers to the inflated perception and idealization processes of an online partner. Recent research (Nowak *et al.* 2005; Yao and Flanagin 2006) empirically supports Walther's hyperpersonal approach.

It should be noted that transference and projective processes that entail the operation of numerous cognitive mechanisms relating to cyberspace ambiguity also serve as typical processes characterizing online counselling – a specific online interaction in which two communicating partners are usually unfamiliar with each other. These processes normally enhance the therapeutic encounter and provide therapists with different approaches – be they psychodynamic, cognitive, narrative, or existential – and significant materials with which to work in the therapeutic encounter (Barak 2004; Rochlen *et al.* 2004). Actually, from a psychoanalytic–psychodynamic point of view, cyberspace is considered an ideal therapeutic environment, as

its ambiguity allows a patient's desired projections and transference processes (Suler 2000; Gabbard 2001; Fenichel *et al.* 2002). In other words, from this psychotherapeutic perspective, the ambiguous virtual environment provides useful psychological grounds for effective transference and countertransference processes (Suler 2000, 2004a); these add a significant, independent dimension – and advantage – to the use of the Internet over both the mere exchange of therapy-relevant information (e.g., Baur 2000) and the application of psychotherapeutic treatment techniques (e.g., Yellowlees 2002; Tate and Zabinski 2004). For example, Gaggioli *et al.* (2003b) proposed the use of avatars in group therapy conducted in a virtual environment, as the avatars would reflect patients' perceived selves and interact with other patients' projected, socially meaningful avatars. The specific choice of avatars, according to this conception, might have significant therapeutic meaning. A related example is a proposal made by Ookita and Tokuda (2001), who supplied an empirical evaluation of an online counselling group based on the participants' 'projective agents', on which they projected their personality characteristics. Suler (1996–2005) listed and described a number of uses of avatars in an online virtual environment, each characterized by some distinctive 'personality', for possible productive use in social interactions in cyberspace.

Several psychological theories account for the basic *motivation* to complement missing or vague information in the ambiguous virtual environment characterizing cyberspace. One model ascribes a major motivational role to the instinctive *need for cognitive orientation*, which refers to the generation of meaning; this includes components of beliefs about self, norms, goals and environment, that are manifested in behavioural intent and planned behaviour (Kreitler 1976; Kreitler and Kreitler 1990). This model has much relevance in the context of cyberspace, as it argues that individuals – based on inherent, instinctive needs – strive for explanations to reduce the strain caused by a lack of cognitive orientation. Consistent with this conception, quite a few studies have found a significant relationship between, on the one hand, the design and navigation of information websites, as well as Web-based communication platforms and, on the other, user satisfaction and performance (e.g., Galimberti et al. 2001; Gamberini and Valentini 2001). These models can explain, for example, van Oostendorp's and van Nimwegen's (1998) finding that variables related to the design and navigability of online newspapers affect users' performance and satisfaction in reading them. Similar findings support the argument that a lack of cognitive orientation is related to personal experiences of inconvenience, which in turn causes behaviours that might subsequently reduce tension.

Another relevant model that pertains to Internet users' motivation to reduce vagueness relates to the *cognitive need for closure* (e.g., Kruglanski and Webster 1996). According to this view, individuals act on a level congruent with their personal need for closure when seeking information consistent with their prior personal knowledge. In this context, Amichai-Hamburger et al. (2004) showed how the need for closure, in addition to a website's level of interactivity, influenced participants' Internet-surfing behaviour (see also Chapter 13 in this volume).

Yet another model that could be adopted to explain individuals' motivation to close gaps and seek clarification in the ambiguity of cyberspace relates to the *personality drive to avoid cognitive dissonance* (Festinger 1957; Harmon-Jones 2001). According to this conception, people who communicate in cyberspace or use online tools for browsing the net and obtaining information tend to distort information or change their attitudes and/or behaviours to maintain cognitive consistency. Accordingly, Czerwinski and Larson (2003) argued that when designing online applications, website planners should consider this consistency factor in order to achieve optimal user performance and satisfaction.

The drive to avoid cognitive dissonance might be related to another theoretical approach, one that reflects the motivation, need, or drive to close gaps in the elevated ambiguity of cyberspace environment – the uncertainty reduction theory. According to this viewpoint (Berger and Calabrese 1975; Berger and Gudykunst 1991), people actively engaged in seeking information about others – by collecting data, conversing, interrogating and using their own judgements – want to reduce uncertainty about other persons. All these activities take place because, as the theory assumes, uncertainty is an unpleasant state

for the individual; hence, they take actions to avoid it. Related to the uncertainty reduction theory is the more comprehensive field of behavioural and emotional reactions in uncertain situations (e.g., Brashers 2001). According to Brashers, 'uncertainty exists when details of situations are ambiguous, complex, unpredictable, or probabilistic; when information is unavailable or inconsistent; and when people feel insecure in their own state of knowledge or the state of knowledge in general' (2001: 478). Based on the cognitive appraisal view of emotion and much research in a variety of areas in behaving under uncertain circumstances, positive (e.g., hope), negative (e.g., anxiety), neutral (e.g., indifference) and combined reactions might occur under these circumstances – all based on the different perceptions, attributions and appraisals of the situation that different people might hold. People, then, may manage uncertainty to reduce and avoid negative or enhance and maintain positive experiences. That is, people may selectively use communication to manipulate uncertainty to suit their personal needs.

Because of either one of the psychological drives and motives just described and under the mental circumstances under the state of ambiguity and uncertainty, it is argued here that an individual strives to put things in place, to make order, to create consistency and harmony, to satisfy curiosity and to feel oriented and reassured in accordance with their personal perceptions, expectations, beliefs, values and other factors relevant to the theoretical motivational model adopted. In other words, the contention is that a person will actively attribute content to objects and make cyberspace a more individually experienced, convenient environment. In cyberspace, stimuli are usually vague, foggy and unclear; it happens, therefore, that close-to-transparent, personal motivations sometimes come into play in order to maintain psychological balance. Cyberspace thus presents a classic environment for filling in gaps through and by virtue of one's personal psychological repertoire. This is where *imagination* and *imagery* are played out. Imagination entails the general cognitive capacity of human beings to fantasize about the nature of others, both people and environments or objects, through ideas, narratives, concepts, explanations, assumptions and beliefs (Thomas 2003). Imagery refers to the visual representation of imagined objects – namely, assigning them forms (Thomas 1999). Thus, imagination and imagery, as two cognitive capacities, bring into play an individual's psychological drives through inherently automatic, unintentional, unwitting and usually unknowing processes. In the context of online communication, in which ambiguity prevails,

> the role of imagination in generating emotions in cyberspace is even greater than in actual-space. The factual information we have about an online partner is usually more limited than our knowledge of an offline partner and our imagination must fill in the gap.

(Ben-Ze'ev 2004: 80)

In experiencing virtual communication in cyberspace through the dynamic operation of the mechanisms and processes of inherent motivations, imagination and imagery, individuals relatively quickly transform communication into *relationships*. That is, they convert an exchange of messages into interpersonal contact, which is accompanied by a broad range of emotions (Galimberti *et al.* 2001; Mantovani 2001a; McKenna and Green 2002; Riva 2002; Sassenberg 2002). Forming relationships in cyberspace creates a social environment. The maintaining of social interactions on the Internet – whether in a dual relationship or with multiple partners – is characterized by many interpersonal attitudes and behaviours typical of offline social relations. Unique social aspects (e.g., flaming), however, have been identified, too (e.g., Joinson 2003), which makes this environment both special and emerging in the context of the social sciences. Indeed, consistently and overwhelmingly, research has found and numerous anecdotal reports have documented – perhaps against common sense or intuitive thinking – that social interactions in cyberspace elicit strong affects, despite (and perhaps because of) the virtual nature of the environment as though one is experiencing actual, Real World occurrences (Ben-Ze'ev 2004; Fenichel 2004).

The nature of online emotions

When communication is basically virtual, based on exchanges of typed messages, frequently between unidentifiable partners and mediated by complicated technology, the interpersonal relationships formed are essentially based on information that, in principle, lacks any external validation. Rather, they rely mainly on data inherent in the communication style – for example use of humour, wittiness, spelling mistakes – and content. That is, the information about and the perception of online partners is commonly based not on actual knowledge, hard facts, or verified details, but on information supplied by a partner either directly by communicating messages or indirectly by retrieving existing online information (e.g., personal details typed in the 'User Details' space in Internet chat profiles or personal information of a blogger). Although relationship-building based on discourse is feasible and actually quite prevalent in current times, it obviously is limited to virtual contacts; its maturing into a more advanced, offline, stable and committed relationship would require additional, less purposeful and subjective and more objective (e.g., physical) information (Baker 2005).

When individuals engage in the common type of virtual relationship, the autonomic operation of the motivational processes on the one hand and imagination and imagery processes on the other cause them to become usually highly immersed in and, therefore, fascinated, preoccupied and captivated by the experience of *flow and presence*. As a result, especially in interpersonal interactions (in contrast to Web browsing as such), people tend to develop certain cognitions: they strongly believe in the validity of their observations and deductions, including their attribution of traits to others (Markey and Wells 2002; Rouse and Hass 2003); they feel various degrees of attraction to others (Williamson *et al.* 2003); they develop assessments of the intentions and attitudes of these others (Light and Wakeman 2001); they form different levels of trust in other Internet users (see Chapter 4, this volume); they build up trust in online advice (see Chapter 22, this volume); and they develop perceptions, expectations, attributions and beliefs that affect their attitudes toward virtual online partners. In addition, these individuals also develop specific attitudes in regard to risk, such as evaluations pertaining to the various degrees of risk of the virtual situation they are experiencing (Zimmer and Hunter 2003) or estimations of the degree of danger of situations in which children are involved (Livingstone 2003; Quigley and Blashki 2003). Such attitudes influence their decisions and reactions vis-à-vis strangers. It is important to note that people who conceive, emotionally react and behave in reaction to various virtual, basically invalidated and unchecked stimuli under uncertain ambiguous circumstances do not do so because of naivety, stupidity, or negligence: on the contrary, their actions are natural and normal for any human being in such a social environment. That is, social cognition is as active online as it is offline in determining various aspects of human functioning (Rafaeli *et al.* 2005).

Personal conviction, which goes hand in hand with imagined scenarios and imageries, with gullibility, as well as with the disinhibition of personal content and behaviours that are normally inhibited, operates quickly and powerfully to develop authentically experienced emotions (Ben-Ze'ev 2003, 2004; McKenna and Seidman 2005). Such emotions include, for example, sincere empathy toward others (Preece 1999; Preece and Ghozati 2001), hate (Lee and Leets 2002; Levin 2002), love (Cornwell and Lundgren 2001; Whitty 2003a, 2003b; Ben-Ze'ev 2004) and aggression (Cunneen and Stubbs 2000).

It should be kept in mind, however, that the emotional experiences are generated, or inflamed, by – in many cases – false, arbitrary, biased, exaggerated, manipulated, misleading, or invalid information that is created by online partners or by self-imagination. Evidently, such experiences are also influenced by stigmatic impressions (Wildermuth 2004), being helped or being offered help (Blair *et al.* 2005), response time (Tyler and Tang 2003), the revelation of deception (Birchmeier *et al.* 2005), judgements of content and style (Savicki *et al.* 2003), perception of gender-role (Dorer 2002), being ignored (Williams *et al.* 2000), the purposive nature of the interactive messages (Lee 2005a) and stereotypes and expectations (Epley and Kruger 2005). These are normal social cognitive processes, similar in nature to people's offline experiences (Riva and Galimberty 1997, 1998, 2001; Riva 2001b, 2002; LaRose *et al.* 2001a; Hofer 2004; Eastin 2005; Rafaeli *et al.* 2005). Thus, in the absence of credible resources – as is typical in cyberspace, especially between strangers – perceived and imagined data fill the role of facts in many instances. Imagined and believed 'facts' become, relatively easily in cyberspace, something that is personally considered true, thereby exchanging 'seeing is believing' with 'believing is believing'. Because of the psychological processes responsible for their generation, emotions based on wishful thinking and deprived needs and expectations, influenced by misinformation or disinformation, together with the massive catalyzing effect of online disinhibition, are personally experienced as though completely well-founded. And, indeed, on the individual's subjective level of experience, these emotions are in no way different from emotions based on actual, genuine relationships (Döring 2002a; Sassenberg 2002). That is, emotional arousal of any sort stemming from incidence encountered in cyberspace with virtual partners is as meaningful and experiential as those with actual, real world partners. This is as relevant and applicable to single, passing incidents as to online relationships developed over time. The essential, central role of the cognitive and personality dynamics systems in generating emotions is overwhelming, regardless of the correctness or reality of objects. Griffiths (2004), highlighting the illusory and personal dynamic-dependent nature of affects generated in online, text-based communication, wrote:

> Words that are originated from within ourselves and received by the computer without contest or contempt may produce the feelings that tell us we are being accommodated. Is this denial of reality or is it the individual's unique reality upon which he or she has managed to create a tool for expression and containment? Relating in this way, it could enable the reclamation of projected parts of 'self' by way of introjections and therefore serve to help the individual with whole relatedness.

(Griffiths 2004: 157)

Thus, the powerful psychological dynamic operating within individuals – reflecting both inner mechanisms and personal processes and content and not necessarily reality – is presumably responsible to a large degree for the various personal emotions experienced in cyberspace. Moreover, as sensual perceptions and cognitive mechanisms are responsible for the subjective processing of external information, the manipulation of these external sources could significantly affect personal experiences. Consequently, online emotions are not only elicited, in principle, by externally invalid stimuli, but they are also unstable and prone to be manoeuvred as a result of the intentions of others.

Impersonation, deception and impression formation

There is a complementary component to the powerful, basically internal circumstances mentioned so far: the psychological existence of a *partner* (or partners) in the cyberspace relationship. In cyberspace, people may choose their own 'identity'. Because of the lack of visibility and identification on the one hand and the absence (or exhausting) of ways of checking and verification on the other, users may create their own identity, fabricating a name, age, gender, origin/ethnicity, appearance, location and so on, in order to optimize their self-presentation (Walther 1996). Technically, identity construction on the Internet – whether through publishing a personal website or blog, communicating by instant messaging, conversing in a chat room, or participating in a forum – is simple and perceived as relatively (compared to offline identity-construction) un-risky to the identity creator (Donath 1999; Wallace 1999; Döring 2002b). The major risk an impersonator faces is the strong reaction of others if or when the impersonation is revealed (Donath 1999; Joinson and Dietz-Uhler 2002; Birchmeier *et al.* 2005). Thus, Internet users may effortlessly construct a *persona* with which they prefer others to observe and perceive them. Obviously, one might devise either a permanent fabricated persona or multiple identities from which to present oneself in any given situation or even more than one identity simultaneously (Joinson and Dietz-Uhler 2002). Identity-management in cyberspace, then, can be exercised and exhibited along several dimensions more or less in one's control and awareness (Suler 2002). This persona might be created for malicious intentions, such as paedophilic bait for children (Quayle and Taylor 2001, 2003) or other types of sexual exploitation (Barak 2005), for psychopathological reasons

(Munchausen by proxy; Feldman 2000), or for more innocent reasons, such as children hiding their real age (Harman *et al.* 2005) or attempting to gain greater appreciation and attraction in an online courtship. In this last incident, the attempt could lead from just flirting (Levine 1998; Cornwell and Lundgren 2001; Ben-Ze'ev 2004) to actual seduction (Mantovani 2001b) as has been observed in various online environments, including lesbian chat rooms (Poster 2002). Another example of the manipulation of online identity is to mask gender through 'gender bending' or gender concealment, an approach often used by women to avoid feelings of inferiority or harassment by men (Jazwinski 2001; Barak 2005). Concealment, incidentally, frequently stimulates guessing a partner's actual gender (Savicki *et al.* 2003), with varying degrees of success (Paasonen 2002). Not surprisingly and consistent with the current view, impression-formation managed through computer-mediated communication was found to be more influential and intensive than if attempted through face-to-face communication (Hancock and Dunham 2001). An extended understanding and examination of this area, however, is still in the making (see a recent proposed model by Carlson *et al.* [2004]). In many instances, the ease with which an online identity may be fabricated generates fear and anger among naive Internet users (Donath 1999), who suspect criminal conduct by those they perceive as online identity thieves and hackers (Kreuter 2003; Voiskounsky and Smyslova 2003; Turgeman-Goldschmidt 2005). For regular users, however, the creation of a persona for a number of purposes, such as gender switching that does not lead to harm, is considered legitimate. It may even be considered psychologically useful as a developmental task in identity experimentation (Suler 1996–2005; Roberts and Parks 2001). Indeed, the use of a persona is expected and even considered normal in cyberspace, where manipulation, impersonation and insincerity are not only possible but in common practice (Joinson 2005).

It should be stressed that constructing a persona – in cyberspace or in general – is not always a conscious or deliberate choice. People often unconsciously act in ways that are not natural for them, but targeted toward achieving a certain goal, usually that of gaining appreciation and high appraisal from others, offline (Schlenker 2003) as well as online (Suler 1996–2005), through a complicated process of self-perception and impression-management (Sherman 2001). An example of this, though some may consider it a constructive manipulation of personal features, is the concealing of a disability in order for a person to be judged as an individual rather than as disabled (Cromby and Standon 1999; Bowker and Tuffin 2002). As Seymour and Lupton put it:

> Online communication exposes people with dis-abilities to the world of strangers. The computer opens the door to a world of new ideas and values. It heightens the possibility that disabled people will come into contact with people who do not share their view of the world and that the communica-tion will take place in a context that is not domi-nated by their 'tragedy'.
>
> (Seymour and Lupton 2004: 300)

Moreover, impression-management online does not always reflect a person's intentions and desires; it may also refer to 'virtual mirroring'. That is, a person often reacts to the mirroring of herself or himself as expressed through part-ners' communications in the 'telecopresence' environment, thus creating a 'digital self' (Zhao 2005). In this way, an even more complicated interaction is created between self-presentation and self-formation and reflected in a persona.

Such behavioural conduct, in reflecting the fluidity and multiplicity of identities, might manifest a postmodern, constructivist view of emerging personality, a fragmented self and multifaceted interpersonal relations (Turkle 1995; Maczewski 2002), which the Internet makes more convenient to achieve. It is a well-known fact among users of online dating websites, for instance – albeit this behaviour pattern character-izes offline dating, too – that people exaggerate, beautify and ennoble self-presentations in order to impress others and, consequently, enhance their chances to gain attention, be contacted and maintain a virtual relationship (Baker 2005). Actually, flirting online typically involves the salient use of impression-formation, which is more easily enabled in cyberspace (Whitty 2004). As another example, it is well documented that

children who interact in online groups present themselves selectively and differently, depending on the nature of the group with which they are interacting (Calvert et al. 2003), in order to feel accepted and appreciated. Valkenburg et al. (2005) found that approximately 50% of a sam-ple of adolescents pretended to be older than their real age in Internet communications, while approximately 10% presented themselves as the opposite gender and 13% played a fantasized figure. These researchers also concluded that the reasons for faked identities were self-explo-ration (to explore how others react), social com-pensation (to compensate for shyness) and social facilitation (to facilitate relationship-for-mation). Moreover, young Internet users, in developing their personal offline identities, identify with specific Internet subcultures that, in turn, influence their online identity in their attempts to belong and accept local norms (Wilson and Atkinson 2005). For immigrants, too, identity-concealing, on the one hand and identifying with the same online affiliation group, on the other, reflect an additional influence on virtual identity-formation as Mitra (2005) recently showed for Indian immigrants in the United States. Online consumers, too, tend to fabricate identity; their behaviour could be explained on several theoretical grounds (Lwin and Williams 2003), but supposedly is due to the desire to avoid commercial spamming later on. Many users of chat rooms tend to lie about themselves either to impress (men) or as a safe-guard (women) (Whitty 2002). The need to mask personal identity may be considered from a psychoanalytic viewpoint, too. Online roman-tic relationships have been analysed from this angle (Seiden 2001) as the construction of a common narrative, based on mutual impulses and narcissistic needs. Here, self-definition expresses self-object for the purpose of loving and being loved, which behaviours are intensi-fied through the ambiguity and illusionary nature of the environment. It should be noted, however, that the formation of an impression is not always invalid or misleading; Vazire and Gosling (2004) found that personal identities created on a personal website were, as perceived by visitors, fairly similar to the actual personali-ties of the site owners. Obviously, this finding does not mean that websites always candidly reflect their owners' true character, only that an online persona might or might not be manipulated as its owner wishes.

Thus, in the virtual environment, in which validation, confirmation and vindication are almost impossible and motivations for identity concealment are plentiful, persona – the made-up, selective, biased self-presentation of a person – is assumed to constitute a major source of information for impression formation. This source of information has a significant added value beyond the style and pattern of behaviour revealed through textual interactions, as reviewed previously. When online, therefore, a person perceives another person as the latter is reflected in that person's frequently artificial, invalid persona and reacts to this image accordingly. As was pointed out, it is a common experience among Internet users, one consistently documented in empirical research (see Barnes 2003a, b) that when online, individuals regularly manipulate their persona, consciously or unconsciously, maliciously or innocently, directly or indirectly and they do so variably according to the online environment and communication channel. Moreover, as Utz (2005) found, different types of identity manipulations – category deception, attractiveness deception and identity concealment – affect differentially and cause perceptions relating to the deceivers' motivation to deceive and purpose of deception.

Almost inevitably, then, many people in cyberspace perceive and refer to others in the manner in which these others manipulate them or elicit their responses (Merkle and Richardson 2000) through the powerful influence and easy, though sophisticated, manipulation of written language (Zhou *et al.* 2004) in interaction with the perceiver's personal psychological load. Deliberate manipulations, targeting a variety of goals, cause trust and openness to intimacy to become major issues in online communication (Clark 1998; Ben-Ze'ev 2003), apparently more than in an offline relationship, where 'seeing is believing' has an overriding effect. Thus the emotions of individuals relate, in principle, to cognitively created figures that these individuals believe reflect the partners with whom they are communicating and interacting. Consequently, they usually behave accordingly. It is ironic to note, however, that a preliminary survey shows

that people admit to lying more in telephone conversations and face-to-face encounters than in emails, though this may be due to the archiving feature of email (New Scientist Online 2004; see also Chapter 19, this volume). This finding is consistent, however, with Hardey's (2002) argument, based on analyses of more than 400 datingwebsite users, that online communication with virtual partners assists in building trust for later offline relationships.

Phantom emotions

The result of the two psychological phenomena described above – the natural tendency, based on personal needs and wishes, to fantasize and so close gaps in subjectively important information in ambiguous situations on the one hand and the common use of a made-up persona to represent one's identity in virtual environments, on the other – unavoidably creates '*phantom emotions*'. This term is chosen to connote the phenomenon in question because it is conceptually parallel to the psychophysiological occurrence of phantom sensations experienced by individuals, such as feeling pain in a body organ that is missing, which is a typical and wellknown sensation for amputees. The point is that an amputee's authentic subjective feeling of an absent limb is palpably experienced even though the valid, external information is false (Fraser 2002; Wade 2003), both physically (it is absent) and psychologically (its absence is recognized). Similar to amputees' supposed feelings, phantom sensations also occur in people who lack a tooth (Tassinari *et al.* 2002), an eye (Soros *et al.* 2003), or smelling sensors (Grouios 2002). The term 'phantom recall' was adopted (Brainerd *et al.* 2003) to designate metaphorically a certain type of vividly experienced, illusory memory; with similar logic, the concept of 'phantom' is adopted here. Thus, like the case of phantom sensations or phantom recall, an individual online genuinely experiences an emotion – be it attraction or repulsion, lust, love, hate, or jealousy – although these emotional sensations are based, in principle, on false objective foundations. Moreover, not only is the external information inaccurate (or entirely false), but the personal emotions are elicited (or triggered) by illusionary objects momentary believed to be authentic and real. Using Russell's (2003) terms in conceptualizing emotion, this means that the *attributional processes* become central and play a major role in creating an emotional episode.

The argument advanced here is that the submerging effects of presence, the inherent psychological processes that individuals go through in such situations owing to various motivational factors and the common behaviour of Internet surfers in managing a fabricated (or deliberately modified) persona, allied with the virtual, ambiguous nature of cyberspace and human communication in this environment, all combine to elicit emotions that, though actually experienced, are determined, in principle, on false grounds, of which the individual is usually unaware. People in cyberspace who authentically feel an attraction to a communication partner, particularly a stranger, go through a phantom sensation phenomenon frequently as soon as a few moments after virtually meeting the partner. However, unlike 'love at first sight', which in a minimal way refers to relatively objective or genuine data (e.g., looks, skin colour, non-verbal communication cues), however preliminary, that elicit this emotion (Soble 1990; Forrest 2004), affective reactions in cyberspace rely, in principle, mostly – sometimes entirely – on rather virtual information. There are other fundamental differences, however, between the occurrence of 'love at first sight' in face-to-face relationships and falling in love with a virtual partner in cyberspace. As Ben-Ze'ev put it:

It should be noted that although beauty has a powerful impact at first sight, the weight of this impact decreases as times goes by and once we know other characteristics of the person. Likewise, wittiness has a powerful impact at first chat, but its impact may be reduced once we know other characteristics of the person. When wittiness is perceived to be superficial and more profound characteristics, such as kindness and wisdom, are found to be wanting, the weight of the positive initial impact of wittiness may vanish. [Moreover] In love at first sight, the high value accorded to the other's external appearance is projected onto [that person's] characteristics. In love at first chat, the high value accorded to the other's writing abilities is projected onto other characteristics, including external appearance. Both are instances of real love that is based on scant information and on imagination that fills the missing gaps.

(Ben-Ze'ev 2004: 177)

That is, as in 'love at first sight' – where a spillover effect causes a cognitive bias in attributing positive and attractive characteristics to a person rated for his or her appearance, documented in psychology research for over half a century as a 'halo effect' (Asch 1946) – virtual interpersonal contact, which is characterized by the unique psychological circumstances described above, also produces a halo effect. Physical attraction, for instance, is replaced by wittiness or 'textual attraction'. However, unlike cognitions elicited offline – that is, with greater inner psychological powers – emotional reactions to an online partner are produced to a major degree by (as proposed here) the way these emotions satisfy personal needs and expectations. In emphasizing cognitive processes, then, the halo effect in virtual interpersonal relationships reflects – apparently differently from the parallel effect in a face-to-face relationship – and refers to a broad spectrum of possible emotions, not only love. These attributions stem from one's personality structure, personal dynamics and current psychological state.

The process embodied in the halo effect could possibly explain a variety of online phenomena, not only those related to interpersonal relationships. For example, the phenomenon of phantom emotions could explain positive cognitive bias (e.g., unrealistic optimism) found when Internet users judge events experienced online when compared with 'an average person' (Campbell *et al.* in press). In this case, overestimation of one's personal coping ability and the desirability and controllability of events might reflect a phantom emotion in that the virtual online event (e.g., being contacted by friend; being robbed of personal ID) produced personal emotions that primarily reflected wishful thinking and beliefs rather than real probabilities. Another example is that of unrealistic perceptions of online information credibility (Metzger *et al.* 2003). Here, too, users' needs and wishful thinking, on the one hand and the seemingly appealing online information, on the other, could explain the phantom emotion responsible for a positive perception bias. This conception may also be applied to explain Rouse and Haas's (2003) finding that users of a chat room develop textual relationships with online strangers in correlation with the personality traits they attribute to these others. The current framework could also be used to account for teenagers' perceptions of the risks and benefits of personal disclosure of information (Youn 2005); phantom emotions – influenced by attractive disclosure benefits – affect their behaviour and attitude toward the protection of privacy online.

Thus, a broad spectrum of emotions, well known to Internet communication users, is subject to the psychological determination process conceptualized and termed here as phantom emotion. By explanations stemming from this model, it is argued that rapidly developing online love and sexual attraction (Levine 2000; Whitty 2003a; Ben-Ze'ev 2004), liking and closeness in online communities (McKenna et al. 2002), extensive altruism and mutual help in online support groups (Chapter 10, this volume), on the one hand and accelerated hate and aggression (Lee and Leets 2002), bullying and harassment (Barak 2005) and negative manipulations and insults (Suler and Phillips 2000), on the other hand, all share a phantom sensation basis. That is, these emotionally based reactions are not generated or induced by real, personally experimented and verifiable factors; rather, they are primarily the result of the fantasized experiences typically characterizing cyberspace.

A phantom emotion is so prevalent and so genuinely felt in cyberspace that many people, perhaps even most Internet users who experience virtual communication, do not notice the difference between the virtual and a substantiated emotion (i.e., an emotion based on valid information and real-life experiences). The emotional experience in cyberspace is subjectively identical to the vivid, authentic feeling of itching, pain, or tickling that an amputee feels in an absent limb. Falling in love with, feeling attracted to, being jealous of, or despising or resenting a virtual partner might be baseless in terms of rational thinking and factual data. The subjective emotion, however, is as intensively, authentically and overwhelmingly experienced as is, say, 'true love' (Ben-Ze'ev 2004) or the rage experienced in typical online flame wars (Thompson 2003; Alonzo and Aiken 2004;

Lee 2005b). What makes these emotions special – phantom – is neither their nature nor their experienced authenticity, but the subjectively biased basis by which they were created.

This phenomenon of 'virtual emotion' actually represents the kind of intensified or double-edged emotional mythology experienced by Pygmalion and his creation, Galatea (Ovid 18 BC). Not only does the sculptor have needs and wishes and therefore modifies his creation accordingly; the sculpture, too, has needs and wishes to be related to in a certain way and so it influences the sculptor's attention and feelings accordingly. This extra dynamic of mutual expectations and subsequent manipulations is magnified in cyberspace – in terms of the intensity of emotions and the speed with which they develop – because of the online disinhibition effect (Suler 2004b) and the elevated expression of 'inner self' (McKenna and Seidman 2005). Consequently, these unique circumstances provide grounds for the powerful, accelerated emotions experienced by individuals in the virtual environment. Since people do not all behave identically in any given environment, their personal differences interact in cyberspace with the reactivity of emotional sensations and with a wide range of behavioural responses (see Chapter 13, this volume).

Similarly, emotional processes are possibly related to and perhaps moderated by, personality dispositions as was shown by Alonzo and Aiken (2004), Lee (2005b) and Thompson (2003) for flaming behaviour, for example. Phantom emotions, however, are prevalent and they overwhelmingly reflect the unique dynamics characterizing cyberspace and the interpersonal relationships and behaviours in the virtual environment. Moreover, because of the foggy atmosphere characterizing cyberspace and its inhabitants, phantom emotions tend to be preserved and empowered, since no external boundaries, control, or feedback is in fact present. Created and maintained online, phantom emotions tend to become perpetuated and even to escalate to the level that best fits personal desires. The construction of experience is possible, then, in terms not only of fantasizing through thoughts but also of complementing these thoughts with authentic, self-fulfilling feelings. Perhaps only full personal awareness, along with strong self-control and self-discipline, can assist individuals to maintain an integrative life with their Real World (Suler 1996–2005) and avoid possible compulsive behaviours online – 'Internet addiction' (Suler 1999; LaRose *et al.* 2003) under its powerful psychological circumstances.

Implications

The current conceptualization of phantom emotions has several important theoretical, research and practical implications. First, this view can shed light on processes that determine – directly or in interaction with other factors – a variety of online behaviours and thus lay advanced theoretical grounds for a better understanding of experiences in cyberspace and for predicting an individual's experiences. By introducing the concept of phantom emotions, a deeper, more accurate understanding of people's behaviour in cyberspace might occur. Thus, adding this rather important psychological factor into a model that aspires to explain and predict online experiences and behaviours necessitates appending variables and measures that will specifically target phantom emotions as a mediator. The explanatory value of this conception is still to be investigated: however, it seems that the present framework is applicable to a variety of online social interaction situations.

It is postulated here that phantom emotions could prove to be of great value in explaining interpersonal group behaviour in virtual communities, where group processes, flaming, coalitions and interpersonal attraction typically take place (McKenna and Bargh 1998; McKenna and Green 2002; Lee 2005a, b; McKenna and Siedman 2005). In contrast to the SIDE model's viewpoint that stresses the role of group salience as a major source of behaviour online (see Chapter 17), the current approach assigns a heavier role to *personal awareness* rather to group awareness (as recently was empirically supported by Yao and Flanagin 2006); on the other hand, phantom emotions might also explain personal sentiments and affects typical of Internet cultures (King 2001; Forster 2004) that produce a broad spectrum of attitudes and behaviours pertaining to commitment, a sense of community, belongingness and group trust. In this regard, it is proposed that personal variables relating to the concept of phantom emotion (e.g., personal

cognitions) be included as a major explanatory factor in addition to the variables that commonly had been used until now. Phantom emotions might be also an important mediator in conceptualizing online work collaboration, in which ongoing negotiations, interpersonal liking and disliking, collaboration and misunderstandings are common (e.g., Hathorn and Ingram 2002). In this context, it might be of significant importance to add a focus on interpersonal perceptions, expectations and attributions, as well as personal wishes, as determinants of phantom emotions, since all these components might significantly contribute to interpersonal (and group) behaviours in this rather specific context. In addition, phantom emotions could be considered an important factor in designing, managing and studying e-learning, for which group cooperation and interpersonal relationships are important for effective learning (Kubo et al. 2002; Kreijns *et al.* 2003). Understanding the nature of learners' psychological dynamics (including needs, wishes and perceptions, all related to the virtual emotive dimension), rather than system-related variables, might prove effective in investigating pedagogical issues in online learning, including its processes and outcomes.

Phantom emotions, as noted earlier, might be of essential value in investigating online dating and romance because of the central role of mutual, but frequently unfounded, attraction in cyberspace (Merkle and Richardson 2000; Cornwell and Lundgren 2001; Seiden 2001; Döring 2002a; Whitty 2003a, b; Ben-Ze'ev 2004, 2005; Baker 2005) and may also shed light on online infidelity (Young *et al.* 2000; Aviram and Amichai-Hamburger 2005). In the area of romantic relationships, the suggestion is to give special weight to variables related to phantom emotions, as the latter seem to be of prime value in determining interpersonal attraction and the maintenance of relationships. Related to online relationship-formation, phantom emotions might be a crucial mediator in the study of cybersex owing to the well-documented phenomenon of obsession with this activity (e.g. Levine 1998; Cooper *et al.* 2000; Mantovani 2001b; Young 2001; Barak and Fisher 2002; Cooper *et al.* 2002; Griffin-Shelley 2003). In this regard, a powerful, perhaps pathological need for pleasure and gratification projected onto virtual partners might provide a theoretical framework for explaining this abnormal behaviour and subsequently treating it. Such a new framework might introduce a change in the focus of quite a few approaches. In the same way, the concept of phantom emotions is of great importance for Internet-based counselling and therapy: the possibility of harnessing the development of these emotions in the context of the client–therapist exchange offers an effective therapeutic process related to transference, thus contributing to the establishment of therapeutic alliance and impact (Cook and Doyle 2002; Barak and Bloch 2006; Barak, 2007). Integrating the concept of phantom emotions into such research attempts could enhance understanding of processes that are essential for establishing online therapeutic contact. The concept could thus become a successful vehicle for moderating therapeutic change (Hsiung 2002; Barak 2004; Rochlen *et al.* 2004a), perhaps interacting with the influence of the level of emotionality on online therapy in general (Rochlen *et al.* 2004b).

Phantom emotions might become a central concept in developing and examining advanced online assessments, too: the differential personal experiencing of phantom emotions in online situational tests may be indicative of a subject's psychological needs and wishes, thus reflecting personality-relevant factors (Barak and Buchanan 2004). Phantom emotions might also be exploited as an important factor for studying online shopping and marketing, which are obviously affected by user's emotions (Mummalaneni 2005), for possible effects on online shopping behaviour (Dholakia and Chiang 2003), rather than concentrating on system and practical factors. Phantom emotions may possibly be identified as a central moderating variable in studying the addiction to and effects of online games, especially by those users who develop a powerful immersion in virtual presence (Griffiths and Wood 2000; Williams and Skoric 2005); this variable may not only contribute to understanding important psychological processes in this regard but also help in developing prevention programs. The concept of phantom emotions could be of significant value in the study of still other behaviours on the Internet that involve interpersonal relationships and personal emotions.

In turn, the present view might contribute to extending an understanding of prevailing concepts of love, attraction, hate and anger in offline environments. In a broader sense, the current conceptualization could be integrated into theoretical attempts to apply social models of cyberspace (e.g., McKenna and Bargh 1999; Rafaeli *et al.* 2005).

Introducing the idea of the phantom basis of online emotions makes it advisable, if not necessary, for researchers to employ perceptual and other cognitive measurements in attempting to give a more valid explanation of human experiences in cyberspace. This is being advised in order to emphasize the crucial nature of the *psychological* factor to an understanding of online behaviours – a factor commonly missed by communication researchers (and those who arrive from related disciplines, such as media studies and journalism, computer sciences, or information systems). An important example in this regard was provided by LaRose *et al.* (2001b) when investigating the alleged link between Internet use and depression. These researchers found that self-efficacy and expectations of stress had significant moderating effects in predicting depressive moods, thus adding a meaningful input into the understanding of prior research in this important area, which has intensively occupied numerous researchers and writers. Consistent with the present view, too, psychological research might have to focus more closely on intra-psychic experiences – rather than solely on overt behaviours or externally observed environmental factors – in order to deepen understanding of the phenomena in question. It might be interesting to pursue psychophysiological brain research in a similar manner to the investigation of the experience of presence in virtual reality (Insko 2003); and, consistent with recent findings concerning brain activity as reflecting emotional (i.e., empathy; Singer *et al.* 2004), cognitive (i.e., placebo effects; Wager *et al.* 2004) and social (Pelphrey *et al.* 2004) phenomena, also to investigate the appearance and correlates of online phantom emotions in brain activity. In another direction, it might prove worthwhile to adopt the current view in conceptualizing and studying online trust in the commercial realm. In this context, it might prove useful to include inner-user psychological processes – consistent with the current conception – to understand, explain and predict users' trust and disclosure on commercial sites and online shopping. This view could add a significant contribution to modifying users' behaviours, much beyond such traditional variables as demographics, personal traits, or culture (see Chapter 13). Similarly and in a broader sense, the current approach may contribute significantly to the study of interpersonal trust in cyberspace (Chapter 4, this volume), in online advice and online information (Chapter 22, this volume) and in online negotiations (Naquin and Paulson 2003), as well as other types of online interpersonal behaviours as recently proposed and explored by Forgas, East and Chan (2007).

The present view has significant implications for various aspects of managing and exploiting online environments and online communication channels. Although existing education and prevention programmes highlight the effects of anonymity, invisibility, impersonation and fabrication on the Internet (Dombrowski et al. 2004), they refrain from including the important, perhaps dominant, factors that relate to users' inner processes, especially the prevailing effect of phantom emotions, as characterizing and significantly affecting online communication and interpersonal contacts. Similarly, psycho-educational programs published on the Internet contain pieces of relevant information and cautions, but they exclude the major impact of emotions – that is, of phantom emotions – that are generated by misleading and frequently malicious information and messages (e.g., GetNetWise at http://www.getnetwise.org; SafeKids.Com at http://www.safekids.com; and NetSmartz at http://www.netsmartz.org). The current approach, however, argues that inner emotional processes, their determinants and a user's self-awareness of them are central to the self-regulation of online behaviour. Similarly, more attention may have to be given to phantom emotions in relation to therapeutic issues when treating problematic Internet use – i.e., 'Internet addiction' (Leung 2004), compulsive online sex consumption (Delmonico et al. 2002), or compulsive online gambling (Griffiths and Cooper 2003). It seems that current theoretical views of these areas (e.g., Morahan-Martin 2005) could gain construct validity by introducing the phantom emotion factor into their models.

This would mean placing greater emphasis on the user's internal awareness and control of cognitive processes relating to unfounded fantasies, as well as perhaps to related psychodynamic processes, in order to help alter problematic behaviours rather than concentrating on stimulus–response behavioural approaches, which might miss crucial components.

Further research may shed more light on the empirical status of these implications and postulates. Acceptance of the proposed conception will contribute to the discipline of psychology by advancing understanding of emerging behaviours in what might be considered a new era for psychology (Barak 1999; Sassenberg et al. 2003). The current conception also concurs with Bargh and McKenna's (2004) notion – parallel to the elevated self-expression and extended unclarity typical of online communication – that 'one's own desires and goals regarding the people with whom one interacts has been found to make a dramatic difference in the assumptions and attributions one makes within that informational void' (2004: 586). In other words, when a person's own mind plays a central role in constructing his or her cognitions, self-produced emotions are invited and, subsequently, prevail.

References

Alcañiz, M., Baños, R., Rotella, C. and Rey, B. (2003). The EMMA project: emotions as a determinant of presence. *Psychology Journal 1*(2), 141–150. Retrieved 10 January 2006 from http://www.psychnology.org.

Alonzo, M. and Aiken, M. (2004). Flaming in electronic communication. *Decision Support Systems 36*, 205–213.

Amichai-Hamburger, Y. (2002). Internet and personality. *Computers in Human Behavior 18*, 1–10.

Amichai-Hamburger, Y., Fine, A. and Goldstein, A. (2004). The impact of Internet interactivity and need for closure on consumer preference. *Computers in Human Behavior 20*, 103–117.

Asch, S. E. (1946). Forming impressions of personality. *Journal of Abnormal and Social Psychology 41*, 258–290.

Aviram, I. and Amichai-Hamburger, Y. (2005). Online infidelity: aspects of dyadic satisfaction, self-disclosure and narcissism. Journal of Computer-Mediated Communication 10(3), article 1. Retrieved 10 January 2006 from http://jcmc.indiana.edu/vo110/issue3/aviram.html.

Baker, A. J. (2005). *Double click: Romance and commitment among online couples.* Cresskill, NJ: Hampton Press.

Barak, A. (1999). Psychological applications on the Internet: a discipline on the threshold of a new millennium. *Applied and Preventive Psychology 8*, 231–246.

Barak, A. (2004). Internet counseling. In C. E. Spielberger (ed.), *Encyclopedia of applied psychology* (pp. 369–378). San Diego, CA: Academic Press.

Barak, A. (2005). Sexual harassment on the Internet. *Social Science Computer Review 23*, 77–92.

Barak, A. (2007). Emotional support and suicide prevention through the Internet. *Computers in Human Behavior 23*, 971–984.

Barak, A. and Bloch, N. (2006). Factors related to perceived helpfulness in supporting highly distressed individuals through an online support chat. *CyberPsychology and Behavior 9*, 60–68.

Barak, A. and Buchanan, T. (2004). Internet-based psychological testing and assessment. In R. Kraus, G. Stricker and J. Zack (eds), *Online counseling: A handbook for mental health professionals* (pp. 217–239). San Diego, CA: Elsevier Academic Press.

Barak, A. and Fisher, W. A. (2002). The future of Internet sexuality. In A. Cooper (ed.), *Sex and the Internet: A guidebook for clinicians* (pp. 263–280). New York: Brunner-Routledge.

Barak, A. and Miron, O. (2005). Writing characteristics of suicidal people on the Internet: a psychological investigation of emerging social environments. *Suicide and Life – Threatening Behavior 35*, 507–524.

Brashers, D. E. (2001). Communication and uncertainty management. *Journal of Communication 51*, 477–497.

Bargh, J. A. and McKenna, K. Y. A. (2004). The Internet and social life. *Annual Review of Psychology 55*, 573–590.

Barnes, S. B. (2003a). *Computer-mediated communication: human-to-human communication across the Internet.* Boston, MA: Pearson Allyn and Bacon.

Barnes, S. (2003b). Cyberspace: creating paradoxes for the ecology of self. In L. Strate, R. L. Jacobson and S. B. Gibson (eds), *Communication and cyberspace: Social interaction in an electronic environment*, 2nd edn. (pp. 229–253). Cresskill, NJ: Hampton Press.

Baur, C. (2000). Limiting factors on the transformative powers of e-mail in patient-physician relationships: a critical analysis. *Health Communication 12*, 239–259.

Ben-Ze'ev, A. (2000). *The subtlety of emotions.* Cambridge, MA: MIT Press.

Ben-Ze'ev, A. (2003). Privacy, emotional closeness and openness in cyberspace. *Computers in Human Behavior 19*, 451–467.

Ben-Ze'ev, A. (2004). *Love online: emotions on the Internet.* Cambridge: Cambridge University Press.

Ben-Ze'ev, A. (2005). 'Detattachment': the unique nature of online romantic relationships. In Y. Amichai-Hamburger (ed.), *The social net: Human behavior in cyberspace* (pp. 115–138). New York: Oxford University Press.

Berger, C. R. and Calabrese, R. J. (1975). Some explorations in initial interaction and beyond: toward a developmental theory of interpersonal communication. *Human Communication Theory 1*, 99–112.

Berger, C. R. and Gudykunst, W. B. (1991). Uncertainty and communication. In B. Dervin and M. Voight (eds), *Progress in communication sciences* (pp. 21–66). Norwood, NJ: Ablex.

Birchmeier, Z., Joinson, A. N. and Dietz-Uhler, B. (2005). Storming and forming a normative response to a deception revealed online. *Social Science Computer Review 23*, 108–121.

Bird, J. (2003). 'I wish to speak to the despisers of the body': the Internet, physicality and psychoanalysis. *Journal for the Psychoanalysis of Culture and Society 8*, 121–126.

Blair, C. A., Thompson, L. F. and Wuensch, K. L. (2005). Electronic helping behavior: the virtual presence of others makes a difference. *Basic and Applied Social Psychology 27*, 171–178.

Blair, I. V. (2002). The malleability of automatic stereotypes and prejudice. *Personality and Social Psychology Review 6*, 242–261.

Bordin, E. S. (1955). Ambiguity as a therapeutic variable. *Journal of Consulting Psychology 19*, 9–15.

Bouchard, S. (2004). Reply to Slater's comments on Robillard *et al. CyberPsychology and Behavior 7*, 123.

Bowker, N. and Tuffin, K. (2002). Disability discourses for online identities. *Disability and Society 17*, 327–344.

Brainerd, C. J., Payne, D. G., Wright, R. and Reyna, V. F. (2003). Phantom recall. *Journal of Memory and Language 48*, 445–467.

Calvert, S. L. (2002). The social impact of virtual environment technology. In K. M. Stanney (ed.), *Handbook of virtual environments: Design, implementation and application* (pp. 663–680). Mahwah, FL: University of Central Florida.

Calvert, S. L., Mahler, B. A., Zehnder, S. M., Jenkins, A. and Lee, M. S. (2003). Gender differences in preadolescent children's online interactions: symbolic modes of self-presentation and self-expression. *Applied Developmental Psychology 24*, 627–644.

Campbell, J., Greenauer, N., Macaluso, K. and End, C. (in press). Unrealistic optimism in internet events. *Computers and Human Behavior.*

Carlson, J. R., George, J. F., Burgoon, J. K., Adkins, M. and White, C. H. (2004). Deception in computer-mediated communication. *Group Decision and Negotiation 13*, 5–28.

Chan, D. K. S., Cheng, G. H. L. and Metts, S. (2004). A comparison of offline and online friendship qualities at different stages of relationship development. *Journal of Social and Personal Relationships 21*, 305–320.

Chen, H. (2006). Flow on the net – detecting Web users' positive affects and their flow states. *Computers in Human Behavior 22*, 221–233.

Chen, H., Wigand, R. and Nilan, M. (2000). Exploring Web users' flow experiences. *Information Technology and People 13*, 263–281.

Cho, H. -K., Trier, M. and Kim, E. (2005). The use of instant messaging in working relationship development: a case study. Journal of Computer-Mediated Communication 10(4), article 17. Retrieved 10 January 2006 from http://jcmc.indiana.edu/vol10/issue4/cho.html.

Civin, M. A. (2000). *Male, female, e-mail: The struggle for relatedness in a paranoid society*. New York: Other Press.

Clark, L. S. (1998). Dating on the Net: teens and the rise in 'pure' relationships. In S. G. Jones (ed.), *Cybersociety 2.0: Revisiting computer-mediated communication and community*, vol. 2 (pp. 159–183).

Cook, J. E. and Doyle, C. (2002). Working alliance in online therapy as compared to face-to-face therapy: preliminary results. *CyberPsychology and Behavior 5*, 95–105.

Cooper, A., Delmonico, D. L and Burg, R. (2000). Cybersex users, abusers and compulsives: new findings and implications. *Sexual Addiction and Compulsivity 7*, 5–29.

Cooper, A., Golden, G. and Kent-Ferraro, J. (2002). Online sexual behaviors in the workplace: how can human resource departments and employee assistance programs respond effectively? *Sexual Addiction and Compulsivity 9*, 149–165.

Cornwell, B. and Lundgren, D. C. (2001). Love on the Internet: involvement and misrepresentation in romantic relationships in cyberspace vs. realspace. *Computers in Human Behavior 17*, 197–211.

Cromby, J. and Standon, P. (1999). Cyborgs and stigma: technology, disability, subjectivity. In A. J. Gordo-Lopez and I. Parker (eds), *Cyberpsychology* (pp. 95–112). New York: Routledge.

Csikszentmihalyi, M. (1975). *Beyond boredom and anxiety*. San Francisco, CA: Jossey-Bass.

Csikszentmihalyi, M. (1982). Towards a psychology of optimal experience. In L. Wheeler (ed.), *Annual Review of Personality and Social Psychology*, vol. 3 (pp. 13–36). Beverly Hills, CA: Sage.

Cunneen, C. and Stubbs, J. (2000). Male violence, male fantasy and the commodification of women through the Internet. *Interactive Review of Victimology 7*, 5–28.

Cupchik, G. C, Leonard, G., Axelrad, E. and Kalin, J. D. (1998). The landscape of emotion in literary encounters. *Cognition and Emotion 12*, 825–847.

Czerwinski, M. P. and Larson, K. (2003). Cognition and the Web: moving from theory to Web design. In J. Ratner (ed.), *Human factors and Web development* (pp. 147–165). Mahwah, NJ: Erlbaum.

Delmonico, D. L., Griffin, E. and Carnes, P. J. (2002). Treating online compulsive sexual behavior: when cybersex is the drug of choice. In A. Cooper (ed.), *Sex and the Internet: A guidebook for clinicians* (pp. 147–167). New York: Brunner-Routledge.

Dholakia, R. R. and Chiang, K. (2003). Shoppers in cyberspace: are they from Venus or Mars and does it matter? *Journal of Consumer Psychology 13*, 171–176.

Dombrowski, S. C., LeMasney, J. W., Ahia, C. E. and Dickson, S. A. (2004). Protecting children from online sexual predators: technological, psychoeducational and legal considerations. *Professional Psychology: Research and Practice 35*, 65–73.

Donath, J. S. (1999). Identity and deception in the virtual community. In P. Kollock and A. S. Smith (eds), *Communities in Cyberspace* (29–59). London, UK: Routledge.

Dorer, J. (2002). Internet and the construction of gender: female professionals and the process of doing gender. In M. Consaluo and S. Paasonen (eds), *Women and everyday uses of the Internet: Agency and identity* (pp. 62–89). New York: Perer Lang Publishing.

Döring, N. (2002a). Studying online-love and cyber-romance. In B. Batinic, U. D. Reips and M. Bosnjak (eds), *Online Social Sciences* (pp. 333–356). Toronto: Hogrefe and Huber.

Döring, N. (2002b). Personal home pages on the Web: a review of research. *Journal of Computer-Mediated Communication 7*(3). Retrieved 10 January 2006 from http://www.ascusc.org/jcmc/vo17/issue3/doering.html.

Douglas, K. M. and McGarty, C. (2001). Identifiability and self-presentation: computer-mediated communication and intergroup interaction. *British Journal of Social Psychology 40*, 399–416.

Epley, N. and Kruger, J. (2005). When what you type isn't what they read: the perseverance of stereotypes and expectancies over e-mail. *Journal of Experimental Social Psychology 41*, 414–422.

Esterling, B. A., L'Abate, L., Murray, E. J., Pennebaker, J. W. (1999). Empirical foundations for writing in prevention and psychotherapy: mental and physical health outcomes. *Clinical Psychology Review 19*, 79–96.

Eastin, M. S. (2005). Teen Internet use: relating social perceptions and cognitive models to behavior. *CyberPsychology and Behavior 8*, 62–75.

Feldman, M. D. (2000). Munchausen by Internet: detecting factitious illness and crisis on the Internet. *Southern Medical Journal 93*, 669–672.

Fenichel, M. A. (2004). Online behavior, communication and experience. In R. Kraus, J. Zack and G. Stricker (eds), *Online counseling: A handbook for mental health professionals* (pp. 3–18). San Diego, CA: Elsevier Academic Press.

Fenichel, M., Suler, J., Barak, A., Zelvin, E., Jones, G., Munro, K., Meunier, V. and Walker-Schmucker, W. (2002). Myths and realities of online clinical work. *CyberPsychology and Behavior 5*, 481–497.

Festinger, L. (1957). *A theory of a cognitive dissonance*. Stanford, CA: Stanford University Press.

Forgas, J. P., East, R. and Chan, N. Y. M. (2007). The use of computer-mediated interaction in exploring affective influences on strategic interpersonal behaviours. *Computers and Human Behavior 23*, 901–919.

Forrest, D. V. (2004). Love at first sight: why you love who you love. *American Journal of Psychiatry 161*, 2337–2338.

Forster, P. M. (2004). Psychological sense of community in groups on the Internet. *Behaviour Change 21*, 141–146.

Fraser, C. (2002). Fact and fiction: a clarification of phantom limb phenomena. *British Journal of Occupational Therapy 65*, 256–260.

Gabbard, G. O. (2001). Cyberpassion: e-rotic transference on the Internet. *Psychoanalytic Quarterly 70*, 719–737.

Gaggioli, A., Bassi, M. and Delle Fave, A. (2003a). Quality of experience in virtual environments. In G. Riva, F. Davide and W. A. IJsselsteijn (eds), *Being there: Concepts, effects and measurements of user presence in synthetic environments* (pp. 121–135). Amsterdam, Holland: IOS Press.

Gaggioli, A., Mantovani, F., Castelnuovo, G., Wiederhold, B. and Riva, G. (2003b). Avatars in clinical psychology: a framework for the clinical use of virtual humans. *CyberPsychology and Behavior 6*, 117–125.

Galimberti, C., Ignazi, S., Vercesi, P. and Riva, G. (2001). Communication and cooperation in networked environments: an experimental analysis. *CyberPsychology and Behavior 4*, 131–146.

Gamberini, L and Valentini, A. (2001). Web usability today: theory, approach and method. In G. Riva and C. Galimberti (eds), *Toward cyberpsychology: Mind, cognitions and society in the Internet age* (pp. 109–125). Amsterdam, Holland: IOS Press.

Granic, I. and Lamey, A. V. (2000). The self-organization of the Internet and changing modes of thought. *New Ideas in Psychology 18*, 93–107.

Griffin-Shelley, E. (2003). The Internet and sexuality: a literature review – 1983–2002. *Sexual and Relationship Therapy 18*, 355–370.

Griffiths, L. (2004). Electronic text-based communication – assumptions and illusions created by the transference phenomena. In G. Bolton, S. Howlett, C. Lago and J. K. Wright (eds), *Writing cures: An introductory handbook of writing in counselling and psychotherapy* (pp. 151–159). Hove, East Sussex: Brunner-Routledge.

Griffiths, M. and Cooper, G. (2003). Online therapy: implications for problem gamblers and clinicians. *British Journal of Guidance and Counselling 31*, 113–135.

Griffiths, M. and Wood, R. T. A. (2000). Risk factors in adolescence: the case of gambling, videogame playing and the Internet. *Journal of Gambling Studies 16*, 199–225.

Grigorovici, D. (2003). Persuasive effects of presence in immersive virtual environments. In G. Riva, F. Davide and W. A. IJsselsteijn (eds), *Being there: Concepts, effects and measurements of user presence in synthetic environments* (pp. 191–207). Amsterdam, Holland: IOS Press.

Grouios, G. (2002). Phantom smelling. *Perceptual and Motor Skills 94*, 841–850.

Hancock, J. T. and Dunham, P. J. (2001). Impression formation in computer-mediated communication revisited: an analysis of the breadth and intensity of impressions. *Communication Research 28*, 325–347.

Hardey, M. (2002). Life beyond the screen: embodiment and identity through the internet. *Sociological Review 50*, 570–585.

Harman, J. P., Hansen, C. E., Cochran, M. E. and Lindsey, C. R. (2005). Liar, Liar: Internet faking but not frequency of use affects social skills, self-esteem, social anxiety and aggression. *CyberPsychology and Behavior 8*, 1–6.

Harmon-Jones, E. (2001). The role of affect in cognitive-dissonance processes. In J. P. Forgas (ed.), *Handbook of affect and social cognition* (pp. 237–255). Mahwah, NJ: Erlbaum.

Hathorn, L. G. and Ingram, A. L. (2002). Online collaboration: making it work. *Educational Technology 42*, 33–40.

Hofer, B. K. (2004). Epistemological understanding as a metacognitive process: thinking aloud during online searching. *Educational Psychologist 39*, 43–55.

Hsiung, R. C. (ed.) (2002). *E-therapy: Case studies, guiding principles and the clinical potential of the Internet.* New York: Norton.

IJsselsteijn, W. A., Freeman, J. and De Ridder, H. (2001). Presence: Where are we? *CyberPsychology and Behavior 4*, 179–182.

IJsselsteijn, W. A. and Riva, G. (2003). Being there: the experience of presence in mediated environments. In G. Riva, F. Davide and W. A. IJsselsteijn (eds), *Being there: Concepts, effects and measurements of user presence in synthetic environments* (pp. 3–16). Amsterdam, Holland: IOS Press.

Insko, B. E. (2003). Measuring presence: subjective, behavioral and physiological methods. In G. Riva, F. Davide and W. A. IJsselsteijn (eds), *Being there: Concepts, effects and measurements of user presence in synthetic environments* (pp. 109–119). Amsterdam, Holland: IOS Press.

Jacobson, D. (2001). Presence revisited: Imagination, competence and activity in text-based virtual worlds. *CyberPsychology and Behavior 4*, 653–673.

Jazwinski, C. H. (2001). Gender identities on the World Wide Web. In C. R. Wolfe (ed.), *Learning and teaching on the World Wide Web* (pp. 171–189). San Diego: CA: Academic Press.

Johns, M. D., Chen, S. S. and Hall, G. J. (eds) (2004). *Online social research: Methods, issues and ethics.* New York: Peter Lang.

Joinson, A. N. (1998). Causes and implication of disinhibited behavior on the Internet. In J. Gackenbach (ed.), *Psychology and the Internet: intrapersonal, interpersonal and transpersonal implications* (pp. 43–60). San Diego, CA: Academic Press.

Joinson, A. N. (1999). Social desirability, anonymity and Internet-based questionnaires. *Behavior and Research Methods, Instruments and Computers 31*, 433–438.

Joinson, A. N. (2001). Self-disclosure in computer-mediated communication: the role of self-awareness and visual anonymity. *European Journal of Social Psychology 31*, 177–192.

Joinson, A. (2003). *Understanding the psychology of Internet behaviour.* Basingstoke, UK: Palgrave Macmillan.

Joinson, A. N. (2005). Deviance and the Internet. *Social Science Computer Review 23*, 5–7.

Joinson, A. N. and Dietz-Uhler, B. (2002). Explanations for the perpetration of and reactions to deception in virtual community. *Social Science Computer Review 20*, 275–289.

Kamada, M., Ambe, M., Hata, K., Yamada, E. and Fujimura, Y. (2005). The effect of the emotion-related channel in 3D virtual communication environments. *PsychNology Journal 3(3)*, 312–327. Retrieved 10 January 2006 from http://www.psychnology.org.

Kenny, D. A. (1994). *Interpersonal perception: A social relations analysis.* New York: Guilford.

King, A. B. (2001). Affective dimensions of Internet culture. *Social Science Computer Review 19*, 414–430.

Kleinke, C. L. (1986). Gaze and eye contact: a research review. *Psychological Bulletin 100*, 78–100.

Knapp, M. L. and Hall, J. A. (2001). *Nonverbal communication in human interaction*. Singapore: Wadsworth.

Kreijns, K., Kirschner, P. A. and Jochems, W. (2003). Identifying the pitfalls for social interaction in computer-supported collaborative learning environments: a review of the research. *Computers in Human Behavior 19*, 335–353.

Kreitler, H. (1976). *Cognitive orientation and behavior*. New York: Springer.

Kreitler, S. and Kreitler, H. (1990). *The cognitive foundations of personality traits*. New York: Plenum.

Kreuter, E. A. (2003). The impact of identity theft through cyberspace. *Forensic Examiner 12*, 30–35.

Kruglanski, A. W. and Webster, D. M. (1996). Motivated closing of the mind: 'seizing' and 'freezing.' *Psychological Review 103*, 263–283.

Kubo, M. M., Tori, R. and Kirner, C. (2002). Interaction in collaborative educational virtual environments. *CyberPsychology and Behavior 5*, 399–407.

LaRose, R., Eastin, M. S. and Gregg, J. (2001b). Reformulating the Internet paradox: social cognitive explanations of Internet use and depression. *Journal of Online Behavior 1*(2) Retrieved 10 January 2006 from: http://www.behavior.net/JOB/v1n2/paradox.html.

LaRose, R., Lin, C. A. and Eastin, M. S. (2003). Unregulated Internet usage: addiction, habit or deficient self-regulation? *Media Psychology 5*, 225–253.

LaRose, R., Mastro, D. and Eastin, M. S. (2001a). Understanding Internet usage – a social-cognitive approach to uses and gratifications. *Social Science Computer Review 19*, 395–413.

Lee, E. and Leets, L. (2002). Persuasive storytelling by hate groups online: examining its effects on adolescents. *American Behavioral Scientist 45*, 927–937.

Lee, H. (2005a). Implosion, virtuality and interaction in an Internet discussion group. *Information, Communication and Society 8*, 47–63.

Lee, H. (2005b). Behavioral strategies for dealing with flaming in an online forum. *Sociological Quarterly 46*, 385–403.

Leung, L. (2004). Net-generation attributes and seductive properties of the Internet as predictors of online activities and Internet addiction. *CyberPsychology and Behavior 7*, 333–348.

Levin, B. (2002). Cyberhate: a legal and historical analysis of extremists' use of computer networks in America. *American Behavioral Scientist 45*, 958–988.

Levine, D. (1998). *The joy of cybersex*. New York: Ballentine Books.

Light, A. and Wakeman, I. (2001). Beyond the interface: users' perceptions of interaction and audience on websites. *Interacting With Computers 13*, 325–351.

Livingstone, S. (2003). Children's use of the Internet. Reflections on the emerging research agenda. *New Media and Society 5*, 147–166.

Lwin, M. O. and Williams, J. D. (2003). A model integrating the multidimensional developmental theory of privacy and theory of planned behavior to examine fabrication of information online. *Marketing Letters 14*, 257–272.

Maczewski, M. (2002). Exploring identities through the Internet: youth experiences online. *Child and Youth Care Forum 31*, 111–129.

Mantovani, F. (2001a). Cyber-attraction: the emergence of computer-mediated communication in the development of interpersonal relationships. In L. Anolli, R. Cieri and G. Riva (eds), *Say not to say: New perspectives on miscommunication* (pp. 236–252). Amsterdam, Holland: IOS Press.

Mantovani, F. (2001b). Networked seduction: a test-bed for the study of strategic communication on the Internet. *CyberPsychology and Behavior 4*, 147–154.

Mantovani, G. (2002). Internet haze: why new artifacts can enhance situation ambiguity. *Culture and Psychology 8*, 307–326.

Markey, P. M. and Wells, S. M. (2002). Interpersonal perception in Internet chat rooms. *Journal of Research in Personality 36*, 134–146.

Mayer, J. D. and Salovey, P. (1997). What is emotional intelligence? In P. Salovey and D. Sluyter (eds), *Emotional development and emotional intelligence: Educational implications* (pp. 3–31). New York: Basic Books.

McKenna, K. Y. A. and Bargh, J. A. (1998). Coming out in the age of the Internet: identity 'demarginalization' through virtual group participation. *Journal of Personality and Social Psychology 75*, 681–694.

McKenna, K. Y. A. and Bargh, J. A. (1999). Causes and consequences of social interaction on the Internet: a conceptual framework. *Media Psychology 1*, 249–269.

McKenna, K. Y. A. and Bargh, J. A. (2000). Plan 9 from cyberspace: the implication of the Internet for personality and social psychology. *Personality and Social Psychology Review 4*, 57–75.

McKenna, K. Y. A. and Green, A. S. (2002). Virtual group dynamics. *Group Dynamics 6*, 116–127.

McKenna, K. Y. A., Green, A. S. and Gleason, M. E. J. (2002). Relationship formation on the Internet: What's the big attraction? *Journal of Social Issues 58*, 9–31.

McKenna, K. Y. A. and Seidman, G. (2005). You, me and we: interpersonal processes in electronic groups. In Y. Amichai-Hamburger (ed.), *The social net: Human behavior in cyberspace* (pp. 191–217). New York: Oxford University Press.

Merkle, E. R. and Richardson, R. A. (2000). Digital dating and virtual relating: conceptualizing computer mediated romantic relationships. *Family Relations: Journal of Applied Family and Child Studies 49*, 187–192.

Metzger, M. J., Flanagin, A. J. and Zwarun, L. (2003). College student Web use, perceptions of information credibility and verification behavior. *Computers and Education 41*, 271–290.

Mitra, A. (2005). Creating immigrant identities in cybernetic space: examples from a non-resident Indian website. *Media, Culture and Society 27*, 371–390.

Morahan-Martin, J. (2005). Internet abuse: Addiction? Disorder? Symptom? Alternative Explanations? *Social Science Computer Review 23*, 39–48.

Mummalaneni, V. (2005). An empirical investigation of web site characteristics, consumer emotional states and on-line shopping behaviors. *Journal of Business Research* 58, 526–532.

Naquin, C. E. and Paulson, G. D. (2003). Online bargaining and interpersonal trust. *Journal of Applied Psychology* 88, 113–120.

New Scientist Online (2004). *People lie more on the phone than by email.* Retrieved 10 January 2006 from http://www.newscientist.com/news/ news.jsp?id=ns99994663.

Newhagen, J. E. and Rafaeli, S. (1996). Why communication researchers should study the Internet: a dialogue. *Journal of Computer-Mediated Communication 1(4).* Retrieved 10 January 2006 from http://www.ascusc.org/jcmc/vol1/issue4/rafaeli.html.

Nicovich, S. G., Boller, G. W. and Cornwell, T. B. (2005). Experienced presence within computer-mediated communications: initial explorations on the effects of gender with respect to empathy and immersion. *Journal of Computer-Mediated Communication 10(2),* article 6. Retrieved 10 January 2006 from http://jcmc.indiana.edu/ vol10/issue2/nicovich.html.

Nowak, K. L. and Rauh, C. (2005). The influence of the avatar on online perceptions of anthropomorphism androgyny, credibility, homophily and attraction. *Journal of Computer-Mediated Communication 11(1),* article 8. Retrieved 10 January 2006 from http://jcmc.indiana.edu/vol11/issue1/nowak.html.

Nowak, K. L., Watt, J. and Walther, J. B. (2005). The influence of synchrony and sensory modality on the person perception process in computer-mediated groups. *Journal of Computer-Mediated Communication 10(3),* article 3. Retrieved 10 January 2006 from http://jcmc.indiana.edu/vol10/issue3/ nowak.html.

Ookita, S. Y. and Tokuda, H. (2001). A virtual therapeutic environment with user projective agents. *CyberPsychology and Behavior 4,* 155–167.

O'Rorke, P. and Ortony, A. (1994). Explaining emotions. *Cognitive Science 18,* 283–323.

Ortony, A., Clore, G. L. and Collins, A. (1988). *The cognitive structure of emotions.* New York: Cambridge University Press.

Ovid (18 BC). Translated by A. D. Melville (1998). *Metamorphoses,* Book X. New York: Oxford University Press.

Paasonen, S. (2002). Gender, identity and (the limits of) play on the Internet. In M. Consaluo and S. Paasonen (eds), *Women and everyday uses of the Internet: Agency and identity* (pp. 21–43). New York: Peter Lang Publishing.

Pelphrey, K. A., Viola, R. J. and McCarthy, G. (2004). When strangers pass: processing of mutual and averted social gaze in the superior temporal sulcus. *Psychological Science 15,* 598–603.

Pennebaker, J. W., Mehl, M. R. and Niederhoffer, K. G. (2003). Psychological aspects of natural language use: our words, our selves. *Annual Review of Psychology 54,* 547–577.

Pew Internet Project (2003). America's online pursuits: the changing picture of who's online and what they do (December, 2003). Retrieved 10 January 2006 from http://www.pewinternet.org/reports/toc.asp?Report=106.

Pew Internet Project (2005). *Internet activities.* Retrieved 10 January 2006 from http://www.pewinternet.org/trends/ Internet_Activities_3.02.05.htm.

Pickett, J. M. (1998). *The acoustics of speech communication: Fundamentals, speech perception theory and technology,* 2nd edn. Boston, MA: Pearson/Allyn and Bacon.

Poster, J. M. (2002). Trouble, pleasure and tactics: anonymity and identity in a lesbian chat room. In M. Consaluo and S. Paasonen (eds), *Women and everyday uses of the Internet: Agency and identity* (pp.21–43). New York: Peter Lang Publishing.

Postmes, T. and Spears, R. (2002). Behavior online: does anonymous computer communication reduce gender inequality? *Personality and Social Psychology Bulletin 28,* 1073–1083.

Preece, J. (1999). Empathic communities: balancing emotional and factual communication. *Interacting with Computers 12,* 63–67.

Preece, J. J. and Ghozati, K. (2001). Experiencing empathy online. In R. E. Rice and J. E. Katz (eds), *The Internet and health communication* (pp. 237–260). Thousand Oaks, CA: Sage.

Prinz, J. J. (2004). *Gut reactions: A perceptual theory of emotion.* New York: Oxford University Press.

Quayle, E. and Taylor, M. (2001) Child seduction and self-representation on the Internet. *CyberPsychology and Behavior 4,* 597–608.

Quayle, E. and Taylor, M. (2003). Model of problematic Internet use in people with a sexual interest in children. *CyberPsychology and Behavior 6,* 93–106.

Quigley, M. and Blashki, K. (2003). Beyond the boundaries of the sacred garden: children and the Internet. *Information Technology in Childhood Education Annual 15,* 309–316.

Rafaeli, S., Raban, D. and Kalman, Y. (2005). Social cognition online. In Y. Amichai-Hamburger (ed.), *The social net: Human behavior in cyberspace* (pp. 57–90). New York: Oxford University Press.

Reeve, J. (2005). *Understanding motivation and emotion,* 4th edn. Hoboken, NJ: Wiley.

Riva, G. (2001a). Communicating in CMC: making order out of miscommunication. In L. Anolli, R. Cieri and G. Riva (eds), *Say not to say: New perspectives on miscommunication* (pp. 204–233). Amsterdam, Holland: IOS Press.

Riva, G. (2001b). From real to virtual communities: cognition, knowledge and intention in the World Wide Web. In C. R. Wolfe (ed.), *Learning and teaching on the World Wide Web* (pp. 131–151). San Diego, CA: Academic Press.

Riva, G. (2002). The sociocognitive psychology of computer-mediated communication: the present and future of technology-based interactions. *CyberPsychology and Behavior 5,* 581–598.

Roberts, L. D. and Parks, M. R. (2001). The social geography of gender-switching in virtual environments on the Internet. In E. Green and A. Adam (eds), *Virtual gender: Technology, Consumption and Identity* (pp. 265–285). London: Routledge.

Robillard, G., Bouchard, S., Fournier, T. and Renaud, P. (2003). Anxiety and presence during VR immersion: a comparative study of the reactions of phobic and non-phobic participants in therapeutic virtual environments derived from computer games. *CyberPsychology and Behavior 6*, 467–476.

Rochlen, A. B., Land, L. N. and Wong, Y. J. (2004b). Male restrictive emotionality and evaluations of online versus face-to-face counseling. *Psychology of Men and Masculinity 5*, 190–200.

Rochlen, A. B., Zack, J. S. and Speyer, C. (2004a). Online therapy: review of relevant definitions, debates and current empirical support. *Journal of Clinical Psychology 60*, 269–283.

Rouse, S. V. and Hass, H. A. (2003). Exploring the accuracies and inaccuracies of personality perception following Internet-mediated communication. *Journal of Research in Personality 37*, 446–467.

Russell, J. A. (2003). Core affect and the psychological construction of emotion. *Psychological Review 110*, 145–172.

Sassenberg, K. (2002). Common bond and common identity groups on the Internet: attachment and normative behavior in on-topic and off-topic chats. *Group Dynamics 6*, 27–37.

Sassenberg, K., Boos, M., Pstmes, T. and Reips, U. D. (2003). Studying the Internet: a challenge for modern psychology. *Swiss Journal of Psychology 62*, 75–77.

Savicki, V., Kelley, M. and Oestrreich, E. (2003). Judgments of gender in computer-mediated communication. *Computers in Human Behavior 15*, 185–194.

Schlenker, B. R. (2003). Self-presentation. In J. P. Tangney and M. R. Leary (eds), *Handbook of self and identity* (pp. 492–518). New York: Guilford.

Seiden, H. M. (2001). Creating passion: an Internet love story. *Journal of Applied Psychoanalytic Studies 3*, 187–195.

Seymour, W. and Lupton, D. (2004). Holding the line online: exploring wired relationships for people with disabilities. *Disability and Society 19*, 291–305.

Sherman, R. C. (2001). The mind's eye in cyberspace: online perceptions of self and others. In G. Riva and C. Galimberti (eds), *Toward cyberPsychology: Mind, cognitions and society in the Internet age* (pp. 53–72). Amsterdam, Holland: IOS Press.

Singer, T., Seymour, B., O'Doherty, J., Kaube, H., Dolan, R. J. and Frith, C. D. (2004). Empathy for pain involves the affective but not sensory components of pain. *Science 303*, 1157–1162.

Slater, M. (2004). Presence and emotions. *CyberPsychology and Behavior 7*, 121.

Smith, C. A. and Kirby, L. D. (2000). Consequences require antecedents: toward a process model of emotion elicitation. In J. P. Forgas (ed.), *Feeling and thinking: The role of affect in social cognition* (pp. 83–106). New York: Cambridge University Press.

Soble, A. (1990). *The structure of love*. New Haven, CT: Yale University Press.

Sohn, D. and Lee B. (2005). Dimensions of interactivity: differential effects of social and psychological factors. *Journal of Computer-Mediated Communication 10*(3), article 6. Retrieved 10 January 2006 from http://jcmc.indiana.edu/vol10/issue3/sohn.html.

Soros, P., Vo, O., Husstedt, I.-W., Evers, S. and Gerding, H. (2003). Phantom eye syndrome: its prevalence, phenomenology and putative mechanisms. *Neurology 60*, 1542–1543.

Spears, R., Postmes, T., Lea, M. and Wolbert, A. (2002). When are net effects gross products? The power of influence and influence of power in computer-mediated communication. *Journal of Social Issues 58*, 91–107.

Strate, L., (2003). Cybertime. In L. Strate, R. L. Jacobson and S. B. Gibson (eds), *Communication and cyberspace: Social interaction in an electronic environment*, 2nd edn. (pp. 361–387). Cresskill, NJ: Hampton Press.

Strate, L., Jacobson, R., L. and Gibson, S. B. (2003). Surveying the electronic landscape: an introduction to *Communication and Cyberspace*. In L. Strate, R. L. Jacobson and S. B. Gibson (eds), *Communication and cyberspace: Social interaction in an electronic environment*, 2nd edn. (pp. 1–26). Cresskill, NJ: Hampton Press.

Strongman, K. T. (2003). *The psychology of emotion: From everyday life to theory*. Chichester: Wiley.

Suler, J. (1996–2005). The psychology of cyberspace. Retrieved 10 January 2006 from http://www.rider.edu/suler/psycyber/.

Suler, J. R. (1999). To get what you need: healthy and pathological Internet use. *CyberPsychology and Behavior 2*, 385–393.

Suler, J. (2000). Psychotherapy in cyberspace: a 5-dimensional model of online and computer-mediated psychotherapy. *CyberPsychology and Behavior 3*, 151–159.

Suler, J. R. (2002). Identity management in cyberspace. *Journal of Applied Psychoanalytic Studies 4*, 455–459.

Suler, J. (2004a). The psychology of text relationships. In R. Kraus, J. Zack and G. Stricker (eds), *Online counseling: A handbook for mental health professionals* (pp. 19–50). San Diego, CA: Academic Press Elsevier.

Suler, J. (2004b). The online disinhibition effect. *CyberPsychology and Behavior 7*, 321–326.

Suler, J. R. and Phillips, W. L. (2000). The bad boys of cyberspace: deviant behavior in a multimedia chat community. *CyberPsychology and Behavior 1*, 275–294.

Sundar, S. S. (2004). Theorizing interactivity's effects. *The Information Society 20*, 385–389.

Tassinari, G., Migliorini, A., Girardini, F. and Luzzani, A. (2002). Reference fields in phantom tooth pain as a marker for remapping in the facial territory. *Functional Neurology: New Trends in Adaptive and Behavioral Disorders 17*, 121–127.

Tate, D. F. and Zabinski, M. F. (2004). Computer and Internet applications for psychological treatment: update for clinicians. *Journal of Clinical Psychology 60*, 209–220.

Thomas, N. J. T. (1999). Are theories of imagery theories of imagination? An active perception approach to conscious mental content. *Cognitive Sciences 23*, 207–245.

Thomas, N. J. T. (2003). Mental imagery, philosophical issues about. In C. L. Nadel (ed.), *Encyclopedia of cognitive science*, vol. 2 (pp. 1147–1153). London, UK: Macmillan.

Thompson, P. A. (2003). What's fueling the flames in cyberspace? A social influence model. In L. Strate, R. L. Jacobson and S. B. Gibson (eds), *Communication and cyberspace: Social interaction in an electronic environment*, 2nd edn. (pp. 329–347). Cresskill, NJ: Hampton Press.

Tidwell, L. C. and Walther, L. B. (2002). Computer-mediated communication effects on disclosure, impressions and interpersonal evaluations: Getting to know one another a bit at a time. *Human Communication Research 28*, 317–348.

Turgeman-Goldschmidt, O. (2005). Hackers' accounts: hacking as a social entertainment. *Social Science Computer Review 23*, 8–23.

Turkle, S. (1995). *Life on the screen*. New York: Touchstone, Simon and Schuster.

Turkle, S. (2004). Whither psychoanalysis in computer culture? *Psychoanalytic Psychology 21*, 16–30.

Tyler, J. R. and Tang, J. C. (2003). When can I expect an email response? A study of rhythms in email usage. *Proceedings of the European Conference of Computer-Supported Cooperative Work: ECSCW*. Helsinki, Finland. Retrieved 10 January 2006 from http://www.hpl.hp.com/research/idl/papers/rhythms/ECSCWFinal.pdf.

Utz, S. (2005). Types of deception and underlying motivation. *Social Science Computer Review 23*, 49–56.

Valkenburg, P. M., Schouten, A. P. and Peter, J. (2005). Adolescents' identity experiments on the Internet. *New Media and Society 7*, 383–402.

Vazire, S. and Gosling, S. D. (2004). E-perceptions: personality impressions based on personal websites. *Journal of Personality and Social Psychology 87*, 123–132.

Viseu, A., Clement, A. and Aspinall, J. (2004). Situating privacy online: complex perceptions and everyday practices. *Information, Communication and Society 7*, 92–114.

Voiskounsky, A. E. and Smyslova, O. V. (2003). Flow-based model of computer hackers' motivation. *CyberPsychology and Behavior 6*, 171–180.

Wade, N. J. (2003). The legacy of phantom limbs. *Perception 32*, 517–524.

Wager, T. D., Rilling, J. K., Smith, E. E., Sokolik, A., Casey, K. L., Davidson, R. J., Kosslyn, S. M., Rose, R. M. and Cohen, J. D. (2004). Placebo-induced changes in fMRI in the anticipation and experience of pain. *Science 303*, 1162–1167.

Wallace, P. (1999). *The psychology of the Internet*. New York: Cambridge University Press.

Walker, B. M., Harper, J., Lloyd, C. and Caputi, P. (2003). Methodologies for the exploration of computer and technology transference. *Computers in Human Behavior 19*, 523–535.

Walther, J. B. (1996). Computer-mediated communication: impersonal, interpersonal and hyperpersonal interaction. *Communication Research 23*, 3–43.

Walther, J. B. and D'Addario, K. P. (2001). The impacts of emoticons on message interpretation in computer-mediated communication. *Social Science Computer Review 19*, 323–345.

Webbink, P. (1986). *The power of the eyes*. New York: Springer.

Weinberg, H. (2002). Community unconscious on the Internet. *Group Analysis 35*, 165–183.

Whittaker, J. (2004). *The cyberspace handbook*. New York: Routledge.

Whitty, M. T. (2002). Liar, liar! An examination of how open, supportive and honest people are in chat rooms. *Computers in Human Behavior 18*, 343–352.

Whitty, M. T. (2003a). Cyber-flirting: playing at love on the Internet. *Theory and Psychology 13*, 339–357.

Whitty, M. (2003b). Logging onto love: an examination of men's and women's flirting behaviour both offline and on the Internet. *Australian Journal of Psychology 55*, 68–86.

Whitty, M. T. (2004). Cyber-flirting: an examination of men's and women's flirting behaviour both offline and on the Internet. *Behaviour Change 21*, 115–126.

Whitty, M. T. and Carr, A. N. (2006). New rules in the workplace: applying object-relations theory to explain problem Internet and email behaviour in the workplace. *Computers in Human Behavior 22*, 235–250.

Wildermuth, S. M. (2004). The effects of stigmatizing discourse on the quality of on-line relationships. *CyberPsychology and Behavior 7*, 73–84.

Williams, D. and Skoric, M. (2005). Internet fantasy violence: a test of aggression in an online game. *Communication Monographs 72*, 217–233.

Williams, K. D., Cheung, C. K. T. and Choi, W. (2000). Cyberostracism: effects of being ignored over the Internet. *Journal of Personality and Social Psychology 79*, 748–762.

Williamson, I. O., Lepak, D. P. and King, J. (2003). The effect of company recruitment web site orientation on individuals' perceptions of organizational attractiveness. *Journal of Vocational Behavior 63*, 242–263.

Wilson, B. and Atkinson, M. (2005). Rave and straightedge, the virtual and the real: exploring online and offline experiences in Canadian youth subcultures. *Youth and Society 36*, 276–311.

Yao, M. Z. and Flanagin, A. J. (2006). A self-awareness approach to computer-mediated communication. *Computers in Human Behavior 22*, 518–544.

Ybarra, M. L. and Mitchell, K. J. (2004). Youth engaging in online harassment: associations with caregiver-child relationships, Internet use and personal characteristics. *Journal of Adolescence 27*, 319–336.

Yellowlees, P. M. (2002). Clinical principles to guide the practice of e-therapy. In R. C. Hsiung (ed.), *e-Therapy: Case studies, guiding principles and the clinical potential of the Internet* (pp. 136–149). New York: Norton.

Youn, S. (2005). Teenagers' perceptions of online privacy and coping behaviors: a risk-benefit appraisal approach. *Journal of Broadcasting and Electronic Media 49*, 86–110.

Young, K. S. (2001). *Cybersex: The secret world of Internet sex.* London, UK: Carlton Books.

Young, K. S., Griffin-Shelley, E., O'Mara, J. and Buchanan, J. (2000). Online infidelity: a new dimension in couple relationships with implications for evaluation and treatment. *Sexual Addiction and Compulsivity 7,* 59–74.

Zhao, S. (2005). The digital self: Through the looking glass of telecopresent others. *Symbolic Interaction 28,* 387–405.

Zhou, L., Burgoon, J. K., Zhang, D. and Nunamaker, J. F. (2004). Language dominance in interpersonal deception in computer-mediated communication. *Computers in Human Behavior 20,* 381–402.

Zimmer, E. A. and Hunter, C. D. (2003). Risk and the Internet: perception and reality. In L. Strate, R. L. Jacobson and S. B. Gibson (eds), *Communication and cyberspace: Social interaction in an electronic environment,* 2nd edn. (pp. 183–202). Cresskill, NJ: Hampton Press.

Zizek, S. (2004). What can psychoanalysis tell us about cyberspace? *Psychoanalytic Review 91,* 801–830.

CHAPTER 21

Internet use and abuse and psychological problems

Janet Morahan-Martin

The Internet is transforming lives. It has become an invaluable tool for communication, information and entertainment. Most Internet users find it indispensable and are using it in ways that enhance their lives (Howard *et al.* 2001; Rainie and Horrigan 2005). However, a small minority are using the Internet in ways that have led to problems in their lives. Among these are some who have been labelled Internet addicts. Almost 10 per cent of adult Internet users in a large online study self-identified themselves as Internet addicts (Cooper *et al.* 2002) and 15 per cent of university students in the United States (US) and Europe claim they know someone is addicted to the Internet (Anderson 1999). Anecdotal accounts of Internet abuse and addiction date to the early 1990s (e.g. Moore 1995; Rheingold 1993). These accounts describe individuals whose Internet behaviour was out of control, with some self-labelling themselves as 'Internet Addicts'. As the Internet expanded to the general population, the popular media began to publicize these concerns (e.g., Wallis 1997). Critics dismissed these claims and the publicity in the popular media that they received (Grohol 1999): however, clinicians began to report that they were seeing cases of Internet-related disturbances, including some patterns with were

called Internet addiction or abuse (Orzack 1999), and established clinics such as the Computer Addiction Service at McLean Hospital, a Harvard University Medical School affiliate. Since then, Internet abuse has been reported worldwide, research on Internet abuse has proliferated, and clinics for Internet addiction have opened in many countries. The South Korean government plans to increase the number of treatment centres for Internet addicts from 40 to 100 by 2010 (South Korea plans more centres to treat Internet addiction 2005) while in the People's Republic of China, the first officially licensed government clinic for Internet addiction was opened in 2004 at the Beijing Military Region Central Hospital (Wired News 2004).

Research and clinical observation have documented that disturbed patterns of Internet use often are associated with other disturbances such as depression (Young and Rodgers 1998; Whang *et al.* 2003), and sexual compulsivity (Cooper *et al.* 1999). This has raised questions about what the relationship is between Internet abuse and other pathologies. Some contend that behaviours that have been labelled as Internet abuse are instead symptomatic of other disorders such as sexual compulsivity. Others argue that there are patterns of disturbed behaviours unique to the Internet that are analogous to substance abuse or impulse control disorders, and have labelled these behaviours with a number of terms such as Internet addiction or abuse, pathological Internet use, Internet abuse, or disturbed Internet behaviours. However, etiology is not clear and etiological explanations of the relationship of Internet abuse and other disturbances differ. Some maintain that that Internet abuse causes problems such as depression, while others maintain that those with pre-existing pathology may be vulnerable to developing disturbed patterns of Internet use.

The primary focus of this chapter is the relationship of Internet abuse to psychological disorders and personality factors. It will first provide an overview of definitions and criticisms of the concept of Internet abuse. Then, it will focus on different approaches to understanding the relationship of Internet abuse to various psychological disorders and personality factors. Finally, it will present emerging theories about the etiology of Internet abuse.

What is Internet abuse?

Internet abuse is a broad term which has varied names and definitions. The terms used include Internet addiction (Young 1998; Bai *et al.* 2001; Pratarelli and Browne 2002; Nalwa and Anand 2003; Chak and Leung 2004; Nichols and Nicki 2004; Simkova and Cincera 2004), Internet dependency (Scherer 1997; Chen *et al.* 2001; Lin and Tsai 2002; Whang *et al.* 2003), Internet abuse (Morahan-Martin 1999, 2001), compulsive Internet use (Greenfield 1999), pathological Internet use (Morahan-Martin and Schumacher 2000; Davis 2001), problematic Internet use (Shapira *et al.* 2000; Caplan 2002; Shapira *et al.* 2003).

In part, these terms reflect varying conceptualizations of Internet abuse. Often, Internet abuse has been treated as a clinical entity with distinct criteria. Some have established criteria by modifying *Diagnostic and Statistical Manual of Psychiatric Disorders (DSM)* (American Psychiatric Association 2000) criteria for substance abuse (Scherer 1997; Nichols and Nicki 2004) or pathological gambling (Young 1998). Others have argued that Internet abuse should

be considered an impulse control disorder not otherwise specified (NOS) (Orzack 1999; Treuer *et al.* 2001; Shapira *et al.* 2003) or as a behavioural or technological addiction (Griffiths 1998). Implicit in these definitions is the assumption that Internet abuse is a specific disorder or disease. This is reflected in use of the term Internet addiction.

However, other researchers do not apply clinical labels and instead approach what has been called Internet abuse as a continuum from normal to disturbed patterns of Internet use (Morahan-Martin and Schumacher 2000; Caplan 2002, 2003, 2004, 2005). These researchers have used terms such as problematic or pathological Internet use.

Despite differences in definitions and specific criteria to assess Internet abuse, there is general agreement that Internet abuse involves use(s) of the Internet that causes marked disturbances in the person's life. Additionally, most agree that it involves preoccupation with using the Internet, symptoms of tolerance and withdrawal, unsuccessful attempts to cut back on use and using the Internet to alter moods (i.e., when down, anxious or as an escape) (Morahan-Martin 2001, 2005). Those who develop these disturbed patterns use the Internet more than others, and some have equated Internet abuse with heavy or excessive use of the Internet. However, excessive Internet use alone does not qualify as Internet abuse because Internet abuse is universally defined in terms of its negative impact on an individual's life.

In this chapter, the term Internet abuse (IA) is used except in reference to other authors' terminology. This term is not meant to imply a specific disease process or addictive behaviour, but rather patterns of using the Internet that result in disturbances in the person's life.

Incidence of IA

IA has been found worldwide, and there have been a number of studies to assess its prevalence. Young's (1998) criteria for IA, which is modelled on criteria for pathological gambling, has been the model for defining IA for most studies. Estimates of the incidence of IA vary widely. Epidemiological studies of adolescents in Finland

and Norway found less than two per cent of all 12–18 year old adolescents had IA. Incidence increased with amount and frequency of Internet use (Johansson and Götestam 2004; Kaltiala-Heino *et al.* 2004). Two studies in Taiwan that used representative samples reported that among those who had ever used the Internet, 12 per cent of high school students had IA (Lin and Tsai 2002; Tsai and Lin 2001). Other studies which have used convenience samples report IA incidence as ranging from 3.5–15 per cent (Scherer 1997; Morahan-Martin and Schumacher 2000; Bai *et al.* 2001; Morahan-Martin 2001; Whang *et al.* 2003; Chak and Leung 2004). Differences in prevalence may represent differences in culture, sampling, age, or criteria used.

Criticism of the concept of IA

The concept of Internet abuse has not been without its critics and many are sceptical about its existence. Detractors have questioned the concept of IA and some have dismissed research on the topic (Grohol 1999; Mitchell 2000; Shaffer *et al.* 2000; Walther and Reid, 2000). Critics also have questioned the appropriateness of applying *any* pathological label for Internet behaviour (Grohol 1999; Walther and Reid, 2000). Grohol (1999) has argued that the Internet is no more addictive or compulsive than other leisure activities such watching television, talking on the telephone and so on. Although people engage in these activities to the point of interrupting other aspects of their lives, there is little alarm about television or telephone addiction (Morahan-Martin 2005). Turkle (1995) argues that widespread alarm about IA may reflect fears about the rapid spread of new technology by people who are intimidated by that technology.

Critics also have contended that focusing blame on the Internet rather than the specific online activity that is causing problems is deceptive. The problem is not the Internet per se, but the specific activities that people pursue online (Shaffer *et al.* 2000). Holmes (1997) cautions:

> People develop problems with certain activities which they do online. There are people who compulsively chat online, people who compulsively download pornography and people who compulsively

play games. If the word 'addiction' is even appropriate, I'd like to suggest that people become 'addicted' to these activities and not to the Internet itself. The term 'sex addict' is not an official diagnostic term, but it is sometimes used to describe someone who is compulsively sexual and seems to be addicted to sex. Many of these people buy pornographic magazines and videos. We don't consider them to be addicted to magazines or videos, but to sex – the content of the magazines and videos.

Other critics also have questioned the appropriateness of applying the addiction model to IA. Walther and Reid (2000) contend that 'we should not use value-laden terms such as addiction to label something we know so little about' (p. B5). Broadening addiction from substances to behaviours is controversial. Since the 1970s, there has been a trend to label disturbed patterns of behaviours such as eating, exercise, gambling, sex, shopping, television, computer games and sex as addictions (e.g., Milkman and Sunderwirth 1982; Jacobs 1986; Cooper *et al.* 1999; Kubey and Csikszentmihalyi 2002). Jaffe (1990) contends that the broadened use of the term 'addiction' trivializes the concept of substance-related addiction, and is detrimental to understanding specific etiology and treatment approaches for substance-related as well as other compulsive, repetitive behaviours, which have been inappropriately called addictions. At an individual level, labelling such behaviour as addiction leads these behaviours 'to grow because it excuses uncontrolled behaviors and predisposes people to interpret their lack of control as the expression of a disease that they can do nothing about' (Peele, cited in Jaffe 1990: 1426).

Yet other critics have questioned whether it is premature to consider IA as a separate diagnostic category. Shaffer *et al.* argue that 'empirical support for the construct validity of computer addiction has yet to emerge, (and) that defining the construct as a unique psychiatric disorder is therefore premature' (2000: 162). Further, they contend that 'in most cases, computer (and Internet) use may be symptomatic of other, more primary disorders' (2000: 162). From this perspective, labeling IA 'as if it were a new diagnostic entity may lead to the misdiagnosis of primary psychiatric disorders for which we have proven therapeutic interventions' (Huang and Alessi, 1997: 890).

Relationship between Internet abuse and other problems

In fact, IA has been associated with a number of other problems including depression (Young and Rodgers, 1998; Whang *et al.* 2003), substance abuse (Bai *et al.* 2001) and sexual compulsivity (Cooper *et al.* 1999). Those with IA are more likely than others to engage in activities such as online gambling and netsex (Young 1998; Greenfield 1999; Morahan-Martin and Schumacher 2000). Personality factors associated with IA include loneliness (Morahan-Martin and Schumacher 2000, 2003; Kubey *et al.* 2001; Caplan 2002; Nalwa and Anand 2003; Whang *et al.* 2003), shyness and social anxiety (Caplan 2002; Chak and Leung 2004; Pratarelli 2005).

Approaches to understanding the relationship of IA to other disorders

The relationship of IA to other disorders has raised a number of questions, and approaches to understanding the relationship between IA and other problems have varied. As indicated earlier, critics maintain that what has been labelled as IA is symptomatic of other disorders. From this perspective, focusing on IA rather than the real disorder is inappropriate. This approach would suggest those labelled with IA have pre-existing disorders. A related approach emphasizes the need to delineate patterns of Internet-related behaviours associated with specific activities that are direct manifestations of established pathologies, such as compulsive sexual behaviour, from a more generalized form of IA, and to study each separately.

Each approach suggests different etiologies to explaining IA or disturbed patterns of Internet use. An overarching issue is the relative role of the Internet and of the individual in the development of disturbed behaviors online and/or IA. To varying degrees, differing approaches maintain that disturbed online behaviours and/or IA may be attributed to either the Internet or the individual user. A diathesis-stress model would suggest that some individuals are vulnerable to developing IA. The unique attributes of the Internet may facilitate the development of disturbed patterns of Internet use, but it is not clear if certain people are more vulnerable to develop Internet-related pathologies such as Internet abuse because of pre-existing problems or vulnerabilities. Drawing on relevant research, the following sections discuss each approach separately.

Pre-existing problems and IA

Limited evidence that those with IA had preexisting problems is provided by a small scale study of 20 individuals with IA who were administered face-to-face (ftf) interviews using the Structured Clinical Interview for Diagnostic and Statistical Manual of Mental Disorders (SCID-IV). The researchers found all 20 participants had at least one lifetime DSM-IV Axis 1 diagnosis in addition to IA with an average of five other diagnoses. Nearly 2/3s (70 per cent) had a lifetime diagnosis of bipolar disorder, 85 per cent had received previous mental health treatment, and 75 per cent had been treated with psychotropic medications (Shapira *et al* 2000).

The pre-existence of other pathologies with IA can be interpreted in several ways. It is possible, as Shaffer *et al* (2000) argue, that focus on IA masks appropriate diagnosis. Symptoms attributed to IA may represent ways of dealing with stress associated with these disorders. Research supports that those with IA are more likely than others to use the Internet to modulate negative affect; they use the Internet to escape pressures, when down, anxious, socially isolated and to control moods (Morahan-Martin and Schumacher 2000; Anderson, 1999). Although this provides support for those who contend that Internet abuse is symptomatic of other problems such as depression, the direction of the relationship is not clear. Comorbidity does not determine direction of the relationship. A number of other disorders are comorbid with depression including substance abuse, pathological gambling, sexual compulsivity, impulse control disorders, chronic loneliness and social anxiety (Becona *et al.* 1996; Cooper *et al.* 1999; Forsyth and Elliott 1999; American Psychiatric Association 2000).

Specific vs. generalized IA

An alternative approach is to delineate subtypes of Internet-related disturbances according to specific online activities. Certain activities associated with IA, such as disturbed patterns of online gambling and compulsive online sexual activity, are more aptly conceptualized as Internet-enabled pathologies and should be distinguished from a more generalized form of IA which is not dependent on specific applications. It is not the Internet itself that is causing problems, but the specific activity (Davis 2001; Morahan-Martin 2005). Davis (2001) proposes two distinct types of IA: specific and generalized. Specific IA involves the overuse or abuse of a content-specific function of the Internet such as downloading pornography or gambling, while generalized IA not linked to any specific content but to abuse of the Internet itself that results in negative consequences. Alternatively, specific IA's should be considered not as forms of IA but as technologically enabled variants of other pathologies such as pathological gambling or compulsive sexuality. The term IA as used in this chapter refers to generalized IA. However, research on IA rarely has distinguished specific forms of IA, so that it is probable that an unknown percentage of those labelled in existing research as having IA should instead be viewed in terms of their specific behavioural disorders.

However, there is a large and growing body of research on patterns of online sexual behaviours and gambling (e.g.; Cooper *et al.* 1999, 2000; Griffiths 2001; Griffiths and Parke 2002; Ladd and Petry 2002; Boies *et al.* 2004). Although this literature is beyond the scope of this chapter, a few findings from research on online sexual behaviours and disturbances are relevant to this discussion because they parallel research on generalized IA. A large scale online study of online sexual activities (OSA) found that about one-sixth (16 per cent) were sexually compulsive but only 1 per cent of all who engaged in OSA were what the authors called online sexual compulsives (Cooper *et al.* 2000). Although there is evidence that those who develop problems from their online sexual behaviours have pre-existing pathology (Schwartz and Southern 2000), Cooper *et al.* (1999) found some who develop problems from their OSA had no prior

history of sexual compulsivity. They speculate that these individuals may have been vulnerable to sexual compulsivity, but 'may never have had difficulty with sexual compulsivity if it were not for the Internet' (p. 85) because they had sufficient internal resources and impulse control to resist acting out these impulses until they went online. This group consists largely of people who are depressed and those who use OSA when they are highly stressed as a way of escaping or distracting themselves from negative feelings associated with stress. Confirmation of the role of using the Internet to deal with stress in the development of problems from OSA was found in second study which compared those with online sexual problems with a matched sample of OSA users. Those who developed problems from their use of OSA were more likely to use OSA to cope with stress and explore sexual fantasies (Cooper *et al.* 2001).

A second factor associated with disturbances arising from OSA is being involved in OSA activities to seek relationships. In a study of OSA among Canadian university students, Boies *et al.* conclude that 'activities facilitating interpersonal contact were most strongly correlated to Internet-related problems suggesting Internet use is related to a need for affiliation in some individuals' (2004: 215).

These findings are similar to research on IA. Both those with IA and those whose use of OSA is disturbed are more likely than others to be depressed and to use the Internet and to use the Internet to deal with stress. For both, online social interactions are an important factor.

Generalized IA and online social interaction

There is a growing consensus that the unique social interactions made possible by the Internet play a major role in the development of IA (Scherer 1997; Young 1998; Young and Rogers 1998; Morahan-Martin and Schumacher 2000; Davis 2001; Weiser 2001; Caplan 2002; Pratarelli and Browne 2002; Leung 2004; Yuen and Lavin 2004). Those with IA are more likely than other Internet users to participate in socially interactive activities such as chat rooms, newsgroups, interactive games (Young 1998; Morahan-Martin and

Schumacher 2000; Chen *et al.* 2001; Weiser 2001; Lin and Tsai 2002; Whang *et al.* 2003; Chak and Leung 2004; Johansson and Götestam 2004; Leung 2004); and to go online to meet new people, talk to others with the same interests, and find emotional support (Morahan-Martin and Schumacher 2000).

Davis (2001) argues that IA occurs when Internet users develop problems due to the unique communicative context of the Internet. Morahan-Martin and Schumacher (2000) found that the social aspects of Internet use consistently differentiate those with IA from other Internet users. Those with IA are more likely to be exhibit increased social confidence online than others. They were more likely to report that going online has made it easier to make friends, that they have a network of online friends, and that they are friendlier and open up more to people online than in real life. Internet abusers also find the Internet to be socially liberating. They are more likely to say that they are more themselves online, have more fun with people they know online, share intimate secrets online and prefer online to ftf communication. Further, those with IA are more likely to say that they know most of their friends from being online, and that their online friends understand them better than other people. The authors conclude that for those with IA, 'the Internet can be socially liberating, the Prozac of social communication' (2000: 20). Similarly, Leung (2004) found anonymity, social ease online and social disinhibition are strong predictors of IA, while Whang *et al.* 2003) found those with IA are more likely to reveal personal concerns to online friends and even to meet online friends ftf. Caplan (2002) found that users' preference for the social benefits available online is an important predictor of IA and concludes that these results suggest that 'preference for computer-mediated social interaction, as opposed to face-to-face interaction, plays a role in the etiology, development and outcomes' of generalized IA.

Loneliness, social anxiety, IA and online social interaction

The appeal of the enhanced social environment online is pertinent in explaining the relationship between IA and loneliness and social anxiety and is central to an emerging theory of generalized IA. As noted earlier, several studies have found that IA is related to loneliness (Morahan-Martin and Schumacher 2000, 2003; Kubey *et al.* 2001; Caplan 2002; Nalwa and Anand, 2003; Whang *et al.* 2003) as well as social anxiety and shyness (Pratarelli and Browne 2002; Caplan 2004; Chak and Leung 2004). However, the direction of these relationships is not clear, especially in the case of loneliness and IA. The following sections explore approaches to understanding the increased incidence of IA among first the lonely, and then the socially anxious. Drawing on literature from personality, communications and Internet use, they describe characteristics of the lonely and socially anxious, how they use the Internet, and why they may be more prone to develop IA. An integrative theory to explain IA follows.

IA and loneliness: two hypotheses

Two hypotheses have been proposed to explain the relationship between loneliness and IA. The first hypothesis claims that loneliness is a result of excessive Internet use and abuse while the second hypothesis claims that lonely individuals are at greater risk for developing Internet-related problems such as IA because the changed social interaction available online can become so compelling that it disrupts users' lives (Morahan-Martin 1999; Morahan-Martin and Schumacher 2003).

Hypothesis 1: the Internet causes loneliness

The first hypothesis contends that loneliness is a by-product of excessive Internet use because time spent online displaces ftf time spent with friends and families, thus isolating individuals and interrupting their sense of connection and belonging in their community (Nie, 2001; Nie and Ebring 2002).

The release of the first wave of the HomeNet study (Kraut *et al.* 1998) provided support for this hypothesis. This study monitored Internet use of new users and found neither depression nor loneliness before starting to use the Internet predicted depression or loneliness after the first 12–18 months of Internet use. However, increased Internet use was associated with higher levels of both depression and loneliness. The authors attribute these increases in depression and loneliness to decreases in family communication, social activities, happiness and the number of individuals in one's social network, which also were associated with increased Internet use. A second study using a time diary also found increases in Internet use led to declines in spending time with family and friends and in attending social events (Nie and Ebring 2002).

The HomeNet study and its findings were widely criticized. However, despite its small and select sample, it is one of a limited number of systematic longitudinal studies which followed the antecedents and consequences when users were introduced to the Internet.

The second wave of the HomeNet study (Kraut *et al.* 2002) contradicted the results from the first. Instead, this study found that after participants had been online for two to three years, loneliness and depression was unrelated to amount of Internet use. However, the impact of Internet use on psychological well-being varies between extroverts and introverts. For extroverts, increased use of the Internet is associated with greater social involvement and 'increased sense of well-being, including decreased levels of loneliness, decreased negative affect, decreased time pressure, and increased self esteem' (2002: 64). Conversely, for introverts, the effects were opposite in each of these measures of self esteem. Separate analyses controlling for previous levels of loneliness and social involvement found increased use of the Internet decreases loneliness and increases social involvement for extroverts, but has the opposite effects for introverts. The authors suggest a 'rich get richer' hypothesis. That is, for extroverts who already have greater social resources, Internet use enhances their well-being while the opposite is true for introverts.

Hypothesis 2: the lonely are drawn to the Internet

The finding that the positive or negative impact of Internet use is dependent upon personality is consistent with the second hypothesis regarding the relationship between loneliness and IA.

This hypothesis asserts that chronically lonely individuals are vulnerable to develop IA and other Internet-related problems. The Internet can provide social networks and a changed social environment that may be especially appealing to those who are chronically lonely, but at the same time, this environment can become so compelling that they spend increasingly more time online to the exclusion of other activities and develop IA (Morahan-Martin 1999; Morahan-Martin and Schumacher 2003). Research on characteristics of the lonely and how they use the Internet provides support for this approach.

This hypothesis views loneliness as a personality trait rather than as a temporary reaction. Being lonely can be a transient, situational state. Seventy-five per cent of first year students in their first two weeks at a large university reported that they had experienced loneliness, with 40 per cent saying that they were moderately to severely lonely (Cutrona 1982). For some, though, loneliness is a chronic state that is considered a stable personality trait (Weeks *et al.* 1980). Chronically lonely people have fewer friends, spend less time with friends, date less and attend less parties than others (Archibald *et al.* 1995). They find it difficult to make friends, participate in groups and initiate social activities (Horowitz and deSales French 1979; Prisbell 1988). Compared to those who are not lonely, lonely individuals report that they are less interested in ftf social activity and perceive ftf social activity to be less rewarding (Prisbell 1988). Chronically lonely tend to be self-conscious, introverted, socially inhibited, and sensitive to rejection (Russell *et al.* 1980; Bruch *et al.* 1988; Solano and Koester 1989). They are inclined to feel close to and spend more time in shallow relationships with strangers than with family and friends (Jones 1981). Lack of social skills and negative expectation about social encounters are major contributors to chronic loneliness (Burger 2004). Those who are lonely are prone to approach social situations pessimistically. They expect rejection and anticipate negative appraisal by others. This often results in their tendency to display minimal interest in getting to know others (Sloane and Solano 1984; Burger 2004). This sensitivity to interpersonal criticism and rejection (Frankel and Prentice-Dunn 1990) underlies their problems initiating social activities (Horowitz and deSales French 1979; Burger, 2004). Additionally, problems in interpersonal style make it difficult for the chronically lonely to cultivate friendships. They tend to adopt a passive interpersonal style (Vitkus and Horowitz 1984) and show a lack of understanding of social rules (Sloane and Solano 1984). They have problems with self-disclosure, either revealing too little about themselves (Sloane and Solano 1984) or too much (Solano and Koester 1989). Not surprisingly, chronically lonely are more likely than others to be depressed (Koenig *et al.* 1995; Joiner *et.* 1999) and have other psychological problems (Booth 2000).

The appeal of the Internet to the lonely

The Internet may provide a safe haven where those who are lonely can interact to a vastly expanded social network in an anonymous, non-ftf environment in which they may be less restrained by existing self-defeating behavioural patterns and cognitions. On the Internet, lonely individuals can control their self presentation and interactions in ways which may alleviate some of their negative expectations and skill deficits. Online anonymity can weaken patterns of social inhibition which plague the chronically lonely. 'Self perceptions of social incompetence may lead lonely . . . people to seek out what they perceive to be a safer and less threatening alternative to ftf interaction' (Caplan 2003: 628). Further, the heightened intimacy which characterizes many online interactions (Bargh *et al.* 2002; Walther 1996) can facilitate lonely individuals' opening up to others. This may lead to their being able to interact at a more intimate level with online acquaintances, which in turn may cause them to find greater social support online and alleviate their sense of isolation. Additionally, the lonely can use the Internet to alleviate depression and other negative feelings associated with loneliness (Morahan-Martin 1998; Caplan 2003; Morahan-Martin and Schumacher 2003). Finally, the very attractiveness of the Internet to the lonely can lead them to depend on it increasingly, leading them to develop IA and other problems in their offline lives (Caplan 2003; Morahan-Martin and Schumacher 2003).

How the lonely use the Internet

Research supports that the lonely use the Internet differently than others in ways that help them cope with some of the deficiencies described above. The lonely are more likely than others to use the Internet to increase their social network (McKenna and Bargh 1998; Morahan-Martin and Schumacher 2003), find others similar to themselves, make friends, and find emotional support (Bonebrake 2002; Morahan-Martin and Schumacher 2003). They show a strong preference for online rather than ftf interactions and find online anonymity liberating (Caplan 2003; Morahan-Martin and Schumacher 2003). Overall, the social behaviour of the lonely is enhanced online. They are friendlier online, find it easier than the non-lonely to open up to others online than off, and are more likely to share intimate secrets with others online (Morahan-Martin and Schumacher 2003; Whang *et al.* 2003). Those who are lonely are 'somewhat more likely to feel they can express their real selves with others on the Internet than they can with those they know offline' (McKenna *et al.* 2002: 28), and believe that they are more themselves online than off (Morahan-Martin and Schumacher 2003). The lonely also are more likely than non-lonely to report improvement in friendships on the Internet. They were more likely to say that

> going online had make it easier to make friends, that they had a network of online friends, and even that most of their friends were online friends. These friendships were positive; lonely individuals were more likely than others to report that they had more fun with their online than ftf friends, and that their online friends understand them better.

> (Morahan-Martin and Schumacher 2003: 20)

Consistent with the model presented above, lonely individuals also are more likely than others to use the Internet to deal with negative feelings. Compared with others, they are more likely to go online to feel better when they are down and anxious, to talk with others when they are isolated, to use the Internet to relax and waste time and to feel totally absorbed when online (Caplan 2002; Gross *et al.* 2002; Morahan-Martin and Schumacher 2003).

For lonely people, the quality of the online relationships that they seek when feeling isolated may be weak. A study of early adolescents that measured daily adjustment levels of loneliness and social anxiety and Internet activities found that when lonely, youth were more likely to communicate online with people with whom they did not have a close affiliation. The authors suggest that

> when they feel connected and comfortable with school-based peers, early adolescents use the Internet to seek out additional opportunities to interact with them. In the case of chronic or even temporary feelings of social discomfort or detachment, however, adolescents may use the Internet to avoid being alone, and, in doing so, turn to people disconnected from their daily life.
>
> (Gross *et al.* 2002: 87)

This tendency may play a role in explaining the paradox that even though the lonely report positive social benefits from their online interactions, they also report that they have missed online social engagements because of online activities (Morahan-Martin and Schumacher 2003). Additionally, despite the benefits derived from online interactions, lonely people are more likely to develop problems in their real life because of their use of the Internet (Caplan 2003; Morahan-Martin and Schumacher 2003).

Social anxiety, shyness, and Internet use and abuse

Social anxiety also has been associated with increased risk of developing IA as has shyness (Pratarelli and Browne 2002; Caplan 2004; Chak and Leung 2004). This is not surprising because the socially interactive aspects of the Internet are ideally suited to those who are socially anxious in ways that are analogous to the appeal of the Internet for the lonely. The characteristics of those who are socially anxious and shy help explain the appeal of the Internet to them.

Social anxiety and shyness are highly correlated with each other. Although some psychologists distinguish between the two (Buss 1980), most researchers refer to the two interchangeably (Rapee 1995; Burger 2004). Social anxiety

exists on a continuum from mild to severe. Clinically, many of those with high degree of social anxiety meet the criteria for social phobia and avoidant personality disorder. Shyness is inversely related to sociability (Bruch *et al.* 1989). Those who are socially anxious tend to have poor social skills, decreased networks of social support (American Psychiatric Association 2000), and difficulty forming and maintaining satisfying social relationships (Leary and Kowalski 1995a). In one study, over 2/3s (69 per cent) of people with social phobia believed that their anxiety interfered with social relationships (Turner *et al.* 1986).

An underlying issue for shyness and social anxiety is evaluation apprehension. That is, socially anxious people are afraid of what others will think of them and are especially sensitive to negative evaluation from others (Leary and Kowalsky 1995b). Subjectively, those who are socially anxious approach social situations with a great deal of apprehension about others' impressions and evaluations of them. They

> tend to interpret the reactions of others as less positive ... (and) are more likely than nonsocially anxious persons to feel rejected even in the absence of any objective indication of exclusion. Relative to non shy people, shy individuals report that their friends are less supportive, accepting, understanding, and attentive.
>
> (Leary and Kowalsky 1995a: 173)

They also tend to be self-preoccupied with their perceived social limitations and deficiencies. This in turn negatively impacts their social behaviour. Socially anxious people tend to have trouble expressing themselves, and their behaviour is often socially inhibited, reticent and socially withdrawn. Many avoid social situations (Leary and Kowalsky 1995a). Interpersonally, socially anxious people disaffiliate, that is, they behave in ways that reduce the amount of social contact they have with others. This social withdrawal results in varying degrees of social avoidance. Often, those who are socially anxious become involved in a vicious cycle. 'Because social anxiety entails heightened self-awareness, socially anxious persons become preoccupied with personal deficiencies and more sensitive to the negative reactions of others lead to a further increase in social anxiety' (Leary and Kowalsky 1995a, pg. 138). Subjectively, social anxiety is a very painful, distressing state. It is often comorbid with other disorders including depression, other anxiety disorders, substance abuse and other escapist behaviours (Leary and Kowalsky 1995a; Rapee 1995; American Psychiatric Association 2000).

> The aversiveness of subjective social anxiety, paired with the negative self-thoughts of socially anxious people, may help explain why people who are socially anxious or social phobic are prone to abuse alcohol and engage in other escapist behaviors.
>
> (Leary and Kowalsky 1995a: 138)

Social anxiety, Internet use and IA

Those who are socially anxious are drawn to the socially interactive aspects of the Internet. They use the Internet more and spend more time using chat rooms than extroverts (Anolli et al. 2005). They are more likely than others to form friendships and intimate relationships with those they meet on the Internet (McKenna and Bargh 1999), and these relationships are intense (Anolli et al 2005). Degree of social anxiety is strongly related to a preference for online over ftf social interactions (Caplan 2003; Erwin et al. 2004). In a study of how those who are socially anxious use the Internet, Erwin et al. (2004) found amount of time socially interacting on the Internet was associated with greater 'comfort initiating and maintaining conversations with others on the Internet than ftf and . . . (preference for) discussing their problems with others on the Internet to interacting ftf socially' (2004: 643). They argue that their findings suggest that a subgroup of individuals with social anxiety disorder have found out a 'separate, more tolerable social world on the Internet' (2004: 643), but, at the same time, 'these gains may prove to be elusive, belying greater isolation, anxiety, and impairment associated with non-cyberspace interactions, and greater misinformation and entrenchment of maladaptive beliefs' (2004: 643).

Similarly, Caplan (2003) has found that an important mediator between social anxiety and

negative outcomes from Internet use is a preference for online over ftf social interaction. This preference for online interactions may be due to reductions in anxiety in online social interactions for those who are shy. Yuen and Lavin (2004) compared those with and without IA in their level of reported shyness in online versus ftf situations. Level of shyness did not differ in ftf and online interactions for those without IA. However, those with IA reported they would feel less shy in online interactions than in ftf interactions. They suggest that

> the Internet provides a safe haven where feelings of social discomfort are alleviated. Online use eliminates the negative and undesirable feelings that accompany ftf communication. Internet dependents may feel more confident when interacting online rather than in ftf situations . . . The attenuation of shyness fosters online dependency.
>
> (Yuen and Lavin 2004: 382)

As reported earlier, longitudinal research also has found Internet-related impairment in adjustment for introverts. That is, for introverts, increased levels of Internet use is associated with decreased sense of well-being, including increased levels of loneliness, negative affect, time pressure and decreased self-esteem. However, the results are opposite for extroverts (Kraut et al. 2002).

Loneliness, social anxiety and IA

There is considerable overlap in loneliness and social anxiety in both their characteristics and how those who are lonely and socially anxious use the Internet. In fact, trait loneliness and social anxiety are highly correlated (Lamm and Stephan 1987; Anderson and Harvey 1988), although the two are considered separate personality constructs (Jones et al. 1990). Caplan (2004) maintains that the relationship between loneliness and IA 'is spurious, an artifact of the influence of social anxiety on both problematic Internet use and loneliness' (2004: 11). Using structural equation modelling, he found that when social anxiety was accounted for, loneliness failed to predict negative outcomes from Internet use.

A cognitive–behavioural model of IA

Thus far, the evidence presented supports that some personality types may be vulnerable to develop IA and other Internet-related problems. From a person by situation approach, research supports that some vulnerable individuals such as those who are lonely or socially anxious find the socially interactive aspects of the Internet so compelling that they begin to use the Internet to the detriment of their everyday life. Still missing is a comprehensive theory which explains the etiology of IA.

In a series of research studies, Caplan has developed a cognitive–behavioural model of IA which advances understanding of the etiology of IA (Caplan 2002, 2003, 2004, 2005). Caplan's model is an extension and refinement of Davis' cognitive–behavioural model of IA (2001) which argues that existing psychosocial problems such as loneliness predispose some Internet users to exhibit maladaptive cognitions and behaviours that result in IA. Caplan maintains that 'a social-skill deficit, along with exposure to the Internet, predisposes an individual to develop a preference for online, rather than ftf, social interaction, which then leads to compulsive Internet use that results in negative outcomes' (2005: 725).

The social skill deficit identified in this theory is a deficit in self-presentational skills, which is the ability to make strategic self-presentation of themselves on others to make positive impressions. Those with well developed self-presentational skills 'are generally adept, tactful, and self confident in social situations and can fit in comfortably in just about any type of social situation' (Riggio 1989: 3). However, those with deficits in self-presentation skills lack confidence in their ability to make effective self-presentations: this includes many who are socially anxious and lonely. People who perceive themselves to have weak self-presentational skills are 'likely to seek out communicative channels that minimize potential costs and enhance their limited abilities' (Caplan 2005). In situations where their self-presentation is threatened, people tend to prefer computer mediated communication (CMC) over ftf communication (O'Sullivan 2002). Online social interactions are well matched for those who have weak self-presentation skills. O'Sullivan argues that CMC is helpful 'for managing self-relevant information in pursuit of self-presentational goals' (2002: 404).

As discussed earlier, many factors related to online social interactions combine to facilitate more effective self-presentation online than ftf. Online communication allows for greater control over self-presentation. Online anonymity can lead to weakened inhibitions and decreased risk in social interactions. Individuals are freed of existing social roles, and can experiment with different ways of interacting. Success and acceptance in online interactions can foster an increased sense of control and self-efficacy in online social interactions. This also reinforces a preference for online over ftf interaction, which is a key cognitive component of IA. Caplan (2003) defines preference for online over ftf social interaction as a 'cognitive individual-difference construct characterized by beliefs that one is safer, more efficacious, more confident and more comfortable with online interpersonal interactions and relationships than with traditional ftf social activities' (2003: 629).

Once individuals develop a preference for online over ftf interactions, they spend increasingly more time and become more emotionally connected with online interactions which weakens ftf interactions. For some, this leads to compulsive Internet use which in turn leads to negative outcomes (Caplan 2005).

This model is pertinent in explaining the relationship between IA and loneliness and social anxiety. Both are characterized by low levels of self-presentation skills and high levels of fear of negative evaluation (Leary and Kowalsky 1995 a, b; Burger 2004) which may make them vulnerable to developing a preference for online over ftf interactions. This preference in turn would lead to compulsive use and negative outcomes including IA.

Conclusions

A small percentage of Internet users become dependent upon the Internet to such an extent that their Internet use is causing serious problems in their lives have been called Internet abusers. Research has found that IA is associated with a number of other disorders. Critics have questioned the concept of IA and maintained that IA may instead be a manifestation of other disorder. Two subgroups of dependent users are identified: the first consists of those who develop problems from their use of specific Internet applications such as online gambling or online sexual activities. In these cases, the Internet has become a new vehicle for other, established pathologies. The second group consists of those who develop problems from a more generalized use of the Internet, a group Davis (2001) describes as suffering from generalized IA. There is strong evidence that the socially interactive aspects of the Internet have strong appeal for those who develop IA and that the development of generalized IA is a result of the unique communication context of the Internet. People with IA are drawn to the experience of being online, and prefer virtual rather than ftf interpersonal communication. Those who are lonely and socially anxious or shy are at higher risk of developing IA. Although it has been suggested that excessive Internet use causes loneliness, research indicates that those who are chronically lonely as well as those who are socially anxious or shy are more likely than others to find socially interactive activities on the Internet so compelling that they increasingly become more emotionally invested online and spend increasing amount of time online which eventually can lead to the development of IA. Caplan's Cognitive–Behavioural Model of Problematic Internet Use provides a framework to understand IA and why those who are lonely and socially anxious may be at higher risk of developing IA. This approach proposes that those with a social skill deficit in self-presentation skills when exposed to the Internet are at risk of developing a preference for online, rather than ftf social interaction, and this can lead to compulsive Internet use and IA (Caplan 2004).

Internet abuse is a fertile area for future research. The Internet is in constant flux. How one can access the Internet, the types of activities available and the population who are online has changed dramatically in the decade since the first studies on IA were published. Future research will need to address these changes. One high priority for future research is to distinguish the specific activities that are associated with disturbed behaviour. Most research on IA has consisted of surveys which have been given to convenience samples; longitudinal studies as well as more experimental studies with more representative samples would provide valuable data.

References

American Psychiatric Association (2000). *Diagnostic and statistical manual*, 4th edn, text revision. Washington, DC: American Psychiatric Association.

Anderson, C. A. and Harvey, R. J. (1988). Discriminating between problems in living: an examination of measures of depression, loneliness, shyness and social anxiety. *Journal of Social and Clinical Psychology 6*, 482–491.

Anderson, K. (1999). Internet dependency among college students: should we be concerned? Paper presented at the 107th annual convention of the American Psychological Association, Boston, MA. Retrieved 21 February 2000 from http://www.rpi.edu/~anderk4/research.html.

Anolli L., Villani, D. and Riva, G. (2005). Personality of people using chat: an on-line research. *CyberPsychology and Behavior 8*, 89–95.

Archibald, F. S., Bartholomew, K. and Marx, R. (1995). Loneliness in early adolescence: a test of the cognitive discrepancy model of loneliness. *Personality and Social Psychology Bulletin 21*, 296–301.

Bai, Y. M., Lin, C. C. and Chen, J. Y. (2001). Internet addiction disorder among clients of a virtual clinic. *Psychiatric Service 52*(10), 1397.

Bargh, J. A., McKenna, K. Y.A. and Fitzsimons, G. M. (2002). Can you see the real me? Activation and expression of the 'True Self' on the Internet. *Journal of Social Issues 58*(1), 33–48.

Wired News (2004) Beijing clinic treats Web addicts. July, retrieved 1 February 2006 from http://www.wired.co/news/culture/1,68081–0.html.

Becona, E., Del Carmen, L. M., Fuentes, M. J. (1996). Pathological gambling and depression. *Psychological Reports 78(2)*, 635–640.

Beyond shyness and stage fright. (2003). *Harvard Mental Health Letter*, 1–3.

Boies, A., Cooper, A. and Osborne, C. S. (2004). Variations in Internet-related problems and psychosocial functioning in online sexual activities: implications for social and sexual development of young adults. *CyberPsychology and Behavior 7*, 207–230.

Bonebrake, K. (2002). College students' Internet use, relationship formation, and personality correlates. *CyberPsychology and Behavior 5*(6), 551–557.

Booth, R. (2000). Loneliness as a component of psychiatric disorders. *Medscape Mental Health 5*(2). Retrieved 14 November 2000 from http://www.medscape.com/medscape/psychiatry/journal/2000/v05.n02/mh3272.boot/mh3272.boot-01/html.

Brashers, D. E. (2001). Communication and uncertainty management. Journal of Communication, 51, 477- 497.

Bruch, M. A., Gorsky, J. M., Collins, T. M. and Burger, P. A. (1989). Shyness and sociability reexamined: a multi-component analysis. *Journal of Personality ad Social Psychology 57*, 904–915.

Bruch, M. A., Kalfowitz, N. G. and Pearl, L. (1988). Mediated and unmediated relationships of personality components to loneliness. *Journal of Social and Clinical Psychology 6,* 346–355.

Burger, J. M. (2004). *Personality,* 6th edn. Belmont, CA: Wadsworth.

Buss, A. H. (1980). *Self-consciousness and social anxiety.* San Francisco, CA: W. H. Freeman.

Caplan, S. E. (2002). Problematic Internet use and psychosocial well-being: Development of a theory-based cognitive-behavioral measurement instrument. *Computers in Human Behavior 18*(5), 553–575.

Caplan, S. E. (2003). Preference of online social interaction: a theory of problematic Internet use and psychosocial well-being. *Communication Research 30*(6), 625–648.

Caplan, S. E. (2004). Refining the cognitive behavioral model of problematic Internet use: a closer look at social skill and compulsive behavior. A paper presented at the annual conference of the National Communication Association, Chicago.

Caplan, S. E. (2005). A social skill account of problematic Internet use. *Journal of Communication 55,* 721–736.

Chak, K. and Leung, L. (2004). Shyness and locus of control as predictors of Internet addiction and Internet use. *CyberPsychology and Behavior 7*(5), 559–570.

Chen, K., Chen, I. and Paul, H. (2001). Explaining online behavioral differences: an Internet dependency perspective. *Journal of Computer Information Systems 41*(3), 59–63.

Civin, M. A. (2000). Male, female, e-mail: The struggle for relatedness in a paranoid society. New York: Other Press.

Cooper, A., Delmonico, D. and Burg, R. (2000). Cybersex users, abusers, and compulsives: new findings and implications. In A. Cooper (ed.), *Cybersex: The dark side of the force* (pp. 5–29). Philadelphia, PA: Brunner Routledge.

Cooper, A., Griffin-Shelley, E., Delmonico, D. and Mathy, R. (2001). Online sexual problems: assessment and predictive variables. *Sexual Addiction and Compulsivity 8,* 267–285.

Cooper, A., Morahan-Martin, J., Mathy, R. and Maheu, M. (2002). Toward an increased understanding of user demographics in online sexual activities. *Journal of Sex and Marital Therapy 28,* 105–129.

Cooper, A., Putman, D., Planchon, L. and Boies, S. (1999). Online sexual compulsivity: getting tangled in the net. *Sexual Addiction and Compulsivity 7,* 5–30.

Cutrona, C. E. (1982). Transition to college: loneliness and the process of social adjustment. In L. A. Peplau and D. Perlman (eds), *Loneliness* (pp. 291–309). New York: Wiley.

Davis, S. (2001). A cognitive-behavioral model of pathological Internet use. *Computers in Human Behavior 17,* 187–195.

Erwin, B. A., Turk, C. L., Heimberg, R. F., Fresco, D. M. and Hantula, D. A. (2004). The Internet: home to a severe population of individuals with social anxiety disorder? *Journal of Anxiety Disorders 18*(5), 629–646.

Forsyth, D. and Elliot, T. (1999). Group dynamics and psychological well being: the impact of groups on adjustment and dysfunction. In R. Kowalski and M. Leary (eds.), *The social psychology of emotional and behavioral problems: interfaces of social and clinical psychology* (pp. 339–361). Washington DC: American Psychological Association.

Frankel, A. and Prentice-Dunn, S. (1990). Loneliness and the processing of self-relevant information. *Journal of Social and clinical Evidence 9,* 303–313.

Greenfield, D. (1999). Psychological characteristics of compulsive Internet use: a preliminary analysis. *Cyber Psychology and Behavior 2,* 403–412.

Griffiths, M. D. (1998). Internet addiction: does it really exist? In J. Gachenbach (ed.), *Psychology and the Internet* (pp. 61–75). San Diego, CA: Academic Press.

Griffiths, M. D. (2001, October). Internet gambling: preliminary results of the first UK prevalence study. *E-Gambling: The Electronic Journal of Gambling Issues* (Issue 5). Retrieved 23 February 2005 from http://www.camh.net/egambling/issue5/research/griffiths_article.html.

Griffiths, M. and Parke, J. (2002). The social impact of Internet gambling. *Social Science Computer Review 20,* 312–320.

Grohol, J. (1999). Too much time online: internet addiction or healthy social interactions. *Cyber Psychology and Behavior, 2,* 395–402.

Gross, E., Juvonen, J. and Gable, S. L. (2002). Internet use and well-being in adolescence. *Journal of Social Issues 58*(1), 75–90.

Holmes, L. (1997). Pathological internet use – some examples. *About: Health Resources* Retrieved 22 March 2005 from http://mentalhealth.about.com/cs/sexaddict/a/intaddict_2.htm.

Horowitz, L. M. and deSales French, R. (1979). Interpersonal problems of people who describe themselves as lonely. *Journal of Consulting and Clinical Psychology 47,* 762–764.

Houston, T. K., Cooper, L. A. and Ford, D. E. (2002). Internet support groups for depression: a 1-year prospective cohort study. *American Journal of Psychiatry 159,* 2062–2068.

Howard, P. R., Rainie, L. and Jones, S. (2001). Days and nights on the Internet: the impact of a diffusing technology. *The American Behavioral Scientist 45,* 383–404.

Huang, M. P. and Alessi, N. E. (1997). Internet addiction, Internet psychotherapy. *American Journal of Psychiatry 153,* 890.

Jacobs, D. (1986). A general theory of addictions. *Journal of Gambling Behavior 2,* 15–31.

Jaffe, J. (1990). Trivializing dependence. *British Journal of Addiction 85,* 1425–1427.

Johansson, A. and Götestam, K. G. (2004). Internet addiction: characteristics of a questionnaire and prevalence in Norwegian youth (12–18 years). *Scandinavian Journal of Psychology 45,* 223–229.

Joiner, T. E., Catanzano, S. J., Rudd, M. D. and Rejab, M. H. (1999). The case for a hierarchical, oblique, and bidimensional structure of loneliness. *Journal of Social and Clinical Psychology 18,* 47–75.

Joinson, A. N. (1998). Causes and implications of disinhibited behavior on the Internet. In J. Gackenbach (ed.), *Psychology and the Internet* (pp. 43–60). San Diego, CA: Academic Press.

Jones, W. H. (1981). Loneliness and social contact. *Journal of Social Psychology 113,* 295–296.

Jones, W. H., Rose, J. A. and Russell, D. (1990). Loneliness and social anxiety. In H. Leitenberg (ed.), *Handbook of social and evaluation anxiety* (pp. 247–266). Plenum, New York.

Kaltiala-Heino, R., Lintonen, T. and Rimpelä, A. (2004). Internet addiction? Potentially problematic use of the internet in a population of 12–18 year old adolescents. *Addiction Research and Theory* 12(1), 89–96.

King, S. and Barak, A. (1999). Compulsive Internet gambling: a new form of an old pathology. *Cyber Psychology and Behavior 2*, 441–456.

Kaltiala-Heino, R., Lintonen, T. and Rimpelä, A. (2004). Internet Addiction? Potentially problematic use of the Internet in a population of 12–18 year old adolescents. *Addiction Research and Theory 12*, 89–96.

Koenig, L. J., Isaacs, A. M. and Schwartz, J. A.J. (1995). Sex differences in adolescent depression and loneliness: why boys are lonelier if boys are more depressed. *Journal of Research in Personality 28*, 27–43.

Kraut, R., Kiesler, S., Boneva, B., Cummings, J., Helgeson, V. and Crawford, A. (2002). Internet paradox revisited. *Journal of Social Issues 58*, 49–74.

Kraut, R., Patterson, M., Landmark, V., Kiesler, S., Mukophadhyay, T. and Scherlis, W. (1998). Internet paradox: a social technology that reduces social involvement and psychological well being? *American Psychologist 53*, 1017–1031.

Kraut, R., Scherlis, W., Mukhopadhyay, T., Manning, and Kiesler, S. (1996). The HomeNet field trial of residential Internet services. *Communications of the ACM 39*, 55–63.

Kubey, R. and Csikszentmihalyi, M. (2002). Television addiction is no mere metaphor. *Scientific American 286*(2), 79–86.

Kubey, R. W., Lavin, M. J. and Barrows, J. R. (2001). Internet use and collegiate academic performance decrements: early findings. *Journal of Communication 51*, 366–382.

Ladd, G. T. and Petry, N. M. (2002). Disordered gambling among university-based medical and dental patients: a focus on Internet gambling. *Psychology of Addictive Behaviors 16*(1), 76–79.

Lamm, H. and Stephan, E. (1987). Loneliness among German university students: some correlates. *Social Behavior and Personality 15*, 161–164.

Leary, M. R. and Kowalsky, R. M. (1995a). *Social anxiety*. New York: Guilford.

Leary, M. R. and Kowalsky, R. M. (1995b). The self-presentation model of social phobia. In R. G. Heimberg, M. R. Liebowitz, D. A. Hope and F. A. Schneier (eds), *Social phobia: Diagnosis, assessment, and treatment* (pp. 94–112). New York: Guilford.

Leung, L. (2004). Net-Generation Attributes and seductive properties of the Internet as predictors of online activities and Internet addiction. *CyberPsychology and Behavior 7*(3), 333–348.

Lin, S. S.J. and Tsai, C. C. (2002). Sensation seeking and internet dependence of Taiwanese high school adolescents. *Computers in Human Behavior 18*, 411–426.

McKenna, K. Y. and Bargh, J. A. (1998). Coming out in the age of the Internet: identity 'demarginalization' through virtual group participation. *Journal of Personality and Social Psychology 75*, 681–694.

McKenna, K. Y. and Bargh, J. A. (1999). Causes and consequences of social interactions on the Internet: a conceptual framework *Media Psychology 1*, 249–269.

McKenna, K. Y., Green, A. S. and Gleason, M. E.J. (2002). Relationship formation on the Internet: what's the big attraction? *Journal of Social Issues 58*(1), 9–31.

Milkman, H. and Sunderwirth, S. (1982). Addictive processes. *Journal of Psychoactive Drugs 14*, 177–192.

Mitchell, P. (2000). Internet addiction: genuine diagnosis or not? *Lancet 355*(9204), 632.

Morahan-Martin, J. (1999). The relationship between loneliness and Internet use and abuse. *CyberPsychology and Behavior 2*, 431–440.

Morahan-Martin, J. (2001). Impact of Internet abuse for college students. In C. Wolfe, ed. *Learning and teaching on the World Wide Web* (pp. 191–219). San Diego, CA: Academic Press.

Morahan-Martin, J. (2005). Internet abuse: Addiction? Disorder? Symptom? Alternative Explanations? *Social Science Computer Review 23*(1), 39–48.

Morahan-Martin, J. and Schumacher, P. (2000). Incidence and correlates of pathological Internet use among college students. *Computers in Human Behavior 16*, 13–29.

Morahan-Martin, J. and Schumacher, P. (2003). Loneliness and social uses of the Internet. *Computers and Human Behavior 19*(6), 659–671.

Moore, D. (1995). *The emperor's virtual clothes: The naked truth about Internet culture.* Chapel Hill, NC: Alogonquin.

Nalwa, K. and Anand, A. P. (2003). Internet addiction in students: A cause of concern. *CyberPsychology and Behavior 6*(6), 653–656.

Nichols, L.A. and Nicki, R. (2004). Development of a psychometrically sound Internet addiction scale: a preliminary step. *Psychology of Addictive Behaviors 18*, 381–384.

Nie, N. H. (2001). Sociability, interpersonal relations, and the Internet: reconciling conflicting findings. *American Behavioral Scientist 45*(3), 426–437.

Nie, H. and Ebring, L. (2002). Internet use, interpersonal relations, and sociability: a time diary study. In B. Wellman and C. Haythornwaite (eds), *Internet and everyday life* (pp. 215–243). London: Blackwell.

Orzack, M. (1999). Computer addiction: IS it real or virtual? *Harvard Mental Health Letter 15*(7), 8.

O'Sullivan, P. (2002). What you don't know won't hurt me: impression management functions of communication channels in relationships. *Human Communication Research 26*, 403–431.

Pratarelli, M. E. (2005). Sex, shyness, and social Internet use. Paper presented at the 113th Annual Convention of the American Psychological Association, Washington, DC.

Pratarelli, M. E. and Browne, B. L. (2002). Confirmatory factor analysis of Internet use and addiction. *CyberPsychology and Behavior 5*(1), 53–64.

Prisbell, M. (1988). Dating competence as related to levels of loneliness. *Communication Report 1*, 54–59.

Rainie, L. and Horrigan, J. (2005). *Internet evolution. A decade of adoption: how the Internet has woven itself into American life.* Washington, DC: Pew Internet and American Life Project. Retrieved 22 February 2005 from http://www.pewinternet.org/PPF/r/148/report_display.asp.

Rapee, R. M. (1995). Descriptive psychopathology of social phobia. In R. G. Heimberg, M. R. Liebowitz, D. A. Hope and F. A. Schneier (eds), *Social phobia: Diagnosis, assessment, and treatment* (pp. 41–66). New York: Guilford.

Rheingold, H. (1993). *The virtual community: Homesteading on the electronic frontier.* Reading, MA: Addison-Wesley.

Riggio, R. (1989). *The social skills inventory manual: Research edition.* Palo Alto, CA: Consulting Psychologists Press.

Russell, D., Peplau, L. A. and Cutrona, C. E. (1980). The Revised UCLA Loneliness Scale: Concurrent and discriminant validity. *Journal of Personality and Social Psychology 39,* 472–480.

Scherer, K. (1997). College life online: healthy and unhealthy Internet use. *Journal of College Student Development 38,* 655–665.

Schwartz, M. F. and Southern, S. (2000). Compulsive cybersex: the new tea room. In A Cooper, ed. *Cybersex: The dark side of the force* (pp. 127–144). Philadelphia, PA: Brunner Routledge.

Shaffer, H. J., Hall, M. N. and Vander Bilt, J. (2000). 'Computer addiction': a critical consideration. *American Journal of Orthopsychiatry 70*(2), 162–168.

Shapira, N. A., Goldsmith, T. D., Keck, P., Khosla, U. and McElroy, S. (2000). Psychiatric features of individuals with problematic Internet use. *Journal of Affective Disorders 66,* 283.

Shapira, N., Lessig, M., Goldsmith, T., Szabo, S., Lazoritz, M., Gold, M. and Stein, D. (2003). Problematic Internet use: proposed classification and diagnostic criteria. *Depression and Anxiety 17,* 207–216.

Simkova, B. and Cincera, J. C. (2004). Internet addiction disorder and chatting in the Czech Republic. *CyberPsychology and Behavior 7,* 536–539.

Sloane, W. W. and Solano, C. H. (1984). The conversational style of lonely males with strangers and roommates. *Personality and Social Psychology Bulletin 10,* 293–301.

Solano, C. H. and Koester, N. H. (1989). Loneliness and communication problems: subjective anxiety or objective skills? *Personality and Social Psychology Bulletin 15,* 126–133.

South Korea plans more centres to treat Internet addiction (2005, September). Retrieved from Lexis/Nexis database.

Treuer, T., Fabian, Z. and Furedi, J. (2001). Internet addiction associated with features of impulse control disorder: Is it a real psychiatric disorder? *Journal of Affective Disorders 66,* 283.

Tsai, C. C. and Lin, S. S. (2001). Analysis of attitudes toward computer networks and Internet addiction of Taiwanese adolescents. *CyberPsychology and Behavior 4*(3), 373–376.

Turkle, S. (1995). *Life on the screen: Identity in the age of the Internet.* New York: Simon and Schuster.

Turner, S. M., Beidel, D. C., Dancu, C. V. and Keyes, D. J. (1986). Psychopathology of social phobia and comparison to avoidant personality disorder. *Journal of Abnormal Psychology 95,* 389–395.

Vitkus, J. and Horowitz, L. M. (1984). Poor social performance of lonely people: lacking a skill or adopting a role? *Journal of Personality and Social Psychology 52,* 1266–1273.

Wallis, D. (1997). Just click no. *The New Yorker 72*(42), 28.

Walther, J. B. (1996). Computer-mediated communication: IMPERSONAL, interpersonal, and hyper personal interaction. *Communication Research 23,* 3–43.

Walther, J. B. and Reid, L. D. (2000). Understanding the allure of the Internet. *Chronicle of Higher Education* 4 February, B4–B5.

Weeks, D. G., Michela, J. L., Peplau, L. A. and Braggs, M. E. (1980). Relation between loneliness and depression: a structural equation model. *Journal of Personality and Social Psychology 39,* 1238–1244.

Weiser, E. B. (2001). The functions of Internet use and their social and psychological consequences. *CyberPsychology and Behavior 4*(6), 723–743.

Whang, L. S., Lee, S. and Chang, G. (2003). Internet over-users' psychological profiles: a behavior sampling analysis on Internet addiction. *CyberPsychology and Behavior 6*(2), 143–150.

Young, K. S. (1996). Pathological Internet use: a case that breaks the stereotype. *Psychological Reports 79,* 899–902.

Young, K. S. (1998). Internet addiction: the emergence of a new clinical disorder. *CyberPsychology and Behavior 1,* 237–244.

Young, K. S. and Rodgers, R. (1998). The relationship between depression and Internet addiction. *Cyber Psychology and Behavior 1,* 25–28.

Yuen, C. N. and Lavin, M. J. (2004). Internet dependence in the collegiate population: the role of shyness. *CyberPsychology and Behavior 7*(4), 379–383.

CHAPTER 22

Examining the role of the Internet in health behaviour

Elizabeth Sillence and Pam Briggs

Introduction

Accessing information about health can now be achieved via the telephone, the Internet or even the television (BBC Online 2004). There are over 70,000 health related websites (Pagliari and Gregor 2004) making the Internet a major source of health information. Worldwide about 4.5 per cent of all Internet searches are for health related information (Morahan-Martin 2004) and it has been estimated that over 68 million people have been influenced by the information provided therein (Pew 2003). The range of topics is increasing and so is availability of sites. Given the range of health advice and information available, patients are faced with decisions about which information and website providers to trust. How do people make decisions about trust in this context and how is this affecting their health behaviour? This chapter aims to explore the role of the Internet in health behaviour placing particular emphasis on the issue of trust and trusting behaviours, as this is seen as key to determining the impact of the Internet on health outcomes. The rest of this chapter is organized as follows: In the next section we discuss the role of the Internet in the context of health information and advice, exploring the broader

issues such as user motivation and outcomes in terms of perceived health benefits as well as interactions with healthcare professionals. We then go on to examine the types of health website available and explore issues of advice and information quality and in the following section examine the context of trust in relation to online health advice and information and present a staged model of trust which helps reconcile differences in the literature. The last section presents a validation of the staged model through in-depth, longitudinal qualitative work. The conclusion draws together the literature and the results of the qualitative work to present some conclusions and considerations for future research.

Why go online for health advice?

Eighty per cent of adult Internet users have gone online in search of health information. In a very recent study of over 1900 Internet users Sillence *et al.* (2006) found that over 1400 had used the Internet for health advice and 76 per cent of these respondents were women. People search online for health information and advice for a number of reasons. Some people want to be better informed, better prepared when meeting the doctor, or are searching for support, alternative answers or reassurance (Rozmovitis and Ziebland 2004). Nearly half of Europeans say they would like to discuss information found on the Internet with their doctor and one in five European consumers has asked their doctor about a symptom or diagnosis after having read information online (WHA 2002). Many people searching online for health advice believe that it will enable them to better deal with their health and will convey health benefits (Mead *et al.* 2003; Sillence *et al.* 2006).

Time constraints in the consulting room have also led to an increase in online searching. The average length of an appointment with a family practitioner is currently about eight minutes, and in this short period of time both the doctor and the patient find it difficult to explain and discuss all their issues. Patients often think doctors do not give them enough information to make sensible choices about how they want to be treated (Carvel 2005) and they often find it difficult to recall the specifics of their discussions with the doctor after the consultation (Kalet *et al.* 1994). Young people in particular are turning to the Internet rather than to a family doctor or a parent to get health information and advice, and the appeal of the Internet is particularly strong for those people who wish advice on important but sensitive matters (Klein and Wilson 2003).

The use of the Internet for health information is not limited to accessing information per se. People are using the Internet in a number of different ways to meet their health needs and the needs of family and friends (Sillence *et al.* 2006). These include self-diagnosis, booking a doctor's appointment or seeking social and emotional support (Nicholas *et al.* 2003). A number of electronic support groups exist online (Joinson 2003) and interact through email or web message boards and may even include face-to-face meetings (Sillence 2005). There are online social support groups for a range of health conditions including sports injuries (Preece 1999), irritable bowel syndrome and breast cancer (Coulson 2005a, b) and groups specifically designed to provide support for friends, family and other caregivers (White and Dorman 2000).

The Internet allows people to communicate and interact with a far greater variety of people across all walks of life. It provides up to date information as well as increased social support (see Eysenbach *et al.* 2004 for a review). Online social support can reduce feelings of isolation and can provide information and emotional support (Preece 1999). The Internet allows information to be shared in the form of text and images and can put people in touch with the most up to date information from some of most eminent sources in the medical profession. It can offer people second and even third opinions and in short can provide information and advice that simply cannot be found anywhere else.

But does the Internet leave patients better informed and does reading online information and following advice lead to better health outcomes? Some studies have indicated that information gained from an online search helps the majority of users to understand more about an illness or injury and in some of these cases the information is sufficient for patients to act upon to improve their health (Nicholas *et al.* 2003). A review of the literature concerning online cancer support suggested that participation in such groups helped people cope more effectively with the disease (Klemm *et al.* 2003). However, other studies have indicated that whilst the Internet can increase patients' knowledge about their health conditions, they can be left feeling too overwhelmed by the information available online to be able to make an informed decision about their own health care (Hart *et al.* 2004). Reviews of quantitative web-based intervention studies have generally indicated beneficial effects of the Internet on health outcomes although issues concerning the methodological quality of such studies remain (Bessell *et al.* 2002). A more recent meta-analysis by Wantland *et al.* (2004) concluded that in the majority of studies, knowledge and or behavioural outcomes improved for participants using web-based health interventions.

One potential outcome of using the Internet for health advice is the resulting impact upon the doctor-patient interaction. Relatively few studies have assessed the Internet's value for improving patients' relationships with health care practitioners. Gerber and Eiser (2001) propose a number of possible scenarios for how the patient-physician relationship might develop in the Internet age. First physicians could direct their patients to certain websites containing information that reinforced their preferred course of action. This scenario however is very physician-controlled. Other scenarios may be more patient-led: for example, a patient may be motivated to become involved in the decision-making process and as such use the Internet prior to any consultation with the physician. This would enable the patient to take a fully active role in the decision making process. Doctors in this scenario must be prepared to discuss alternatives ideas that the patient may have come across and to help 'process' rather than simply 'provide' information (Hart *et al.* 2004). Other patients may want to be better informed about their illness but are happy to leave any decisions up to their doctors. The Internet, however, may still have a role to play in this kind of scenario. Patients may benefit from following up the consultation with an Internet search, leaving them reassured and feeling more comfortable with the physician's decision.

What do physicians think of these scenarios? Time appears to be the most important issue. Bastian (2003) argues that the knowledgeable patient is taking up more than their fair share of the physician's time and adding to health inequalities by leaving needier patients waiting. Potts and Wyatt (2002) asked doctors about their patients' use of the Internet. The doctors reported that the overall experience for their patients was neutral with 43 per cent reporting benefits and 23 per cent reporting problems. Benefits included patients being better informed about their condition and getting helpful advice from patient support groups. Problems centred around patients being misinformed about their condition. Doctors noted problems associated with too much good information rather than problems of poor quality information. Consultations which involved viewing material from the Internet were often very useful but also very time-consuming.

Assessing the quality of online health information and advice

If online information and advice is going to affect health behaviour then a key issue is the extent to which users recognize quality advice and information. Whether this information comes from a recognized medical source or from an online support group, its perceived usefulness and credibility is important in determining whether or not people will trust the information and act upon it. Assessing the quality of information online is a daunting task, not least because the range of health topics and the number of different websites is so enormous. Health information online covers topics as diverse as cancer, thyroid problems, sexual health and restless leg syndrome with the most popular search topics being cancer, alternative health and diet/slimming (Sillence and Briggs, 2007).

To indicate the range of different sites available, Table 22.1 provides an overview of three

Table 22.1 Health websites and range of features/services

	Netdoctor www.netdoctor.co.uk	Dipex www.dipex.org	NHS direct www.nhsdirect.nhs.uk
Domain	General health	General health	General health
Owner	Web provider	Charity	Government
Type of advice	Patient fact sheets 'Ask the doctor' service News Discussion boards	Personal accounts Medical information Frequently asked questions	Health encyclopaedia Self-help guide Clinical evidence-based research reports
Commercial aspects	Health-related advertising	Donations requested	None
Notable features	SMS alert service e.g. contraceptive pill reminder Discussion boards	Video clips Links to support groups	Locate nearest NHS services facility

different UK-based sites, highlighting their main features and the range of services available on each site.

It is not only the health topics that vary widely but also the nature of the websites themselves. There are variations in authorship, scope and features. Health information and advice online covers discussion groups, chat rooms as well as static pages and is written and produced by leading researchers through to enthusiastic patients. Given this huge variation, how does one begin to assess quality? Most expert discussions of quality have taken a purely medical perspective. There have been numerous detailed assessments of the quality of health information on the Web embracing diverse topics such as Viagra, rheumatoid arthritis and diabetes. A systematic review of these evaluations found that the most frequently used quality criteria were accuracy, completeness, readability and design. Of the 79 studies reviewed, 70 per cent concluded that quality is a problem on the Internet (Eysenbach et al. 2002).

Given the inherent difficulties associated with controlling the content on the Internet, many see that it is imperative that consumers know how to search for trustworthy information and avoid untrustworthy information (Peterson et al. 2003). Seals of approval or trustmarks have been suggested as a strategy to help consumers in identifying high quality information. Most seals act as proxy indicators of quality by requiring websites to, for example, disclose any commercial interests they might have. The codes, however, do not offer any direct assessment of content. Unfortunately the presence of such codes and awards appears to have no significant effect on the credibility or retention of health information on a web page (Shon et al. 2000). Furthermore, consumer expectations of such health seals are often incongruent with practice (Burkell 2004).

Other researchers have been interested in empowering health consumers to judge the quality of the information they find on the Internet for themselves. The Judge project (Childs 2005) provides guidelines for support groups on how to produce good quality information and guidelines for consumers on how to judge the quality of a website. These guidelines are particularly helpful for consumers because they recognize the importance of alternative sources of advice,

for example, support groups, which may differ from traditional medical opinion and advice.

So how are genuine consumers searching for and evaluating the trustworthiness and quality of health websites? The large body of research on online health advice belies the fact that very little is known about how health consumers seek advice. As we have already indicated, almost all of the existing studies have evaluated the quality of information and advice available on the Internet from a medical perspective (Smart and Burling 2001). This is a problem, because we know that ordinary consumers search for and appraise information in a different way to experts. They are more likely to be influenced by the attractiveness of the design (Stanford et al. 2002) and they will begin their search for advice from a general information portal (Briggs et al. 2002) which means that they gain access to information indiscriminately. Eysenbach and Köhler (2002) noted that consumers (as opposed to experts) failed to check the authorship or owners of the website or read disclosure statements, despite suggesting these as important quality markers beforehand. However their study made use of an experimental search task and the authors suggested that people in a 'real setting' with a greater stake in the outcome may well pay more attention to the content of the websites, in terms of markers of quality. There is thus a real need for systematic explorations of the ways in which people evaluate the trustworthiness of health information and advice online in order to better understand how it influences their health behaviour.

Trust and mistrust of health advice online

Surveys of Internet users suggest that trust is an important issue in the health domain (Williams et al. 2003), yet attempts to unpack the concept of trust with respect to online information and advice reveal a multifaceted, complex concept. The literature regarding trust in an e-commerce setting provides a useful starting point for exploring the ways in which people evaluate the trustworthiness of health information and advice online (see Grabner-Krauter and Kaluscha 2003 for a recent review.) Based on this literature we can assume that various factors are likely to govern the extent to which individuals feel they can trust health advice online. First, they may be influenced by the look and feel of the site – trusting, for example, those sites rated high in visual appeal and mistrusting those sites with poor visual design or with unprofessional errors. Secondly, they may be influenced by the branding of the site or by the presence of familiar images or trusted logos. Thirdly, they may be influenced by the quality of information available on the site, trusting those sites with greater perceived expertise, and fourthly, they may be influenced by the extent to which the advice is personalised to the individual – i.e. the extent to which the advice appears to come from and be directed to similar individuals (i.e. those with a shared social identity).

While these different factors appear to be important, researchers disagree over their relative importance in fostering trust. For example, some researchers argue that consumer trust (or a related construct, credibility) is primarily driven by an attractive and professional design (Fogg et al. 2002; Stanford et al. 2002,) or is influenced by the presence or absence of visual anchors or prominent features such as a photograph or trust seal (Riegelsberger et al. 2003). Others argue that trust reflects the perceived competence, integrity predictability and/or benevolence of the site (McKnight and Chervany 2001; Bhattacherjee 2002). A few authors also highlight the importance of personalization in the formation of trust judgements (Briggs et al. 2004) or the notion of good relationship management (Egger 2000).

One way of reconciling these different findings is to consider a developmental model of trust or the way in which trust develops over time. For example it is worth distinguishing between the kinds of trust that support transient interactions and those that support longer-term relationships (Meyerson et al. 1996). A number of authors (Egger 2000, 2001; Sillence et al. 2004a) have suggested that three phases are important: a phase of initial trust followed by a more involved exchange which then may or may not lead to a longer-term trusting relationship. If one considers trust in this developmental context then some of the findings in the literature make more sense. In particular, consideration of a developmental context helps to reconcile the tension between those models of trust which suggest that it is a concept grounded in careful judgement of institution and process factors such as vendor expertise and experience, process predictability, degree of personalization and communication integrity and those models that suggest trust decisions depend much more heavily on the attractiveness and professional feel of a site.

Drawing on the social psychology literature, a staged model of trust (see Figure 22.1) makes it possible to distinguish between relatively 'hasty' and more 'considered' processing strategies for the evaluation of trust in high and low risk environments. Chaiken (1980) identified two processing strategies by which an evaluation of trustworthiness may be made: first a heuristic strategy which follows a 'cognitive miser' principle – where people base decisions on only the most obvious or apparent information; and secondly, a systematic strategy that involves the detailed processing of message content. A number of other studies in the persuasion literature support the two-process model, namely that people use cognitively intense analytical processing when the task is an important or particularly engaging one, whereas they use affect or other simple heuristics to guide their decisions when they lack the motivation

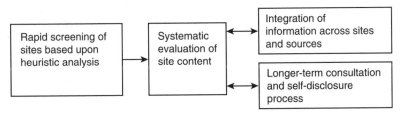

Figure 22.1 The staged model of trust.

or capacity to think properly about the issues involved. Such different processing strategies also reflect the distinction between the preliminary stage of (i) *intention to trust* and the later stage of (ii) *trusting activity* (McKnight and Chervany 2001).

The process does not stop there however, and a more realistic assessment of the development of trust should include a third stage in which a trusting relationship develops between the consumer and the website. This final stage has been rather overlooked in the trust literature, although it was originally proposed in the Cheskin/Sapient report (1999) and also appears in MoTEC (a Model of Trust for E-Commerce) (Egger 2000, 2001) where the authors described a stage of trust maintenance. In the health literature Rozmovits and Ziebland (2004) noted that cancer patients' use of the Internet was primarily concerned with the exchange of long-term support. The Internet was often used to share experience and advice, and to contact support groups and chat rooms. In other health domains, e.g. hypertension, personal experiences are also important (Sillence *et al.* 2004). The online community literature also suggests that long-term relationships online are based upon a sense of trust which develops through the exchange of information which is often highly personal. The ability to personalize content and to build personalized content is important in developing empathy within health-based communities (Preece and Ghozahti 2001).

A methodology for examining health consumers' use of the Internet

A novel methodology was developed in order to examine how genuine health consumers search for and appraise online health information and advice. It allows for the examination of people's decision-making processes, in particular with respect to trust, observed through the first few seconds of interaction with a website to one year of engagement.

Three longitudinal studies examining groups of people faced with risky health decisions were undertaken. The health topics were menopause and hormone replacement therapy (HRT), hypertension and healthy living. In addition a

small-scale study examining MMR was also carried out. For the purposes of clarity one such study is outlined below: all four studies followed a similar agenda.

Fifteen women at various stages of the menopause participated in the study (mean age 49 years). All the women were interested in finding out more about the menopause and all used the Internet at least once a week. Each participant attended a total of four two-hour sessions held in an Internet café in Newcastle-upon-Tyne, UK. During all four sessions, participants used the Internet to search for information and advice on the menopause, followed by a group discussion with a facilitator. Participants were told to freely surf the Web during sessions 1 and 4, and were directed to specific websites during sessions 2 and 3. These specific sites were chosen for their trust design elements. Earlier focus group work had identified a number of issues that people anticipated would be important in terms of trusting online health advice. The issues were primarily content- and provider-based. They included the site being provided by a well-known organization, contact details on the website, simple easy to understand language and up-to-date information. These requirements are in line with those found by Eysenbach and Köhler (2002). They found that consumers wanted a reputable source of information, a professional layout and some sort of endorsement or quality seal. In this current study, the sites that the participants were directed to in weeks 2 and 3 contained a range of provider, content and design features varied for trust.

The longitudinal studies were spilt into two phases. During each phase of the study a number of different records were taken.

Phase 1

Participants' actions online were automatically logged. All the websites visited by the participants were logged and the amount of time spent on each site was recorded. Secondly (and concurrently) participants engaged in verbal protocols or 'thinking aloud' as they searched through some of the sites. Thirdly, the participants were asked to record their perceptions of each site visited in a logbook and use this information during subsequent discussion sessions. Fourthly, following the online period, participants engaged in guided group discussion using themes piloted during earlier focus groups. The discussion guide covered the following main areas:

1. current information sources
2. search strategies
3. trusted and mistrusted websites
4. first impressions, and
5. revisiting websites.

Phase 2

At the end of the fourth week the participants were given diaries in order to record their ongoing information and advice searches both online and offline. Participants kept these diaries over a six-month period. Following the return of the diaries all of the participants in the menopause/HRT study were invited to take part in a final, follow-up interview. This structured interview examined the ways in which the Internet sources affected the patients' experiences of the menopause both in terms of decision-making and communications with their doctor.

Results

The results for each phase of the study are described below along with the forms of data analysis undertaken. In phase 1 the data logs were analysed to provide a timeline of rejected sites. The rejected sites were also classified in terms of their content. All the discussions and verbal protocols from phase 1 were recorded on audiotape and then transcribed. The transcripts were scrutinized for extracts describing trust and mistrust and then were coded by one member of the research team under several anticipated themes (for example, first impressions of websites, source credibility) and emergent themes (such as social identity markers and mistrust and confusion surrounding risk information). Then at least one other research team member read the transcripts and considered the codes. Constant comparison was used in the analysis to ensure that the thematic analysis represented all perspectives. Discrepancies between coders were resolved through discussion and mutual agreement before analysis.

In phase 2 the diaries were analysed according to the thematic analysis method described above.

The diary entries were coded under several themes including search motivation and decision-making. Examples of online–offline integration of information were also noted. The structured interviews were analysed according to the specific questions put to the participants and in terms of emergent themes. Once again a constant comparison method was used in the analysis to ensure that the thematic analysis represented all perspectives.

Phase 1 results

Search behaviour

Participants' search strategies varied considerably depending on the individuals' specific interests and became more refined and sophisticated over time (Sillence et al. 2004a, 2004b). During the hypertension study sessions most participants began by entering simple search terms such as 'high blood pressure' or 'hypertension' into a search engine. Over the following weeks their searches became more subtle with participants making use of explicit Boolean operators (in most cases 'AND'). One participant searched for 'hypertension AND alcohol' whilst several others searched specifically using the name of their hypertension medication, e.g. 'atenenol'. This confirms earlier work by Briggs et al. (2002) that showed that 'average' users often started their searches from general search engines or portals. Peterson et al. (2003) also noted that most health consumers had a single favourite search engine that they would always use. The results also illustrate, however, that genuine consumers can become increasingly sophisticated searchers over time. This fact is often overlooked in attempts to artificially replicate the search pattern of an average user for the purposes of quality assessment (Dunn et al. 2001; Reed and Anderson 2002).

Timeline analysis

To begin with we examined what users were doing within the first few seconds or minutes of searching online. The data from the website logs showed that people spent different amounts of time on different websites: 80 sites were logged automatically as being viewed, only 34 of which, however, were recorded in the logbooks as being viewed by the participants (despite clear instructions to record ALL sites visited). The 46 remaining sites were rejected by participants at different times. A significant finding was that any site viewed for less than two minutes was not recorded in the log book. To try and understand why this might be an analysis of the content of websites rejected at different stages was carried out. The analysis highlighted the effectiveness of rapid heuristic processing of information. Within a 30-second window, participants were able to efficiently sift information – recognizing and rejecting general portals and sales sites quickly. This may be because such sites have distinctive design features associated with them, but some content processing is also underway.

During the first ten seconds of scanning websites participants are keen to find something that is immediately relevant to them and to find content that they can 'latch onto'. Many of the rejected sites at this stage were portal sites. Portal sites often require participants to carry out a deeper search or to input additional search terms.

At 30 seconds, the largest category of sites rejected at this point were sales-based. Participants were clearly able to detect and reject signs of commercial activity and a sales orientation very rapidly. At two minutes, many sites rejected at this stage were either sales-based or were classified as 'other related'. Some sales sites do not reveal their commercial element until the user has explored the site in some detail. Participants may search through the site and then make a decision to reject the site after discovering its commercial motivation.

The speed with which consumers reject information should provide a salutary lesson regarding the importance of providing the right cues to site content in a highly visible manner. Participants missed out on some potentially good sites with useful information because of poor design.

Rejecting or selecting health websites

The transcripts from the group discussions and the verbal protocols were examined in terms of the selection (trust) or rejection (mistrust) of websites. A number of themes relating to the first impressions of the website and characteristics of trustworthy sites emerged. In terms of rejection the overwhelming majority of comments related to the design of the website. The look and feel of the website was clearly important to the participants. Visual appeal, plus design issues relevant to site navigation appeared to exert a strong influence on people's first impressions of the site. Poor interface design was particularly associated with rapid rejection and mistrust of a website. In cases where the participants did not like some aspect of the design the site was often not explored further than the homepage and was not considered suitable for revisiting at a later date. Negative comments included inappropriate name for the website, complex busy layout, lack of navigational aids, poor use of colour and pop-up adverts.

The participants mentioned a number of factors in terms of the sites they had selected to explore in more depth. The participants liked sites that contained a great deal of information that was presented in such a manner that an individual could quickly pinpoint their own specific areas of interest. Participants trusted the selected sites because they demonstrated an in-depth knowledge of a wide variety of relevant topics and put forward unbiased clear information. Participants were more likely to trust the information if they could verify it and cross check it with other websites. Most individuals preferred sites that were run by reputable organizations or had a medical or expert feel about them. They trusted the information on such websites especially when the credentials of the site and its authors were made explicit. Most participants showed some distrust of the advice and information on websites sponsored by pharmaceutical companies or those explicitly selling products. Participants were looking for sites that were written by people similar to themselves, who shared similar interests.

Phase 2 results

We asked the participants in our longitudinal studies to keep diaries over a six-month period in order to assess how they followed up the information and advice they had read online and to see how it affected their health behaviour. The participants were asked to record any sites that they visited during that time and to make a note of what prompted them to go online. We also asked them to note any 'offline' interactions concerning this particular health topic, for example, interactions with health professionals and friends and family. They were asked to make a note of any other resources they had used, for example, television, radio, or newspapers.

We were interested to find out when and where the Internet becomes involved in the decision-making process and to assess whether or not information integration had occurred. We noted that the Internet was affecting decision-making concerning treatments and lifestyle issues differentially across health topics and across individuals. For some participants, online information and advice was affecting their thinking on week by week basis. For others their decision-making processes were affected in an ongoing manner over the course of the following year. Below are three examples which illustrate how participants used the information online, how it was integrated with other sources and overall how it affected outcomes in terms of decision-making.

1. ST took part in the MMR study. Prior to using the Internet she had already discussed the issue at length with her family and with her doctor and health visitor. Her thinking was very much influenced by what she read during each week's session. At the end of the second week, in which she had examined pro-vaccination websites she felt more convinced about giving her child the MMR vaccination. However, during the third week she encountered material relating to both sides of the debate and in particular information on risk. At the end of this week ST had changed her mind and was convinced that she no longer wanted to give her child the MMR vaccination. During the fourth and final week ST carried out a free search and concluded at the end of that week to go ahead with the vaccination.

2. DB took part in the hypertension study. He was taking medication for his high blood pressure and was unhappy with what he saw as the debilitating side effects. Discussions prior to the study had left him frustrated since his doctor had advised him that side-effects were very unusual for this medication. DB was convinced his symptoms were not normal. During the sessions he came across one site in particular which detailed other people's experiences of side-effects while taking this particular medication. During the group discussions he

told everyone of his findings and his intention to show these results to his doctor. The diaries indicated that he returned to the website several times before visited his doctor. In consultation with his doctor he had agreed a change in his medication.

3. JP took part in the HRT study. At the time of the study she was taking HRT but was thinking about stopping. At the end of the four-week study she reported that she intended to visit her doctor to discuss coming off HRT and trying alternative remedies. Her diary indicated that she saw her doctor the week after the sessions ended and decided to come off HRT. Over the next six months she consulted several websites concerned with alternative remedies and sought the opinion of a relative, a homeopath. By the time the follow-up interview was carried out, however, she had returned to HRT. She found the alternative remedies were not helping her symptoms and agreed with her doctor to go back on the HRT but at a reduced dosage.

Implications

Implications for the staged model of trust

The findings of the qualitative studies reported above provide support for a staged model of trust. Within the first ten seconds of viewing a website people are already engaged in rapid heuristic processing. Participants carried out a rapid screening process rejecting sites they did not trust. Poor design relates to the rapid rejection and mistrust of health sites. Participants then selected sites to engage with further and to evaluate in more depth. Credibility of information and personalization of content predicted selection (trust) of advice sites. In terms of longer-term engagement with a site both elements are likely to be influential. As Hassenzahl and Trautmann (2001) suggest, the 'character' of a website, meaning its visual design and its content, affects users' interpretation, acceptance and further interaction with the site. These findings have already proved useful in the development of guidelines for improving the trustworthiness of health websites (Sillence et al. 2005b).

Implications for our understanding of consumer evaluation of health websites

Previous studies have been overly keen to point out that average consumers are poor evaluators of content too interested in the visual appeal of the website. Our studies (Sillence *et al.* 2004a, b) have highlighted that genuine consumers' 'wish lists' for health websites do not differ that greatly from the comments made by experts in other evaluation studies e.g. (Stanford *et al.* 2002).

As predicted the participants in our studies, with a greater stake in the outcome of their web searches, paid close attention to the content of selected sites and were careful and critical evaluators of the information. We can presume that for these users faced with genuine health risks associated with taking the online advice involvement with the site was high. This is important when we consider trust and it reflects the work of Chaiken (1980) who described two experiments that show the degree of *involvement* in an issue affects processing strategy – those participants with low involvement adopted a heuristic approach to evaluating a message and were primarily influenced by its attractiveness, whereas those with high involvement adopted a systematic approach – presenting more arguments to support their judgement.

It is perhaps not that surprising that people express wishes about the content-based features of online advice prior to searching and then, at least initially, fall back on visual appeal factors in terms of rejecting poor sites. The majority of comments made by genuine consumers, and indeed experts, concerning ideal online advice relate to content features such as ownership, quality and depth of information and personalization. Once online searching commences, however, consumers are often overloaded with the sheer volume of results and so have to make use of some simple heuristics, involving low cognitive effort, based on visual appeal to sift out and reject poor sites (Peterson *et al.* 2003; Sillence *et al.* 2004a). The sites they then choose to engage with and act upon are once more related to issues of content and quality. While not so unlike 'experts' in many senses it is important to remember that consumers may still want different things from websites than experts. Medical experts, for example, are not the same

as people with genuine health concerns who may want support and empathy in addition to purely medical content.

Implications for health behaviours and interactions with doctors

The examples from the follow-up diaries and interviews illustrate how the influence of the Internet in health behaviour can be immediate and reactionary. However the Internet can also influence health behaviour through a process of careful reflection, cross-checking of information and discussion with the doctor, family and friends. While some decisions are irreversible others can be altered in response to new information. In general, the diaries and telephone interviews indicate that once viewpoints have been established and decisions made searching online ceases or at least diminishes greatly. In fact many of the participants spent little time looking online over the six month period of the diaries. In the interviews participants indicated that they only searched online as and when an issue arose. This could be in response to a change of symptoms or to the publication of a new, relevant piece of research. Williams *et al.* (2003) found that the Internet is used both as way of enhancing the doctor-patient relationship and as a counterbalance to information (or the lack of it) provided by the doctor. Our findings support this notion and concur with work of Hart *et al.* (2004) who suggest that talk of widespread cyberchondria may be exaggerated and that hype surrounding Internet use by patients appears to exceed the reality of its use. At the moment, it seems that while a lot of people have looked online for health advice, not many have actually taken their findings with them to the consulting room. Hart *et al.* (2004) found that even people who had looked up information online prior to their consultation often did not tell their doctor they had done so.

During the follow-up interviews all the participants expressed the opinion that they were now more careful evaluators of online and offline content. They also reported a new-found confidence with respect to doctors and medical information. The Internet afforded increased feelings of social support and identity and gave the participants valuable time to explore alternative approaches to healthcare. The influence of the Internet in health behaviour is more commonly felt as part of an integrated process of health care management. The Internet affects health behaviour through interaction with other information sources, family, friends and the medical profession.

Conclusions and future considerations

The British Government is keen to promote a more informed patient population and health information online may be one way of achieving this aim. Current patterns of Internet use, however, may not reflect those most at need in terms of health information. Over two-thirds of UK users are from more affluent social groups and nearly half are aged under 35 years (Which Online 2001). Mead *et al.* (2003) reported on a project designed to encourage the use of online health information among socially disadvantaged patients. Despite free Internet access uptake was very poor, suggesting that increasing access to the Internet is necessary but not sufficient to get people using online health information and advice. In a follow-up study Rogers and Mead (2004) found that peoples' motivations and expectations regarding the Internet for health advice were far greater predictors of uptake. Interestingly they noted that confidence in e-health information was linked to pre-existing styles of interaction with health professionals. People who already took an active role in their own health decisions and used other sources of health were far more likely to use the Internet for health advice.

Not everyone wants to use the Internet for health information and advice, but for those motivated to do so it can prove a rewarding and satisfying experience. In our studies participants were faced with risky health decisions and the influence of the Internet in the decision-making process varied for these men and women. For some people the Internet provided vital knowledge with which to make their choice, for others it challenged assumptions and prompted further doctor consultations. For the remaining participants the Internet confirmed previously held beliefs and provided justification for their choices.

Despite the ongoing concerns regarding quality of online information our studies and others (e.g. Hardy 1999) have shown that it is the users

of Internet information rather than authors or professional experts who decide what and how material is accessed and used. Ultimately decisions concerning the selection of online material, and evaluations of its trustworthiness and quality will always be influenced by peoples' own particular motivations and cognitive biases (issues that we are currently investigating). Online information highlights the struggle over expertise in the health domain. How the Internet affects health behaviour depends in part on the existing nature of the patient-physician relationship and in part on the patients existing attitude towards his or health. As the Internet becomes more integrated into health care so it promises to transform relationships between doctors and their patients.

References

Bastian, H. (2003). Just how demanding can we get before we blow it? *BMJ 326*, 1277–1278.

BBC Online (2004). Health advice 'through your TV'. Available at http://news.bbc.co.uk/go/pr/fr/-/1/hi/health/4100717.htm Accessed 11 January 2005.

Bessell, T., McDonald, S., Silagy, S., Anderson, J., Hiller, J. and Sansom, L. (2002). Do Internet interventions for consumers cause more harm than good? A systematic review. *Health Expectations 5*(1), 28–37.

Bhattacherjee, A. (2002). Individual trust in online firms: scale development and initial test. *Journal of Management Information Systems 19*(1), 211–241.

Briggs, P., Burford, B., De Angeli, A., and Lynch, P. (2002). Trust in online advice. *Social Science Computer Review 20*(3), 321–332.

Briggs, P., de Angeli, A. and Simpson, B. (2004). Personalisation and trust: a reciprocal relationship? In M. C. Karat, J. Blom and J. Karat (eds), *Designing personalized user experiences for ecommerce*. Dortrecht: Kluwer 39–56.

Burkell, J. (2004). Health information seals of approval: what do they Signify? *Information, Communication and Society 7*(4), 491–509.

Carvel, J. (2005). Lack of information worries NHS patients. *The Guardian*, 21 February, p. 10.

Chaiken, S. (1980). Heuristic versus systematic information processing and the use of source versus message cues in persuasion. *Journal of Personality and Social Psychology 39*, 752–766.

Cheskin Research and Studio Archetype/Sapient (1999). Ecommerce trust study. Retrieved 16 July 2003 from http://www.cheskin.com/p/ar.asp?mlid=7andarid=40andart=0andisu=1.

Childs, S. (2005). Judging the quality of Internet-based health information. *Performance Measurement and Metrics 6*(2), 80–96.

Coulson, N. (2005a). Receiving social support online: an analysis of a computer-mediated support group for individuals living with irritable bowel syndrome. *CyberPsychology and Behavior 8*, 580–584.

Coulson, N. (2005b) Coping with breast cancer in cyberspace: understanding the role of the online support group. Proceedings of the European Health Psychology Society. Galway, Ireland, August 2005.

Dunn, A., Victor, R. G. and Vaeth, P. A. C. (2001). Alternative remedies dominate the lay literature about hypertension on the Internet. *American Journal of Hypertension 14*(4, Part 2), A30.

Egger, F. N. (2000). 'Trust me, I'm an online vendor': towards a model of trust for e-commerce system design. *Proceedings of CHI 2000* (pp. 000–000). New York: ACM Press.

Egger, F. N. (2001). Affective design of e-commerce user interfaces: how to maximise perceived trustworthiness. *Proceedings of CAHD: Conference on Affective Human Factors Design* (pp. 317–324).

Eysenbach, G., Powell, J., Englesakis, M., Rizo, C. and Stern, A. (2004). Health related virtual communities and electronic support groups: systematic review of the effects of online peer to peer interactions. *BMJ 328*, 1166–1170.

Eysenbach, G. Powell, J., Kuss, O., and Sa, E-R. (2002). Empirical studies assessing the quality of health information for consumers on the world wide web, a systematic review. *Journal of the American Medical Association 287*(20), 2691–2700.

Eysenbach, G. and Köhler, C. (2002). How do consumers search for and appraise health information on the world wide web? Qualitative study using focus groups, usability tests and in-depth interviews. *BMJ 324*, 573–577.

Fogg, B. J., Kameda, T., Boyd, J., Marchall, J., Sethi,R., Sockol, M. and Trowbridge, T.(2002). *Stanford-Makovsky Web Credibiltiy Study 2002: Investigating what makes Web sites credible today*. A Research Report by the Stanford Persuasive Technology Lab and Makovsky and Company, Stanford University. Retrieved from http://www.webcredibility.org.

Gerber, B. S. and Eiser, A. R. (2001). The patient-physician relationship in the Internet age: future prospects and the research agenda. *Journal Medical Internet Research 3*(2), e15.

Grabner-Krauter, S. and Kaluscha, E. A. (2003). Empirical research in online-trust: a review and critical assessment. *International Journal of Human-Computer Studies 58*, 783–812.

Hardy, M. (1999). Doctor in the house: the Internet as a source of lay health knowledge and the challenge to expertise. *Sociology of Health and Illness 21*(6), 820–835.

Hart, A., Henwood, F., and Wyatt, S. (2004). The role of the Internet in patient practitioner relationships: findings from a qualitative research study. *J Med Internet Res 6*(3), e36.

Hassenzahl, M. and Trautmann, T. (2001). Analysis of web sites with the repertory grid technique. *Proceedings of CHI 2001* (pp. 167–168). Seattle, WA: ACM Press.

Joinson, A. N. (2003). *Understanding the psychology of Internet behaviour: Virtual world, real lives*. Basingstoke and New York: Palgrave Macmillan.

Kalet, A, Roberts, J. C. and Fletcher, R. (1994). How do physicians talk with their patients about risks? *Journal of General Internal Medicine 9*, 402–404.

Klein, J. D. and Wilson, K. M. (2003). Delivering quality care: adolescents' discussion of health risks with their providers. *Journal of Adolescent Health 30*(3), 190–195.

Klemm, P, Bunnell, D., Cullen, M., Soneji, R, Gibbons, P., Holecek, A. (2003). Online cancer support groups: a review of the research literature. *Comput Inform Nurs 21*(3), 136–42.

McKnight, D. H. and Chervany, N. L. (2001). Trust and distrust definitions: one bite at a time. In R. Falcone, M. Singh and Y.-H. Tan (eds), *Trust in cybersocieties* (pp. 000–000). Berlin: Springer-Verlag.

Mead, N., Varnam, R., Rogers, A. and Roland, M. (2003). What predicts patients' interest in the Internet as a health resource in primary care in England? *Journal of Health Services Research and Policy 8*(1), 33–39.

Meyerson, D., Weick, K. E. and Kramer, R. M. (1996). Swift trust and temporary groups. In R. M. Kramer and T. R. Tyler (eds), *Trust in organizations: Frontiers of theory and research* (pp. 166–195). Thousand Oaks, CA: Sage Publications.

Morahan-Martin, J. M. (2004). How Internet users find, evaluate and use online health information: a cross-cultural review. *CyberPsychology and behaviour 7*(5), 497–510.

Nicholas, D. Huntington, P. Gunter, B., Russell, C. and Withey, R. (2003). The British and their use of the web for health information and advice: a survey. *Aslib Proceedings 55*(5/6), 261–276.

Pagliari C and Gregor P. (2004). Literature review of traditional research databases. Available at www.sdo.lshtm.ac.uk/ehealth.html.

Peterson, G., Aslani, P., and Williams, K. A. (2003). How do consumers search for and appraise information on medicines on the Internet? A qualitative study using focus groups. *Journal of Medical Internet Research 5*(4), e33.

Pew (2003). Health searches and email have become more common place, but there is room for improvement in searches and overall Internet access. Available at http://www.pewinternet.org/.

Potts, H. W. W. and Wyatt, J. C. (2002). Online survey of doctors' experience of patients using the Internet. *Journal of Medical Internet Research 4*(1), e5.

Preece, J. (1999). Empathic communities: balancing emotional and factual communication. *Interacting with Computers 12*(1), 63–77.

Preece, J. and Ghozati, K. (2001). Observations and explorations of empathy online. In R. R. Rice and J.E. Katz (eds), *The Internet and health communications: Experience and expectations* (pp. 237–260). Thousand Oaks, CA: Sage Publications Inc.

Reed, M. and Anderson, C. (2002). Evaluation of patient information Internet web sites about menopause and hormone replacement therapy. *Maturitas 4*, 135–154.

Riegelsberger, J., Sasse, M. A., and McCarthy, J. (2003). Shiny happy people building trust? Photos on e-commerce websites and consumer trust. *Proceedings of CHI 2003* (pp. 121–128). New York: ACM Press.

Rogers, A. and Mead, N. (2004). More than technology and access: primary care patients' views on the use and non use of health information in the Internet age. *Health and Social Care in the Community 12*(2), 102–110.

Rozmovits, L. and Ziebland, S. (2004).What do patients with prostate or breast cancer want from an Internet site? A qualitative study of information needs. *Patient Education and Counselling 53*, 57–64.

Shon, J., Marshall, J. and Musen, M. A. (2000). The impact of displayed awards on the credibility and retention of web site information. *Proceedings of the AMIA Symposium* (pp. 794–798).

Sillence, E., Briggs, P., Fishwick, L. and Harris, P. (2004a). Trust and mistrust of online health sites. *Proceedings of CHI 2004* (pp. 663–670) New York: ACM Press.

Sillence, E., Briggs, P. and Herxheimer, A. (2004b). Personal experiences matter: what patients think about hypertension information online. *He@lth Information on the Internet 42*, December, 3–5.

Sillence, E. Briggs, P. Fishwick, L. and Harris, P. (2005b). Guidelines for developing trust in health websites. Poster presented at the 14th International WWW conference. Chiba, Japan, 11–14 May 2005.

Sillence, E. and Briggs, P. (2007). Please advise. Using the Internet for health and financial advice. *Computers in Human Behavior,* January, 2007, 728–748.

Sillence, E. Briggs, P. Harris, P. and Fishwick, L. (2006). Changes in online health usage over the last 5 years. *Proceedings of CHI 2006* (pp. 1331–1336) New York: ACM Press.

Sillence, E. (2005). Beyond the web: integrated digital communities. *Int J Web Based Communities 1*(3), 360–371.

Smart, J. M. and Burling, D. (2001). Radiology and the Internet: a systematic review of patient information resources. *Clinical Radiology 56*(11), 867–870.

Stanford, J., Tauber, E., Fogg, B. J. and Marable, L. (2002). Experts vs. online consumers: a comparative credibility study of health and finance web sites. *Consumer Web Watch Research Report* Retrieved August 2003 from http://www.consumerwebwatch.org/news/ report3_credibilityresearch/slicedbread_abstract.htm.

Wantland, D., Portillo J., Holzemer W., Slaughter R. and McGhee, E. (2004). The effectiveness of web-based vs. non-web-based interventions: a meta-analysis of behavioral change outcomes. *J Med Internet Res 6*(4), e40.

WHA (2002). Internet transforming the doctor patient relationship. Available at http://www.w-h-a.org/ wha2/index.asp.

Which? Online (2001). *Annual Internet Survey*. Available at http://wwww.which.net/surveys/intro.htm.

White, M. H. and Dorman, S. M. (2000). Online support for caregivers. analysis of an Internet alzheimer mailgroup. *Comput Nurs 18*(4), 168–76.

Williams, P. Huntington, P. and Nicholas, D. (2003). Health information on the Internet: a qualitative study of NHS Direct Online users. *Aslib proceedings 55*(5/6), 304–312.

CHAPTER 23

Tokyo youth at leisure

Online support of leisure outings

Diane J. Schiano, Ame Elliott and Victoria Bellotti

The Internet is not just for PCs anymore; it's going mobile, and it's doing so especially rapidly in Japan. There, mobile phone ('keitai') ownership is essentially ubiquitous – over 70 per cent of the entire population and over 90 per cent of young adults own keitai (Matsunaga 2005). Most keitai owners – 72 per cent and growing in 2002 – subscribe to mobile Internet services and have done so for years (Matsuda 2005). Carried on one's person, the keitai is a continuously available personal technology, in contrast to the PC in Japan, which tends to be a more limited family resource (Dobashi 2005). This chapter describes some suggestive findings on how young adults in Tokyo use mobile- and PC-based Internet resources outside of work or school. Our primary interest was in exploring leisure activities – and most notably, leisure outings – and how they are supported online. The findings presented here are initial results from an extensive research project designed to explore how Tokyo youth spend leisure time, and how they tend to coordinate, plan and otherwise support leisure activities. The ultimate goal of the project is to help identify issues and opportunities for designing new online media to support leisure activities, especially leisure outings. Yet even these early findings suggest some important emerging issues regarding how and why people use online technologies to support leisure practices, and we focus on these findings here.

We chose to study leisure practices of Tokyo youth for several reasons. While young people in Japan have more free time than mid-career adults or school children, coordination of leisure outings in Tokyo is quite complex. Schedules are tight, commutes are long and friends might easily live over an hour's train ride away. Also, keitai have permeated Japanese society for well over a decade now, and social practices around their use have solidified perhaps more in Japan than elsewhere (Kashimura 2005; Okada 2005). Moreover, mobile device design is especially highly advanced in Japan, and keitai are rapidly acquiring advanced features and the functionality of multipurpose PCs. Newer keitai may have such features as videophone-call capability, an MP3 player, a radio, a personal calendar/scheduler, games and a camera. Mobile Internet access began in Japan in 1993; higher-data rate 'third generation' services started in 2001 (Matsunaga 2005). Proprietary services like DoCoMo's i-mode and KDDI/au's ez-web offer such leisure-relevant information as train schedules, weather reports, restaurant recommendations and movie listings. In short, young adults in Tokyo are technologically savvy and in the vanguard of those using new mobile Internet technologies. Studying their attitudes and behaviours should serve as a good point of departure for understanding issues and opportunities around the design of new online leisure support technologies.

Historically, research on technology use has long focused primarily on work- or education-related activities. More recent studies have begun to look at entertainment of various types, including, for example: digital music (e.g., Voida *et al.* 2005), photographs (e.g., Schiano *et al.* 2002a) and games (e.g., Brown and Bell 2004; Ducheneaut and Moore 2004), as well as new-media approaches to fun (Barkhuus *et al.* 2005; Flintham *et al.* 2003) and experiencing the 'street' (Paulos and Jenkins 2005). However, little research on leisure pursuits has directly explored issues around supporting people in planning and engaging in typical leisure activities such as meeting friends for dinner at a restaurant (Pousman *et al.*'s [2004] event planner is one exception).

Communication clearly plays an important role in leisure, and a large, growing body of literature has been devoted to documenting the ever-increasing use of person-to-person communication media around the world, including voice calls, short text messaging (SMS), instant messaging (IM) and mobile email (Grinter and Eldgridge 2001; Schiano *et al.* 2002; Grintner and Palen 2002; Kasesniemi 2003; Ling 2004; Ito and Okabe 2005). A major use of such personal communication media – and mobile media in particular – appears to centre around coordinating schedules and managing expectations for forthcoming face-to-face appointments (Rheingold 2003; Ling 2004). This topic has been extensively explored by sociologists in Europe, including most notably Richard Ling. One study estimates that at least 34 per cent of SMSing on mobile phones in Norway primarily concerns coordination of this kind (Ling 2004). Work by Ito and colleagues (Ito and Okabe 2005) and others suggests that a similar pattern also holds for mobile email use in Japan.

Beyond communication, new research from Japan notes that the mobile Internet services on the keitai currently provide access to a vast wealth of information previously only available via PC, and have been doing so for some time now.

One report suggests that Japanese young people are starting to view the keitai as primarily an information-gathering – rather than a communication – device. In this study, the keitai is described as 'fast for getting information anytime, anywhere' (McVeigh 2003).

The present research builds on such findings, while focusing on creating a more complete characterization of leisure behaviour in particular. Our concern is with behaviours around leisure outing planning and practice, and how online technology is – and can be – used to support leisure activities. We also identify some important emerging issues around the design and use of new leisure support media.

Method

This project represents a large exploratory research effort, involving several studies and multiple methods. In this paper, we aim only to provide an overview of methods and initial patterns of results across studies; analyses are still in progress. The work was conducted in Tokyo in two phases. The first phase was designed to get a broad sense of issues around leisure from a population with a wide age-range – 16–33 year-olds. It involved two major studies: (1) an initial (preQ) survey and (2) an in-depth interview study. Certain patterns of findings from the first phase suggested that focusing on 19–25 year olds, those of university age, would be most promising (they have more leisure time, fewer constraints and tend to go out more; they may also be more comfortable with new technology). In this second phase of the research, all participants were drawn from this revised target population. Five studies were conducted:

1. an online survey

2. an in-depth interview study

3. a follow-up (i.e., post-interview) focus-group

4. a focus-group study specifically on mobile phone use, and

5. a keitai diary study of leisure activities throughout one leisure day.

These studies are described below, though very briefly due to space constraints. Further information is available by contacting the first author.

Background research

Background research included extensive reading of leisure guide content on- and off-line, informal field observations of popular youth 'hangouts' in Tokyo, interviews with editors of major leisure publications, and discussions with especially technically savvy university students.

Two surveys: preQ and online survey

Two survey studies were performed, a small preQuestionnaire (or 'preQ') given prior to the first interview study, and a large online survey given before the remaining studies in the second phase. The 'preQ' survey was completed in paper form by 20 interview participants (16–33 years of age), shortly before the interview session in the first phase of this research. The preQ comprised ~30 open-ended and multiple-choice questions on typical daily schedules, amount of leisure time, leisure planning resources, leisure activities and technology use. Participants' responses were used to support detailed discussions of leisure practices during the interview session.

The online survey was designed to gather more extensive demographic, behavioural, and attitudinal data on leisure practices of Tokyo 19–25-year-olds (our revised target population) in the second phase of this research. It was designed to be very similar to the preQ (although some items were redesigned for structured rather than open-ended responses). In all, there were ~40 numerical response and multiple-choice items – additional items largely concerned keitai use. A popular online club that rewards survey participants with shopping 'points' made the online survey available to members for three days in April 2005. Six hundred and ninety-seven people responded and served as participants in the online survey. Twenty-three online survey respondents living in central Tokyo were recruited to participate in further studies.

Two interview studies

An individual in-depth interview study was performed in each phase of the research. The first interview study involved twenty participants aged 16–33. The second involved twelve 19–25-year-old participants recruited from the online survey. Each interview session lasted about two hours. Both studies featured detailed discussions of how leisure time was spent and why, as well as descriptions of specific recent leisure outings and the details of how they were planned and executed. Towards the end of the study session, some early design concepts for leisure support technologies were also discussed. The first interview study took place in a classic market-research office. In the second study, we used the more naturalistic contexts of a local café or restaurant. For each study, translators were required, and a concerted effort was made to protect privacy.

Interview follow-up focus groups

All participants in the second interview study met in one of two interview follow-up focus group (IFFG) sessions. Sessions were spent clarifying issues and attempting to test and extend our initial impressions from the individual interviews. We also gained some additional feedback on the leisure-support design concepts discussed in the interview sessions.

Mobile phone focus groups

Two mobile phone focus group (MPFG) sessions explored how keitai use was related to leisure practices. Eleven people aged 19–25 participated in total. They were also recruited from the online survey, but did not participate in the interview or follow-up sessions. Sessions were semi-structured to promote discussion. Participants brought their keitai and began by describing their phone, why they bought it and its best and worst features. They later chose three general concepts that best related to their phone use – for example, dating, style, convenience – and explained how this was so. Comparisons of experience were elicited.

Mobile phone photo diaries

Ten participants recruited from the MPFG study sent an email message about their current leisure activities via keitai every hour of one Sunday in May. They documented where they were, who they were with and what they were doing, adding an illustrative photo. Hourly email reminders about these mobile phone photo diaries (MPPD) promoted compliance.

Results and discussion

In this section we consider some emerging patterns of findings suggesting issues to inform further research in understanding both leisure behaviour and technology design. We first discuss findings on leisure practice in general, and then proceed to those on mobile phone use in particular.

Findings on leisure practices

Typical leisure activities

An open-ended preQ question asked participants to list their top (i.e., most frequently engaged in) three typical leisure activities. A content analysis showed that the most frequent responses centred on the following concepts:

♦ TV – 28 per cent,
♦ (Being with) friends – 23 per cent,
♦ Email – 10 per cent,
♦ Internet – 7 per cent, and
♦ Shopping – 5 per cent.

Note that using email and the Internet were among the top leisure activities mentioned. An age analysis on the preQ results showed 19–25-year-olds were most likely to mention going out or outings of some kind.

In the online survey 19–25 year olds rated how often they engaged in a variety of activities for leisure, on a scale of 0–5 (never–multiple times per day; see Table 23.1). 'Non-outing' activities tended to be rated as more frequent than those involving outings; this converges with interview and MPPD (photo diary study) findings that much leisure time is spent indoors, often at home and often (but not always) alone. This is also consistent with survey respondents'

estimates that a great deal of their leisure time was spent at home – 40 per cent in the preQ, 49 per cent in the online survey. Strikingly, the top frequency ratings were given to online activities, WWW/PC, email/mobile and email/PC.

For leisure outings, shopping ranked highest, followed by going out with friends. Interviewees' descriptions of specific recent leisure activities suggest typical outings (typically done with friends): shopping, window-shopping, café/restaurant, movies, karaoke, bowling, sports events, concerts and hobby or club-related activities. The photo diary study results are consistent with this (especially shopping, café/restaurant and movies). Special leisure outing activities include visiting 'back home', going to hot springs, going to an amusement park, ski trips, music festivals (or special concerts), school or club field trips and tourism (mostly within Japan). Both survey and interview responses suggest that companionship may be the most important factor in leisure outings; precisely what to do or where to go is of only secondary importance. In the online survey weekdays were estimated as accounting for 25.4 per cent of leisure time overall, Saturdays for 36.3 per cent and Sundays for 38.3 per cent.

Resources for leisure discovery and planning

The preQ included an open-ended question about the top three resources used to learn about and plan leisure activities. Table 23.2 shows the results in terms of frequency of mention of each kind of resource. Friends and family were mentioned most often, followed by television. However, Internet search engines in specific and using the Internet/WWW on the PC came in third and fourth, respectively. Note that if the results from these last two – and those from the

Table 23.1 Mean frequency ratings of top leisure activities (non-outings and outings) in the online survey

Non-outings					
Mean rating [0–5]	WWW/ PC 4.55	Email/mobile 4.53	Email/PC 4.36	Live TV, home 4.21	Music, home 3.43
Outings					
Mean rating [0–5]	Shopping 2.57	Out with friends 2.02	Restaurant 1.96	Dating 1.53	Sports 1.43

Table 23.2 Frequency of mention of top leisure planning resources in PreQ

Resources	Frequency of mention in PreQ (%)
Friends/family	27
TV	18
Search engine	17
Internet/PC	12
Other magazines (not leisure guides)	08
Ads/promotions	08
Leisure Magazines	03
Free papers	03
Internet/mobile	02
Newspapers	02

'Internet/mobile' category – were combined, the result would be in first place. Clearly the Internet functions as a major leisure resource. Notably, however, this is overwhelmingly on the PC – the mobile Internet was only mentioned in 2 per cent of the responses.

In the online survey 19–25 year old respondents ranked their top three leisure planning resources from an existing list. Results in terms of rankings of weighted scores are shown in Table 23.3. PC-based online resources came in first (accessing web via PC) and second (Internet search engines on the PC) place, followed by friends and family and television. Since the survey was performed online, we might expect to see some bias towards using online resources. Yet accessing the Web via the keitai received the lowest ranking, coming in last out of 11 options, underscoring the fact that the mobile Internet is not a primary leisure planning resource. The list of the most commonly mentioned resources

(if not their precise relative ordering) was remarkably similar across the two studies.

Spontaneous discovery and focused research

The findings above and our interview discussions suggest that people initially encounter information about potential leisure activities in a fairly effortless, even serendipitous way. Leisure topics tend to 'come up naturally' in conversations with friends or family members, or while TV is playing in the 'background'. This initial serendipitous discovery seems to be primarily done offline, although a few interviewees mentioned learning of a new leisure activity because something 'caught my eye' online (e.g., on Yahoo!'s Front Page). Recommendations from friends' and family's personal experience are seen as most 'reliable', and most likely to match one's own tastes. Moreover, they are easy to obtain with minimal work. Still, even recommendations from unknown individuals online seem to be trusted more than those from marketers, who are understood to be out to make a profit. TV shows and ads, while not trusted as much as personal recommendations, can still provide timely information on the newest movies and trends that friends and family may or may not be aware of yet.

Once an interesting option is encountered, engaging in research to plan a specific outing is common, especially for group outings. This process does appear to commonly involve online resources. The Internet – and especially search engines – is a familiar tool for Tokyo youth, and is especially well-suited to this research task. Online research can be used to find a particular place on a given theme or in a given area (e.g., a karaoke bar nearby), or for specific information on a known place (e.g., maps, train schedules). We find it striking that while most keitai support Internet access and while there is a great

Table 23.3 Rankings of weighted scores of 'top leisure planning resources' in online survey

	WWW/PC	Internet search engine/PC	Friends/family	TV	Leisure magazines
Ranking weighted of score	1	2	3	4	5

deal of leisure-related information available on the mobile web, keitai are apparently not frequently used for Internet researching of leisure-time activities. They are certainly poor browsing tools compared to the PC, with its larger screen and keyboard, and most of this sort of research probably takes place before embarking on an outing, and not while engaged in one. In addition, the cost of wireless Internet access favours intermittent short connections for email message transfer over constantly connected web page data access. Moreover, there is limited Internet access between stops on the subway, where people might otherwise spend time browsing web pages. Finally, phone carriers make anything other than proprietary-network-specific content access difficult, which our MPFG focus group participants found especially frustrating. Easy-look-up mobile Internet information like train timetables and weather reports seem to be the killer keitai web applications for this population.

Organizing and coordinating group activities

As noted earlier, companionship is a key element of leisure outings. Almost all of the specific recent outings described in both interview studies included at least one companion, and often a small group (4–6 persons on average). This is also consistent with the photo diary study findings. In describing how group outings are planned and organized, we found that it was common for one member of a group to take on the work of researching and planning, typically on the PC, as described above. Then the information gained (including URLs) is shared with the group, largely through email. Coordination of schedules also tends to take place via email, typically on the keitai. Thus the keitai is used to communicate and coordinate with information gathered on the PC.

Leisure time spent using online resources

In the online survey, participants were asked to estimate how many hours of week they spent using various online resources for leisure, 'outside of work or school' (see Table 23.4). These young online respondents estimated that they accessed the Web via PC about 15 hours per week in their leisure time. (This estimate may be inflated a bit by the tendency for students to spend a lot of time online in any case). The next

Table 23.4 Mean estimates of hours of use per week of online resource in online survey

Resources	Hours per week
WWW/PC	14.86
Email/PC	03.61
Email/keitai	03.13
Chat/PC	01.54
Voice/keitai	01.30
WWW/keitai	01.51
Voice/home phone	00.53
Chat/keitai	00.11

highest use estimate was for email accessed via PC, at a much lower rate of 3.6 hours/week, similar to that for email accessed via keitai (3.1 hours/ week). Accessing the Web via keitai came in at 1.3 hours per week. Again, the high estimates of online resource use may reflect the online proclivities of this sample, which was recruited online and largely comprised university students – who are more likely to own their own computers than most other Japanese. Still, the pattern is very suggestive. It supports our findings discussed above, that these students are familiar with the Web, that the keitai is used primarily for communication (email and voice) and much less so much for accessing Internet information, for which the PC is overwhelmingly the resource of choice. It also underscores the importance of communication for this population, whether via PC or phone, in voice or in text.

In the next section we discuss leisure uses of mobile phones. The findings add to the previous literature on keitai use, providing a more detailed and nuanced understanding of issues around using the keitai in leisure practices.

Findings on leisure uses of mobile phones

As noted earlier, keitai are ubiquitous among Japanese youth: 97.3 per cent of the online survey respondents currently owned one. While many studies have explored keitai use, the present project is more concerned with the keitai's role in leisure practice. MPFG (focus group) findings show that keitai are often used to 'kill time', especially during train commutes. Entertainment content can include games, music and even video. In the focus groups, young men talked more than women about using games and other advanced features on the keitai, although their usage patterns in the survey data did not differ substantially. Our survey and focus results also suggest that communication (the core keitai functionality) can serve as a leisure activity in itself; that is, communication itself can be entertaining. This may be especially true for young women. Gender differences were discussed extensively in both focus group sessions; the consensus was that young women focus more on communication, sending more, longer and more 'emotive' messages. While men also primarily use the keitai for communication, they seem less interested in extended email conversations.

With regard to mobile communication, a striking finding from the focus groups is the sense that the keitai is now considered a social 'necessity': 'if you want to live in today's life – in today's society, you are expected to have a mobile phone' (see also Ling 2004; Kato 2005). Survey results show communication functionality ('email' followed by 'voice'), as the top-rated keitai features. In the focus groups, email and voice were the primary features used, and some people – notably women – said they used nothing else. As noted earlier, online survey estimates of keitai use per week 'outside of work or school' averaged around 6 hours; use of email (3.1 hours) was double that of voice (1.5 hours) functionality. Focus group discussions suggest fairly short bursts of use, mostly exchanging messages among fairly close friends and family, with multitasking common.

Hyperconnectivity

The keitai (with email) makes communication cheap, fast and easy. Carried on one's person (typically in a pocket or purse) and 'always on', it is a continuously available personal technology. Ling (2004) has described 'hypercoordination' among mobile phone users, and we certainly found that keitai are used to coordinate leisure outings (largely through email). However, we see hypercoordination as falling under a more general phenomenon which we call 'hyperconnectivity', a sense of essentially continual real-time connection. Hyperconnectivity is illustrated in

bold relief by one interviewee who 'communicate(s) by e-mail [with his girlfriend] on the mobile phone ... it amounts to about 20 messages per day'. Focus group estimates of typical use was 5–10 messages on an average day (although sometimes much more). Other researchers have also found that short text messages tend to be exchanged among youth at least a few times a day with a small number of intimates in one's social network (Grinter and Eldgridge 2001; Grintner and Palen 2002; Schiano et al. 2002; Kasesniemi 2003; Ling 2004; Ito and Okabe 2005). Our sense from the focus group and interview discussions is that the social 'necessity' of the keitai goes far beyond mere coordination and communication. Continual connection seems to function essentially as form of co-presence, or virtual companionship. The tendency to keep phones 'always on' (some participants claimed to do so even while asleep), and making contact even when they 'don't have anything to say' makes sense in this context as well (see also Puro 2002). Thus a small group of close friends or family members are essentially in constant contact. This may be especially common among young people in Japan, for whom association with peers is so important, but difficult to achieve for logistical reasons. Researchers studying young Japanese keitai users in particular have referred to this behaviour as essentially producing a 'full-time intimate community' transcending spatial boundaries (Nakajimia et al. 1999; Matsuda 2005); Habachi (2005) refers to it as 'telecocooning'.

Hyperconnectivity is clearly something that people choose to pursue, yet it also has negative consequences. These include:

1. 'shallow' friendships conducted more by mobile email than in person (see also McVeigh 2003)

2. new forms of 'rudeness' (e.g., abusing constant connection as permission to be indecisive or late, using the phone while ignoring those around you) and social faux pas (e.g., inadvertently sending casual messages to work superiors), and

3. new conventions to avoid rudeness (e.g., using the silent mode in public, not using the phone with others present; see also Ito 2003).

In addition, while hyperconnectivity seems intended to assuage loneliness, it can also engender new forms of loneliness, as some focus group participants mentioned:

> The other day I had a day I did not receive any emails or phone calls. Then I felt loneliness. But [the] loneliness was special by having a mobile phone ... if it does not ring, it's not broken it should ring but it doesn't. Maybe it's an insecure feeling but when I did not have a mobile phone I did not feel this way, this kind of loneliness.

And

> When you are with your friend and she or he receives mail or phone calls and you are left alone I feel loneliness. Then I start sending mails and then sometimes I feel even though we are together now we don't even talk. That's *really* lonely!

Privacy paradox

Coordination is clearly an important part of leisure communication, as discussed above. We therefore expected participants to be receptive to design suggestions to support coordination, such as a shared calendar tool. Yet despite their commitment to hyperconnectivity, we found a strong reticence among our participants to share information about themselves online in forms other than email, including a shared calendar. Most participants found having access to other people's schedules 'convenient', but also found it quite worrisome to think about others having access to theirs. For one participant, 'concerning the schedule she doesn't know if it's good for other to people to look at their friends' schedules, but if possible, it would be convenient because she would know what they're doing and what time is open for them'. Words like 'scared', 'worried', 'hesitant', 'uneasy' and 'bothered' came up repeatedly in this context. We explored a variety of concerns in this context. Major issues included:

1. maintaining privacy (not wanting others to be able to see everything that one is doing)
2. keeping up appearances (the desire to maintain an image of being socially active, even if one's calendar is empty), and
3. plausible deniability (the desire to avoid causing offense by turning down an invitation, even when one is not busy).

The strong concern suggested here about keeping one's own information private, despite a clear willingness to see others' information – indeed, despite a desire for hyperconnectivity with at least a small number of others – appears paradoxical at first glace, but may well reflect some deep yet conflicting social psychological motivations (as in 'the tragedy of the commons'; Hardin [1968]). Some – but by no means all – of these concerns might be assuaged by limiting full calendar information or shared access to only the limited group of intimates one is in constant contact with (i.e., one's telecocoon). We find this topic intriguing; more systematic research is clearly needed.

Further considerations

We began our fieldwork expecting to learn about a culture of using mobile phones as multipurpose Internet PCs, but discovered that they are still primarily used as interpersonal communication tools. Our young study participants, though largely recruited from an online resource, still see communication as the keitai's primary function, and did not make extensive use of keitai-based Internet information.

Our findings on leisure activity discovery and planning suggest a 'division of labour' in which PCs are used for intensive Internet search in planning of leisure activities and keitai are used for discussing and coordinating leisure in email (supplemented perhaps by mobile web fact-finding during the activity, especially perhaps checking train connections). This may have partly to do with the fact that Internet access is cheaper on a PC, and easy access to much wider content than carriers' services enable is possible. However, it is also clear that, when one is not on the go, a larger screen is likely to be more convenient for browsing for and researching things to do. Further, some participants explicitly pointed to the fact that using the Internet on the keitai is very unwieldy, although that could be due to poor interface design or current limitations of keitai content.

The use of the PC to do research, frequently followed by use of the keitai email to coordinate, points to a design imperative to in some way connect the keitai and the PC in better support of leisure, although our participants made no mention of any technology that currently attempts to do this. Facilitating easy transfer of information researched and gathered on the PC onto the keitai and using it in combination with phone capabilities is intriguing from a design perspective, and one that could support both advanced planning and serendipitous discovery.

The primary use of the mobile Internet among our study participants was for mobile email. The way in which people described their use patterns suggests a quest for constant social connection, which we called 'hyperconnectivity'. We discussed this phenomenon in some detail, and noted that it stands in apparently paradoxical relation with the strong concern for privacy that many interviewees also expressed.

We should mention in this context the emergence of an interesting new form of online leisure publication, which blurs the distinction between communication and information on the mobile Internet. Tokyo-based Xavel's Girls Walker has been strikingly successful in Japan, with about 2 million users in 2003 (Nakada 2003). It depends largely on the contributions of girls (in their late teens to twenties) for content. Readers submit blog entries and subscribe to receive updates on their keitai. The interaction is inherently social, and the interface is quite similar to that for email messaging. The publication gets revenue from advertising and shopping on the keitai and has been growing rapidly in popularity. Thus despite the concerns we heard in our studies about keeping one's own activities private, the Girls Walker success suggests that Japanese youth are starting to adopt new-media-based opportunities for sharing information about their interests and opinions with strangers. Based on our background research into the leisure time content industry, we feel it is likely that, as it becomes possible to aggregate the thoughts and experiences of multiple people (perhaps within one's social network, perhaps beyond it), end-user-generated content – particularly from keitai users – will become increasingly popular as a leisure information source. This is in part because our participants mentioned that they tended to trust private individuals more than profit-making commercial entities as sources of information. In addition, if designed well, this kind of social content creation may be seen more as a form of communication than as an information tool, and as such may be acceptable to more people. It may also lower the bar to more extensive use of the mobile web. We are currently investigating opportunities to leverage this kind of content creation in our ongoing research.

Conclusions

This chapter presents a set of very suggestive findings on how online resources are used to support leisure outings among young adults in Tokyo. An extensive body of data was gathered from several studies in a large research project on leisure practices; we report here on initial findings of particular relevance to Internet use. While we began our fieldwork expecting to learn about a culture of using mobile phones as multipurpose Internet PCs, we discovered that they are still primarily used as interpersonal communication tools. Our young study participants, though largely recruited from an online resource, still see communication as the primary function of the mobile phone (or 'keitai'), and did not make much use of available mobile Internet information besides simple look-ups like train timetables. Our results also suggest specific patterns of leisure discovery (serendipitously), planning (via PC-based Internet search) and coordination (largely through email, often via keitai). Of particular interest is the strong emphasis we found on remaining in constant communication while mobile, and the apparent tension between engaging in this sort of hyperconnectivity and maintaining a sense of personal privacy online. While further work is clearly needed, many of the issues we uncover here should be of timely interest to a wide audience in the applied psychology community.

Acknowledgements

We thank the many participants who kindly shared information about their leisure time practices with us. We also thank our research sponsors at Dai Nippon Printing Co. Ltd., and several on-location support organizations.

References

Barkhuus, L., Chalmers, M., Tennent, P., Bell, M., Hall, M., Sherwood, S. and Brown, B. (2005). Picking pockets on the lawn: the development of tactics and strategies in a mobile game. In *Proceedings of UbiComp 2005* (pp. 358–374). Springer.

Brown, B. and Bell, M. (2004). CSCW at play: 'There' as a collaborative virtual environment. In *Proceedings of CSCW 2004* (pp. 350–359). New York: ACM Press.

Caspary, C. and Manzenreiter, W. (2003). From subculture to cyberculture. In N. Gottleib and M. McLelland (eds), *Japanese cybercultures* (pp. 60–74). Routledge.

Dobashi, S. (2005). The gendered use of *keitai* in domestic contexts. In M. Ito, D. Okabe and M. Matsuda (eds), *Personal, portable, pedestrian: Mobile phones in Japanese life* (pp. 219–236). Cambridge, MA: MIT Press.

Ducheneaut, N. and Moore, R. J. (2004). The social side of gaming. In *Proceedings of CSCW 2004* (pp. 360–369). New York: ACM Press.

Flintham, M., Anastasi, R., Benford, S., Hemmings, T., Crabtree, A., Greenhalgh, C., Rodden, T., Tandavanitj, N., Adams, M. and Row-Farr, J. (2003). Where on-line meets on-the-streets. In *Proceedings of CHI 2003* (pp. 569–576). New York: ACM Press.

Grinter, R. E. and Eldridge, M. A. (2001). y do tngrs luv 2 txt msg? In *Proceedings of ECSCW 2001* (pp. 219–238). New York: ACM Press.

Grinter, R. E. and Palen, L. (2002). Instant messaging in teen life. In *Proceedings of CSCW 2002* (pp. 21–30). New York: ACM Press.

Habuchi, I. (2005). Accelerating reflexivity. In M. Ito, D. Okabe and M. Matsuda (eds), *Personal, portable, pedestrian: Mobile phones in Japanese life* (pp. 165–182). Cambridge, MA: MIT Press.

Hardin, G. (1968). The tragedy of the commons. *Science* 162, 1243–1248.

Ito, M. (2003). A new set of social rules for a newly wireless society. *Japan Media Review* Available at http://www.ojr.org/japan/.

Ito, M. and Okabe, D. (2005). Technosocial situations: emergent structuring of mobile e-mail use. In M. Ito, D. Okabe and M. Matsuda (eds), *Personal, portable, pedestrian: Mobile phones in Japanese life* (pp. 257–273). Cambridge, MA: MIT Press.

Kasesniemi, E.-L. (2003). *Mobile messages: Young people and a new communication culture*. Tampere University Press.

Kashimura, A. (2005). Daitaiteki seikatsu sekaitei communication no tenkai (Development of alternative lifeworld communication). In S. Tanabe and S. Shimazono (eds), *Tsumagarino Naka no Iyashi (Healing in the Connection)* (pp. 211–249). Senshu Daigaku Shuppan Kyoku.

Kato, H. (2005). Japanese youth and the imaging of *keitai*. In M. Ito, D. Okabe and M. Matsuda (eds), *Personal, portable, pedestrian: Mobile phones in Japanese life* (pp. 103–119). Cambridge, MA: MIT Press.

Ling, R. (2004). The mobile connection: The cell phone's impact on society. Elsevier.

Matsunaga, A. (2005). Overview of 'keitai' (mobile phone) services in Japan. IEEE International Symposium on Wearable Computers 2005. Osaka, Japan.

Matsuda, M. (2005). Mobile community and selective sociality. In M. Ito, D. Okabe and M. Matsuda (eds), *Personal, portable, pedestrian: Mobile phones in Japanese life* (pp. 124–142). Cambridge, MA: MIT Press.

McVeigh, B. (2003). Individuation, individuality and the Internet. In N. Gottleib and M. McLelland (eds), *Japanese cybercultures* (pp. 19–33). Routledge.

Mobile Communications Research Group (MCRG) (2002). Keitai Denwa Riyo no Shinka to Sono Eikyo (The Evolution of the Uses of Keitai and its Influences). Cited in Ito, M., Okabe, D. and Matsuda, M. (Eds) *Personal, portable, pedestrain: mobile phones in Japanese life*. Cambridge, MA: MIT Press.

Nakada, G. (2003). Shopping on the small screen: *Girls Walker* shows that young women are ready and willing to buy via *keitai. Japan Inc.* Available at http://www.japaninc.net/article.php?articleID=1039.

NHK Broadcasting Culture Research (2002). *NHK databook 2000: National time use survey*. Tokyo: Japan Broadcast Publishing Company.

Nakajimia, I., Himeeo, K., and Yoshii, H. (1999). Diffusion of cellular phones and PHS and its social meanings (trans.). *Joho Tsuushin Gakkai-shi 16*, 79–92.

Okabe, D. and Ito, M. (2005). *Keitai* in public transportation. In M. Ito, D. Okabe and M. Matsuda (eds), *Personal, portable, pedestrian: Mobile phones in Japanese life* (pp. 205–217). Cambridge, MA: MIT Press.

Okada, T. (2005). Youth culture and the shaping of Japanese mobile media. In M. Ito, D. Okabe and M. Matsuda (eds), *Personal, portable, pedestrian: Mobile phones in Japanese life* (pp. 41–60). Cambridge, MA: MIT Press.

Paulos, E. and Jenkins, T. (2005). Urban probes: encountering our emerging urban atmospheres. In *Proceedings of CHI 2005* (pp. 241–350) New York: ACM Press.

Puro. J.-K. (2002). Finland: a mobile culture. In J. E. Katz and M. Aakhus (eds), *Perpetual contact: Mobile communications, private talk, public performance.* Cambridge University Press.

Pousman, Z., Iachello, G., Fithian, R., Moghazy, J. and Stasko, J. (2004). Design iterations for a location-aware event planner. *Personal Ubiquitous Computing 8*, 117–125.

Qiu, J. (2004). NTT DoCoMo: review of a case. *Japan Media Review* Available at http://www.ojr.org/japan/.

Rheingold, H. (2003). *Smart mobs: The next social revolution*. Perseus Publishing.

Rutledge, B. (2003). Cell phone companies set their sights on senior citizens. *Japan Media Review* Available at http://www.ojr.org/japan/.

Schiano, D. J., Chen, C. P. and Isaacs, E. (2002). How teens take, view, share, and store photos. *CSCW 2002* Interactive Poster.

Schiano, D. J., Chen, C. P. and Isaacs, E. (2002). How teens take, view, share, and store photos. In *Proceedings of CSCW 2002* (pp. 000–000). New York: ACM Press.

Voida, A., Grinter, R. E., Ducheneaut, N., Edwards, K. E. and Newman, M. W. (2005). Listening in: practices surrounding iTunes music sharing. In *Proceedings of CHI 2005* (pp. 191–200). New York: ACM Press.

PART 5

Internet-Based Research

CHAPTER 24

The methodology of Internet-based experiments

Ulf-Dietrich Reips

Introduction

This chapter contains information about methods and techniques, procedures and tools that have been found to be necessary or useful in Internet-based experimenting.[1] While the focus is on experiments, many of the methods apply to other types of Internet-based research as well.

The Internet-based experimental method lends itself easily to research in particular areas of psychology, more so in some than in others. For example, it is straightforward to use the method in judgement and decision-making research (Birnbaum 2001; Schulte-Mecklenbeck and Neun 2005) and other areas of cognition, while there are limitations to Internet-based research in neuropsychology (see Erlanger *et al.* [2003] for a noteworthy exemption). Interestingly,

it could be shown empirically that the distribution of usage among subfields of psychology remains constant over the years. Reips and Lengler (2005) analysed data from submissions by experimenters to one of the largest web portals for Internet-based experiments, the Web Experiment List,[2] and compared the results with those from a web survey conducted by Musch and Reips (2000) in 1998 and 1999 among the early web experimenters. Table 24.1 shows their results. Note that social psychology rivals cognition in number of Internet-based studies.

It has also repeatedly been noted that the number of Internet-based experiments conducted is increasing exponentially or nearly exponentially (Reips 2002c; Birnbaum 2004; Birnbaum and Reips 2005). In a recent analysis of data from the Web experiment list this description of the trend turned out to be appropriate (see Figure 24.1) (Reips, 2006a). The number of web experiments in the list is now (July 2006) at 400.

Given the widespread and increasing use of the method it is surprising that most universities are not yet fully prepared to teach students how to conduct this type of research properly.

---

[1] The term 'Internet-based experiment' is largely synonymous with the widely used terms 'Web experiment', 'Internet experiment', 'on(-)line experiment', 'web-based experiment', and 'WWW experiment', because experiments using Internet services other than the WWW (such as email, Telnet, ICQ, Gopher, FTP etc.) are rarely conducted. Because most experiments on the Internet are based on web pages the term 'web experiment' is used most often in this chapter.

[2] http://genpsylab-wexlist.unizh.ch/.

Table 24.1 Number and percentage of web experiments by field in two studies, from the end of the 1990s and 2005

Field	Web survey in 1998/9 (Musch and Reips, 2000)	Web experiment list (Reips and Lengler, 2005)
Cognitive Psychology	10 (56%)	100 (40%)
Social Psychology	4 (22%)	90 (36%)
Perception	1 (5%)	25 (10%)
Internet Science	1 (5%)	10 (4%)
Personality Psychology	1 (5%)	10 (4%)
Clinical Psychology	-	10 (4%)
Development Psychology	-	3
Neuropsychology	1 (5%)	2
Sum	18	250

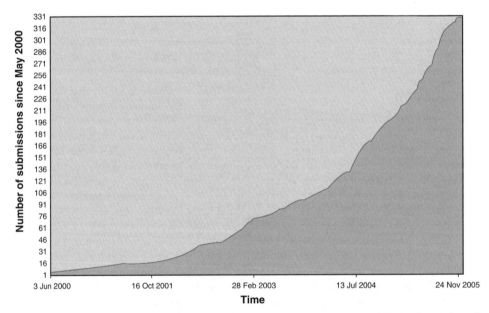

Figure 24.1 Number of submissions of web experiments to the Web Experiment List by time (adapted from Reips, 2006a).

One of the reasons may be that most researchers and teachers received their own methods training during a time when the Internet was little more than an obscure military network. As a result of the widespread lack of education in Internet-based research methods and the misconception that Internet-based research can be conducted by applying laboratory techniques in a 1:1 fashion, many web-based studies appear on the Internet and in manuscripts that do not meet basic methodological standards[3] (Reips, under review).

For example, Reips (2002b) describes a number of frequent 'configuration errors' that may lead

---

[3] Currently, some of these may pass the review process, because many reviewers are no exemption to the situation, which in many ways parallels the time when statistical testing was introduced to research.

to (often undetected) methodological and/or ethical problems. *Configuration errors I and II* describe how just by design of the Web study confidential participant data may accidentally end up in the wrong hands.[4] In the case of *configuration error V* one of the legitimate responses to a question is erroneously preselected. This happens easily if the experimenter thinks in terms of usual procedures in paper-based questionnaires, where a range of categories is listed for the participant to choose from. For example, 'below 10' may end up as a preselected option in a drop-down menu near a question that asks the participant to select his or her age. Rather than simply transferring the question format from paper to the Internet, it is important to preselect an option that says something like 'please choose here' that returns a 'missing' code unless the participant makes a choice. If, however, a legitimate answer is preselected the experimenter will be unable to distinguish real data from those that result when participants fail to respond to the item – quite a frequent behaviour on web pages. In the example above, the sample would appear to contain a surprisingly high number of children.

How to counter the problem of frequent flaws in Internet-based studies? There are at least three solutions: one way will be to include Internet-based research methodology in curricula. This requires colleges to employ teachers who are savvy of Internet-based research and change their course programmes. A second possibility is the use of software that automatically implements techniques that maximize the advantages of Internet-based data collection and prevent the experimenter from pitfalls arising from the particularities of conducting research via the Internet – for example WEXTOR for web experiments (see Reips and Neuhaus, 2002, and http://psych-wextor.unizh.ch/wextor/en/). Finally, the knowledge about Internet-based research methods needs to be disseminated to an interested readership – an aim this section of this book will hopefully meet.

[4] In routinely checking requests for enlistment of studies on the Web experiment list, the Web survey list, and the Web Experimental Psychology Lab the author frequently encounters instances of these configuration errors. Most recently, he was able to download a data set that included personal information from 65,000 participants in a study. These data, including email addresses, were also accessible to spammers.

The current chapter is structured in a step-by-step fashion, guiding the reader through the various stages of setting up and conducting a web experiment. Apart from *general issues* the relevant steps begin with *planning, generating,* and *pre-testing* an experiment. They continue with *recruitment* and *monitoring,* then *analysis and archiving.*

General issues

It should be noted that conducting Internet-based experiments requires knowledge of and familiarity with methodological and technological particularities that relate to the networked structure of the Internet. Not only is it necessary to understand the basics of HTML (the code web pages are made of), the workings of the TCP/IP protocol (the Internet's address and transportation system), and the meshwork of technical components in a web experiment (e.g. Reips 2000; Schmidt, Chapter 29 this volume) but how participant behaviour changes in Internet-based studies.

Much of what we know from research in computer-mediated communication (CMC) can be applied to the participant situation in Internet-based research, because in this type of research participants use a computer by definition (even if it is a mobile phone or PDA). At least five issues are critical in CMC:

1. cues transmitted,
2. bandwidth,
3. cost constraints,
4. level and type of anonymity,
5. synchronicity and exclusivity (Joinson 2003).

In comparison to a laboratory situation and depending on the exact Internet service used, Internet-based research may thus primarily differ on these dimensions, and suffer or profit from their impact on the information transmission and on the psychology of the participant.

One of the reasons why the methods of Internet-based experimenting became widely used is the *fundamental asymmetry of accessibility* (Reips 2002c, 2006b). What is programmed to be accessible from any Internet-connected computer in the world will surely also be accessible in a university laboratory, but what is programmed to work in a local computer lab may not necessarily be accessible anywhere else. A laboratory experiment cannot simply be turned into a web experiment, because it may be programmed in a stand-alone programming language and lack Internet-based research methodology, but any web experiment can also be used by connecting the laboratory computer to the Internet. Consequently, it is a good strategy to design a study web-based, if possible.

Web-based methods offer several benefits to the researcher (for summaries, see Birnbaum 2004; Reips 2000, 2002c). The main advantages are that:

- it is possible to test large numbers of participants quickly;
- it is possible to recruit large heterogeneous samples and people with rare characteristics (Schmidt 1997); and
- web-based methods are more cost-effective in administration, time, space, and labor in comparison with laboratory research.

Methodological analyses and studies reveal that web-based methods are usually valid (e.g., Krantz and Dalal 2000) and sometimes even generate higher quality data than laboratory studies (Buchanan and Smith 1999; Reips 2000; Birnbaum 2001). They facilitate research in previously inaccessible areas (e.g., Bordia 1996; Coomber 1997; Rodgers et al. 2001).

Other benefits of web-based methods are

- the ease of access for participants (bringing the experiment to the participant instead of the opposite);
- the ease of access to participants from different cultures, given Internet access and the availability of the Web experiment in the respective languages – for instance, Bohner, Danner, Siebler, and Samson (2002) conducted a study in three languages with 440 women from more than nine countries;
- truly voluntary participation (unless participants are required to visit the Website);
- detectability of confounding with motivational aspects of study participation;
- the better generalizability of findings to the general population (e.g., Brenner 2002; Horswill and Coster 2001);
- the generalizability of findings to more settings and situations because of high external validity – Laugwitz (2001), for instance, was able to show that a colour perception effect in

software ergonomics persisted despite the large variance of conditions of lighting, monitor calibration, etc. in participants' settings;

- the avoidance of time constraints;
- the simultaneous participation of large numbers of participants is possible;
- the reduction of experimenter effects (even in automated computer-based assessments there is often some kind of personal contact, but this is not so in most web-based assessments);
- the reduction of demand characteristics (see Orne 1962);
- greater visibility of the research process (web-based studies can be visited by others, and their links can be published in articles resulting from the research);
- the access to the number of people who see the announcement link to the study, but decide not to participate;
- the ease of cross-mode comparison – comparing results with results from a sample tested in the laboratory;
- greater external validity through greater technical variance; and
- the heightened public control of ethical standards.

In preparation of conducting a web experiment it is important to adhere to good research ethics and Internet etiquette. Ess (Chapter 31 this volume) discusses a number of general principles and issues. Birnbaum and Reips (2005) give a set of recommendations for good practice in all stages of conducting a study via the Internet. They also stress putting dangers from this type of research into perspective, i.e. that 'it is difficult to injure someone via the Web, except by dishonesty, so the fundamental ethical principle for web-based research is honesty' (2005: 488). Their recommendations include:

- keeping up with promises (e.g. regarding renumeration, information);
- avoiding anything that resembles a chain letter, commercial advertising, or spamming;
- taking care of security and confidentiality;
- polite and careful communication with participants and intermediaries (e.g. administrators of mailing lists and newsgroups that are contacted for recruitment).

Generally, the Internet researcher should be aware of the technological basis, i.e. networking, protocols, software, hardware and the resulting technical variance (Reips 2000, 2002b, 2002c; Chapter 29 this volume). One also needs to know that technology may interact with a study's topic and/or participant demography (Buchanan and Reips 2001). Finally, there may be mode effects – participants with computer anxiety will be less likely to join web studies, tests may turn out to need re-validation (Buchanan, Chapter 28 this volume), and response behaviour with a mouse arrow on a web page differs in many ways from response behaviour with a pencil on paper (see Bosnjak 2001; Reips 2002a).

Planning a web experiment

Setting up a web experiment for the first time means an investment. Less so in terms of infrastructure: nowadays it is fairly easy to set up and maintain a web server with web pages on it and record the data in a data base or a log file for later analysis, most new computers come with the necessary software pre-installed.[5] More likely an investment for researchers is to take the time and consider, learn and implement proper methodologies for Internet-based research. Alternatively, one may use a web service that automatically implements these methodologies (see 'Generating a web experiment'). The iScience Server at http://psych-iscience.unizh.ch/ (see Figure 24.2) serves as a portal to a number of such services.

Techniques for handling of dropout

Dropout (attrition) is built into Internet-based research. An Internet scientist can choose

[5] Mac OS X is currently, and has been, particularly comfortable and safe for setting up Internet-based research.

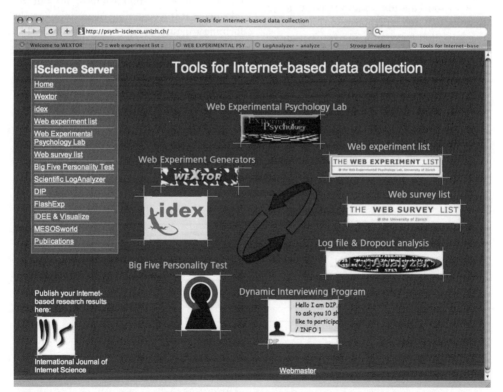

Figure 24.2 Main page of the iScience Server at the University of Zürich (http://psych-iscience.unizh.ch/), with links to web experiment generators (WEXTOR, idex), recruitment portals (Web Experimental Psychology Lab, Web Experiment List, Web Survey List), Scientific LogAnalyzer, DIP, and an online Big Five personality test.

among four strategies of dealing with it: use it, control it, avoid it or suppress it. Reips (2002b) recommends using dropout as a dependent variable and describes how it may be used for detecting *motivational confounding* by looking at dropout curves by experimental condition. If there is higher dropout in one condition, then it can be concluded that the condition is more boring or otherwise less attractive to the participants. Comparisons of experimental conditions on other dependent variables would therefore be hampered by confounding. Figure 24.3 shows dropout curves for two conditions that would indicate motivational confounding, if the experiment were to be conducted in the laboratory.

The *high entrance barrier* or *high hurdle technique* (Reips 2000, 2002d) is a control procedure that can be applied to provoke dropout to happen early and ensure continued participation after someone makes the decision to stay. This means bundling of demotivating factors (i.e. long loading times from large images, long texts) at the very beginning of a web experiment, so visitors with a low motivation for continued participation will likely drop out early. Motivating factors should be implemented increasingly thereafter, enticing participants to continue with the experiment. Reips (2000: 110–111) recommends several measures that are likely to support this strategy:

♦ Tell participants participation is serious, and that science needs good data.

♦ Personalize – ask for an email address and/or phone number.

♦ Tell them you can trace them (via their computer's IP address).

♦ Be credible: tell them who you are, and your institutional affiliation.

♦ Tell them how long the Web experiment will take.

♦ Prepare them for any sensitive aspects of your experiment (e.g. 'you will be asked about your financial situation').

♦ Introduce your experimental manipulation after a warm-up phase.

♦ Tell them what software they will need (and provide them with hyperlinks to get it).

♦ Perform Java, Javascript, and plug in tests (but avoid Active-X).

♦ Make compliance a prerequisite for winning the reward.

Participant dropout during a web experiment can be avoided via the *warm-up technique*. It is based on the observation that most dropout will take place at the beginning of an online study, forming a 'natural dropout curve' (Reips 2002d). A main reason for the initial dropout is the short orientation period many participants show before making a final decision on their participation.

Finally, the most simple and elegant technique of avoiding a large portion of the dropout, namely one that results from mere curiosity, is the *seriousness technique*. Participants are merely asked 'How do you intend to browse the Web pages of this study?' and are given the two options 'I would like to seriously participate now' and 'I would like

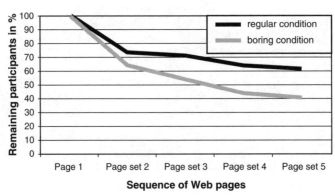

Figure 24.3 Dropout curves for two conditions that differ in attractiveness and may therefore cause motivational confounding if conducted as a laboratory experiment.

to look at the pages only.' By far the largest proportion of those who later drop out will indicate so by choosing the latter option.

Meta-tagging techniques

Meta tags are snippets of information beginning with '<meta' that are located in the 'head' section of the source code of web pages.[6] Meta tags can be used for a variety of tasks, here the focus is on guiding participants' Web browsers, so-called 'proxy caches', and search engines.

The first meta tag displayed in Table 24.2 (<meta name='ROBOTS' content='NONE'>) will keep search engines from indexing pages subsequent to the designated entry page, preventing scores of participants entering on pages where they will be asked for their sex and other delicate questions. The meta tag will be obeyed by most of the indexing requests (called 'robots', 'bots', 'spiders', or 'crawlers') sent by search engines, but unfortunately there are exemptions.

The second meta tag displayed in Table 24.2 keeps caches and proxy servers from serving old

---

[6] The source code of a web page can easily be viewed by choosing the respective option on the 'View' menu in most web browsers.

Table 24.2 Use of meta tags in pages after the entry page of a web study

<HTML>
<HEAD>
<meta name='ROBOTS' content='NONE'>
<meta http-equiv='pragma' content='no-cache'>
<meta http-equiv='expires' content='Thursday, 1-Jan-1991 01:01:01 GMT'>
<TITLE> </TITLE>
</HEAD>
(followed by the body of the web page)

Note. This method can be used to keep search engines from indexing pages subsequent to the first page of a web experiment, and to prevent caches and proxy servers from serving old versions of research materials. (These meta tags are automatically added to pages in web experiments created with WEXTOR.)

versions of research materials. As will be seen in 'Pre-testing of web experiments' below, it rarely happens that a newly designed web experiment is without errors. During pre-testing, a study needs to be updated frequently, as new versions are developed and tested again. The pragma no-cache meta tag tells servers that function as intermediary storages spaces (caches) for web content flowing in and out of institutions to skip the content of the current web page. If the content were stored (cached) old versions of the research materials would go to all participants using computers in the respective institution until the cache is updated. Here the third meta tag is asked to play its role. It suggests that the content of the current web page has long expired, triggering servers to delete the content from their caches.

Other techniques to consider in the planning stage

Password techniques (e.g. Schmidt 1997) provide web experimenters with ways of limiting access to the study that may be important, for example if a clearly defined sample is required. If passwords are individualized there is a very good chance that indeed the individual using the password is the person it was given to. On an even higher level of security, passwords expire after they have been used once. Some ways of conducting Internet-based experiments, for example in online panels, automatically include authentication (see Göritz, Chapter 30 this volume).

Birnbaum and Reips (2005) recommend building some redundancy and cross-examination into questionnaires on the Internet. A number of techniques can be used to re-examine answers before sending people to different questionnaires. For example, Javascript can provide cross-examination when a person clicks a link to identify his or her gender. If the person clicks 'male', the prompt opens a new box with the question, 'is it correct: you are male?' requiring a yes/no answer before the person can continue. A similar check cross-examines those who click 'female'. A similar technique is to provide HTML links that provide a 'second chance' to link to the correct gender. The person who clicks 'male' then receives a page with a link to click 'if you are female', which would send the person to the female questionnaire, where there is also a chance to revert.

One of the most helpful measures in planning an experiment is to visualize the design. WEXTOR, the experiment generator for web and lab described further below, includes visualization of experimental designs and procedures. In addition, it automatically implements most of the techniques discussed above.

Generating a web experiment

The simplest way to create a web experiment is by creating a series of web pages or parallel strings of web pages that contain experimental materials (instructions, pictures, sound files etc.) and measures (scales made from radio buttons etc.) and implement random distribution to conditions. There are a number of options for the latter:

1. Client-side scripting, meaning that a snippet of script code is included with a web page and tells the web browser to run certain processes on the participant's computer as soon as the web page is opened and the script code is started;

2. Server-side scripting, by which all of the computing is done on the server and only the result is sent to the client;

3. HTML-based pseudo-randomization, for example the birthday technique, where participants select their experimental conditions by mouse-clicking on their birthday or -month (e.g., Birnbaum and Reips 2005).

Client-side versus server-side

Client-side scripting can be an advantage, in that it frees the server from making calculations and having a lot of traffic delays sending information back and forth. It can also be a disadvantage, if the participant computer or web browser does not understand the scripting language or has it turned off. At a time when Internet Explorer used an error-prone version of a Javascript compiler and some people had turned it off (fearing to allow other people's programs to run on one's own machine), Schwarz and

Reips (2001) found that Javascript caused a higher rate of dropout in web studies compared with methods that did not require client-side scripting. However, in recent years, Javascript is so prevalent in websites that few people have it turned off.

By doing the computing on the server side, one guarantees that any participant at a web browser can complete the study (Schmidt 2000 see Chapter 29, this volume). On the other hand, server-side programs may introduce delays as the participant waits for a response from the server. When there are delays, some participants may become frustrated or think the program has stopped, and may terminate their participation. There are, however, certain tasks that can and should only be done by the server, such as saving data or handling issues of security (e.g., passwords, using an exam key to score a test, etc.). Perl and PHP are the two most popular programming languages that can be used to write server-side programs. Of course, to program a server, one needs to have access to the server and the knowledge to program it.

An example for client-side scripting is Javascript, it is used by WEXTOR, the (web) experiment generator that will now be described.

WEXTOR

There are not many software systems for Internet-based experimenting yet, and even some of these few are not freely available. In the following a system is presented that integrates many of the Internet-based research methods discussed in this chapter. WEXTOR is a free web service that serves as an experiment generator and teaching tool on the WWW that can be used to design laboratory experiments and web experiments in a guided step-by-step process. Web services are WWW-based 'software', a new type of interactive application that is accessible wherever one has access to the Web. WEXTOR dynamically creates the custom-tailored web pages and Javascripts needed for the experimental procedure, and it provides the experimenter with a print-ready visual display of the experimental design. WEXTOR flexibly supports complete and incomplete factorial designs with between-subjects, within-subject, and quasi-experimental factors as well as mixed designs.

The software implements both client-side and server-side time measurement and contains a content wizard for the creation of interactive materials as well as dependent measures (visual analogue and radio button scales, multiple choice items, etc.) on the experiment pages, but its aim is not to replace a full-fledged HTML editor. Several of the methodological features described in this chapter that are specifically necessary in web experimental design have been implemented in the Web-based tool, for example the seriousness check technique and the high hurdle technique. WEXTOR is platform-independent, so it runs on any type of operating system in any type of web browser, as long as Javascript is supported. The created web pages can be uploaded to any type of web server, where data may be recorded in log files or via database, or they can simply be served from the WEXTOR website, where hosting of the experiment is offered as an additional service.

Many human factors considerations are built into WEXTOR, and it automatically prevents several methodological pitfalls in Internet-based research. This web service uses non-obvious file naming, automatic avoidance of page number confounding, Javascript test and redirect functionality to minimize drop-out and randomized distribution of participants to experimental conditions. Different from the usual practice in many offline studies, demographic questions by default are asked at the *beginning* of a web experiment, because this procedural sequence has been shown to produce less dropout and better data quality (Frick et al. 2001), and asking contact information early reduces the ethical and procedural problem that participants who drop before providing the information can't be contacted. WEXTOR also provides for optional assignment to levels of quasi-experimental factors, optional client-side response time measurement, randomly generated continuous user IDs for enhanced multiple submission control, and it automatically includes the meta tags described in this chapter. In addition, WEXTOR implements the warm-up technique for dropout control mentioned above and provides for interactive creation of dependent measures and materials. The hosting facility supports download of the original log file (raw data) and a data file ready for import to Excel or SPSS.

WEXTOR's current version may be used freely for educational and non-commercial uses. Its web address http://psych-wextor.unizh.ch/wextor/.

Pre-testing a web experiment

Internet-based experiments offer so many advantages in comparison with laboratory experiments (Reips 2000, 2002c) that some of the challenges may easily be overlooked. In Internet-based studies the experimenter's control over the participant setting is much reduced. Often, it is not possible or desirous to communicate with the participants during the experiment. As a result, there may be questions or misunderstandings with some participants regarding the experimental materials or procedure that can not be corrected, and technical errors may go undetected. (Chapter 29, this volume). Consequently it pays off to invest much time and effort into pre-testing the Internet-based experiment.

Experiments generated with WEXTOR offer the usability advantages of self-containment of the experiment files and a one-to-one correspondence of files and folders to screens and conditions.

Procedures to apply in pre-testing

Pre-testing begins with repeated tests by the experimenter. These should be conducted with different web browsers, and possibly from different computers. Most important are checks of the correspondence between surface and deep structure of the web pages: Is a response to a radio button recorded as intended and consistent throughout the study materials, e.g. will a 'Yes' response to the question 'Do you wear glasses?' always be recorded as '1', even if the order of responses is varied?

Pre-tests are best to be continued with a small number of friends and acquaintances who will not hesitate in helping the experimenter in improving the study. Other possible procedures include unobtrusive observation of volunteers in the lab and trying the experiment on different web browsers and on a number of computers with a variety of monitors. The final stage of pre-testing should always be a limited 'live' online test.

What to discover and how to prevent

Some issues are frequently discovered during pre-testing, others may go undetected until the data from test trials are downloaded and analysed.

If text fields or text areas are used as input devices on web pages, it may sometimes be forgotten to limit the number of characters that can be filled into these spaces. In the case of asking for a percentage it makes sense to limit the number of digits to three. Otherwise, the data file may later contain entries saying 'one hundred' or '58.99999' or even a ten page excerpt from a googled dissertation on the 'understanding of the probability format'. Such entries cause a lot of work and possibly methodological issues during analysis, and may in some cases even crash the Web server. The content of a text field can be limited by using the maxlength tag 'e.g. writing 'maxlength=3' for limiting input to three characters'.

Web experimenters are forced to make some critical decisions while planning their experiments. It is necessary to decide if a certain functionality is worth the additional technologies, potential methodological disadvantages and the psychological impact that is associated with it. For example, Schwarz and Reips (2001) found certain Javascript routines to dramatically increase the dropout in a web experiment by comparing a non-Javascript version with an otherwise identical version of the experiment that used these routines. Furthermore, Buchanan and Reips (2001) showed that sampling may get biased depending on technology used in Internet-based research. In their web-based personality study (also see Chapter 28 this volume) they observed respondents to indicate a higher level of education in the non-Javascript version, probably indicating a higher awareness of Internet security problems in more educated persons. They also observed personality differences between people accessing the study on a Mac versus a PC.

A problem that can occur if one codes the web pages used in an Internet-based experiment by hand: the value used for missing data is the same as a code used for real data (Birnbaum and Reips 2005). For example, the authors describe a survey on the Web in which the participants were asked to identify their nationalities. In this case, the same code value (99) was assigned to India as to the preselected 'missing' value. If not warned, the researcher might have concluded that there had been a large number of participants from India.

Recruitment

Internet-based studies appeal to many people, because they are curious about research or they see it as a way to learn something about their psychological self, as in self-tests in magazines. It has been found that material incentives are not of highest importance when recruiting participants (Göritz 2006), but small incentives do have an impact on dropout and data quality (Frick et al. 2001).

How to find participants for Internet-based experiments? Of course, one may always contact family and friends. However, these people often have particular knowledge and motivations towards the experimenter, they may bias the results. As such, this group is ideal for pre-testing the experiment (see above), because they will likely tend to talk freely about the technical problems they encountered or the way they (mis)understood the instructions.

Web portals and lists

Free recruitment is available from portals and lists for web experimentation. The largest such sites are 'Psychological Research on the Net' by John Krantz (http://psych.hanover.edu/research/exponnet.html) and the criterion-searchable web experiment list shown in Figure 24.4 (http://genpsylab-wexlist.unizh.ch/) (Reips and Lengler 2005). Entries can be requested via a web form, each entry will be checked by an administrator who is knowledgeable in Internet-based research. The highly awarded Web Experimental Psychology Lab (http://tinyurl.com/dwcpx [Reips 2001], founded in 1995, is the oldest website for recruitment of participants and resembles a virtual laboratory. More web experiments can be found at the Online Social Psychology Studies site by Scott Plous (http://www.socialpsychology.org/expts.htm).

Mailing lists, forums, and newsgroups

One very effective way of recruiting participants are emails to mailing lists or messages to forums and newsgroups of people who don't mind

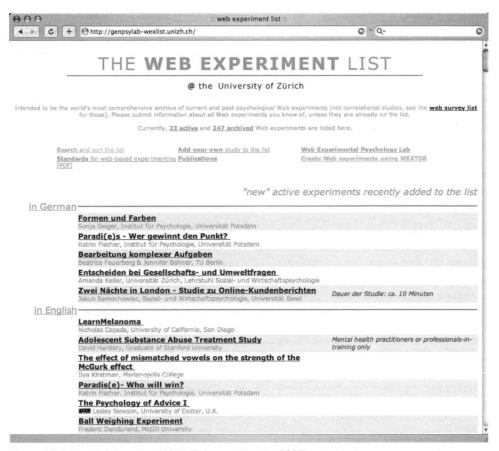

Figure 24.4 The Web Experiment List (Reips and Lengler 2005), entry page.

receiving messages with information about studies for participation (e.g. mailing lists for psychology students). At a conference on decision-making (SPUDM, Zürich 2003), the author heard an interesting paper on the first day of the conference, and decided to replicate that study overnight. He was able to include the results in his talk on the second day of the conference, in order to demonstrate the efficiency of web-based research (see Reips 2006b). Within eight hours, complete data sets from 162 participants (compared to 64 in the original study) were recorded in the Web experiment, most of which were recruited via three mailing lists.

Recruiting via mailing lists, forums or newsgroups should be done with care, because some of the readers/recipients of the recruitment message may see it as spam. Therefore, it is best to ask the group's moderator or administrator for permission to send the message or even convince the moderator to endorse it and send it.

Participant pools and online panels

Often, researchers are keen on knowing who is part of the population they are sampling from. Well-kept participant pools or online panels are a way of approximating this goal, and potentially having hundreds or thousands of motivated participants ready for participation (see Göritz 2006 and Chapter 30 this volume; Reips, 2000). However, there is discussion about panellists getting used to or even burnt out on the panel. They may know how to work their way through studies without paying much attention to it or even abuse the panel, in particular if they receive incentives for being a member. Also, panels likely become targets for manipulation attempts, if they are used in market research (Geissler *et al.* 2005).

Search engines and banners

Meta tags (see Planning of web experiments) can be used for recruitment via search engines. This type of recruitment is only suitable in long-term studies, though, because it usually takes several weeks for the search engines to become aware of the new web pages and list them. Two meta tags to be used are shown in the following example of a fictitious study targeted at people with protanopia, a particular subtype of red–green colour blindness.

<HTML>

<HEAD>

<META NAME='keywords' CONTENT= 'protanopia, red-green colour blindness, survey, experiences, psychology, research>

<META NAME='description' CONTENT= 'research psychologists invite people with protanopia (a particular variant of red-green colour blindness) to complete a survey of their experiences that we hope will contribute to understanding this condition'

<TITLE>Survey of persons with protanopia </TITLE>

</HEAD>

<BODY>

(Further information on the study and a link to the study would be placed here)

</BODY>

</HTML>

Compared with other methods of recruitment, search engines are usually much less effective. This also applies to banner advertisements, which recently are often linked with search engines. Because banners usually represent commercial advertising, a banner ad for a scientific study is hard to distinguish from a deceptive link to a commercial message. Tuten *et al.* (2000) found banner advertisement to be ineffective in web research.

Offline recruitment

An alternative to any type of Internet-based recruitment is traditional recruitment offline. If an experiment is conducted both in the laboratory and on the Web, random allocation to the mode condition is essential for acceptable mode comparisons.

Multiple site entry technique

Depending on the chosen recruitment strategy the sample will be more or less heterogeneous and more or less known. In some cases, experimenters may prefer a homogeneous sample, for example to reduce error variance, or to better be able to compare results with past research (*ca.* 80 per cent of samples in psychological research are made up from young psychology undergraduates: Reips 2000). In other cases, sample composition may simply be not important to experimenters, or only as a distant boundary condition to generalizability. A heuristic strategy that can be used to estimate the influence of sampling and self-selection effects on results is the *multiple site entry technique* (Reips, 2000, 2002c). One implements the technique by advertising the Web experiment in different locations on the Internet or offline. Each link is formed differently, to later allow the separation of sources during data analysis. For example, the URL of the Web experiment could be amended by '. . . index.html?source=studlist' in the version that is sent to a student mailing list, and by '. . . index.html?source=sport' if a link is placed on a website dealing with sports. In the resulting data file there will be a column 'source', in which each participant has one entry 'studlist' or 'sport' or else.

Monitoring a web experiment

Once a web experiment is up and running and participants have been recruited it is important to monitor the study. For example it is necessary to note one's own test accesses to the website in order not to let these contaminate the data. Ways of doing this are:

◆ Record ones own IP address each time one logs into the experiment, unless one has a static IP

◆ Record the times of one's test accesses

◆ Whenever one logs on, one enters 'TEST' or similar into one of the text fields on the web pages belonging to the Web experiment.

With all of these methods, the critical data sets can be identified during preparation of data analysis.

Free tracking services are available for monitoring site traffic, and with a little bit of installation work of freeware this can be done on one's web server too. Monitoring site traffic allows the researcher to detect sudden changes in the frequency of visits to the Web experiment. For example, a press note or a link from a highly frequented site may increase number of visits, and technical problems may be the reason for a sudden decrease in traffic. Detailed monitoring of site traffic allows further diagnoses. Via the so-called 'referer' information it can be determined how much traffic came from which website linking to the experiment. Tracking services sometimes offer visualization of location of participants. Figure 24.5 shows a participant's location, visiting time, provider, type of connection, operating system, type of web browser, screen resolution, screen colour depth and Javascript status on a map, here near the White House in Washington, DC. At maximum resolution of the zoomable map the picture would show two buildings.

Data analysis

Data handling and analysis in Internet-based experimenting requires particular attention to three phenomena: *requests and entries not coming from human participants, technical variance,* and *high rates of non-response*. These are never or only rarely seen in offline studies and may therefore easily be overlooked by experimenters untrained in Internet-based research.

Inclusion criteria

In psychological offline studies it would be regarded as highly unusual to consider data entries coming from other than human participants. At most, an experimenter needs to be aware of test trials by staff members and take appropriate steps to keep those from contaminating the data. In Internet-based experimenting, the latter remains an issue, and the former requires attention as well. In many web-based studies the majority of unique requests and entries do not come from human participants, but from bots (spiders, crawlers or robots)[7]

[7] Examples are msnbot, googlebot, spider.search.ch, npbot, f-bot testpilot, jetbot, turnitinbot, psbot, HenryTheMirageRobot, Gaisbot, Nutch-bot, Exabot, WISEnutbot, itbot.

mentioned above, including bots from search engines or those looking for specific exploits in a web server. The prevalence of bot requests has increased from *ca.* 6 per cent in 1996 to *ca.* 65 per cent in 2005, and the number of different types of robots has increased almost eightfold (Reips, 2007).

Visits generated by bots, test visits by experimenters, and other undesirable entries in the data file need systematic attention before the analysis process, resulting in the following check list of inclusion criteria:

1. no visits by experimenters
2. no visits generated by bots
3. no multiple visits from same IP address (e.g. exclude every entry after first one)
4. if identification of log entries by one participant depends on IP addresses only, then it is recommended to exclude entries from Internet providers with dynamic IP addressing (Reips 2002c)
5. no 'snoopers', only include those that make it beyond the experiment's start page (or are assigned to an experimental condition)
6. only those that answer a certain number/ percentage of items or those items that are essential to the study.

The respective entries are marked and not included in the main data analysis. Because the number of cases is often substantial, it should become a standard procedure to report figures for types of in- or exclusions at the beginning of the Results section in articles about Internet-based research (Reips 2002c).

Checking for technical variance

Technical variance is built into Internet-based research (Reips, 2000; Schmidt, Chapter 29, this volume) and may influence results if it is overlooked (Reips 2002b). Conducting experiments over the Internet involves a worldwide network of cables, routers (computers at cross-points of Internet traffic), plugs, and participants use a wide range of computers, monitors, keyboards, mice, speakers or ear phones, web browsers and net connections. Technical variance is not necessarily of disadvantage, its impact depends on the study design (Reips 2000, 2002b, 2002c, see also Chapter 25 and 29, this volume). In an

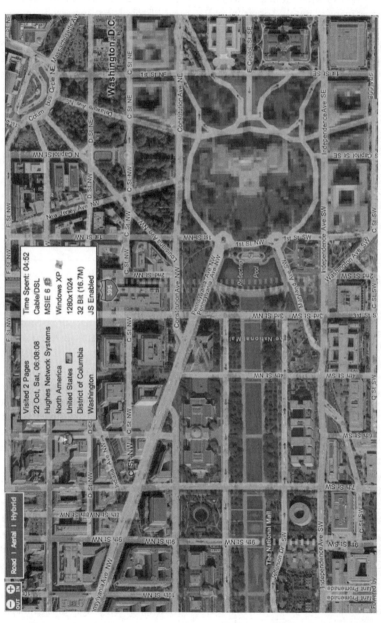

Figure 24.5 Visualization of participant location (left of information box) and additional information offered by tracking services for website traffic.

Internet-based experiment tight experimental control and the associated dependency on a fully functional and unbiased equipment available in a laboratory are replaced by random technical variance, and therefore generalizability of the resulting effects is increased, if the error noise allows for the detection of effects (Reips, 2000). In support of the trade-off, Krantz (2000, 2001) has shown effects of technical variance in computer monitors and Plant *et al.* (2003) alerted the scientific community to how choice of mouse may affect response timing in psychological studies.

Incompatibilities with particular technologies may systematically bias the sample. Buchanan and Reips (2001) showed that technology used in the implementation of an Internet-based study may interact with demography or personality. In their study they showed that the average education level was higher in a web-based test if no JavaScript was used, and that Mac users scored significantly higher on Openness than PC users. Consequently, one of the first standard procedures in data analysis in Internet-based research is to compare dropout and values on dependent variables for the different types of technologies the HTTP protocol provides information for. These are the type of operating system, type and version of web browser and connection speed. Additional information can be collected via JavaScript or Java, e.g. JavaScript compatibility, screen resolution, colour depth. These control analyses for technical variance can be combined in one analysis step with those from the multiple site entry technique (see above).

Dropout analysis

Internet-based research in general shows high rates of non-response. These may therefore be used as dependent variables (Reips 2000, 2002b, 2002c).

A dropout analysis is typically carried out with all included data sets plus those mentioned in inclusion criterion 6 above. The point of a dropout analysis is to see where and how many participants left the study (e.g. for use as a dependent variable) and to find out whether the dropout may be systematic. If dropout coincides with an experimental manipulation, then motivational confounding may be at work and the study is severely compromised (Reips 2000, 2002b), see Figure 24.3 above.

What dropout rate to expect? Musch and Reips (2000) found that the average dropout rate in Internet-based experiments is 34 per cent (median = 35 per cent), with a range from 1–87 per cent. The large range suggests that there are other motivational factors that influence dropout, some of which were since examined empirically. Musch and Reips showed that the completion rate of Internet-based experiments was 86 per cent if some form of reward (individual payments or lottery prizes) was offered, up from 55 per cent without such rewards. In a follow-up experiment Frick *et al.* (2001) tested the influence of two variables on dropout: placement of assessment of personal information and information about financial incentives for participation on dropout rates. They found the following dropout rates: 5.7 per cent for participants who were asked personal information and information about financial incentives at the beginning of the experiment, 21.9 per cent in the condition with both at the end. Dropout rates in the other conditions were in-between (13.2 and 14.9 per cent).

Dropout can be analysed and reported in four ways that differ in information: overall, as rates, and curves, and as trees (Reips 2002b, Reips and Stieger 2004). *Overall* dropout is the percentage of total participants in a study that did not complete it. Usually this information will not suffice in manuscripts submitted to good journals where editors and reviewers are aware of the high rates of non-response in Internet-based research. Dropout *rates* provide summary information by experimental condition, just as in the example above this paragraph. Often this level of information will suffice in reports. Figure 24.3 shows the visually most informative way of reporting dropout, as *curves*. Dropout curves provide information by condition about dropout over time and – if these are marked – in relation to particular events during the experiment. Finally, dropout can also be reported in a *tree* format, see Figure 24.6. Such dropout trees are generated by the Scientific LogAnalyzer (Reips and Stieger 2004), online they can interactively be manipulated by mouse-clicking the '–'– and '+'–squares to expand and collapse the tree's branches. A branch shows the absolute numbers of participants, and their proportion relative to the mother branch, that chose to visit the web page.

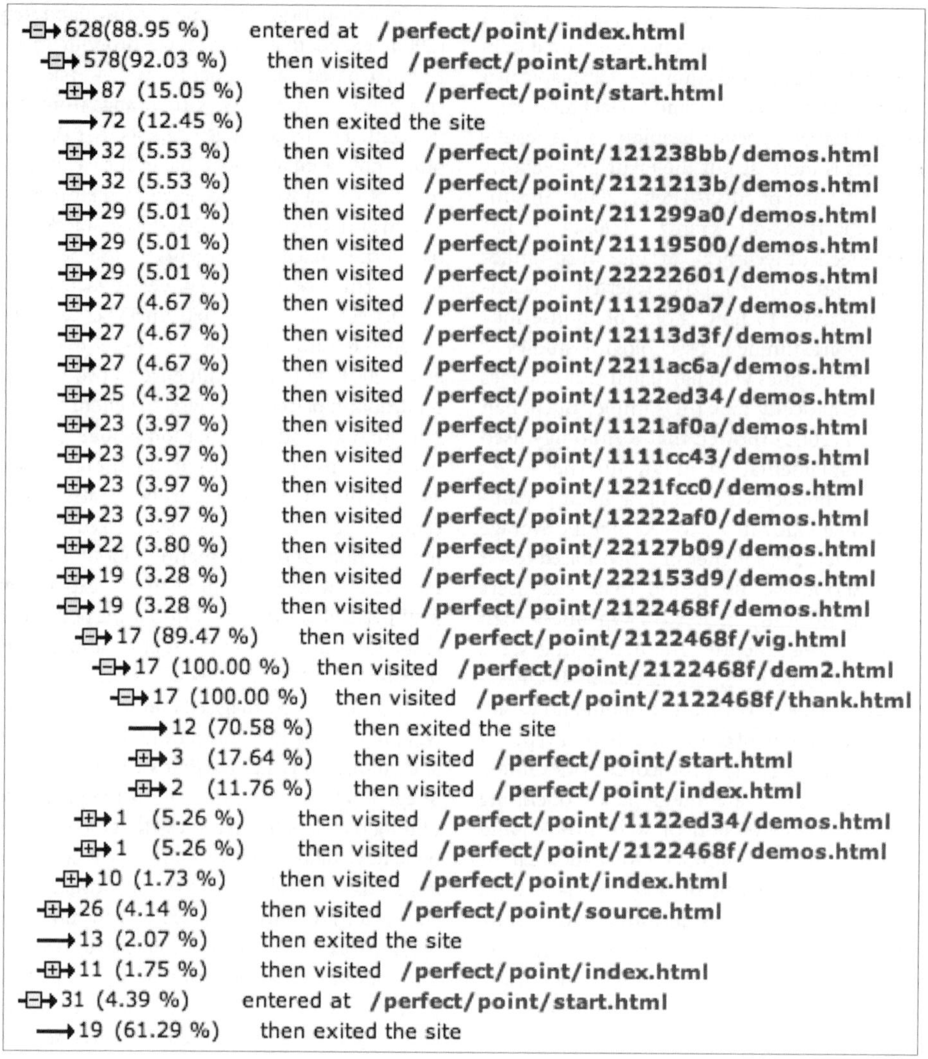

```
⊟▸ 628(88.95 %)      entered at  /perfect/point/index.html
 ⊟▸ 578(92.03 %)      then visited  /perfect/point/start.html
  ⊞▸ 87 (15.05 %)     then visited  /perfect/point/start.html
  ──▸ 72 (12.45 %)    then exited the site
  ⊞▸ 32 (5.53 %)      then visited  /perfect/point/121238bb/demos.html
  ⊞▸ 32 (5.53 %)      then visited  /perfect/point/2121213b/demos.html
  ⊞▸ 29 (5.01 %)      then visited  /perfect/point/211299a0/demos.html
  ⊞▸ 29 (5.01 %)      then visited  /perfect/point/21119500/demos.html
  ⊞▸ 29 (5.01 %)      then visited  /perfect/point/22222601/demos.html
  ⊞▸ 27 (4.67 %)      then visited  /perfect/point/111290a7/demos.html
  ⊞▸ 27 (4.67 %)      then visited  /perfect/point/12113d3f/demos.html
  ⊞▸ 27 (4.67 %)      then visited  /perfect/point/2211ac6a/demos.html
  ⊞▸ 25 (4.32 %)      then visited  /perfect/point/1122ed34/demos.html
  ⊞▸ 23 (3.97 %)      then visited  /perfect/point/1121af0a/demos.html
  ⊞▸ 23 (3.97 %)      then visited  /perfect/point/1111cc43/demos.html
  ⊞▸ 23 (3.97 %)      then visited  /perfect/point/1221fcc0/demos.html
  ⊞▸ 23 (3.97 %)      then visited  /perfect/point/12222af0/demos.html
  ⊞▸ 22 (3.80 %)      then visited  /perfect/point/22127b09/demos.html
  ⊞▸ 19 (3.28 %)      then visited  /perfect/point/222153d9/demos.html
  ⊟▸ 19 (3.28 %)      then visited  /perfect/point/2122468f/demos.html
    ⊟▸ 17 (89.47 %)    then visited  /perfect/point/2122468f/vig.html
     ⊟▸ 17 (100.00 %)  then visited  /perfect/point/2122468f/dem2.html
      ⊟▸ 17 (100.00 %)  then visited  /perfect/point/2122468f/thank.html
       ──▸ 12 (70.58 %)   then exited the site
       ⊞▸ 3  (17.64 %)    then visited  /perfect/point/start.html
       ⊞▸ 2  (11.76 %)    then visited  /perfect/point/index.html
    ⊞▸ 1  (5.26 %)     then visited  /perfect/point/1122ed34/demos.html
    ⊞▸ 1  (5.26 %)     then visited  /perfect/point/2122468f/demos.html
   ⊞▸ 10 (1.73 %)      then visited  /perfect/point/index.html
  ⊞▸ 26 (4.14 %)      then visited  /perfect/point/source.html
  ──▸ 13 (2.07 %)    then exited the site
  ⊞▸ 11 (1.75 %)      then visited  /perfect/point/index.html
 ⊟▸ 31 (4.39 %)      entered at  /perfect/point/start.html
  ──▸ 19 (61.29 %)    then exited the site
```

Figure 24.6 A dropout tree created with Scientific LogAnalyzer (Reips and Stieger 2004).

Archiving of web experiments

One of the chief advantages of Internet-based experimenting is the public visibility and availability of the materials. Reips (2002c) defines public archiving as one of sixteen standards for Internet-based experimenting: 'The experimental materials should be kept available on the Internet, as they will often give a much better impression of what was done than any verbal description could convey.' (p. 254). Archived web experiments may serve readers of publications as helpful illustration, given that the web address is provided in the publication. Furthermore, archived web experiments may be used as teaching materials for students in psychology and related sciences. Finally, materials that are available online can be used by researchers to easily create variants of experiments, significantly speeding up the research cycle (Reips 2000; Birnbaum 2004).

Internet-based experiments can be archived in the Web experiment list that was earlier described as a website for the recruitment of participants. The site contains a search function that will generate lists of web experiments by field, status (active versus archived), time, language (English or German), and combinations thereof.

Conclusion

It has been noted that Internet-based experimenting is neither similar to nor different from laboratory experiments (Reips 2002c). There are a number of particular methodological issues that may be general or associated with the tasks of planning, generating, pre-testing, recruitment, monitoring, analysis, and archiving of an experiment. Some of the issues are related to technology and its proper use (see Chapter 29, this volume), some to experimental design (see Chapter 25, this volume) others are due to the psychological effects of various aspects of the vast social sphere that continues to build up: the Internet.

Hopefully, this chapter provides a helpful collection of techniques, recommendations, and pointers to those who will soon conduct their first Internet-based experiment, and to those who continue to learn about research on the Internet.

References

Birnbaum, M. H. (2001). A Web-based program of research on decision making. In U.-D. Reips and M. Bosnjak (eds), *Dimensions of internet science* (pp. 23–55). Lengerich: Pabst Science.

Birnbaum, M. H. (2004). Human research and data collection via the internet. *Annual Review of Psychology 55*, 803–832.

Birnbaum, M. H. and Reips, U.-D. (2005). Behavioral research and data collection via the internet. In R. W. Proctor and K.-P. L. Vu (eds), *The handbook of human factors in Web design* (pp. 471–492). Mahwah, NJ: Erlbaum.

Bohner, G., Danner, U. N., Siebler, F. and Samson, G. B. (2002). Rape myth acceptance and judgments of vulnerability to sexual assault: an internet experiment. *Experimental Psychology 49*(4), 257–269.

Bordia, P. (1996). Studying verbal interaction on the internet: the case of rumor transmission research. *Behavior Research Methods Instruments and Computers 28*(2), 149–151.

Bosnjak, M. (2001). Participation in non-restricted web surveys: a typology and explanatory model for item non-response. In U.-D. Reips, and M. Bosnjak, (eds), *Dimensions of Internet Science* (pp. 193–208). Lengerich: Pabst Science.

Brenner, V. (2002). Generalizability issues in internet-based survey research: implications for the internet addiction controversy. In B. Batinic, U.-D. Reips and M. Bosnjak (eds.), *Online social sciences* (pp. 93–114). Seattle, WA: Hogrefe and Huber.

Buchanan, T. and Reips, U.-D. (2001). Platform-dependent biases in online research: do Mac users really think different? In K. J. Jonas, P. Breuer, B. Schauenburg and M. Boos (eds), *Perspectives on internet research: Concepts and methods*. Retrieved 27 December 2001 from http:\\server3.uni-psych.gwdg.de/gor/contrib/buchanan-tom.

Buchanan, T. and Smith, J. L. (1999). Research on the internet: validation of a world-wide web mediated personality scale. *Behavior Research Methods Instruments and Computers 31*(4), 565–571.

Coomber, R. (1997). Using the Internet for survey research. *Sociological Research Online 2*(2), 14–23.

Erlanger, D., Feldman, D., Kutner, K., Kaushik, T., Kroger, H., Festa, J., *et al.* (2003). Development and validation of a web-based neuropsychological test protocol for sports-related return-to-play decision-making. *Archives of Clinical Neuropsychology 18*(3), 293–316.

Frick, A., Bächtiger, M. T. and Reips, U.-D. (2001). Financial incentives, personal information and dropout in online studies. In U.-D. Reips and M. Bosnjak (eds), *Dimensions of internet science* (pp. 209–219). Lengerich: Pabst Science.

Geissler, H., Loewe, G., Göritz, A., Irmer, C., Baierl, M., von Heesen, B., Schwabl, T., Wagner, F. and Knapp, F. (2005). *Current relevance and future of online access panels*. Panel discussion at 7th General Online Research (GOR) Conference, March 21–23, Zürich Switzerland. Available at http://gor.de/gor05/podiumsdiskussion_en.htm.

Göritz, A. S. (2006). Incentives in web studies: methodological issues and a review. *International Journal of Internet Science 1*(1), 58–70.

Horswill, M. S. and Coster, M. E. (2001). User-controlled photographic animations, photograph-based questions and questionnaires: three instruments for measuring drivers' risk-taking behavior on the internet. *Behavior Research Methods, Instruments and Computers 33*, 46–58.

Joinson, A. (2003). *Understanding the psychology of Internet behaviour: Virtual worlds, real lives*. Houndmills: Palgrave Macmillan.

Krantz, J. H. (2000). Tell me, what did you see? The stimulus on computers. *Behavior Research Methods, Instruments and Computers 32*, 221–229.

Krantz, J. H. (2001). Stimulus delivery on the web: what can be presented when calibration isn't possible. In U.-D. Reips, and M. Bosnjak, (eds.), *Dimensions of internet science* (pp. 113–130). Lengerich: Pabst Science.

Krantz, J. H. and Dalal, R. S. (2000). Validity of web-based psychological research. In M. H. Birnbaum (ed.), *Psychology experiments on the internet* (pp. 35–60). San Diego, CA: Academic Press.

Laugwitz, B. (2001). A web-experiment on colour harmony principles applied to computer user interface design. In U.-D. Reips and M. Bosnjak (eds), *Dimensions of internet science* (pp. 131–145). Lengerich: Pabst Science.

Musch, J. and Reips, U.-D. (2000). A brief history of web experimenting. In M. H. Birnbaum (ed.), *Psychological experiments on the internet* (pp. 61–88). San Diego, CA: Academic Press.

Orne, M. T. (1962). On the social psychology of the psychological experiment: with particular reference to demand characteristics and their implications. *American Psychologist 17*, 776–783.

Plant, R. R., Hammond, N. and Whitehouse, T. (2003). How choice of mouse may affect response timing in psychological studies. *Behavior Research Methods, Instruments and Computers 35*(2), 276–284.

Reips, U.-D. (2007). Collecting data in surfer's paradise: internet-mediated research yesterday, now and tomorrow. Manuscript submitted for publication.

Reips, U.-D. (2006a). Internet-basierte Methoden [Internet-based methods]. In F. Petermann and M. Eid (Hrsg.), *Handbuch der Psychologischen Diagnostik* (pp. 218–225). Göttingen: Hogrefe.

Reips, U.-D. (2000). The web experiment method: advantages, disadvantages and solutions. In M. H. Birnbaum (ed.), *Psychological experiments on the internet* (pp. 89–114). San Diego, CA: Academic Press.

Reips, U.-D. (2001). The web experimental psychology lab: five years of data collection on the internet. *Behavior Research Methods, Instruments and Computers 33*, 201–211.

Reips, U.-D. (2002a). Context effects in web surveys. In B. Batinic, U.-D. Reips and M. Bosnjak (eds.), *Online social sciences* (pp. 69–79). Seattle, WA: Hogrefe and Huber.

Reips, U.-D. (2002b). Internet-based psychological experimenting: five dos and five don'ts. *Social Science Computer Review 20*(3), 241–249.

Reips, U.-D. (2002c). Standards for internet-based experimenting. *Experimental Psychology 49*(4), 243–256.

Reips, U.-D. (2002d). Theory and techniques of web experimenting. In B. Batinic, U.-D. Reips and M. Bosnjak (eds.), *Online social sciences* (pp. 229–250). Seattle, WA: Hogrefe and Huber.

Reips, U.-D. (2006b). Web-based methods. In M. Eid and E. Diener (eds.), *Handbook of multimethod measurement in psychology* (pp. 73–85). Washington, DC: American Psychological Association.

Reips, U.-D. and Lengler, R. (2005). The web experiment list: a web service for the recruitment of participants and archiving of internet-based experiments. *Behavior Research Methods 37*, 287–292.

Reips, U.-D. and Neuhaus, C. (2002). WEXTOR: a web-based tool for generating and visualizing experimental designs and procedures. *Behavior Research Methods, Instruments and Computers 34*, 234–240.

Reips, U.-D. and Stieger, S. (2004). Scientific log analyzer: a web-based tool for analyses of server log files in psychological research. *Behavior Research Methods, Instruments and Computers 36*(2), 304–311.

Rodgers, J., Buchanan, T., Scholey, A. B., Heffernan, T. M., Ling, J. and Parrott, A. (2001). Differential effects of ecstasy and cannabis on self-reports of memory ability: a web-based study. *Human Psychopharmacology: Clinical and Experimental 16*(8), 619–625.

Schmidt, W. C. (1997). World-wide web survey research: benefits, potential problems and solutions. *Behavior Research Methods, Instruments and Computers 29*, 274–279.

Schmidt, W. C. (2000). The server-side of psychology web experiments. In M. H. Birnbaum (ed.), *Psychological experiments on the internet* (pp. 285–310). San Diego, CA: Academic Press.

Schulte-Mecklenbeck, M. and Neun, M. (2005). WebDiP: a tool for information search experiments on the world-wide web. *Behavior Research Methods 37*(2), 293–300.

Schwarz, S. and Reips, U.-D. (2001). CGI versus Javascript: a web experiment on the reversed hindsight bias. In U.–D. Reips and M. Bosnjak (eds.), *Dimensions of internet science* (pp. 75–90). Lengerich: Pabst Science.

Tuten, T. L., Bosnjak, M. and Bandilla, W. (2000). Banner-advertised web surveys. *Marketing Research 11*(4), 17–21.

CHAPTER 25

Designing online experiments

Michael H. Birnbaum

Theory

A psychological theory is a set of statements that satisfies five philosophical criteria. The first criterion is that the proposed explanation can be used to deduce the behavioural phenomena to be explained. For example, suppose someone asks, 'Why is bread good to eat?' We use operational definitions of 'bread' and 'good to eat' in order to link these concepts to the world of observations. Define a substance as 'good to eat' if more than 75 per cent of 1-year-old rats given access to water and that substance under standard lab conditions survive on this diet for six months. Define 'bread' as what comes from the market in a package marked 'Weber's bread'.

The following argument illustrates deduction:

P1: Bread is made of cyanide

P2: Everything made of cyanide is good to eat

C: Bread is good to eat.

If both premises are true, then the conclusion follows by logic. This example illustrates deduction. It also shows that one can deduce a true conclusion from false premises. Thus, a true conclusion does not 'prove' the premises to be true. However, if the conclusion is false, at least one of the premises must be false. For this reason, we speak of *testing* theories rather than 'proving' them.

The second criterion of a theory is that it should not be meaningless. The empirical meaning of a statement is equivalent to the set of specifiable, testable implications. If a statement has no testable implications, then it is devoid of empirical meaning. Unfortunately, many so-called theories, like psychoanalysis, are built on entities such as subconscious conflicts that cannot be observed empirically. By definition, the contents of a mind are private, which means that only one mind can observe the contents of that mind. By definition, the contents of the subconscious mind cannot be observed by that mind itself. Unless concepts are linked to events and objects that can be observed, measured, or tested, they fall outside the world of science and into the pages of poetry. So, if we theorize that all rats have subconscious conflicts and whenever an organism has a subconscious conflict, bread is good to eat, we have a deductive theory, but one that is meaningless, except for its conclusion.

The third criterion of a theory is that it is predictive. In principle, if one knew the theory in advance, one could have predicted the behaviour or events to be explained. A system that is deductive, meaningful and predictive is a called a *predictive system*. An example of a predictive system is Kepler's laws of astronomy. Kepler postulated that planets travel in elliptical orbits around the sun with the sun at one focus and that they sweep out equal areas in the ellipse in equal time. He also assumed that the squares of the periods of revolution are proportional to the cubes of the average distance from the sun.

From these three assumptions and geometry, one can make many predictions of the future. For example, one can accurately predict the positions of Sun, Moon, Venus, Mars, Jupiter and Saturn as seen against the stars for any date in the next thousand years, predict when these planets will go into retrograde motion, and predict eclipses of both sun and moon.

Although a predictive system can be valuable, we usually want more from an explanation than just prediction. The fourth criterion of an explanation is that it should contain a causal argument. That means that the explanation provides a way, in principle, to control the behaviour to be explained. In other words, we can predict the results of manipulation of variables. Whereas correlational relationships allow one to predict ongoing behaviour, it is causal statements that allow us to predict what would happen if we introduced changes in the system. Kepler's astronomy does not predict what would happen if we could change the mass of the sun, for example, but Newton's laws do allow such 'what if' calculations.

The difference between correlation and causation is the difference between prediction and control. Both are useful concepts, but they lead to different uses and they can appear to be opposites. For example, a correlational survey would find that people who received antibiotics last year are more likely to be dead this year than people who received no antibiotics last year. So we can use antibiotics to predict death. However, by means of an experiment, we can randomly assign people with infections to two groups, one that receives antibiotics and the other receives a placebo. The results of such studies show that antibiotics cause a reduction in the death rate. So, we find that receiving antibiotics is positively correlated with death in surveys and receiving antibiotics is negatively correlated with death in an experiment. Although paradoxical, there is no contradiction.

Both correlational and causal relations are interesting and useful, even when they seem to say the opposite things. Suppose you have a life insurance company; you sell insurance that pays out when a person dies. Before you sell someone insurance, you could ask if they have been taking antibiotics. If yes, you do not want to sell them insurance because they are likely to die.

However, if you already sold a policy to a client and that person becomes sick, you would like them to take antibiotics because it causes a reduction in the death rate.

Correlation has been called the 'instrument of the Devil' when evidence of a correlation is used to argue for a causal conclusion. For example, it has been shown that students in small classes do worse in high school than students in large classes. What class in a high school is the smallest? It is the class for 'special education' students, students who have behaviour problems or are mentally retarded. So, small classes size is correlated with poor performance. Those who misunderstand this correlation argue that all classes should be large, because larger classes get better performance.

The fifth criterion of an explanation is that it is general. A general explanation for one phenomenon can also be used to explain other phenomena. Put another way, the premises of an explanation have the characteristics of scientific laws, statements that hold in general. This means that good explanations lead to new testable implications. Although we can't change the mass of our sun in practice, we can bring objects of different masses together on earth and measure the forces between them. Newton's laws are considered very general because they can be used to make many predictions for objects in space and on earth including falling bodies, trajectories of cannon balls, collisions and thousands of other calculations useful in mechanical and structural engineering.

Experiments test among theories

Psychology is the study of alternative explanations of behaviour. The purpose of an experiment is to test between alternative theories. Students sometimes talk about trying to 'prove' a theory, as if they could somehow show that a theory is 'true'. Such thinking leads to bad research. For example, consider a person who thinks that bread is good to eat because it is made of cyanide, and everything made of cyanide is good to eat. To 'prove' the theory, the person eats bread and argues that this 'proves' the theory true, since if the theory is true, bread should be good to eat. I assume the reader can think of some different experiments that would refute these premises.

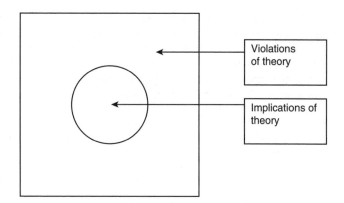

Figure 25.1 Set representation of results of studies to test a theory. It is argued that people should devise experiments to look outside the circle of implications of the theory.

Consider the diagram of Figure 25.1. Suppose the box represents the universe of all possible results of experimental tests, and the elements inside the circle represent data that would be consistent with the theory. Many researchers conduct experiments to look inside the circle; that is, they look for confirmations of their theory. For example, a person might eat bread to 'prove' their theory. Instead, what researchers should do is devise experiments to test the theory by looking outside the circle; that is, they should look for results that would refute the theory. For example, test if bread is really made of cyanide and test if cyanide is really good to eat.

The fallacy that one should try to 'prove' one's theory leads to bad research. To avoid this problem, I suggest that researchers think in terms of comparing at least two theories, and searching for implications to test that would be consistent with one theory and that would refute the other. If both theories qualify as theories of the behaviour in question, one should be able to devise a test that would refute at least one of them.

Example: expected value theory

Suppose a researcher wanted to test the theory that people evaluate gambles by their expected values. In particular, let $G = (x_1, p_1; x_2, p_2; \dots ; x_n, p_n)$ represent a gamble with n mutually exclusive, exhaustive outcomes, which pay cash prizes of x_i with probabilities, p_i, where $\sum_{i=1}^{n} p_i = 1$. Let $G \succ F$ represent systematic preference for gamble G over gamble F. The concept of systematic preference is given the following operational definition: we can reject the hypothesis that the probability of

choosing F over G is less than or equal to 1/2 in favour of the hypothesis that the probability of choosing G over F exceeds 1/2.

Now suppose we have the following theory:

$$G \succ F \Leftrightarrow U(G) > U(F) \Leftrightarrow EV(G) > EV(F), \quad (1)$$

$$EV(G) = \sum_{i=1}^{n} p_i x_i \quad (2)$$

According to this theory, increasing the expected value of a gamble should improve it. So, consider the following two gambles: $G = (\$100, 0.5; \$0, 0.5)$, a 'fifty-fifty' gamble to win either $100 or $0, and $F = (\$100, 0.2; \$0, 0.8)$, a 20 per cent chance to win $100 otherwise $0. The expected values are $EV(G) = \$50$ and $EV(F) = \$20$, so people should prefer G over F. Indeed, few people would not prefer G to F. Similarly, people should prefer $G = (\$100, 0.5; \$0, 0.5)$ over $F' = (\$50, 0.5; \$0, 0.5)$ because $EV(G') = \$50$ and $EV(F') = \$25$. We could continue doing such 'confirming' experiments for years and continue to find evidence consistent with ('for') EV. However, such research is not very informative – it is like eating bread to prove that bread is made of cyanide. To test a theory, we should think of how it can be refuted rather than on how it might succeed.

According to EV theory, two gambles with the same EV should be equally attractive. Consider $G = (\$100, 0.5; \$0, 0.5)$ and $F'' = (\$55, 0.5; \$45, 0.5)$ which both have EV = $50. When these gambles are presented for comparison, most people prefer

$F'' \succ G$, so this result is not consistent with EV. Indeed, most people prefer $45 for sure to gamble G, which has a higher EV of $50. By looking for exceptions to the theory, we find that EV is systematically violated. Not only do people prefer 'safe' gambles with lower EV over 'risky' ones with higher EV, it has been known for about 300 years that people even prefer a small amount of cash to certain gambles with infinite expected value.

The St Petersburg paradox involves a gamble with infinite expected value. Suppose we toss a coin and if it is heads you win $2, but if it is tails we toss again, and now if heads occurs you win $4, but if tails, we toss again. If the coin shows heads on the third toss, the prize is $8, but if tails, we toss again. The prize for heads doubles each time tails occurs. When heads shows the prize is given and the game ends. This gamble has infinite expected value because

$$EV = \sum_{i=1}^{\infty} p_i x_i = \frac{1}{2}\$2 + \frac{1}{4}\$4 + \frac{1}{8}\$8 +$$
$$= 1 + 1 + 1 + \quad = \infty \qquad (3)$$

However, most people say they would prefer $10 for sure over a chance to play the game once. This preference was known as a 'paradox' because mathematicians who accepted expected value as the 'fair' price of a gamble also thought it was reasonable to prefer a small amount of cash over this gamble.

Bernoulli (1738) proposed expected utility (EU) as an explanation for the St Petersburg paradox and showed how this theory could explain why people might buy and sell gambles and insurance. Expected utility of gamble $G = (x_1, p_1; x_2, p_2; \ldots ; x_n, p_n)$ can be written as follows:

$$EU(G) = \sum_{i=1}^{n} p_i u(x_i) \qquad (4)$$

where u(x) is the utility of a cash prize of x. Whereas x is the objective cash value, Bernoulli assumed that utility of money is not linearly related to money. In particular, Bernoulli suggested that utility is a logarithmic function of wealth. If so, the St Petersburg gamble has finite expected utility (equivalent to the utility of $4)

even though it has infinite EV. Bernoulli showed how EU implies a poor person would not be ill-advised to sell a 50–50 chance to win 20,000 ducats to a rich man for less than its expected value, and how a rich person should be happy to buy it for that price.

Expected utility theory is a theory that is more general than EV in the sense that EV is a special case of EU in which $u(x) = x$. Therefore, evidence consistent with EV is also consistent with EU, but EU can predict phenomena that cannot be explained by EV. This situation is shown in Figure 25.2. In a sense, it seems almost 'unfair' in that there is no observation that can refute EU in favour of EV but there are results that can refute EV in favour of EU.

Allais' paradoxes refute EU

Allais (1953) proposed two paradoxes that violated EU. These were combinations of choices that cannot be reconciled with either EU or EV. They are known as the 'constant ratio' paradox and the 'constant consequence' paradox. The constant ratio paradox can be illustrated by the following two choices (Birnbaum, 2001):

A:	B:	
0.5 to win $100	sure to win $50	89.5%
0.5 to win $0		chose B
C:	D:	
0.01 to win $100	0.02 to win $50	34.9%
0.99 to win $0	0.98 to win $0	chose D

According to expected utility, $A \prec B \Leftrightarrow C \prec D$ From EU, $A \prec B \Leftrightarrow EU(A) < EU(B)$. $EU(A) = 0.5u(\$100) + 0.5u(\$0)$; $EU(B) = u(\$50)$. Because most people choose B over A, we have, $0.5u(\$100) + 0.5u(\$0) < u(\$50)$. Multiplying both sides of the inequality by 0.02, we have $0.01u(\$100) < 0.02u(\$50)$; subtracting $0.01u(\$0)$ from both sides, we have, $0.01u(\$100) < 0.02u(\$50) - 0.01u(\$0)$; adding $0.99u(\$0)$ to both sides, we have, $0.01u(\$100) + 0.99u(\$0) < 0.02u(\$50) + 0.98u(\$0)$, which holds if and only if $C \prec D$. Consistent with Allais' paradox, which has been replicated many times (Kahneman and Tversky 1979), Birnbaum (2001) found that most people violate EU. Indeed, of the 743 participants who

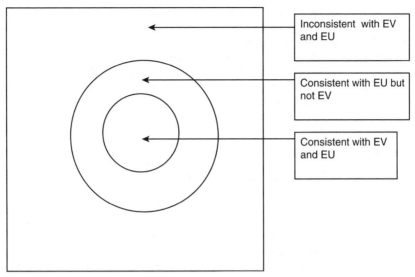

Figure 25.2 Relationship between EV and EU theories. EV is a special case of EU.

made both choices, 426 (57 per cent) chose $A \prec B$ and $C \succ D$ and only 20 (2.7 per cent) had the opposite pattern of preferences.

The constant consequence paradox can be illustrated with the following two choices:

E: 15 to win $500,000 85 to win $11	F: 10 to win $1,000,000 90 to win $11	70% chose F
G: sure to win $500,000	H: 10 to win $1,000,000 85 to win $500,000 05 to win $11	29% chose H

Birnbaum (in press) tested 200 participants who made each choice twice. According to EU theory, $E \prec F \Leftrightarrow G \prec H$. This implication follows from EU because $E \prec F \Leftrightarrow EU(E) < EU(F)$. $EU(E) = 0.15u\,(\$0.5M) + 0.85u\,(\$11) < EU(F) = 0.1u(\$1M) + 0.9u(\$11)$. We can subtract $0.85u\,(\$11)$ from both sides and add $0.85u(\$0.5M)$, so, $u(\$0.5M) < 0.1u(\$1M) + 0.85u(0.5M) + 0.05u(\$11)$, which holds if and only if $G \prec H$. Therefore, the fact that significantly more than half the participants preferred F over E and significantly more than half preferred G over H is inconsistent with EU theory.

In the illustration of Figure 25.2, the Allais paradoxes fall outside the circles representing EU and EV theory. These results refute both EV and EU. A number of theories were proposed to account for the Allais paradoxes and new paradoxes have been devised to test among these new theories. The point of this example is to illustrate how the Allais paradoxes led to refutation of EU theory.

To pick up the modern thread of this story, which includes the development of prospect theories to account for the Allais paradoxes (Kahneman and Tversky, 1979; Tversky and Kahneman, 1992), see Birnbaum (2004a, b, 2005a, b; in press 2006; Birnbaum & Bahra, in press). Although the prospect theories can explain the classic Allais paradoxes, Birnbaum showed that a series of 'new' paradoxes refute both versions of prospect theory. The new paradoxes remain consistent with a model by Birnbaum, which awaits the invention of new paradoxes to refute it.

Between versus within-subjects designs

Suppose we want to manipulate a variable to determine its causal effect. For example, to test EV theory, we might want to compare gambles with equal EV that have different variances.

This could be done by randomly assigning participants to groups that receive different levels of the variable or by manipulating the variable for each person. When we randomly assign people to different groups, it is called a *between-subjects design*, and when the same person receives two or more levels of the independent variable, it is called a *within-subjects design*.

Confounded contexts

It is important to realize that when the dependent variable of an experiment is a judgement, within and between-subjects designs often yield opposite conclusions. For example, Birnbaum (1999) randomly assigned participants to two groups, each of which was instructed to judge 'how big' a number was. One group judged the size of the number 9, and the other group judged the number 221. It was found that 9 is significantly 'bigger' than 221. Of course, no single participant ever said that 9 is greater than 221, but by the rules of between-subjects designs, an experimenter would conclude that 9 is 'subjectively' bigger than 221. This conclusion should seem silly, but some investigators studied less obvious examples to draw odd inferences.

The problem with between-subjects research is that the context for judgement and the stimulus are completely confounded. Although people have seen numbers both larger and smaller than 9 and 221 before participating, they do not have a context for comparison so they must supply it themselves. Apparently, the number 221 brings to mind a context that includes larger numbers (among which 221 seems 'small') compared to the context evoked by the number 9. This example was devised to create a situation in which few would argue that the conclusion is that 9 'really is' subjectively bigger than 221.

There are many different areas of psychology in which between-subjects designs have been used to reach conclusions that are reversed in within-subjects designs. For example, Jones and Aronson (1973) found that respectable victims are rated more at fault for their own rape than less respectable victims. In particular, women described as a 'virgin' or 'married' were rated more blameworthy than those described as 'divorced'. Jones and Aronson theorized that in order to believe in a 'just world', a respectable victim would

not deserve to be raped and therefore she must have done something to deserve it. However, this conclusion is reversed in a within-subjects design. When participants rate both victims or even when they rate both victim and perpetrator, the divorced woman is judged more at fault than the virgin or married woman (Birnbaum 1982).

In the area of human judgement, it has been argued that people 'neglect' base rate, based on the small effects observed when this variable is manipulated between-subjects (Kahneman and Tversky 1979). Similarly, people supposedly fail to distinguish sources of information that differ in validity when making predictions. However, when these variables are manipulated within-subjects, people do attend to base rate and to source credibility (Birnbaum 1976; Birnbaum and Mellers 1983).

Kahneman has argued that the world is 'more like' a between-subjects design than a within-subjects design. So, when results from these designs conflict, he prefers the between-subjects design. If you believe that 9 is subjectively 'bigger' than 221, then you might accept these arguments for between-subjects designs, but if you think otherwise, you should be sceptical of results until they are confirmed or reversed by within-subjects tests.

Dropouts in between-subjects designs

Many investigators are attracted to web research because of the possibility of testing large numbers of subjects. Between-subjects designs require large numbers of participants, so web-based research might seem a good way to do such research. For example, if a person has a simple $2 \times 2 \times 2$ design with 50 participants in each condition, it requires 400 participants. This requirement might exceed a semester's quota an experimenter might be able to receive from the 'subject pool' of many universities. So, experimenters designing between-subjects studies are attracted to the idea of recruiting large numbers of participants via the Web (Birnbaum, 2000; 2004).

However, web-based experiments have higher dropout rates than lab studies. In lab studies, a participant would have to tell someone they are leaving, so there is some social pressure to stick it out to the end. Via the Web, however, people feel no qualms about just clicking another button to leave a boring task (Birnbaum 2004b, c; Birnbaum and Reips, 2005). For studies of who quits, when and why, see Frick *et al.* (2001). See also Reips (2000, 2002a, b; Reips and Stieger 2004) for suggestions about how to minimize dropout and how to analyse the causes of dropout. When there are dropouts, even when dropout rates are equal in all groups, the data can give a misleading picture of the actual effects of a variable.

For example, Birnbaum and Mellers (1989) showed that a treatment intended to improve test scores (e.g., workshops intended to prepare people to take the Graduate Record Exam [GRE]) could appear to be beneficial by simply including a sample test at the end of the treatment. Suppose that the treatment actually lowers test scores, but people who do poorly on the sample test are less likely to take the GRE at the next test date. Because those who would score low decide not to take the test, a harmful treatment could appear to produce a beneficial gain compared to the control group, when all it did was increase the correlation between preparation and the decision to retake the test. See Birnbaum and Mellers for a detailed numerical example of how this can happen.

Dropouts are still a problem but a less serious problem for within-subjects studies because dropping out is not confounded with the manipulated independent variable – everyone who completes the study provides a separate test of the two conditions. To test for the effects of a GRE workshop, each participant receives both the treatment condition and the control condition, with half the participants receiving the two treatments in each of the possible orders. Participants in both groups will receive the sample test. This mixed design allows both between-subjects comparisons for the effects of treatment orders and within-subject comparisons for the effects of the treatment. The test also provides two dependent variables, the test score after the first treatment and the test score following the second treatment.

Representative design

Brunswik (1956) argued that between-subjects designs should be avoided because they create situations that are not representative of the environment to which generalization is desired. He also argued against systematic designs (such as one factor designs and factorial designs), in which the independent variables are made to have zero correlations with other variables and with each other. If people use the distribution of the variables including the variance and covariance of the independent variables, then systematic research creates situations in which important variables influencing judgement will have been fixed to unrealistic levels.

Brusnwik (1956) argued that the only basis for generalization from experiments is the theory of statistical sampling. If we wish to know the mean in a population, for example, and if we have random samples, we can use statistical theory of random sampling to estimate and make inferences about that population mean. Similarly, if we want to know the effect of an independent variable, we should sample that variable randomly as well. If the effect of a variable depends on its levels and correlation with other variables in the textured environment, we need to sample randomly from that environment if we hope to generalize our results to that environment.

Brunswik went on to argue that if for practical reasons we cannot sample randomly, the next best approach is to sample representatively.

For example, suppose we wished to predict the outcome of a district election in the USA, and we know that republicans and democrats favour different candidates. Suppose 55 per cent of those who vote in this district are democrats. It would certainly be unrepresentative if our sample included 90 per cent republicans. To achieve a more representative sample, we can make sure that the percentage of democrats in our sample matches the percentage of democrats among those we think likely to vote. The same could be done for age, gender, and other variables that we think might affect the outcome. Representativeness is not a very precise concept; indeed, random samples are often not representative. Nevertheless, some scientists are content to treat samples that they believe are representative as if they were random and apply the same statistics.

Brunswik theorized that people are sensitive to the ecological validities of cues in perception. The ecological validity of a cue is the correlation between that cue and the distal state of nature that the perceiver is trying to infer. For example, in order to know how large an object is, one must not only use its proximal size (the size of the retinal image), one needs to know its distance.

But there are many cues to distance; among them are binocular disparity (relative separations in the retinal positions of objects in the two eyes), height in the visual field, geometric perspective and many others. Usually, objects that are higher in the visual field are farther away than objects lower in the field. For example, the horizon is both farther away and higher in the visual field than one's foot on the ground, so this cue has ecological validity in predicting distance.

Suppose an experimenter sets up a study to make height in the visual field independent of all the other variables. If so, that experimenter has made the ecological validity of that cue zero, because in a systematic study of one variable, height in the visual field no longer correlates with actual distance or anything else. If people are sensitive to the ecological validity of a cue, and cue intercorrelations, they should stop using height in the visual field in this experiment, because it no longer has validity as a predictor of distance. In other words, when an experimenter makes this variable independent of all other variables, the experimenter has changed the situation to one from which one cannot generalize. To Brunswik, trying to use this experiment to predict the effect of height in the visual field would be like trying to predict an election with a sample of all republicans.

Figure 25.3 shows a diagram of a factorial design in which each level of variable X is paired with each of the five levels of independent variable Y. This makes X and Y uncorrelated. If this correlation is itself an important determinant of behaviour, this experiment sets this variable to a level that may not be representative of the natural ecology of the person tested.

Brunswik proposed using representative design, in which variables were to be studied in the natural environment. Statistical analyses would then be required to tease apart the effects of confounded variables. Unfortunately, these ideas led to the use of multiple linear regression as both a data analysis device and substantive theory of human judgement. Multiple linear regression is

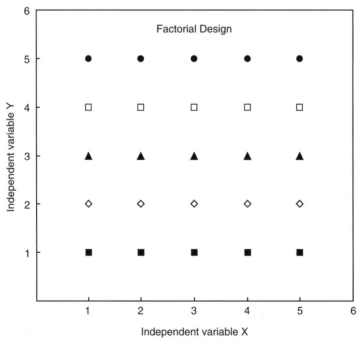

Figure 25.3 Factorial design. Variables X and Y are independent, producing a zero correlation, but suppose the correlation is not zero in the natural environment and suppose it affects behaviour; if so, then this design sets this factor to an unrealistic value.

known to have many flaws, which are exacerbated when variables are correlated. As a data analysis device, it is not well-understood by those who use it, who often draw inappropriate conclusions from its calculations.

It is unfortunate that some people took Brunswik's term, ecological validity, and changed its definition as if it referred to a characteristic of an experiment, a theory, a task, or of results. In Brunswik's terminology, ecological validity is an objective concept and it can be calculated. When this term is misued, it usually refers to someone's mushy intuitive judgement of how 'good' or 'bad' someone's study is with respect to how well it psychologically resembles somebody's idea of some 'real world'. When the term 'ecological validity' is used in reference to an experiment, one can simply rewrite the sentence, 'the study has low ecological validity', as follows: 'this study does not appeal to me'. For another view of representative design and the misuse of terms, see Hammond (1998): http://www.albany.edu/cpr/brunswik/notes/essay2.html.

Brunswik also discussed the use of a hybrid design in which a factorial design is modified by leaving out certain combinations that are unusual, creating correlations among variables. But this approach assumes that presentation of these combinations would affect the responses to other combinations and allows no way to test that proposition. Figure 25.4 shows an example of hybrid design. In this case, it was assumed that the environmental correlation between X and Y is positive, so the experimenter has removed some of the cells of the factorial design that are rare in nature to preserve this correlation in the experiment.

Systextual design

A criticism of representative design is that it assumes an empirical theory to determine a methodological approach that prevents testing of the empirical theory upon which the method is founded (Birnbaum and Veit 1973, 1974; Birnbaum 1975). An alternative approach is to

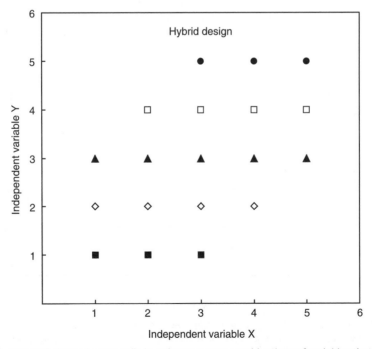

Figure 25.4 Brunswik deleted some cells in order to remove combinations of variables that were not representative of the natural environment, calling the remaining design a 'hybrid' design. This design still holds the correlation between variables fixed.

use systextual design rather than representative design. Systextual design requires systematic manipulation of the research design itself, including all aspects of the environment that are thought important to behaviour. This method allows us to determine if these variables are important and it allows us to use theory supported by evidence to generalize to new environments, including ones not found in nature.

The theory that people are influenced by cue correlations and intercorrelations is a theory that can be tested by systextual design, which involves systematic manipulation of the context in an experiment. Birnbaum (1975) shows how one can use contextual stimuli to manipulate the correlation between two variables while using a factorial design nested within the overall correlation to analyse the effects of the variables, including the correlation. Several studies reported that the effect of a variable can be altered and

even reversed by manipulation of its correlation with a third variable (Birnbaum, 1975; Birnbaum, Kobernick & Veit, 1974; Birnbaum & Veit, 1973).

Figure 25.5 illustrates an example of systextual design that allows an experimenter to manipulate cue intercorrelation and still use a factorial design to analyze the data. In this case, the factorial combinations form a 5 × 5, X by Y factorial design. In order to manipulate the correlation between X and Y, some additional cue combinations are added to create a correlation. To create a positive correlation between X and Y, the experimenter could present stimuli shown in the figure as '+' symbols. To create a negative correlation, the experimenter can present those combinations indicated by '−', and to create a zero correlation while keeping the range and marginal distributions of X and Y the same, the experimenter can alternate presentations of the cue-combinations labeled '−' and '+'.

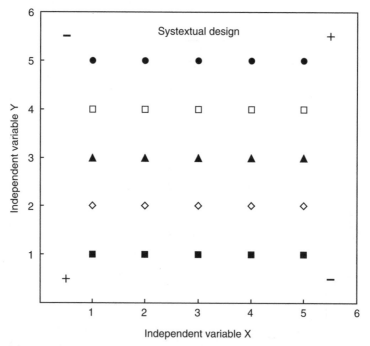

Figure 25.5 Systextual design. In systextual design, additional cells are added to manipulate the correlation between the independent variables. In this case, adding the combinations denoted plus (+) creates a positive correlation between the variables; adding only the combinations marked with a minus (−) creates a negative correlation, and by presenting both sets of contextual combinations, one maintains a zero correlation. Thus, a factorial design can be nested within an overall correlation.

Using this approach, Birnbaum and Veit (1973) showed that the effect of variable X on judgements can be reversed by manipulating its correlation with Y. They manipulated the correlation between the number of dots on a card and the size of the card. Participants were instructed to judge the subjective numerosity of the dots on the cards. Participants saw the size of each card before it was turned over to show the number of dots. When there was no correlation between size and actual number, ratings of numerosity were lower on larger backgrounds, as if people expected more dots on larger cards. When the correlation was positive, this effect was magnified. However, when the correlation was negative, judgements were increased in larger areas, showing contrast with a reversed expectancy.

So Brunswik's empirical assumption is not unfounded: people do react to correlations among variables. However, by means of systextual design we can test theories of the effect of these correlations. It is not sampling but theory that is the basis for generalization. By knowing how correlation affects behaviour, we can develop theories that enable us to generalize to any new environment in which the correlations might be different. Brunswik was right to be concerned that cue intercorrelation can influence behaviour, but his advice to use representative design does not allow the scientist to test that proposition or to generalize to a new situation with any correlation, which is possible via theory combined with systextual design.

Parducci (1995) summarizes a research programme investigating the effects of the spacing and probability distribution of independent variables. He has shown that the relationship between physical stimuli and judgements of those stimuli depends on the stimulus distribution, and that this effect is not linear but follows instead a range-frequency compromise. Indeed, this theory was used by Birnbaum (1982) in his analysis of between-subjects studies.

Another literature that involves a systematic manipulation of context is reviewed and summarized by Rieskamp et al. (2006). They review studies in which the probability of choosing A over B depends on the other alternatives in the choice set.

Ordóñez (1998) manipulated the correlation between price and quality by means of a systextual design. It is usually the case that goods of higher quality come at higher prices, but not always, and when the price is fixed, the components of quality are often negatively correlated. For cameras of the same price, one digital camera might have a higher powered optical zoom and another might have a higher resolution. If these correlations were perfect, one would need only to decide how much to pay for an item and one would automatically find the best quality for that price. But these correlations are not perfect, so buyers must compare products.

Fasolo et al. (2005) studied how consumers use websites that allow comparisons of goods like digital cameras. They investigated consumer behaviour by means of systextual design and found that people indeed adapt to and use the correlation between cues when they use websites to make decisions about consumer goods. This web-based study examined ways that products can be described on the Web, the effects of decision-aiding tools intended to help people make decisions, and the effect of quality intercorrelations on the way people search for information about the goods. They found that people are sensitive to the correlation structure when they search for information about products. Two decision aids were compared: a compensatory model that aggregated the attribute information and an elimination by aspects model that set thresholds for quality on the attributes. In the negative correlation condition, with the compensatory aid, people clicked on more options. With the elimination by aspects aid, people made more attribute clicks with the negative than positive correlation.

Thus, how people search for information to compare products should not be thought of as a fixed process. It is not the case that people look at attributes for each option or compare the options on a given attribute. Instead, the manner in which people search for information depends on the structure of the environment. In particular, the correlation among the attributes as well as the decision aids available influence how people search for information.

Conclusions

There is a famous question that is asked at nearly all doctoral oral examinations. This question is some variation of the following: 'I see that your results agree with the theory that you proposed. What would it have been like if your theory were wrong?' As one might expect, the student who passes the final orals should be able to describe what would have convinced them that their theory was wrong and who can show that the study was capable of disproving that theory. Unless one attends to devising a test of at least one theory (and preferably at least two), the effort may be viewed as another case of a person eating bread.

The results of psychological experiments can and do depend on the experimental designs used to establish causal effects. For example, the effect of a variable can be opposite in within- as opposed to between-subjects designs; indeed, in between-subjects, we find that the number 9 is 'bigger' than 221, whereas within-subjects, everyone says 221 is bigger than 9. Between subjects designs are also vulnerable to experimental dropouts, so use of these methods should be avoided if possible in web research, where participants find it easy to drop in and drop out. If a between-subjects design is absolutely required, it is suggested that the experimenter do everything possible to reduce the dropout rate to an absolute minimum.

The effect of a variable can also be reversed when the correlations among independent variables are manipulated via systextual design. These findings mean that the conclusions one draws need to be restricted to the type of experimental design used until one has established the effects of experimental designs themselves. Whereas the representative design uses the theory of sampling to generalize to a particular context, this article advocates the use of psychological theory to generalize to any context.

Acknowledgements

Support was received from National Science Foundation Grants, SBR-9410572, SES 99–86436, and BCS-0129453.

References

Allais, M. (1953). Le comportement de l'homme rationnel devant le risque: Critique des postulats et axiomes de l'école Américaine. *Econometrica 21*, 503–546.

Bernoulli, D. (1738). Specimen theoriae novae de mensura sortis. *Commentarii Academiae Scientiarum Imperialis Petropoliannae 5*, 175–192. Translated by L. S. (1954). Exposition of a new theory on the measurement of risk. *Econometrica 22*, 23–36.

Birnbaum, M. H. (1975). Expectancy and judgment. In F. Restle, R. Shiffrin, N. J. Castellan, H. Lindman and D. Pisoni (eds), *Cognitive theory* (pp. 107–118). Hillsdale, NJ: Lawrence Erlbaum Associates.

Birnbaum, M. H. (1976). Intuitive numerical prediction. *American Journal of Psychology 89*, 417–429.

Birnbaum, M. H. (1982). Controversies in psychological measurement. In B. Wegener (eds), *Social attitudes and psychophysical measurement* (pp. 401–485). Hillsdale, NJ: Erlbaum.

Birnbaum, M. H. (1999). How to show that 9 > 221: collect judgments in a between-subjects design. *Psychological Methods 4*(3), 243–249.

Birnbaum, M. H. (ed.) (2000). *Psychological experiments on the internet.* San Diego, CA: Academic Press.

Birnbaum, M. H. (2001). A Web-based program of research on decision making. In U.-D. Reips and M. Bosnjak (eds), *Dimensions of Internet science* (pp. 23–55). Lengerich, Germany: Pabst Science Publishers.

Birnbaum, M. H. (2004). Human research and data collection via the internet. *Annual Review of Psychology 55*, 803–832.

Birnbaum, M. H. (2004a). Causes of Allais common consequence paradoxes: an experimental dissection. *Journal of Mathematical Psychology 48*(2), 87–106.

Birnbaum, M. H. (2004b). Methodological and ethical issues in conducting social psychology research via the Internet. In C. Sansone, C. C. Morf and A. T. Panter (eds), *Handbook of methods in social psychology* (pp. 359–382). Thousand Oaks, CA: Sage.

Birnbaum, M. H. (2004c). Tests of rank-dependent utility and cumulative prospect theory in gambles represented by natural frequencies: effects of format, event framing and branch splitting. *Organizational Behavior and Human Decision Processes 95*, 40–65.

Birnbaum, M. H. (2005a). A comparison of five models that predict violations of first-order stochastic dominance in risky decision making. *Journal of Risk and Uncertainty 31*, 263–287.

Birnbaum, M. H. (2005b). Three new tests of independence that differentiate models of risky decision making. *Management Science 51*, 1346–1358.

Birnbaum, M. H. (2006). Evidence against prospect theories in gambles with positive, negative and mixed consequences. *Journal of Economic Psychology, 27*, 737–761.

Birnbaum, M. H. (in press). Tests of branch splitting and branch-splitting independence in Allais paradoxes with positive and mixed consequences. *Organizational Behavior and Human Decision Processes.*

Birnbaum, M. H. and Bahra, J. (in press). Gain-loss separability and coalescing in risky decision making. *Management Science.*

Birnbaum, M. H., Kobernick, M. and Veit, C. T. (1974). Subjective correlation and the size-numerosity illusion. *Journal of Experimental Psychology 102*, 537–539.

Birnbaum, M. H. and Mellers, B. A. (1983). Bayesian inference: combining base rates with opinions of sources who vary in credibility. *Journal of Personality and Social Psychology 45*, 792–804.

Birnbaum, M. H. and Mellers, B. A. (1989). Mediated models for the analysis of confounded variables and self-selected samples. *Journal of Educational Statistics 14*, 146–158.

Birnbaum, M. H. and Reips, U.-D. (2005). Behavioral research and data collection via the Internet. In R. W. Proctor and K.-P. L. Vu (eds), *Handbook of human factors in web design* (pp. 471–491). Mahwah, NJ: Lawrence Erlbaum Associates.

Birnbaum, M. H. and Veit, C. T. (1973). Judgmental illusion produced by contrast with expectancy. *Perception and Psychophysics 13*, 149–152.

Birnbaum, M. H. and Veit, C. T. (1974). Scale-free tests of an averaging model for the size-weight illusion. *Perception and Psychophysics 16*, 276–282.

Brunswik, E. (1956). *Perception and the representative design of psychological experiments*, 2nd edn. Berkeley, CA: University of California Press.

Fasolo, B., McClelland, G. H. and Lange, K. A. (2005). The effect of site design and interattribute correlations on interactive web-based decisions. In C. P. Haugtvedt, K. Machleit and R. Yalch (eds), *Online consumer psychology: understanding and influencing behavior in the virtual world* (pp. 325–344). Mahwah, NJ: Lawrence Erlbaum Associates, Inc.

Frick, A., Bächtiger, M. T. and Reips, U.-D. (2001). Financial incentives, personal information and drop-out in online studies. In U.-D. Reips and M. Bosnjak (eds), *Dimensions of internet science* (pp. 209–219). Lengerich: Pabst Science Publishers.

Hammond, K. R. (1998). Ecological validity: Then and now. Available at http://www.albany.edu/cpr/brunswik/notes/essay2.html, retrieved 12 ed June 2006.

Jones, C. and Aronson, E. (1973). Attribution of fault to a rape victim as a function of respectability of the victim. *Journal of Personality and Social Psychology 26*, 415–419.

Kahneman, D. and Tversky, A. (1979). Prospect theory: an analysis of decision under risk. *Econometrica 47*, 263–291.

Ordóñez, L. D. (1998). The effect of correlation between price and quality on consumer choice. *Organizational Behavior and Human Decision Processes, 75*, 258–273.

Parducci, A. (1995). *Happiness, pleasure and judgment.* Mahwah, NJ: Lawrence Erlbaum Associates.

Reips, U.-D. (2000). The web experiment method: advantages, disadvantages and solutions. In M. H. Birnbaum (eds), *Psychological experiments on the internet* (pp. 89–117). San Diego, CA: Academic Press.

Reips, U.-D. (2002a). Standards for internet experimenting. *Experimental Psychology 49*(4), 243–256.

Reips, U.-D. (2002b). Theory and techniques of conducting web experiments. In B. Batinic, U.-D. Reips and M. Bosnjak (eds), *Online Social Sciences* (pp. 219–249). Seattle, WA: Hogrefe and Huber.

Reips, U.-D. and Stieger, S. (2004). LogAnalyzer- analyze your logfile. Available at http://genpsylab-logcrunsh.unizh.ch/index.html: Retrieved 1 June 2004.

Rieskamp, J., Busemeyer, J. R. and Mellers, B. A. (2006). Extending the bounds of rationality: evidence and theories of preferential choice. *Journal of Economic Literature, 35*, 631–661.

Tversky, A. and Kahneman, D. (1992). Advances in prospect theory: Cumulative representation of uncertainty. *Journal of Risk and Uncertainty, 5*, 297–323.

CHAPTER 26

Gathering data on the Internet

Qualitative approaches and possibilities for mixed methods research

Claire Hewson

Introduction

This chapter first outlines the scope for implementing qualitative data-gathering techniques on the Internet, considering the tools, technologies and procedures available, their advantages and disadvantages (compared with each other and with traditional approaches) and some ethical issues which emerge. Possibilities for conducting interviews, observation and document analysis on the Internet are considered, these having been identified as the main tools of data collection used by qualitative researchers (Mann and Stewart 2000). In the course of the chapter, specific procedures and technologies will be described, with reference to web resources (such as free software, databases, etc.) which may be of use to the qualitative researcher. A precise and robust distinction between qualitative and quantitative research is not easily derived (Mann and Stewart 2000), but for current purposes qualitative approaches are seen as characterized by an emphasis on gathering rich,

elaborate, meaningful, language- or image-based data amenable to a 'thick' interpretive description. Quantitative approaches in contrast are characterized as those which aim to generate numerical data amenable to statistical analysis, with an emphasis on generalizability, validity and reliability. Qualitative researchers are essentially concerned with questions about how people construct meanings, and how these meanings may vary over different historical, cultural and individual contexts. Political, social and action/change-oriented strategies may often be integral to qualitative approaches (e.g. feminist research; action research). Qualitative researchers also tend to recognize and welcome subjectivity as part of the research process, emphasizing the importance of researcher reflexivity. Quantitative researchers, on the other hand, tend to strive for objectivity and aim to derive context-free generalizations which cut across historical and cultural boundaries. While the methods described in the present chapter (interviews, observation, document analysis) may be applied in a more qualitative or quantitative manner (it is probably most useful to view qualitative and quantitative approaches as opposite poles of a continuum), interest here is in a fully qualitative research orientation, as just characterized. After a thorough consideration of the range of qualitative research techniques which the Internet can support, the chapter concludes with some comments on the scope for conducting mixed methods research on the Internet. Mixed methods approaches often combine both qualitative and quantitative techniques, and are becoming increasingly advocated by social science researchers (e.g. Johnson *et al.* 2004). The benefits of adopting a mixed methods approach will be further considered in the final section of this chapter. Quantitative methods (e.g. structured surveys, experiments, structured observation), though integral to mixed methods approaches, are not considered in any depth in the present chapter, since they are well-covered elsewhere in the current volume.

Online interviews

Tools, technologies and procedures

Synchronous approaches

Traditionally, interviews are conducted face-to-face (ftf) or via telephone (Mann and Stewart 2000). These approaches are *synchronous*, in that they take place in real time. Conducting synchronous interviews via the Internet is possible using online 'chat' facilities, such as Internet Relay Chat (IRC). This allows users to log on to a server and communicate with others in a text-based conversational environment, typically referred to as a chat room. Individuals communicate by typing in text, which is then displayed in a discussion window, viewable by all participants. On a practical level, both researcher and interviewee must have access to the relevant equipment (a computer and Internet connection), appropriate software program (IRC client, which enables connection to an IRC server), and the necessary experience and skills needed to be able to communicate via this medium. A number of IRC clients are available, either freely or commercially; for example, the popular 'mIRC' (available at http://www.mirc.com/), though a one-off payment ($20, at the time of writing) is required in order to continue using this software

after the 30-day trial period. Other IRC clients, including some 'freeware' (meaning no payment is required) packages, are listed and available for download at the very useful 'Tucows' website (http://www.tucows.com).[1] Online synchronous chat is also supported by several other more general software packages, such as Virtual Learning Environments (VLEs). Both the freely available, open source VLE 'Moodle' (http://www.moodle.org), and the more expensive, commercial package 'WebCT' (http://www.WebCT.com)[2] allow users to take part in synchronous online discussion sessions.

Chat rooms tend to involve discussion amongst groups of several participants, though many also provide scope for 'going private', thus supporting dyadic interactions. An alternative option for one-to-one (and perhaps multi-user) discussions, however, is offered by Instant Messaging (IM) software. Here, users who are logged on at the same time are able to send messages rapidly back and forth, thus creating what may be considered a close approximation to a real-time conversation. Both conversational partners will need to have appropriate software installed on their computer; free IM packages include Microsoft's MSN Messenger for Windows (available at http://messenger.msn.com/), and ICQ ('I Seek You', available at http://www.icq.com/) which supports both Windows and Macintosh platforms.

The range of technologies described above makes conducting both one-to-one and larger 'focus group' style interviews online feasible (focus groups are interviews involving more than one participant, moderated by the researcher). A number of researchers to date have reported making use of these Internet technologies to support interview-based approaches, with differing levels of success. Davis *et al.* (2004) report a study looking at gay mens' experiences of seeking sex via the Internet, with particular focus on

[1] Tucows provides information about a large range of software resources: searching the website for 'IRC clients' should bring up a list of those currently available.

[2] At the time of writing, WebCT is in the process of merging with what has to date been the other main commercially available VLE – Blackboard – with plans to continue trading under the Blackboard brand name (see: http://www.blackboard.com/webct/merger/index, retrieved 6 February 2006).

their awareness of, attitudes towards, and practice of safe and risky sex. These researchers used IRC style software to carry out one-to-one online synchronous interviews in private chat rooms in 'Gay.com'. Though the procedure was somewhat successful, in that participants were able to log on and engage in discussion with the researcher (probably aided by the fact that they were already experienced Internet users), Davis et al. report finding the data generated by this method impoverished and limited, due to the tendency for superficial, non-elaborate and brief exchanges. Madge and O'Connor (2002), on the other hand, report greater success. In contrast to Davis et al.'s approach of using an existing chat room environment, Madge and O'Connor set up their own synchronous discussion forum, on a web server, specifically designed for the purpose of supporting their 'Cyberparents' research project. Participants were recruited from an existing online community of new and soon-to-be parents (at http://www.babyworld.co.uk), and online focus groups were conducted after volunteers had received and installed the necessary software for accessing the researchers' discussion forum. Madge and O'Connor report that the online focus groups were successful in generating rich, elaborate data, in which participants were forthcoming in sharing their views, experiences and feelings relating to issues surrounding childbirth and parenting. Possible reasons for the different experiences of these researchers are explored further below.

The possibilities for conducting online synchronous interviews, as described above, does of course impose the constraint that any discussion must proceed in entirely text-based format. Thus the types of non-verbal (e.g. body language) and paralinguistic (e.g. tone of voice) cues which are typically present in ftf contexts are not available in the online interview (the implications of which are discussed later). Technologies do exist, though, for incorporating audio and video capabilities into online real-time chat, thus allowing possibilities for creating what may be the closest approximation to a ftf interview without direct spatial proximity (see for example Apple's iSight at www.apple.com). However, at present many Internet users are unlikely to have ready access to the equipment necessary for implementing such an approach, i.e. a microphone and speakers (for audio), and a webcam (for video), and this will thus severely restrict the types of samples that can be obtained using this method. Furthermore, the use of audio and video in online communication is at present hampered by a range of technical difficulties, which makes the approach currently unfeasible for conducting online interviews (see also Chapter 29, this volume). These problems include low reliability and sound/image quality, due to the need to transfer large amounts of data using relatively limited bandwidths (for most users at least),[3] which can lead to 'packet loss' (Apostolopoulos 2001), and produce jerky video and inaudible sound (Hewson et al. 2003). Even assuming the availability of a high-speed Internet connection, data transmission can still be impeded by the unpredictable effects of the volume of network traffic, and the resulting fluctuation in bandwidths that this can cause. The impact of varying data transmission rates in online communications using audio and video has been explored by Yoshini et al. (2001), in a context which has relevance for online interview approaches. These researchers conducted online clinical assessment interviews, using both low (128 kilobits/s) and high (2 megabits/s) bandwidths, and found that the high bandwidth online-assessment interviews generated greater agreement with ftf interviews than did the low bandwidth assessment interviews. In the low bandwidth condition, raters reported problems with the audio and video quality, and the near impossibility of observing facial expressions (Yoshini et al. 2001). While many Internet users in the UK will now likely have Internet connection speeds of greater than 128 kilobytes/s, many will not yet have speeds of 2 megabytes/s. However, increasingly fast Internet connection speeds are clearly becoming more available, and at decreasing cost.

---

[3] 'Bandwidth' refers to the amount of data that can be transferred in a fixed time, usually measured as bytes (or kilobytes, or megabytes) per second. Broadband is becoming increasingly widespread, compared to the previously common dial-up connection, which uses a standard phone line and has comparatively limited bandwidth. Broadband companies are now offering as standard bandwidths up to 2 megabytes/s, though the typical UK broadband user is likely to have a bandwidth nearer 512 kilobytes/s (costing from around £15 per month). Cable Internet access can offer even higher bandwidths, up to as much as 24 megabytes/s.

As well as bandwidth issues, other factors may influence the ability to transfer audio and video data reliably via the Internet. Firewalls, for example, can prevent data transmission. Also, the technical specification of a user's local computer can have an impact, with relatively high processing speeds and high-quality hardware (e.g. webcam, monitor), being needed to produce good quality images and sound. The upshot of all these considerations is that, at present, incorporating sound and video into online interviews is not advisable, except possibly in well-controlled environments where it is known that participants have suitable equipment, and where steps are taken to maximize reliability (Hewson *et al.* 2003). Even then, interruptions such as the loss of a connection, or slow data transmission rates, are likely to occur. The extent and impact of such technical difficulties remains to be explored; to date, online interviewers have tended to stick to the more reliable text-based approaches.

Asynchronous approaches

The Internet may also be used to support asynchronous interviews. Indeed, a particularly interesting feature of the Internet is the possibilities it creates for novel forms of asynchronous communication, email probably being the most widely known and used technology. While in some ways analogous to postal mail, emails travel much more swiftly than letters, arriving at the recipient's mail server account only seconds after the sender has pressed the send button.[4] Thus, in theory, a response can be returned within a matter of minutes; in practice, email exchanges are often punctuated with periods of hours, days or even weeks intervening (e.g. Murray and Sixsmith 1998). Email thus provides a potentially useful tool for conducting online *asynchronous* interviews, due to the typically more relaxed timing of email exchanges compared with the tools mentioned above (IM, online chat), whose typically more 'interactive' contexts of usage, and the expectation for an instantaneous response, make them more suitable for conducting *synchronous* interviews. In order to conduct an email interview, both interviewer and interviewee need

access to the appropriate technologies: a computer with an email client installed (e.g. Pegasus, Eudora, Outlook), an 'email account' on a mail server (provided by an ISP, or Internet Service Provider) and an Internet connection (e.g. via dial-up, ADSL broadband, or cable). Having made initial contact (see below for a discussion of sampling possibilities) and gained consent for participation, the interviewer may initiate the interview by sending questions or topics for discussion in the body of an email message, to which the interviewee can respond in their own time. Follow-up questions and responses can then create an ongoing interview-type dialogue, expanding over a time period negotiated by the participants. Given the asynchronous nature of this approach, it may well be appropriate to extend the interview over a period of several weeks in order to allow sufficient exploration of the topic at hand, depending on the time frequency of exchanges. However, it has been noted that it is the researcher's responsibility to impose a time limit for completion of email interviews, to avoid the process dragging out the duration of a research study (Murray and Sixsmith 1998).

Probably one of the earliest attempts to use email to conduct asynchronous interviews has been reported by Murray and Sixsmith (1998). In a study of people's experiences of prosthesis use, these researchers recruited participants via topic-relevant specialist listserv discussion groups (or mailing lists, discussed further below) and then conducted one-to-one email interviews with individuals who volunteered to take part. From their experiences, they conclude that the email interview presents a viable and valuable approach, alongside traditional ftf interview methods. Bowker and Tuffin (2004) have more recently adopted a similar approach, recruiting disabled people who were already using the Internet and/or email, and conducting one-to-one email interviews with these participants in order to find out about their perceptions of the Internet as a source of information and support on disability issues. Again, these authors report overall success in using this method, describing the email interview as offering an 'effective and appropriate approach for accessing discourse about the online experiences of people with disabilities' (Bowker and Tuffin 2004: 228).

---

[4] Though it should be noted that several factors may delay or prevent entirely emails from reaching the intended recipient, including spam filters and DNS resolve delay.

As well as the possibilities email offers for conducting one-to-one asynchronous interviews, the ease of emailing to several respondents simultaneously also provides scope for conducting asynchronous online focus groups. Most simply, online focus groups may be conducted by instructing all participants to send their email messages to all other group members. If the group moderator (researcher) starts by sending an introductory email to everyone in the group, then it is a simple matter for any individual recipient to hit the 'reply all' button in their mail client in order to post a comment to the whole group. However, probably a more reliable and efficient approach (e.g. some participants may forget to mail everyone in the group) would be to make use of specialist software available for managing dissemination of individuals' email postings to all members of a group. Listserv[5] is probably the most well-known software application for managing group mailing lists, which are also referred to as 'discussion lists' or 'discussion groups' (the latter not to be confused with Usenet discussion groups or 'newsgroups' which are described later, but which serve a similar purpose). Thousands of mailing lists exist on the Internet, each one managed by a listserver, covering topics ranging from mountain biking to quantum theories of consciousness. Some of these lists will have a moderator who monitors the messages before they are posted to list members and can thus intercept messages which are deemed off-topic or inappropriate in any other way; unmoderated lists do not have a moderator and messages are automatically relayed to all subscribers. If a list is 'open' (which many are) all a user needs to do to join is send a subscribe email to the relevant listserver address, and the Listserv software will add them automatically. For further details on how to locate and subscribe to lists on particular topics see the listserv primer in Appendix A. Catalist (http://www.lsoft.com/catalist.html) is a convenient web-based resource which provides access to a large searchable database of mailing lists, some of which allow subscription via a web browser.

Mailing lists thus provide a potential resource for implementing online asynchronous focus groups, though in many cases it will not be viable for a researcher to simply jump into an existing list and ask to conduct a focus group interview. Aside from the impracticalities concerning distinguishing the research focus group's discussion (involving those who have agreed to participate) from the larger group's discussion, it is generally considered impolite to join a group and post off-topic requests or comments.[6] Of course, in much qualitative research the aim is to target special interest groups and elicit their views on a shared topic of interest, such as in the work of Murray and Sixsmith (1998) and Bowker and Tuffin (2004) mentioned above, who did recruit people for one-to-one email interviews via specialist mailing list discussion groups. Such on-topic requests, projected via a mailing list moderator, should not be problematic, and are unlikely to cause offence. Several researchers have successfully adopted this approach to recruit participants for online asynchronous focus group interviews. Gaiser (1997), for example, reports posting requests (via moderators) to existing listserv discussion groups, and then making use of a private distribution list set up for research purposes in which to conduct focus group discussions with volunteers. This approach requires access to Listserver software, and the required level of technical expertise (or assistance) to set up a dedicated mailing list. For more information and guidance on how to do this see the *Introductory List Owners Guide* and other related documents available at http://www.lsoft.com/resources/manuals.asp (accessed 15 March 2005).

Other software applications which serve a very similar purpose to mailing lists may also prove useful for conducting asynchronous online focus groups. These include Bulletin Board System (BBS) software, which as the name suggests aims to provide a virtual bulletin

---

[5] 'Listserv' was originally developed in the mid 1980s for the Bitnet computer network, but the term has now come to be used to refer to any software application which manages mailing lists (http://www.answers.com).

[6] Researchers should always be mindful of 'Netiquette': the rules and conventions which govern what is considered acceptable behaviour online, when undertaking any IMR study. Respecting these principles is essential, not only in protecting the reputation of an individual researcher or research group, but the wider academic research community in general. As well, of course, as protecting potential participants. For a summary of the key principles of Netiquette, see http://www.albion.com/netiquette/.

board on which users can post messages which are then readable by anyone who has access to the board (and this can be restricted, e.g. via a user-name/password). Yahoo! provides a list of BBSs at: http://uk.dir.yahoo.com/Computers_and_Internet/Internet/Chats_and_Forums/Bulletin_Board_System__BBS_/.[7] Usenet has been referred to as a 'giant distributed bulletin board system'; it uses the Internet to provide access to thousands of newsgroups, which are essentially like massive bulletin boards which may have hundreds of readers.[8] Anyone can subscribe to and post messages to these discussion boards if they have a computer with the appropriate software for accessing a news server (to which they must be subscribed[9]) on which these newsgroups reside. While some groups will be set up to restrict access, most are open. Many web browsers are able to act as newsreaders (e.g. versions of Firefox, Explorer, and Safari). Also, Usenet groups can be accessed and managed at the web-based interface: http://groups.google.com/, using a web browser without the need for any additional newsreader software, or access to a news server. This web-based interface allows users to create new groups, selecting from several different access options (e.g. public, invitation only), very easily in a matter of minutes, with minimal levels of user expertise. Given their massive distributed nature, and the particular customs, rules, goals

and agendas of the online communities they support, many existing Usenet newsgroups are unlikely to prove useful for conducting online focus group interviews (for the same types of reasons as outlined above in relation to mailing list discussion groups). However, as just noted new specialist and restricted access groups can easily be created. The larger, existing groups may provide a useful source of access to participants, as well as a potential resource for online observational research (as discussed below).

Other software packages, such as the VLEs mentioned earlier, will also often incorporate asynchronous (as well as synchronous) discussion tools which function very much like the online discussion forums just mentioned. These may thus provide another alternative tool for researchers wishing to conduct online interviews, who have access to such packages. Kenny (2005) has reported successfully using the VLE WebCT, and its integrated multithread discussion board, to conduct an online asynchronous focus group interview with 38 Australian nurses.

Finally, a more recent development serving essentially the same function as Usenet groups is the World Wide Web (WWW) forum. WWW forums are discussion forums hosted on a web server, and having the advantage that they do not typically require any specialist software (e.g. a newsreader) for access and participation other than a basic web browser and Internet connection. A searchable database of WWW forums is available at: http://www.ezboard.com. Information on how to set up a WWW forum is also available at the ezboard website; registering is free and setting up and maintaining a board, or 'online community', costs around $4 a month (after a 30-day free trial period). Setting up a WWW forum may thus be the easiest way for a researcher to conduct an online focus group, in terms of the levels of equipment, software, expertise and experience required.

Advantages of online interviews

A number of general advantages of Internet-mediated research (IMR) have by now become well recognized, and many of these apply to the qualitative data-gathering techniques (interviews, observation and document analysis) considered in the present chapter. These advantages

---

[7] BBSs have been around since the 1970s, and started off as a single computer connected to a phone line via a modem, running appropriate software which allowed other computers to dial-up and connect via their modem/phone line (http://www.bbsdocumentary.com/). Setting up a dedicated BBS does require some level of expertise, and with the advent of the Internet the alternative methods now available for creating online discussion forums will probably prove more efficient and accessible to the majority of users.

[8] A key difference between mailing lists and BBSs and newsgroups, despite their similar functions as discussion forums, is that mailing lists deliver messages to individual subscribers' mailboxes, whereas messages posted to BBSs and newsgroups are stored on a news server (or computer) where they can then be accessed by subscribers as and when they chose. Thus BBSs/newsgroups may be considered less imposing than mailing lists, which could be seen to have implications (though not necessarily) for different levels of commitment, interest and engagement in the discussion topic by subscribers of these two related technologies.

[9] Most Internet Service Providers (ISPs) will provide access to a news server as part of their package.

include increased cost and time efficiency (due to automation of procedural aspects and data input, and cost-effective recruitment procedures), broad geographical reach and access to specialist groups, potential for enhanced candidness in online communications, and reduced biases resulting from perceptions of biosocial attributes (see, for example, the summaries provided in Hewson [2003] and Reips [2000]). Several potential advantages are especially salient in relation to qualitative online interviewing approaches, including increased candidness and a greater willingness to discuss sensitive topics, increased depth and reflexivity, more balanced power relationships and facilitation of participation for otherwise difficult-to-access groups.

Enhanced candour and self-disclosure

The increased levels of anonymity typical in an online interview setting, compared with ftf contexts, may result in participants being more open and willing to disclose personal and sensitive information. Heightened anonymity emerges due to the lack of readily available information about biosocial attributes (e.g. age, sex, social class, and ethnic origin); though some such information can often be inferred from, for example, usernames, this information can be inaccurate or deliberately misleading and is typically unverifiable. Thus online interviewees may experience enhanced perceptions of privacy, since they are able to choose to conceal or disclose as much information about themselves as they wish. This may plausibly lead to a greater willingness to disclose information that may otherwise be withheld in a ftf setting. Also, the lack of social context cues available in the online interview, due to both greater levels of anonymity and a lack of paralinguistic information (body language, tone of voice, facial expression, etc.), may contribute to enhanced levels of self-disclosure, since participants may have less of a sense of being observed, and judged. In computer-mediated communication (CMC) in general (of which online communication is a specific instance), evidence has been presented for both higher levels of self-disclosure (e.g. Bargh et al. 2002; Joinson 2001) and reduced levels of socially desirable responding (e.g. Joinson 1999), compared with ftf communication contexts. Though there is evidence that these effects may be constrained

to *visually anonymous* (i.e. excluding approaches making use of a video link, which were discussed above) CMC (Joinson 2001). Overall, there seems to be compelling evidence that CMC in general, and online communication in particular, does lead to enhanced levels of disclosure of sensitive and personal information (see Joinson and Paine, Chapter 16 this volume).

With regards to online interviews (compared with ftf approaches) several authors have confirmed these effects. Thus Murray and Sixsmith (1998) note that their online asynchronous interviews with prosthesis users were more effective in eliciting information on personal and intimate topics, such as respondents' sex lives, than were their ftf interviews. These authors suggest that in the latter context the direct physical proximity of the researcher is more likely to cause embarrassment to participants when personal topics are raised. Madge and O'Connor (2002) also report what they perceived as the disinhibiting effects of the online environment during their online synchronous focus group interviews with new parents, noting that on some occasions participants were observed to engage in flirtatious behaviours, with each other and the researchers, which it was felt would likely not have occurred in a ftf setting. For a more comprehensive discussion of issues relating to levels of disclosure, privacy, anonymity and social regulation in CMC, across a broader range of contexts, the interested reader is referred to Joinson (2003), Spears et al. (2002), and Chapter 16 this volume.

Depth and reflexivity

A further possible advantage of online interviews, particularly in asynchronous contexts, is the scope for elicitating deeper, more reflective, detailed and accurate responses. The timescale of an asynchronous email interview can allow participants scope for reflection, in a way not achievable in synchronous (online or offline) approaches. Further, since a ready log of the conversation is automatically archived during an email exchange, participants (and researchers) can reflect back over the points and comments that have already been made at their leisure, which could serve to enhance levels of accuracy and reflection. Participants engaged in email or other asynchronous online interviews also have greater scope for checking the accuracy of information provided, e.g. by reference to documents, diaries, etc. Synchronous online interview approaches seem to offer less scope for allowing depthy, reflective responses, due to their less relaxed timescale, although they may share the feature of providing a readily available log of previous conversational elements, as the comments typed by each participant will often remain visible as they scroll up the chat window. This adds a further dimension to online synchronous interviews, compared with offline synchronous approaches, the implications of which requires further exploration. Overall, it is likely that asynchronous online interviews will be better able to generate the kind of deep, detailed, rich and reflective data typically desired by qualitative researchers, than online, and perhaps also offline, synchronous approaches.

Researchers using asynchronous online interviews have typically reported success in generating rich and reflective data (e.g. Murray and Sixsmith 1998; Bowker and Tuffin 2004; Kenny 2005). Bowker and Tuffin (2004) used both asynchronous and synchronous approaches within the same study, and report that the former were more successful in generating rich, detailed data; these authors suggest that the extended timescale of an email interview may account for this effect by inducing a 'reduced sense of urgency', thus allowing for more considered and lengthy responses. Online interview approaches may also lead to greater levels of researcher *reflexivity*, since the anonymous nature of the interaction can encourage participants to direct probing questions at the researcher (Ward 1999).

Balanced power relationships

There is some evidence that online, compared with ftf, interviews may lead to more balanced power relationships between researcher and participant, as well as between research participants themselves (e.g. in online focus groups). Factors which have been identified to account for this include the typically heightened levels of anonymity in online communication, as noted above, and the greater levels of participant control over where and when to participate (Madge and O'Connor 2002). Evidence for such effects has been reported by Murray and Sixsmith

(1998), who note that their online interviews proceeded in a manner whereby researcher and participant acted largely as co-researchers, an outcome often desired in qualitative research. Thus these researchers found that their online interviewees asserted themselves, and took on an active role in directing the flow[10] and direction of the interview, in a way which did not occur with their ftf interviewees. A third factor which has been highlighted as contributing to the enhanced empowerment of online interviewees relates to the increased scope for participants to become involved in the interpretative process, an ideal often advocated in qualitative research but rarely achieved. Murray and Sixsmith (1998) explain how the extended timescale of their asynchronous email interviews allowed them to maintain several ongoing interviews with different participants simultaneously, which in turn created possibilities for what they refer to as a 'cross-fertilisation of ideas'; that is, the sharing (via the researcher) of comments between participants. The extended timescale involved also allowed the researchers to reflect upon and present their own interpretations of the interview data to participants, giving participants the opportunity to feed back their own reflections on these interpretations, thus leading to their greater involvement in the research process. Also relevant to the issue of more balanced power relationships in online communication, due to enhanced levels of anonymity, is Hewson *et al.*'s (1996) suggestion that the lack of ready access to biosocial information in online interactions may help to reduce interpersonal perceptual biases, such as those due to the application of stereotypical assumptions relating to gender, social class or ethnicity (Hewson *et al.* 1996). The potential for such biases in traditional ftf interviews has long been recognized (Murray and Sixsmith 1998). The possible elimination, or reduction, of such biases in online interviews may contribute towards creating more balanced power relationships than may be possible in

---

[10] The meaning of conversational 'flow' can vary depending upon context and focus. Here the term probably most aptly refers to the topics covered, links drawn between sub-themes, and the timescale of the interview dialogue. Other relevant usages of the term 'flow' will be described at relevant points in the chapter.

many offline ftf settings (though see the further discussion on this topic below for an alternative perspective).

Facilitating participation

The ability to respond remotely, as opposed to having to travel to an interview site, and in one's own timeframe, may have particular relevance in terms of facilitating participation for certain groups, such as disabled people (Bowker and Tuffin 2004), or new mothers (Madge and O'Connor 2002). This may help give a voice to, and thereby empower, groups who may otherwise be under-represented due to participation barriers. Also, the possibilities for the 'cross-fertilisation of ideas' in email interviews (Murray and Sixsmith 1998), as mentioned above, may allow these to function somewhat like a focus group, yet without requiring the presence of all group members simultaneously. This could confer benefits in facilitating participation from, and interaction amongst, respondents across different geographical regions and time zones in a way not practicable in ftf contexts. These outcomes are less likely to be applicable to synchronous approaches, however, since these demand participation at a set time, and certain skills and abilities, such as typing dexterity/speed, visual acuity, etc. These constraints in synchronous interviews may thus create participation barriers for certain groups, such as those with a physical disability which makes them less able to type speedy responses.

Overall, there is evidence that online interviews can offer the advantages of encouraging more candid responses from participants, and a willingness to discuss personal and sensitive topics, compared with ftf approaches, due to the effects of anonymity and a lack of paralinguistic social cues. Also, they may encourage more balanced power relations, due to less information being available about personal characteristics (sex, class, race, etc.), and interviewees' greater control over the participation context. Asynchronous approaches may have an advantage over synchronous approaches, both online and offline, in facilitating the generation of richer data, due to a more relaxed timescale. Asynchronous approaches may also help facilitate participation from a broader range of participants.

Disadvantages of online interviews

Online interviews are also susceptible to the general disadvantages which have been identified with IMR (as noted above, see Hewson [2003], and Reips [2000] for summaries). The main issues concern restrictions on who can participate, due to the need for technological equipment and levels of expertise (of both researchers and participants) and the possibly biased nature of the Internet User Population (IUP) and subpopulations; threats to reliability and validity due to a lack of researcher control over and knowledge of procedural details; and difficulty in implementing appropriate ethical procedures in an online context. All these factors may affect online interviews, though reliability and validity issues are generally of more relevance in quantitative than qualitative research. Nevertheless, greater difficulty in verifying who has responded, and whether responses are genuine and honest, may constitute a disadvantage of online interview approaches, compared with ftf alternatives. In relation to participation restrictions, given the more widespread use of asynchronous communication tools, such as email, mailing lists, and WWW forums, than synchronous communication facilities, it would seem that synchronous online interview approaches must inevitably impose greater constraints on who can participate. While techniques are available for arriving at reasonable estimates of the IUP, i.e. by counting the number of accessible Internet hosts and IP addresses (Hewson *et al.* 2003), estimating the relative size and diversity of synchronous and asynchronous user populations is more difficult, and any such estimates will likely be inaccurate. Recent figures estimate the number of Internet-accessible hosts to be 353 million in July 2005, up from 147 million in January 2002 (Internet software consortium, http://www.isc.org/). Estimates of the number of Internet users will be much higher than the number of hosts; recent figures suggest around 1 billion users (e.g. Computer Industry Almanac Inc., http://www.c-i-a.com/pr0106.htm, accessed February 2006). What is clear from examination of the resources and tools outlined above is that both synchronous and asynchronous Internet communication technologies support vast communities of users, whatever actual proportion of the currently estimated number of Internet users each represents. The synchronous user population will no doubt be smaller, since whereas most synchronous users will also use asynchronous communication tools, the reverse is not true.

Several disadvantages of IMR seem to be of particular relevance for online interview approaches, including barriers in establishing rapport; reduced depth and greater levels of ambiguity due to the text-only nature of the communication medium; and difficulty in implementing ethical procedures.

Establishing rapport

Enhanced levels of anonymity in online communication, and a lack of paralinguistic cues, were mentioned earlier in terms of the potential benefits for reducing bias, balancing power relations, and enhancing levels of candidness and self-disclosure. However, these features may also embody the disadvantage of making it more difficult to establish rapport with participants in an online interview, due to the less 'personal' tone of the interaction. Researchers conducting online interviews have recognized and addressed this issue in a number of ways. One approach has been to adopt a strategy of (researcher) self-disclosure in order to encourage levels of trust from participants, and thus help establish levels of rapport. Madge and O'Connor (2002) adopted this approach, posting pictures and biographies of themselves on their research project website, and engaging in preliminary one-to-one email interactions with focus group volunteers prior to the actual synchronous focus group sessions. The subsequent reported success in generating good rapport with participants, who were recruited via the website www.babyworld.com, may also have been aided by fact that the researchers were themselves new mothers, and thus shared a common identity with the participants. Bowker and Tuffin (2004) also used self-disclosure to try and encourage rapport in their asynchronous email interviews, but comment that establishing relational development did take longer than in ftf approaches. Though being able to meet participants ftf in advance, or being already casually acquainted, did help facilitate relational development, and the depth and 'flow' (here most appropriately referring to 'fluency'

and 'continuity') of the conversation. Gaiser (1997) has reported successfully making use of 'introductory exercises' as a precursor to an asynchronous focus group session, in order to encourage group cohesion, bonding and participant ease. These examples all suggest that levels of rapport comparable to those which can be achieved in offline contexts are possible in online interviews. However, some researchers have reported less positive experiences. Strickland *et al.* (2003) report conducting online asynchronous focus groups with perimenopausal women, using an online discussion board set up for research purposes. Several groups were conducted, each consisting of between four and eight participants. However, these researchers found that participation was slow, and group members failed to spontaneously post to the discussion board, requiring reminders and prompts from the researcher. Also, some participants tended to get locked into one-to-one discussions with each other, while ignoring the researcher's prompts and questions. Perhaps of significance, compared with the above more successful reports, is that Strickland *et al.* do not report using any special strategies for building rapport, such as self-disclosure, or the use of personally engaging exercises; rather the researcher/moderator posted an initial welcome to the group along with a set of questions.

Further research is clearly needed to determine which factors may enhance or inhibit levels of rapport in online interviews. The above illustrations highlight some possible contributing factors, including the nature of the sample (in the above accounts, the studies where rapport was more readily developed utilized recruitment methods more likely to obtain participants who had greater familiarity with the online communication tools utilized in the study), and the use of strategies for building rapport and levels of relational development. Also, making some kind of preliminary contact, e.g. ftf or by email, or being acquainted, may help. Individual communication style may also play a role in the way an online interview progresses (Bowker and Tuffin 2004). Whether synchronous or asynchronous approaches have different implications in terms of establishing rapport is to date unclear, and as the examples noted above indicate, success has been achieved in both contexts.

Impoverished and ambiguous data

One implication of failing to establish good levels of rapport with online interview participants is a possible reduction in the frequency, depth and reflectivity of the responses obtained, due to a lack of engagement in the interview process (as was experienced by Strickland et al. 2003). As noted earlier, there is evidence that asynchronous approaches, at least, have the potential to encourage more reflective and detailed responses from interviewees. However, failure to establish good levels of rapport in online interviews could inhibit this effect. Another factor which may act as a barrier to obtaining rich and meaningful data in online interviews is the lack of paralinguistic information available, noted above as potentially beneficial in relation to the positive consequences of enhanced levels of anonymity. However, a potential disadvantage of this lack of paralinguistic information is reduced depth, and greater ambiguity, due to the inability to utilize cues such as facial expressions, body language, tone of voice and so on. Given that synchronous online interviews do not benefit from a relaxed timescale, and, enhanced participant control which may play a role in encouraging depth and reflectivity, the limitations due to a lack of paralinguistic information may be particularly problematic for these approaches. There is evidence that this is the case. Researchers have reported that synchronous online interviews generate less text than ftf approaches, even though they take longer (Schneider et al. 2002; Davis et al. 2004), and interviewees' responses tend to convey 'information', but lack depth and meaning (Davis et al. 2004). Ambiguities have also been found to emerge in synchronous (e.g. Davis et al. 2004), and asynchronous (e.g. Bowker and Tuffin 2004) online interviews. Gaiser (1997) has suggested that because online chat is typically expected to be playful and superficial, it may be of limited value as an interview medium where detailed, sincere, thoughtful responses are desired. However, as noted above, Madge and O'Connor (2002) have been able to generate rich, detailed, reflective data using online synchronous focus groups. Aside from the rapport-building techniques these researchers used, other factors may have contributed to their greater success in generating rich, elaborative data.

For one thing, the focus groups consisted entirely of women, and women have been shown to typically engage in more personal, cooperative and supportive styles of communication than men (e.g. see the chapters in Coates 1998). Secondly, a relatively novel approach was adopted in which one researcher took on the role of typist, using pre-prepared chunks of text to cut and paste into the discussion window, while the other acted as discussion group moderator. In any case, this example illustrates that rich, meaningful data can be achieved in synchronous contexts. Researchers should be especially aware of using techniques which may encourage this process.

While it has been taken for granted in the above discussion that online communication precludes possibilities for the use of paralinguistic information, 'emoticons' (e.g. smile: :-), wink and smile: ;-), kiss: :-*) and acronyms (e.g. LOL: 'laughing out loud', ROTFL: 'rolling on the floor laughing') can provide textual/graphical representations of facial expressions and/or body language. Using capital letters is taken to indicate shouting. Although perhaps a rather crude substitute for actual paralinguistic cues in ftf interactions, such textual/graphical linguistic devices can actually make online communication far richer than those who are unfamiliar with such devices might imagine. For experienced and fluent users these devices can both speed up and enrich the online communication experience. They may also serve the function of reducing ambiguities, which may otherwise arise in interpreting purely textual expressions; for example a smile may clarify whether an utterance is intended as hostile or friendly. Of course, naive users who are unfamiliar with the use of such online paralinguistic devices will find them awkward to use and interpret, at first. While commonly used in online synchronous chatroom discussions, such cues are probably used less liberally in asynchronous settings, such as email, where they are likely less necessary since the extended timescale allows for the use of richer and more descriptive language. Thus, while a lack of paralinguistic information in the online interview has been seen as particularly problematic for synchronous interviews, the use of emoticons and acronyms by experienced users may serve to create richer and less ambiguous communication. A further possible consequence of the lack of paralinguistic cues in both synchronous and asynchronous online interviews, which cannot be resolved by the use of online paralinguistic substitutes, is the greater ease afforded to interviewees to deceive the researcher. For example, online interviewees may easily lie about their age, gender or emotional state (Murray and Sixsmith 1998), or whether there is a third party present guiding their responses (Bowker and Tuffin 2004).

One possible disadvantage of asynchronous over synchronous approaches in online interviewing is the decreased sense of continuity and 'flow' which can characterize the discussion, as a result of the extended timescale. This may potentially lead to reduced clarity, and instances of ambiguity. 'Flow' in this sense refers roughly to the perceived links between conversational elements, such as questions from the interviewer. For example, if the interviewer has just asked 'would you consider yourself racist?', and then asks 'what ethnic backgrounds do your friends have?', these questions will likely be seen as linked in a synchronous exchange, but the connections may be less likely to be made in an asynchronous exchange. Murray and Sixsmith (1998) have indicated experiencing a lack of such continuity and flow in their asynchronous online interviews, referring to the 'slow and interrupted flow of information'. Bowker and Tuffin (2004) have similarly commented on the interruptions which can occur in asynchronous communication settings, noting the frustration that would sometimes emerge from not knowing when their email interviewees might respond.

Ethical issues

Several novel ethical issues emerge in online interviewing, which also occur as more general concerns in Internet-mediated research. These include how to obtain informed consent (e.g. Kraut *et al.* 2004) and how to maintain data security and confidentiality (e.g. Gaiser 1997; Hessler *et al.* 2003). The latter issue is especially problematic in email-based approaches, where data travels across a number of servers (Internet-connected computers) and thus has the potential to be intercepted and viewed by a third party at a number of stages. Some issues will demand technological solutions, such as how to store participants' responses securely, so that they are safe from hackers, for example. This particular issue will, of course, be more pertinent to qualitative research eliciting data on sensitive and personal topics. Other issues emerge in the form of new questions and dilemmas for which there are no existing guidelines. In relation to interview-based approaches, these include questions about what is appropriate and acceptable behaviour online, e.g. is it okay to post unsolicited participation requests to selected newsgroups? To date, a comprehensive set of established guidelines on ethics in IMR has not been developed. However, there are a number of useful and informative publications on the topic (e.g. Kraut *et al.* 2004; Peden and Flashinski 2004; Birnbaum and Reips 2005). For a detailed discussion of ethical issues in online research see Ess (Chapter 31 this volume).

Sampling approaches for online interviews

A number of approaches are possible in recruiting online interview participants. As noted above, researchers have placed advertisements on existing websites (e.g. Madge and O'Connor 2002), and posted invitations to newsgroups or mailing lists (e.g. Gaiser 1997; Murray and Sixsmith 1997).

Gaiser (1997) has suggested that recruiting all members of a focus group from the same list may not be optimal, due to the likelihood of thus obtaining a homogenous group of participants who are well-acquainted with each other (though in some instances this may be what is wanted). Other researchers have used email (e.g. Strickland *et al.* 2003), or made use of offline recruitment methods (e.g. Kenny 2005) or both offline and online methods (e.g. Strickland *et al.* 2003).

There has been some general concern about levels of bias inherent in the Internet user population (e.g. Bordia 1996; Schmidt 1997), though more recently it is becoming recognized that with the rapid growth and changing composition of the IUP, ever more diverse samples are achievable (Hewson 2003). The problems in obtaining probability samples via the Internet, arising due to difficulties in specifying a sampling frame, and implementing effective random selection procedures, has also received discussion (e.g. Dillman and Bowker 2001). It is especially difficult to verify that an individual has received a participation request in Internet-based methods, given the fluctuating nature of the IUP, changing and dormant email addresses, and so on. However, this issue is less of a problem in qualitative research where obtaining probability samples which can lead to broadly generalizable, representative data is typically less important than generating rich, meaningful responses which give insight into participants' own understandings (Hewson *et al.* 2003). The ready access to small, specialist, and difficult-to-access populations, compared with accessibility to these via traditional offline sampling methods, is a particular strength of Internet-mediated sampling approaches, relevant to the goals of much qualitative research. These populations can be accessed via specialist discussion groups, mailing lists, and topic-specific websites. Indeed, some researchers have found the Internet useful as a source of access to participants who are then asked to take part in a study offline; Parsons *et al.* (2004), for example, recruited a specialist sample of male escorts who used the Internet as a point of access to clients, since this population was of key interest to their research goals (comparing the experiences of these men with those of previously studied male escorts who traded in offline contexts). These men were contacted by obtaining their email addresses, through America Online user profiles, and male escort websites. Clearly the sampling approach adopted will influence the type of sample obtained, and in qualitative research the Internet can be especially useful in this respect. Several points are important when recruiting participants by any of the methods suggested above, including directing any requests to discussion groups via moderators where possible (Murray and Sixsmith 1998) and, in general, respecting principles of netiquette and codes of professional conduct (e.g. those set out by the British Psychological Society). A more detailed discussion of the sampling procedures available to online interviewers can be found in Mann and Stewart (2000).

Obviously samples recruited online will be restricted in certain ways. They will probably be particularly interested in the research study topic (though this may often be desirable). They will be already fairly well-acquainted with online technologies, and possess a level of computer literacy (as well as access to the relevant equipment and technologies) not representative of the population at large. Though recruiting participants already well-versed in Internet communication technologies may have the advantage of facilitating the interview process, as noted above. For any study, levels of participant selectivity will depend on both the sampling procedures employed and the procedural and technological demands imposed. Email interviews are likely to enable the widest level of participation, whereas synchronous real-time chat approaches will impose greater restrictions. Nevertheless, the broad geographical reach afforded in IMR has been noted as advantageous by a number of online interviewers (e.g. Murray and Sixsmith 1998; Gaiser 1997; Strickland *et al.* 2003). In many cases online approaches may be able to facilitate research which would otherwise be difficult or impossible, such as running focus group sessions with people from diverse locations around the world.[11]

Summary of online interview approaches

In summary it would appear that both asynchronous and synchronous approaches in online interviewing may have their own benefits and drawbacks, and often trade-offs will be apparent, e.g. features leading to higher levels of anonymity in online interviews may encourage more candid, open responses, but also impede relational development, rapport-building, and richness of data. Similarly, the extended timescale of asynchronous interviews may serve both to allow for deeper, considered responses, and hinder conversational flow. Thus the researcher must make appropriate choices depending on the research context and goals. In general, asynchronous approaches seem to offer the advantages of being able to cut across geographical time zones, being easier for participants who are less fluent typists, and providing greater scope for detailed and reflective responses. Synchronous approaches may allow for a more flowing dialogue, and perhaps make establishing rapport more rapid

---

[11] Though this would not be practicable using synchronous approaches, due to the issue of different time zones.

(Bowker and Tuffin 2004). Synchronous approaches may also offer greater scope for making use of paralinguistic information. It is worth noting, however, that the distinction between synchronous and asynchronous approaches in online communication may not always be clear. Email, for example, is generally considered an asynchronous mode of communication, but it is certainly possible for email exchanges to be very rapid. Likewise online chat technologies can be used more or less synchronously (e.g. a participant may be distracted or multi-tasking). Perhaps the most useful approach may be to view Internet-based forms of communication as lying somewhere on a continuum between synchronous and asynchronous.

Online observation and document analysis

Observational approaches and the analysis of documents are closely related in an Internet-mediated research context, since both may involve the analysis of stored records available online. These will be logs of text-based verbal exchanges between people in the case of observational research, e.g. from archives of discussion forums, mailing lists, and so on (e.g. Bordia 1996; Herring *et al.* 1998) and 'documents' created for the purpose of publishing on the WWW, in the case of document analysis (e.g. Schütz and Machilek 2003). Thus the distinction between observational research and document analysis can become a little blurred in an IMR context, compared with traditional offline approaches where the observational researcher typically observes behaviour in real-time (often creating a log of this behaviour in the form of a video or audio recording for subsequent playback and analysis) while the document analyst makes use of existing text- or image-based records. The nature of the Internet, and the types of communication systems it supports, is such that many online interactions will be automatically logged, thus eliminating the need for the observational researcher to actively engage in this part of the data-gathering process, having only to locate and access the already available archives of online interactions. For the purposes of the current discussion, a working definition will be adopted of online observational research as that which uses logs of *interactions* (typically verbal exchanges) between participants, as opposed to document analysis which makes use of static records constructed specifically for the purpose of dissemination via the Internet, and whose primary purpose is not to facilitate an ongoing dialogue-type communication between individuals. Of course, observation of online interactions in real-time is also a possibility, and clearly a case of observational research.

Tools, technologies and procedures for online observation and document analysis

Observation

Qualitative researchers have been inclined to use 'naturalistic' observation, that is, observation of behaviour in a typical everyday setting familiar to participants, as opposed to the more controlled, artificial, experimental environments commonly used by quantitative researchers, since this is more likely to produce rich and informative data in which participants' own understandings, meanings and perspectives can emerge within a real-world context. The scope for conducting such observational research online clearly has some limitations, being primarily restricted to observation of 'linguistic behaviour'. Observation of paralinguistic features, body language and spatial behaviours (e.g. interpersonal proximity) is not readily available online, though as already mentioned emoticons and other paralinguistic substitutes may be informative, as may conversational turn-taking and timings and pauses, in a real-time synchronous conversational context. Further, interaction and navigation within an online 'virtual environment' may open up possibilities for observing spatial and other non-linguistic behaviours (e.g. see Givaty *et al.* 1998), though the extent to which this may be considered 'naturalistic' observation is debatable. This does not make the approach uninteresting, however, and the implications of the detached embodiment in such settings is a topic worthy of study in itself. Qualitative researchers, however, are coming to view language as of increasing importance in supporting approaches such as ethnomethodological research – the study of shared social meanings – and have developed various techniques (e.g. conversational and discourse analysis) which focus essentially upon the way people use language. The Internet with its wealth of such data thus provides a valuable resource for these forms of qualitative research in which language plays a primary role. As already noted in relation to online interviewing techniques, the Internet creates possibilities for both synchronous and asynchronous forms of verbal interaction, each of which can be useful in online observational research.

Observation of asynchronous online communication is possible using the archives of discussion groups, such as Usenet newsgroups, and listserv mailing lists, as described earlier in relation to online interview approaches. In observational studies very similar techniques can be used, but instead of using these tools to interact with participants and generate data, the researcher may use them to gain access to archived logs of discussions that have taken place. Discussion group archives can be accessed using the technologies and websites already mentioned; for example, listserv archives can be searched at the Catalist website. Bordia (1996) has made use of discussion archives (on Usenet, Internet and Bitnet) to search for and unobtrusively observe naturalistic rumour transmission, in a way previously not possible using offline approaches (Bordia 1996). Susan Herring and colleagues (e.g. Herring *et al.* 1998) have adopted a similar approach, using mailing list discussions to study gender issues in online verbal interactions, though in contrast to Bordia (1996) these authors appear to have followed and logged discussions as they occurred, rather than searching archives for a specific topic after the discussion had taken place. Sotillo and Wang-Gempp (2004) report a study in which they downloaded archives of political discussions on a public bulletin board in order to produce a corpus of texts which they then subjected to both quantitative and qualitative analyses. Stegbauer and Rausch (2002) have observed the behaviour of lurkers in mailing lists.

Observation of online synchronous interaction is possible using online chat, or instant messenger, programs (such as IRC, ICQ, etc.), which can be observed in real time, or by accessing archives of synchronous discussions. In the former approach the researcher will need to create a log of the interaction for subsequent analysis, and this can be done by cutting and pasting the discussion into a text document for storage (Davis *et al.* 2004 used this approach in their online synchronous interviews), or by making use of recording software which automatically logs and stores the conversation in a data file. Some software programs which support online synchronous chat will incorporate a recording facility (e.g. WebCT). However, currently most do not allow playback in real time, so timing information will be lost. Some researchers have reported successfully using online streamed chat (e.g. IRC) to study online conversations (e.g. Rodino 1997). Many IRC programs allow for time-stamping of contributions to the chats.

In both synchronous and asynchronous online observation contexts, the researcher has the option of adopting a participant or non-participant approach. Asynchronous approaches which make use of discussion archives, such as that used by Bordia (1996), are useful for non-participant observation where the researcher does not wish to be intrusive. Alternatively, a researcher may subscribe to a discussion forum or mailing list, either disclosing their presence or not, and contributing or not to the discussion as they wish. It is possible to 'lurk' (observe silently, without revealing one's presence) in asynchronous discussions, but this is not easy in synchronous settings since the presence of all chat forum members is readily available, as their username appears in the chat window when they join the discussion. However, the availability of logs of synchronous online chat allows the possibility of a non-participant undisclosed approach in this context, also, though unlike asynchronous conversations many synchronous discussions will not be automatically recorded and archived (a WWW search should locate some that have). For research on lurkers in mailing lists see Stegbauer and Rausch (2002); for a framework of these and other 'non-responders' see Bosnjak (2001).

A further option for online observational research, as noted above, moves beyond purely text-based approaches: this is made possible by the existence of online virtual environments, known generically as MU environments. These include MUDs (multi-user dungeons, since they started off as places where users played the role-playing game Dungeons and Dragons), MUSEs '(multi-user simulated environments)', MOOs '(MUD-object-oriented)', etc. These online environments support virtual communities who meet up and interact in a virtual world, often based on a fantasy role-playing game of one sort or another. They may often incorporate graphics as well as text, allowing users to wander around in rooms, and interact with objects as well as each other. Observation of behaviour in these environments could give a fascinating insight into role-playing in environments that couldn't possibly be created offline, as well as insight into the way people can entertain multiple alternative identities, for example. The researcher may make use of the existing virtual reality environments available, as a disclosed or undisclosed participant observer (e.g. see the list at: http://uk.dir.yahoo.com/Recreation/Games/Video_Games/Internet_Games/MUDs__MUSHes__MOOs__etc_/), or set up their own environment specifically to suit their own research context (which would require some greater level of expertise). The former approach may be considered more naturalistic, though the extent to which behaviour in these types of virtual environments relates to offline behaviour is a research area in its own right.

Document analysis

Document analysis in IMR is similar to some forms of observation, which make use of online archives, but here the records accessed are not logs of interactions but documents which have been purposely placed on the WWW. The Internet provides a massive resource of all sorts of online documents. These include personal home pages with informational or artistic content, theoretical and scientific articles, news articles, stories (fiction or non-fiction), poetry and bibliographies. A fairly recent phenomenon is the emergence of 'blogs' ('weblogs'), which started out as online personal diaries which (strangely enough) individuals post in the public domain, via a website, with the intention that other web users may access and read them. Since blogs are intended to function as regularly updated personal diaries, they are not simply static documents, so the extent to which they constitute data for observational research or document analysis is unclear. Again the continuum between asynchronous

and synchronous interactions online raises some new and interesting issues. Based on the earlier definition provided, online personal diaries would probably be classified as documents, since they involve monologues rather than records of interactions between individuals. Having said this, as they have emerged and evolved, blogs are now also becoming used like open bulletin boards. See the Yahoo! list of blogs for examples: http://buzz.yahoo.com/buzz_log/entry/2005/03/08/1300/. In which case, they may be considered appropriate for linguistic observation research.

Schütz and Machilek (2003) have carried out research on personal homepages, and provide a useful discussion of the various sampling approaches which may be used to locate these pages. While their focus is on obtaining a representative sample, which may be less relevant to the goals of many qualitative research studies, a number of useful techniques are described, including using directories with which home pages have been registered (e.g. the Yahoo! directory of English language personal home pages: http://dir.yahoo.com/Society_and_Culture/People/; the directory of Women Internet Researchers, maintained by Nicola Döring: http://www.nicola-doering.de/women.htm), sampling via lists of home pages provided by ISPs, and using search engines (such as http://www.google.co.uk). Qualitative researchers may find the latter approach particularly useful, if for example pages on a specific topic are desired. Whether or not home pages can provide rich and elaborate data of the type typically required by qualitative researchers remains to be further explored; to date, analysis of personal home pages seems to have been carried out largely within a quantitative methodological framework (e.g. Schütz and Machilek 2003), though some researchers have also adopted a qualitative approach (e.g. Karlsson 1998). Heinz et al. (2002) report a qualitative study in which they carried out a rhetorical–critical examination of texts and images on a selection of gay, lesbian, bisexual and transgender websites. Sites were chosen based on their popularity and relevance to the research question: global and local constructions of gay identities on WWW sites.

As well as making use of those resources which are already available online, document analysts may choose to solicit documents, such as personal diaries. Hessler *et al.* (2003) have taken this approach in a qualitative study on adolescent risk behaviour. These authors report successfully eliciting daily diary entries from participants by email, and thereby generating 'rich and extensive narratives of everyday life as seen through adolescent eyes' (Hessler *et al.* 2003: 111).

Advantages of online observation and document analysis

There is considerable overlap in the issues affecting online observation and document analysis. Both inherit the general advantages of IMR which have been outlined earlier (cost/time savings, broad geographical reach, ready access to potentially very large pools of data, enhanced disclosure and candidness). Hessler *et al.* (2003), for example, note both the cost-effectiveness of their elicitation of online diaries from adolescents, as well as the success in generating more candid responses and establishing better rapport, than has previously been possible in ftf settings, likely due to the nameless, faceless nature of the interaction. The potential for more equitable power relations in the online environment, including facilitation of participation for some marginalized groups, and enhanced possibilities for unobtrusive observation are also particularly relevant.

Ready access to large volumes of data

A key advantage for both observation and document analysis using the Internet is the ready availability of online resources, their ease of accessibility, and the ability to quickly search for and locate topic-relevant sources. In relation to observation studies, this applies to the availability of data trails of interactive communication on the Internet; for document analysis it applies to the enormous range of static documents available (web pages etc., as discussed above). While researchers may need to be carefully selective in determining which of these sources may provide data suitable for a research study, several authors have successfully located and utilized relevant sources using an IMR approach (refer to the examples above). As Bordia (1996) has noted, the sheer volume of archives of online discussions available creates the potential

for gaining easy access to information which may in offline contexts be difficult and time-consuming to obtain. Bordia's success in obtaining transcripts of rumour transmission, in a way that would not have been possible with such ease and efficiency using traditional methods (where the researcher may have to observe numerous conversations before coming across a topic-relevant discussion) illustrates this point well. Ward (1999) has noted the advantage of the online environment for observational research in allowing extended periods for observation, compared with offline approaches.

Unobtrusiveness

A further advantage of online *observation* methods in particular, also highlighted by Bordia (1996), is the enhanced possibilities for unobtrusive observation. Unlike in offline contexts, a researcher can easily lurk (i.e. observe without taking part) in asynchronous communication contexts, including discussion groups and mailing lists, without their presence being known. In synchronous contexts such lurking is still possible, though an individual's presence can be observed (when they log on and enter a chat forum); in large conversational groups this presence may go unnoticed or ignored but in smaller groups it may not and lurking will often attract direct comments requesting at least an introduction. Some researchers report simply not reacting to any such comments, and seem to have successfully gathered records of synchronous text-based interactions by this method (e.g. Al-Sa'Di and Hamdan 2005), though this approach could also be expected to provoke a hostile response from chat room members, depending on the setting. Hudson and Bruckman (2004) provide evidence on this; they found that upon entering IRC chatrooms and posting a message either stating that they were recording participants, or asking people to opt in, or to opt out of being recorded, they were kicked out of the chat room in 63.3 per cent of cases. However, if they simply lurked in the chat room without posting any message (but still recorded participants) they were kicked out on only 29 per cent of occasions. These authors also note that only a tiny proportion of chat room participants consented to being recorded when asked to opt in, and thus conclude that obtaining consent in this type of real time online observational research is impracticable. However, whether lurking and recording participants without obtaining consent meets appropriate ethical standards is open to debate. Nevertheless, the contexts which the Internet offers do potentially expand the possibilities for carrying out undisclosed observational research.

Power relationships

The aforementioned features of anonymity and enhanced participant control in online communication, which may serve to provide more balanced power relations between interviewer and interviewee (as well as amongst interviewees themselves), may also extend to power relations between participants in non-specifically research-oriented online contexts, such as those drawn upon in observation research, as described above (i.e. chat forums, etc.). Indeed, the effect of the online communication medium on power relationships is an interesting area for study. While some authors have claimed a 'democratizing' effect in Internet interaction, due to the lack of readily available cues about gender, race, socio-economic status, and so on, various strands of evidence have challenged this view (for a thorough and informed discussion of this issue see Mann and Stewart [2000], Chapter 7). For one thing, online researchers have found that people will direct probing questions where such biosocial and demographic information is not provided (e.g. Ward 1999), as well as make assumptions about the personal characteristics of those they meet online (Kendall 1999). The language a person uses may give clues about themselves; there is evidence that characteristic 'gendered' communication styles are transported to online settings (e.g. Herring 1993; Postmes and Spears 2002). Further, discriminatory and oppressive behaviours can occur online as well as offline, and perhaps more so, given the possible disinhibiting effects of the online medium, mentioned earlier. For example, women have reported experiencing sexual harassment by men in online interactions where their gender was disclosed (Mann and Stewart 2000). Thus Internet-based communication may be far from achieving the democratizing effects which some have claimed. However, perhaps online contexts can offer greater scope for reducing some of the biases often found in ftf interactions.

Disadvantages of online observation and document analysis

The general disadvantages of IMR outlined earlier also apply to observation and document analysis (participation restrictions due to the nature of the IUP and technological requirements; lack of researcher control; difficulty in implementing ethical procedures). Those issues highlighted as especially pertinent to online interactive communication contexts also affect observational approaches (potentially greater ambiguity, poorer relational development and more impoverished data due to a lack of paralinguistic cues). In considering the relative merits of observing interactions in asynchronous or synchronous online contexts, many of the same points discussed above in relation to online interviews apply. However, some of the ethical considerations relevant to observation and document analysis in IMR differ slightly from those which have already been highlighted in relation to online interviewing, as now discussed.

Ethical issues

Ethical issues relevant to online observation and document analysis are well-covered in Ess (Chapter 31 this volume). The key issues include ambiguity over the public/private domain distinction in online contexts; anonymity, protecting participant identity and the use of online pseudonyms; and copyright and the appropriate attribution of authorship for online sources. The present discussion is brief, and the reader is referred to the aforementioned well-informed account, as well as other available more detailed discussions of these issues (e.g. Kraut *et al.* 2004, and others mentioned earlier). In relation to the distinction between the public and private domain, there has been some disagreement concerning the extent to which researchers should feel free to utilize online discussion archives, or log synchronous chat room conversations. Earlier, the possibilities for undisclosed observation via lurking were noted, but it has been unclear in which contexts this does not constitute an invasion of privacy. 'Private' online chat discussions are quite clearly out of bounds for the observational researcher (who would have difficulty accessing these anyway) without first gaining informed consent. This is certainly possible; Al-Sa'Di and Hamdan (2005) have reported using online synchronous chat logs provided by consenting participants who had already recorded their own private conversations. In other settings, however, appropriate standards are less clear. Several authors have considered materials, including logs of online discussions, made available online as in the public domain (e.g. Bordia 1996). A stricter view would advocate that informed consent is required for use of any such archives. However, gaining such consent raises practical problems since tracing participants who have taken part in archived online discussions can be difficult: users may leave a discussion group, email addresses may change, be left unchecked, and so on. Of course, asking for participation consent prior to observing an online real-time conversation may have obvious implications for the naturalness of the subsequent discussion. In the absence of a consistent and officially recognized set of guidelines, currently, researchers will need to make their own judgements on these issues.

While protecting participants' identities by the use of pseudonyms may be considered a sufficient procedure in addressing concerns about whether to, for example, publish individuals' comments in research reports, the issue emerges of the extent to which online identities can be considered anonymous. Some authors have argued that individuals often invest a lot into their online personas, and that these can reveal personal information about their offline identities; thus these online identities should be protected in the same way as offline identities (Frankel and Siang 1999). Copyright issues also emerge (Bowker and Tuffin 2004). Researchers may be obliged to cite the author of a text, yet this may compromise anonymity (and potentially cause harm, even if the author of the text agreed to or requested the citation). Confidentiality may be jeopardized in IMR, since it may be relatively easy to locate the author of an anonymous quote using Internet search facilities, compared with offline settings (Bowker and Tuffin 2004). Because of these issues surrounding anonymity, confidentiality and privacy in online observation research, some researchers have chosen to use online interviews, in which informed consent can more easily be obtained (e.g. Bowker and Tuffin 2004). In cases where documents are solicited, gaining informed consent resolves the public/private domain issue. As noted, Hessler

et al. (2003) used solicited documents in a study in which adolescents were asked to send daily diary entries via email. In this study informed consent was clearly required, and careful measures were taken to protect identity and data security as far as was practically possible.

Mixed methods possibilities in IMR

In the social sciences generally researchers are becoming increasingly aware of the possibilities and benefits of a *mixed methods* research strategy; that is, one which uses both quantitative and qualitative methodologies within the same study in order to address a single research question (Hewson 2006). This approach is facilitated by the recognition that the long-standing perceived division between qualitative and quantitative research approaches, and the belief that they are incompatible, is not useful (e.g. Johnson and Onwuegbuzie 2004; Eid and Diener 2006). The mixed method strategy is underpinned by a *pragmatist* philosophical position, which denies the incompatibility of qualitative and quantitative approaches, and urges recognition that both approaches have their own strengths and weaknesses and may be usefully combined in informing a single thread of enquiry. An important concept associated with mixed methods approaches is 'triangulation', which refers to the strategy of exploring an issue from several angles in order to cross-validate and corroborate different strands of evidence. In this way a more comprehensive and complete account may be possible. The possibilities, merits and drawbacks of mixed methods approaches are now becoming widely discussed (e.g. Johnson and Onwuegbuzie 2004), though some authors remain opposed to this orientation on philosophical grounds (see Smith [1983] for further discussion of the compatibility or otherwise of quantitative and qualitative approaches). Nevertheless, there is no doubt that mixed methods approaches are becoming more and more widely recognized and used by social science researchers, as is apparent from both the increasing number of published research reports adopting this methodology, and the appearance of chapters and books devoted to the approach in key research methodology texts (e.g. Creswell 2003; Eid and Diener 2006).

For a detailed and well-informed account of mixed methodology approaches see Tashakkori and Teddlie (1998). Tashakkori and Teddlie have noted the distinction between mixed methods approaches, which mix qualitative and quantitative approaches in the *methodology* of a study, and mixed model approaches, which combine both approaches across all stages of the research process. The present focus is on mixed methods research in IMR, since it is the use of the Internet as a *data-gathering* tool that is under consideration. Mixed mode approaches, in which data is gathered via two or more modes (e.g. via both a computer terminal, and pen and paper questionnaire), will also be briefly considered since these approaches have been useful in IMR.

Internet-mediated mixed methods studies

Mann and Stewart (2000) provide some discussion of the potential for implementing mixed methods approaches in IMR, referring to examples of research studies which have adopted the approach in an IMR medium. Mixed methods research takes place in one of two major modes: *sequential* or *concurrent* (Creswell 2003[12]). An example of a sequential approach would be administration of (qualitative) semi-structured interviews, the results of which provide a basis for constructing a follow-up (quantitative) structured questionnaire. Concurrent approaches may involve, for example, collecting both behavioural and self-report data simultaneously, such as during a problem-solving task. Within these designs, the respective (quantitative and qualitative) methods can be given greater or lesser importance, depending on the researcher's orientation and goals.

Several authors have implemented sequential mixed methods approaches in IMR. Madge and O'Connor (2002) used a combination of online methods, including a web-based survey[13] and synchronous online interviews, in their study looking at new parents' experiences and reasons

for using the website babyworld.co.uk. The survey was posted on the website and follow-up interviews were conducted with respondents who volunteered to take part, after receiving an email request sent to them upon completion of the survey. Fifteen out of 155 survey respondents volunteered to take part in group interviews. Herring's research (e.g. Herring 1993; Herring et al. 1998) on online gendered communication has also made use of mixed methods approaches. For example, several months after carrying out observation of postings to a mailing list discussion thread, an open-ended survey was posted to the list in order to compare participants perceptions' of what had occurred during the discussion thread with what had been observed by the researchers (Herring et al. 1998). Interestingly, the two accounts were quite discrepant,[14] illustrating the value of this type of mixed methods approach. Kendall (1999) has also pointed out the advantage of being able to readily combine observations of actual behaviour with self-report data in an IMR context, having made use of this approach using ftf interviews, group participation sessions and information gathered via newsgroups and mailing lists. Simultaneous online mixed methods research has also been carried out. Ward's (1999) 'cyberethnographic' study of online communities made use of both observation and semi-structured interview approaches, carried out simultaneously over an extended period, using BBS and email. Ward reports the approach as successful in being able to generate a rich understanding of these online communities' perceptions and experiences.

A number of *mixed mode* studies have been conducted in IMR, largely with the purpose of validating Internet-mediated research procedures, though they may also be seen as serving to validate offline approaches, e.g. by testing the robustness of psychological test instruments with different samples, or in different participation contexts (Hewson and Charlton 2005). Buchanan (Chapter 28 this volume) discusses

---

[12] Creswell also refers to 'transformational' mixed methods designs.

[13] Which can be viewed at http://www.geog.le.ac.uk/baby/babyworldform.asp (accessed 19 February 2005).

[14] Although contrary to what had actually occurred, Herring found men perceived women as having dominated the discussion; in actual fact men had contributed more than women both in terms of length and number of postings (Herring et al. 1998).

such approaches; see also the collections in Reips and Bosjnak (2001) and Birnbaum (2000). Such mixed mode approaches typically compare Internet versus laboratory or pen and paper implementations of the same survey, questionnaire or experimental procedure. Other mixed mode studies, which have not explicitly focused on the goal of validiating online and offline methods, can also be useful. For example, Workman (1992) reports how he used electronic media to support participant observation fieldwork; while the electronic media did not replace traditional methods, it was useful for scheduling meetings, and gaining additional information from e.g. BBSs and mailing lists. Davis *et al.* (2004), though recognizing the limitations of their data generated via online synchronous chat interviews (due mainly to problems with ambiguity, and a lack of deep, detailed descriptions), suggested that such approaches could be useful when combined with other offline methods (e.g. ftf interviews, which were also used in the same study). Mixed mode studies may also be useful due to the diverse and readily available pool of potential participants accessible via online methods, e.g. psychological research has traditionally relied on access to psychology undergraduates as a participant pool, who tend to consist largely of females. The often-cited bias towards males in online contexts[15] may thus be useful in serving to redress this gender imbalance, by using a mixed mode approach which samples by both traditional and online methods (Hewson 2003).

Advantages of using the Internet in mixed methods research

A number of advantages of using online methods to facilitate mixed methods research seem apparent, including the general advantages of IMR approaches already noted above. Of particular relevance to mixed methods approaches, which tend to involve lengthy and costly data collection procedures, is the digitizing of data

which occurs in IMR, thus rendering it in a format which can be readily transported between different data management software packages, including both those designed for qualitative and quantitative forms of analysis (Mann and Stewart 2000). As well as the cost- and time-saving benefits to the researcher, online mixed methods approaches can reduce demands on participants, due to the greater control offered over when and where to respond. Of course, mixed methods approaches will inherit all the advantages and disadvantages of the respective data-gathering methods they employ, as discussed throughout this chapter. Another key advantage of mixed methods approaches in IMR is that, given the strengths and weaknesses of different online approaches, e.g. synchronous and asynchronous interviews, a strategy in which several approaches are utilized together in a single study may provide an overall richer exploration of a research topic, by combining the strengths of the respective approaches. Thus, in these early days of IMR, where the relative advantages and disadvantages of the various procedures available are still being uncovered (e.g. Reips 2002), and where trade-offs are clearly apparent in making choices about which approach to use, it would seem sensible to suggest making use of more than one approach. Especially given the particularly salient feature of Internet-mediated data gathering approaches that they typically lead to substantial time and cost savings.

In summary, Internet-mediated research is still young, and mixed methods approaches just coming to fruition and widespread recognition; as more researchers join those pioneers of IMR mixed methods research mentioned here, the benefits and drawbacks of marrying these two approaches will become more apparent.

Conclusions

This chapter has outlined the range of possibilities for conducting qualitative interview, observation and document analysis data-gathering procedures in an Internet-mediated research context. The range of approaches, tools and technologies for supporting such research has been considered, as well as the advantages and disadvantages incurred in using the different techniques. Finally, it has been argued that mixed

---

[15] It is likely that this gender bias may be decreasing, in relation to the demographics of the entire IUP at least, though of course different sampling approaches may still be more or less likely to recruit either males or females.

methods approaches are valuable, and that these may benefit particularly from being adapted to an IMR environment, since the cost and time savings that IMR affords may be especially useful in supporting research which is typically high in resource demands. Further exploration of mixed methods IMR is now an important research avenue.

Acknowledgements

The author would like to thank Immo Fritsche and Zak Birchmeier for providing very helpful, thorough and detailed comments in reviewing an earlier draft of this chapter. Also Ulf-Dietrich Reips whose guidance and feedback on earlier versions has been extremely valuable.

References

Al-Sa'Di, R. A. and Hamdan, J. M. (2005). 'Synchronous online chat' English: computer-mediated communication. *World English 24*(4), 409–424.

Apostolopoulos, J. G. (2001). Reliable video communication over lossy packet networks using multiple state encoding and path diversity. *Visual Communications and Image Processing 4310*, 24–26.

Bargh, J. A., McKenna, K. Y. A. and Fitzsimons, G. M. (2002). Can you see the real me? Activation and expression of the 'True Self' on the internet. *Journal of Social Issues 58(1)*, 33–48.

Birnbaum, M. H. (ed.) (2000). *Psychological experiments on the Internet*. San Diego, CA: Academic Press.

Birnbaum, M. H. and Reips, U.-D. (2005). Behavioral research and data collection via the internet. In R. W. Proctor and K.-P. L. Vu (eds), *The handbook of human factors in Web design* (pp. 471–492). Mahwah, NJ: Erlbaum.

Bordia, P. (1996). Studying verbal interaction on the internet: the case of rumour transmission research. *Behavior Research Methods, Instruments and Computers 28*, 149–151.

Bosnjak, M. (2001). Participation in non-restricted web surveys: a typology and explanatory model for item non-response. In U.-D. Reips and M. Bosnjak (eds), *Dimensions of Internet science* (pp. 193–208). Lengerich: Pabst.

Bowker, N. and Tuffin, K. (2004). Using the online medium for discursive research about people with disabilities. *Social Science Computer Review 22*(2), 228–241.

Coates, D. (ed.). (1998). *Language and gender: a reader*. Blackwell, Oxford.

Creswell, J. W. (2003). Research design: *Qualitative, quantitative and mixed methods approaches*. 2nd edition, Thousand Oaks, CA: Sage.

Davis, M., Bolding, G., Hart, G., Sherr, L. and Elford, J. (2004). Reflecting on the experience of interviewing online: perspectives from the internet and HIV study in London. *AIDS CARE 16*(8), 944–952.

Dillman, D. A. and Bowker, D. K. (2001). The web questionnaire challenge to survey methodologists. In Reips, U. -D. and Bosnjak, M. (eds), *Dimensions of internet science* (pp. 159–178). Pabst Science Publishers, Lengerich, Germany. Available at http://survey.sesrc.wsu.edu/dillmans/papers.htm.

Eid, M. and Diener, E. (eds) (2005). *Handbook of multimethod measurement in psychology*. Washington, DC: American Psychological Association. Available at http://www.apa.org/books/4316063.html.

Frankel, M. and Siang, S. (1999). *Ethical and legal issues of human subjects research on the internet – report of a workshop*. Washington, DC: American Association for the Advancement of Science. Available at http://www.aaas.org/spp/sfrl/projects/intres/report.pdf.

Gaiser, T. (1997). Conducting online focus groups: a methodological discussion. *Social Science Computer Review 15*(2), 135–44.

Givaty, G., Hendrick, A. H.C., van Vaan, Christou, C. and Heinrigh, H. Bulthoff (1998). Tele-experiments – experiments on spatial cognition using VRML-based multimedia. Available at www.ece.uwaterloo.ca/vrm198/cdrom/papers/givaty/givaty.pdf.

Heinz, B., Gu, L., Inuzuka, A. and Zender, R. (2002). Under the rainbow flag: webbing global gay identities. *International Journal of Sexuality and Gender Studies 7*(2/3), 107–124.

Herring, S. C. (1993). Gender and democracy in computer-mediated communication. *Electronic Journal of Communication 3*(2), Available at http://ella.slis.indiana.edu/~herring/ejc.txt.

Herring, S. C., Johnson, D. A. and DiBenedetto, T. (1998). Participation in electronic discourse in a 'feminist' field. In J. Coates (ed.), *Language and gender: a reader* (pp. 197–210). Blackwell Publishers Ltd, Oxford.

Hessler, R. M., Downing J., Beltz C., Pelliccio A., Powell M. and Vale W. (2003). Qualitative research on adolescent risk using email: a methodological assessment. *Qualitative Sociology 26*(1), 111–124.

Hewson, C. M., Laurent, D. and Vogel, C. M. (1996). Proper methodologies for psychological and sociological studies conducted via the Internet. *Behavior Research Methods, Instruments and Computers 32*, 186–191.

Hewson, C. M., Yule, P., Laurent, D. and Vogel, C. M. (2003). *Internet research methods: A practical guide for the social and behavioral sciences*. London: Sage.

Hewson, C. (2003). Conducting psychological research on the internet. *The Psychologist 16*(6), 290–292.

Hewson, C. (2006), Mixed methods research. In V. Jupp (ed.) *The Sage dictionary of social research methods*. London: Sage.

Hewson, C. and Charlton, J. P. (2005). Measuring health beliefs on the internet: a comparison of paper and internet administrations of the multidimensional health locus of control scale. *Behavior Research Methods, Instruments and Computers 37(4)*, 691–702.

Hudson, J. and Bruckman, A. (2004). 'Go away': participant objections to being studied and the ethics of chatroom research. *The Information Society 20*(2), 127–139.

Johnson, R. B. and Onwuegbuzie, A. J. (2004). Mixed methods research: a research paradigm whose time has come. *Educational Researcher 33*(7), 14–26.

Joinson, A. N. (1999). Social desirability, anonymity and internet-based questionnaires. *Behavior Research Methods, Instruments and Computers 31*, 433–438.

Joinson, A. N. (2001). Self-disclosure in computer-mediated communication: the role of self-awareness and visual anonymity. *European Journal of Social Psychology 31*, 177–192.

Joinson, A. N. (2003). *Understanding the psychology of Internet behaviour: Virtual worlds, real lives.* Basingstoke and New York: Palgrave Macmillan.

Karlsson, A-M. (1998). Selves, frames and functions of two Swedish teenagers' personal home pages. Paper presented at the 6th International Pragmatics Conference, Reims/Frankreich. [Online]. Available at http://www.nordiska.su.se/personal/karlsson-a-m/ipra.htm.

Kendall, L. (1999). Recontextualising 'cyberspace': methodological considerations for on-line research. In S. Jones (ed.), *Doing Internet research: Critical issues and methods for examining the Net.* London: Sage.

Kenny, A. J. (2005). Interaction in cyberspace: An online focus group. *Journal of Advanced Nursing, 49*(4), 414–422.

Kraut, R., Olson, J., Banaji, M., Bruckman, A., Cohen, J. and Couper, M. (2004). Psychological research online: report of board of scientific affairs' advisory group on the conduct of research on the internet. *American Psychologist 59*(2), 105–117.

Madge, C. and O'Connor, H. (2002). On-line with e-mums: exploring the internet as a medium for research. *Area 34*(1), 92–102.

Mann, C. and Stewart, F. (2000). *Internet communication and qualitative research: A handbook for researching online.* London: Sage.

Murray, C. D. and Sixsmith, J. (1998). Email: a qualitative research medium for interviewing? *International Journal of Social Research Methodology: Theory and Practice 1*(2), 103–121.

Parsons, J. T., Koken, J. A. and Bimbi, D. S. (2004). The use of the internet by gay and bisexual male escorts: sex workers as sex educators. *AIDS CARE 16*(8), 1021–1035.

Peden, B. F. and Flashinski, D. P. (2004). Virtual research ethics: a content analysis of surveys and experiments online. In E. Buchanan (ed.), *Readings in virtual research ethics: Issues and controversies.* Hershey, PA: Information Science Pub. Also available at http://www.idea-group.com/downloads/excerpts/1591401526E.pdf.

Postmes, T. and Spears, R. (2002). Behaviour online: does anonymous computer communication reduce gender inequality? *Personality and Social Psychology Bulletin 28*(8), 1073–1083.

Reips, U.-D. (2000). The web experiment method: advantages, disadvantages and solutions. In M. H. Birnbaum (ed.), *Psychological experiments on the Internet* (pp. 89–120). San Diego, CA: Academic Press.

Reips, U.-D. and Bosnjak, M. (eds) (2001). *Dimensions of internet science.* Pabst Science Publishers, Lengerich, Germany.

Reips, U.-D. (2002). Internet-based psychological experimenting: five dos and five don'ts. *Social Science Computer Review 20*(3), 241–249.

Rodino, M. (1997). Breaking out of binaries: reconceptualizing gender and its relationship to language. *Journal of Computer-Mediated Communication 3*(3). Available at http://www.ascusc.org/jcmc/vol3/issue3/rodino.html

Schmidt, W. C. (1997) World-wide web survey research: benefits, potential, problems and solutions. *Behavior Research Methods, Instruments and Computers 29*, 274–279.

Schneider, S. J., Kerwin, J., Frechtling, J. and Vivari, B. A. (2002). Characteristics of the discussion in online and face-to-face focus groups. *Social Science Computer Review 20*(1), 31–42.

Schütz, A. and Machilek, F. (2003). Who owns a personal home page? A discussion of sampling problems and a strategy based on a search engine. *Swiss Journal of Psychology 62*(2), 121–129.

Smith, J. K. (1983). Quantitative versus qualitative research: an attempt to clarify the issues. *Educational Research 12*, 6–13.

Sotillo, S. M. and Wang-Gempp, J. (2004). Using corpus linguistics to investigate class, ideology and discursive practices in online political discussions. In V. Connor and T. A. Upton (eds) *Applied corpus linguistics. A multidimensional perspective* (pp. 91–122). Rodopi, Amsterdam & Atlanta.

Spears, R., Postmes, T., Lea, M. and Wolbert, A. (2002). When are net effects gross products? The power of influence and the influence of power in computer-mediated communication. *Journal of Social Issues 58*(1), 91–107.

Stegbauer, C. and Rausch, A. (2002). Lurkers in mailing lists. In B. Batinic, U.-D. Reips and M. Bosnjak (eds), *Online Social Sciences* (pp. 263–274). Seattle, WA: Hogrefe and Huber.

Strickland, O. L., Moloney, M. F., Dietrich, A. S., Myerburg, J. D., Cotsonis, G. A. and Johnson, R. (2003). Measurement issues related to data collection on the world wide web. *Advances in Nursing Science 26*(4), 246–256.

Tashakkori, A. and Teddlie, C. (1998) *Mixed methodology: Combining qualitative and quantitative approaches.* Thousand Oaks, CA: Sage.

Ward, K. J. (1999). The cyber-ethnographic (re)construction of two feminist online communities. *Sociological Research Online 4*(1). Available at http://www.socresearchonline.org.uk/socresearchonline/4/1/ward.html.

Workman, J. P. (1992). Use of electronic media in a participant observation study. *Qualitative Sociology 15*(4), 419–425.

Yoshini, A., Shigemura, J., Kobayashi, Y., Nomura, S., Shishikura, K., Den, R., Wakisaka, H., Kamata, S. and Ashida, H. (2001). Telepsychiatry: assessment of televideo psychiatric interview reliability with present- and next-generation internet infrastructures. *Acta Psychiatrica Scandinavica* *104*, 223–226.

Appendix A: listserv primer

How to access and search messages on discussion lists

You will need: an Internet connection, and an email client or web browser. The email method is described in Hewson *et al.* (2003); send an email to listserv@listserv.net, leaving the subject line blank and writing 'list global' in the body. You will get back an email stating that there are around 48,000 (at the time of writing) listserv lists available, and that you should narrow your search (using e.g. 'list global punk'). Alternatively, using a web browser access the Catalist interface available at: http://www.lsoft.com/catalist.html. Using the latter method, a search for 'punk' in the list title will return around three hits. Email searches will return a similar number of hits, but the two methods will not always return identical results. Subscription information is provided either in the returned email, or by following the list link on the Catalist webpage. Many lists have a web archive interface which allows a direct search of messages in that list. Let's suppose we wanted to find out more about 'panpsychism' and thought that a consciousness search result: PSY-CHE-L@LISTSERV.UH.EDU might contain postings on this topic. Via the web interface, searching all postings from February 1993 to November 2004, eight matches are returned (search conducted 23 February 2005).

CHAPTER 27

Context effects in Internet surveys

New issues and evidence

Jolene D. Smyth, Don A. Dillman, and Leah Melani Christian

Introduction

When one asks another person, 'Is it cold in here?' the answer is undoubtedly affected by the situation or context in which the question is posed. If it is winter and one is talking to a live-in partner, the question may refer to whether or not it is colder in the room than usual. If that same question is asked to a guest, however, it can take on a totally different meaning: 'Is the room as warm as you would like or expect it to be?' The answer that the guest gives might be affected by other contextual factors such as norms of politeness, expectations of what actions the person asking might take given a certain answer and whether the guest knows the questioner's preference for room temperature. If the question is posed while standing in a walk-in freezer, it takes on yet another meaning as the definition of cold now refers to temperatures sufficiently low to preserve food. In this context, the fact that one prefers rooms to be at a comfortable 22°; Celsius (71.6° Fahrenheit) is largely irrelevant to the question at hand. In yet another context this question may not actually refer to temperature at all and, in fact, it may be more of a statement than a question. For example, if, following a particularly rude comment, one asks, 'Is it cold

in here?' the question, in this context, becomes an evaluation of the actions of another person in the room and can serve as an admonition for unacceptable behaviour.

Context matters in normal conversation. Everything from the relationship between participants in the conversation to the physical setting, history of interaction, and presence or absence of others is combined to form the context of everyday conversations. This context affects how simple statements are interpreted and responded to, oftentimes giving to statements meaning that would not be immediately obvious without it. Context also matters in how people interpret and respond to survey questions. During the latter part of the twentieth century, evidence accumulated that a wide variety of contextual factors, such as previous questions and interviewer presence, influence the answers people choose to give to survey questions (e.g., Schuman and Presser 1981; Schuman 1992; Sudman et al. 1996). More recently, research has shown that factors such as visual layout of questions influence people's answers (Christian and Dillman 2004; Tourangeau et al. 2004; Smyth et al. 2006a). Although our knowledge about the mechanisms through which context effects occur is limited, we now know that the interpretation and answering of survey questions is influenced by much more than the wording of individual queries.

It is becoming increasingly clear that many of the context effects found in paper and telephone modes extend to surveys conducted via the Internet as well. However, the substantial variability that is possible in Internet survey design means that the Internet does not provide a unified survey mode in the same way mail and telephone do. This variability in design possibilities corresponds to equally complex variability in possible context effects that result from the use and combination of specific design features. For example, under some circumstances Internet surveys closely resemble mail surveys, such as when they contain only visual stimulus, but under other circumstances, such as when they incorporate aural stimulus or interactive response feedback, they more closely resemble telephone surveys. In still another instance a combination of telephone- and Internet-like features may be included in a design, resulting in complex patterns of context effects. As a result of the myriad possibilities introduced by the Internet, it is becoming increasingly important to approach the examination of context effects from the more specific vantage point of features of survey modes. From this vantage point we can examine when and how context effects in Internet surveys resemble those in mail and telephone surveys and also look at new sources of context effects found only in Internet surveys. The infancy of Internet surveying, seldom used prior to 1998, means that these effects are only now being studied and many important issues have yet to be systematically addressed.

Our purpose in this chapter is to first present a definition of context effects that eliminates from consideration factors beyond the control of survey researchers yet is sufficiently broad to incorporate diverse but related sources of survey context. We then examine four types of context effects that have been documented in mail and telephone surveys with an eye toward identifying new concerns that have arisen or may arise as a result of conducting Internet surveys. The four sources of context effects discussed are: the survey mode used to pose questions to respondents, the order in which questions are asked, the ordering of response options, and the choice of response scale. In addition to reviewing previous research, we report results of new context experiments in which we manipulate response scales across Internet and telephone modes.

What are context effects?

Survey researchers often use the term 'context effects' narrowly to refer to the effects of prior questions on responses to subsequent questions (Schuman and Presser 1981; Schuman 1992; Sudman *et al.* 1996; Tourangeau *et al.* 2000). For example, Schuman and Presser (1981) include context effects, which they define as transfers of meaning between questions, under a broader umbrella of question order effects. However, as Tourangeau *et al.* (2000) point out, the treatment of context as synonymous with question order is largely one of practicality.

> In principle, of course, question context could have a much broader meaning, reflecting the purposes of the survey (as these were presented to the respondent), the climate of opinion at the time of the survey, the presence of other people during the interview, the characteristics of the interviewer, or even the weather at the time of the interview. As a practical matter, though, most research on question context has focused on the effects of earlier questions on answers to later ones.
>
> (Tourangeau *et al.* 2000: 200)

Although they largely limit their discussion of context effects to question order effects, Tourangeau *et al.* (2000) point out that many aspects of the survey instrument as well as the respondents' surroundings, moods and experiences can provide context that may affect how questions are interpreted and answered. The ubiquitous nature of context effects poses a dilemma for researchers of defining such effects so broadly that the term, context, loses its utility for describing such effects, or defining it so narrowly (e.g., only question order effects) that it captures only a small and incomplete aspect of an important phenomenon. With this dilemma in mind, we use the term 'context effects' in this chapter to describe influences on question answers that occur because of information passed on to the respondent *from the survey environment* in which the question is answered. This definition allows us to eliminate superfluous influences that are beyond the control of the researcher (i.e., the weather, past experiences and in many instances setting and mood) and would weaken the explanatory power of the concept, but to broaden the definition beyond question order effects.

The need to broaden the definition of context effects in this way is suggested by the work of Schwarz (1996) and Schwarz et al. (1998) in which, using Grice's (1975) logic of conversation, they argue that respondents approach survey questionnaires as if they are engaged in cooperative conversations. Within this framework, respondents treat formal features of the questionnaire, which represent the contribution of the researcher to the conversation and are assumed to be guided by Grice's (1975) maxims of communication,[1] as communicating the researcher's expectations. Thus, all formal features of the questionnaire or survey process can form context that is used by respondents to make sense of and answer questions, resulting in context effects.

Context effects as a result of survey mode

To the extent that certain response options or questions are presented in differing, but seemingly mode-appropriate ways, different survey modes are bound to produce different response distributions (Dillman and Christian 2005). For example, it is customary in telephone surveys to avoid presenting a 'don't know' option to respondents, but to record don't know answers if they are volunteered (Dillman 2000); to present scales with only the end-points labelled (Dillman and Christian 2005 and Christian 2003); and to use a forced-choice (yes/no) format for multiple-answer questions (Smyth et al. 2006b, c). In contrast, those administering self-administered surveys often include don't know as an explicit option, present scales with all scale points labeled, and present multiple-answer questions

in the check-all-that-apply format. With increasing use of Internet surveys, these practices raise questions about when Internet queries should be matched more closely to the telephone formats, when they should be matched more closely to the mail formats, and in what instances Internet-specific formats should be developed and deployed. Perhaps more important though, are the questions they raise about data quality in increasingly common mixed- or multi-mode research designs. The extent to which such changes across modes alter the survey context and results are empirical questions in need of additional research. Nonetheless, setting aside issues of question format differences, we can still expect context effects related to other features of various survey modes.

The presence or absence of interviewers

Researchers have long recognized that the influence of social desirability on responses to sensitive or embarrassing questions – for example physical health or criminal activity and substance abuse (Phillips and Clancy 1970; Aquilino 1994) is higher in interviewer-administered than self-administered survey modes (Tourangeau and Smith 1996); the presence of interviewers makes norms about interaction and concern with presentation of self much more salient (Dillman and Tarni 1991; de Leeuw 1992; Krysan et al. 1994). To avoid this problem, some face-to-face interviews include self-administered forms of data collection for the sensitive questions (de Leeuw 2005).

Given previous research, we can expect both mail and the Internet to produce fewer socially desirable responses because they are self-administered modes. For both mail and Internet surveys, however, this expectation is contingent on respondents' trust in the survey situation (e.g., Do they believe confidentiality statements and do they think their submitted answers are identifiable to the researchers?) and whether or not they are alone when they complete the questionnaire. In addition, for the Internet it is further contingent on respondents' perceptions of and trust in computer and Internet technology in general (i.e., Can information be stored on their computer without them knowing? Does the Internet provide a confidential vehicle for transmitting sensitive information?) (Couper 2000).

---

[1] The Maxim of Quantity – contributions are meant to be as informative as possible without giving too much information; The Maxim of Quality – contributions are true and can be backed up by evidence; and The Maxim of Manner – contributions are to be clear, unambiguous, brief, and orderly (Grice 1975: 45–46).

While more research is needed in this area, preliminary evidence indicates that Internet surveys do produce less social desirability than telephone surveys (Chang 2001; Taylor *et al.* 2005).

Another way that an interviewer-present survey context may lead to altered responses is through acquiescence or the tendency to give agreeable responses regardless of what the true response might be; it is easier and more polite in most cultures to agree than to disagree (Javeline 1999; Dillman 2000). An example of acquiescence can be seen in findings showing that 60 per cent of respondents in one group agreed with a statement blaming crime and lawlessness on individuals while 57 per cent of respondents in another group agreed that social conditions were to blame from crime and lawlessness (Schuman and Presser 1981). Five months later respondents were re-interviewed, but given the opposite question. Results indicated that over the two interviews about 25 per cent of respondents agreed to both versions of the question.

As was the case with social desirability, since acquiescence is a norm-based phenomenon we expect to find higher degrees of it in interviewer-administered modes where social norms are invoked and lower degrees in self-administered modes where social norms can more easily be ignored. This expectation has been confirmed by some (Dillman and Tarni 1991), but disconfirmed by others (de Leeuw 1992), leaving it an open question for further research, research that must now address the extent to which acquiescence is a problem in Internet surveys as well as telephone, mail, and other modes (see Smyth *et al.* [2006b] for discussion of acquiescence in multiple-answer questions in Internet surveys).

Control of the survey process

Modal differences in who has control over the survey process can also lead to context effects in response distributions. In telephone and face-to-face surveys an interviewer has control over the survey process and can regulate both the order in which respondents receive questions and the speed with which the survey is completed. Telephone interviews tend to be conducted at relatively quick paces, thus limiting the amount of time that respondents have to process questions and formulate answers (Krosnick and Alwin 1987) and leading to more use of pre-formed responses and previously accessed information (Dillman *et al.* 1996). In mail surveys, on the other hand, the respondent maintains complete control over the speed of the survey and the order in which questions are processed (Dillman 2000).

Internet surveys, however, can be designed to give respondents varying levels of control over survey speed and question order. Some Internet surveys, for example, impose time constraints by timing out if left idle for specified periods of time; others have no such constraints. In one comparison in which the Internet had no imposed time constraints, Christian et al. (forthcoming) found that respondents to the Internet mode took substantially longer to complete a 25 question survey (a mean of 21.4 minutes) than did respondents to the telephone mode (12.1 minutes). Varying levels of time pressure may result in respondents experiencing surveys in different contexts: however, empirical research into the exact mechanisms behind time pressure differences and the consequences of these differences remains scarce.

With respect to question order, scrollable Internet surveys where all the questions appear on one page give the respondent full control over what they process and when, making this type of Internet survey quite similar to mail surveys. In contrast, page-by-page survey construction allows researchers to impose various levels of control over the order in which questions are read, ranging from very little (like mail) to full control (like face-to-face and telephone). For example, Internet survey designers can control whether respondents are allowed to advance through the survey if they have not adequately answered a question and whether they can move backward through the survey to return to previous questions. Context effects associated with question order will be considered in more depth below. Suffice it to say here that having full control over the order in which questions are read and processed allows researchers to at least anticipate, and in some instances eliminate, context effects due to question order effects.

Aural vs. visual communication

A final fundamental mode difference that can affect responses is the basic form of communication that makes up the modes. Whereas interviewer-administered surveys are almost always (with the exception of show cards) based on aural communication, paper surveys are based entirely on visual communication. Internet surveys, however, can be designed entirely visually so that they emulate paper surveys or they can be designed using features such as sound and video clips, moving them closer to telephone and face-to-face interviews.

The distinction between these two types of communication is important because they provide different cues from which respondents infer information about the survey and the response task. For example, visual grouping and subgrouping in self-administered questionnaires may communicate to respondents that questions (and/or response options) are related, leading to question order effects, a topic that will be discussed below. When the same questions are read over the telephone, respondents may not make the same connections between them. A number of recent studies have produced evidence that respondents to self-administered, visually based surveys rely on visual cues in addition to the verbal messages on the page/screen to interpret and answer survey questions (Christian and Dillman 2004; Couper et al. 2004b; Smyth et al. 2004, 2006a; Tourangeau et al. 2004).

New mode context effects introduced by Internet surveys

In addition to the factors that they share in common with either mail or telephone surveys, Internet surveys are also complicated by a number of Internet-specific factors that can lead to alterations in context. The landscape orientation of most computer screens, for example, may encourage a horizontally oriented design, such as when response options are double- or triple-banked to take advantage of horizontal space. Moving response options into multiple columns may interrupt the linear flow of scales or make some options appear more prominent than others, thus altering the interpretation and answering of the question. For example, Christian and Dillman (2004) report a tendency for respondents to focus on the top line of options when they are double- or triple-banked (also see Christian 2003; Dillman and Christian 2005).

In addition, varying hardware and software configurations introduce the complication that what the designer creates may not actually be what the respondent receives. While steps can be taken to minimize alterations to the questionnaire as a result of hardware and software configurations (see Chapter 29, this volume), none are effective in all situations and some respondents will inevitably receive the questionnaire with altered visual effects (e.g., changes in font, colour or spacing) that may then affect their interpretation and answering of questions. Survey compatibility with old or less common browsers and the likelihood that some respondents disable JavaScript (i.e., a scripting programming language commonly used in designing Internet surveys) also pose significant challenges for the Internet mode (see Schmidt, Chapter 29 this volume). Perhaps more troublesome though is that different hardware and software configurations are likely to be associated with various demographic factors such as age and socio-economic status, thus introducing systematic bias into results (Buchanan and Reips 2001).

The Internet also introduces a number of technical innovations that may have context effects, some of which are as yet unknown. Researchers have virtually unlimited ability to use colour, graphics, and, as mentioned previously, even sound and video clips in Internet surveys. The effects of such technical features on survey responses has barely begun to be explored although there is some evidence that such features may increase download time, promoting early termination (Couper 2002). One such component that has received some research attention is the effect of including progress indicators in Internet surveys. Couper et al. (2001) report only slight, and not significant, increases in completion rates when progress indicators are present in Internet surveys: however, they speculate that some of the gain in completion rates is offset by early terminations due to increased download times. Another innovative component that has received some research attention is the effects of using photos in Internet surveys (Couper et al. 2004b, 2005; Witte et al. 2004). The findings here generally indicate that respondents take into account the information in the photos when formulating their responses and that results are significantly altered by the presence of the photos. Finally, researchers are beginning to examine the effects of new question formats that are possible in Internet surveys. For example, one study indicates that when drop-down menus require respondents to scroll down to reveal all available answers, the options that appear initially are more prone to endorsement (Couper *et al.* 2004a).

Context effects as a result of question order

The most commonly studied type of survey context effects are question order effects whereby previous questions and the answers given to them affect how respondents interpret and answer subsequent questions. Question order effects become increasingly likely to occur the closer questions are to one another, in terms of both topic and location in the questionnaire. When they do occur, question order effects can be categorized as either assimilation effects, where responses to two or more question become more highly correlated, or contrast effects, where responses become less correlated. Since others (Schuman and Presser 1981; Strack 1992; Tourangeau 1992; Tourangeau *et al.* 2000) have reviewed question order effects in substantial depth, our discussion of them here is more limited and is meant only to provide a general framework for understanding potential question order effects in Internet surveys.

Oftentimes question order effects occur when a prior question brings to mind considerations that are then more accessible for use in interpreting and responding to a subsequent question – a priming function (see Schwarz and Clore 1983; Tourangeau *et al.* 1989; Schwarz and Bless 1992). The result of priming is likely to be an assimilation effect when the information brought to mind is used to form a representation of the object being inquired about. In contrast, if the information brought to mind is used to form the referent or standard to which the respondent compares the object of inquiry, the result could be either a contrast or an assimilation effect depending on how the referent is formulated. For example, we would expect a contrast effect if the standard of comparison for a question asking about one's current quality of life was a particularly bad event in the past, such as a divorce process or a period of homelessness (both are extreme values on the dimension of judgement). If that same question were asked, in a context where the standard of comparison was an average of previous 'measures' of quality

of life, we would expect an assimilation effect (Tourangeau *et al.* 2000).

A previous question may also influence responses to subsequent questions by invoking a norm or cultural value. Oftentimes, but not always, the norms/values invoked are the norms of cooperative communication sketched out in Grice's maxims of communication. For this type of effect to occur, the respondent must perceive the two questions as being related topically, or, in other words, as belonging to the same conversational context. For example, respondents following Grice's maxims of communication might perceive questions as related because they expect them to be relevant to the conversation as it has been occurring. In this instance we might expect an assimilation effect (carry-over effect) because seeing the questions as topically linked would lead to the use of similar considerations in formulating responses (for examples see Schuman and Presser 1981; Tourangeau and Rasinski 1988; Strack *et al.* 1991). However, if the respondents invoke the norm of non-redundancy, they may assume that later answers should exclude information already used or reported in earlier answers. Following this conversational norm would result in a contrast effect, more specifically, a subtraction effect (for examples see Schuman and Presser 1981; Schwarz *et al.* 1991b; Tourangeau *et al.* 1991; Mason *et al.* 1994). This type of order effect is particularly common in part-whole question sequences (i.e., marital satisfaction and general satisfaction sequences).

Respondents may also invoke cultural norms and values that are not necessarily part of the logic of conversation. For example, norms of fairness (reciprocity or even-handedness), consistency and neutrality can be invoked in answering survey questions. The effects of the norm of even-handedness on survey responses was demonstrated in a classic study by Hyman and Sheatsley (1950) and replicated by Schuman and Presser (1981). In both instances, researchers found that respondents were significantly more likely to answer a question asking whether communist reporters should be allowed to report on visits to the United States affirmatively after having answered affirmatively to a similar question about allowing US reporters to report on visits to the Soviet Union. Similarly, research has shown that placing somewhat related items together in a questionnaire can result in assimilation effects because respondents don't want to appear inconsistent in their responses (Smith 1983). Finally, fear of taking extreme positions on highly polarized topics may lead to contrast effects as respondents attempt to appear neutral and non-partisan by selecting some items but rejecting others (Tourangeau 1992).

New question order context effects introduced by computerized and Internet surveys

Much of the above research and theorizing about question order effects predates the expansion of Internet surveying. While it is highly likely that the same types of order effects occur in Internet surveys for the same reasons as cited above, computerized surveying and its ease of use via the Internet also introduces a number of factors not found in other modes that may impact question order effects. For example, in Internet surveys it is easy to vary how the question order is presented to respondents; this manipulation can range from simply flipping the order of two questions to complete randomization of all questions. However, the extent to which these are viable options depends greatly on the purpose and methodology – single vs. mixed mode, cross-sectional vs. longitudinal vs. panel, etc. – of the study.

As mentioned previously, researchers also have the option of presenting all of the questions on one screen, making the questionnaire more similar to a paper survey, or presenting questions on separate screens (page-by-page construction), making it more similar to a telephone survey. The choice that researchers make between these two options may have important implications for question order effects. Presenting all of the questions on one screen allows respondents to easily scroll back and forth throughout the survey to remind themselves of the context of the conversation and to re-examine relationships between questions, but doing so may increase the likelihood of context effects and the likelihood that the effects flow both forward and backward (i.e., early question affect later questions and visa versa). Using page-by-page construction, on the other hand, should reduce the likelihood of context effects by making the relationships between questions less obvious.

As in telephone surveys, the extent to which early questions can affect later questions in a page-by-page design depends on respondents' memory capacity. However, the danger in page-by-page design is that the respondent may lose track of the relationships between questions so much that they lose a sense of continuity in the survey and questions seem isolated.

The expectation of increased context effects when multiple questions appear on one screen has been confirmed in at least three published studies. Couper et al. (2001) found that item correlations were higher among items when they appeared together on a screen as opposed to on separate screens, but that the differences were not large enough to be statistically significant. Reips (2002) found that two items on spending (for a better Internet connection vs. charity) influenced each other when presented on the same screen. And, Tourangeau et al. (2004) presented respondents with eight related items regarding diet all together on one screen, separated in groups of four on two screens, or each on its own screen. They found that the eight items were most highly correlated when all eight were on one screen followed by the two-screen (four items per screen) treatment and then the treatment in which all items appeared on their own page. While the context effects reported in these studies are assimilation effects, it is likely that presenting part-whole question sequences together on a screen would produce contrast effects.

Context effects resulting from response category order

Similarly to question order effects, the order in which response categories are presented can also influence the answers given to questions. Typically response order effects come in two types: primacy effects, in which options are more likely to be endorsed when they appear early in the list, and recency effects, in which options are more likely to be selected when they appear late in the list. Current research suggests several mechanisms that may underlie response order effects. The evidence seems to indicate that none of these factors can account for all of the nuances of response order effects, but instead multiple factors may oftentimes work in concert to produce or to obscure evidence of primacy and recency effects.

Memory limitations and response order effects

In early work researchers proposed memory limitations as an explanation for response order effects (Schuman and Presser 1981; Krosnick and Alwin 1987). The theory of memory limitations predicts recency effects, especially in questions with long or complex lists of options, because respondents have an easier time recalling response options that are stored in their short-term memory, the last options read or heard, than those stored in their long-term memory, the first options read or heard. Response options in the middle of lists are the least likely to be remembered. This theory, however, has been called into question based on findings of primacy effects (Mueller 1970; Krosnick and Alwin 1987) and response order effects in questions with only two or three response options (Schuman and Presser 1981; Schwarz et al. 1992).

The cognitive elaboration model of response order effects

More recent work has led to the development of the cognitive elaboration perspective in which a three-way interaction between response option order, presentation mode and item plausibility is theorized (Schwarz et al. 1992; Sudman et al. 1996). This perspective relies on the underlying assumption that each response option is a short persuasive communication that brings to mind for the respondent either confirming or disconfirming cognitive elaborations. The more time respondents have to consider an option the more confirming or disconfirming information they will think of, making them more likely to endorse or reject the option. The amount of time that respondents have to consider an option depends on both its serial position in the list and the survey presentation mode (visual vs. aural) (Krosnick and Alwin 1987; Schwarz et al. 1992).

In visually based survey modes respondents can deeply process items appearing early in the list, but as they move through the list their minds become more cluttered and their ability to process options becomes increasingly limited. Thus, respondents give options appearing later in the list less processing time and energy (Krosnick and Alwin 1987). If early response options are plausible, bringing to mind confirmatory thoughts, they are more likely to be endorsed than those appearing later, resulting in primacy effects. However, if early items are implausible, bringing to mind disconfirming thoughts, they are less likely to be selected, resulting in recency effects.

In contrast, in aurally based survey modes, interviewers control the pace of the survey and tend to move rapidly through the response options, not allowing long pauses until the end of the list. Respondents, therefore, have more time to process response options appearing later in lists. Processing-time limitations combined with memory limitations lead to deeper processing of later items. If the later options are plausible a recency effect is expected as they will be more likely to be selected, but if they are implausible respondents will avoid selecting them, resulting in a primacy effect. Under typical survey conditions, where researchers try to avoid providing implausible response options, we would expect primacy effects in visually based surveys and recency effects in aurally based surveys.

Evidence supporting these expectations was found in research by Schwarz et al. (1992). In their experiments, the visual presentation format produced primacy effects while the aural presentation format produced recency effects. Based on the theory that response order effects depend on the confirming or disconfirming thoughts respondents have about the response options, Schwarz et al. (1992) hypothesized that they could eliminate response order effects by stimulating respondents to think about the specific content of response options in previous questions. In this way, they primed the respondent so that processing time limitations would have less influence; the respondent had already processed a lot of information about the topic by the time they got to the response options of interest. They found that including relevant context questions in this way entirely eliminated response order effects, a result that supports the cognitive elaboration model of response order effects.

Satisficing as an alternative explanation for response order effects

While the cognitive elaboration model seems to accurately account for response order effects,

Tourangeau *et al.* (2000) point out that response order effects could be explained equally well by another more parsimonious perspective, Krosnick's (1991, 1999) theory of satisficing. According to this theory, respondents avoid expending the energy to provide an optimal answer by making a dichotomous judgement (i.e., yes/no) about each response option. They proceed through the options until they come to one they consider satisfactory and then endorse that option and discontinue their consideration of subsequent options. In visual modes, respondents can be expected to work from the top of the list down and in aural modes from the bottom of the list up for the same reasons discussed above.

A complicating factor: anchoring effects

Researchers also recognize that other mechanisms unrelated to memory, cognitive elaboration, or satisficing response strategies may underlie response order effects. For example, when respondents are asked to evaluate options on some dimension of judgement – degree of typicality, degree of appeal, etc. – one option may stand out as a standard or anchor against which all others are compared. If the option used as the standard sets a high expectation, then the moderate options that follow it will become less likely to be endorsed (primacy effect). If it sets a low expectation the moderate options that follow it become more likely to be endorsed (recency effect). In one example, respondents were asked which of the foods potatoes, noodles and rice, were 'typically German.' Significantly more respondents marked potatoes and noodles as 'typically German' when rice was presented at the beginning of the list than when rice appeared after these other options (Noelle-Neumann 1970). Contrast effects such as these can greatly complicate predictions and interpretations of primacy and recency effects.

New response position effects introduced by Internet surveys

To date very little research on the effects of response position order in Internet surveys has been done. The research that has been done, however, indicates that Internet surveys are prone to similar types of response option position effects as paper surveys. For example, Couper *et al.* (2004a) asked respondents to report which of twelve nutrients is the most important when selecting a breakfast cereal and found that options have significantly higher endorsement rates when they appear in the top five positions of the list. A second question asking about the most important feature in decisions about automobile purchases produced similar patterns of primacy. Perhaps more importantly though, their results showed that response option position effects were magnified under specific design conditions that are unique to Internet surveys. In particular, in what they refer to as the 'visibility principle' response options that were immediately visible, in this case the first items in drop-down menus, were more likely to be selected than those that respondents had to scroll down to reveal.

While the Internet appears to present similar response option position effects as paper surveys, it also provides innovative design features that might be used more easily and cost effectively to address such effects. Most importantly, Internet survey designers can vary the order that response options appear for each respondent up to the point of fully randomizing them in order to mitigate response option position effects. Again, the possibility of taking advantage of this ability greatly depends on the purpose of the study and its design.

Response option scale effects

In addition to considering the possibility of response position and order effects, survey designers must attempt to avoid response scale effects. Scale effects occur when the choice of scale provided to answer a question affects the answers given. Tourangeau *et al.* (2000) offer a useful summary of five ways in which response scales can alter the way respondents answer questions:

1. Positivity or leniency bias – respondents avoid the negative end of rating scales;

2. Scale label effects – respondents avoid negative numbers because they imply more extreme judgements than low positive numbers (Schwarz *et al.* 1991a);

3. Response contraction bias – responses clump toward the middle of scales because respondents attempt to avoid extreme categories;

4. Reference point effects – specific numbers (0, 10, 50, 100 etc.) have predetermined cultural connotations that either encourage or discourage their selection (i.e., the number zero implies absence of); and

5. Scale range effects – the range of a scale either
   (a) changes definitions of the topic at hand (i.e., when asked about frequency of anger low scales may imply that only serious anger incidences should be counted and high scales may imply that less serious incidences are relevant) or
   (b) changes definitions of the distribution of the characteristic in the general public which are then used as a reference for the respondent in judging their own situation (i.e., low scales imply that average people don't get angry very often while high scales imply higher incidence of anger among average people) (Schwarz *et al.* 1991a: 248).

In addition the visual presentation of scales may influence and interact with these five scale effects. Research by Dillman and Christian (2005) and Christian and Dillman (2004) has shown that the answers respondents provide to both paper and Internet surveys are influenced by the visual presentation of scales.

The first two effects, positivity bias and scale label effects, are demonstrated in face-to-face and paper surveys by Schwarz *et al.* (1991a). When respondents were asked to rate how successful they had been in life, 34 per cent of those who received a scale ranging from 0–10 rated themselves between 0 and 5 while only 13 per cent of those who received a scale ranging from –5 to 5 (with the same end point labels) rated themselves on equivalent values (–5 to 0). Further experimentation revealed that respondents determined the meaning of the scale labels based on the numbers associated with them. The label 'not at all successful' associated with a score of 0 can be interpreted to mean an absence of success, but the same label associated with a negative number (–5) may refer to the presence of explicit failure (also see Schwarz *et al.* 1998).

This finding has recently been extended to Internet surveys (Tourangeau *et al.* 2006).

The third effect, the tendency for respondents to prefer middle categories, is confirmed in recent research on Internet surveys by Tourangeau *et al.* (2004). In fact, these researchers found that respondents are drawn toward the visual midpoint of scales, not necessarily the conceptual midpoint. In one experiment, respondents were presented with scales that included nonsubstantive response options ('no opinion' or 'don't know'). These response options were visually separated from the scale for some respondents, but not for others. When they were not visually separated, responses tended to fall lower on the scale, toward the visual midpoint. When they were visually separated, responses tended to be higher, again toward the visual midpoint (which had moved up when the nonsubstantive responses were separated from the scale). In additional experiments, spacing between scale items was manipulated such that in some treatments the conceptual and visual midpoints of the scale were aligned and in others they were not. Results were similar in that respondents tended to be drawn toward the visual midpoint over the conceptual midpoint.

Several studies have addressed the fifth effect, scale range effects. This body of research is largely based on an early study by Schwarz *et al.* (1985). They found that when respondents were asked how many hours of television they watch per day only about 16 per cent reported watching more than 2½ hours when they were presented with a scale ranging from 'up to ½ hour' to 'more than 2½ hours'. In comparison, about 38 per cent reported watching more than 2½ hours when they were presented with a scale ranging from 'up to 2½ hours' to 'more than 4½ hours' (Schwarz *et al.* 1985). In addition, respondents given the low scale range estimated that others watch television significantly less than did respondents given the high scale range did (2.7 hours vs. 3.2 hours). These findings indicate that respondents use information in scales to inform their answers; they may assume that the scale represents the most common answers or even that the midpoint of the scale represents the response of a 'typical' respondent. Given such information, respondents may then formulate their answer based on how typical they think they are.

Schwarz and colleagues' (1985) findings were replicated and extended by Rockwood *et al.* (1997). These researchers found that the range provided in response options has significant effects for questions about frequent and mundane behaviours (hours students spend studying or watching television), but does not have significant effects for questions about more rare topics (such as grade point average), suggesting that the scale range is more influential when respondents have to estimate frequencies rather than simply recall factual information. In addition, they established that response option effects such as these occur in both mail and telephone surveys and that in telephone surveys they can be confounded by other factors such as social desirability and pace of the interview (see the research example below for an extension to Internet surveys).

New response scale effects introduced by Internet surveys

Because Internet surveys are generally visually based they are not plagued by the same memory limitations as telephone surveys. As a result, unlike telephone surveyors, Internet surveyors can use fully labelled scales, a practice that has the potential to eliminate vagueness in some scales, thus reducing the amount of interpreting and inferring that the respondent has to do and thereby reducing context effects. This practice seems preferable, but again, may be limited by any mixed-mode considerations.

The Internet also introduces the opportunity to utilize new and innovative ways of displaying response options, the effects of which are largely unknown as of yet. We have already discussed the use of drop-down menus. Another example is the sliding scale in which the respondent uses the mouse to drag a marker along a scale and drop it at the point on the scale that they feel best represents them or their opinion. Bayer and Thomas (2004) compared seven-point sliding scales to conventional scales constructed using radio buttons. They found that the sliding scales took significantly more time to complete and that they resulted in higher mean values because respondents with sliding scales were more likely

to endorse the highest point on the scale than were those with radio button scales. While Bayer and Thomas' (2004) sliding scales limited respondents to seven possible scale points, others have examined visual analogue scales in which the respondent can mark any point on the scale resulting in interval level scalar data (Funke and Reips 2006). Results indicate that visual analogue scales (when linearly transformed) also produce more extreme responses than categorical scales. As more and more innovative scalar designs are developed for Internet surveys it will be important to study the effects they have on respondent answers systematically.

A research example: how the estimation of routine behaviours is influenced by mode and response scale contexts

A survey conducted in autumn 2004 emulated the Schwarz *et al.* (1985) and Rockwood *et al.* (1997) studies by asking a randomly selected sample of Washington State University undergraduate students how many hours per day they typically study, spend on a computer, and watch television. Students were randomly assigned to receive a low estimate scale (½ hour or less to more than 2½ hours), a high estimate scale (2½ hours or less to more than 4½ hours) or an open-ended answer box (not reported in depth here since it is not the main interest of the chapter) in either the Internet or telephone mode (see Table 27.1 for response rates and Figure 27.1 for treatments). This study extends past research by examining scale range effects in the Internet mode and by considering the extent to which such questions are affected by the Internet context relative to the telephone context.

Results

Response distributions and significance tests for the low- and high-range scales are shown in Table 27.1. These results indicate that Internet surveys are prone to the same type of scale effects reported by Schwarz *et al.* (1985) and Rockwood *et al.* (1997). When asked how many

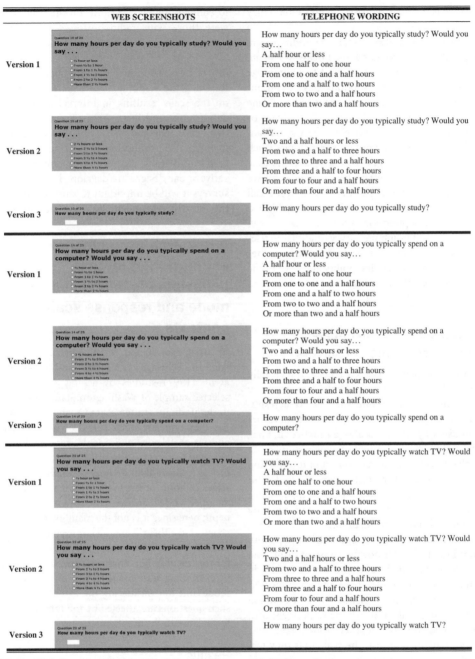

Figure 27.1 Experimental treatments as they appeared in each mode.

hours per day they study, 29.8 per cent of Internet respondents to the low-range scale and 71.1 per cent of Internet respondents to the high-range scale reported studying over 2.5 hours per day, a difference of 41.3 percentage points! Similarly, only 29.2 per cent of low range scale respondents reported over 2.5 hours of computing per day while 66.0 per cent of high range scale respondents reported this amount of computing and only 8.4 per cent of low range scale respondents reported watching over 2.5 hours of television per day compared to 21.3 per cent

Table 27.1 Percentage of respondents reporting spending up to 2.5 hours and over 2.5 hours/day studying, computing, and watching TV by mode

	Web sample			Telephone sample		
	Low range	High range	Significance tests	Low range	High range	Significance tests
Study						
≤ 2½ hours	70.2	28.9	$\chi^2 = 123.38$	65.8	26.5	$\chi^2 = 96.60$
> 2½ hours	29.8	71.1	$p = 0.000$	34.2	73.6	$p = 0.000$
Computer						
≤ 2½ hours	70.8	34.1	$\chi^2 = 96.75$	74.6	48.9	$\chi^2 = 43.56$
> 2½ hours	29.2	66.0	$p = 0.000$	25.4	51.1	$p = 0.000$
TV						
≤ 2½ hours	91.6	78.8	$\chi^2 = 22.99$	93.6	82.3	$\chi^2 = 18.57$
> 2½ hours	8.4	21.3	$p = 0.000$	6.4	17.7	$p = 0.000$
Response rate	351/600	379/600		311/536	311/536	
	(58.5%)	(63.2%)		(58.0%)	(58.0%)	

of high-range scale respondents. Results are similar within the telephone mode. Of the respondents who received the low scale 34.2 per cent reported spending over 2.5 hours studying, 25.4 per cent reported spending over 2.5 hours on a computer, and 6.4 per cent reported spending over 2.5 hours watching television. In comparison, among those receiving the high scale 73.6 per cent reported studying, 51.1 per cent reported computing, and 17.7 per cent reported watching television over 2.5 hours per day. All of these differences across scale ranges for both the Internet and telephone modes are highly significant ($p = 0.000$).

These results indicate that the scales used provided different contexts resulting in different responses: however, they do not address whether or not survey mode context effects occurred either independently or in conjunction with the scale effects. For the three questions analysed here, logistic regressions were conducted to estimate the likelihood of reporting greater than 2.5 hours of activity based on mode and question form. The logistic regression results allow us to do three things that the chi-square analyses reported above do not: (1) test for the significance of response scale effects while controlling for mode effects and visa versa, (2) examine whether response scale effects and mode effects

depend on each other (interaction effects), and (3) estimate the magnitude of the scale and mode effects.

The findings of the logistic regression equations (Table 27.2) confirm the findings reported above. Respondents were 5.35 times more likely to report studying, 3.07 times more likely to report computing, and 3.13 times more likely to report watching TV over 2.5 hours per day if they received the high-range scale, rather than the low-range scale. Respondents to all three questions were also more likely to report spending over 2.5 hours per day on these activities if they received the open-ended response format, although this format did not have as large of effects as the high-range scale (studying = 1.99 times, computing = 1.60 times, and TV = 2.82 times).

With regard to mode effects, the findings of the logistic regressions indicate that mode did not have an independent effect on the results of any of the three questions analysed. However, significant interaction effects were found between mode and the open-ended response format for both the study time and computing time questions, indicating that the effect of the open-ended response format depends on survey mode. In particular, Internet respondents to the open-ended question format (compared to the low scale range respondents) were 3.62 times more

Table 27.2 Logistic regression results of the effects of response option format and survey mode

	Odds ratio	Standard error	z	p
Q10: Study time				
High scale	5.35	0.941	9.54	0.000
Open-ended	1.99	0.326	4.18	0.000
Mode (web)	0.82	0.137	−1.21	0.227
High * Mode	1.08	0.260	0.34	0.736
Open * Mode	1.63	0.373	2.13	0.033
N				2,006
Q14: Computer time				
High scale	3.07	0.531	6.50	0.000
Open-ended	1.60	0.279	2.67	0.008
Mode (web)	1.21	0.212	1.09	0.277
High * Mode	1.52	0.361	1.80	0.072
Open * Mode	1.62	0.384	2.04	0.042
N				2,004
Q23: TV time				
High scale	3.13	0.859	4.15	0.000
Open-ended	2.82	0.780	3.75	0.000
Mode (web)	1.34	0.403	0.96	0.338
High * Mode	0.94	0.338	−0.17	0.865
Open * Mode	1.05	0.380	0.13	0.898
N				1,996

* denotes interaction terms between the two variables listed.

likely to report over 2.5 hours of studying per day while their telephone counterparts were only 1.99 times more likely to report this much studying. Similarly, Internet respondents to the open-ended format were 3.22 times more likely to report over 2.5 hours of computing per day while their telephone counterparts were only 1.60 times more likely to report this much computing. Additionally, although it did not reach significance, the interaction effect of the high-range scale and survey mode did approach significance for the computing time question.

It is possible that the apparent mode effects in these models are actually due to mode-related non-response if respondents who spend a lot of time studying or using computers were more likely to respond to the Internet mode than to the telephone mode. In analyses not shown here this alternative explanation was explored. At the final phase of data collection 600 telephone non-responders were re-contacted and asked to complete the survey via the Internet mode; 144 (24 per cent) did so. If high study or computing time respondents are more likely to respond to the Internet than the telephone mode these 'converted' respondents should report higher study and/or computing time than those who initially responded to the telephone mode. However, this does not appear to be the case, as the percentages of respondents reporting over 2.5 hours of each activity per day do not significantly differ between these two groups. These results suggest that the mode differences in these questions are not due to mode-related non-response bias.

Overall then, the results of the present experiment confirm the findings of Schwarz *et al.* (1985) and Rockwood *et al.* (1997) with respect to low- and high-range scales and extend those findings to the Internet mode. Internet respondents also rely on the information they gather from the context of the survey process, in this case from both the range of the scales provided and the mode in which the survey is conducted, to help them formulate their responses to questions. As a result, it seems advisable to minimize context in an effort to get unbiased responses from respondents. To that end, Schwarz et al. (1985) recommended the use of open-ended response formats instead of scalar formats for behaviour frequency questions. While this strategy may reduce response option context effects, the data presented here indicate that the open-ended format was more prone to mode context effects than the other formats. In fact, the most important finding of this experiment might be that the effects of different contexts do not always happen independently of each other. The complex relationships and potential trade-offs between different types of survey context is a topic in need of much further study.

Conclusion

In everyday conversation, we encounter countless seemingly simple questions such as: what time is it? What should I do next? Are we headed in the correct direction? Do I have enough money? We oftentimes fail to explicitly realize that our understanding of these questions and the answers we provide to them are based on far more than the meaning of the words that form them; they also depend on the context of our everyday conversations. The task of answering a survey question shares common elements with the task of answering any one of the questions we face everyday. Context matters in our everyday and survey conversations; whether the question is, 'Is it cold in here?' or 'How many hours do you typically study per day?'

Within survey methodology the term context effects has long been used in a limited way to refer to question order effects. However, more recent work has begun to recognize that other survey characteristics, such as mode and presentation of response options, also play an important role in setting the survey context. We argue that the definition of context effects within survey methodology should be broadened to include multiple factors that influence the survey context; however, this expanded definition should exclude factors external to the survey process itself that are out of the researcher's control to maintain the usefulness of the concept to survey methodologists.

In this chapter, we have reviewed four major types of context effects: survey mode, question order, response option order and response scales. We focused on how these four types of context effects manifest themselves in Internet surveys and also discussed relevant research on paper and telephone surveys that enhances our understanding of the causes and consequences of context effects in Internet surveys.

One of the most important themes to emerge from the developing body of research using Internet surveys is that context effects can vary widely depending on the specific design features employed in the survey. The flexibility and ability to combine features from various other survey modes when designing Internet surveys means that it is not accurate to assume Internet surveys will perform similarly to paper or telephone surveys. Whether the context of an Internet survey more closely resembles a paper survey or a telephone survey, depends on what specific features are employed in its design and implementation. To understand context effects in Internet surveys it is important to isolate which features they share with other survey modes as well as new features and combinations that are unique to Internet surveys.

Even though the four types of context effects are summarized separately, the research example at the end of the chapter reveals how multiple types of context effects work together to influence the question-answer process. The experiment highlights the fact that different types of context effects oftentimes occur in conjunction with one another; sometimes reducing one type of context effect (e.g., using open-ended answer spaces to avoid the suggestive information in conventional scales) may increase another (e.g., response differences due to the contexts of web and telephone modes). As surveys become more and more complex, understanding how different types of context effects occur independently and/or in conjunction with each other becomes important in reducing measurement error.

References

Aquilino, W. S. (1994). Interview mode effects in surveys of drug and alcohol use: a field experiment. *Public Opinion Quarterly 58*, 210–240.

Bayer, L. R. and Thomas, R. K. (2004). A comparison of sliding scales with other scale types in online surveys. Paper presented at RC33 6th International Conference on Social Methodology. August, 2004.

Buchanan, T. and Reips, U.-D. (2001). Platform-dependent biases in online research: do Mac users really think different? In K. J. Jonas, P. Breuer, B. Schauenburg and M. Boos (eds), *Perspectives on internet research: concepts and methods.* Retrieved 8 June 2006 from http://www.psych.uni-goettingen.de/congress/gor-2001/contrib/contrib/buchanan-tom/buchanan-tom.

Chang, L. (2001). A comparison of samples and response quality obtained from RDD telephone survey methodology and internet survey methodology. Doctoral Dissertation. Department of Psychology. The Ohio State University, Columbus, OH.

Christian, L. M. (2003). The influence of visual layout on scalar questions in web surveys. Master's Thesis: Washington State University, Pullman, WA.

Christian, L. M. and Dillman, D. A. (2004). The influence of graphical and symbolic language manipulations on responses to self-administered questions. *Public Opinion Quarterly 68*, 1, 57–80.

Christian, L. M., Dillman, D. A. and Smyth, J. D. (Forthcoming). The effects of mode and format on answers to scalar questions in telephone and web surveys. In J. Lepkowski, C. Tucker, M. Brick, E. DeLeeuw, L. Japec, P. Lavrakas, M. Link, and R. Sangster (eds), Advances in telephone survey methodology. New York: Wiley-Interscience.

Couper, M. P. (2000). Web surveys: a review of issues and approaches. *Public Opinion Quarterly 64*, 464–494.

Couper, M. P. (2002). New technologies and survey data collection: challenges and opportunities. Presented at the International Conference on Improving Surveys, Copenhagen, Denmark. August, 2002.

Couper, M. P., Conrad, F. G. and Tourangeau, R. (2005). Visual effects in web surveys. Paper presented at the American Association of Public Opinion Research. Miami, Florida, May 2005.

Couper, M. P., Traugott, M. W. and Lamias, M. J. (2001). Web survey design and administration. *Public Opinion Quarterly 65*, 230–254.

Couper, M. P., Tourangeau, R., Conrad, F. G. and Crawford, S. D. (2004a). What they see is what we get: response options for web surveys. *Social Science Computer Review 22*(1), 111–127.

Couper, M. P., Tourangeau, R. and Kenyon, K. (2004b). Picture this! exploring visual effects in web surveys. *Public Opinion Quarterly 68*, 255–266.

De Leeuw, E. D. (1992). *Data quality in mail, telephone and face to face surveys.* Amsterdam: TT Publications.

De Leeuw, E. D. (2005). To mix or not to mix data collection modes in surveys. *Journal of Official Statistics 21*, 233–255.

Dillman, D. A. (2000). *Mail and internet surveys: the tailored design method.* New York: John Wiley and Sons.

Dillman, D. A. and Christian, L. M. (2005). Survey mode as a source of instability in responses across surveys. *Field Methods 17*(1), 30–52.

Dillman, D. A., Sangster, R. L., Tarni, J. and Rockwood, T. H. (1996). Understanding differences in people's answers to telephone and mail surveys. In M. T. Braverman and J. K. Slater (eds), *New directions for evaluation series*, 70, Advances in survey research (pp. 45–62). San Francisco, CA: Jossey-Bass.

Dillman, D. A. and Tarni, J. (1991). Mode effects of cognitively-designed recall questions: a comparison of answers to telephone and mail surveys. In P. P. Biemer, R. M. Groves, L. E. Lyberg, N. A. Mathiowetz and S. Sudman (eds), *Measurement errors in surveys* (pp. 73–93). New York: Wiley.

Funke, F. and Reips U.-D. (2006) Visual analogue scales in online surveys: non-linear data categorization by transformation with reduced extremes. Presented at the 8th International Conference GOR06, March 21-22, 2006, Bielefeld, Germany. Retrieved 6/20/06 at http://www.frederikfunke.de/papers/gor2006.htm.

Grice, H. P. (1975). Logic and conversation. In P. Cole and J. L. Morgan (eds), *Syntax and semantics, 3: speech acts* (pp. 41–58). New York: Academic Press.

Hyman, H. H. and Sheatsley, P. B. (1950). The current status of American public opinion. In J. C. Payne (ed.), *The teaching of contemporary affairs: twenty-first yearbook of the National Council for the Social Studies* (pp. 11–34). New York: National Education Association.

Javeline, D. (1999). Response effects in polite cultures: a test of acquiescence in Kazakhstan. *Public Opinion Quarterly 63*, 1–28.

Krosnick, Jon A. (1991). Response strategies for coping with the cognitive demands of attitude measures in surveys. *Applied Cognitive Psychology 5*, 213–236.

Krosnick, Jon A. (1999). Survey research. *Annual Review of Psychology 50*, 537–567.

Krosnick, J. A. and Alwin, D. F. (1987). An evaluation of a cognitive theory of response order effects in survey measurement. *Public Opinion Quarterly 51*, 201–219.

Krysan, M., Schuman, H., Scott, L. J. and Beatty, P. (1994). Response rates and response content in mail versus face-to-face surveys. *Public Opinion Quarterly 58*, 381–399.

Mason, R., Carlson, J. E. and Tourangeau, R. (1994). Contrast effects and subtraction in part-whole questions. *Public Opinion Quarterly 58*, 569–578.

Mueller, J. E. (1970). Choosing among 133 candidates. *Public Opinion Quarterly 34*(3), 395–402.

Noelle-Neumann, E. (1970). Wanted: rules for wording structured questionnaires. *Public Opinion Quarterly 34*(2), 191–201.

Phillips, D. L. and Clancy, K. J. (1970). Response biases in field studies of mental illness. *American Sociological Review 36*, 512–514.

Reips, U.-D. (2002) Context effects in web surveys. In B. Batinic, U.-D. Reips and M. Bosnjak (eds), *Online social sciences* (pp. 69–79). Seattle, WA: Hogrefe and Huber.

Rockwood, T. H., Sangster, R. L. and Dillman, D. A. (1997). The effect of response categories in questionnaire answers: context and mode effects. *Sociological Methods and Research 26*(1), 118–140.

Schuman, H. (1992). Context effects: state of the past/state of the art. In N. Schwarz and S. Sudman (eds), *Context effects in social and psychological research* (pp. 5–20). New York: Springer-Verlag.

Schuman, H. and Presser, S. (1981). *Questions and answers in attitude surveys: experiments on question form, wording and context*. New York: Academic Press.

Schwarz, N. (1996). *Cognition and communication: judgmental biases, research methods and the logic of conversation*. Mahwah, NJ: Lawrence Erlbaum.

Schwarz, N. and Bless, H. (1992). Scandals and public trust in politicians: assimilation and contrast effects. *Personality and Social Psychology Bulletin 18*, 574–579.

Schwarz, N. and Clore, G. L. (1983). Mood, misattribution and judgments of well-being: informative and directive functions of affective states. *Journal of Personality and Social Psychology 45*, 513–523.

Schwarz, N., Grayson, C. E., Knäuper, B. (1998). Formal features of rating scales and the interpretation of question meaning. *International Journal of Public Opinion Research 10*(2), 177–183.

Schwarz, N., Hippler, H. J., Deutsch, B. and Strack, F. (1985). Response scales: effects of category range on reported behavior and comparative judgments. *Public Opinion Quarterly 49*(3), 388–395.

Schwarz, N., Hippler, H. J., Noelle-Neumann, E. (1992). A cognitive model of response order effects in survey measurement. In N. Schwarz and S. Sudman (eds), *Context effects in social and psychological research* (pp. 187–201). New York: Springer-Verlag.

Schwarz, N., Knäuper, B. Hippler, H. J., Noelle-Neumann, E. and Clark, L. (1991a). Rating scales: numeric values may change the meaning of scale labels. *Public Opinion Quarterly 55*(4), 570–582.

Schwarz, N., Strack, F. and Mai, H. (1991b). Assimilation and contrast effects in part-whole question sequences: a conversational logic analysis. *Public Opinion Quarterly 55*, 3–23.

Smith, T. W. (1983). An experimental comparison between clustered and scattered scale items. *Social Psychology Quarterly 46*, 163–168.

Smyth, J. D., Dillman, D. A., Christian, L. M. and Stern, M. J. (2004). *How visual grouping influences answers to internet surveys*. Social and Economic Sciences Research Center Technical Report #04-023. Pullman, WA: Washington State University.

Smyth, J. D., Dillman, D. A., Christian, L. M. and Stern, M. J. (2006a). Effects of using visual design principles to group response options in web surveys. *International Journal of Internet Science 1*, 6–16.

Smyth, J. D., Dillman, D. A., Christian, L. M. and Stern, M. J. (2006b). Comparing check-all and forced-choice question formats in web surveys. *Public Opinion Quarterly 70*, 66–77.

Smyth, J. D., Dillman, D. A. and Christian, L. M. (2006c). Does 'yes or no' on the telephone mean the same as 'check-all-that-apply' on the web? Paper presented at the Second International Conference on Telephone Survey Methodology. Miami, Florida, January 12–15, 2006.

Strack, F. (1992). 'Order effects' in survey research: activation and information functions of preceding questions. In N. Schwarz and S. Sudman (eds), *Context effects in social and psychological research* (pp. 23–34). New York: Springer-Verlag.

Strack, F., Schwarz, N. and Wänke, M. (1991). Semantic and pragmatic aspects of context effects in social and psychological research. *Social Cognition 9*, 111–125.

Sudman, S., Bradburn, N. and Schwarz, N. (1996). *Thinking about answers*. San Francisco, CA: Josey-Bass.

Taylor, H., Krane, D. and Thomas, R. K., (2005). How does social desirability affect responses?: differences in telephone and online surveys. Paper presented at the American Association for Public Opinion Research. Miami, Florida, May 2005.

Tourangeau, R. (1992). Context effects on responses to attitude questions: attitudes as memory structures. In N. Schwarz and S. Sudman (eds) *Context effects in social and psychological research* (pp. 35–47). New York: Springer-Verlag.

Tourangeau, R., Couper, M. P. and Conrad, F. (2004). Spacing, position and order: interpretive heuristcs for visual features of survey questions. *Public Opinion Quarterly 68*(3), 368–393.

Tourangeau, R., Couper, M. P. and Conrad, F. (2006) Color, labels and interpretive heuristics for response scales. Paper presented at the American Association of Public Opinion Research, Montreal, Quebec, Canada, May 18–21, 2006.

Tourangeau, R. and Rasinski, K. A. (1988). Cognitive processes underlying context effects in attitude measurement. *Psychological Bulletin 103*, 299–314.

Tourangeau, R., Rasinski, K. and Bradburn, N. (1991). Measuring happiness in surveys: a test of the subtraction hypothesis. *Public Opinion Quarterly 55*, 255–266.

Tourangeau, R., Rasinski, K., Bradburn, N. and D'Andrade, R. (1989). Carry-over effects in attitude surveys. *Public Opinion Quarterly 53*, 495–524.

Tourangeau, R., Rips, L. J. and Rasinski, K. (2000). *The psychology of survey response*. New York: Cambridge University Press.

Tourangeau, R. and Smith, T. W. (1996). Asking sensitive questions: the impact of data collection mode, question format and question context. *Public Opinion Quarterly 60*, 275–304.

Witte, J. C., Pargas, R. P., Mobley, C. and Hawdon, J. (2004). Instrument effects of images in web surveys: a research note. *Social Science Computer Review 22*, 363–369.

CHAPTER 28

Personality testing on the Internet

What we know, and what we do not

Tom Buchanan

Online personality tests, where psychological scales are administered through the medium of networked computers, appear to be here to stay. From the mid-1990s onwards, psychologists have sought to implement personality tests via the Internet, with the items of traditional paper and pencil inventories initially reproduced as HTML forms on web pages, and more recently with more sophisticated technologies and innovative presentation formats.

From early visions of what might be possible (e.g. Bartram 1998) and empirical investigations of whether it might work (e.g. Pasveer and Ellard 1998; Buchanan and Smith 1999), online psychological assessment has grown rapidly in research, commercial, clinical and amateur fields. In a survey of Internet testing practices, Coyne *et al.* noted that 'most of the well-known personality tests in the UK were represented' (2003: 4) among the instruments being delivered online by major test publishers. However, the speed and scale of development may have outstripped fundamental research on the psychometric properties of Internet-mediated assessments – something that may prove to be problematic in various applied contexts.

The aims of this chapter are to provide an overview of some of the key issues in online personality assessment, to provide practical advice for people planning to use such tests in research or applied settings, and to flag up some priorities for future research. As well as personality inventories, the chapter will mention other forms of self-report questionnaire-based psychological assessment that may reflect relatively stable individual differences but not strictly fall into traditional models of personality. For example, these will also be considered in the discussion of equivalence between online and offline tests, because it is likely that any psychological processes affecting the completion of online personality tests (e.g. increased self-disclosure) will be shared with these instruments as well. In terms of methodology, if not the constructs being measured, there are strong similarities that will inform discussion of issues such as equivalence. The same is true of research on online survey methodology – again, there are valuable lessons to be learned from that body of literature.

Why use the Internet for personality assessment?

There are a number of compelling reasons for psychologists to use the Internet as a medium for psychological testing (see, for example, Bartram 1998; Buchanan and Smith 1999; Barak and English 2002; Fouladi *et al.* 2002; Wilhelm and McKnight 2002; Riva *et al.* 2003; Naglieri *et al.* 2004 and a number of other authors). These include the potential speed and efficiency of test administration and data collection – information can be gathered from large numbers of people automatically. Data entry requirements (and associated costs and time delays) are largely eliminated, and the potential for errors in data entry is reduced. Analyses and sometimes even the generation of interpretive reports can be automated and immediate feedback on test scores generated.

While some of these characteristics are shared with 'traditional' computer-based testing, where inventories are administered via stand-alone machines, there are other unique attributes of online measures that confer additional advantages. For example, Internet-based tests are easily scalable: there is little difference in the cost, effort or infrastructure required by a test administrator whether their instruments are completed by five people each week or by five hundred. Online tests can be easily updated and revised: for instance, if it becomes apparent that a change to a test's instructions is required, then the files on a centralized server can be updated very rapidly and at very little cost. Consider an equivalent exercise with a traditional test – updates would need to be sent to large numbers of test users, at considerable cost and inconvenience.

Use of the Internet as a mediating technology removes the requirement for direct interaction and physical proximity between a test administrator and a test-taker. For example, it is entirely possible for a test hosted and scored on a machine in Switzerland to be completed by a person in Arizona as part of an application procedure for a job in Germany. Barriers of distance, and to some extent time, can thus become less important than would be the case with traditional testing procedures (though removal of these barriers and the changes incurred in the relationship between test-taker and administrator may also introduce practical and ethical complications).

As well as the answers they give to test items, computerized testing procedures can also give us metadata related to how people complete the tests – how long do they dwell on particular items? Do they go back and change answers? How do they move their mouse pointer over the various options? Sophisticated programming techniques can allow these questions to be answered and may be informative. For example, time taken to complete a test (or parts thereof) could be used to detect impression management (e.g. where a test-taker is faking good or bad in a high-stakes assessment, they may spend longer on items they think are related to the way they wish to depict themselves). This has been demonstrated in the context of both offline computerised tests (Brunetti *et al.* 1998) and also for Internet-mediated instruments (Buckley and Williams 2002). While acquisition of such data is clearly possible and useful in the case of offline, stand-alone computerized tests, when combined with the other advantages described above it adds even more to the possible strengths of Internet mediated testing.

Each of these advantages may be more or less relevant to various applied contexts in which one might want to use Internet-mediated tests. In the context of clinical psychology, there is increasing interest in behavioural telehealth applications where mental health services are remotely delivered to clients for whom it would otherwise be inconvenient or impossible to use the services of a psychologist or a counsellor (e.g. living in a remote rural area or housebound). Online psychological tests may have roles to play in such situations, informing clinical diagnoses or assessing the outcome of therapeutic procedures (Buchanan 2002, 2003; Barak and Buchanan 2004).[1] The potential value of online data acquisition for psychological research has been well documented (e.g. Hewson *et al.* 1996; Schmidt 1997; Smith and Leigh 1997; Pasveer and Ellard

---

[1] It is important to note that there are important ethical and practical issues associated with this application of online tests (Buchanan 2002, 2003). Also, Naglieri *et al.* (2004) point out that psychological testing is only one part of an assessment procedure. The extent to which full assessment procedures may be implemented via the Internet remains to be seen. For a more general discussion of the ethics of online data collection, see Ess, Chapter 31 this volume.

1998; Buchanan and Smith 1999; Reips 2000). Researchers can gather information from very large numbers of remote participants in a manner that is inexpensive and convenient for both parties. For psychologists providing commercial assessment services (e.g. for occupational selection purposes) there is a potential for new modes of service delivery (e.g. Bartram 1998; Buckley and Williams 2002; Barak 2003).

Online tests are also increasingly being used in activities outwith the tradition domain of the psychologist. For instance, they are seeing use in what one might call 'social networking' technologies – matchmaking sites, for example, where members are paired and dates arranged on the basis of desired characteristics. There is also wide use of online tests for non-professional self-development and self-exploration purposes (Barak and Buchanan 2004). The proliferation of amateur testing sites on the Internet, and the high traffic that free personality test sites receive, provides evidence that there is a real hunger for this kind of information among at least some elements of society.

Why not use the Internet for personality assessment?

Despite all the potential advantages of online testing, there are also a number of problematic issues one must be aware of (e.g. Barak and Buchanan 2004; Naglieri et al. 2004). Most of these are related to diminished control over the testing situation. Psychometric tests are usually designed to be administered under controlled circumstances, under the supervision of a test administrator. This is usually not achievable with tests delivered via the Internet, giving rise to both practical and psychological issues.

From a practical perspective, there are likely to be problems with security. This refers both to test content and the data generated by online tests. It is important that the contents of tests used for important real-life purposes do not become public knowledge – if that were to happen, their usefulness as assessment instruments would be seriously compromised. Unfortunately, this does appear to be happening – it is even easy to find websites describing how one might go about influencing the results of various tests,

and copyright violations appear to be frequent. For legal and ethical reasons, test administrators also need to consider data security issues: the use of secure sites to protect the confidentiality of personal data is important (Naglieri et al. 2004). There is evidence (Reips 2002a) that security issues are frequently overlooked in online data collection, with the result that test respondents' confidentiality may be compromised. Where the data collected is sensitive in nature, or contains personal identifiers, this is a serious problem.

Another potential problem revolves around the issue of identity verification. For some people using online tests, it is not necessary to know exactly who is completing it (indeed, in research settings that may be a good thing, permitting respondents complete anonymity). For others, though, it is very important to ensure that the person completing an online test is really who they say they are. In a high-stakes assessment, what is to stop someone 'cheating' on an online test, or even getting someone else to do it for them? However, there are ways of dealing with this. For example, in a selection situation, one could initially screen applicants via the Web, then retest candidates with a shortened version of the test when they are physically present for an interview. Other solutions such as proctored administration at test centres are also possible and may be desirable for high-stakes assessments. Realistically, however, the issue of cheating and identity misrepresentation is more likely to be an issue for tests of maximal performance (ability or achievement tests) than for measures of typical performance (personality). The cheating we are more likely to encounter with personality tests is impression management and manipulation of self-presentation (templating, faking good, faking bad and so on). As already outlined, it may be possible to detect such behaviour using information such as item response latencies.[2]

In addition to these largely practical concerns, there are also questions that relate more to what might be called the psychological side of testing, and in particular to the validity of online tests as measures of the intended constructs. This issue

[2] Issues of protocol validity are addressed by Schmidt, Chapter 29 this volume and Johnson (2005).

arises because there are a number of factors that might influence the way people respond to online scales.

One such issue is environmental variance. Online testers have no control over the settings in which their instruments are completed – a noisy workplace during the lunch hour, a crowded computer laboratory, or at home late at night when the respondent is tired and may have had a glass of wine with their evening meal. This environmental variance may well affect responses. Some authors (e.g. Reips 2000) have suggested this is actually a good thing: we are able to measure people in their own self-selected environments, rather than an artificially constrained situation such as a research laboratory or assessment centre. It may well be that ecological validity of assessments is thus increased by environmental variance. However, it is still an issue that could influence the way people respond to Internet tests.

There have also been suggestions that the assessment medium itself could affect the way people respond. This has its roots in the computer-mediated communication literature, and the idea that people may be more willing to disclose sensitive information to computerized questionnaires than they would be to other people (Weisband and Kiesler 1996). Along with evidence that people may respond in a less socially desirable manner when tested via the Internet (Joinson 1999) this has led to the suggestion that responses to online tests may be characterized by higher levels of self-disclosure and candour than would paper questionnaires administered in person (e.g. Buchanan *et al.* 2002; Herrero and Meneses 2006). Along with other suggested effects revolving around anonymity, differences in motivation and absence of experimenter effects (e.g. Hewson *et al.* 1996; Buchanan and Smith 1999) these observations raise the very real possibility that people may respond to online questionnaires in different ways than they would to traditional measures.

Taken together, these practical and psychological issues give pause for thought. They do not mean that we should not use the Internet for personality testing, but they do mean that there are some questions we need to address when doing so. The practical issues may be relatively straightforward (if not easy or inexpensive) to resolve. However, the psychological issues, which potentially affect the ability of online tests to validly measure personality, may be considerably more perplexing and important. This has prompted a number of authors to examine the validity of online personality tests in some detail.

The issue of equivalence

In much of the literature concerning online tests that has been published to date, a key theme has been comparison of online tests with traditional paper and pencil versions. There are a number of reasons for this. The first is that in the early days of online data collection, there was a high level of concern about the extent to which Internet-mediated data would prove to be usable (e.g. Pasveer and Ellard 1998; Buchanan and Smith 1999; Davis 1999; Krantz and Dalal 2000). Could the results from online studies be valid? Would they be the same as the findings of traditional research? Would personality tests work the same way when placed on the Web?

This issue of equivalence between online and offline versions of tests is an important one. The main reason for this is that the majority of online tests (at least those being used for serious purposes, rather than novelty items created by amateurs) are direct translations of existing paper and pencil measures. For this reason, it is important to establish whether online tests are reliable, valid and measure the same constructs. A number of studies have been conducted with this goal in mind. The research to date has led some authors to argue that equivalence has been demonstrated and is no longer a priority for future work (e.g. Epstein and Klinkenberg 2001) while others (e.g. Buchanan *et al.* 2005) argue that this is only the case for some instruments, not all.

As the discipline of psychometric testing advances, the equivalence issue is likely to become less important. Because of the numerous advantages of online tests, it is easy to imagine a future where virtually all testing is conducted online. This may be done using web browsers on conventional computers, or via advanced devices such as hand-held computers, personal digital assistants, mobile phones or even network-enabled gaming consoles. In such a scenario, tests would be developed and validated online, and the old technology of paper and pencil questionnaires either relegated to a historical curiosity or only used in special cases where there is a compelling reason to use paper (e.g. situations with limited technological infrastructure). There will be little need to consider equivalence if everything is computerized, and in the special cases where paper tests are used then one will need to ask the question whether *they* are equivalent to the standard, computerized, method of choice.

However, we have not yet reached that stage. Even as more individuals and organizations move towards online testing, it is clear that a century's worth of offline psychometric testing is not going to disappear overnight. This is largely because there are a large number of widely used, well-validated measures of various psychological constructs available. If one wishes to measure, say, neuroticism then rather than constructing a new test it is easiest to simply use a traditional instrument converted to an electronic format. This applies both to public domain instruments and commercially copyrighted tests controlled by test publishers. For such instruments, there is often a long history of research use that provides evidence of construct validity. If we can demonstrate that the online version is equivalent to the offline version, then it is possible to argue that all this validation data applies to the new instrument as well: evidence that it does do what it claims.

Second, in many applications it is useful to compare individuals' scores with normative data (for example, deciding whether a score on an anxiety scale indicates the likely presence of a clinically significant problem). For many traditional instruments, there are very large sets of normative data available. Are these offline normative data usable for interpretation of test scores derived from online instruments?

Third, it is sometimes convenient to use mixed-mode tests, for example allowing people to respond to a questionnaire online, on paper, or via computer-assisted telephone interviews. If data gathered in various ways are to be pooled or compared, then we need to know that the various technologies used provide comparable data.

For these reasons, the issue of equivalence between online and offline versions of tests may still be an important one, depending on what one plans to do with the data gathered. Furthermore, knowing about similarities and differences in the ways people respond to online and offline measures informs research on Internet-mediated behaviour, and the psychological processes that may operate in differentially mediated domains of human–computer and human–human interaction.

Types of equivalence

There are different types of equivalence that have different implications. Drawing on the work of van der Vijver and Harsveld (1994), Preckel and Thieman (2003) distinguish between qualitative and quantitative equivalence: 'Whereas qualitative equivalence refers to construct validity, quantitative equivalence addresses mainly the question whether the norm data of one test version can be applied to the other test version' (2003: 132).

Along similar lines, Meyerson and Tryon (2003) have a nice discussion of psychometric equivalence in the context of online tests. Drawing on the work of Ghiselli *et al.* (1981) they note that there are three criteria on which online and offline versions of tests must prove comparable before they can be considered parallel (equivalent). These criteria are equality of means; equality of variances; and similarity of correlations with other variables (e.g. demonstrated by comparison of the correlation matrices of each test with a number of validation scales). Essentially, the requirements with respect to means and variances are what Preckel and Thieman (2003) described as quantitative equivalence, while the third criterion is an index of qualitative equivalence.

Of the two, qualitative equivalence is the most important. Quantitative equivalence is important to know about, but can be adjusted. As Meyerson and Tryon suggest, two forms of a test that are quantitatively different can be rendered parallel by adding or subtracting constants to the means, or transformation of the score distributions (e.g. equipercentile transformation). As long as we know that there are differences in score distributions, individual scores can be modified so that (for example) a score derived from an online test could be interpreted in the context of offline norms. However, if the two measures are not qualitatively equivalent, then no amount of transformation can render them parallel: essentially, at least one of the measures cannot be a valid index of the construct of interest.

Empirical evidence pertaining to equivalence

Studies published to date have adopted a number of approaches to establishing qualitative equivalence. These involve different levels of difficulty and sophistication, and provide different levels of evidence. Approaches adopted to date include comparisons of internal consistency, comparisons of latent structure through exploratory or confirmatory factor analyses, examination of correlations with theoretically related constructs, comparisons of criterion groups who should differ on various constructs, item response theory analyses and multivariate comparison of the covariance matrices between the scale of interest and other measures obtained with online and offline samples.

One of the reasons advanced for observed differences between online and offline versions of tests is the existence of sampling bias, or differences between the samples compared (Herrero and Meneses 2006). For example, Buchanan (2003) describes the comparison of scores on an online measure of depression and anxiety with normative data obtained with the pencil and paper version. The participants in the online sample were self-selected individuals who had chosen to do and sought out an online personality inventory. In contrast, those in the traditional comparison sample had received a diagnosis of cancer. One would expect differences in the mean scores of these samples, and differences were indeed observed (the interesting thing about that study, though, is that the differences were not what one would predict: the scores of the Internet sample were considerably higher than those of the cancer patients!). Clearly, if one is to address the issue of quantitative equivalence then like must be compared with like. The same is likely to be true of some methods of establishing qualitative equivalence. For example, consider the comparison of latent structures of an inventory in two samples. One should be aware that if

one sample is relatively homogenous on the construct of interest, then a different picture of its latent structure may be obtained than would be the case for a more heterogeneous sample as inter-item correlations may be attenuated due to restricted range (see Buchanan and Smith [1999] for a similar argument).

Due to the possible effects of sampling biases, the best evidence pertaining to equivalence comes from studies where participants drawn from the same source are randomly assigned to either online or offline conditions. Joinson (1999) is an early example of the most common approach to matching samples in this body of research – assigning traditionally recruited participants (the ubiquitous student participant) to either condition. Indeed, Joinson's finding that his online participants scored lower on a measure of social desirability has had an important influence on suggestions that people may respond differently to online and offline tests.

What follows is not a comprehensive review of the literature, but an attempt to synthesize typical findings from studies that permit quantitative as well as qualitative comparisons: studies that have used equivalent samples randomly assigned to conditions. Inevitably there is a degree of compromise here: by limiting the participants to what are effectively traditional captive undergraduate student samples, some ecological validity is sacrificed. There have been a number of studies using unmatched or Internet-only samples that have provided important evidence of qualitative equivalence (and difference, on occasion). However, for current purposes a selective account of several studies that additionally permit evaluation of quantitative equivalence will serve to demonstrate some of the key issues arising from the literature to date.

Fouladi et al. (2002) compared findings from three questionnaires measuring, respectively, attachment to father and to mother, perceived ability to reduce negative mood and awareness of mood and mood regulation strategies. These were administered either online or in paper and pencil format, with traditionally recruited participants randomly assigned to conditions. Although psychometric properties and latent structures were in general very similar, there were some small differences between the Internet-mediated and traditional versions of the instruments. Mean scores on two of the mood-related scales differed significantly, there were differences in means and variances on a number of items and there were some distributional differences. Fouladi *et al.* argued that although their findings demonstrate that Internet administration of psychological measures is clearly viable, they also indicate the need for further evaluation and refinement of such measures.

Herrero and Meneses (2006) randomly assigned students to either web-based or paper questionnaire conditions for the completion of brief measures of depression and stress. Test completion was unsupervised in each case. A MANOVA using the individual items of the stress scale as dependent variables indicated there was a significant main effect of administration format, with participants tested via the Web reporting less stress (however, post-hoc analyses suggest this was due to scores on a single item). Administration format did not significantly affect depression scores. Further analyses pertained to qualitative equivalence: comparison of reliability and factor structures for the two samples indicated that the psychometric properties of the scales were invariant across conditions.

In Fouladi *et al.*'s study, participants in the offline condition completed the questionnaires under the supervision of an experimenter. In the offline condition, they were alone and unsupervised. Herrero and Meneses' participants, on the other hand, completed the measures unsupervised in both conditions. It is possible that in cases like Fouladi *et al.* or Joinson (1999), the observed differences were not due to paper vs. Internet mediation, but to the presence of a test administrator in the pencil and paper condition (supervised or proctored administration). A small number of studies have discussed this issue, and attempted to disentangle these two variables.

Cronk and West (2002) assigned student participants to complete a morality questionnaire in either paper and pencil or web-based format; either in class or alone at a time of their own choosing (take-home condition). Neither the format nor setting in which the scale was completed had any effect on the mean scores obtained (the design probably had sufficient power to detect such an effect were it present). However, Cronk and West report higher variance when questionnaires were completed via the Web in the take-home setting.[3] They note that this is inconsistent with other studies such as Pasveer and Ellard (1998) which report higher variance in web conditions – however, in those other studies, the Web condition was effectively the same as the take-home/web cell in Cronk and West's design. Their findings are thus consistent with earlier work and suggest that there is something about the *interaction* between mediating technology and completion setting that influences responses. It was also found that response rates were significantly lower in the take-home/web cell. This suggests that there may be motivational differences between participants in the different conditions, which may in turn have some influence on the way they respond to the questionnaire.

Chuah *et al.* (2006) randomly assigned students participants to one of three conditions: paper and pencil (supervised), web-based (supervised – in computer lab) and web-based (unsupervised). This design includes three of the four cells in the designs used by Cronk and West (2002) and Buchanan (2005), with the missing condition being paper and pencil (unsupervised): a take-home paper questionnaire. Using a set of Big 5 personality markers – emotional stability, extraversion, openness, agreeableness and conscientiousness – derived from the International Personality Item Pool (IPIP) (Goldberg 1999) and also a health behaviours checklist, they compared conditions in a number of ways.

For four of the Big 5 dimensions, Item Response Theory (IRT) analyses indicated that items functioned the same way for the three groups and no substantive differences across modality were indicated (the Big 5 openness scale was not examined because preliminary analyses indicated that the set of items used violated the assumption of unidimensionality).

For these four dimensions, factor analyses suggested that the same model provided a good fit to the latent structure of the inventory in

---

[3] Variances in the Web/in class and the two paper cells were comparable, and lower than the Web/take-home cell.

each of the three conditions. Furthermore, one-way ANOVAs indicated there were no mean differences once a Bonferroni adjustment was applied. Finally, correlations between personality variables and health behaviour criteria were largely equivalent across the three conditions. Given that the vast majority of their analyses were indicative of equivalence, Chuah *et al.* conclude that there were no systematic differences between the pencil and paper and Internet administrations of the measure they used.

A study by Buchanan (2005) also used an inventory derived from the IPIP, and previously validated for use on the Internet (Buchanan *et al.* 2005). This was a different measure from the one used by Chuah *et al.* (2006) but addressed the same underlying constructs. Like Cronk and West (2002) this study also crossed the factors of supervision and mediation format. Like Herrero and Meneses (2006) it also employed a measure of depression.

Undergraduate student volunteers were randomly assigned to one of four experimental conditions: completion of measures in either web- or paper-based formats, alone or under supervision. Participants anonymously completed the Hospital Anxiety and Depression Scale (HADS) (Zigmond and Snaith 1983) and a Five Factor personality inventory (measuring openness to experience, conscientiousness, extraversion, agreeableness and neuroticism). Previous work using these measures has shown elevated online scores on anxiety, depression and neuroticism in online samples when compared to existing paper and pencil norms (Buchanan 2003; Buchanan and Joinson 2004). Participants also rated the extent to which they believed they as individuals could be linked to the data they provided (perceived anonymity). A series of two-way ANCOVAs indicated that HADS depression scores were higher in the online conditions. Contrary to expectations, assessment medium did not significantly affect either anxiety or neuroticism. For the other variables, there were no significant main effects. However, there was a significant interaction between medium and supervision for both openness to experience and perceived anonymity. For openness, supervision did not seem to make a difference in the paper-based conditions, but did in the web-based conditions with people in the online-supervised condition scoring lowest. For perceived

anonymity, supervision did not seem to affect the extent to which people felt they were identifiable in the Web condition, but in the paper-based condition people completing the questionnaires under supervision considered themselves more likely to be identifiable.

Implications of research to date

So what do the somewhat contradictory results of these studies tell us about equivalence? The message seems to be that when online tests are compared with paper and pencil versions of the same instruments, in general they are qualitatively (psychometrically) equivalent, though small differences are sometimes observed. For those that are qualitatively equivalent, sometimes they are quantitatively equivalent (in terms of means and other distributional properties) and sometimes they are not. The effect sizes for those quantitative differences that have been found are relatively small. For example, Glass' d for the online/offline difference in depression scores reported by Buchanan 2005, was 0.26; in the multivariate online/offline comparisons reported by Fouladi *et al.* 2002, values of epsilon squared for the scales that differed significantly ranged from 0.051 to 0.142. The practical significance of these differences will vary depending on how the tests are to be used.

The qualitative differences between online and offline versions of tests, when observed, tend to be relatively minor – a couple of items here and there with the 'wrong' factor loadings and so on. The extent to which such minor differences are important is debatable. For example, Buchanan *et al.* (2005) created a revised version of the IPIP inventory they used due to the presence of 'rogue items' in the original. However, when correlations of the original and revised scales with validation criterion measures were examined, the two versions were almost identical in their average predictive power. Sometimes, therefore, the differences may be trivial in terms of the usability of the scales in the real world. The research published so far would seem to suggest that most personality inventories fall into this category. However, it would be dangerous to assume that this will always be the case. For example, Buchanan *et al.* (2005) describe the factor analysis of a memory questionnaire that proved to have a latent structure very different to what was expected when it was administered online. While the instrument evaluated by Buchanan *et al.* (2005) is not a personality inventory, it is a clear demonstration that online tests may not always have the expected psychometric properties.

If some tests are affected by Internet mediation and others are not, why is that the case? Measurement of which specific psychological constructs (or domains of constructs) are likely to be affected, in what ways, and to what extent? What underlying mechanisms or processes lead people to respond differentially to questionnaires depending on the technology through which they are administered?

Reflecting on these questions is a little bit like being a detective who is fairly sure that a crime has been committed, but is not sure what it is or who should be on his list of suspects. The 'Internet mediation' effect is somewhat elusive: sometimes it is observed, and sometimes it is not – even when the same constructs seem to be being measured (e.g. depression or neuroticism, as shown in the examples above). However, there do appear to be some likely suspects whose possible guilt makes further investigation worthwhile. Two substantive questions seem to arise from the literature cited. The first is why some studies find quantitative differences and others do not.

For the first question, there may be explanations that are relatively mundane. For example, Joinson *et al.* (2007) have demonstrated that relatively minor manipulations of the way a questionnaire is presented to a respondent can influence the extent to which they disclose personal information. Could such differences between the studies cited above give rise to the inconsistency of findings?

Alternatively, there may be differences between the studies that affect the extent to which underlying processes operate. For example, one might suggest that online–offline differences occur because in the online conditions participants are anonymous (or at least *feel* more anonymous than in the offline condition). In the study conducted by Buchanan (2005), no identifying information was requested from participants in any condition (yet there were still differences in the extent to which they felt anonymous). However, in Chuah *et al.*'s (2006) study,

Internet participants entered a unique username and password. Herrero and Meneses (2006) used a similar procedure. Could this be why Buchanan (2005) found online–offline differences, while these other studies found none, even though the same constructs were being addressed?

The second question that arises is why online–offline differences exist, if and when they do occur. A good candidate for the answer is anonymity, which is likely to play a mediating role. Richman *et al.* (1999) found that anonymity decreased socially desirable responding, and Joinson (1999) has shown a similar effect when comparing online and offline test administrations. This social desirability effect may contribute to higher levels of self-disclosure to online questionnaires and thus differences in test scores. However, Buchanan and Joinson (2004) found that online–offline differences in neuroticism scores were not accompanied by similar differences in a measure of self-disclosure. Clearly this is a question further work is required to address.

Another possible mediating factor is computer anxiety. While this is possibly a less salient issue than it once was (due to the modern ubiquity of computers and information technology), it may still have a role to play in that people with higher levels of computer anxiety may respond to an Internet-mediated test in different ways to those who are more comfortable with the technology. For example, Tseng *et al.* (1998) have shown that levels of computer anxiety can affect participants' responses in different ways depending on the technology used to gather data (PC versus pen-based personal digital assistant).

Other forms of assessment

One issue not so far discussed is the development of novel forms of psychometric assessment. All the instruments considered are essentially traditional questionnaires converted to an electronic format. However, web presentation (and computerization in general) creates possibilities for assessment instruments to take other forms.

It has been argued (Barrett and Ebbeling 2003) that questionnaires represent outdated technology and that the psychometrics of personality cannot significantly advance without innovation and reconceptualization of measurement techniques. Barrett's approach has been to construct single statements reflecting the 'meaning' of particular personality traits, then get respondents to rate these on a sliding scale using a graphical interface. The technique seems to be efficient and is liked by respondents, and appears to 'work' – although the extent to which it is better or worse than traditional techniques still requires evaluation. However, versions of this technique are already seeing commercial use and it is likely that we will see other alternative psychometric procedures in the future. Some may be improvements on what already exists; others may not.

Another procedure that has been widely used on the Internet and aroused considerable interest is the Implicit Association Test (IAT) (Greenwald *et al.* 1998), a tool that can be used to measure implicit attitudes. In this methodology, the time taken for participants to assign stimuli (words, images) to categories is measured. The procedure gives indices of the strength of association between concepts and attributes, and permits measurement of attitudes that people may be unable or unwilling to self-report. Most applications of the IAT lie within the domain of social psychology (its use in research on racial prejudice is probably best known at present), but the methodology is also applicable to measurement of individual differences in personality.

As new technologies, scripting languages, browser plugins and so on become available, it becomes possible to create very technically sophisticated measurement tools. When an assessment becomes reliant on the test-taker having a particular hardware or software configuration, though, problems may arise. For example, consider the application of tests within behavioural telehealth contexts. One of the advantages they offer is that clients otherwise unable to access services may be able to remotely complete assessment instruments. However, if those clients lack the facilities to do so (e.g. don't have a particular piece of software installed on their home computer) then that advantage may be lost for some people, and further inequities in access to healthcare may arise. This was demonstrated in a study by Buchanan and Reips (2001) that found differences in personality between users of different computing platforms, and differences in demographic characteristics (education) of people who did or did not have the scripting language Javascript enabled on their machines. This suggests that if web-based applications rely on particular technologies, then some people may not be able to access them. This may have ethical and legal implications in some applied fields (consider equal opportunities legislation) and also have the effect of biasing samples in research conducted via the Internet. There is a lesson to be learned from the survey literature, where Dillman *et al.* (1998) demonstrated that using 'fancy' online questionnaire layout was associated with higher dropout rates. The lesson is simple: the more complicated one makes things, the more likely one is to encounter difficulties. Tests should be kept as simple as possible, and created using the most basic and ubiquitous technologies with which they can be realistically implemented.

Unanswered questions

As indicated above, there are a number of issues that require further attention, and a number of things we do not know about online personality testing. Perhaps the biggest of these unanswered questions, as already discussed, is why some studies find differences between online and offline tests. Under what circumstances are such differences observed, and what causes them? While some ideas have arisen from research conducted to date (e.g. anonymity, social desirability, self-disclosure, motivation differences and others), further systematic research is required.

In addition, literature on Internet-mediated questionnaire-based assessment is somewhat fragmented at present, and the evidence base is rather small with only a limited number of well-controlled studies having been conducted. Research relevant to the important methodological questions is located in pockets of activity among psychologists, survey methodology researchers, social scientists, medical professionals, career counsellors and other disciplines. A comprehensive survey or meta-analysis of findings from research across a number of areas where online and offline tests could be compared would likely be very informative.

Another area that requires research revolves around non-professional or amateur tests. A web search for 'personality tests' will result in a huge number of hits, and personality testing sites are easy to find. Probably the majority of these are constructed by non-psychologists, and might be best described as rubbish, bearing no relationship to established psychological theory or psychometric practice. However, given the fact that there seems to an enormous public interest in self-discovery and assessment (Barak and Buchanan 2004), it is inevitable that large numbers of people are using these instruments. In many (most?) cases this is likely to be for entertainment purposes, and little attention may be paid to feedback and test scores. However, it is also likely that some people will pay a lot of attention to feedback and may potentially be upset by it (Buchanan 2003) or make faulty life decisions based on it. Given the proliferation of these instruments, it would seem wise for professional psychologists to examine the extent to which non-professional 'tests' are being used, and what effects they may be having.

General advice

In closing, it appears that a number of recommendations can be derived from the literature published to date. These should not be considered as a comprehensive or rigid set of guidelines, more as a number of things one should think about when considering the use of an online personality test. Many of these principles are also applicable to other forms of psychological questionnaire (e.g. surveys, measures of clinical constructs, cognitive tests) that one might also wish to implement online. A number of authors have produced recommendations for best practice in online data collection (e.g. Birnbaum 2001; Reips 2002b; Hewson et al. 2003; Chapter 24 this volume) and readers are encouraged to consult these for additional advice.

Online personality tests are becoming widely used, and have the potential to be extremely useful in a number of applied contexts. It is becoming clear that they can 'work' and provide valid measures of the constructs they are intended to address. However, there are instances where they do not behave quite as expected, and there are a number of potential pitfalls that need to be considered.

In any application where tests exist in multiple formats (e.g. where the online test is derived from an existing paper and pencil instrument) the issue of equivalence must be considered. When a test is used for the first time on the Internet, care must be taken to ensure that it is a valid measure of the intended construct. The fact that it is a scale that had good psychometric properties in a paper and pencil format may mean nothing; the psychometric properties of the online version need to be independently established. Even if an online test does prove to be psychometrically equivalent to an offline version, that does not mean that score distributions will be the same. While it is entirely possible that existing traditional norms will be suitable for use in interpreting scores obtained on an online test, it is also entirely possible that they will not. Anyone seeking to use norms in this fashion should take pains to establish equivalence of typical score distributions, or to establish exactly how they differ so that scores can be modified and the tests made parallel by addition or subtraction of constants or use of transformations (Meyerson and Tryon 2003). Failure to consider these issues may lead to misinterpretation of test scores or use of essentially meaningless data. For researchers this would be unfortunate and embarrassing. For applied practitioners in (e.g.) clinical or occupational settings, it could lead to flawed decisions that have negative impacts on the lives of clients and give rise to ethical and potentially legal difficulties. The same observations apply to situations where one might wish to use data gathered in multiple ways (e.g. via both a website and a postal survey). It is possible that data gathered using multiple techniques will not be directly comparable.

Where possible, the use of metadata should be considered: for example, measurement of response latency as an index of impression management. However, this should not be done at the expense of simplicity: introducing sophisticated technology or software may be counterproductive if it means some people will be unable to complete the tests.

Finally, it should be recognized that there are many unanswered questions about the ways in which people respond to online personality tests. More work is required to answer a number of important questions. As previously mentioned, the development and application of online tests has proceeded faster than basic research on their measurement properties and factors that might influence how people respond to them. It is time for the research to catch up.

References

Barak, A. (2003). Ethical and professional issues in career assessment on the Internet. *Journal of Career Assessment,* 11, 3–21.

Barak, A. and Buchanan, T. (2004). Internet-based psychological testing and assessment. In R. Krause, G. Stricker and J. Zack (Eds), *Online counseling: a handbook for mental health professionals* (pp. 217–239). San Diego, CA: Elsevier Academic Press.

Barak, A. and English, N. (2002). Prospects and limitations of psychological testing on the Internet. *Journal of Technology in Human Services* 19, 65–89.

Barrett, P. and Ebbeling, N. (2003). Personality assessment via a graphical profiler. Paper presented at NZ Annual Psychology Conference, Palmerston North, New Zealand.

Bartram, D. (1998). Distance Assessment: Psychological assessment through the Internet. Paper presented at the British Psychological Society Division of Occupational Psychology Conference.

Birnbaum, M. H. (2001). *Introduction to behavioral research on the Internet.* Upper Saddle River, NJ: Prentice Hall.

Brunetti, D. G., Schlottmann, A. B. S. and Hollrah, J. L. (1998). Instructed faking and MMPI-2 response latencies: the potential for assessing response validity. *Journal of Clinical Psychology* 54, 143–153.

Buchanan, T. (2002). Online assessment: desirable or dangerous? *Professional Psychology: Research and Practice,* 33, 148–154.

Buchanan, T. (2003). Internet-based questionnaire assessment: appropriate use in clinical contexts. *Cognitive Behaviour Therapy* 32, 100–109.

Buchanan, T. (2005). Equivalence of Internet-administered and traditional personality tests: What experimental evidence shows. Paper presented at the meeting of the Society for Computers in Psychology, Toronto, Canada, 10 November 2005.

Buchanan, T. and Joinson, A. N. (2004). Are online–offline differences in personality test scores due to increased self-disclosure? Paper presented at German Online Research 2004, Duisburg, Germany, 30 March.

Buchanan, T. and Reips, U. -D. (2001). Platform-dependent biases in online research: do Mac users really think different? Paper presented at German Online Research 2001, Gottingen, Germany.

Buchanan, T. and Smith, J. L. (1999). Using the Internet for psychological research: personality testing on the World-Wide Web. *British Journal of Psychology* 90, 125–144.

Buchanan, T., Johnson, J. A. and Goldberg, L. (2005). Implementing a five-factor personality inventory for use on the Internet. *European Journal of Psychological Assessment 21,* 115–127.

Buchanan, T., Joinson, A. N. and Ali, T. (2002). *Development of a behavioural measure of self-disclosure for use in online research.* Paper presented at German Online Research 2002, Hohenheim, Germany.

Buchanan, T., Ali, T., Heffernan, T. M., Ling, J., Parrott, A. C., Rodgers, J. and Scholey, A. B. (2005). Non-equivalence of online and paper-and-pencil psychological tests: the case of the Prospective Memory Questionnaire. *Behavior Research Methods 37,* 148–154.

Buckley, N. and Williams, R. (2002). Testing on the web – response patterns and image management. *Selection and Development Review 18,* 3–8.

Chuah, S. C., Drasgow, F. and Roberts, B. W. (2006). Personality assessment: does the medium matter? No. *Journal of Research in Personality, 40,* 359–376.

Coyne, I., Bartram, D. and Smith-Lee Chong, P. (2003). Survey of good practice issues: Internet-delivered personality testing in the UK. *Selection Development Review 19,* 3–6.

Cronk, B. C. and West, J. L. (2002). Personality research on the Internet: a comparison of web-based and traditional instruments in take-home and in-class settings. *Behavior Research Methods, Instrument, and Computers 34,* 177–180.

Davis, R. N. (1999). Web-based administration of a personality questionnaire: comparison with traditional methods. *Behavior Research Methods, Instruments, and Computers 31,* 572–577.

Dillman, D. A., Tortora, R. D., Conradt, J. and Bowker, D. (1998). Influence of plain vs. fancy design on response rates for web surveys. Paper presented at Joint Statistical Meetings, Dallas, Texas.

Epstein, J. and Klinkenberg, W. D. (2001). From Eliza to Internet: a brief history of computerized assessment. *Computers in Human Behavior 17,* 295–314.

Fouladi, R. T., McCarthy, C. J. and Moller, N. P. (2002). Paper-and-pencil or online? Evaluating mode effects on measures of emotional functioning and attachment. *Assessment 9,* 204–215.

Ghiselli, E. E., Campbell, J. P. and Zedeck, S. (1981). *Measurement theory for the behavioral sciences.* New York: W. H. Freeman.

Goldberg, L. R. (1999). A broad-bandwidth, public-domain, personality inventory measuring the lower-level facets of several five-factor models. In I. Mervielde, I. J. Deary, F. De Fruyt and F. Ostendorf (eds), *Personality psychology in Europe,* vol. 7 (pp. 7–28). Tilburg, The Netherlands: Tilburg University Press.

Greenwald, A. G., McGhee, D. E. and Schwarz, J. L. K. (1998). Measuring individual differences in implicit cognition: The Implicit Association Test. *Journal of Personality and Social Psychology 74,* 1464–1480.

Herrero, J. and Meneses, J. (2006). Short Web-based versions of the perceived stress (PSS) and Center for Epidemiological Studies-Depression (CESD) Scales: a comparison to pencil and paper responses among Internet users. *Computers in Human Behavior 22,* 830–846.

Hewson, C. M., Laurent, D. and Vogel, C. M. (1996). Proper methodologies for psychological studies conducted via the Internet. *Behavior Research Methods, Instruments, and Computers 28,* 186–191.

Hewson, C., Yule, P., Laurent, C. and Vogel, D. (2003). *Internet research methods: A practical guide for the social and behavioural sciences.* London: Sage.

Johnson, J. A. (2005). Ascertaining the validity of web-based personality inventories. *Journal of Research in Personality* 39, 103–129.

Joinson, A. N. (1999). Anonymity, disinhibition and social desirability on the Internet. *Behavior Research Methods, Instruments, and Computers* 31, 433–438.

Joinson, A. N., Woodley, A. and Reips, U. -D. (2007). Personalization, authentication and self-disclosure in self-administered Internet surveys. *Computers in Human Behavior, 23,* 275–285.

Krantz, J. H. and Dalal, R. (2000). Validity of Web-based psychological research. In M. H. Birnbaum (ed.), *Psychological experiments on the Internet* (pp. 35–60). San Diego, CA: Academic Press.

Meyerson, P. and Tryon, W. W. (2003). Validating Internet research: a test of the psychometric equivalence of Internet and in-person samples. *Behavior Research Methods, Instruments and Computers* 35, 614–620.

Naglieri, J. A., Drasgow, F., Schmit, M., Handler, L., Prifitera, A., Margolis, A. and Velasquez, R. (2004). Psychological testing on the Internet: new problems, old issues. *American Psychologist* 59, 150–162.

Pasveer, K. A. and Ellard, J. H. (1998). The making of a personality inventory: help from the WWW. *Behavior Research Methods, Instruments, and Computers* 30, 309–313.

Preckel, F. and Thieman, H. (2003). Online- versus paper-pencil-version of a high potential intelligence test. *Swiss Journal of Psychology* 62, 131–138.

Reips, U. -D. (2000). The Web experiment method: advantages, disadvantages, and solutions. In M. H. Birnbaum (ed.), *Psychological experiments on the Internet* (pp. 89–117). San Diego, CA: Academic Press.

Reips, U. -D. (2002a). Internet-based psychological experimenting: five dos and five don'ts. *Social Science Computer Review* 20, 241–249.

Reips, U. -D. (2002b). Standards for Internet-based experimenting. *Experimental Psychology* 49, 243–256.

Richman, W. L., Weisband, S., Kiesler, S. and Drasgow, F. (1999). A meta-analytic study of social desirability response distortion in computer-administered and traditional questionnaires and interviews. *Journal of Applied Psychology* 84, 754–775.

Riva, G., Teruzzi, T. and Anolli, L. (2003). The use of the Internet in psychological research: comparison of online and offline questionnaires. *CyberPsychology and Behavior* 6, 73–80.

Schmidt, W. C. (1997). World-Wide Web survey research: benefits, potential problems, and solutions. *Behavior Research Methods, Instruments, and Computers* 29, 274–279.

Smith, M. A. and Leigh, B. (1997). Virtual subjects: using the Internet as an alternative source of subjects and research environment. *Behavior Research Methods, Instruments, and Computers* 29, 496–505.

Tseng, H. M., Tiplady, B., Macleod, H. A. and Wright, P. W. (1998). Computer anxiety: a comparison of pen-based personal digital assistants, conventional computer and paper assessment of mood and performance. *British Journal of Psychology* 89, 599–610.

van de Vijver, F. J. R. and Harsveld, M. (1994). The incomplete equivalence of the paper-and-pencil and computerized versions of the general aptitude test battery. *Journal of Applied Psychology* 79, 852–859.

Weisband, S. and Kiesler, S. (1996). Self disclosure on computer forms: meta-analysis and implications. In M. J. Tauber, (ed.), *Proceedings of the SIGCHI Conference on Human Factors in Computing Systems: Common Ground* (pp. 3–10). New York, NY: ACM Press.

Wilhelm, O. and McKnight, P. E. (2002). Ability and achievement testing on the World Wide Web. In B. Batinic, U. -D. Reips and M. Bosnjak (eds), *Online social sciences* (pp. 151–180). Seattle, WA: Hogrefe and Huber.

Zigmond, A. S. and Snaith, R. P. (1983). The Hospital Anxiety and Depression Scale. *Acta Psychiatrica Scandinavica* 67, 361–370.

CHAPTER 29

Technical considerations when implementing online research

William C. Schmidt

A s this volume attests, the online medium can be harnessed in the service of carrying out a great variety of intriguing research that would not have been possible just a decade earlier. While there is no ignoring use of the Internet medium for future research, in order to obtain trustable, reproducible and representative data, and in order to do so with minimal setbacks and wasted effort, researchers need to be aware of some of the technical factors involved. Without technical knowledge there is room for mistakes, misapplication, and the undermining of the credibility of the data collected. Knowledge of Internet-based research methods is beneficial even if only used during peer review or assessing other researchers' findings.

Although humbling, practically all researchers who have used the Internet to collect data, will have a story to tell about technical errors they encountered after having launched an Internet-based research study. Even researchers familiar with the medium and methods can have difficulty controlling factors that may lead to respondent non-response (the failure of participants to supply requested data), dropout (prematurely terminating participation) or denial of participation (a willing participant is prevented from

contributing data) due to technical reasons. It is not necessarily the researcher's fault either – day-to-day changes in technology can render a study that was previously programmed and working flawlessly to become a victim of software updates.

The goal of the current chapter is to introduce to the novice, some of the rudimentary underlying concepts of how the Internet works, and to point out a number of caveats that can influence the quality of collected data. It is hoped that after becoming familiar with the information herein, researchers will be capable of determining whether the research application they are interested in pursuing is fit for the Internet medium, or whether technical issues will pose problems that threaten the validity of the work. It is hoped too, that more expert researchers will gain some insight into problems they may have been unlucky enough to encounter or to gain an awareness of problems they may not yet have experienced.

Internet basics

The Internet is a communications medium, which like the telephone has a vast network of interconnected units – in this case, computers. Unlike the telephone, multiple connections can be made at any point in time so that information can be gathered from (or delivered to) multiple sources from anywhere on the network. Even multiple exchanges of information between connected computers takes just fractions of a second.

Clients and servers

Like other communication media, the Internet has talkers and listeners. Talkers are known as 'servers' because they deliver information, either when spoken to through an information request, or without having been spoken to – by forcing the information out to other listeners. Listeners are 'clients' or users of information – they can either request information from a server or receive information being delivered by a server.

Pull and push

Some other terms that are used in the context of Internet communications are 'push' and 'pull'. The default and most polite way of communicating is client-pull – the client makes a request to the server for some specific piece of information and pulls it off of the server. Less polite is server-push in which the server starts talking to the client and forces some piece of information on the client whether they want it or not. Luckily, the majority of interactions on the Internet are client pull – the information must be specifically requested before it can be delivered. Server-push still has its uses however, such as in applications like chat where the client specifically opens up to the prospect of having information pushed at them from another user. Server-push is generally not obtrusive, but it can be such as the uninvited messages, usually of an advertising nature, that readers may have experienced through instant messaging software.

IP numbers, MAC addresses and domain names

For human communication to occur, talker and listeners have to be active at the same time and aware that information will be exchanged. Before talking to somebody on the telephone for instance, one must connect to a telephone receiver near them via their phone number. The phone number is crucial because it instructs the telephone network how to direct voice information.

With computer systems on the Internet things operate similarly. Before a client can make a request for information, and before a server can send information to a client, the physical address of the communicators needs to be known.

Each computational system on the Internet has a unique identifying number built into its hardware (the MAC address) that enables the specific routing of information between machines. An IP address (Internet protocol address) of the form xxx.xxx.xxx.xxx corresponds to one or more MAC addresses (xxx is an integer between 0 and 255). The IP address is somewhat like a phone number for a machine or group of machines. This way information can be sent between groups of machines and routed to the specific one of interest using the MAC address. Also just like phone numbers, when one physical address (the MAC address) is no longer using an IP number, it is available to be reassigned to another address.

To make machine contact information easier to remember than a bunch of numbers, or perhaps to make the likely server name for some types of information guessable, machines are also named in a directory that maps mnemonic names onto computers. This directory is the domain name service or DNS, and is actually the only level of computer naming that most Internet users encounter (i.e., www.whatever.com). In summary, each computer on the Internet has a MAC address, an IP number and often a corresponding domain name in the DNS.

Communication protocols

There is one other major requirement for communication. Humans need to have some shared background in terms of how to syntactically process and interpret the noises that are coming at them from other humans. Humans communicate because speakers have common experience, usually with similar dialects of a language. Without implicit or explicit agreement on syntax, messages do not get transmitted clearly. Similarly with the Internet, different computer systems need to be able to break apart and process the information that is being sent to them, or to package information in a way that other computers will be able to disassemble. The term used for this information format is the communication 'protocol'. Just as humans speak a wide variety of languages, there are essentially an infinite number of possible protocols for machine communication.

Uniform resource locator or URL

Putting all of the above together demonstrates that in order for one computer to communicate with another, requires a combination of being hooked up on the Internet, an appropriate shared protocol, a client on one system asking for a resource and a server responding, at least the name of the server computer to be known, and knowing what resource to ask for. Together this is all specified in the URL or universal resource locator, which is of the form 'protocol://servername/resource'. For the Web, the protocol is hypertext-transfer protocol or 'http'. Sometimes it is a digitally encoded secure 'https' format that hides the content being transferred (more on this later).

To summarize, the Internet is a medium of interconnected systems that allows communication between devices that are connected to it. The chapter will now turn to technical problems that can arise at each level of this communication and implications for data collection.

Technical problems

For any social science researcher who has first-hand experience in trying to recruit people to participate in a study, the possibility of acquiring hundreds or thousands or even tens of thousands of participants in an automated fashion is astoundingly tempting. Anecdotes about friends-of-friends who used the Internet to acquire some unbelievable amount of data surface repeatedly. Furthermore, the seamless ease that people have in opening a Web browser and acquiring information from servers anywhere in the world makes it seem plausible that Internet-based research shouldn't be difficult.

The problem with preparing an Internet application is that Murphy's law governs all Web interactions. To phrase it more technically, the combinatorial explosion of interacting sources of undesirable side-effects ensures that any Web application is unlikely to work for every potential participant. To keep such side-effects to a minimum, thereby controlling the online session in order to maximize the collection of valid

and usable data, researchers should take steps to ensure that as few things go wrong in the client–server interaction as possible. Even if data are collected, the quality and content of those data will be affected by technical decisions made by the researcher. Variability in the data obtained that is attributable to technical aspects of data collection has been termed 'technical variance' by Reips (2002a). Technical variance can arise from a wide variety of sources ranging from the obvious such as the speed of the user's Internet connection to the subtleties of the settings or manufacture of their computer monitors (Krantz 2000).

Denial of participation

The combination of likely participants and the technology that they will probably be using to access an Internet study should be considered when implementing a Web-based research study. As an example, consider a visually handicapped user. Currently, popular text-to-speech converters for Web access are reliant on a text-based Web browser known as Lynx. Any Web page therefore that cannot be rendered by Lynx, or that is awkwardly rendered by Lynx, will increase the chances that this class of Web user will not participate – not because they chose not to, but because they were deprived of the ability as a result of the technology used to implement the research paradigm. The researcher will have no indication as to the reasons that the individual did not participate and will be unable to discern disinterest on the part of the participant from denial of participation on the part of the researcher.

Depending on what is being studied, the unpredicted, yet systematic exclusion of subpopulations of participants because of technical factors could affect the content of the data obtained and conclusions drawn on the basis of such data. Note that although data will be obtained it would, in the instance just mentioned, be systematically under-representing visually handicapped Web users. Similarly, for any technical error in online research, the possibility remains that some systematic exclusion of participation may be occurring, thereby affecting data quality. As noted by others, dropout is rather high in Web applications (Piper 1998) and can mask trends that really exist, and distort conclusions that are drawn (Birnbaum 2001; Reips 2000, 2002a).

Technical decisions affect data quality and content

It is important to stress that no matter how many technical errors a researcher makes, in all likelihood, data will be obtained. The important issue is whether there are confounds introduced in the data because of technical decisions made by the researcher. For instance, Javascript is a popular client-side browser scripting language that allows more advanced tasks to be accomplished on the potential respondent's computer. Being client-side means that the program administering the Web application is being run on the respondent's, not the researcher's, computer. Some Web-based research paradigms are written entirely in Javascript, presenting stimuli and questions to the respondent and delivering the research paradigm. The technical decision to use Javascript in one's research however, comes at the price of excluding any potential respondents with Web browsers that do not support Javascript (i.e., the visually impaired users mentioned earlier), who may have disabled Javascript, or who may have an outdated version of a Web browser that does not properly run the Javascript code. There may even be users participating by cell phone browsers, personal digital assistants or other Internet-connected devices – where Javascript isn't necessarily an option.

At issue is whether the exclusion of such potential respondents will unnecessarily bias the sample frame, indirectly skewing data on the topic of study. Buchanan and Reips (2001) reported that in their study on the issue respondents with Javascript enabled had lower average education levels than those who could or did not have Javascript enabled in their browsers. Similarly, Mac users scored different (sic) than others on the personality variable of 'openness'. These findings reveal first hand that technical decisions made by the researcher can unwittingly influence who participates and thereby alter the data obtained in unpredictable ways.

As different types of Web browser programs (of different versions, or on different operating systems, or on differently configured computers) rarely display content identically, the presentation of a study to potential respondents may vary. As long as this does not influence who responds or how they respond, then this variability is unlikely to present a problem. However, even subtle formatting differences can yield different trends in data drawn from the same participant pool (Baron and Siepmann 2000; Smyth *et al.* 2006).

A final consideration regarding technical variability concerns the applicability of between-subjects designs. As others have noted (Reips 2000; Eichstaedt 2002), differential vulnerability to systematic dropout between experimental groups of participants can misleadingly confound experimental manipulations. There is no principled reason why such confounds would not similarly arise from denial of participation factors that could unintentionally affect one experimental group versus another. For this reason and others (see Birnbaum 1999), within-subjects designs are preferable. If between-subjects designs must be used then the reporting of extra measures (such as dropout as a function of browser type used for initial access) may be desirable to ensure that systematic dropout or denial of participation is not skewing the data.

Programming for the lowest common technology

Interactions in collected data that are influenced by technological considerations suggest that a lowest common denominator approach to technology ought to be adopted by researchers. This approach will similarly minimize denial of participation. Having a respondent visit an online research site with the possible intention of participating, and then indirectly denying that participation is not good for public relations, nor does it allow the researcher a full analysis of the data that were obtained, because data are missing.

Internet connectivity issues

Some researchers have noted that variability introduced by poor Internet connectivity can result in frustrated users or increased dropout. A graphics-intensive website made with no regard toward minimizing the amount of data required to be transferred from the server to the client, introduces a technical bias against the participation of users with slow speed Internet connections (Reips 2002a). These are people likely to be low in socio-economic status, perhaps of older age, or other factors that may correlate with variables that are of importance. For this reason it has been suggested that file size for pictures and other components that may need to be transmitted should be minimized (McGraw *et al.* 2000a; Schmidt 2001).

Similarly, it may be worth investigating the speed of the Internet connection from which any web application is hosted. The closer the server is to major Internet backbones, the faster each exchange will be between the server and the client, and the less waiting participants may have to endure. For research paradigms requiring very few client–server interactions and few downloaded resources, this is unlikely to be a major factor, but if the application requires multiple client–server interactions, every reduction in time reduces the likelihood of dropout due to impatient participants.

The best way to investigate how centrally located an Internet service provider is, is to use a *traceroute* tool to count the number of hops between a server computer and various computer installations around the world (just trace the route from the server to known hosts in distant lands (i.e., from the host to china.com). The fewer the number of hops the better, and the faster each hop and the total time for the interaction, the better. Should a researcher discover that their server is not well-connected, they should consider hosting their research paradigm from a service provider's server farm that is better positioned to provide potential participants with fast and easy access. Such hosting is unlikely to incur much more than a small cost, and could result in more trustworthy data.

Client configuration issues

Just as download intensive research paradigms may result in participant exclusion, technologies requiring that participants have a high-powered computer, or the ability to install, verify or modify software settings before participating, will similarly exclude some potential respondents. This will be a result of willing participants not having the technical expertise required to participate, not possessing required equipment or dropping out as they become frustrated by delays or annoyed by the technical hassles required just to qualify to participate.

Client-side interpreters

An interpreter is the software that translates between the code that is delivered by the server into the actions that are taken on the client computer – such as rendering a graphic or presenting text in a particular format. Because client-side technologies have themselves matured along with web browser technology, some versions of these languages have features or capabilities that earlier versions did not. If a researcher takes advantage of such features, then a particular version of an interpreter may be required to access the research paradigm.

Some examples of technologies with interpreters built into the browser software include HTML, DHTML, Javascript or Java. Hyper-text markup language (HTML) has gone through several revisions, and DHTML (dynamic HTML) is a more recent expansion of the language to include animation and interactivity. Javascript (or JScript on Microsoft browsers) include a range of programming capabilities to perform math functions, animations or manipulation of web page components. Browsers additionally provide an interface to Java – a full-fledged programming language interpreter that can carry out an even wider range of tasks on the client computer. Finally, a plugin interface allows browsers to be extended by specialized interpreters that exist now or that may be created in the future, but require that users install these extra software interpreter components so that they can access special content from a particular website.

Requiring a particular minimum version of an interpreter technology in order to participate in social science research means that user effort may be required to enable their participation. Although not a realistic example nowadays, consider the introduction of HTML 2.0 in 1995 which added forms components to HTML, thereby providing a standard interface for sending information from the client back to the server. Users accessing a web application programmed using HTML 2.0 with a browser having an HTML 1.0 interpreter would be unable to participate due to the server technology exceeding the web client capabilities.

Java

In the case of Java – a full featured client-side language – Microsoft's Windows operating systems and its Internet Explorer web browser shipped for a long period of time without any Java capabilities, leaving potential users of this technology on their own to know or discover how to locate, download and install the Java interpreter. Although the Java language itself is free, the installation requires a sizeable download plus knowledge about how to obtain and install the language. As a result of Microsoft's large market share in desktop operating systems, this meant that the majority of computer systems deployed were without the Java technology.

Even if Java does come preinstalled and preconfigured within a browser, if a web-based research paradigm uses the latest features of the language, not all users with Java installed will have an adequate version. As with the basic installation of Java, updating requires either a full installation of the language or in easier cases, an Internet-delivered update. Regardless, there is a substantial download required that can take very long for users with slower Internet connections.

Javascript and HTML/DHTML

Javascript, and advanced features of HTML and DHTML are technologies built into the web browser software itself, meaning that if a particular minimal version of any of these is required, then the user will have to update their browser software. This involves locating the appropriate browser software, obtaining the installer (usually through a lengthy download), quitting their web browser and installing the new browser software, followed by running the browser and returning to the originating website.

Plugins

Macromedia's *Authorware* is capable of delivering some very sophisticated experimental designs involving graphics and a high level of interactivity (McGraw *et al.* 2000a, b). This technology requires that the Authorware web player plugin be installed. Although the web player is free, it requires a substantial download and installation that technologically unsophisticated users may

be hesitant to make. Furthermore, Authorware performance and accuracy seems to scale with the client's processor speed (Schmidt 2001), making it a technology that is ideally suited for the collection of data from a networked computer lab environment that is likely to have fast Internet access and a technician to ensure that all technical requirements have been met.

Macromedia *Flash* is one major plugin technology that is widely supported across many types of browser running under multiple operating systems. More recently, this browser plugin is automatically preloaded and configured with the installation of many web browsers, making its market penetration wide. In fact, Macromedia has claimed that 97 per cent of web users have Flash installed. This number, however, is guaranteed to be lower among older operating system and web browser combinations, and the technology itself is incompatible with web readers for the visually impaired. Nonetheless, this medium is ideally suited for dazzling graphics delivery where the timing of stimulus delivery is not of utmost importance (Schmidt 2001).

Ramifications of client-side technology

Given the hesitance of many computer users to substantially reconfigure any part of a working operating system, it is reasonable to assume that users should not be relied on to possess this type of technical expertise just to qualify for a study. Although willingness to reconfigure their system and return to a site to contribute data to a social science research project indicates a high level of motivation, deemed 'voluntariness' by Reips (2002a), such subjects are unlikely to be representative of the general population. That is, it is unreasonable to expect that the average or even modal individual of most populations (e.g., the general population or even many special populations being sampled) has either the means or the motivation to go out of their way for the altruistic opportunity of contributing data.

Although the data acquired from individuals high in voluntariness is arguably of a higher quality than data from subjects who did not have to overcome obstacles to participation (Reips 2002a), this probably reflects that subjects took their task seriously, having demonstrated their desire to contribute and being invested in the task. This in itself implies the presence of a selection bias and therefore questions the generalizability of the informational content of the data obtained. Whether the researcher wishes to generalize to the general population (e.g., citizens of the EU) or even to a specially selected subset (e.g., citizens of the EU referred from a particular advertising campaign), a selection bias will still exist in the sample obtained – namely a selection bias based on technical skill that would not be equally present had the researcher used a method of data collection that did not rely on participants requiring such skills.

Test, test, test

A minimum software requirement is necessary for all client-side technologies, and it is not always clear what proportion of users can be expected to meet technical hardware and software requirements. Where multiple versions of client-side software are involved, it is incumbent upon the researcher to thoroughly verify that their web application works on as wide a variety of software and operating system combinations as possible. Many examples of reusable code are freely available on the web for client-side interpreters such as DHTML, Javascript and Java. Of some assistance, such websites often provide information about browser compatibility for the code snippets they provide. This gives programmers and researchers reasonable expectations regarding system, browser and interpreter requirements.

Despite having an idea about compatibility of one's web code, testing web applications on a wide range of operating system and browser configurations is still important. Like all software, different browsers and interpreters running the same code may have unexpected side effects and may not always perform according to specifications. Software bugs can produce some of the least predictable denials of participation.

From a participant's point of view, perhaps the worst kind of implementation error is one in which data can be contributed only up to a certain point before participation is denied – when this occurs, participants invest their time and effort only to be excluded from making that

effort usable. Such occurrences not only frustrate the participant, but may reduce the likelihood that such a person will attempt donating their time and effort toward online research studies in the future. A poorly implemented web study is likely to result in frustrated respondents and the loss of valuable information.

Unfortunately, many errors in programming are often discovered after a study has begun, at which time the researcher/programmer is left scrambling to track down the source of the problem and to create a correction for it that does not introduce other problems. Widespread testing – or even holding a brief trial period before collecting data outright – is critical to prevent unforeseen denial of participation problems. From the researcher's point of view, saving data as the participant proceeds through an online session is a wise approach in order to maximize data collected – even if it is incomplete. Such data may end up being usable for partially answering some questions of interest, and it acts as a record that can be examined to assist in evaluating whether participants were denied participation and at what point in the session problems may have arisen.

Browser bugs

Some browser bugs that the author has personally encountered include limits on the number of form items that can be displayed on a single web page (Netscape 2.0 running under Windows), or a lack of appropriate information being passed from the web browser to the server regarding the last page visited (any Windows XP browser when the Service Pack 2 firewall is enabled).

Several versions of Internet Explorer under Windows 98 fail to update web pages when the URL to a CGI program has not changed from one server response to the next. That is, even though the web server would supply new web page content, because the URL is identical to one viewed before, the browser simply shows the server's previous and therefore unchanged response. This browser bug can be overcome by having programmers include a randomly generated string at the end of every URL after the CGI program's name, thereby tricking the browser into treating the information request as new.

Yet another browser error involves the manual refresh of a web page in some versions of Netscape as a result of the user moving or resizing the browser window. This can result in the resubmission of data or a server interaction that was not initiated by the browser user. Other browser errors involve the web browser supplying the server with information about the last web page visited even though the user did not recently click on a link (Internet Explorer 5 under MacOS 8–9).

Although each of the above browser bugs may seem minor, if a web application is programmed to rely on any of the information to accurately determine the user's intent for purposes of interacting with the server, then browser bugs guarantee that unintended consequences will arise for any of the users of affected web clients. Browser bugs such as these can prevent participation resulting in selection biases introduced by the research paradigm. Similarly, such bugs may affect the quality of data that is collected through denial of participation, or incomplete data.

Server side and data security issues

Having discussed many of the technical problems that can arise as a result of client-side technological issues, it seems appropriate to consider server-side issues. The predominant concerns on the server-side relate to data security, though see Schmidt (2000) for an overview of the information available for server side programming and suggestions for controlling web sessions through server-side programming.

Server intrusions

One common question regarding web research relates to whether the data can be publicly accessed or whether they are safe from prying eyes. There are several levels of answers relating to this issue. First, in these days of sophisticated entry techniques where even top-level international security agencies have been 'hacked', it is a possibility that a meager server for some social science web-based research is vulnerable to a similar fate. However, one needs to consider whether there would be motivation for such an intruder to go to the effort of accomplishing such a feat. Similarly, would individuals interested in influencing the

outcome of a social science web application have the sophistication to break into a web server in the first place? The majority of server intrusions are not for data so much as to install undetected Trojan software that can be used to spam others, collect personal financial information or to participate in denial of service attacks.

The best way to prevent server intrusions – and this should be done regardless of concern for protecting collected data – is to ensure that all of the operating system patches available for the operating system that the server software is running on have been applied. Keeping the server and operating system software up to date guards against known vulnerabilities and is the best step in data protection.

Data interceptions

A second part of the answer regarding data security concerns interception of data during transmission. Technically, eavesdropping could occur at every connection between the server and the participant. However, this requires that the data involved a particular transmission be picked out of the billions of other transmissions passing through major Internet hubs. Further, data snooping requires that the eavesdropper have direct physical access to the network at some point where the data are being passed between the client and the server, and that they have some way of picking out specific information from the information flow. Again, this is a lot of trouble to go through to access data from a social science web application.

To guard against the worries of intercepted data, the researcher can run a server that encrypts the information being passed between it and the client. Such a 'secure server' uses the https:// protocol rather than the http:// protocol, and requires that the client's web browser be capable of accessing securely encrypted documents. Most browsers released in the last five years have this functionality built in. Even should a third party intercept the data being passed from the client to the server, it is encoded with an encryption algorithm that requires a large amount of computational effort to decode, making it unlikely to be worth anyone's effort to go to the trouble of trying to break the encryption in the first place.

Should an online research program opt to use a secure server, the server can be configured so that it automatically uses non-encrypted communication should a potential participant's web browser be incapable of secure communication. If the web server is not configured this way, then users with non-secure browsers will be denied participation, thereby introducing a selection bias that arises for technical reasons.

Physical server theft

A third way that data can become vulnerable to theft concerns the physical location of the server. What can be stolen through off site access can also be stolen on site. Hence it may be of interest to investigate security of an Internet service provider's server farm or to reconsider the physical security of the server hardware.

Some operating systems (i.e., recent versions of MacOS) can encrypt data as it is written to files so that even if some third party should gain access to the file or the hardware, they will need to decrypt such information before it can become useful. As with data encryption during transmission, the effort and computational power required to break the encryption is usually beyond being easily compromised by the thieves.

Researcher carelessness

The fourth and most likely security violation dealing with online research data is due to sloppy handling by the researcher. Leaving data on an office computer, portable storage unit or some such method exposing it to easy access by others, is far more likely to result in others gaining access to it via the network through deviant means.

Similarly, leaving data files exposed in directories that are readable by the web server program make it possible for others to either guess the data file's name and thereby gain access to downloading it. Even more transparently, if directory browsing is enabled and the data are in a publicly accessible directory, then the data can be easily accessed. For this reason it is advisable to disable directory browsing on the server (Reips 2002a, b).

Precautions should be taken to protect data on multiple user machines, as these may allow data to be accessed by other legitimate accounts (which may or may not have been hacked) on the machine. Modern multi-user operating systems rely on various flags associated with accounts, files and directories to determine which users and applications are authorized to access a particular data file. The 'file permissions', if too leniently set, could allow other users to read, copy, delete or modify information either intentionally or unintentionally. For this reason, it is important for web applications that make use of multiple user machines to check file permissions ensuring that data are safeguarded.

Databases are becoming increasingly popular for data management in online social research. The free MySQL database provides a powerful, yet easy to use, free solution. However, administrators should be aware that the database needs to be secured after installation. Standard configurations of MySQL on several different operating systems include access to the database with no password protection on several sample databases and accounts (e.g., test), and do not have the database administrator password set. These loopholes are there for testing purposes after installation, but require that the database's true administrator modify their settings to prevent others from being able to store, modify or delete data (or databases) from the machine.

Server-side programming

Apart from data security issues, the only other real caveat concerning the server side of web research is the language or method that one uses to program the server-side of the client-server interaction. In order to store any data whatsoever, there needs to be some minimal amount of server programming. Any language that can create an executable program can be used to do this programming, though some text manipulation languages provide the tools to do this quickly and easily. PERL for instance (Practical Extraction and Report Language) provides a wide range of text processing capabilities making it a favorite for programming on the server side. Other specific applications have been created for this purpose as well – active server pages, PHP scripts, Cold Fusion scripts, Web Objects, Java Servlets and the list goes on. Any one of these methods works just fine.

One caution regarding server-side programming however, again relates to security. One way that hackers compromise server computer systems is by directing large amounts of data into server-side programs in hope that the unanticipated size or nature of the input will cause the program to crash, resulting in direct passing of information, such as commands, to the operating system of the server. To prevent against these types of intrusions, some interpreted languages on servers ensure that inputs to the programs can never be executed (i.e., the –t option in Perl). This way any sort of information coming from external sources is kept strictly independent of programs that are run, preventing hackers from executing any commands in the operating system. Programs written in languages that have no run-time checking (i.e. C) may pose more of a security risk if researchers are not careful to validate the input.

Limits of precision

Research methods relying on precise stimulus delivery conditions present a particular problem for many web-delivered research paradigms that are open to public participation. Many environmental factors in web applications cannot be controlled such as background noise, lighting, viewing angles and sizes (Hecht *et al.* 1999). Similarly, computer set-ups provide widely variable precision in stimulus delivery with sources of variability ranging from the software level, how the operating system interacts with running programs (MacInnes and Taylor 2001), the speed of the central processing unit (CPU) (Schmidt 2001), and even the minute details of how an image is rendered on the display (Krantz 2000).

Technical variability between subjects

Some work has gone into measuring the degree of variability that is introduced by having different hardware and/or software combinations (Myors 1999; Krantz 2000; Schmidt 2001) and methods for overcoming or controlling some of them have been proposed for the lab (MacInnes and Taylor 2001). Krantz (2000) observed a high degree of variability in cathode ray tube (CRT) monitor output, while others have reported error in the measurement reported by the operating system (Myors 1999; Eichstaedt 2001; MacInnes and Taylor 2001). Similarly, variability introduced by

the nature of input devices such as keyboards and mice (Plant *et al.* 2003) compound inaccuracies in measurement. All of these methods relied on reports of timing returned in software.

Particularly targeting web-based visual stimulus delivery, Schmidt (2001) compared the obtained performance of multiple web animation methods across a variety of operating systems, browsers and CPU speeds. Timing reported by the software was frequently returned as accurate, though the objectively measured output on the monitor as measured through optical detection, showed high variability. This variable was referred to as presentation accuracy to differentiate it from the accuracy levels returned at the level of the software. The latter could not be trusted as the accuracy measuring software was itself inaccurate by variability that went undetected.

Timing in Web-based visual stimulus delivery

Java-based animation was the method most robust against variability in CPU speed and computer system type, whereas methods such as Flash animation, Javascript/JScript, Authorware and animated GIF all scaled in error with the speed of processor (Schmidt 2001). This suggests that the client's processor speed is an important factor in determining presentation accuracy, with the least variable data coming from faster computer systems. Given that not all participants will have fast and up-to-date computer systems, Java should produce the least variable data as it is robust against variability due to CPU speed.

The various methods had different minimal presentation durations as well, with Java being the clear winner, off by no more than one monitor refresh cycle for a 100 msec presentation, even on slow systems. For slow systems, the minimal presentation duration achieved when a 100 msec duration was programmed, ranged from 240–945 msec. This suggests that when CPU speed is not taken into account and a method other than Java is used for animation, the minimal achievable duration is about a quarter of a second. When data from faster systems only are considered, Authorware, Java and Javascript/JScript performed quite accurately.

Further strengthening the rationale for using Java-based animation for research in which timing is important, are routines developed by Eichstaedt (2001) that run a separate threaded process whose sole task is to verify that the timing returned by the delivery program is accurate. Because the largest source of timing variability results from hogging of the processor by other processes in the middle of a time-critical trial, Eichstaedt (2001) reasoned that researchers could determine if a timing error occurred on a given trial by comparing the time taken as reported by a process delivering the trial against the trial time as measured by another process. If the two were discrepant, then the processor must have been interrupted by the operating system and the trial data suspect. By running extra trials, a valid set of data could be obtained. Of course it is up to the researcher to determine if trial frequency is an important issue and to separately track this variable and its effects.

Just as the aforementioned method omits trials that may produce contaminated data, participants whose data come from an operating system assessed as inadequate can also be omitted. Note that this is not denial of participation on the part of the researcher as individuals are allowed to participate; their data however, may simply not be included in analyses that seek to keep variability low.

Whether the concerns over accuracy are warranted is a serious question that begs to be better investigated. McGraw *et al.* (2000b) reported the results from a variety of Authorware experiments that were graphics intensive and in which timing played an important role. They replicated a large number of offline studies and were able to reproduce response times, measured in milliseconds, that rivaled traditional data collection methods. The conclusion drawn from this is that the increased power one gets from large sample sizes more than makes up for between subject sources of variability. Just how large an N is required for these methods to be accurate is an important question.

Knowing when to use the Web

As the current chapter demonstrates, a wide range of technical issues can affect the data that is obtained when collecting social science data online. While the number of such issues is large, each is unlikely to prevent the collection of data.

Hence it is doubly important to be aware of the issues surrounding technical variance to assist in understanding trends that are occurring in data collected, to avoid pitfalls, and to ensure that conclusions drawn from such data are valid.

Before getting carried away with the possibilities of collecting enormous amounts of data, researchers should closely consider the quality of data they are likely to acquire using web-based versus traditional methods and to weigh this against the efforts required to gather that data. In particular, researchers should consider whether the data acquired are likely to answer the research questions that they wish to answer, and whether the required commitment to mastering the technology will pay off because of the larger numbers or specialized types of participants that it will enable them to access. These factors should be compared to traditional research methods to determine which is best for a particular application.

References

Baron, J. and Siepmann, M. (2000). Techniques for creating and using web questionnaires in research and teaching. In M. H. Birnbaum (eds), *Psychological experiments on the Internet* (pp. 235–265). San Diego, CA: Academic Press.

Birnbaum, M. H. (1999). How to show that 9 > 221: collect judgments in a between-subjects design. *Psychological Methods* 4(3), 243–249.

Birnbaum, M. H. (2001). *Introduction to behavioral research on the Internet.* Upper Saddle River, NJ: Prentice Hall.

Buchanan, T. and Reips, U.-D. (2001). Platform-dependent biases in online research: do Mac users really think different? In K. J. Jonas, P. Breuer, B. Schauenburg and M. Boos (eds), *Perspectives on Internet research: Concepts and methods.* Available at http://www.gor.de/gor01/proceedings/.

Eichstaedt, J. (2001). An inaccurate-timing filter for reaction time measurement by JAVA applets implementing Internet-based experiments. *Behavior Research Methods, Instruments and Computers 33,* 179–186.

Eichstaedt, J. (2002). Measuring differences in pre-activation on the Internet: the content category superiority effect. *Experimental Psychology 49,* 283–291.

Hecht, H., Oesker, M., Kaiser, A., Civelek, H. and Stecker, T. (1999). A perception experiment with time-critical graphics animation on the World-Wide Web. *Behavior Research Methods, Instruments and Computers 31,* 439–445.

Krantz, J. H. (2000). Tell me, what did you see? The stimulus on computers. *Behavior Research Methods, Instruments and Computers 32,* 221–229.

MacInnes, W. J. and Taylor, T. L. (2001). Millisecond timing on PCs and Macs. *Behavioral Research Methods, Instruments and Computers 33*, 174–178.

McGraw, K. O., Tew, M. D. and Williams, J. E. (2000a). PsychExps: an on-line psychology laboratory. In M. H. Birnbaum (ed.), *Psychological Experiments on the Internet* (pp. 219–233). San Diego, CA: Academic Press.

McGraw, K. O., Tew, M. D. and Williams, J. E. (2000b). The integrity of web-delivered experiments: can you trust the data? *Psychological Science 11*, 502–506.

Myors, B. (1999). Timing accuracy of PC programs running under DOS and Windows. *Behavior Research Methods, Instruments and Computers 31*, 322–328.

Piper, A. I. (1998). Conducting social science laboratory experiments on the Word Wide Web. *Library and Information Science Research 20*, 5–21.

Plant, R. R., Hammond, N. and Whitehouse, T. (2003). How choice of mouse may affect response timing in psychological studies. *Behavior Research Methods, Instruments and Computers 35*(2), 276–284.

Reips, U. -D. (2000). The Web experiment method: advantages, disadvantages and solutions. In M. H. Birnbaum (ed.), *Psychological experiments on the Internet* (pp. 89–117). San Diego, CA: Academic Press.

Reips, U. -D. (2002a). Standards for Internet-based experimenting. *Experimental Psychology 49*, 243–256.

Reips, U.-D. (2002b). Internet-based psychological experimenting: five do's and five don'ts. *Social Science Computer Review 20*(3), 241–249.

Schmidt, W. C. (2000). The server-side of psychology Web experiments. In M. H. Birnbaum (ed.), *Psychological experiments on the Internet* (pp. 285–310). San Diego, CA: Academic Press.

Schmidt, W. C. (2001). Presentation accuracy of Web animation methods. *Behavior Research Methods, Instruments and Computers 33*, 187–200.

Smyth, J. D., Dillman, D. A., Christian, L. M. and Stern, M. J. (2006). Effects of using visual design principles to group response options in Web surveys. *International Journal of Internet Science 1*, 6–16.

CHAPTER 30

Using online panels in psychological research

Anja S. Göritz

Introduction

The objective of this chapter is to give an overview of the current state of use of online panels (OPs). The chapter explains what OPs are, what type of OPs there are, how OPs work from a technological point of view, and what their advantages and disadvantages are. Moreover, the chapter reviews the current body of methodological findings of doing research with OPs. Based on this evidence, recommendations are given as to how the quality of data that are collected in OPs can be augmented. The chapter is relevant for psychologists seeking to gather data in OPs as well as to build and maintain their own OP.

What an online panel is

OPs are an important form of web-based data collection, as is illustrated by their widespread use: in the Autumn of 1999, Göritz et al. (2000) identified 64 OPs in a comprehensive web search. In August 2000, Couper (2000) found over 80 OPs listed on the website www.money4surveys.com. Today this site lists 110 panels. As of December 2004, Batinic and Moser (2005) estimated the number of existing OPs at 650–750 worldwide.

In the classical sense, a panel is a longitudinal study in which the same information is collected from the same individuals at different points in time. In contrast to that, an OP has come to denote a pool of registered people who have agreed to occasionally take part in web-based studies. Thus with OPs, the traditional understanding of a panel as a longitudinal study is broadened because an OP can be employed as a sampling source for both longitudinal and cross-sectional studies. OPs are therefore more properly referred to as 'online access panels'. Because the term 'OP' has been well established, it will be used in this chapter. It should be kept in mind, however, that it is not necessarily a longitudinal study but a pool of readily available participants for different kinds of studies.

There are several types of OPs. One criterion for distinction is the medium in which the panel is operated. There is a continuum between online and offline panels. With pure OPs, the panel is operated entirely via the Internet (i.e., the recruitment of panellists, the studies, and the maintenance of the panel all take place online), whereas with offline panels, all processes are carried out offline. With mixed mode panels, some processes are implemented online, some offline, and some processes may even be implemented in both modes. Moreover, OPs can be distinguished according to the type of panellists they hold. For example, there are specialist panels such as dentist panels or child panels, and there are panels that are open to people from all walks of life. Moreover, panels can be characterized by the studies that are run in them: on one end of the continuum, there are panels to conduct scientific studies. They are most often based in universities. On the other end of the continuum, there are commercial OPs, which are usually maintained by market research firms.

Another distinction among OPs regards to how the panellists were sampled (cf. Couper 2000). On one end of the spectrum there are volunteer opt-in panels, which are the most common form of OPs. Such panels have been built on the basis of non-probability sampling. Typically, appeals for signing up with such a panel are posted in newsgroups, mailing lists, on websites via links or banners, or announcements are disseminated in offline media or by word of mouth. Despite attempts to weight or stratify the participants in subsequent panel studies, the initial sample remains one of volunteers who have selected themselves from an unknown population. Hence, attempted generalizations to a target population are based on leaps of faith rather than sound statistical principles. Volunteer opt-in panels need to be distinguished from pre-recruited panels. On the one hand there are pre-recruited panels with probability sampling of panellists. These panels are drawn from a (hopefully unbiased) sampling frame of the desired population. On the other hand, there are pre-recruited list-based panels where the entire population and not only a sample is integrated into the panel (e.g., the student body of a university or the employees of a company). However, because in practice list members' awareness and agreement to take part in research may be more or less explicit, with many such lists the distinction is blurred whether they are merely databases of students, customers, employees etc. or whether they can rightly be called OPs.

Benefits and threats for psychological research

Computer-based and Internet-based studies offer numerous advantages compared to more traditional techniques of offline data collection (cf. Göritz and Schumacher 2000; Reips 2000; Fricker and Schonlau 2002; Birnbaum 2004). For instance, computer-based research allows multimedial stimuli to be combined within the same study, the data come in electronic form, and often

there are less costs for interviewers and consumables. In addition to that, using the Internet as a research platform allows field times to be short, study participation independent of the time of day and geographical location, and more cost savings because there are no expenses for interviewers and laboratories. In addition to these general benefits, OPs offer specific methodological and economic advantages when compared to offline studies on one hand and to unrestricted online studies (i.e., with ad hoc recruitment) on the other hand. For instance, from an OP researchers can draw variable samples, be it for cross-sectional, trend-, panel- and other designs (Göritz *et al.* 2002). Moreover, participants are readily available because of their pre-recruitment, so field times can be even shorter than with unrestricted web surveys.

Another benefit of gathering data within a panel is that the profile data of the panellists and – unless they are new to the panel – their data from earlier studies are known. On the basis of these profile and historical data, target samples can be drawn without elaborate screening, questionnaires can be limited to novel items, which also means that panellists need not be bored with the same questions again and again, newly collected data can be checked for reliability and consistency by matching them to existing data. Furthermore, the percentage and characteristics of people who refuse to take part in a given study can be assessed. In addition, with OPs it is easier than in unrestricted surveys to prevent multiple registration and study participation by the same person. Finally, there are ethical advantages of OPs when compared to unrestricted surveys: panellists can be informed as early as at their sign-up that they may be invited to studies whose purpose cannot be disclosed before the research is concluded. Also, panellists who have abandoned a study prematurely can still be debriefed because they are accessible via email, whereas ad hoc recruited dropouts can usually not be debriefed (Göritz 2002).

A challenge that is unique to panel or longitudinal surveys is that of *panel conditioning*, also called *panel bias*. Panel conditioning occurs through panellists' ongoing survey participation (cf. Couper 2000; Kalton and Citro 1993). Given panellists' experience with the survey over time, their responses may increasingly differ from the responses given by people answering the same survey for the first time. Although with an OP, the surveys may vary over time, the mere act of participating in an ongoing panel may change respondents' behaviour and attitudes. However, panel conditioning does not necessarily falsify responses, but can cause them to become closer to the 'true values'. For example, practice reduces the unfamiliarity with the survey material or the uneasiness with the interviewing situation. Panel conditioning can be addressed if a rotating panel design is used, that is, if information is not collected every time from the same panellists but alternately from different panel subgroups. Dennis (2001) reports several case studies from an OP where no noteworthy effects of panel conditioning could be established. However, he notes that speciality and longitudinal panels, where panellists are repeatedly surveyed on the same topic and often with a long questionnaire, are at a higher risk of creating 'professional respondents'.

Especially panels that offer lucrative rewards for study participation face the challenge of identifying and barring respondents who lie about themselves in order to fit into the target sample. In such panels, respondents should be covertly screened for study eligibility, and consistency checks should be employed on a regular basis.

Function, structure and infrastructure of an online panel

To describe what is going on in an OP, one can break down the stages of an OP into the recruitment of the panellists, sampling and invitation for the studies, data collection within studies, and rewarding of respondents (cf. Figure 30.1).

The recruitment varies with the type of sampling used and with the medium of solicitation. With opt-in panels, the process starts with the potential panellists arriving at the panel website, where they can find information about the panel such as the terms and conditions. Interested people can enroll as panellists by filling out a registration form. In this registration form various profile data are gathered (e.g., socio-demographic information) and fed into a database.

Multiple registrations can be thwarted by matching new registrations to existing profiles (see also Chapter 24 in this volume for details on the identification of duplicates). According to Gräf (2001), 0.6 per cent of the sign-ups in OPs are duplicates. Between the years 2000 and 2005 in the OP at the author's university (www.wisopanel.uni-erlangen.de), 242 of 3925 sign-ups (6.2 per cent) were duplicates. This figure is higher than that reported by Gräf (2001) because in the early years of this panel panellists were required to log onto the panel website in order to take part in a study. On these occasions, many panellists confounded logging-on with signing-up and registered anew. In sum, these figures from different panels suggest that few panellists register multiple times, and most of them seem to do so innocently.

Besides signing-up multiple times, panellists might inadvertently or deliberately fill in wrong information in the registration form. Whether a signed-up panellist of a specified name truly lives at the specified address can only be ascertained by falling back on offline contacts. A simple method

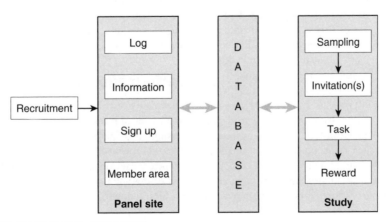

Figure 30.1 Structure of an online panel.

is to send new panellists a welcome letter or gift. Gräf (2001) has reported only two returned welcome letters out of 1000 (0.2 per cent). In Göritz (2008), six out of 204 mousepads (2.9 per cent) sent to newly registered panellists were undeliverable. Hence, despite often-heard concerns to be otherwise, only a small fraction of panellists seems to provide false contact data. However, to draw reliable conclusions, more data are needed.

As an additional component, many panel sites feature a password-protected personal area (cf. Göritz et al. 2002). Panellists can log on to this area to update their profile, to check their account of earned rewards or to find other information such as study results or the names of winners of panel lotteries. In the background, all user activities on the panel site are recorded in server log files (see Reips and Stieger 2004). These log files can be analysed to gauge the amount of traffic on the panel site as well as identify weaknesses in the usability of the site (e.g., broken links).

Once a sufficient total number of panellists or a satisfactory number of target persons have enrolled, a sample can be drawn and invited to a study. Usually, the invitation to a study is sent by email. Compared to postal mail, inviting panellists by email is extremely fast and virtually free of charge. As a downside, email invitations bounce quite often due to exceeded disk quotas and outdated email addresses. In the panel at the author's university, between November 2000 and December 2005, 518 of 3925 email addresses were invalid at registration or expired later on. This amounts to an average annual loss of 2.6 per cent of the panellists due to invalid email addresses. Similarly, according to Gräf (2001) 2.7 per cent of the panellists register with an invalid email address. These figures illustrate that it is useful not only to collect a panellist's email address at sign-up but also their postal address or their phone number or an alternative email address. If the primary email account is invalid an otherwise lost panellist can thus be recovered.

Besides a unique hyperlink to the study, an invitation email usually contains other pieces of information such as the topic, duration and closing date of the study. If panellists fail to take part in a study by a certain deadline, it is possible to send them one or more reminders. Moreover, in order to keep non-response and dropout low, panellists are normally compensated for their participation. Possible incentives, which can also be used in combination, are per-capita payments, redeemable loyalty points, tickets for lotteries, donations to charity, gifts, or study results.

The management of the panel in general and the allocation of rewards in particular are rendered more convenient if the panel manager can avail of a web-based administration interface that is coupled with the panel database. Panel management software is available from different companies. A web search will bring up websites of relevant companies, and the reader can look up up-to-date information about the costs involved. Professional panel management software seems to be widespread among commercial OPs. By contrast, academic OPs mostly rely on home-made solutions. To the author's knowledge, there does not exist any share- or freeware for maintaining OPs. That is why she is programming an open source tool for OP management (for details see www.goeritz.net/panelware/).

When choosing or home-developing a panel software one should make sure it supports the following functionalities: search panellists; view, modify, export, and delete profile data; display panel statistics; identify duplicates; draw samples; send emails; create and manage email templates. Professional software often provides features beyond these basics, such as parameterization as to the maximal number of surveys to send panellists, integration of online survey software to create and conduct studies seamlessly, and real-time reporting of field data and survey results. As a rule of thumb, the higher the number of people who work with an OP, the less familiar these people are with databases, and the more frequently studies are conducted the more advisable to invest in professional panel management software.

Performance and quality

The quality of collected data can be augmented by an array of measures such as logging and processing participants' paradata (e.g., IP address, relevant browser and computer settings, response latencies; see Couper 2005 and Chapters 24, 26 and 29, this volume), regular updates of panellists' profiles, following-up of unheeded invitations, reliability and consistency checks of answers to questionnaire items and identity checks through offline contact (Göritz *et al.* 2002). Respondents' motivation can generally be enhanced by wakening their interest, reducing respondent burden and creating an atmosphere of mutual trust. Some possible measures toward these aims are sending personalized invitations to studies (see Joinson and Reips, 2007; Joinson *et al.* 2007), sending birthday and Christmas cards, providing background information on the research conducted, offering material incentives, ensuring data security and confidentiality, facilitating participation through lean questionnaires, a reasonable frequency of studies and a careful selection of questions with regard to wording, complexity and intrusiveness (Dillman 1978; Klein and Porst 2000; Göritz *et al.* 2002). However, because at this stage the effectiveness of most of these measures is merely plausible or has been extrapolated from findings in the offline realm, their actual effectiveness needs to be demonstrated in controlled studies.

Recruitment and sampling

Internet-based studies that aim at the estimation of population parameters would only be feasible if each member of the target population had access to the Internet and is addressable online (e.g., via email or Instant Messaging). As a consequence, web surveys with self-selected respondents or those conducted in volunteer opt-in panels are not suited to derive parameter estimates for the general population because of the under-representation of certain strata of the general population in the subpopulation of Internet users and because of the lack of an appropriate sampling frame (Göritz and Moser 2000).

A possible way out is to use pre-recruited panels. As mentioned above, one form of a pre-recruited panel is a list-based panel. Here, a circumscribed population of interest is integrated into the panel (i.e., a census is conducted). The higher the Internet penetration among such a population the less coverage error occurs and/or the smaller the cost to provide Internet access for those who are not yet connected to the Internet. If study participation is mandatory with such list-based panels (and given the absence of technical problems in taking part in a study) there are no non-response problems. Of course, data obtained with list-based panels cannot be generalized to other populations.

Another form of a pre-recruited panel is one with probability sampling of panellists. Such a panel is based on random samples drawn from an unbiased sampling frame. As there is no register of all Internet users, people for such a panel need to be sampled and contacted offline, for example by Random Digit Dialling. Depending on the population to which inference is sought, either the Internet users or all persons of the contacted sample are solicited to join the panel. If people are solicited regardless of their online connection status, in order to reduce coverage error those who are not yet online need to be provided with access to the Internet (which is prohibitively expensive if the share of Internet users is small).

A key problem with pre-recruited panels with probability sampling has been the low initial response rate to the recruitment interview and the low number of interviewees who subsequently agree to participate in the panel. For example, Weßels and Zimmermann (2001) recruited online panellists by phoning a random household sample. Of all 8615 interviewees, 8.3 per cent became panellists. Hellwig *et al.* (2003) recruited panellists by Random Digit Dialling as well. Of all 2021 interviewees, only 2.1 per cent became panellists. Venningen (2002) recruited online panellists by mailing 50001 invitations to a random household sample. Only 1.1 per cent of the successfully contacted people registered with the panel. Loosveldt and Heerwegh (2004) invited 3094 people from a public database to take part in a web survey, at which end they were asked to take part in future studies. Of the contacted sample, 18.8 per cent agreed to take part in the future, and 13.1 per cent actually participated in the first study thereafter. Joinson and Reips (2007) emailed a stratified sample of 9294 adult students an invitation to join a student panel. Of those, 1405 people (15.1 per cent) registered with the panel. Moreover, these authors found that women were more likely to sign up than men. Finally, Göritz (2004a) compared random email sampling from a volunteer web-based sampling frame (a white pages service), random letter sampling, random fax sampling, and flier based convenience sampling as solicitation methods for an OP. With email, 25.5 per cent of invitations resulted in panel registrations, with fax 7.7 per cent, with flier 7.0 per cent, and with letter only 1.3 per cent. The composition of the samples differed according to solicitation method: fax-recruited individuals were older than flier- and email-recruited ones. Panellists recruited via email had been using the Internet longer than flier- and fax-recruited ones, and they used the Internet more often than fax-recruited ones. After their recruitment, panellists were followed up in the first two studies run in the panel. Their probability to call up and to complete these studies was independent of the method by which they had been recruited. The same study examined whether recruitment success was augmented by material incentives. Half of each sample's invitations mentioned a cash lottery into which new panellists would be entered. The lottery was effective with fliers but not with email, fax, and letter. Müller-Peters *et al.* (2001) have shown that after a face-to-face solicitation people are more inclined to sign-up with a market research panel if cash compared to no incentive is offered and if a cheque versus inclusion in a lottery is offered.

To sum up, pre-recruited panels with probability sampling are the most expensive form of web surveys because they require considerable resources for both recruitment and panel maintenance. There are few studies that have evaluated whether these expenses are justified by an improved quality obtained from the probability based approach. Faas (2003) compared a web survey in an OP with probability sampled Internet users with a paper and pencil interview of a random sample of Internet users. Despite large efforts that had been taken to recruit the OP, there were considerable differences in the results. Besides differences in political attitudes, the panel sample was significantly younger, more educated and more experienced with the Internet. It should be noted, however, that the two surveys also differed in mode.

However, not all research questions require representative samples. Many studies in psychology are suitable to be carried out with a volunteer sample (Mook 1983), for example, developments of psychometric scales (cf. Buchanan and Smith

1999), explorations and feasibility studies, longitudinal and cross-sectional experiments (cf. Reips 2002), as well as qualitative and casuistic studies. For some of such studies, the Internet is not merely an alternative but a superior platform for data collection because of the cost savings and because samples drawn from the Internet tend to be more heterogeneous and hence yield more robust results than ubiquitous student samples (Reips 2000).

Response and dropout rates

Besides sample bias, another source of error is *non-response*. Non-response threatens the validity of the survey data because responding people and non-respondents often differ in a number of characteristics (Rosnow and Rosenthal 1976). In a panel context one can distinguish unit-non-response and attrition. Unit-non-response occurs if an invited panellist fails to take part in a particular survey, whereas attrition occurs if the panellist leaves the panel or remains permanently inactive. An OP can shrink for a multitude of reasons such as natural mortality, non-accessibility due to invalid email addresses, or refusal due to waning interest or concerns with data security.

Depending on the panel as well as the length and topic of the survey at hand the response rate (i.e., of all invited persons the number of people who call up the first survey page) and the dropout rate (i.e., of all persons who have called up the first survey page the number of people who do not reach the last survey page) vary to a great extent. For example, Batinic and Moser (2005) obtained an average response rate of 73.9 per cent and an average dropout rate of 3.1 per cent in 70 studies that were conducted in four different OPs. Earlier, Gräf (2001) observed typical dropout rates between 0.3 per cent and 4.5 per cent in different OPs, and Venningen (2002) yielded a response rate of 80.3 per cent in the first study in a new market research panel. Loosveldt and Heerwegh (2004), in the first two studies in their new university-based panel yielded response rates of 69.8 per cent and 55.9 per cent and dropout rates of 4.2 per cent and 2 per cent, respectively. In a study in an adult student panel, Joinson and Reips (2007) observed response rates ranging from 40.1 per cent to 53.4 per cent depending on experimental condition. In the same panel but another study, Joinson *et al.* (2007) observed response rates ranging from 44.1 per cent to 48.8 per cent, depending on experimental condition. In both instances, they found that if a powerful source issues the invitation to a study a personal salutation elicits a higher response rate than an impersonal salutation. Leopold (2004: 68) reports a study that yielded a response rate of 45.4 per cent and a dropout rate of 9.4 per cent. He notices that respondents predominantly drop out at the beginning of a questionnaire or at the first occurrence of a new question format such as open-ended or grid questions (2004: 68, 110). Finally, in studies run in the panel at the University of Erlangen-Nuremberg response rates usually vary between 40 per cent and 70 per cent and dropout rates between 5 per cent and 20 per cent. As one can imagine, response rates tend to be much higher in studies that are conducted in a new panel or after having swept the panel (i.e., panellists who fail to update their profiles by a particular deadline are deleted).

With regard to the question which panellists are more likely to heed a request for participation, in Leopold (2004: 198) women compared to men were more likely to take part in several studies in a market research OP. In contrast to these results, the sexes did not differ in their likelihood to take part in the two studies in Göritz (2005). However, in one study in Göritz (2005) women were indeed more likely to heed a request for participation than men ($\varphi = -0.19$, $N = 166$, $p = 0.02$). In sum, there seems to exist a tendency that female panellists are more willing to take part in studies than male panellists. The volatility of this effect in the studies mentioned points to the existence of moderators (e.g., study topic, length of study, etc.). Such moderators should be identified through further research.

Reminders

To increase the response rate researchers may send one or several reminder emails to panellists who have not heeded the original invitation to a study. In a study the author conducted in a market research panel, before sending a reminder the response rate was 48.7 per cent while after

the reminder it went up to 64.2 per cent. In four studies that were conducted in the panel at the University of Erlangen-Nuremberg, response rates before the reminder were 55.8 per cent, 58.4 per cent, 69.2 per cent, and 41.3 per cent. After the reminder they went up to 74.1 per cent, 75.9 per cent, 70.8 per cent, and 52.4 per cent, respectively (Göritz 2005). Leopold (2004: 111) reports similar results for a market research panel study: The response rate was 39.9 per cent before the reminder and went up to 53.6 per cent after the reminder. Furthermore, there is evidence that people who participate before a reminder drop out of the study less likely than those who participate after a reminder. The dropout rates in the five studies quoted above (Göritz 2005) were 4.3 per cent for unreminded versus 7.6 per cent for reminded panellists, 1.1 per cent versus 27.6 per cent, 11.3 per cent versus 13.8 per cent, 15.6 per cent versus 100 per cent, and 26.5 per cent versus 25.8 per cent, respectively. With Leopold's study (2004: 111), 2.9 per cent of unreminded participants abandoned the survey prematurely compared to 8.0 per cent of reminded participants.

Although these figures suggest that reminders may be worthwhile, one should not draw premature conclusions because there has been no systematic study of the effectiveness of reminders in OPs if employed on a regular basis. Because reminders are intrusive – as long as there are no probative data that urge a different approach – it is prudent to use reminders sparingly to maintain panellists' long-term willingness to participate.

Field times

In three studies that were conducted in the panel at the author's university, invited panellists were informed about the study's field time in advance. Figure 30.2 shows the typical logarithmic pattern of returns. As expected, participation in Study 2, with a field time of 24 days, was more evenly spread over time than in Studies 1 and 3 where the field time was eight days. However, in all three studies by the close of the third day, 75 per cent or more of the final participants had already taken part.

In corroboration, Welker (2001) has observed that most survey responses to email invitations occur within nine days. In addition, Gräf (2001)

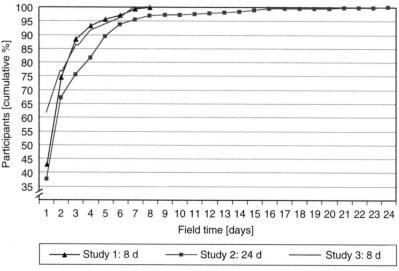

Figure 30.2 Cumulative return rates in three online panel studies.

has reported five studies with field times of two or three days where 24 hours after sending out the invitation two-thirds of the invited people had already taken part. In these studies, the final response rate was higher among panellists who at their sign-up had indicated using the Internet daily (77.3 per cent average response rate across the five studies) than among panellists who had indicated to use the Internet on two to five days a week (65.4 per cent average response rate). In a similar vein, Leopold (2004: 91f.) has shown that late respondents to a survey use the Internet more infrequently than early birds.

Because the available studies have not systematically varied the field time and its announcement, no definite recommendations can be derived as to what field times are reasonable. However, the available results show that especially in studies that require above average computer skills and Internet knowledge, deadlines should not be too tight. Still, the relative shortness of field times permits the frequency of surveys or panel waves to be higher than in offline panels. Ideally, the frequency of surveys in a panel is not too high in order to prevent participation fatigue and panel conditioning, while it is also not too low in order to keep panellists committed.

Incentives

A comparatively well-studied measure to keep non-response at bay is to offer respondents material and non-material incentives, for example, money, gifts, survey results, redeemable loyalty points, lotteries and contributions to charity. In a meta-analysis of online incentive experiments (Göritz 2006a), there were 32 comparisons between a material incentive and a no-incentive control group on response and 26 comparisons on retention (the retention rate is 100 minus dropout rate). A moderator test revealed that the incentive effects on response did not significantly differ ($Q < 0.01, p = 0.94$) if a study involved a list-based sample (odds ratio [OR] = 1.19, $n = 26$) or an undefined sample (OR = 1.19, $n = 4$). The situation was similar with retention as a dependent variable: The incentive effects did not significantly differ ($Q < 0.01, p = 0.97$) between list-based (OR = 1.28, $n = 18$) and undefined samples (OR = 1.27, $n = 7$). An additional moderator test undertaken for this chapter contrasted OP studies (i.e., studies in which list members had explicitly agreed to occasionally take part in research) with studies not conducted in an OP. When response was the dependent measure, the incentive effect in OP studies (OR = 1.23,

$n = 15$) did not significantly differ ($Q = 0.36$, $p = 0.55$) from the incentive effect in studies not conducted in an OP (OR $= 1.18$, $n = 15$). The same picture was found with retention: the incentive effect in OP studies (OR $= 1.18$, $n = 15$) did not significantly differ ($Q = 0.34$, $p = 0.56$) from the incentive effect in studies not conducted in an OP (OR $= 1.30$, $n = 10$).

These results demonstrate that incentives per se tend to be effective when used in list-based as well as in OP studies. However, more detailed reviews of incentive effects in OP studies that take into account background variables (e.g. type and amount of incentive, timing of the incentive, characteristics of the study and the sample) require more experiments. To this end, an extension of this meta-analysis is planned, and readers are invited to contribute their own study results by filling out the form at www.goeritz.net/incentives.htm. The next paragraphs look at individual studies that allows for finer-grained analyses.

In an experiment conducted in a market research OP that was not included in the meta-analysis for lack of a no-incentive control group (Göritz 2004b), the response rate was slightly higher when loyalty points were used as incentives (82.4 per cent) than if cash (78.0 per cent) or trinkets (78.6 per cent) were raffled. In addition, loyalty points brought about less dropout than the cash lottery. Furthermore, the more loyalty points were awarded the less dropout occurred. By contrast, the total payout of the lottery and into how many cash prizes the payout was split did not influence response, dropout, panellists' conscientiousness when filling out the questionnaire, survey outcome, and sample composition. In the same vein, in a second experiment in a non-profit panel (Göritz 2004b), response, dropout, conscientiousness, survey outcome and sample composition did not differ across four lotteries that differed in total payout and/or number of prizes.

Another six experiments were conducted in a non-profit OP to examine the effectiveness of cash lotteries in particular (Göritz 2006b). In each of the six studies, the cash lottery was offered in two versions, either the total payout of the lottery was mentioned or the lottery was split into multiple prizes. The control group was not offered any incentive whatsoever. A cash lottery

relative to no incentive did not increase response or decrease dropout; neither did it make a difference if one large prize or multiple smaller prizes were raffled. It remains an interesting question whether these null effects are restricted to non-profit panels with occasional studies. In non-profit panels, panellists may take surveys primarily out of curiosity or a desire to help in research. Moreover, occasional study participation is conducive to frame one's engagement in the panel as a leisure activity. By contrast, participating in studies frequently is burdensome and such an effort may only be elicited if invitees are externally rewarded, for example through a cash lottery.

Neither of the summarized studies has examined the effectiveness of offering a donation to charity on behalf of the panellists in exchange for their participation in a study. If effective, donations to charity would be a suitable incentive to be used in OPs, because they incur almost no transaction costs. When used in offline studies, donations tend to be ineffective (Hubbard and Little 1988; Warriner et al. 1996). In our university panel, the offer to donate €0.5 or €1 to charity per participating panellist was contrasted with the offer to include the participant in a 5 × €20 cash lottery. The response rate with the lottery (46.1 per cent) was significantly higher than with the €0.5 (37.3 per cent) or €1 donation (35.1 per cent). The two donation conditions did not significantly differ. However, before putting donations down as ineffective incentives, more experiments are needed.

A simple and cost-free option is to mention in the study invitation that the reception of an incentive is contingent upon the submission of a completely filled out questionnaire. Restricting the eligibility for an incentive in this way might lead to a better data quality because participants may make a stronger effort to fill out the questionnaire more completely and more conscientiously in order to be eligible for the incentive. Five experiments (Göritz 2005), of which four were carried out in a university-based and one in a market research OP, examined the effectiveness of this technique. Four times the incentive was a cash lottery and once it was a personal gift. A meta-analysis of the five experiments revealed that contingent relative to unconditional incentives decrease response to a survey (odds ratio = 0.81). Thus, it is not recommended to frame the incentive as being contingent upon the completion of the questionnaire.

Because most hitherto presented evidence stems from cross-sectional OP studies, the generalizability of these findings to repeated surveys is questionable. Knowledge on how to motivate panellists to participate in the long run is especially salient in the context of OPs because it lies in the nature of OPs that participants are requested to take part in surveys repeatedly. To find out more about the long-term impact of incentives on participation, an experiment consisting of five waves was conducted in a market research panel (Göritz, 2008). After registration with the panel, one group of panellists was sent an advance gift; the other group did not receive a gift. For participation in the studies, half of the panellists were repeatedly offered redeemable loyalty points. The others were offered to be included in cash lotteries. At the beginning, the advance gift significantly increased participation, but this effect dwindled linearly throughout the waves of the study. Moreover, initially there was no difference in response between people with loyalty points and those offered to be included in the cash lottery. Over time though, loyalty points relative to the cash lotteries became more attractive. In Wave 1, the advance gift was especially useful when combined with the lottery. This effect faded in the course of the longitudinal study. The study also showed that low-income panellists were more susceptible to the advance gift than well-off people.

A second longitudinal experiment examined the influence of a lottery of gift certificates on response and dropout in four studies in a university OP (Göritz and Wolff 2007). Independent of the lottery, panellists who responded in a given wave were more likely to respond in the next wave. This process was characterized as a first-order Markov chain. There was a direct positive effect of the lottery on response only at the first wave of the study. However, mediated by the Markov process, the positive effect of the lottery on response at the first wave was carried over into later waves. The lottery did not have any effect on dropout. Furthermore, it was found that dropout at a given wave is a reliable predictor for unit-non-response in the next wave. This information could be used by survey managers to diagnose and act on any impending non-response.

To sum up, despite the varying effectiveness of different types of incentives, overall it seems worthwhile to employ incentives in OPs. However, possible gains in response need to be balanced against the extra costs for the incentive and its distribution. Moreover, there are ethical issues when using incentives. Without there being a difference in effort on the part of the participants, a group of participants is sometimes offered a certain incentive while other groups are offered a less valuable incentive or no incentive at all. This apparent violation of the principles of equality and equity regularly occurs (1) in incentive experiments, (2) if some respondents are more valuable to the researcher than others (e.g., low-incidence versus ubiquitous segments of the population), or (3) if respondents who have expressed their reluctance or have actually refused are offered a refusal conversion incentive but cooperative respondents are not.

The way some of these instances might be justifiable depends on the ethical paradigm (cf. Ess, Chapter 31 this volume). For example, a deontologist might point out the right of the researcher to the pursuit of knowledge, whereas a consequentialist might point out the study's contribution to the greatest good for the greatest number. Two studies (Groves *et al.* 1999; Singer *et al.* 1999) have empirically examined participants' reactions to learning about the differential use of incentives. The first study was done in the laboratory with community volunteers using self-administered responses. The second study was a field study using face-to-face interviews. The laboratory experiments resulted in significant negative effects of disclosing differential incentives to participants on their expressed willingness to participate in the survey. This finding was not replicated in the field study, nor were respondents in the field study to whom differential incentives had been disclosed significantly less likely to respond to a new survey request from an ostensibly different organization a year later.

Professional codes do not go into much detail on ethical issues of using incentives. The *Ethical principles of psychologists and code of conduct* issued by the American Psychological Association (2002) forbids unfair discrimination based on age, gender, gender identity, race, ethnicity, culture, national origin, religion, sexual orientation, disability, socio-economic status, or any basis proscribed by law. When offering inducements for research participation psychologists ought to make reasonable efforts to avoid offering excessive or inappropriate financial or other inducements for research participation when such inducements are likely to coerce participation. The *Quality Assurance Standards for Online Questionnaires* (Arbeitskreis Deutscher Markt- und Sozialforschungsinstitute *et al.* 2001), which is a joint declaration by several German professional associations concerned with market and opinion research, states that incentives should merely be a compensation for respondents' effort in terms of time and money to participate in the study. It further states that with one-time studies the reception of the incentive must be contingent upon the formally correct participation in the study alone. By contrast, with OPs it is permissible to award loyalty points for participation that may be accumulated and – upon reaching a threshold – redeemed against an incentive.

The future of online panels

The Internet is now reaching into three in four households in the Western world, and it continues to expand. Besides the rising penetration of the Internet, the general increase in bandwidth and its ensuing possibilities to collect data in even more sophisticated ways is a promising outlook for web-based and therefore OP-based data collection. For studies that allow field times of several months or for smaller studies that require up to one or two hundred participants it is usually unnecessary to recruit via OPs. Instead one can use free-of-charge recruitment lists (see Chapter 26, this volume). However, as a rule of thumb, if the field time must not exceed a few weeks or even days or one needs more than two hundred participants, recruitment of respondents via email lists (e.g., Birnbaum and Reips 2005) or via OPs is indispensable to keep the study affordable. Because of their benefits, OPs are likely to become the dominant form of web-based data collection in the long run.

However, this optimistic outlook is somewhat dampened by the ongoing inability to avoid coverage error associated with doing web surveys of the general public, which is likely to persist for the foreseeable future (Dillman and Bowker 2001). Moreover, many practical and methodological questions of how to collect data of the highest possible quality at the lowest possible cost remain unanswered. For instance, virtually nothing web-specific is known about panel conditioning and the effectiveness of some response-enhancing measures such as sending greeting cards, informing about issues of data security and confidentiality, or about the most favourable frequency at which to run studies in a panel. These questions should bring about more systematic studies in the future.

References

American Psychological Association (2002). *Ethical principles of psychologists and code of conduct.* Retrieved May 29 2006 from http://www.apa.org/ethics/.

Arbeitskreis Deutscher Markt- und Sozialforschungsinstitute, Arbeitsgemeinschaft Sozialwissenschaftlicher Institute, Berufsverband Deutscher Markt- und Sozialforscher and Deutsche Gesellschaft für Online-Forschung. (2001). *Standards zur Qualitätssicherung für Online-Befragungen* [Quality Assurance Standards for Online Questionnaires]. Retrieved May 29 2006 from http://www.adm-ev.de/quali_online.html.

Batinic, B. and Moser, K. (2005). Determinanten der Rücklaufquote in Online-Panels [Determinants of response rates in online panels]. *Zeitschrift für Medienpsychologie 17*, 64–74.

Birnbaum, M. H. (2004). Human research and data collection via the Internet. *Annual Review of Psychology 55*, 803–832.

Birnbaum, M. H. and Reips, U.-D. (2005). Behavioral research and data collection via the Internet. In R. W. Proctor and K.-P. L. Vu (eds), *The handbook of human factors in Web design* (pp. 471–492). Mahwah, NJ: Erlbaum.

Buchanan, T. and Smith, J. L. (1999). Using the Internet for psychological research. Personality testing on the World-Wide Web. *British Journal of Psychology 90*, 125–144.

Couper, M. P. (2000). Web surveys: a review of issues and approaches. *Public Opinion Quarterly 64*, 464–494.

Couper, M. P. (2005). Technology trends in survey data collection. *Social Science Computer Review 23*(4), 486–501.

Dennis, J. M. (2001). Are Internet panels creating professional respondents? A study of panel effects. *Marketing Research 13*(2), 34–38.

Dillman, D. A. (1978). *Mail and telephone surveys. The total design method.* New York: Wiley.

Dillman, D. A. and Bowker, D. K. (2001). The web questionnaire challenge to survey methodologists.

In U.-D. Reips and M. Bosnjak (eds), *Dimensions of Internet science* (pp. 159–178). Lengerich: Pabst.

Faas, T. (2003). Offline rekrutierte Access Panels: Königsweg der Online-Forschung? [Offline-recruited access panels: Silver bullet of online research?] *ZUMA-Nachrichten 53*(27), 58–76.

Fricker, R. D. (Jr.) and Schonlau, M. (2002). Advantages and disadvantages of Internet research surveys: Evidence from the literature. *Field Methods 14*(4), 347–367.

Göritz, A. S. (2002). Stimmungsinduktion über das WWW [Mood induction via the WWW]. *Report Psychologie 3*, 192–202.

Göritz, A. S. (2004a). Recruitment for online access panels. *International Journal of Market Research 46*(4), 411–425.

Göritz, A. S. (2004b). The impact of material incentives on response quantity, response quality, sample composition, survey outcome and cost in online access panels. *International Journal of Market Research 46*(3), 327–345.

Göritz, A. S. (2005). Contingent versus unconditional incentives in WWW-studies. *Metodološki zvezki – Advances in Methodology and Statistics 2*(1), 1–14.

Göritz, A. S. (2006a). Incentives in Web studies: methodological issues and a review. *International Journal of Internet Science 1*(1), 58–70.

Göritz, A. S. (2006b). Cash lotteries as incentives in online panels. *Social Science Computer Review. 24*(4), 445–452.

Göritz, A. S. (2008). The long-term effect of material incentives on participation in online panels. *Field Methods 20*(3), 211–225.

Göritz, A. S. and Moser, K. (2000). Repräsentativität im Online-Panel [Representativeness in online panels]. *Der Markt 155*, 156–162.

Göritz, A. S. and Schumacher, J. (2000). The WWW as a research medium: An illustrative survey on paranormal belief. *Perceptual and Motor Skills 90*, 1195–1206.

Göritz, A. S. and Wolff, H.-G. (2007). Lotteries as incentives in longitudinal web studies. *Social Science Computer Review. 25*(1), forthcoming.

Göritz, A. S., Reinhold, N. and Batinic, B. (2002). Online Panels. In B. Batinic, U. Reips and M. Bosnjak (eds), *Online Social Sciences* (pp. 27–47). Seattle, WA: Hogrefe and Huber.

Gräf, L. (2001). Internet Access Panels in der Praxis [Internet access panels in practice]. In A. Theobald, M. Dreyer and T. Starsetzki (eds), Online-Marktforschung (pp. 319–334). Wiesbaden: Gabler.

Groves, R. M., Singer, E., Corning, A. D. and Bowers, A. (1999). A laboratory approach to measuring the effects on survey participation of interview length, incentives, differential incentives and refusal conversion. *Journal of Official Statistics 15*, 251–268.

Hellwig, J. O., von Heesen, B. and Bouwmeester, R. (2003) Rekrutierungsunterschiede bei Online-Panels und ihre Folgen [Differences in recruitment with online panels and their consequences]. In A. Theobald, M. Dreyer and T. Starsetzki (eds), Online-Marktforschung –

Theoretische Grundlagen und praktische Erfahrungen (pp. 241–254). Wiesbaden: Gabler.

Hubbard, R. and Little, E. L. (1988). Promised contributions to charity and mail survey responses: Replication with extension. *Public Opinion Quarterly 52*, 223–230.

Joinson, A. N. and Reips, U.-D. (2007). Personalized salutation, power of sender and response rates to Web-based surveys. *Computers in Human Behavior 23*(3), 1372–1383.

Joinson, A. N., Woodley, A. and Reips, U.-D. (2007). Personalization, authentication and self-disclosure in self-administered Internet surveys. *Computers in Human Behavior, 23*, 275–285.

Kalton, G. and Citro, C. F. (1993). Panel surveys: adding the fourth dimension. *Survey Methodology 19*(2), 205–215.

Klein, S. and Porst, R. (2000). Mail Surveys. Ein Literaturbericht [Mail surveys. A literature review]. *ZUMA-Technischer Bericht, 10*. Retrieved January 24, 2006, from http://www.social-science-gesis.de/ Publikationen/Berichte/ZUMA_Methodenberichte/ documents/pdfs/tb00_10.pdf.

Leopold, H. (2004). Rücklauf bei Online Befragungen im Online Access Panel [Response in online surveys in online access panels]. Hamburg: Kovac.

Loosveldt, G. and Heerwegh, D. (2004). Unit non response in face-to-face and web surveys. Some comparisons. Paper presented at the Lazarsfeld Symposium, Brussels, Belgium.

Mook, D. G. (1983). In defense of external invalidity. *American Psychologist 38*, 379–387.

Müller-Peters, A., Kern, O. and Geißler, H. (2001). Die Wirkungsweise unterschiedlicher Incentivierungssysteme auf Rekrutierungserfolg und Stichprobenqualität [The effect of incentives on recruitment and sample quality]. Paper presented at the German Online Research conference, Göttingen, Germany.

Reips, U.-D. (2000). The Web experiment method: advantages, disadvantages and solutions. In M. H. Birnbaum (ed.), *Psychological experiments on the Internet* (pp. 89–117). San Diego, CA: Academic Press.

Reips, U.-D. (2002). Standards for Internet-based experimenting. *Experimental Psychology 49*, 243–256.

Reips, U.-D. and Stieger, S. (2004). Scientific LogAnalyzer: a web-based tool for analyses of server log files in psychological research. *Behavior Research Methods, Instruments and Computers 36*(2), 304–311.

Rosnow, R. and Rosenthal, R. (1976). The volunteer subject revisited. *Australian Journal of Psychology 28*(2), 97–108.

Singer, E., Groves, R. M. and Corning, A. D. (1999). Differential incentives: beliefs about practices, perceptions of equity and effects on survey participation. *Public Opinion Quarterly 63*, 251–260.

Venningen, H. (2002). Offline Rekrutierung für ein OP [Offline recruitment for an online panel]. Unpublished final thesis (Diplomarbeit), University of Salzburg, Austria.

Warriner, G. K., Goyder, J., Gjertsen, H., Hohner, P. and McSpurren, K. (1996). Charities, no; lotteries, no; cash, yes. Main effects and interactions in a Canadian incentives experiment. *Public Opinion Quarterly* 60, 542–561.

Welker, M. (2001). Email surveys: non-response figures reflected. In U.-D. Reips and M. Bosnjak (eds), *Dimensions of Internet Science* (pp. 231–237). Lengerich: Pabst.

Weßels, M. and Zimmermann, M. (2001). *Offline-rekrutierte Access-Panels als Königsweg der panelbasierten Online-Forschung?* [Are offline-recruited access panels the silver bullet of panel-based online research?]. Paper presented at the German Online Research conference, Göttingen, Germany.

CHAPTER 31

Internet research ethics

Charles Ess

Introduction: why Internet research ethics?

Gold mines and/or land mines? Promises and problems in Internet research

As the Internet both developed and exponentially extended its reach – first within the United States and then well beyond its borders (though not, of course, without disparities and inequalities) – researchers from a range of disciplines, including psychology, communication, sociology, anthropology and the humanities, quickly recognized that the various venues of the Internet (email, listservs, USENET groups, MUDs and MOOs, web pages, ICQ and its descendents such as Instant Messenger, etc.) facilitated distinctive new ways for human beings to interact with one another. These new places and modes of interaction deserved careful study. Moreover, the ready-made data sets automatically generated, for example, by listserv and USENET archives, the accessibility of venues, and, in many cases, the anonymity researchers could enjoy as 'lurkers', made study of human interactions in these new contexts seem like a researcher's dream.

Like much of the other early Internet euphoria and utopianism, researchers' early enthusiasm soon encountered new difficulties – including new sorts of ethical problems. Of course, ethical difficulties in research involving human subjects are nothing new. As is well-known, following clear abuse of human beings in the name of research

both during the Second World War and in other (in)famous cases – for example the Tuskegee Institute study (Pence 1990: 184–205)—professional ethics codes, declarations and national and international laws emerged intended to protect basic human rights, beginning with the right to informed consent to experimental procedures on one's own body.[1] At the same time, however, while such codes were well established especially in the United States – and enforced, for example, by its distinctive matrix of Institutional Review Boards[2] – prevailing views of the Internet emphasized its creating a new 'Cyberspace' and attendant forms of human communication and

[1] These basic rights include familiar rights to informed consent, anonymity, privacy, and protection of confidentiality, as well as the requirement that researchers minimize the risk of harm to research subjects. These requirements have been developed since the Nuremberg Code (1947) through the Belmont Report (1972) to the US Code of Federal Regulations to the Office for Protection from Research Risks (1991). The most important international declaration of these rights is the World Medical Association Declaration of Helsinki (2004).

[2] Such boards are required by the Federal codes in the United States (cf.. Walther 2002) and are a part of every college and university that undertakes research involving human subjects. They certainly have their counterparts in the English-speaking world – such as the 'Research Ethics Boards' (National Research Council, Canada), external Learning and Teaching Support Networks' subject centres and internal Academic Standards and Policy committees in the UK, the National Health and Medical Research Council (Australia) and the Australian Research Council. By contrast, such oversight authorities are absent, for example, in Danish universities. See also Johns *et al.* (2004).

identity that were radically different from the offline world – first of all, because human beings could precisely escape their material bodies to develop and play with new forms of 'virtual' identity online. Especially as almost all communication online involved texts generated by virtual identities that may have been entirely untraceable to an offline person – it was by no means clear that the human subjects protections codes, developed in medicine and the social sciences to prevent harm to offline persons and minds, had any relevance to research on online communication and interaction.[3]

But research history repeated itself – first of all, as a number of incidents and cases made clear that it is indeed possible to harm minds and identities, if not bodies, online. In the US/English-speaking context, for example, a male psychologist made bad research history by pretending to be a disfigured and handicapped female while chatting with women, ostensibly in the name of better understanding female psychology and interaction patterns (Van Gelder [1985], 1991; cf. Mann 2003: 36). When he revealed his 'real' (i.e., offline/embodied) self to be male, predictable outrage followed – first of all, from the women participants who (rightly) felt deceived into relationships of trust and intimacy online in which they revealed aspects of themselves that they otherwise would not have shared with a male psychologist. Even more spectacularly, the (in)famous 'rape in cyberspace' (Dibbell 1993) opened up extensive discussion, for example, as to whether words and speech *could*, in at least extreme instances, indeed harm real human beings in ethically unacceptable ways. The emergent discussion of Internet research ethics (IRE) then crystallized in a watershed special issue of *The Information Society* (e.g., Herring 1996; King 1996), followed by a national-level workshop on IRE in 1999, organized by the US NIH Office for Protection from Research Risks and the American Association for the Advancement of Science (Frankel and Siang 1999). Within the discipline of psychology alone, as Peden and Flashinski point out, Michalak and Szabo (1998) attempted to develop guidelines for Internet researchers based on general standards, personal experience and the 1992 ethical standards established by the American Psychological Association (Peden and Flashinski 2004: 3). In 2000, Azar focused on the difficulties of informed consent and debriefing in online research – along with the problem that conducting a study online makes public a researcher's procedures and methods, thus opening up the possibility of intellectual piracy (Azar 2000, cited in Peden and Flashinski 2004: 5) In that same year, finally, Peden and Flashinski note the publication of Reips' guidelines (Reips 2000) – which they in turn use to evaluate a range of online surveys and experiments. They found that while many Internet-based experiments and surveys complied with requirements for avoiding deception and excessive inducements, they did less well with regard to assessing informed consent and debriefing (Peden and Flashinski 2004: 14). In addition, while 45% of the studies and experiments asked for personal information (e.g., name, phone number) – only 20% used secure sites, and only 19% created separate data files for personal information and responses (2004: 15). They comment: 'Although psychologists are expected to protect confidential information, our results indicate considerable room for improvement' (2004: 15).

More broadly, a growing body of literature, composed primarily of working researchers' reflections on the ethical difficulties they encountered in their online research (e.g., Sveningsson 2001) further added to the resources then taken up by the ethics working committee of the Association of Internet Researchers (AoIR), charged in 2000 with developing interdisciplinary and international guidelines for online research. The first version of these guidelines was approved by the AoIR membership in 2002, and has found

---

[3] As one example from 1994: 'If the research does not involve identifiable subjects, there is no risk to subjects, and therefore the protection of these rights and interests no longer applies' (Jones 1994: 33, cited in Lawson 2004: 84). More recently, Dzeyk, for example, flatly states that 'Denn es ist kaum vorstellbar, dass bei netzbasierten humanexperimentellen Untersuchungen Versuchspersonen z.B. in Lebensangst versetzt werden könnten' [It is scarcely imaginable that experimental subjects could experience any anxiety about their lives in net-based experimental research] – in order to argue that *deontological* codes (e.g., those that emphasize motives, ethical principles, etc. without regard for consequences) hence do not apply to online research (Dzeyk 2001: 5). As we are about to see, however, the possibility of online research resulting in serious harm to human subjects started to become apparent as early as 1985.

extensive use in the English-speaking world (see AoIR 2002; Ess 2004). More specifically, the German Society for Online Research and others has established a set of guidelines for Internet-based surveys that include ethical considerations (Arbeitskreis Deutscher Markt- und Sozialforschungsinstitute et al. 2001).

Some basic issues in IRE

Sources, frameworks, and initial considerations

The development of IRE in Western countries has drawn from four major sources:

1. The models of human subjects research and human subjects protections in the life sciences – i.e., medical ethics, bioethics, etc. – and social sciences – e.g., psychology (Kraut et al. 2004);

2. Professional ethics – including codes for computer-related professions (e.g., Association for Computing Machinery 1992 etc.);

3. Ethical codes in the social sciences and the humanities – where the latter do not see human beings online as 'subjects' to be protected, but rather as authors or amateur artists whose work is public and needs only the protection of copyright, but not, for example, anonymity, informed consent, etc. (e.g., Bruckman 2002); and

4. The philosophical work on philosophy of information and information ethics (e.g., Floridi 2003).

Underlying these more specific approaches are a number of Western ethical frameworks that require at least brief definition. *Deontology*, associated in the modern era especially with Kant, emphasizes the primary importance of respecting the basic rights of human beings as autonomous beings – i.e., free and thereby capable of establishing their own moral norms and rules. The primary requirement to respect this essential freedom then issues in a range of rights, duties, obligations, and principles – including those central to shared conceptions of human subjects' protections, i.e., rights to privacy, confidentiality, anonymity, and informed consent – and the correlative duties of researchers to respect and protect these rights, no matter the

'costs' of doing so (e.g., increased complexity in research design and implementation – or even, in a worst-case scenario, the necessity to abandon a research project because it would unavoidably violate these basic rights and duties). This philosophical orientation appears to be emphasized, for example, in approaches to research ethics in many (but by no means all) European countries – by contrast, that is, with *consequentialist* approaches, including the *utilitarianism* characteristic of ethical decision-making in the Anglo-American spheres. Utilitarianism stresses an effort to balance real and potential costs (usually, to a few) and benefits (usually, to the many): from a utilitarian perspective, if research is likely to contribute to the greatest good for the greatest number (e.g., in terms of improvements in health, social welfare, the environment, etc.), such benefits may ethically trump their costs – even such costs as subjects' experiencing suffering, the loss of rights and autonomy, etc., during the course of a research project. So in the US and the UK, for example, if the anticipated outcomes of research are likely to benefit the larger society (including, in some cases, precisely the research subjects themselves, as research may uncover new cures, etc.), research codes typically emphasize the importance of *minimizing* risks to research subjects. Deontologists counter, however, that 'the greatest good for the greatest number' can – as historical examples such as the Tuskegee Institute study unfortunately illustrate – justify extreme suffering and even the deaths of 'the few', i.e., a relatively limited number of human beings now treated precisely as *subjects*, i.e., no longer as autonomous human beings. In addition to these two large poles, contemporary ethical approaches further include, for example, feminist and communitarian approaches that emphasize (as complements to, not opposites of, the strictly rational principles of deontology and consequentialism) the ethical importance of personal relationships and care between researchers and those engaged as 'subjects'. In doing so, these ethical approaches come closer to utilizing forms of 'the Golden Rule' – i.e., asking researchers to consider how they themselves would *feel* if they found themselves treated in the ways they proposed to treat their subjects? Moreover, these approaches characteristically expand the ethical focus from the research subject as autonomous individual to his/her circle of close relationships, so that the researcher may be obliged, as in the NESH (2002) guidelines, for example, to protect the anonymity and confidentiality of not simply a given subject, but also those of their close friends and intimate partner(s): see Johns et al. (2004). Our responses to specific ethical issues in research can thus be shaded in significantly different ways, depending on which of these frameworks we take as primary (cf. AoIR 2002; Ess 2003).

More specifically, contrary to the 1990s arguments *against* applying human subjects protection models, such models prevail both in contemporary discussions of IRE and the three extant ethical guidelines intended to address a large range of ethical issues in online research (i.e., AoIR 2002; NESH 2003; Kraut et al. 2004). Rooted in both national and international declarations of human rights (Reidenburg 2000; Michelfelder 2001), these models stress protecting the integrity and dignity of human persons first of all through an emphasis on rights to informed consent and to privacy as protected by guarantees of confidentiality and anonymity. The right to privacy, moreover, is reinforced especially in the philosophical discussions of information ethics – e.g., as such privacy is seen as instrumental to the personal development of the human being as a free and rational being, and as a participant in a democratic society (Johnson 2001; Bizer 2003).

In addition to this strong focus on human subjects protections (as drawn primarily from medical and social science approaches), contemporary IRE may also take up copyright issues (as reflecting more humanistic approaches that stress the producer of a text as an *author* rather than as a 'subject'). Especially given that in the US context, anything appearing on the Web is immediately considered protected by copyright – researchers who take this approach to, say, studying websites, USENET postings, etc., – will have a second set of ethical issues to consider, including what counts as 'fair use' of such texts, acknowledging copyright holders (not always obvious), and, in some cases, acquiring permission for direct citations. Especially this last requirement, when it emerges, confronts researchers with a set of both rights (i.e., authorship as protected by copyright, etc.) and costs to consider (e.g., the time and labour required to track down ostensible authors, to certify that they are indeed the authors and thus copyright-holders of a specific text, to acquire consent in ways that overcome the possibility, heightened in the online context, of ensuring that the consent comes from the proper author, etc.)

These emphases on the rights of participants must be considered further alongside other important rights and values – including (deontological) emphases on the importance of knowledge developed through research, and (more utilitarian) emphases on research knowledge as contributing to public policy and debate, along with researchers' rights and interests in pursuing knowledge, in enjoying free expression of their views, etc.

A large matrix thus emerges (see Table 31.1) – one made up of possible but contrasting *ethical* approaches such as deontology, consequentialism, virtue ethics, etc., coupled to large ranges of

Table 31.1 Continua/considerations in Internet research ethics

Ethical frameworks	*Deontology* – rights, duties, obligations, principles as paramount (can override even significant promises of benefit from research) *Utilitarianism* – costs and risks of research may be justified in light of 'greater good' to be gained for the greater number → emphasis on minimizing (rather than eliminating) risks to research participants *Feminist/communitarian* – the human being as a member of a 'web of relationships' → ethical obligations not only to the individual implicated in research, but also their circle of close friends, relations *Good Samaritan* – ethical choices beyond an 'ethical minimum' as established by extant professional codes, laws

Continued

Table 31.1 Continua/considerations in Internet research ethics *cont.*

Disciplinary frameworks/Who is the participant?	*Medical/social sciences* → participant as *research subject* → Human Subjects Protections (anonymity, confidentiality, informed consent)	*Humanities* → poster as *author* → copyright protections, fair use provisions
Tensional rights and interests	Participants' (*deontological*) rights to privacy, copyright, etc. vis-à-vis . . . potential (*utilitarian*) public benefits of research; (*deontological*) researchers' rights to free speech (including public debate, democratic governance), pursuit of knowledge . . .	
Question: online vs. offline research?	*Utilitarian*: costs/benefits of online vs. offline – e.g., greater scope, ease in research data gathering online vs. greater *risks* to privacy, greater difficulty in determining identity, acquiring informed consent, etc. *Deontological*: *greater* difficulties in especially fulfilling Human Subjects protections online	
Considerations, venues frameworks:	*Expectations* of participants – i.e., public – private space? Announcements, postings, etc., defining whether or not space is public/private?	
Example	**Greater risks ↔ lesser risks** Less sensitive ↔ more sensitive – information involved? (greater ↔ lesser need for privacy, confidentiality) Larger (less private) ↔ smaller (more private)? Synchronous – Asynchronous? (harder to/easier to acquire informed consent, etc.) Subjects/posters as *less* vulnerable ↔ *more* vulnerable? **Utilitarian:** benefits of research may override *minimal* risks to participants ↔ **Deontology:** protection of some rights (e.g., privacy) is an absolute duty **Feminist/communitarian:** *may* emphasize participants' rights, *feelings* more strongly *large chatroom*: if identity is protected, no need for informed consent ↔ *small listserv* – e.g., on health issues: anonymity + informed consent likely necessary	
Specific issues	Protecting privacy online (including links, cookies, IP addresses, etc.) → greater attention to securing data, especially if shared online Research with vulnerable populations/encountering sensitive, disturbing information online (e.g., suicidal language) → greater researcher responsibility to intervene	
Methodology-specific	Discourse analysis – greater need for verbatim quotes → greater need for researcher independence (e.g., from participants' preferences regarding publication, etc.)	Participant–observation, feminist–communitarian – closer relation between researcher/subject → greater ethical responsibility/ sensitivity to participants

NB: this table is intended to serve both as an initial orientation, in the form of a conceptual map, and as a summary of some of the main ethical considerations raised in this chapter. It does not intend to imply reductionism of any sort – nor simple either/or's (e.g., between the poster as author vis-à-vis participant as subject: rather, these distinctions – as the arrows seek to show – are intended as points along lines of continua.

recognized ethical issues shaped by whether we regard the persons implicated in our online research primarily as participants (thus calling into play the ethical codes primarily characteristic of medical and social sciences) or authors (thereby calling into play humanities approaches and issues of copyright, etc.). Within this matrix, researchers may begin by considering first of all whether online research is indeed preferable to offline research, precisely for ethical reasons. For example – and beginning from a consequentialist perspective – offline research may offer certain ethically relevant advantages, including potentially greater security for confidential data stored in physical rather than electronic formats. At the same time, however, research online – including web-based experiments, surveys, etc. – offers a distinctive set of advantages and potential benefits (see Chapters 24, 26, 28 and 30, this volume). Online researchers, for example, can much more easily acquire responses from those in remote areas, those whose disabilities might prevent them from physically travelling to a university campus or research centre, etc. To do so, moreover, researchers in some cases may make use of online surveys as well as automated programs (including data-gathering robots or 'bots'), for example, that can track web use (including through the use of cookies) – thereby developing data sets on dramatically new and potentially very significant scales. In turn, these potential advantages must be further weighed against the distinctive costs and risks of online research, including: *greater risks to individual privacy and confidentiality* (because of greater accessibility of information online regarding individuals, groups, and their communications – and in ways that may prevent subjects from knowing that their behaviours and communications are being observed and recorded); *greater challenges to researchers* because of greater difficulty in obtaining informed consent; and *greater difficulty of ascertaining subjects' identity* because of use of pseudonyms, multiple online identities, etc. As well, the diversity of research venues (email, chat rooms, web pages), various forms of synchronous communication (such as Instant Messaging, IRC, audio- and video-chat, and so forth) present a wide range of distinctive ethical challenges – all of which is further complicated in international collaborations that thereby involve both subjects and

researchers from countries with contrasting, if not conflicting, ethical and legal requirements, for example regarding privacy (cf. AoIR 2002). Finally, the use of cookies, bots, various forms of data mining, etc., while simplifying the researcher's work in many ways as they simultaneously expand the potential scale and scope of research, thereby introduce distinctive ethical issues of their own (cf. Allen et al. 2006). Even from a strictly consequentialist perspective, sorting out these complex ranges of the potential benefits and costs of online vis-à-vis offline research, is not always an easy matter (cf. Reips 1997, 2000, 2002).

Human subjects protections online? Informed consent, privacy, confidentiality, anonymity

Given that researchers choose to undertake online rather than offline research – those undertaking primarily social science approaches must then consider carefully how to apply human subjects protections online. Informed consent, for example, is notoriously difficult to obtain in such venues as a large chat room, in which participants – using pseudonyms – come and go with breathtaking speed. In some specific contexts, however, there appears to be little ethical difficulty: consistent with the AoIR guidelines (2002), the most recent guidelines in psychology argue that there in what are analogized as public spaces such as large chat rooms, especially if users are informed from the outset that their communication is *not* confidential, and if researchers record these communications in ways that protect the anonymity (and thus privacy) of individuals, there is no need for informed consent (Kraut et al. 2004; cf. Cousineau et al. 2005).

Informed consent becomes imperative, however, with regard to research and observation involving more clearly private communications and personal information. In the European Union states, in fact, data privacy protection laws define personal information[4] and insist that data

---

[4] Article 2 (a) of the Directive states:
'personal data' shall mean any information relating to an identified or identifiable natural person ('data subject'); an identifiable person is one who can be identified, directly or indirectly, in particular by reference to an identification number or to one or more factors specific to his physical, physiological, mental, economic, cultural or social identity.

subjects must: unambiguously give consent for personal information to be gathered online; be given notice as to why data is being collected about them; be able to correct erroneous data; be able to opt-out of data collection; and be protected from having their data transferred to countries with less stringent privacy protections (European Union 1995).

In between these two relatively clear poles, of course, are the multiple grey areas in which the fine details of context, as well as the larger frameworks of disciplinary ethics, national laws (if any), and national and cultural traditions of ethical decision-making shape both what participants and researchers see as ethical issues and difficulties and the *judgements* ultimately made in the face of those difficulties.[5] For example, what if the chat room you're observing is relatively small and stable, so that participants develop a sense of one another's identities and personalities? What if the chat room, moreover, is populated by persons primarily from a smaller community (or, for that matter, country) – so that the chances are quite good that one or more of the participants know one another offline as well as online? And what if the chat room is devoted to sensitive issues – e.g., the exploration of lesbian sexuality? As Janne Bromseth has carefully explored, a researcher's ethical obligations to protect the identity and privacy of participants under these sorts of circumstances vary across a continuum

of contexts, including cultural ones: Norway, as we will see more fully below, enjoys a higher expectation of privacy and privacy protection than even the EU countries, much less the US (2002). Multiple other examples could be adduced here (e.g., Danet 2002), but the point is that ethical judgements must attend to just such a complex range of contextual details and frameworks – and they will vary in part from country to country.

Specific issues in privacy

As noted above, different Western countries take different views regarding how far the right to privacy is to be protected. In the US and the UK, extant codes and guidelines make clear that such rights are *not* absolute, in the sense that they may be overridden *if* it can be demonstrated that (a) the risks to the subjects in such cases are minimal rather than maximal (as might be the case, for example, if one were to reveal a subject's identity who was infected with HIV) and that (b) such minimal risks are outweighed by the promise of greater good for the greater number as the hoped-for benefit of the research (Office for Protection from Research Risks 1991; Social Research Association 2002). By contrast, the NESH guidelines, for example, emphasize *not* the utilitarian benefit of scientific research, but its intrinsic good (2001: A.1), but even this stronger ethical status does not, in their view, justify overriding rights to privacy. On the contrary, such rights are, if anything, even more extensively protected – especially in the sense that not only are the individual's rights to privacy, confidentiality, etc., to be protected, but also those of their close relations (NESH 2001: para. 40; cf. Bromseth 2002: 36).[6]

Relatedly, a major issue in IRE raises the question, 'when does the private become public'. To begin with, web pages and archives 'publicly'

---

[5] At least since Confucius and Aristotle, philosophers in both Eastern and Western cultures have recognized that ethical judgment is *not* a matter of developing general principles that can then be applied algorithmically to specific issues. Rather, a central reason for why ethical reflection and discussion are both so complex and so necessary is just that *judgement* is involved – where such judgement must decide, for example, *which* general principles may indeed apply to a specific case and context. Aristotle refers to this form of ethical judgement as *phronesis*, and argues that it – along with ethics and political philosophy more generally – require years of experience in the effort to apply ethical norms in *praxis*, as well as of theoretical reflection on both the apparent successes and failures of such effort, in order to be shaped and 'taught' (e.g., *Nichomachean Ethics* 1968, 9 [1094b29–1095a12], 337 [1140a32–1140b7]. His teacher, Plato, used the example of the ship's pilot – the *cybernetes* (from which, in fact, 'cybernetics' derives) – as the model of the ethical person (*Republic* [1968] 1991, 9 [Book I, 332e], 169 [VI, 489c]. More recently, to paraphrase Simone de Beauvoir – ethics is not a matter of general rules and recipes; it is more like the arts, in which one can focus on methods (1948: 134).

[6] As we have seen, Dzeyk notes the distinction between deontological and utilitarian positions, and argues that only utilitarian positions are relevant for online research ethics (2001: 5, cf. note 4). But his own position in fact reflects a mixture of deontological and utilitarian considerations. For example, he recommends first of all attention to protection of private information as required by the German data privacy law [*Bundesdatenschutzgesetz*] – and further notes that this privacy protection derives from the right to 'informational self-determination' [*informationelle Selbstbestimmung*] (13f.). He seems to assume that these basic rights are *not* to be overridden by any possible

posted on the Web are considered under US law to be public documents and 'automatically' copyrighted by the author. But the line between public and private can quickly blur here – for example, as a USENET poster originally submits a message in a forum believed to be private, only to discover years later that the entire USENET archive has been made publicly available online.

Other threats to privacy online are more intrinsic to the media. Even experienced and conscientious researchers, for example, can make a significant blunder when they write up their research: even if they seek to protect privacy by ensuring the anonymity of their research subjects – if they nonetheless include a direct quote from an archive that is publicly available and thus easily found through a search engine such as Google, they thereby make it trivially easy for anyone to determine the author's identity (cf. Eysenbach and Till 2001; Bromseth 2002: 44). Moreover, Reips points out the further problems of researchers who make participant data available online. In keeping with Peden and Flashinski's observations (above), researchers may make no effort to protect the identity of participants in data files: but when these files are made available online – in contrast, that is, with being stored on a secure server with restricted access – such data then become available not simply to other interested researchers (which already violates basic protections of confidentiality and anonymity), but also, indeed, to anyone

who happens to stumble across such files on the Web. In order to protect confidentiality, Reips adds, not only obvious personal identifiers (name, age, address, etc.) but also other information such as web links, IP addresses, etc. should be treated carefully as well, insofar as such information may also be used to trace the identities of research participants (Reips 2002).

Indeed, sophisticated users have at their fingertips a range of technologies, from automated analysis software to programs for 'trapping' Internet transmissions in their entirety, that seem to make online privacy an oxymoron (Hunsinger 2003). In light of the difficulty of establishing and sustaining privacy online, it may well be asked whether or not there is any meaningful ethical obligation to do so? Responses here again vary by country and culture. Roughly, US-based researchers – consistent with the greater willingness in US-based codes and laws to accept at least minimum risks to subjects – seem more comfortable with reduced or eliminated obligations to protect subjects' rights to privacy and confidentiality. By contrast, European researchers – consistent with the shared assumption that the state exists in part precisely to protect basic rights through law, as well as with the generally stronger data privacy protection laws already in place – are more likely to see law and its enforcement as a primary means of articulating and protecting such rights.

As a general, international guideline: in light of this greater difficulty to protect privacy, confidentiality and anonymity online, it is safest to not only anonymize subjects but also to paraphrase any citations or quotes. As we will see in greater detail below, however, in some forms of research such as discourse analysis and ethnography, direct quotes – and, perhaps, the 'real' pseudonyms of their authors – are necessary to support or illustrate a claim. There is some agreement that when such direct quotes and real pseudonyms are used, informed consent is de facto necessary (e.g., Lawson 2004). At the same time, however, in the US context, an Institutional Review Board might waive the requirement for informed consent in such a case, but only if it could be demonstrated that risks posed to the author(s), should their identity become known, would be minimal.

Beyond this first guideline – an additional consideration for researchers is whether or not

---

benefits of research. As such, the affirmation of such basic rights over any consequentialist considerations of possible research benefit counts as a deontological commitment, not a consequentialist one.

As a second example, Dzeyk further recommends Döring's approach: 'Döring empfiehlt beispielsweise ein kontextspezifisches Vorgehen: Ein expliziter Wunsch nach Privatheit sollte in jedem Fall beachtet werden; dies spielt insbesondere bei sensiblen Themen (wie z.B. Missbrauch) eine große Rolle (vgl. Döring, 1999: S. 204)'. That is, any explicit wishes for privacy are to be respected in every case – most especially in connection with sensitive issues such as abuse. But it is precisely this respect for explicit wishes – more broadly, *expectations* – that I would further count as deontological, not consequentialist. Insofar as Dzeyk's position may be representative of German approaches to research ethics, then it would be fairly characterized as one that blends both deontological and consequentialist approaches – and thereby, as something of a middle between more consequentialist approaches in the US and the UK and more deontological approaches in Norway, for example.

they will choose to meet what may be considered the ethical *minimum*, i.e., what is explicitly required by extant professional codes, relevant laws, etc., and/or whether they may choose to pursue a more stringent ethical standard that is above and beyond such minimal requirements. The choice for the latter can be referred to as 'Good Samaritan ethics,' following Judith Jarvis Thomson's development of this distinction in her discussion of abortion (1971). That is, as we will see more fully below, researchers will often decide to protect privacy in stronger ways, to ask for informed consent when perhaps not entirely necessary, etc. – *despite* the greater costs and complications of doing so – as these ethical choices follow from their own personal ethical framework. In contrast with the minimal ethical requirements that are incumbent upon all researchers (especially from *utilitarian* considerations that allow for at least minimal risk to subjects as justified by research benefits for the many) such 'Good Samaritan' choices are by definition exceptional and exemplary (and often rooted in more *deontological* recognitions of the absolute importance of basic rights, respect for subjects as persons, etc. – even if recognizing these in the *praxis* of a specific research design entails greater costs). While such choices are *possible* options for researchers to consider in the face of pressing ethical dilemmas, such 'Good Samaritan' choices are *not* compelling in the same ways as the more common, shared, but comparatively minimal ethical requirements incumbent upon all researchers as professionals in a given discipline, as citizens in a given country, etc. Nonetheless, researchers may find it helpful to review their own ethical dilemmas in part in terms of whether their dilemma represents just such a contrast between the requirements of professional ethics and law, on the one hand, and, as a number of researchers eloquently articulate, their own personal but more demanding ethical frameworks.

Risk to participants

Researchers are thus minimally obligated to attend to the ethical codes of their own disciplines and the state and national legal requirements of their citizenship. While countries vary, as we have seen, regarding their stress on deontological vis-à-vis consequentialist approaches – since consequentialist approaches are widely taken up (e.g., in the US and the UK and, to some extent, Germany), it is further critical to consider with some care the *risks* that human beings face as they participate in online research.

Chris Mann (2003) has helpfully detailed the distinctive risks of online research. Her list includes *technical risks* such as lack of security – because of crashes, poor network set-up, buggy software, sloppy password selection and use, viruses, hackers, etc. – and lack of privacy, and *legal risks* – primarily in the form of people failing to understand the prevailing legal requirements, including copyright laws and data protection laws. In particular, she notes that 'the lack of clarity about which legal systems apply in cross-cultural research means it is difficult to know which laws will apply' (2003: 43). Moreover, her list of participants' personal risks includes: *lack of protection from harassment, abuse and deception; lack of debriefing possibilities; lack of protection from exposure* (i.e., violation of privacy, confidentiality, anonymity – leading to harm to reputation and self-esteem); *lack of knowledge about the potential for exposure* – first of all, as 'Newcomers are not always aware of [the] public nature [of online venues]' (2003: 43); and, finally, *lack of protection for the most vulnerable*, i.e., children and adolescents, the elderly or institutionalized, those with learning disabilities – and, perhaps most risky of all, people with 'serious psychiatric conditions' such as depression or panic attacks (2003: 43f.).

Arguably, many of these risks are *greater* in online research than offline. For example, because of the lack of direct physical contact between researchers and participants, some forms of deception online are easier to carry out. And as the early example of the male psychologist masquerading as a female illustrates, such deception may be experienced as great harm indeed (Van Gelder [1985] 1991). Similarly, especially as technologies for capturing others' information continue to advance (Hunsinger 2003), risks to privacy online – and thus the attendant risks of damage to self-esteem, reputation, private life (and, as the NESH guidelines remind us, close relations) likewise seem greater in online environments than in physical environments where research documents may be strongly safeguarded.

By the same token, newcomers – as those most naive about online environments, their technological construction, and attendant risks – often simply do not know enough to know what risks they thus face. This vulnerability, finally, is only amplified among the groups Mann describes – generally, those whose experiential and/or cognitive limitations render them even more open to inadvertent or intentional exploitation.

This last set of risks, in fact, are not merely theoretical. Rather, risks to adolescents – and the concomitant ethical difficulties confronting researchers – are now well-documented and discussed (e.g., Reips 1999; Stern 2003; Bober 2004; Löfberg 2004). While discussion of this particular dimension of IRE is only at its early stages, there is quickly emerging here a consensus that, indeed, researchers have a greater responsibility to protect such participants from harm – including potential harms, for example, that may befall an adolescent girl who naively posts her home address and the times her parents will be away (Ridderstrøm 2003). Similarly, Susannah Stern argues, based on her own encounters with home pages revealing low self-esteem and suicide fantasies – followed by the real-world suicide of one of the authors of such a home page – that researchers should take such discussions very seriously and consider intervening, if possible, even at the cost of tainting or rendering their research unusable (Stern 2004, 2005). Stern's position may be seen as still another example of Good Samaritan ethics rather than as a requirement for all researchers: in any case, it is an option to be considered seriously.

Whether or not such risks are greater in online research than more everyday risks – such as those faced by every user of CMC (e.g., by having their consumer preferences mined though the use of cookies during frequent visits to a website), or those facing participants in physical research settings – is a critical consideration. That is, researchers will have to assess such risks, and then make their ethical judgements depending on three further issues. One, ethicists – as well as national laws – generally agree that our duties to protect others increase in relation to their vulnerability: the greater the vulnerability – e.g., of a child – the greater our obligation to protect a person from harm. Especially if it seems that vulnerability to such risk of harm is greater in online research environments, then it would appear that researchers have a correspondingly greater

obligation to protect their research participants. Two, as we have seen, countries vary in terms of taking more deontological or consequentialist approaches to research ethics. Researchers – and their collaborators – from more consequentialist countries will have to consider whether these potentially greater risks to participants can be overcome, first of all as risks to participants must be offset by greater *benefits* promised by research. Moreover, given that this claim of greater benefit can be made, even in the consequentialist countries relevant codes require that risks to subjects be *minimized*. Judgements will have to be made as to whether the research design can indeed minimize such risks – and at a cost that in turn can be justified by potential research benefits. Researchers – and their collaborators – in more deontologically oriented countries will recognize in the possibility of greater risk to participants in online research a greater burden of proof: their research design will have to strongly protect their participants against such risks. Finally, if research involves collaboration between colleagues in (more) consequentialist and (more) deontological countries (and corresponding legal traditions), these collaborators will likely need to meet the more stringent requirements of their deontological colleagues – for example, as they would be required to do so by EU data privacy protection laws that would prevent researchers from sharing personal information data with colleagues in countries with less strict data privacy protection, such as the US.

Meta-ethical issues

'Meta-ethical' refers here to those issues, concepts, assumptions, etc., that are otherwise tacitly assumed 'underneath' more straightforward ethical discussion and debate regarding specific ethical conflicts and problems. We have already reviewed two of these – (1) *Offline vis-à-vis online worlds* – how 'real' is the virtual, and thus how far do offline extent codes and guidelines apply to online research? And (2): given that much of Internet research is interdisciplinary – how do we deal with sometimes serious differences between ethical codes of the specific disciplines involved, beginning, as we have seen, with the considerable differences between social science approaches that follow medical models of human subjects protections and humanities disciplines that may treat posters, for example, as authors (e.g., White 2002)?[7]

Methodologies and ethics

The issue of interdisciplinary approaches points to a further meta-ethical issue – that is, how research ethics is intimately interwoven with the specific *methodology/ies* used in a given project.

As a first example, consider online experiments that, like their offline counterparts, frequently offer incentives to attract and retain participants. Obviously, providing rewards such as a lottery prize, credit (for students), or money, requires the researcher to know the identity and important personal information of his or her participants. This requirement for identity, as we have seen, is complicated in the online environment first of all because it may be difficult, if not impossible for a researcher to confirm or correct the real-world details of a participant's identity whom s/he never meets face-to-face. Moreover, if the design of the experiment requires that participants remain anonymous – how is the researcher to both maintain the anonymity of participants *and* their individual identity for the sake of providing them promised incentives (cf. Peden and Flashinski 2004: 2)? More broadly, Danielle Lawson points out that participants 'may hesitate to chat simply for the sake of "research purposes"' such as an Internet-based experiment (2004: 92): indeed, she notes that Elizabeth Reid discovered that participants who were made aware of her research intentions through the informed consent process consciously crafted their textual production in hopes of getting quoted – leading Reid to argue that non-disclosure may be both necessary and justified (Reid 1996: 171, cited in Lawson 2004: 92).

Lawson identifies additional ethical problems associated with specific methodological approaches. On the one hand, researchers may undertake more objectivist methodologies that emphasize classical scientific norms such as replicatability. Such methodologies thus require publication of participant characteristics such as gender, age, etc. – but such publication can run the risk of violating participant confidentiality and anonymity, especially if additional information is published, such as *verbatim* quotes that may be subsequently traced (as available in a publicly accessible archive, etc.). Moreover, as researchers adopt methodologies that emphasize, for example, Geertz's 'thick description' and/or, as we shall see in more detail shortly, participant-observation approaches, the resulting need for publishing more details regarding research participants and their interactions thereby increases the threat to their anonymity and confidentiality (Lawson 2004: 91).

In response to these tensions, Lawson offers a range of possible options that researchers can offer to participants:

1. consent to having their nickname and communicative text used for data analysis only (no publication of name or text);

2. consent to having either their nickname or text published in an academic work, but never together (i.e., no identifiers);

3. consent to having either their nickname or text published in an academic work, but never together (i.e., no identifiers) and providing they get to see the 'write up' prior to publication;

4. consent to having both their nickname and text published in academic work, thereby being credited as the authors of their own words; or

5. consent to having both their nickname and text published in academic work, thereby being credited as the authors of their own words, providing they get to see the 'write up' prior to publication.

The last two options deal directly with the issue of CMC copyright (Lawson 2004: 93). But as Lawson notes, giving participants the option of final approval of a proposed publication has been criticized by researchers such as Lynn Cherny (1999): in particular, Susan Herring objects that critical theorizing will be hampered

[7] A specific example of this conflict is provided by Bassett and O'Riordan (2002) who describe their careful efforts (following the social science guidelines for protecting privacy, etc.) to disguise participants and even the name of a forum dedicated to topics of lesbian sexuality – only to be roundly chastised by the forum owners: such anonymization, etc., in their view only colluded with the larger social marginalization of lesbians and lesbian sexuality, and thus seemed a *violation* of their rights and expectations, not, as intended, the protection and fulfillment thereof.

if participants have, in effect, veto power over the final research publication (1996, cited in Lawson 2004: 94). In response to these sometimes intractable tensions, Lawson concludes that 'Thus, it is up to the researcher to determine how much influence participants' criticisms will have over the final product' (2004: 94). In ethical terms, this means that researchers, in the end, will have to make difficult judgements regarding the tension between protecting anonymity, gaining informed consent, etc., and the scientific requirements of their particular methodology.

Participant observation and discourse analysis

Virtual ethnography and its ethical challenges have received considerable attention in IRE. Katherine M. Clegg Smith, for example, examines some of the central ethical challenges in virtual ethnography vis-à-vis her own research on 'ListX', beginning with whether or not a researcher 'lurking' (i.e., unannounced and unidentified) in a listserv is more akin to a researcher taking notes on a public bench vs. doing so while hiding in a bush? (2004: 230. See also Chapter 26, this volume.) Clegg Smith argues that her participant observation approach – at least in relation to a public list whose introductory message to new members emphasizes that the list is public and all messages are archived – meant that she was not required to announce her 'listening' to postings; nor did she request informed consent (2004: 231–235). Finally, in wanting to include text as data in her research publication, Clegg Smith thus wrestled with whether to treat posters of text as subjects whose anonymity and confidentiality must be protected, and/or as authors who would want credit for their work – choosing, in the end, to keep them anonymous (2004: 230–235; see also Svenningson 2001; Bromseth 2002; Markham 2004).

As a further instance: as Nadia Olivero and Peter Lunt argue, methodologies of participant observation and discourse analysis in online environments *heighten* the importance of privacy, informed consent, and ethical issues surrounding the use of participants' texts (2004: 102). Their review of CMC research literature supports their contention that 'reduced social context cues and technological-induced anonymity can *increase* self-awareness' (2004: 104; my emphasis) – as can

the asynchronous medium of email. This and other considerations lead Olivero and Lunt to endorse an egalitarian relationship between researchers and their informants – considerations reinforced, finally, by the distinctive characteristics of the email venue: because the interviewee can 'disconnect' from email contact with the interviewer at any time – it is even more important in this venue to foster the active and engaged involvement of the interviewee by offering significant reward in the form of 'the gratifying trusted, reciprocal exchange indicated by the feminist perspective' (2004: 107). In somewhat similar ways, but with reference on online support groups, Mary Walstrom (2004) develops a feminist, communitarian ethic in conjunction with participant-observation and discourse analysis research, specifically by way of appeal to Bakhtin – as have G. John Hall, Douglas Frederick, and Mark D. Johns (2004).

As we have seen, Judith Jarvis Thomson introduces the distinction between minimal ethical requirements and those actions and choices – such as those of the Good Samaritan – that are admirable precisely because they go beyond our everyday expectations and codes. But this further means for Thomson that while such actions and choices are exemplary – they cannot, however, be *required* of everyone in every circumstance, e.g., by code or law (1971). Here we can note that such ethical Good Samaritanism seems to emerge frequently among researchers undertaking participant-observation methodology. A number of such researchers have recognized that the usual professional ethical and legal requirements – e.g., as *not* obliging a researcher to protect the privacy and identity of participants in a listserv as a public space – did not meet up to their own ethical standards. Rather, these researchers – as more directly engaged with their participants and thus more directly empathic with the possible harms that loss of privacy might entail – have chosen to take a more stringent ethical stance, for example, by insisting on protecting privacy even though such protection complicated their research, made greater demands on their time and resources, etc. (see King 1996; Reid 1996; Smith 2004). Such ethical Good Samaritanism may be fostered as well among researchers, such as Walstrom (2004) and Hall, Frederick and Johns who, as we have seen, are committed to a feminist communitarian ethics (drawn from Denzin 1997) that emphasizes the central importance of sustaining the web of personal relationships that emerge in the research project (2004: 247–252). (For further discussion of the correlation between distinctive research approaches and their correlative ethical difficulties, see Bakardjieva und Feenberg [2001]; Markham [2003].)

A global Internet research ethics?

A further meta-ethical issue is raised by the global reach of the Internet: in light of often significant national differences such as we've already seen in Western nations between those stressing more deontological and more consequentialist approaches – how might we develop a research ethics that is legitimate for researchers and participants from more than one nation?

Projects such as the AoIR ethical guidelines and the RESPECT project suggest that researchers from a diversity of countries and traditions of ethical decision-making can in fact agree upon a range of basic values and issues – and at the same time preserve local differences in the interpretation and implementation of those values through a strategy of *ethical pluralism*.[8] In fact, while discussion of Internet research ethics is very young in Asia, at least three examples drawn from contemporary praxis articulate strong ethical pluralisms between Western and Eastern approaches. For example, Japanese researcher Tamura Takanori, in a recent study of messages exchanged in a forum, chose what he described as a 'more cautious way' – one that included: asking for consent to use forum exchanges from the forum coordinator; using pseudonyms when referring to specific authors; and using paraphrases, rather than direct quotes (Tamura 2004). To be sure, there are clear and striking differences between Western and Japanese understandings of privacy (see Ess 2005; Nakada and Tamura 2005). Nonetheless, Mr Tamura's approach here is strikingly consistent with several elements of Western IRE. To begin with,

Tamura notes that with regard to web pages, for example, even though they are public documents, their authors often express the desire that they be notified of any links to their pages. By analogy, Tamura's approach to protecting the privacy of the forum participants shows a basic respect for the *expectations* of their authors – a respect that is a cornerstone for especially Western deontological ethics (AoIR 2002: footnote 7). Such expectations are also important for an approach rooted in a Western feminist ethics, specifically an 'ethics of care'. In addition, Tamura's 'more cautious way' (one that in particular contrasts with the less protective approach adopted by other researchers) resonates with a Good Samaritan ethic that, as we have seen, goes beyond the *minimal* requirements of prevailing law and practices. Finally, Tamura's more cautious way is strikingly consistent with Western (again, *deontological*) approaches that emphasize the rights of the subject, including protection against possible harm, above possible benefits of research.

This example thus articulates an ethical pluralism as a structure of shared norms held alongside the irreducible differences that define distinctive cultures. Similar examples can be described with regard to notions of self-regulation in China and some Western countries, and with regard to the central ethical concept of privacy, alongside emerging data privacy protection laws (Ess 2005, forthcoming). While not all cultural differences in research ethics will be resolvable through such pluralisms – nonetheless, these examples suggest that a global IRE may possibly emerge as information ethics and research ethics traditions in both East and West become ever more developed.

Conclusion

Internet research ethics promises to become an ever more robust and significant field within information ethics, on the one hand, and research ethics more broadly, on the other. Especially as new venues emerge for human–human and human–machine interaction (including interaction with increasingly sophisticated programs that may eventually approximate human sentience – and thus, many would argue, would deserve some modicum of ethical respect), it

[8] See especially AoIR (2002: 4), including footnotes 6 and 7, as well as Addendum 2. In addition, I have argued for such a pluralism at work in emerging conceptions of privacy and data privacy protection in China and Hong Kong: see Ess (2005, 2006).

seems certain that new ethical conundrums will emerge. But as I hope is clear in the above, the overall history of Internet research ethics includes at least some convergence on key values and rights, while at the same time preserving important local differences with regard to approaches to ethical decision-making and implementation of basic rights and principles – even across East–West divides. This trajectory suggests not the certainty of finding resolutions to every ethical problem that comes along – but rather the sense of finding such resolutions in the face of new difficulties with sufficient frequency and success as to encourage our further efforts to do so.

Acknowledgements

I wish to express my deep gratitude to more people than I can name – including the members of the AoIR ethics working group and the numerous presenters and participants in AoIR panels and workshops on Internet Research Ethics whose insights and ethical sensibilities are reflected in this chapter. I am especially grateful to Elizabeth Buchanan, Ulf-Dietrich Reips, and two anonymous reviewers whose insightful criticisms and suggestions helped significantly improve this chapter.

References

Allen, G., Burk, D. and Ess, C. (2006). Ethical approaches to robotic data gathering. *Ethics and Information Technology*.

American Psychological Association. (1992). Ethical principles of psychologists and code of conduct. *American Psychologist 47*, 1597–1611.

American Psychological Association (2002). *Ethical Principles of Psychologists and Code of Conduct 2002*. Available at http://www.apa.org/ethics/.

Arbeitskreis Deutscher Markt- und Sozialforschungsinstitute, Arbeitsgemeinschaft Sozialwissenschaftlicher Institute, Berufsverband Deutscher Markt- und Sozialforscher, and Deutsche Gesellschaft für Online-Forschung. (2001). *Standards zur Qualitätssicherung für Online-Befragungen* [Quality Assurance Standards for Online Questionnaires]. Retrieved 10 January 2006 from http://www.adm-ev.de/quali_online.html.

Aristotle (1968). *Nichomachean Ethics* (H. Rackham, Trans.). Cambridge, MA: Harvard University Press.

Association for Computing Machinery (1992). *ACM Code of Ethics and Professional Conduct*. Retrieved 10 January 2006 from http://www.acm.org/constitution/code.html.

AoIR (Association of Internet Researchers) (2002). *Ethical Guidelines for Internet Research*. Retrieved 10 January 2006 from http://www.aoir.org/reports/ethics.pdf.

Azar, B. (2000). Online experiments: ethically fair or foul? *Monitor on Psychology 31*(4), 50–52.

Bakardjieva, M. and Feenberg, A. (2001). Involving the virtual subject: conceptual, methodological and ethical dimensions. *Ethics and Information Technology 2*(4), 233–40.

Bassett, E. H. and O'Riordan, K. (2002). Ethics of Internet research: contesting the human subjects research model. *Ethics and Information Technology 4*(3), 233–247. Available at http://www.nyu.edu/projects/nissenbaum/ethics_bassett.html.

de Beauvoir, S. (1948). *The Ethics of Ambiguity*. New York: The Philosophical Library.

Bizer, J. (2003). Grundrechte im Netz: Von der freien Meinungsaußerung bis zum Recht auf Eigentum. In C. Schulzki-Haddouti (Hrsg.), *Bürgerrechte im Netz* (pp. 21–29). Bonn: Bundeszentrale für politische Bildung. Available at http://www.bpb.de/publikationen/UZX6DW,,0,B%fcrgerrechte_im_Netz.html.

Bober, M. (2004). Virtual youth research: an exploration of methodologies and ethical dilemmas from a British perspective. In E. Buchanan (ed.), *Readings in virtual research ethics: Issues and controversies* (pp. 288–315). Hershey, PA: Information Science.

Bromseth, J. C. H. (2002). Public places – public activities? Methodological approaches and ethical dilemmas in research on computer-mediated communication contexts. In A. Morrison (ed.), *Researching ICTs in Context* (pp. 33–61). Inter/Media Report 3/2002. Oslo: University of Oslo. Available at http://www.intermedia.uio.no/konferanser/skikt-02/docs/Researching_ICTs_in_context-Ch3-Bromseth.pdf.

Buchanan, E. (ed.) (2004). *Readings in virtual research ethics: Issues and controversies*. Hershey, PA: Information Science.

Cherny, L. (1999). *Conversation and community: Chat in a virtual world*. Stanford: Center for the Study of Language and Information.

Clegg Smith, K. M. (2004). 'Electronic eavesdropping': the ethical issues involved in conducting a virtual ethnography. In M. D. Johns, S. S. Chen and G. J. Hall (eds.), *Online social research: Methods, issues, and ethics* (pp. 223–238). New York: Peter Lang.

Cousineau, T. M., Green, T. C. and Rancourt, D. (2005). Web chatter before and after the women's health initiative results: A content analysis of online menopause message boards. *Journal of Health Communication 11*(2), 131–147.

Danet, B. (2002). *Studies of cyberpl@y: Ethical and methodological aspects*. Retrieved 10 March 10 2004 from http://atar.mscc.huji.ac.il/~msdanet/papers/ethics2.pdf.

Denzin, N. K. (1997) *Interpretive ethnography: Ethnographic practices for the 21st century*. Thousand Oaks, CA: Sage.

Directive 95/46/EC of the European Parliament and of the Council of 24 October 1995 on the Protection of Individuals with Regard to the Processing of Personal

Data and on the Free Movement of Such Data. Retrieved 10 January 2006 from http://europa.eu.int/comm/justice_home/fsj/privacy/law/index_en.htm.

Döring, N. (1999). *Sozialpsychologie des Internet*. Göttingen: Hogrefe.

Döring, O. (2003). China's struggle for practical regulations in medical ethics. *Nature Reviews | Genetics* 4(March), 233–239.

Dzeyk, W. (2001). Ethische Dimensionen der Online-Forschung. *Kölner Psychologische Studien*, VI(1), 1–30. Available at http://www.allg-psych.uni-koeln.de/dzeyk/home/docs/ethdimon.pdf.

Ess, C. (2003). The cathedral or the bazaar? The AoIR document on Internet Research Ethics as an exercise in open source ethics In M. Consolvo (ed.), *Internet research annual volume 1: Selected papers from the Association of Internet Researchers Conferences 2000–2002* (pp. 95–103). New York: Peter Lang.

Ess, C. (2005). 'Lost in translation'? Intercultural dialogues on privacy and information ethics (introduction to special issue on privacy and data privacy protection in Asia). *Ethics and Information Technology* 7(1), 1–6.

Ess, C. (forthcoming). Culture and communication on global networks: cultural diversity, moral relativism, and hope for a global ethic? In J. Weckert and J. van den Hoven (eds.), *Information technology and moral philosophy*. Cambridge: Cambridge University Press.

Eysenbach, G. and Till, J. (2001). Information in practice. Ethical issues in qualitative research on internet communities. *BMJ 323*(10 November), 1103–1105. Available at http://bmj.bmjjournals.com/cgi/reprint/323/7321/1103.

Floridi, L. (ed.) (2003). *Blackwell guide to the philosophy of information and computing*. Oxford: Blackwell.

Hall, G. J, Frederick, D. and Johns, M. D. (2004). 'NEED HELP ASAP!!!': A feminist communitarian approach to online research ethics. In M. D. Johns, S. S. Chen and G. J. Hall (eds), *Online social research: Methods, issues, and ethics* (pp. 239–252). New York: Peter Lang.

Herring, S. (1996). Linguistic and critical analysis of computer-mediated communication: some ethical and scholarly considerations. *The Information Society 12*, 153–168.

Hunsinger, J. (2003). Privacy online? Retrieved 10 March 2004 from http://www.sun.psci.vt.edu/ethicsv1.mov.

Jones, R. A. (1994). The ethics of research in cyberspace. *Internet Research 4*(3), 30–35.

Johns, M. D., Chen, S. S. and Hall, G. J. (eds.) (2004). *Online social research: Methods, issues, and ethics*. New York: Peter Lang.

Johnson, D. (2001). *Computer ethics*, 3rd edn. Upper Saddle River, NJ: Prentice-Hall.

King, S. (1996). Researching Internet communities: proposed ethical guidelines for the reporting of results. *The Information Society 12*(2), 119–128.

Kraut, R., Olson, J., Banaji, M., Bruckman, A., Cohen, J. and Couper, M. (2004). Psychological research online: report of the scientific affairs' advisory group on the conduct of research on the Internet. *American Psychologist 59*(2), 105–117.

Lawson, D. (2004). Blurring the boundaries: ethical considerations for online research using synchronous CMC forums. In E. Buchanan (ed.), *Readings in virtual research ethics: Issues and controversies* (pp. 80–100). Hershey, PA: Information Science.

Löfberg, C. (2003). Ethical and methodological dilemmas in research with/on children and youths on the Net. In M. Thorseth (ed.), *Applied ethics in Internet research* (pp. 141–154). (Programme for Applied Ethics, Publication Series No. 1.) Trondheim: Norwegian University of Science and Technology.

Mann, C. (2003). Generating data online: ethical concerns and challenges for the C21 researcher. In M. Thorseth (ed.), *Applied ethics in Internet research* (pp. 31–49). (Programme for Applied Ethics, Publication Series No. 1.) Trondheim: Norwegian University of Science and Technology.

Markham, A. (2003). Critical junctures and ethical choices in Internet ethnography. In M. Thorseth (ed.), *Applied ethics in Internet research* (pp. 51–63). (Programme for Applied Ethics, Publication Series No. 1.) Trondheim: Norwegian University of Science and Technology.

Markham, A. (2004). Representation in online ethnographies: a matter of context sensitivity. In M. D. Johns, S. S. Chen and G. J. Hall (eds.), *Online social research: Methods, issues, and ethics* (pp. 141–155). New York: Peter Lang.

Michelfelder, D. (2001). The moral value of informational privacy in cyberspace. *Ethics and Information Technology* 3(2), 129–135.

Nakada, M. and Tamura, T. (2005). Japanese conceptions of privacy: an intercultural perspective. *Ethics and Information Technology* 7(1), 27–36.

NESH (National Committee for Research Ethics in the Social Sciences and the Humanities) (2001). *Guidelines for research ethics in the social sciences, law and the humanities*. Retrieved 10 January 2006 from http://www.etikkom.no/English/NESH/index.txt.

NESH (National Committee for Research Ethics in the Social Sciences and the Humanities) (2003). *Research ethics guidelines for Internet research*. Retrieved 10 January 2006 from http://www.etikkom.no/English/Publications/internet03.

Office for Protection from Research Risks, National Institutes of Health, Department Of Health And Human Services (1991). *Code of Federal Regulations, 1991*. Title 45, Part 46, 'Protection of Human Subjects'. Retrieved 10 January 2006 from http://ohsr.od.nih.gov/guidelines/45cfr46.html.

Olivero, N. and Lunt, P. (2004). When the ethic is functional to the method: the case of e-mail qualitative interviews. In E. Buchanan (ed.), *Readings in virtual research ethics: Issues and controversies* (pp. 101–113). Hershey, PA: Information Science.

Peden, B. and Flashinski, D. P. (2004). Virtual research ethics: a content analysis of surveys and experiments online. In E. Buchanan (ed.), *Readings in virtual research ethics: Issues and controversies* (pp. 1–26). Hershey, PA: Information Science.

Pence, G. E. (1990). *Classic cases in medical ethics: Accounts of the cases that have shaped medical ethics, with philosophical, legal, and historical backgrounds.* New York: McGraw-Hill.

Plato [1968] (1991). *The Republic of Plato*, 2nd edn. Translated with notes and an interpretive essay by Allan Bloom. New York: Basic Books.

Reid, E. (1996). Informed consent in the study of on-line communities: a reflection on the effects of computer-mediated social research. *The Information Society 12*(2), 169–174.

Reidenberg, J. R. (2000). Resolving conflicting international data privacy rules in cyberspace. *Stanford Law Review 52*, 1315–1376.

Reips, U.-D. (1999). Online research with children. In U.-D. Reips, B. Batinic, W. Bandilla, M. Bosnjak, L. Gräf, K. Moser and A. Werner. (eds), *Current Internet science – trends, techniques, results. Aktuelle Online-Forschung – Trends, Techniken, Ergebnisse.* Zürich: Online Press. Available at http://dgof.de/tband99/pdfs/q_z/reips.pdf.

Reips, U.-D. (2000). The Web experiment method: advantages, disadvantages, and solutions. In M. H. Birnbaum (ed.), *Psychological experiments on the Internet* (pp. 89–117). New York: Academic Press.

Reips, U.-D. (2002). Internet-Based psychological experimenting: five dos and five don'ts. *Social Science Computer Review 20*(3), 241–249. Available at http://www.psychologie.unizh.ch/sowi/team/reips/papers/Reips2002.pdf.

RESPECT Project (2004). Retrieved 10 January 2006 from http://www.respectproject.org/main/index.php.

Ridderstrøm, H. (2003). Ethical challenges in research on youths' personal home pages. In Thorseth (ed.), *Applied ethics in Internet research* (pp. 155–169). (Programme for Applied Ethics, Publication Series No. 1.) Trondheim: Norwegian University of Science and Technology.

Social Research Association (2002). *Ethical guidelines.* Retrieved 10 March 2004 from http://www.the-sra.org.uk/Ethicals.htm.

Stern, S. R. (2003). Encountering distressing information in online research: a consideration of legal and ethical responsibilities. *New Media and Society 5*(2), 249–266.

Stern, S. R. (2004). Studying adolescents online: a consideration of ethical issues. In E. Buchanan (ed.), *Readings in virtual research ethics: Issues and controversies* (pp. 274–287). Hershey, PA: Information Science.

Stern, S. R. (2005). Expecting the unexpected: ethical issues in Internet research. Panel presentation, Internet Research Ethics, Association of Internet Researchers annual conference, Chicago, Illinois, 5 October 2005.

Sveningsson, M. (2001). Creating a sense of community: Experiences from a Swedish web chat (dissertation). The Tema Institute – Department of Communication Studies. Linköping University. Linköping, Sweden.

Sveningsson, M. (2004). Ethics in Internet ethnography. In Buchanan (ed.), *Readings in virtual research ethics: Issues and controversies* (pp. 45–61). Hershey, PA: Information Science.

Tamura, T. (2004). *Internet research ethics in Japan.* Unpublished report.

Tang, R. (2002). *Approaches to privacy – the Hong Kong experience.* Retrieved 10 January 2006 from http://www.pco.org.hk/english/infocentre/speech_20020222.html.

Thomson, J. J. (1971). A defense of abortion. *Philosophy and Public Affairs 1*(1), 47–66.

Thorseth, M. (ed.) (2003). *Applied ethics in Internet research.* (Programme for Applied Ethics, Publication Series No. 1.) Trondheim: Norwegian University of Science and Technology.

Van Gelder, L. [1985] (1991). The strange case of the electronic lover. In C. Dunlap and R. Kling (eds.), *Computerization and controversy: Value conflicts and social choices* (pp. 364–375). New York: Academic Press.

Walstrom, M. (2004). Ethics and engagement in communication scholarship: analyzing public, online support groups as researcher/participant-experiencer. In Buchanan (ed.), *Readings in virtual research ethics: Issues and controversies* (pp. 174–202). Hershey, PA: Information Science.

Walther, J. (2002). Research ethics in Internet-enabled research: human subjects issues and methodological myopia. *Ethics and Information Technology 4*(3), 205–216. Available at www.nyu.edu/projects/nissenbaum/ethics_walther.html.

White, M. Representations or people? (2002). *Ethics and Information Technology 4*(3), 249–266. Available at www.nyu.edu/projects/nissenbaum/ethics_white.html.

World Medical Association Declaration of Helsinki (1964) 2004. *Ethical principles for medical research involving human subjects.* Retrieved 10 January 2006 from http://www.wma.net/e/policy/b3.htm.

Index